Fundamentals of Programming in BASIC

A Structured Approach

Fundamentals of Programming in **BASIC**

A Structured Approach
Second Edition

Robert C. Nickerson
San Francisco State University

Little, Brown and Company

Boston   Toronto

Library of Congress Cataloging-in-Publication Data

Nickerson, Robert C., 1946–
    Fundamentals of programming in BASIC.

    Includes index.
    1. BASIC (Computer program language)   I. Title.
QA76.73.B3N53   1985   005.13′3   85-23090
ISBN 0-316-60655-3

Library of Congress Catalog Card Number 85-23090

ISBN 0-316-60655-3

9 8 7 6 5 4 3 2 1

MU

Published simultaneously in Canada by Little, Brown & Company (Canada) Limited

Printed in the United States of America

Acknowledgment

Apple is a registered trademark of Apple Computer, Inc.; Microsoft is a
registered trademark of Microsoft Corporation; True BASIC is a trademark
of True BASIC Inc.; VAX-11 and BASIC PLUS are trademarks of Digital
Equipment Corporation.

Preface

The objective of this book is to provide a carefully paced introduction to computer programming in the BASIC language. To accomplish this objective the book systematically introduces the features of BASIC as they are needed for various processing situations. Structured programming and problem-solving concepts are developed along with the presentation of language features. Program examples and sample problems drawn from areas that most readers will readily recognize illustrate the topics. As a result, the reader not only learns the BASIC language but also gains an understanding of the need for and use of each language element and learns how to develop well-structured programs in BASIC to solve a variety of problems.

The features of BASIC covered in the book are those found in the most common versions of the language including ANS BASIC and versions of BASIC available on common microcomputers and minicomputers. When a particular characteristic of the language varies from one version to another, this is noted in the text and a table is usually given that shows the differences. The following versions of BASIC are compared in these tables:

> ANS minimal BASIC
> ANS BASIC (proposed)†
> Microsoft BASIC (IBM PC)
> Applesoft BASIC (Apple IIe and IIc)
> True BASIC (IBM PC)
> BASIC-PLUS (DEC PDP-11)
> VAX-11 BASIC (DEC VAX-11)

Sections in the book that describe features of BASIC that are not found in some versions of the language are marked with asterisks. These sections may be skipped without loss of continuity.

Language features are covered in conjunction with problem-solving and program-development concepts. These concepts are introduced in the first chapter and expanded in subsequent chapters. Program structure is discussed early with complete chapters on decision logic (Chapter 3) and loop control (Chapter 4). Nested decisions and loops are described fully in these chapters. The programming process is covered in detail in Chapter 6. Topics such as program design, testing, debugging, and documentation are discussed at appropriate points and illustrated with sample problems. Program style and understandability are emphasized throughout the book. The use of subroutines in the top-down design and development of large programs is covered in Chapter 11. Upon completion of this book the reader should be able to systematically develop well-structured, understandable, and correct programs in BASIC.

The book is organized into two parts. The first part, consisting of Chapters 1 through 6, introduces the fundamental elements of the language and develops basic programming methodology. These chapters cover BASIC language elements needed for input and output, numeric data processing, decision logic, and loop control. Almost

---

† At the time this is being written, the new standard has not yet been finally approved. The material on ANS BASIC in this book is based on the proposed standard.

all programming methodology topics covered in the book are introduced in these chapters. Chapter 6 can be thought of as a capstone for these first chapters because it brings together and explains in detail many concepts about program development. Chapter 6 is also a transition to the second part of the book, which consists of Chapters 7 through 12. These chapters describe additional topics including BASIC functions, string processing, array processing, subroutines and user-defined functions, and files (sequential and random). The material in these chapters can be read in different sequences and some of the topics can be covered along with earlier chapters. (The chapter prerequisite structure is described in the instructor's manual.)

A number of features make the book especially useful. These include the following:

- The first section of Chapter 1 contains a discussion of essential computer concepts. This can be used as an introduction to these topics for readers with no previous background or as a review by readers who have prior experience with computers.
- Chapter 1 contains general explanations of program development using microcomputers and using minicomputers (time-sharing). Consequently, the book can be used with both types of computers and even with mainframe computers. Appendix B lists system commands for several common computers.
- The book is designed so that programming can begin as early as possible. After finishing Chapter 2, the reader can write complete programs of his or her own design. After each succeeding chapter increasingly more complex programs can be developed.
- Many examples and illustrative programs are provided throughout the book. The examples are nonmathematical in nature and oriented toward applications the reader should easily understand. Complete lists of input and output are shown with most sample programs. Input data entered by the user is shown in color in examples and figures; output displayed by the computer is in black.†
- Chapters 2 through 6 each contain a complete solution to a sample problem. The solution is developed systematically from a problem definition, through the program design, coding, and testing, to the final documentation.
- Flowcharting is discussed completely. Flowcharts are introduced in Chapter 1 and used for all sample problems and many illustrative programs.
- Interactive program design is covered in detail. Early examples demonstrate such programs. Characteristics that make an interactive program easy to use are explained and illustrated in Chapter 5. The design of large menu-driven programs is covered in Chapter 11.
- Many common algorithms are described in the book. Included are algorithms for sequential and binary searching, sorting, sequential file updating, and random file processing.
- Each chapter contains questions to review the material covered in that chapter. The answers to approximately half of the review questions are found in Appendix C.
- All chapters except the first contain a substantial number of programming problems. Most problems require only a minimal mathematical background and emphasize nontechnical areas. Included are many problems related to business fields. Some problems are designed for math, science, and engineering students. The programming problems range in difficulty from

---

† All names of persons, companies, and organizations in examples, problems, and questions in this book are fictitious and are used for illustrative purposes only.

relatively easy to very difficult and challenging. Test data is provided with most problems.

- The syntax of the BASIC language covered in the book is summarized in Appendix A.

A separate student workbook is available. The workbook contains additional material to assist the student in understanding and applying the chapter topics. Included for each chapter are objectives, formats of the BASIC language elements covered in the chapter, study comments, practice exercises with answers, and review exercises without answers that can be completed by the student for evaluation by the instructor. A glossary is also included in the workbook.

An instructor's manual is available that contains teaching suggestions, course schedules, chapter objectives, lists of terms and BASIC language elements, complete lecture notes, answers to end-of-chapter review questions, answers to review exercises in the student workbook, and test questions and answers. Also available is a set of transparency masters. Approximately half of the transparency masters are figures from the book; the other half are new illustrations. By using the lecture notes and transparencies made from the masters, a complete course in programming in BASIC can be taught.

Many of the ideas for this edition of the book came from reviews by users of the first edition. I greatly appreciate their effort. My special appreciation goes to Gary Hammerstrom who made many excellent suggestions. The manuscript reviewers did a thorough job and their comments were especially useful. I would like to thank Jack Baroudi of New York University, Henry A. Etlinger of the Rochester Institute of Technology, Richard Fleming of North Lake Community College, Betty Hwang of Purdue University, G. Ron Jongeward of Hawaii Pacific College, James F. La Salle of the University of Arizona, and Eileen M. Trauth of Boston University for their participation in the reviewing process. Many of their suggestions have been incorporated into the book.

Finally, I would like to thank my family for their support and help during the writing of this book.

Contents

1 Introduction to Programming in BASIC   **1**

    1-1   Computer Concepts   1
    1-2   The BASIC Language   9
    1-3   Fundamentals of BASIC   10
    1-4   A Sample Program   13
    1-5   Running a BASIC Program   16
    1-6   Problem Solving and the Programming Process   24
         Review Questions   28
         Computer Exercises   29

2 Essential Elements of BASIC   **30**

    2-1   Constants and Variables   30
    2-2   Numeric Data Processing   34
    2-3   Writing Complete Programs   41
    2-4   Program Style   54
    2-5   A Sample Problem   55
         Review Questions   58
         Programming Problems   60

3 Programming for Decisions   **64**

    3-1   The IF Statement   64
    3-2   Program Logic for Decision Making   69
    3-3   Nested Decisions   75
    3-4   A Sample Problem   79
  *3-5   Variations of the IF Statement   84
    3-6   The ON-GOTO Statement   95
         Review Questions   97
         Programming Problems   99

* Sections marked with an asterisk describe features that are not available in some versions of BASIC.

4   Programming for Repetition   **105**

      4-1   Controlling Loops   105
      4-2   Nested Loops   118
      4-3   FOR Loops   121
      4-4   A Sample Problem   132
     *4-5   WHILE Loops   137
             Review Questions   141
             Programming Problems   143

5   Input and Output Programming   **147**

      5-1   Output Programming   147
      5-2   Interactive Program Design   153
      5-3   The READ, DATA, and RESTORE Statements   156
      5-4   A Sample Problem   160
     *5-5   The PRINT USING Statement   167
             Review Questions   172
             Programming Problems   173

6   Program Development   **176**

      6-1   Program Structure   176
      6-2   Program Understandability   179
      6-3   Program Style   180
      6-4   Program Refinement   183
      6-5   The Programming Process   186
      6-6   Conclusion   204
             Review Questions   204
             Programming Problems   205

7   BASIC Functions   **210**

      7-1   General Characteristics   210
      7-2   The Integer Function   212
      7-3   Random Numbers   214
      7-4   Computer Games   218
      7-5   Computer-Assisted Instruction   221
      7-6   Computer Simulation   224
             Review Questions   229
             Programming Problems   230

8 Strings   234

8-1   String Data   234
8-2   Comparing String Data   239
*8-3   Processing String Data   245
8-4   The READ and DATA Statements with String Data   253
*8-5   The PRINT USING Statement with String Output   254
       Review Questions   255
       Programming Problems   256

9 Arrays   260

9-1   Arrays and Array Elements   260
9-2   Input and Output of Array Data   266
9-3   Array-Processing Techniques   269
9-4   Array Searching   272
9-5   Array Sorting   278
9-6   String Arrays   285
       Review Questions   287
       Programming Problems   288

10 Two-Dimensional Arrays and Matrix Operations   295

10-1   Two-Dimensional Array Concepts   295
10-2   Input and Output of Two-Dimensional Array Data   299
10-3   Processing Two-Dimensional Arrays   301
10-4   An Illustrative Program   306
10-5   Two-Dimensional String Arrays   309
*10-6   Matrix Operations   309
        Review Questions   322
        Programming Problems   323

11 Subroutines and User-Defined Functions   329

11-1   Subroutines   329
11-2   User-Defined Functions   335
*11-3   Multiple-Line Functions   340
*11-4   Subprograms   342
11-5   Developing Large Programs   346
11-6   Interactive Program Design Revisited   356
        Review Questions   365
        Programming Problems   366

12 Files   371

12-1   File Concepts 372
*12-2   Statements for Sequential File Processing 375
*12-3   Sequential File Creation and Access 380
*12-4   Sequential File Updating 387
*12-5   Random Files 393
*12-6   Chaining 410
        Review Questions 412
        Programming Problems 413

Appendices   417

A   Summary of BASIC 417
B   System Commands 424
C   Answers to Selected Review Questions 436

Index   445

Chapter 1

Introduction to programming in BASIC

A computer is a device that is used to solve problems. The process of instructing a computer how to solve a problem is called programming. Programming involves combining words and symbols that are part of a special language. BASIC is a language that is commonly used for programming solutions to many types of problems.

This book is about programming in the BASIC language. The book describes the main rules of BASIC and explains the general process of computer programming. It also presents many programming examples for different types of problems. As a result, you should not only learn the fundamentals of the BASIC language but also gain an understanding of the programming process and an insight into different types of problems that can be solved with a computer.

In this chapter we cover the background necessary to begin studying programming in BASIC. First we explain elementary computer concepts. Then we introduce the BASIC language and describe how programming in BASIC is done on a computer. Finally, we examine problem solving and the programming process in general. After completing this chapter you should have the background needed to begin learning to program in BASIC. Later chapters go into detail about the BASIC language, the programming process, and computer solutions to problems.

1-1 Computer concepts

Before describing BASIC, we need to explain three topics: computers, programs, and data. A *computer* is an electronic device that processes data by following the instructions in a program. A *program* is a set of instructions that is stored in the computer and performed automatically by the computer. *Data*† is facts, figures, numbers, and words that are stored in the computer and processed according to the program's instructions.

Computers

A computer consists of several interconnected devices or components. One way of viewing the organization of a computer is shown in Figure 1-1. In this diagram, boxes represent the different components of the computer and lines with arrowheads

---

† The word "data" is most correctly used as a plural noun. The singular of data is "datum." The usual practice, however, is to use the word data in a singular as well as plural sense. We will follow that practice in this book.

Figure 1-1. The organization of a computer

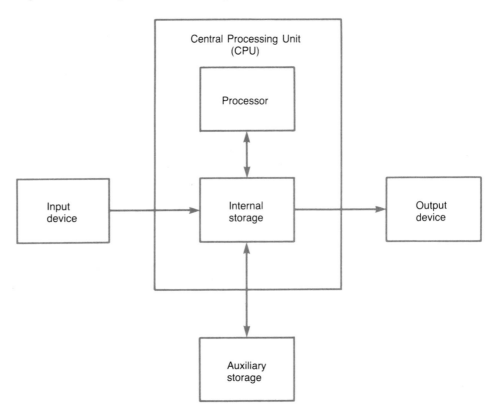

show the paths taken within the computer by data and program instructions. There are five basic components: the input device, the output device, the internal storage, the processor, and the auxiliary storage. Sometimes the internal storage and processor together are called the central processing unit or CPU.

In this subsection we describe each of the components diagrammed in Figure 1-1. Figures 1-2, 1-3, 1-4, and 1-5 show actual computers with the components discussed here.

Input and output devices. An *input device* is a mechanism that accepts data from outside the computer and converts it into an electronic form understandable to the computer. The data that is accepted is called *input data,* or simply *input.* For example, a common input device is a typewriter-like *keyboard.* Each time a key on the keyboard is pressed, the electronic form of the symbol on the key is sent into the computer. Input data is entered by pressing the keys that correspond to the data.

An *output device* performs the opposite function of an input device. An output device converts data from its electronic form inside the computer to a form that can be used outside. The converted data is called *output data* or simply *output.* For example, one common output device is a TV-like screen. The output is displayed as images on the screen. In general, such a video display device is called a *CRT* for cathode *ray tube* (another name for a TV tube). With some small computers a standard television set can be used as a CRT, but usually a special CRT called a *monitor* is used. Another common output device is called a *printer.* This device converts data from the computer into printed symbols to produce a paper copy of the output. We often call this type of output a *report* or computer *printout.*

A CRT or a printer is often combined with a keyboard to form a unit called a *terminal.* A terminal consists of keyboard input *and* either CRT output or printer output.

Figure 1-2. A microcomputer. This is an IBM Personal Computer. (Courtesy of IBM Corp.)

Input and output devices are often referred to together as input/output or *I/O devices*. Most computers have several I/O devices attached at one time. For example, a medium-sized computer may have many terminals plus several printers as well as other types of I/O devices. Some small computers, however, have only one input device and one or two output devices (such as a keyboard, a CRT, and a printer).

Figure 1-3. A microcomputer. This is an Apple IIe. (Courtesy of Apple Computer, Inc.)

Figure 1-4. A minicomputer. This is a Digital VAX 11/785. (Courtesy of Digital Equipment Corp.)

Figure 1-5. A mainframe computer. This is an IBM 3081. (Courtesy of IBM Corp.)

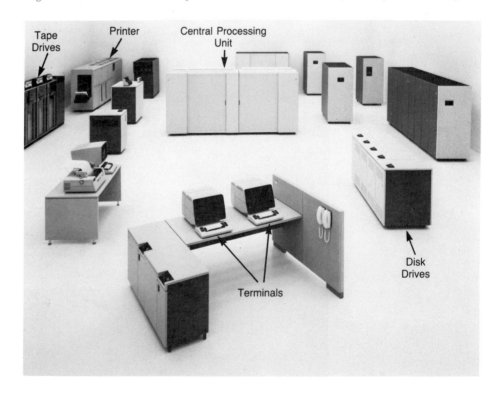

The central processing unit. Between the input devices and the output devices is the component of the computer that does the actual computing or processing. This is the *central processing unit* or *CPU*. (See Figure 1-1.) Input data is converted into an electronic form by an input device and sent to the central processing unit where the data is stored. In the CPU the data is used in calculations and other types of processing to produce the solution to the desired problem. After processing is completed, the results are sent to an output device where the data is converted into the final output.

The central processing unit contains two basic units: the internal storage and the processor. The *internal storage* is the "memory" of the computer. Data currently being processed is stored in this part of the CPU. Instructions in the program being performed are also stored in the internal storage.

The *processor* is the unit that carries out the instructions in the program. Among other things, the processor contains electronic circuits that do arithmetic and perform logical operations. A computer can do the basic arithmetic tasks that a human can do; that is, it can add, subtract, multiply, and divide. The logical operations that a computer can do are usually limited to comparing two values to determine whether they are equal or whether one is greater than or less than the other. Complex processing is accomplished by long sequences of these basic operations.

The processor contains electronic circuits that control the other parts of the computer. These control circuits perform their function by following the instructions in the program. The program is stored in the computer's internal storage. During processing, each instruction in the program is brought from the internal storage to the processor. The control circuits in the processor analyze the instruction and send signals to the other units based on what the instruction tells the computer to do. Performing one instruction may involve actions in any of the other parts of the computer. After one instruction in the programmed sequence is performed, the next is brought from internal storage to the processor and performed. This continues until all the instructions in the program have been carried out.

Auxiliary storage. The final component of a computer is the *auxiliary storage*. This component stores data that is not currently being processed by the computer and programs that are not currently being performed. It differs from internal storage, which stores the data and instructions that are being processed at the time by the computer. Sometimes internal storage is called *primary storage* and auxiliary storage is called *secondary storage* or *mass storage*.

A common type of auxiliary storage is a *magnetic disk,* or simply *disk,* which resembles a phonograph record. Disks are available in different sizes: some as small as $3\frac{1}{2}$ inches in diameter and others as large as 14 inches across. Some disks are made of plastic with a metallic coating; these are called *floppy disks* because they are flexible. Other disks are made of metal; these are commonly called *hard disks*. No matter what type of disk is used, information is recorded on its surface by patterns of magnetism. A *disk drive* is a device for recording data on magnetic disks and for retrieving data from the disks.

Another type of auxiliary storage is *magnetic tape,* or simply *tape,* which is much like audio recording tape. Magnetic tape comes in reels of various sizes and in cassettes and cartridges. Data is recorded on the surface of the tape by patterns of magnetism. A *tape drive* is a device that records data on magnetic tape and retrieves data from the tape.

Most computers have several auxiliary storage devices attached at one time. For example, a computer may have four disk drives and two tape drives. Other types of auxiliary storage can also be used, but disk and tape are the most common.

Computer hardware. The physical equipment that makes up a computer system is called *hardware*. Computer hardware consists of keyboards, CRTs, printers, terminals,

CPUs, disk drives, tape drives, and other pieces of equipment. Figures 1-2, 1-3, 1-4, and 1-5 show typical computers with the hardware that we have described.

Figures 1-2 and 1-3 show examples of small computers called *microcomputers*. Each of the computers in these figures has a keyboard for input and a CRT and printer for output. The computer in Figure 1-2 has two disk drives that use floppy disks for auxiliary storage, whereas the computer in Figure 1-3 has only one floppy disk drive. These microcomputers can execute only one program and be used by only one person at a time.

Figure 1-4 shows a medium-size computer commonly called a *minicomputer*. It is larger and faster than a microcomputer. The computer in the figure has several terminals for input and output and has disk drives that use hard disks for auxiliary storage. This computer can process several programs at a time, and several people can use it simultaneously.

Figure 1-5 shows a large computer, usually called a *mainframe* computer. It has a printer, several CRT terminals, and other devices for input and output. Auxiliary storage consists of a number of disk drives that use hard disks and several tape drives. A computer such as this one usually executes numerous programs concurrently and can be used by many people at one time.

Programs

A computer program is a set of instructions that tells the computer how to solve a problem. A program is prepared by a person, called a *programmer,* who is familiar with the different things a computer can do. First the programmer must understand the problem to be solved. Next he or she determines the steps the computer has to go through to solve the problem. Then the programmer prepares the instructions for the computer program that solves the problem.

To illustrate, assume that we want to use a computer to solve the problem of finding the sum of two numbers. To do this, the computer must go through a sequence of steps. First it must get two numbers from an input device. Then it must add the numbers to find their sum. Finally it must send the sum to an output device, such as a CRT or printer, so that we can see the result. Thus, a computer program to solve this problem would have three instructions:

1. Get two numbers.
2. Add the numbers.
3. Send the result.

The instructions would be prepared in a form the computer could understand. Then they could be performed by the computer. When the computer performs the instructions, we say that it *executes* the program.

In the remainder of this subsection we explain how such a program is executed, what languages are used to prepare programs, and what types of programs are needed.

Program execution. To execute a computer program, we must enter the instructions in the program into the computer using an input device. Usually, the instructions are keyed in using a keyboard. The program is then stored in the computer's internal storage.

In executing a program the computer goes through the instructions one at a time in the sequence in which they are stored. For example, assume that the program to find the sum of two numbers has been entered into the computer and is stored in internal storage. The computer would bring the first instruction in the program from internal storage to the processor. Then execution would proceed as follows:

1. Get two numbers. The processor examines this instruction and sends a signal to the input device that causes two numbers (input data) to be transferred to internal storage. The second instruction is then brought to the processor.
2. Add the numbers. To execute this instruction the processor issues a signal to internal storage that causes the two numbers to be sent to the arithmetic circuit in the processor. The numbers are added and the result is stored in internal storage. The last instruction is then brought to the processor.
3. Send the result. To execute this instruction the processor gives a signal to internal storage to transfer the result to the output device. Then the output device displays or prints the output data.

Two important concepts are illustrated by this example. The first is that internal storage is used to store both program instructions and data. All instructions in the program are stored in internal storage before the program begins execution. Data is brought into internal storage as the program executes.

The second important concept is that the instructions in the program are executed in the sequence in which they are written. The sequence must be such that, when executed, the problem is correctly solved. If the instructions are out of order, the computer cannot figure out what the right sequence should be. In such a case, the computer would follow the instructions in the order in which they are given and thus produce an incorrect result.

Computer programming languages. A program must be written in a form that a computer can understand. Every instruction must be prepared according to specific rules. The rules form a language that we use to instruct the computer. Humans use *natural languages* such as English and Spanish to communicate with each other. When we communicate with a computer we use a *computer programming language*.

To write a sentence in a natural human language, we form words, phrases, and sentences from letters and other symbols. The construction of the sentence is determined by the grammar rules of the language. The meaning of the sentence depends on what words are used and how they are organized. A computer programming language also has rules that describe how to form valid instructions. These rules are called the *syntax* of the language. The meanings or effects of the instructions are called the *semantics* of the language. For example, the *syntax* of a particular computer language may say that one type of instruction has the following form:

```
ln LET variable = numeric expression
```

That is, the instruction consists of a line number (abbreviated *ln*) followed by the word LET, then a *variable,* an equal sign, and finally a *numeric expression.* (Of course, we must know what a line number, a variable, and a numeric expression are in order to complete the instruction.) The *semantics* of the language tells us that this instruction means that the value of the numeric expression on the right of the equal sign is to be assigned to the variable on the left. (We will study this instruction in detail in Chapter 2.)

In this book we discuss the syntax and semantics of the BASIC computer programming language. BASIC is just one of many programming languages. In fact, there are several groups of languages and many different languages in each group.

One group of languages is called *machine language.* A machine language is the one in which a computer actually does its processing. To a computer, a program in machine language is a series of electronic impulses. A programmer expresses programs in this language by using binary numbers — that is, by a series of ones and zeros. Each type of computer has its own machine language; because there are many different types of computers, there many machine languages. It is important to know, however, that the machine language for any particular computer is the *only language that computer can understand*. Every program for a computer must be either written in that computer's machine language, or written in another language and then translated into its machine language.

We think of machine language as a low-level computer language because it is the basic language of a computer. There are also many *high-level languages* for computers. These languages are called "high level" because they are closer to languages humans use than to machine language. BASIC is an example of a high-level language.

All high-level languages have one characteristic in common: any program written in a high-level language must first be translated into the machine language of the computer being used. Only then can the program take control of the computer. For BASIC the translation process is called *compilation* or *interpretation,* depending on how it is done. (The difference between these is not important here.) The translation is performed by a special translator program called a *compiler* or an *interpreter*. First a program is written in BASIC. Then the BASIC program is translated by the translator program into an equivalent machine-language program. Finally the machine language program is executed. (In Section 1-5 we discuss the process of BASIC translation in more detail.)

Computer software. Hardware is the general term for the physical equipment that makes up a computer system. *Software* is the term for programs used with a computer. The software for a computer is any program that can be executed by that computer.

There are two main types of software: application software and system software. *Application software* consists of programs that are written to solve specific problems. For example, a program that prepares the payroll for a business is an application program. Similarly, a program that analyzes an engineering problem is an example of application software.

System software refers to general programs that are designed to make the computer easier to use. A system program does not solve a problem for a specific application but rather makes it easier to develop the necessary application program. Language translators (compilers and interpreters) are examples of system software; they help to prepare high-level language application programs by translating the programs into machine language.

Another example of system software is an *operating system*. This is a set of programs that controls the basic operation of the computer. For example, the operating system determines where an application program is stored in the computer's internal storage. The operating system is always in control of the computer when some other program (such as a language translator or an application program) is not executing.

BASIC is used for programming application software, so all of our examples will show application programs. However, we use system software — including a language translator and an operating system — to help in the development of application programs.

Data

Computers process data. A computer gets data from input devices and sends data to output devices. It stores data in internal storage and in auxiliary storage. It performs computations and makes logical decisions using data. The instructions in a program tell the computer how to process the data.

There are two basic ways, or modes, of processing data on a computer: batch processing and interactive processing. In *batch processing,* all of the data that is to be processed is prepared in some form understandable to the computer prior to the actual processing. For example, all of the data to be processed may be stored in auxiliary storage. Then the batch of data is processed by the computer and the resulting output is received in a batch. An example of batch processing is the preparation of the weekly payroll for a business. At the end of the week each employee turns in a time sheet. The data from each sheet is keyed into the computer. Once all of the data is ready, it is processed in a batch by a payroll program to produce the paychecks and other payroll information.

With *interactive processing* a human interacts with the computer through a keyboard and CRT or other I/O device at the time that the processing is done. Each set of data is entered directly into the computer, processed, and the output is received before the next input data is supplied. An airline reservation system is an example of this type of processing. When a customer requests a ticket for a particular flight, the reservation clerk enters the data directly into the computer using a keyboard. The computer processing includes determining if there is a seat available on the requested flight. The output comes back immediately to the CRT so that the customer will know whether or not the reservation is confirmed.

Sometimes the word *time-sharing* is used instead of interactive processing. In fact, time-sharing is a mechanism used by a computer to interact with several different computer users at one time. With time-sharing the computer allows each user a small amount of time for processing before going on to the next user. In effect, the computer "shares its time" among the people trying to interact with it. With time-sharing it is possible for many people using different I/O devices to interact with the computer at one time.

Interactive processing does not always involve time-sharing. For example, most microcomputers have only one keyboard and one CRT and can interact with just one person at a time. In this situation time-sharing is not needed.

The type of programming discussed in this book is most often used for programs that do interactive processing. Most of the examples emphasize interactive keyboard input and CRT output. Many of the techniques and concepts, however, are applicable to programs that do batch processing. Some of the examples illustrate this type of processing.

1-2 The BASIC language

One of the most widely used high-level languages is *BASIC,* which stands for Beginner's All-purpose Symbolic Instruction Code. Originally developed at Dartmouth College in the mid-1960s, BASIC was designed to make it easy for beginning students to learn programming. Its popularity and ease of use have resulted in its being applied to a wide variety of computer problem-solving situations. It is especially well suited for interactive processing and is probably the most commonly used language on microcomputers.

Since its original development, BASIC has undergone a number of modifications and improvements. Frequently a computer manufacturer or software developer would add features or make changes in the language, so that BASIC on one computer would be slightly different from BASIC on another computer. As a consequence, many different "dialects" or *versions* of BASIC were developed. This created a problem because, in general, it was not possible to write a program in BASIC for one computer and then use it on a different computer without making some modifications in the program.

Table 1-1. BASIC versions

BASIC version	Computer systems
ANS minimal BASIC	—
ANS BASIC (proposed)	—
Microsoft® BASIC	IBM PC and compatible computers
Applesoft© BASIC	Apple IIe and IIc
True BASIC™	IBM PC and compatible computers
BASIC-PLUS™	DEC PDP-11
VAX-11 BASIC™	DEC VAX-11

In order to overcome this problem of incompatibility among different versions of BASIC, the American National Standards Institute (or ANSI) in 1978 developed a standard version of BASIC. This version is called *American National Standard* (or *ANS*) *minimal BASIC*. It contains the most commonly used elements of BASIC but not many of the advanced features that are available on a number of computers. A program written in ANS minimal BASIC should be able to be processed on a variety of computers without changes in the program.

In 1984 ANSI proposed a more complete version of BASIC called *American National Standard* (or *ANS*) *BASIC*.† This version of BASIC contains most of the features of ANS minimal BASIC plus many advanced features. Almost any program written in ANS minimal BASIC should be able to be processed as an ANS BASIC program without change, but a program written in ANS BASIC may not necessarily be processed as an ANS minimal BASIC program.

Most versions of BASIC developed by computer manufacturers and software developers are similar, but not identical, to one or both of the ANS versions of BASIC. In this book we describe the characteristics of BASIC that are common to many versions of the language, including the ANS versions and the versions developed for commonly used computers. When a particular characteristic of the language varies from one version to another, this is noted in the text and a table is usually given that shows the differences. Table 1-1 lists the versions of BASIC that are compared in the book along with the computer systems with which these versions are used. Any section that emphasizes features not found in some versions of BASIC is marked with an asterisk. These sections can be skipped. Appendix A summarizes the elements of the language described in this book.

The characteristics of BASIC described in this book may or may not be the same as those of the version of BASIC for the computer being used. Whenever there is a question, the appropriate reference manual must be consulted to determine the exact requirements.

1-3 Fundamentals of BASIC

Figure 1-6 shows a sample BASIC program. This program performs a simple calculation to find the total and average of three numbers. In the next section we explain how

† At the time this is being written the new standard has not yet been finally approved. The material on ANS BASIC in this book is based on the proposed standard. The standard that is finally approved may be different.

Figure 1-6. A sample program

```
10 REM - TOTAL AND AVERAGE PROGRAM
20 INPUT X,Y,Z
30   LET T=X+Y+Z
40   LET A=T/3
50   PRINT X,Y,Z,T,A
60 GOTO 20
70 END
```

this program works, but for now we are interested only in the language concepts it illustrates.

BASIC statements

Each instruction in a BASIC program is called a *statement*. A BASIC statement tells the computer something about the processing that is to be done in the program. In the sample program in Figure 1-6, each line is a statement. A BASIC *program* is a sequence of BASIC statements that describes some computing process. To prepare a BASIC program, the programmer must know how to form statements in the BASIC language and what each statement means.

One rule of BASIC is that every statement must begin with a *line number*. The line number can vary within a certain range that depends on the version of BASIC. (See Table 1-2.) No two statements, however, can have the same number, and the numbers must be in *increasing* numerical order. (Line numbers are optional in some versions of BASIC.)

Besides these rules, there are no restrictions on line numbers. Thus, we can number the statements in a program 1, 2, 3, 4, . . . , or 10, 20, 30, 40, . . . (as in the sample program in Figure 1-6), or 18, 37, 108, 256, ... The usual practice, however, is to number the statements by tens as in the sample program. This approach makes it easy to add statements to the program. For example, if we wish to add a new statement between lines 30 and 40, we can number it 35 and not change any other numbers. If the statements were numbered by ones, we would have to renumber all statements following the new statement.

Another good practice is to make the line numbers in a program the same length; that is, all line numbers are either two digits, three digits, or four digits. This makes the program easier to read. If the program has fewer than ten statements, we start the numbers at 10 (e.g., 10, 20, 30, . . .). For longer programs, we start the line numbers at 100 or 1000 (e.g., 100, 110, 120, . . .). We will see examples of programs with longer line numbers in later chapters.

Table 1-2. Line-number differences

BASIC version	Line-number range
ANS Minimal BASIC	1–9999
ANS BASIC	1–50000
Microsoft BASIC	0–65529
Applesoft BASIC	0–63999
True BASIC	1–999999 (Line numbers are optional)
BASIC-PLUS	1–32767
VAX-11 BASIC	1–32767

Following the line number in a BASIC statement must be at least one blank space and then a special word called a *keyword*. (In some versions of BASIC the space is optional.) Extra spaces can always be included and are often used to make the program more readable. The keyword identifies the statement and indicates what type of processing is to take place. In the sample program in Figure 1-6, the keywords are REM, INPUT, LET, PRINT, GOTO, and END. Each has a special meaning in BASIC. There must be at least one space after the keyword. (Again, this space is optional in some versions of BASIC.)

Constants, variables, and expressions

In addition to a keyword, a BASIC statement often contains constants, variables, and expressions. Here we give an overview of each of these. We will explain each in detail in Chapter 2.

A *constant* is a fixed data value in a program. A number (other than a line number) is a constant. For example, 3, 6.5, −37, .0012, and −78.36 are constants that might appear in a program. In the sample program in Figure 1-6, the number 3 in the statement numbered 40 is a constant. (The number 20 in statement 60 is *not* a constant, as we will see.)

A *variable* is a name that is used to refer to data that can change in a program. For the time being, we can think of the internal storage of the computer as being composed of twenty-six boxes. (See Figure 1-7). The boxes are called *storage locations*. Each storage location is identified by a letter of the alphabet, which is the variable, and can store a single numeric value. By using the letter (i.e., the variable) for a storage location, we tell the computer to use the value in the location identified by the letter. Thus if we tell the computer to add X and Y, we mean add the values found in the storage locations identified by X and Y. We can change the value in a location by using the letter (variable) for the location in such a way that the value

Figure 1-7. Variables in BASIC

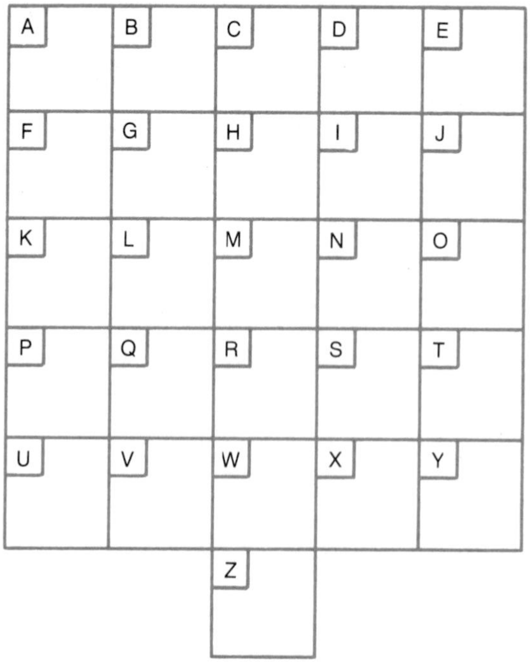

is replaced. In the sample program in Figure 1-6, the variables are X, Y, Z, T, and A.

We combine constants and variables with other symbols to form *expressions*. An expression is an instruction to the computer to perform some operation with data. Usually these are arithmetic operations such as addition, subtraction, multiplication, and division. In the sample program in Figure 1-6 there are two expressions — $X + Y + Z$ and $T/3$. The first expression tells the computer to add the values of the variables X, Y, and Z. The second expression tells the computer to divide the value of the variable T by the constant 3.

1-4 A sample program

We can now begin to understand what the sample program in Figure 1-6 does. Its purpose is to find the total and average of three numbers. The numbers might represent, for example, a student's scores on three tests. The input data is the three test scores. The program gets the scores from an input device, adds the scores to find the total, calculates the average by dividing the total by three, and sends the results of the calculations to an output device.

The actual execution of the program on a computer is shown in Figure 1-8. As we will see, the lines with the question marks contain the input data, which is shown in color in this figure. The other lines are the output. Note that in figures and other examples throughout this book, input data we enter is shown in color; output displayed by the computer is in black.

The first statement in the sample program in Figure 1-6 is a REM statement. This statement is used to put an explanatory comment or remark in a program. In the program in Figure 1-6 the remark in the REM statement identifies the program. As we will see later, REM statements are used often in programs to help explain what a program does and how it works.

The next statement in the program is an INPUT statement. This statement instructs the computer to get some data from an input device and to store the data in the computer's internal storage. We say that the program "accepts" the data from an input device, which, for most programs, is a keyboard. The input data is typed in and stored in the storage locations that are associated with the variables in the INPUT statement. These are the variables X, Y, and Z in the sample program.

The actual effect during execution of the INPUT statement is illustrated in the first line of Figure 1-8. When the INPUT statement is encountered, a question mark is displayed by the computer on the CRT screen. After the question mark appears, the person at the keyboard must type the input data — in this case, three numbers. The numbers must be separated by commas. For example, in the first line of Figure 1-8 the input data that is typed is the numbers 78, 95, and 82. The computer then stores these numbers in the storage locations in the computer's internal storage identified by the letters X, Y, and Z. Thus, after execution of the INPUT statement with the input data shown in Figure 1-8, the value of the variable X is 78, Y is 95, and Z is 82.

Figure 1-8. The result of executing the sample program

```
? 78,95,82
   78          95          82          255         85
? 100,84,92
   100         84          92          276         92
? 78,65,72
   78          65          72          215         71.6667
?
```

Following the INPUT statement in the sample program in Figure 1-6 are two statements that perform calculations. These are called LET statements. The first LET statement instructs the computer to add the values of X, Y, and Z. The result of the calculation (i.e., the total) is stored in the storage location identified by the letter T. The next statement then tells the computer to divide the total just calculated by 3 to obtain the average, which becomes the value of the variable A.

Figure 1-9 summarizes the execution sequence so far by showing the values of the variables at different points in the program. Before the program is executed, the values of the variables (X, Y, Z, T, and A) are unknown. This is shown in Figure 1-9(a). (Some versions of BASIC set all variables to zero before executing the program.) After statement 20 (the INPUT statement) is executed with the data in the first line of Figure 1-8, the values of the variables are as shown in Figure 1-9(b). Notice that X, Y, and Z are equal to 78, 95, and 82, respectively (i.e., the input data), but the values of T and A are still unknown. After the first LET statement (statement 30) is executed, the value of T is the total of X, Y, and Z. This is shown in Figure 1-9(c). With the execution of the second LET statement (statement 40), the average is computed and stored in the storage location identified by the letter A, as shown in Figure 1-9(d).

Statement 50 in the sample program in Figure 1-6 is called a PRINT statement. This statement causes the computer to send the values of all variables given in the PRINT statement to an output device. We say that the program "displays" or "prints" the output on an output device. In this case the values of X, Y, Z, T, and A are displayed on the CRT screen. The second line in Figure 1-8 shows how the output data is displayed. Notice that the data is the current values of the variables shown in Figure 1-9(d).

Following the PRINT statement is a GOTO statement. The number 20 in this statement is the line number of another statement in the program. The effect

Figure 1-9. Variables during the execution of the sample program

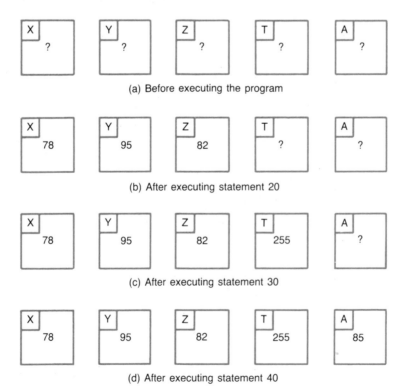

(a) Before executing the program

(b) After executing statement 20

(c) After executing statement 30

(d) After executing statement 40

of execution of this statement is to cause the computer to go to the statement numbered 20 and to continue execution from that point. In this case, the program is repeated from the second statement.

Repeating the program causes the INPUT statement to be executed again. Thus, new input data must be supplied. This is shown in the third line of Figure 1-8. The new input values are the numbers 100, 84, and 92. Before the INPUT statement is executed for the second time, the values of all variables are those remaining from the first execution of the program as shown in Figure 1-10(a). Then the new input data replaces the old values of X, Y, and Z as shown in Figure 1-10(b). Notice that the values of T and A are as yet unchanged. Execution of statement 30 causes a new total to be calculated, replacing the value of T [Figure 1-10(c)]. A new average is then calculated with statement 40, replacing the previous value of A [Figure 1-10(d)]. Finally, the new results are displayed as shown in the fourth line of Figure 1-8.

The program is then repeated a third time with more input data. In fact, the program will continue as long as input data is supplied each time the INPUT statement is executed. The program stops only after a special control character is entered through the keyboard. (This will be described in greater detail in the next section.)

There is one final statement in the sample program — the END statement — which contains only the keyword END. Every BASIC program must have an END statement as its last statement; that is, the highest-numbered statement in a program must be an END statement. The END statement indicates the end of the program to the computer. We will see later how it can be used to stop execution of a program.

These statements make up a complete BASIC program. The statements are performed in the order in which they are written. Thus it is important that they be written in a logical order. For example, the order of the two LET statements cannot be reversed, because the total is used in the calculation of the average and therefore must be calculated first.

Figure 1-10. Variables during the second repetition of the sample program

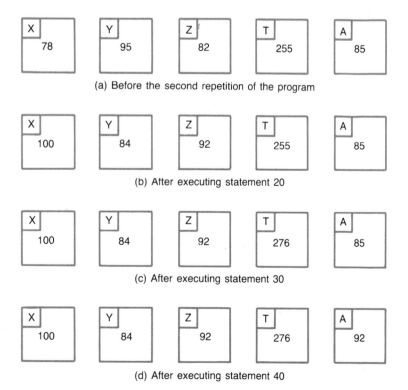

(a) Before the second repetition of the program

(b) After executing statement 20

(c) After executing statement 30

(d) After executing statement 40

Notice that most of the statements in the program are fairly easy to understand. This is especially true of the LET statements, which are written very much like a mathematical formula. Beginning with Chapter 2, we will explain in detail how to write different types of BASIC statements.

1-5 Running a BASIC program

The BASIC program in Figure 1-6 is complete and can be processed or run on a computer. Running a program involves entering the program into the computer, translating the program into machine language, and executing the translated program. In this section we describe how this is done. First we describe program translation and execution. Then we explain how a program is run on two types of computer systems: a microcomputer used by one person at a time and a time-sharing minicomputer used by many people at one time. The explanations are general; the details vary from one computer to another. Finally we discuss error detection.

Program translation and execution

As we have seen, a program written in a high-level language must be translated into machine language before it can take control of the computer. For BASIC the translation process is called either *compilation* or *interpretation,* depending on how it is done. The translation is performed by a special translator program called a *compiler* or an *interpreter.*

As a simple analogy, assume that we have a business with an employee who speaks only French and that we speak only English. Each day when the employee comes to work we must give him or her a list of what we want done during the day. Because we speak only English, we have to prepare the list in English and then have it translated into French. For this purpose we hire an English-to-French translator. This person speaks French but also has an English-to-French dictionary and a grammar book for English. With this information the translator is able to take our list of English-language instructions for the day's work and translate it into an equivalent list in French. Then the French-speaking employee can follow the instructions in the list, performing the task that we want done. This process is illustrated in Figure 1-11.

Essentially the same idea lies behind the translation and execution of a BASIC program. The steps are shown in Figure 1-12. The BASIC program that is prepared by the programmer is called the *source program.* The programmer enters the source program into the computer by typing it on a keyboard. Then the translator program (which is a machine-language program) translates the BASIC program into machine language. The resulting machine-language equivalent of the source program is called the *object program.* After translation, the object program is executed. This often involves getting input data, using the data in calculations and other types of processing, and producing output.

Although the translation of a BASIC program into an object program may seem complicated, to a large extent it is handled automatically by the computer. Most programmers never see their object programs. Instead, the programmer prepares the BASIC source program and the data, and the computer does everything else. It is important to remember, however, that this translation process is required for every BASIC program that is run on a computer.

Figure 1-11. English-to-French translation

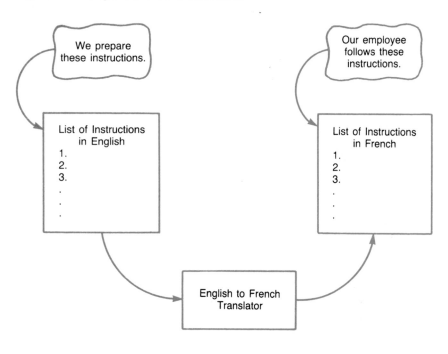

Figure 1-12. BASIC translation and execution

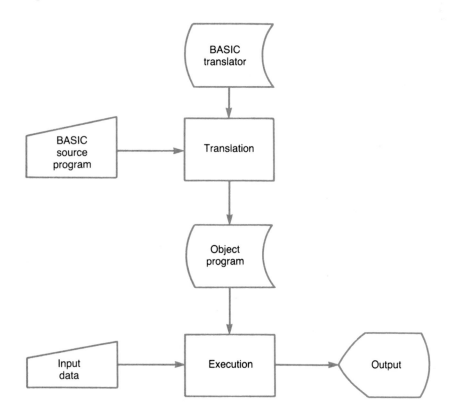

Using a microcomputer†

Most microcomputers are used by one person at a time. In this subsection we describe the general procedures for running a BASIC program on a microcomputer.

Using a keyboard. With a microcomputer, programs and input data are typed in using the keyboard attached to the computer. Each key that is pressed causes the corresponding character (i.e., letter, digit, or special symbol) to be sent into the computer. Each key that is pressed is also displayed on the CRT screen attached to the computer. The space bar is used to advance, just as with a typewriter. If a keying error is made, the error can be corrected by pressing a special key marked BACKSPACE or ← and then keying the correct character.

Only a certain number of characters can be entered on each line. The limit depends on the type of microcomputer being used; typical limits are 40 and 80 characters per line. After a line is typed, a special key that is marked RETURN, ENTER, or ↵ *must* be pressed. This indicates the end of the line to the computer.

Booting the system. Before using a microcomputer it is necessary to turn on the power to the computer. Then the operating system must be stored in the computer's internal storage. This is called "booting" the system. (Recall that the operating system is the set of programs that controls the basic operation of the computer.) The operating system is usually stored on a floppy disk. This disk must be inserted into the appropriate disk drive after the power is turned on. (On some computers the disk is inserted before the power is turned on.) With some computers a special combination of keys has to be pressed to boot the system; with other computers this is not necessary. When the system boots, the computer usually responds by displaying a message. With some computers the symbols A> appear on the screen to indicate that we can continue.

Starting BASIC. After the system is booted it may be necessary to indicate that the BASIC language is going to be used. This may be done by typing the word BASIC or by selecting BASIC from a list of options. After this is done, the computer usually displays a word or symbol such as Ok or] to indicate that it is ready for the next task. Some microcomputers automatically assume that BASIC will be used, in which case this step is not needed.

Various instructions can now be given to the microcomputer. These instructions are called *system commands* and are different from BASIC statements. As we have seen, all BASIC statements begin with a line number. System commands, however, do not have line numbers. In addition, BASIC statements are executed only after all statements in the program have been entered, whereas system commands are executed immediately. There are many system commands; the remainder of this section explains some of these.

Running an existing program. Sometimes we wish to execute an existing program. Usually existing programs are stored in the auxiliary storage, and each is given a unique name to identify it. A program can be executed only if it is in internal storage. Thus we first have to bring the program into the internal storage of the computer. This is done by typing a system command such as LOAD followed by the name of the program in quotation marks. (The quotation marks are not required by some microcomputers.) For example, assume that a program's name is PROGX. We would use the command LOAD "PROGX" to bring this program into the computer's internal

---

† This subsection may be skipped if a different type of computer is used.

storage from auxiliary storage. We can now run the program by typing the command RUN. This command causes the program to be translated *and* executed. During the execution of the program we may have to supply input data. The input data must be separated by commas, and the RETURN or ENTER key must be pressed after the data has been typed.

Entering and running a new program. If we wish to enter and run our own program, we begin by typing a command that clears out any existing program in internal storage. This command is usually the word NEW. If we have just booted the system, this step is not necessary because no program exists in internal storage.

We can now begin to enter a BASIC program. Each line of the program is typed exactly as it is written. In most cases it doesn't matter whether upper or lowercase is used; the computer converts lowercase letters to uppercase. With some computers, however, everything must be typed in uppercase. Keying mistakes are corrected by backspacing and rekeying. If an entire line is wrong, we can simply retype the line and the computer will replace the old line with the new one. A line can be erased completely by typing its line number. Although the line numbers must be in increasing sequence in the program, we can enter the lines out of order and the computer will rearrange them. For example, we can first enter line 10, then line 30, and finally line 20. The computer will arrange the lines in the proper numerical sequence.

After we have entered part or all of the program, we can list the program on the CRT screen by using the system command LIST. We can list the program on the printer by using a command such as LLIST. Any errors that were corrected while the program was being entered will not appear in the listing.

To run the program we type the command RUN. This causes the computer to translate and execute the statements in the program in sequence, beginning with the first. While the program is running, we may have to supply input data (as in the sample program in Figure 1-6). To stop the program from running (for example, when we do not want to enter any more input data), we use a special control character. On some computers this involves holding down the key marked Ctrl (for control) and pressing the key marked Break (called a "control break"). This is how the sample program was stopped in the last line of Figure 1-8.

Saving a program. If we wish to save a program for future use, we type the system command SAVE followed by a name for the program in quotation marks. (The quotation marks are not required by some microcomputers.) Typically a program name can be no more than six to eight characters. For example, we may wish to save the program in internal storage with the name PROGY. This would be accomplished by typing the command SAVE "PROGY". This stores the program that is currently in internal storage in auxiliary storage and identifies it by the name. (If a program is not saved, it will be lost when we finish using BASIC or when we start a new program.) We can retrieve a saved program at some time in the future by using the LOAD command discussed earlier. We can replace a saved program with the program in internal storage by using the SAVE command. If we want to destroy a previously saved program, we type a command such as KILL followed by the name of the program in quotation marks. (The quotation marks are not required by some microcomputers.)

Ending BASIC. When we are done, it is necessary with some microcomputers to indicate that the BASIC language will no longer be used. This is accomplished by a command such as the word SYSTEM. With many computers this step is not necessary.

After we are finished, the computer can be turned off. The disk containing the operating system should be removed from the disk drive and then the power turned off. (On some computers the disk is removed after the power is turned off.)

Summary of system commands. Figure 1-13 shows an example of the display that results from entering and running a program on a typical microcomputer. In this figure, items we enter are shown in color; items displayed by the computer are in black. We assume in the sequence in Figure 1-13 that the computer has been turned on and the system has been booted. First we indicate that the BASIC language is going to be used by typing the command BASIC. Then we enter a new program. After the program is entered, we run it. While the program is running, an error is detected. (We will discuss error detection later.) We correct the error and list the corrected version of the program. Next we run the program, supplying input data and getting output. Finally, we save the program for future use and end the use of BASIC with the SYSTEM command.

The system commands that we have described here vary from one computer to another, although their basic functions are the same. In addition, there are usually many other commands that we have not discussed. Appendix B lists the system commands for several common computers. The programmer will have to determine the exact form of each command for the computer being used.

Using a minicomputer (time-sharing)†

Minicomputers are usually used by many people at one time. This is accomplished by the process called time-sharing, which we discussed earlier. In this subsection we describe the general procedures for running a BASIC program on a time-sharing minicomputer. The concepts also apply to many mainframe computers and to some large microcomputers.

Using a terminal. With a minicomputer, programs and input data are typed in through the keyboard of a terminal. Each time a key is pressed, the corresponding character (i.e., letter, digit, or special symbol) is sent to the computer. Each keyed character is also displayed on the terminal's CRT screen. The space bar can be used to advance just as with a typewriter. If a keying error is made, it is possible to backspace by pressing a special key that is marked RUBOUT, DELETE, or something similar. The correct character can then be keyed.

Only a certain number of characters can be entered on each line. The limit depends on the type of terminal being used, but typically it is 80 characters per line. At the end of each line, a special key that is usually marked RETURN *must* be pressed. This indicates the end of the line to the computer.

Logging in. Before using the computer through a terminal, we must perform a procedure called "logging in" to connect the terminal to the computer. The actual procedure that is used depends on the computer, but typically it involves pressing the RETURN key or typing a certain word such as HELLO. Then a user ID number or account number is entered, followed by a special word called a password. (The account number and password are normally supplied by the computer center that operates the computer.) It is important to remember that after anything is entered into the computer, the RETURN key on the keyboard must be pressed. If the log-in procedure is followed correctly, the computer will usually respond by displaying a message signifying that we can proceed. Sometimes a symbol such as a dollar sign ($) appears to indicate that we can continue.

Starting BASIC. After logging in, it is sometimes necessary to indicate that the BASIC language is going to be used. This is usually done by typing the word BASIC or

---

† This subsection may be skipped if a different type of computer is used.

Figure 1-13. Entering and running a BASIC program on a microcomputer

```
A>BASIC

Ok
10 REM - TOTAL AND AVERAGE PROGRAM
20 INPUT X,Y,Z
30    LET T=X+Y+Z
40    LET A-T/3
50    PRINT X,Y,Z,T,A
60 GOTO 20
70 END
RUN
? 78,95,82
Syntax error in 40
Ok
40    LET A=T/3
LIST
10 REM - TOTAL AND AVERAGE PROGRAM
20 INPUT X,Y,Z
30    LET T=X+Y+Z
40    LET A=T/3
50    PRINT X,Y,Z,T,A
60 GOTO 20
70 END
Ok
RUN
? 78,95,82
 78             95          82          255         85
? 76,39,84
 76             39          84          199         66.3333
?
Break in 20
Ok
SAVE "DEMO1"
Ok
SYSTEM

A>
```

something similar. After this is typed, the computer usually displays a word such as Ready to indicate that it is ready for the next task. Some computers automatically assume that BASIC will be used, in which case this step is not needed.

Various instructions can now be given to the computer. These instructions are called *system commands* and are different from BASIC statements. As we have seen, all BASIC statements begin with a line number. System commands, however, do not have line numbers. In addition, BASIC statements are executed only after all statements in the program have been entered, whereas system commands are executed immediately. There are many system commands; the remainder of this section explains some of them.

Running an existing program. On occasion we may wish to execute an existing program. Usually existing programs are stored in auxiliary storage, and each is given a unique name to identify it. A program can be executed only if it is in internal storage. Thus, we first have to bring the program into the internal storage of the computer. This is done by typing a system command such as OLD followed by the name of the program. For example, assume that the program's name is PROGX. We would use the command OLD PROGX to bring this program into the computer's internal storage from auxiliary storage. We can now run this program by typing the command RUN. This command causes the program to be translated *and* executed. During the execution of the program we may have to supply input data. Input data must be separated by commas, and the RETURN key must be pressed after the data has been typed.

Entering and running a new program. If we wish to enter and run our own program, we begin by typing a command that clears out any old program in the internal storage and indicates that a new program is about to be entered. This command is usually the word NEW. Following this we give the new program a name. Typically a program name can be no more than six or eight characters long. The name is usually typed after the word NEW (e.g., NEW PROGY).

We can now begin to enter a BASIC program. Each line of the program is typed exactly as it is written. In most cases it doesn't matter whether upper or lowercase is used; the computer converts lowercase letters to uppercase. If keying mistakes are made, they can be corrected by backspacing and rekeying. If an entire line is wrong, we can simply retype the line and the computer will replace the old line with the new one. A line can be erased completely just by typing its line number. Although the line numbers must be in increasing order, we can enter the lines out of sequence and the computer will rearrange them. For example, we can first enter line 10, then line 30, and finally line 20. The computer will arrange the lines in the proper numerical sequence.

After we have entered part or all of the program, we can list the program on the CRT screen by using the system command LIST. Depending on the computer system being used, the LIST command or a different command or sometimes several commands are needed to list the program on the printer. Any errors that were corrected while the program was being entered will not appear in the listing.

To run the program we type the command RUN. This causes the computer to translate and execute the statements in the program in sequence beginning with the first statement. While the program is running, we may have to supply input data (as in the sample program in Figure 1-6). To stop the program from running (for example, when we do not want to enter any more input data), we use a special control character. On many computers this involves holding down a key marked CTRL (for control) and pressing the letter C (called a "control C"). This is how the sample program was stopped in the last line of Figure 1-8.

Saving a program. If we wish to save a program for future use, we type the system command SAVE. This stores the program in auxiliary storage and identifies it by the name that we gave it earlier. (If a program is not saved, it will be lost when we disconnect the terminal from the computer or when we start a new program.) We can retrieve a saved program at some time in the future by using the OLD command described earlier. We can replace a saved program with the program in internal storage by using a command such as REPLACE. If we want to destroy a previously saved program, we type a command such as UNSAVE followed by the name of the program.

Ending BASIC. When we are done, it is necessary with some computers to indicate that the BASIC language will no longer be used. This is accomplished by a command such as the word EXIT. With many computers this step is not necessary.

Logging out. After we have finished using the computer, we must disconnect the terminal. This is often called "logging out" and is usually done by typing the word BYE or the word LOGOUT. After doing this, we must log in if we wish to use the computer again.

Summary of system commands. Figure 1-14 shows an example of the display that results from entering and running a program on a typical computer. In this figure,

Figure 1-14. Entering and running a BASIC program on a minicomputer

```
User: 12,34
Password: ABCD

Ready

NEW DEMO1

Ready

10 REM - TOTAL AND AVERAGE PROGRAM
20 INPUT X,Y,Z
30    LET T=X+Y+Z
40    LET A=
?Syntax error at line 40

Ready

40    LET A=T/3
50    PRINT X,Y,Z,T,A
60 GOTO 20
70 END
LIST
DEMO1
10 REM - TOTAL AND AVERAGE PROGRAM
20 INPUT X,Y,Z
30    LET T=X+Y+Z
40    LET A=T/3
50    PRINT X,Y,Z,T,A
60 GOTO 20
70 END

Ready

RUN
DEMO1
? 78,95,82
 78          95          82          255         85
? 76,39,84
 76          39          84          199         66.3333
?

Ready

SAVE

Ready

BYE
```

items we enter are shown in color; items displayed by the computer are in black. In the sequence shown in Figure 1-14, we first log in with the required account number and password. (Usually the password does not show on the CRT.) Then we start a new program, giving it an appropriate name. While entering the program, we correct a line with an error by retyping the line entirely. (We will discuss error detection later.) We then list the corrected version of the program. Next we run the program, supplying input data and getting output. Finally, we save the program for future use and log out.

The system commands that we have described here vary from one computer to another, although their basic functions are the same. In addition, there are usually many other commands that we have not discussed. Appendix B lists the system commands for several common computers. The programmer will have to determine the exact form of each command for the computer being used.

Error detection

In our description of the running of a BASIC program we assumed that the program contains no errors. In fact, one of the biggest problems that a programmer faces is the detection and correction of errors. More often than not, the program does not complete its run successfully. It is the programmer's responsibility to locate and correct any errors in the program.

There are three times that errors may be detected in the processing of the program: during translation, during execution, and after execution. The computer can detect errors that occur during the first two times, but the programmer must detect any errors during the third.

Errors can be discovered by the computer when the program is being translated into machine language. These are usually errors that the programmer has made in the use of the language and are called *syntax errors*. For example, spelling a keyword incorrectly is a syntax error. When such an error is detected, a message that describes the error and indicates the error's location in the program is displayed. The message may appear after the RUN command is typed (see Figure 1-13) or it may be displayed immediately after the line that contains the error is entered (see Figure 1-14). Even though an error has been detected, it cannot be corrected by the computer and the program will not execute. The programmer must correct any syntax errors that are detected.

If the program has no syntax errors, the computer can execute it. During execution, other errors may appear. These are called *execution errors*. For example, an attempt to divide a number by zero causes an execution error. Whenever an execution error is detected, the computer displays an error code or error message and stops executing the program. The programmer must correct the error.

The final type of error is detected only after the program has been executed. If the output from the program does not agree with what is expected, there is a *logic error* in the program. For example, if, in the sample program in Figure 1-6, the first LET statement (statement 30) had been incorrectly written as

```
30 LET T=X-Y-Z
```

then no syntax or execution error would be detected. The final output would be incorrect, however, because the total of three numbers is found by adding the numbers, not by subtracting them. This error is in the logic of the program. The computer cannot detect such an error because it does not know what the logic of the program should be.

It is the programmer's responsibility to detect logic errors in the program. This is done by making up input data to test the program. The programmer figures out what output should be produced by the program using this test data. Then the output from running the program with the test idea is compared with the expected output. Any discrepancy indicates an error that must be corrected. This procedure is called *program testing;* we will have more to say about it later.

Any error in a computer program is called a *bug*. The process of locating and correcting bugs in a program is called *debugging*. Only after a program has been debugged completely can the programmer be reasonably sure that the program is correct.

1-6 Problem solving and the programming process

At the beginning of this chapter we said that programming involves preparing a computer program to solve a problem. It is important to emphasize that programming is a problem-solving process; that is, given a particular problem, how do we develop a computer program that solves the problem? In this section we discuss problem solving and the programming process. First, however, we need to understand the concept of an algorithm.

Algorithms

An *algorithm* is a set of steps that, if carried out, results in the solution of a problem. For example, consider the problem of finding the total and average of sets of data where each set consists of three numbers. Figure 1-15 shows an algorithm that solves this problem. This algorithm corresponds to the logic of the sample program in Figure 1-6. If this algorithm is properly carried out, the total and average problem will be solved.

One of the main tasks in programming is to develop an algorithm to solve the required problem. Given a problem, the programmer must figure out what steps the computer has to go through to solve it. Only after these steps are determined can the program be written. This task of developing an algorithm can be one of the most difficult in the programming process, and we will have more to say about it later.

An algorithm can be expressed in many forms. It may be written in English, described in mathematical notation, or drawn in a diagram. Figure 1-15 shows one way of expressing an algorithm. A computer program written in a programming language is also a representation of an algorithm.

Flowcharts. A tool that is sometimes used to express an algorithm is a *flowchart*. This is a diagram of an algorithm for a computer program. For example, Figure 1-16 shows a flowchart of the algorithm for the sample program in Figure 1-6. The flowchart is drawn using special symbols connected by lines. Within each symbol is written a phrase that describes the activity at that step. The lines connecting the symbols show the sequence in which the steps take place. The flowchart in Figure 1-16 depicts the sequence of steps in the program in Figure 1-6.

In a flowchart, the shape of the symbol indicates the type of activity that is to take place. Figure 1-17 shows the standard program flowchart symbols adopted by the American National Standards Institute (ANSI). The *terminal point symbol* appears at the beginning and at the end of the flowchart. The *input/output symbol* is used for any step that involves input or output of data. The *process symbol* is used to represent any general processing activity such as an arithmetic calculation or a manipulation of data. The *decision symbol* is used whenever a decision is made in the program. The *connector symbol* is used to connect parts of a flowchart. Finally, *flowlines* show the direction of the flow of logic in the flowchart.

The flowchart in Figure 1-16 illustrates some of these symbols. The terminal point symbol is used to mark the point where the flowchart logic starts and where it ends. The input/output symbol shows where the input data is accepted and the output is displayed. The process symbol is used for the calculation steps. Notice that the flowchart symbols do not necessarily correspond directly to individual instructions in the program. For example, the process symbol in the flowchart in Figure 1-16 corresponds to two arithmetic calculations in the program. The *sequence* of symbols, however, does follow exactly the *sequence* of steps in the algorithm, which is the

Figure 1-15. Algorithm for the total and average problem

Repeat the following until there is no more data:
    Accept three numbers.
    Compute the total and average of the numbers.
    Display the three numbers, total, and average.

Figure 1-16. Flowchart of the sample program

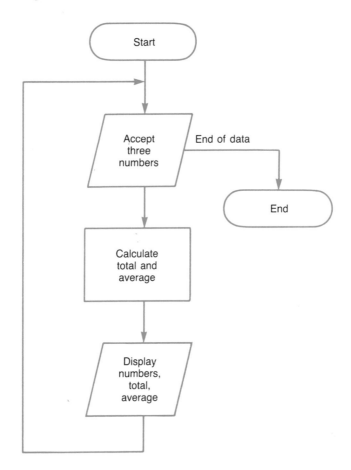

same as the sequence of instructions in the program. By beginning with the symbol marked START and following the flowlines through the flowchart to the END symbol, we can understand the algorithm for the program.

Some of the flowchart symbols in Figure 1-17 are not used in the example in Figure 1-16. In later chapters we will discuss the use of these other symbols.

The programming process

When preparing a computer program to solve a particular problem, a programmer performs several tasks. One is to write the instructions in the program. This, however, is only one activity in the programming process. In fact, five main activities must be completed:

1. Understand and define the problem
2. Design the program
3. Code the program
4. Show that the program is correct
5. Document the program

In this subsection we briefly describe each of these activities. In later chapters we will have more to say about each.

Problem definition. The first step in the programming process is to understand and define the problem to be solved. Understanding the problem involves determining

Figure 1-17. ANSI flowchart symbols

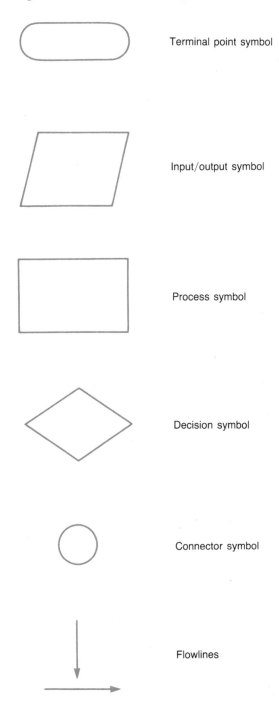

Terminal point symbol

Input/output symbol

Process symbol

Decision symbol

Connector symbol

Flowlines

its requirements and how they can be met. The programmer must know what the program is required to do. This usually means understanding what output it must produce and what computations it must perform. In addition, the programmer must determine what resources are available to meet these requirements. This includes determining the available input. Specifying the input, computation, and output requirements forms the problem definition.

Program design. Having gained an understanding of the problem, the programmer can begin to design a program to solve it. The sequence of steps that is necessary to solve the problem must be carefully planned. This sequence forms the algorithm for the program solution. The programmer may express the algorithm in a flowchart or may use some other technique. This program-designing activity does *not* involve writing the instructions for the program. Before the program can be written, the programmer must develop the algorithm to solve the problem.

Program coding. After the algorithm to solve the problem has been planned, the program can be written. This is called *coding* the program. The programmer uses his or her knowledge of the computer language, an understanding of the problem to be solved, and the algorithm determined previously. With this background the programmer codes the program to solve the problem by writing the necessary computer-language instructions.

Program correctness. The next step is to test the program by running it on the computer with some input data. The output produced is then compared with the expected output; any discrepancy indicates an error which must be corrected. Testing the program in this manner will not necessarily find all the errors, but it will usually point out any serious problems. The actual process of determining the correctness of a program involves much more than just testing the program on a computer. A program is correct because it makes sense logically. The programmer makes sure of this as he or she plans and codes the program.

Program documentation. Finally, the programming process is completed by bringing together all the material that describes the program. This is called *documenting* the program, and the result is the program's *documentation.* Included in the documentation are the program listing, descriptions of the input and output data, and a flowchart. Documentation enables other programmers to understand how the program functions. Often it is necessary to return to the program after a period of time and to make corrections or changes. With adequate documentation it is much easier to understand a program's operation.

   Throughout the next few chapters of this book we will discuss different aspects of these five activities of the programming process. In Chapter 6 we will examine the programming process in detail.

Review questions

1. What are the five basic components of a computer?
2. Data to be processed by a computer is called _____; the result produced by a computer is called _____.
3. Name one input device and two output devices.
4. The unit of a computer that does the actual computing or processing is the _____.
5. What units of the computer are found in the CPU?
6. What is the difference in function between internal storage and auxiliary storage?
7. Name two common forms of auxiliary storage.
8. What is a computer program?
9. What happens in the CPU during the execution of a program?
10. The rules that describe how the instructions of a computer programming language are formed are called the _____ of the language. The meanings or effects of the instructions in a computer programming language are called the _____ of the language.
11. What is the difference between a machine-language program and a high-level language program?
12. Translation of a program written in a high-level language into machine language is called _____.

13. What is the difference between application software and system software?
14. What is an operating system?
15. Explain the difference between batch processing and interactive processing. Give an example of each.
16. What is time-sharing?
17. Can a program that is written in BASIC be processed on different types of computers? Explain.
18. Each instruction in a BASIC program is called a _____.
19. Each statement in a BASIC program must begin with a _____.
20. What are keywords?
21. What is the difference between a constant and a variable?
22. What is the difference between a source program and an object program?
23. What is the function of system commands? Are they part of the BASIC language?
24. Explain the difference between syntax errors, execution errors, and logic errors.
25. Explain the process of program testing.
26. An error in a program is called a _____.
27. What is an algorithm?
28. A diagram of an algorithm for a computer program is called a _____.
29. The process of writing the instructions in a computer program is called _____.
30. What are the five activities in the programming process?

Computer exercises

1. Investigate the computer that you will use to process programs that you will prepare. Who manufactured the computer and what model is it? What input and output devices are available? What type of auxiliary storage does it use? Is it a mainframe, mini, or microcomputer? What operating system does it use? What version of BASIC will you be using? What computer languages other than BASIC are available on the computer?

2. The program shown in Figure 1-6 is complete and can be run on a computer. Doing so will help you to become familiar with the structure of BASIC, the system commands, and the procedures for entering and running a program.

   If you are using a microcomputer, boot the system. If you are using a minicomputer, log in. Then follow the procedure necessary to indicate that the BASIC language is going to be used. (This step may not be needed.) Next enter the sample program exactly as it is shown in Figure 1-6. Any syntax errors that occur are probably the result of keying mistakes and must be corrected. After any errors are corrected, list the program. Then run the program with the input data shown in Figure 1-8. Check the output to be certain it is correct. Finally, run the program with several additional sets of input data.

Chapter 2

Essential elements of BASIC

When we write a computer program to solve a problem, we prepare a sequence of instructions for the computer to follow. Many different sequences can be used, depending on the problem to be solved. One *pattern,* however, appears over and over again. This pattern is simply

input → process → output

That is, first the computer accepts some input data to be used in the problem solution. Then the processing and computation necessary to solve the problem using the input data is carried out. Finally, the output data that represents the results of the processing is produced.

For example, in Chapter 1 we saw a sample program that computes the total and average of three numbers. The first step in this program was to accept the three numbers (i.e., the input data). Then the processing involved calculating the total and average of the numbers. Finally, the results were displayed.

Many other patterns appear in computer programs, but this is one of the most common. The input, process, and output steps may each be quite complex, especially the process step.

In this chapter we describe the elements of BASIC that are essential for practically all programs. These elements include the statements necessary for simple input and output, for numeric data processing, and for program repetition. After completing this chapter you should be able to write programs that involve input, output, and numeric computations. In later chapters we will discuss various other types of processing that can be done in a BASIC program.

2-1 Constants and variables

In Chapter 1 we introduced the ideas of constants and variables in a program. In this section we elaborate on these ideas and give specific rules for constants and variables in BASIC.

Simple constants

A *constant* is a fixed data value that is used in a program. For the time being we will be concerned only with constants that are numbers. A constant is formed from digits (0, 1, 2, . . . , 9) and may include a decimal point and possibly a plus or minus sign. For example, the following are valid constants in BASIC:

```
482.59        0.00056
25            +16
-18           0.0
+5.1083       -128.9
0             5280
```

Note that a constant *cannot* contain a comma or a space. Thus, the number 5,280 is not a valid constant in BASIC.

E-notation constants

Sometimes it is necessary to write very large or very small constants. For example, we may wish to use the following constants in a program:

```
-128460000000000
0.000000000008203
```

Although we can use constants such as these, it is tedious to write them. Therefore, we use a shorthand notation, called *E-notation*.

E-notation is similar to scientific notation. To write a number in scientific notation, we shift the decimal point until it is just after the first nonzero digit. We then multiply the number obtained by the power of ten necessary to shift the decimal point back to its correct place. For example, the two numbers above can be written in scientific notation as follows:

$$-1.2846 \times 10^{14}$$
$$8.203 \times 10^{-12}$$

Notice that the exponent (i.e., the power of ten) is the number of places that the decimal point is shifted. If, in converting from standard form to scientific notation, the decimal point is shifted to the left, the exponent is positive; if it is shifted to the right, the exponent is negative.

In BASIC we write a constant in E-notation by substituting the letter E for the symbols "$\times 10$" in the scientific notation. Then the exponent is written immediately after the E. For example, the two numbers given earlier are written as follows in E-notation:

```
-1.2846E14
 8.203E-12
```

The E means "times ten to the power". Thus, the first constant is -1.2846 times ten to the power 14 and the second constant is 8.203 times ten to the power -12.

In writing an E-notation constant, we can place the decimal point anywhere, as long as we adjust the exponent appropriately. For example, the following are all equivalent to the first example above:

```
-0.12846E15
-128.46E12
-12846.0E10
-12846E10
```

In the last of these, the decimal point is omitted, in which case it is assumed to be to the right of the last digit. Note also that the exponent must have a minus sign if it is negative (as in $8.203E-12$), but a plus sign is optional for a positive exponent. Thus, $-1.2846E14$ and $-1.2846E+14$ are equivalent.

As we will see, E-notation is important not only because it is used for constants in a program, but also because output is sometimes displayed in E-notation. The programmer can convert a number in E-notation to its standard form by remembering that the exponent indicates the number of places that the decimal point is shifted. If the exponent of an E-notation number is positive, the decimal point should be shifted to the right the number of places given by the exponent to convert the number to standard form. If the exponent is negative, the decimal point should be shifted to the left the number of places given by the exponent.

The following are additional examples of constants written with and without E-notation:

Simple constant	E-notation constant
48003600	4.80036E7
$-.000003921$	$-3.921E-6$
-5863.25	$-.586325E+4$
1000000000	1E9
$+.0000087$	$+0.87E-5$

Variables

A *variable* is a name that refers to data in a program. For the time being we will be concerned only with variables that refer to numeric data. As we saw in Chapter 1, a variable identifies a storage location in the computer's internal storage. Each storage location can store one number. Depending on how the variable for a particular storage location is used, we can retrieve the number that is stored in the location or change the value that is stored there.

In Chapter 1 we indicated that the twenty-six letters of the alphabet can be used for variables. In fact, for many programs we need more than twenty-six variables. To make this possible, BASIC syntax allows variables consisting of a letter or a letter followed by a single digit (0, 1, 2, ..., 9). Thus, the following are valid variables in BASIC:

A	H1
A0	J4
A3	M2
A7	S8
A9	Z5

Notice that a letter (e.g., A) and the same letter followed by a digit (e.g., A3) are *different* variables referring to *different* storage locations. The fact that two variables begin with the same letter does not make them the same.

A variable must always begin with a letter and cannot contain a blank space. Thus the following are *not* valid variables in BASIC for the reasons given:

3Z	(does not begin with a letter)
X 5	(contains a blank space)

Depending on the version of BASIC, variables with more than one letter or more than one digit may not be permitted. Other symbols also may not be allowed in a variable. Thus, the following may not be valid variables in BASIC for the reasons given:

```
A27     (contains two digits)
XY      (contains more than one letter)
B.      (contains a period)
```

Long variables. The syntax of variables in some versions of BASIC may be different than that given here. (See Table 2-1.) Often variables are allowed to have many letters and digits plus special characters such as periods or underlines. Sometimes we call these "long" variables. For example, the following are valid variables in different versions of BASIC:

```
AMOUNT
UNIT_PRICE
TOTAL.AMOUNT.DUE
X37Z
M...N
A$5_Z.X9
```

Note that a variable may never contain a blank space and must always begin with a letter.

Using long variables that stand for the data which they identify can make a program easier to read. For example, instead of using the variables T and A for the total and average we could use the variables TOTAL and AVERAGE. If permitted, special characters such as periods may be used where we might want to put a blank space to make the variable easier to read. For example, the variable TOTAL.AMOUNT.DUE is easy to read and understand.

Because long variables are not available in all versions of BASIC and because, when available, their syntax rules vary considerably, we will use only variables that

Table 2-1. Variable differences

BASIC version	Variable syntax
ANS minimal BASIC	A letter or a letter followed by a single digit
ANS BASIC	1 to 31 letters, digits, and underlines beginning with a letter
Microsoft BASIC	Any number of letters, digits, and periods beginning with a letter; only the first 40 characters are used to distinguish variables
Applesoft BASIC	1 to 239 letters and digits beginning with a letter; only the first two characters are used to distinguish variables
True BASIC	1 to 31 letters, digits, and underlines beginning with a letter
BASIC-PLUS	NOEXTEND mode: a letter or a letter followed by a single digit EXTEND mode: 1 to 30 letters, digits, and periods beginning with a letter
VAX-11 BASIC	1 to 31 letters, digits, dollar signs, underlines, and periods beginning with a letter

satisfy the simple syntax rules given earlier in our examples. If long variables are available, however, they should usually be used so that the program is easier to read.

Limitations on data values

The BASIC language does not set a limit on the size of numbers that can be used for constants or that can be assigned to variables. Computers, however, have limited capacities, so there are limits to the values that can be used with any particular computer. We will illustrate these limitations with a typical computer, but details will vary from one machine to another.

Usually all numbers used in BASIC are stored in the computer in a form similar to E-notation. In this form, known as *floating-point notation,* the number is converted to E-notation with the decimal point just to the left of the first nonzero digit. Thus, the number 28.35 would be converted to .2835E2 and the number .058 would be converted to .58E $-$ 1. The limitations on sizes of numbers are expressed in terms of the maximum number of digits between the decimal point and the E (called the fraction) and in terms of the maximum and minimum exponent.

On a typical computer there can be at most six digits in the fraction (i.e., between the decimal point and the E). If a number is written with more than six digits, it is rounded off to six digits and all other digits are converted to zeros. For example, the constant 123456789 would be rounded off to 123457000 and stored in E-notation as .123457E9.

The exponent on a typical computer can range between $+38$ and -38 (i.e., the number can have a magnitude between 10^{+38} and 10^{-38}). For example, the constant .987654E36 is acceptable, as is the constant .234567E $-$ 37. If, however, an exponent is outside this range, the constant is usually not valid. For example, the constant .192837E45 is invalid and results in an error.

The limitations on data values apply to all numeric values used in a program. Thus, all constants, the values of all variables, and all input and output data must be within the limits for the computer being used.

2-2 Numeric data processing

Numeric data processing involves computations with numbers. For example, computing an employee's pay or calculating the trajectory of a rocket involves processing numeric data. In this section we describe the elements of BASIC that are essential for this type of computation. These elements include numeric expressions and the LET statement.

Numeric operators and simple numeric expressions

A *numeric expression* is an instruction to the computer to perform arithmetic. Numeric expressions are formed from constants, variables, and numeric operators.

Numeric operators are symbols that indicate what form of arithmetic is to be performed. The symbols used in BASIC and their meanings are as follows:

Numeric operator	Meaning
+	Add
–	Subtract
*	Multiply
/	Divide
^	Exponentiate (i.e., raise to a power)

To form a simple numeric expression using these symbols, we write an unsigned constant or variable on each side of the operator. For example, the following are valid numeric expressions in BASIC:

```
A+B
X−Y
2*K
T/3
X^2
```

Each of these expressions tells the computer to perform the indicated operation using the values of the variables and constants. For example, A+B means add the value of A and the value of B. If A is 8.3 and B is 5.2, then the value of A+B is 13.5. With subtraction, the value on the right of the subtraction operator is subtracted from the value on the left. Thus, X−Y means subtract the value of Y from the value of X. Notice that multiplication is indicated by the asterisk symbol. Hence, 2*K means multiply the value of K by the constant 2. With division, the value on the left of the division operator is divided by the value on the right. Thus, T/3 means divide the value of T by 3. Exponentiation means raise the value on the left of the operator to the power of the value on the right. Hence, X^2 means raise the value of X to the second power (i.e., square the value of X).

Any variable and any type of constant can be used in a numeric expression. This includes variables composed of more than one symbol (such as X5) and E-notation constants. For example, the following are valid numeric expressions:

```
X5−Z3
A/3.7E15
B7*3E8
```

It is important not to confuse an E-notation constant with the exponentiation operator. For example, 3E8 is the constant 300000000, whereas 3^8 means raise three to the eighth power (which is 6561).

The plus and minus signs may be used alone in front of a single constant or variable to form a numeric expression. In fact, a variable or a constant by itself is considered to be a numeric expression. Hence, each of the following is a numeric expression:

```
3
J
+7.5
+P
−.0063
−A
```

In the last example, if the value of A is −6.2, then the value of the numeric expression is −(−6.2) or 6.2.

Evaluation of complex numeric expressions

To form more complex numeric expressions, several numeric operators are used. For example, the following are valid numeric expressions:

```
E5/F3+2.5
8−I*J
A*X^2+B*X−C
3.14159*R^2
−B+B/2/A
```

With complex numeric expressions the order in which the operations are performed is very important. The order is as follows:

1. All exponentiation is performed.
2. All multiplication and division is performed left-to-right.
3. All addition and subtraction is performed left-to-right.

For example, consider the following expression:

```
8.7-A*2.4/B+C^2+D
```

Figure 2-1 shows how this expression is evaluated if the value of A is 6.0, B is 4.0, C is 2.0, and D is 1.0. The expression is evaluated in the following order:

1. The values of all variables are substituted in the expression.
2. The value of C is raised to the second power.
3. The value of A is multiplied by 2.4.
4. The result from step 3 is divided by the value of B.
5. The result from step 4 is subtracted from 8.7.
6. The result from step 5 is added to the result from step 2.
7. The value of D is added to the result from step 6.

In algebraic notation, the expression is as follows:

$$8.7 - \frac{A \times 2.4}{B} + C^2 + D$$

To change the order of evaluation, numeric expressions can be enclosed in parentheses and combined with other expressions. When this is done, expressions in parentheses are evaluated before operations outside the parentheses are performed. For example, consider the following modification of the previous expression:

```
8.7-A*2.4/(B+C^2)+D
```

Figure 2-1. Evaluation of a numeric expression

Expression	8.7 − A * 2.4 / B + C ^ 2 + D
1. Substitute	8.7 − 6.0 * 2.4 / 4.0 + 2.0 ^ 2 + 1.0
2. Exponentiate	2.0 ^ 2
3. Multiply	6.0 * 2.4
4. Divide	14.4 / 4.0
5. Subtract	8.7 − 3.6
6. Add	5.1 + 4.0
7. Add	9.1 + 1.0
Final result	10.1

The expression B+C^2 is enclosed in parentheses and is evaluated before any other operations are carried out. Thus, the computer first raises the value of C to the second power and adds the result to the value of B. Next, the value of A is multiplied by 2.4, and the result is divided by the value of B+C^2. Finally, the other addition and subtraction are performed. Figure 2-2 shows the evaluation sequence for the data given earlier. The equivalent expression in algebraic notation is as follows:

$$8.7 - \frac{A \times 2.4}{B + C^2} + D$$

Numeric expressions in parentheses may be imbedded in other parenthetic expressions. When this is done, the computer evaluates the expression in the innermost parentheses before continuing with the expression in the next level of parentheses. For example, consider the following:

    8.7-A*(2.4/(B+C^2)+D)

First the computer evaluates B+C^2. The result is divided into 2.4 and the value of D is added. The final multiplication by A and subtraction from 8.7 are then performed. In algebraic notation, this expression is as follows:

$$8.7 - A \times \left(\frac{2.4}{B + C^2} + D \right)$$

When using parentheses, as in these examples, each left parenthesis must have a matching right parenthesis. Extra sets of parentheses that do not change the order of evaluation can always be used. Brackets are not allowed in numeric expressions in BASIC.

A common mistake when writing a numeric expression is to forget that certain operations are performed before others. For example, assume that the programmer must write a numeric expression in BASIC for the following algebraic expression:

$$\frac{A + B}{C + D}$$

Figure 2-2. Evaluation of a numeric expression containing parentheses

Expression	8.7 − A * 2.4 / (B + C ^ 2) + D
1. Substitute	8.7 − 6.0 * 2.4 / (4.0 + 2.0 ^ 2) + 1.0
2. Exponentiate	2.0 ^ 2
3. Add	4.0 + 4.0
4. Multiply	6.0 * 2.4
5. Divide	14.4 / 8.0
6. Subtract	8.7 − 1.8
7. Add	6.9 + 1.0
Final result	7.9

In coding the expression, the programmer may hastily write the following:

    A+B/C+D

This is incorrect because division is done before addition, and this numeric expression is therefore interpreted as follows:

$$A + \frac{B}{C} + D$$

To force the additions to be done before the division, the programmer must use parentheses. The correct numeric expression is as follows:

    (A+B)/(C+D)

It is important to remember that when there is a series of multiplications and divisions, the order of evaluations is left-to-right. Thus, in the expressions A/B*C the division is performed first and the result is multiplied by C. Hence, in algebraic notation the expression is

$$\frac{A}{B} \times C$$

If we wish to write the algebraic expression

$$\frac{A}{B \times C}$$

in BASIC, we must use parentheses to have the multiplication done before the division. Thus, the equivalent BASIC expression for this example is

    A/(B*C)

The left-to-right evaluation also applies to addition and subtraction. For example, in the expression $J-K+L$ the subtraction is done first, followed by the addition. If J is 3, K is 2, and L is 1, the value of this expression is 2. Had we interpreted the expression incorrectly and assumed that the addition was done first, we would get 0 as the result. But because of the left-to-right order of evaluation this is incorrect. To change the order we would have to use parentheses and write the expression as $J-(K+L)$.

With a series of exponentiations, the order of evaluation is also left-to-right. Hence, the expression X^Y^Z is interpreted as (X^Y)^Z. If we want to have the computer evaluate the expression right-to-left, we must use parentheses and write the expression as X^(Y^Z).

Omitting a numeric operator does not, as in algebra, mean multiplication. For example, 3K is invalid and must be written 3*K. Similarly, parentheses cannot be used to imply multiplication. For example, (A+B)(C+D) is invalid and must be written (A+B)*(C+D).

Two numeric operators may not appear adjacent to each other. For example, $A/-B$ is invalid. (In some versions of BASIC this expression is valid, as discussed in the next paragraph.) However, $-B$ by itself is a numeric expression and may therefore be enclosed in parentheses to give it meaning. This example can be written correctly as $A/(-B)$. The same does not hold true for the invalid expression A*/B; there is no way of making this expression meaningful.

In some versions of BASIC a subtraction symbol may come immediately after another numeric operator. (See Table 2-2.) For example, the expression $A/-B$ is valid in these versions of BASIC. In such an expression, the subtraction is done before the

Table 2-2. Numeric expression differences

BASIC version	Subtraction symbol permitted after another numeric operator
ANS minimal BASIC	No
ANS BASIC	No
Microsoft BASIC	Yes
Applesoft BASIC	Yes
True BASIC	No
BASIC-PLUS	Yes
VAX-11 BASIC	Yes

other operation, no matter what the other operation is. Thus, the expression $A/-B$ is interpreted as $A/(-B)$.

The LET statement

A numeric expression by itself is not a BASIC statement. Rather, a numeric expression is part of a statement that is then used in a program. The most common statement in which a numeric expression appears is the LET statement. This statement causes the computer to evaluate a numeric expression and then to assign the result to a variable.

The syntax of the LET statement is as follows:

```
ln LET variable = numeric expression
```

This form shows what must appear in the different parts of the statement. The abbreviation *ln* stands for *line number*. Thus, the first thing in the statement must be a line number (as is the case with all statements in BASIC). Following this is the keyword LET. Then there must be a *variable,* followed by an equal sign, and finally a *numeric expression*. For example, the following are valid LET statements:

```
 30 LET T=X+Y+Z
 40 LET A=T/3
 90 LET Y=A*X^2+B*X+C
100 LET A=3.14159*(D/2)^2
150 LET X3=Z7-3.5E15/Y5
160 LET M9=.0083/A^2
```

In a LET statement, the computer uses the current values of the variables to evaluate the numeric expression. The result is then stored at the storage location identified by the variable on the left side of the equal sign. For example, in the statement

```
 30 LET T=X+Y+Z
```

if the value of X is 78, Y is 95, and Z is 82, then after the execution of this statement the value of T is 255. This value replaces the previous value of T and is the value that is retrieved with any subsequent use of the variable T. Notice that the values of X, Y, and Z are unchanged by the execution of this statement; only the value of T is affected.

The equal sign in a LET statement does not mean equality; it means *assignment*. That is, the equal sign tells the computer that the value of the expression on the right is to be *assigned* to the left-hand variable (i.e., stored in the storage location identified by the variable). This is why there must be one variable on the left of the equal sign. For example, the statement

```
200 LET A+B=X+Y
```

is invalid because it would mean assign the value of X + Y to the expression A + B. Because the left-hand expression is not a single storage location, such assignment is meaningless and therefore not allowed. There must always be a single variable on the left.

A further consequence of this concept of assignment is that some algebraically invalid equations become valid statements in BASIC. For example, the following statement is valid and often useful:

```
70 LET K=K+1
```

The meaning of this statement is that 1 is added to the current value of K and the result is returned to the storage location reserved for K. (See Figure 2-3.) Thus, the value of K is increased by 1. Similarly, the following statement causes the current value of A to be replaced by a value that is five times as large:

```
80 LET A=5*A
```

As we know, a constant or a variable, with or without a sign, is considered to be a numeric expression. Hence, we can use the LET statement to assign a constant to a variable or to assign the value of one variable to another. For example, the statement

```
120 LET M=3
```

assigns the value of 3 to the variable M. Similarly, the statement

```
130 LET N=−M
```

assigns the negative of the value of M to N. If M is equal to 3 before this statement is executed, N will be −3 afterward. Notice also that this assignment does *not* change the value of M; it is still equal to 3 after statement 130 is executed.

In some versions of BASIC the keyword LET is optional in the LET statement. (See Table 2-3.) For example, in these versions the following statements are equivalent:

```
30 LET T=X+Y+Z
30 T=X+Y+Z
```

Figure 2-3. Evaluation of the statement LET K = K + 1

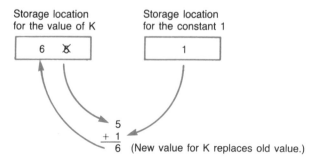

Table 2-3. LET statement differences

BASIC version	*Keyword* **LET** *optional*
ANS minimal BASIC	No
ANS BASIC	No
Microsoft BASIC	Yes
Applesoft BASIC	Yes
True BASIC	No
BASIC-PLUS	Yes
VAX-11 BASIC	Yes

Note that if the keyword LET is not included, there still can be only a single variable on the left of the equal sign.

The LET statement is the fundamental statement that is used in BASIC for numeric data processing. The sample program in Chapter 1 (Figure 1-6) illustrated its use in a program. In the next section we will see more examples of the use of the LET statement in programs.

2-3 Writing complete programs

We can now begin to write complete programs in BASIC. Using sequences of LET statements, we can develop programs that perform numeric computations.

As an example, suppose we wish to compute the amount of interest that a bank deposit will earn in a year. Assume that we put $500 in a bank account at an interest rate of 6%. How much interest do we earn in a year, and what is the total amount we have in the bank at the end of the year?

Figure 2-4 shows part of a program to solve this problem. In this example, B is the original bank balance ($500) and R is the interest rate expressed in decimal form (.06). These variables are assigned values in statements 10 and 20, respectively. Statement 30 then computes the interest, I, by multiplying B by R. Finally, in statement 40 we add the interest to the initial bank balance to obtain the balance at the end of the year (B1).

Notice the sequential order of the execution of the statements in this example. The statements are always executed in the order in which they are written, one statement after another. This order must be carefully planned when the program is designed so that it correctly solves the problem.

The END statement

The example in Figure 2-4 is not a complete program because it does not have an END statement. The last statement in a BASIC program must be an END statement which has the following syntax:

```
1n END
```

The line number in the END statement must be the highest line number in the program. When the END statement is reached, execution of the program stops. Figure 2-5 shows the complete interest-calculation program with the END statement.

Figure 2-4. Statements for a simple interest calculation

```
10 LET B=500
20 LET R=.06
30 LET I=B*R
40 LET B1=B+I
```

Figure 2-5. A simple interest-calculation program

```
10 LET B=500
20 LET R=.06
30 LET I=B*R
40 LET B1=B+I
50 END
```

The PRINT statement

The program in Figure 2-5 is correct and can be run on a computer. However, it is not a very useful program because there is no way to determine the answer to the problem. What are the interest and end-of-year balance? To obtain this information we need to display the values of I and B1. This is accomplished with the PRINT statement.

The syntax of the PRINT statement is as follows:

```
ln PRINT list of variables separated by commas
```

For example, the following are valid PRINT statements:

```
75 PRINT A
85 PRINT P,Q,R
95 PRINT B5,X7,Z8,A9,C2
```

The effect of the PRINT statement is to cause the computer to display on the CRT screen the values of all variables listed in the statement. In the examples just given, statement 75 causes the value of A to be displayed; statement 85 causes the values of P, Q, and R to be displayed; statement 95 displays the values of five variables. Whatever values are currently assigned to the variables in the computer's internal storage are displayed.

Each PRINT statement causes a line to be displayed. A CRT line has a fixed number of spaces for output called *print positions*. The number of print positions in a line depends on the CRT, but typical limits are 40 and 80. The print positions are divided into areas called *print zones*. Each print zone contains a certain number of print positions that depends on the version of BASIC. (See Table 2-4.) The number of print zones depends on the number of print positions in a line and the number of print positions in each print zone. Typically, there are five print zones, each fourteen print positions wide, as shown in Figure 2-6. We will assume this is the case in our examples.

When a PRINT statement is executed, the values of the variables are displayed in successive zones. For example, assume that the value of X is 10, Y is -75.5, and Z is .003, and that the following PRINT statement is executed:

```
105 PRINT X,Y,Z
```

Table 2-4. PRINT statement differences

BASIC version	Print zone width
ANS minimal BASIC	Not specified
ANS BASIC	Not specified
Microsoft BASIC	14 print positions
Applesoft BASIC	16 print positions
True BASIC	16 print positions
BASIC-PLUS	14 print positions
VAX-11 BASIC	14 print positions

Then the output appears as follows:

```
(Print Zone 1)|(Print Zone 2)|(Print Zone 3)|(Print Zone 4)|(Print Zone 5)
 10            |-75.5         |.003          |              |
```

Because there are three variables in the PRINT statement, the values are displayed in the first three print zones. The remaining print zones are left blank. (Of course, just the numbers appear in the output; the vertical lines and the words identifying the print zones are not displayed.)

Each PRINT statement starts a new line. Thus, if three PRINT statements are executed in sequence, each with five or fewer variables, three lines are displayed.

If there are more variables in the PRINT statement than there are print

Figure 2-6. Print zones on a CRT screen

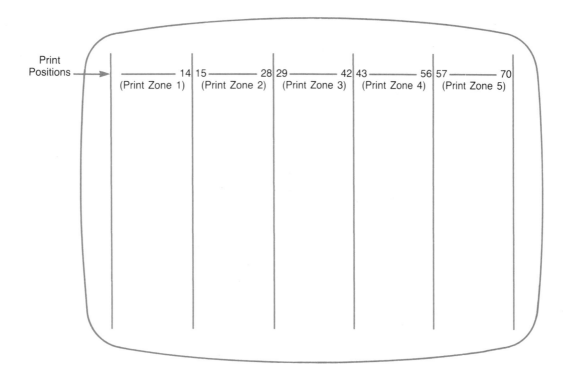

Print Positions

```
—— 14|15 ——— 28|29 ——— 42|43 ——— 56|57 ——— 70
(Print Zone 1)  (Print Zone 2)  (Print Zone 3)  (Print Zone 4)  (Print Zone 5)
```

zones in a line, a new line is started after the last print zone is filled. For example, consider the following statement:

```
115 PRINT A,B,C,D,E,F,G
```

When this statement is executed, the values of the first five variables are displayed on one line. The values of the remaining two variables are then displayed in the first two print zones of the next line.

The form of the output depends on the number being displayed. If the number is an integer (i.e., a whole number) such as 10 or -385, the number is displayed without a decimal point. A negative sign is displayed before a negative number; a blank space precedes a positive number. Most numbers with fractional parts are displayed with a decimal point as we would normally write them. For example, the numbers 289.372 and .000461 would be displayed in these forms. If the number is very large or very small, however, it is displayed in E-notation. For example, assume that the value of A is 84023600000 and B is .0000000000296042 and that the following PRINT statement is executed:

```
125 PRINT A,B
```

The output appears as follows:

(Print Zone 1)	(Print Zone 2)	(Print Zone 3)	(Print Zone 4)	(Print Zone 5)
8.40236E 10	2.96042E-11			

We can now write a more complete version of the interest-calculation program discussed earlier. Assume that we want to display the original bank balance, the year's interest, and the end-of-year balance. The program in Figure 2-7(a) accomplishes this. Notice that the PRINT statement contains the variables that we want displayed. The output from running this program is shown in Figure 2-7(b).

Printer output. The PRINT statement is used to display output on a CRT screen. Depending on the version of BASIC, this statement may also be used to print output on paper with a printer. (See Table 2-5.) When the PRINT statement is used for printer output, special system commands or other steps may be needed to direct the output to the printer. Sometimes a terminal with a printer instead of a CRT is used

Figure 2-7. The interest-calculation program with a PRINT statement

```
10 LET B=500
20 LET R=.06
30 LET I=B*R
40 LET B1=B+I
50 PRINT B,I,B1
60 END
```

(a) The program

```
500          30          530
```

(b) Output

Table 2-5. Printer output differences

BASIC version	Printer output statement
ANS minimal BASIC	PRINT statement
ANS BASIC	PRINT statement
Microsoft BASIC	LPRINT statement
Applesoft BASIC	PRINT statement

True BASIC	Use the statement
	    `OPEN #1:PRINTER`
	at the beginning of the program.
	Then use the statement
	    `PRINT #1:list of variables`
	to print output with the printer.

BASIC-PLUS	PRINT statement
VAX-11 BASIC	PRINT statement

to get printed output. With some computers the output can be displayed on the CRT screen and then printed with the printer by pressing a special key or combination of keys on the keyboard.

Some versions of BASIC have a special statement, the LPRINT statement, for printing on the printer. The syntax of the LPRINT statement is the same as the PRINT statement except the keyword LPRINT is used instead of PRINT. For example, in a version of BASIC with the LPRINT statement, the program in Figure 2-7 can be modified to print the output on the printer by replacing statement 50 with the following:

```
50 LPRINT B,I,Bl
```

The output is the same except that it is printed with the printer and not displayed on the CRT screen.

The INPUT statement

The program in Figure 2-7 is still not very useful. The difficulty is that it solves the interest problem for only one bank balance ($500) and one interest rate (6%). If we wish to change either of these, we must change the program. A better approach is to design the program so that the values of B and R can be supplied when the program is run without modifying the actual program. This is accomplished with the INPUT statement.

The purpose of the INPUT statement is to accept input data from the keyboard. The syntax of this statement is as follows:

```
ln INPUT list of variables separated by commas
```

For example, the following are valid INPUT statements:

```
15 INPUT A
25 INPUT P,Q,R
35 INPUT B5,X7,Z8,A9,C2
```

When an INPUT statement is encountered during the execution of a program, the computer displays a question mark on the CRT and waits for input data to be typed. The question mark is called a *prompt* and it indicates that input data must be entered. The person running the program must type one number after the question mark for each variable in the INPUT statement. The numbers must be separated by commas. After the input data is typed, the RETURN or ENTER key must be pressed.

For example, assume that we are running a program that contains the following INPUT statement:

```
45 INPUT X,Y,Z
```

This statement requires three input values because there are three variables. When the statement is executed, a question mark prompt is displayed, and we then type three numbers separated by commas. For example, we might enter the data after the prompt as follows:

```
? 10,-75.5,.003
```

After the RETURN or ENTER key is pressed, the computer accepts these numbers and assigns them in order to the variables in the INPUT statement. Thus, 10 would be assigned to X, -75.5 would be assigned to Y, and .003 would be assigned to Z.

The input data that is entered must follow the rules for constants in BASIC. The numbers can be positive or negative, contain decimal points or be whole numbers, or be written in E-notation. A comma cannot appear in an input value because commas are used to separate the data.

One value must be entered for each variable in the INPUT statement. If too little or too much data is entered, the computer displays a message indicating the error. All data must then be reentered. (With some computers, if too little data is entered, we need only type the additional data, and if too much data is entered, any excess data is ignored.)

With the addition of an INPUT statement, the interest-calculation program can be designed to compute the interest for any bank balance and any interest rate. The program is shown in Figure 2-8(a). Notice that the program no longer assigns values to B and R; these variables appear in the INPUT statement. Whatever values are entered when the program is run are used in the calculation. Thus, if we type the data after the prompt as follows:

```
? 500,.06
```

the program gives the same answer as before (i.e., the interest on $500 at 6%). However, if we type

```
? 2000,.075
```

the program computes the interest on $2000 at 7.5%. This is shown in Figure 2-8(b).

It is important to recognize the general nature of the program in Figure 2-8(a). The program solves the problem of finding the interest on a bank deposit without knowing the actual values of B and R. These values are supplied when the program is run. At that time, a specific instance of the problem is solved.

This program also illustrates the idea of interactive processing. A person interacts with the computer by supplying input data when a prompt is displayed. Then the output is displayed almost immediately.

Figure 2-8. The interest-calculation program with an INPUT statement

```
10 INPUT B,R
20 LET I=B*R
30 LET B1=B+I
40 PRINT B,I,B1
50 END
```

(a) The program

```
? 2000,.075
  2000           150           2150
```

(b) Input and output

Program repetition

The program in Figure 2-8 solves the interest-calculation problem for one set of input data. If we want to solve the problem for more data, we can run the program again. An easier approach, however, is to design the program so that it automatically repeats.

We accomplish program repetition in BASIC by using the GOTO statement. The syntax of this statement is as follows:

> *ln* GOTO *ln*

The first line number is the number of the GOTO statement. The second line number, after the keyword GOTO, must be the number of another statement in the program. For example, the following is a valid GOTO statement:

```
75 GOTO 150
```

The keyword GOTO usually can be entered as GO TO with a space, but then the space may be deleted by the computer.

The effect of the GOTO statement is to cause the computer to interrupt the normal sequential execution of the program and to continue execution at the statement whose number is given in the GOTO statement. This process of breaking the execution of the program at a certain point and continuing elsewhere is called *branching* or *transferring control*. For example, the GOTO statement just given causes the computer to branch to statement 150. Execution then continues from that point.

It is possible to branch from a point in a program either in the direction of the end of the program (i.e., "down" the program) or toward the beginning of the program (i.e., "up" the program). In later chapters we will discuss examples of branching down the program. For now, however, we will concentrate on branching up.

A GOTO statement can cause the computer to branch up a program so that a series of statements is repeatedly executed. When this is done, the group of statements that is repeated is called a *loop* and the process is called *looping*.

We can include a GOTO statement in the interest-calculation program to create a loop. Figure 2-9(a) shows how this is done. Statement 50 is a GOTO statement that causes the computer to branch to statement 10. Because of this, statements 10 through 50 are repeatedly executed and thus form a loop. Notice that the statements

Figure 2-9. The interest-calculation program with a loop

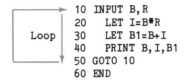

```
10  INPUT B,R
20    LET I=B*R
30    LET B1=B+I
40    PRINT B,I,B1
50  GOTO 10
60  END
```

(a) The program

```
? 500,.06
  500              30              530
? 2000,.075
  2000            150             2150
? 1250,.055
  1250           68.75          1318.75
?
```

(b) Input and output

in the loop, except the first and the last, are indented. This is a common style that, although not required, is usually used in programs so that the loop is clearly shown in the program.

The first time that the loop is executed, the INPUT statement accepts input data for B and R. The calculations are performed with this data and the PRINT statement displays the output. The GOTO statement then causes the computer to go back to the INPUT statement. This causes new input values to be accepted for B and R, replacing the previous values. This new data is then used in the calculations and the output is displayed. Then the GOTO statement causes the program to be repeated again. In fact, the program will continue to repeat as long as we supply it with input data. Figure 2-9(b) shows the input and output for this program for several repetitions.

The biggest problem with looping in a program is not how to create a loop, but rather how to stop the computer from looping. In the program in Figure 2-9, this is done by typing a special control character following the input prompt. When the computer senses that the control character has been entered, it branches to the END statement. This causes the computer to stop execution of the program. (In Chapter 4 we will discuss other ways of stopping a loop.)

The REM statement

A statement that is not required by the language but usually used in BASIC programs is the REM, or remarks, statement. The syntax of the REM statement is as follows:

```
ln REM any comments or remarks
```

We can include any comments or remarks that we want in a REM statement. For example, the following is a valid REM statement:

```
10 REM - INTEREST CALCULATION PROGRAM
```

REM statements can go anywhere in the program before the END statement. During execution of the program, the computer ignores all REM statements; that is, whenever it encounters a REM statement the computer passes over it and continues with the next statement in sequence.

The purpose of the REM statement is to allow the programmer to include explanatory comments or remarks in the program. Such remarks are often used to identify the program, to describe the variables used in the program, and to explain the processing that is done. Remarks like these help other programmers to understand and use the program. REM statements with no comments in them are sometimes used to separate parts of a program. Figure 2-10 shows the interest-calculation program with REM statements. (Notice that because this program is longer than the previous examples, we have begun the line numbers at 100 rather than 10. This is done so that all line numbers are the same length.)

Special form of remarks. In some versions of BASIC remarks may be included in a program by using a special form in addition to using a REM statement. (See Table 2-6.) For example, in one version of BASIC a remark may begin with an apostrophe ('). A remark in this form may be on a line by itself or may come at the end of a line following a statement. The following are examples of this form of a remark:

```
10 'INTEREST CALCULATION PROGRAM
20 INPUT B,R 'ACCEPT BALANCE AND RATE
```

Character output

Most programs display not only the results of processing but also words and phrases that describe the output. This is so that a person reading the output will know what the data represents. Sometimes a word or phrase is displayed followed by the results of a computation. At other times, headings are displayed above columns of output. Many variations are used to make the output more readable. We call this type of output *character output* because it consists of symbols (characters) other than just numbers.†

To produce character output we put the words to be displayed in quotation marks in the PRINT statement. For example, consider the following statement:

```
80 PRINT "THE ANSWER IS",X
```

Execution of this statement causes the computer to display the phrase THE ANSWER IS, followed by the value of the variable X. For example, if X is 125.25, the output appears as follows:

```
THE ANSWER IS  125.25
```

The quotation marks are *not* displayed; only the characters between the quotation marks appear in the output.

There may be as many words or phrases in a PRINT statement as are needed. For example, the following statement displays two separate phrases and the values of two variables:

```
180 PRINT "AMOUNT =",A,"COUNT =",C
```

† In Section 8-1 we will see that character output is a type of data called a string.

Figure 2-10. The interest-calculation program with remarks

```
100 REM - INTEREST CALCULATION PROGRAM
110 REM - VARIABLES:
120 REM      B  = BEGINNING BALANCE
130 REM      R  = INTEREST RATE
140 REM      I  = INTEREST
150 REM      B1 = ENDING BALANCE
160 INPUT B,R
170    LET I=B*R
180    LET B1=B+I
190    PRINT B,I,B1
200 GOTO 160
210 END
```

If A is 250 and C is 9, the output is as follows:

(Print Zone 1)	(Print Zone 2)	(Print Zone 3)	(Print Zone 4)
AMOUNT =	250	COUNT =	9

Notice that the output in this example is spread out. This is because each value begins in the next print zone. The phrase AMOUNT = is displayed in the first zone, the value of A is displayed in the second zone, COUNT = is displayed in the third zone, and the value of C is displayed in the fourth zone.

If the word or phrase to be displayed is longer then one print zone, it continues into the next zone. Anything else to be displayed starts in the next zone. For example, consider the following statement:

```
280 PRINT X,"IS NOT GREATER THAN",Y
```

In this case the value of X is displayed in the first print zone. Then the phrase IS NOT GREATER THAN is displayed beginning in the second zone. Because this phrase requires nineteen print positions, the output continues into the third print zone. Finally, the value of Y is displayed in the fourth zone. If X is 5 and Y is 6, the output appears as follows:

(Print Zone 1)	(Print Zone 2)	(Print Zone 3)	(Print Zone 4)
5	IS NOT GREATER	THAN	6

Table 2-6. Remarks differences

BASIC version	*Special form of remarks*
ANS minimal BASIC Applesoft BASIC	No special form.
ANS BASIC True BASIC BASIC-PLUS VAX-11 BASIC	A remark may begin with an exclamation point (!) and may be on a line by itself or at the end of a line following a statement.
Microsoft BASIC	A remark may begin with an apostrophe (') and may be on a line by itself or at the end of a line following a statement.

We can use the PRINT statement to display just a word or a phrase without displaying any other data. The following statement illustrates this:

```
380 PRINT "STATISTICAL DATA"
```

The effect of the execution of this statement is that the only output displayed is the phrase STATISTICAL DATA. This approach is often used to display a *heading* to describe the output that follows.

Character output such as in the last example begins on the left of the CRT screen. If we want to shift the output to the right several spaces, we can include blanks at the beginning of the character output after the quotation mark. For example, the following statement displays the heading STATISTICAL DATA indented three spaces:

```
380 PRINT "   STATISTICAL DATA"
```

Print zones can be used to arrange headings above columns of output. For example, if we wish to display two columns of data in the first two print zones with the titles AMOUNT and COUNT, the following statement can be used:

```
480 PRINT "AMOUNT","COUNT"
```

Because the words to be displayed appear separately in the PRINT statement, they are displayed in separate zones. AMOUNT is displayed in the first print zone and COUNT in the second zone.

Any characters except quotation marks can be displayed with a PRINT statement. Letters, digits, and special characters including blanks are all permitted. Letters may be upper and lowercase. Quotation marks are not allowed because they are used to set off the words to be displayed. (Some versions of BASIC have provisions for displaying quotation marks.)

With the PRINT statement we can also display a line that contains nothing. This is accomplished by using a PRINT statement with nothing following the keyword PRINT, as in the following example:

```
580 PRINT
```

This tells the computer to skip to the next line, which has the effect of displaying a line of blank spaces. This technique is often used to double-space output.

Figure 2-11(a) shows the interest-calculation program with character output. For each set of input, the program displays a heading (statement 200) and three lines of output with descriptive phrases (statements 220, 230, and 240). Blank lines are displayed to make the output easier to read (statements 190, 210, and 250). Notice that many PRINT statements are needed to produce the output. The input and output that result from running the program are shown in Figure 2-11(b).

Character output can be printed on paper with a printer. As discussed earlier, the approach used for printer output depends on the version of BASIC. Character output can be used with any approach, including the LPRINT statement.

It is important to understand the difference between character output and remarks in a program. Character output, which is displayed by using a PRINT statement, is for the benefit of the person running the program so that the *output* is easier to understand. Remarks, which are in the program in REM statements, are for the benefit of the programmer so that the *program* is easier to understand. Both character output and remarks are important in a well-designed program.

Figure 2-11. The interest-calculation program with character output

```
100 REM - INTEREST CALCULATION PROGRAM
110 REM - VARIABLES:
120 REM      B  = BEGINNING BALANCE
130 REM      R  = INTEREST RATE
140 REM      I  = INTEREST
150 REM      B1 = ENDING BALANCE
160 INPUT B,R
170    LET I=B*R
180    LET B1=B+I
190    PRINT
200    PRINT "INTEREST CALCULATION"
210    PRINT
220    PRINT "BEGINNING BAL",B
230    PRINT "INTEREST",I
240    PRINT "ENDING BAL",B1
250    PRINT
260 GOTO 160
270 END
```

(a) The program

```
? 500,.06

INTEREST CALCULATION

BEGINNING BAL   500
INTEREST         30
ENDING BAL      530

? 2000,.075

INTEREST CALCULATION

BEGINNING BAL   2000
INTEREST         150
ENDING BAL      2150

? 1250,.055

INTEREST CALCULATION

BEGINNING BAL   1250
INTEREST         68.75
ENDING BAL      1318.75

?
```

(b) Input and output

Flowcharts of complete programs

The program in Figure 2-8 is a simple version of the interest-calculation program. The logic of this version involves input, calculations, and output, but no loop. The flowchart for this program is shown in Figure 2-12. The flowchart uses the terminal point symbol for the beginning and end of the flowchart logic, the input/output symbol for the steps where the input is accepted and the output displayed, and the process

Figure 2-12. Flowchart of a simple interest-calculation program

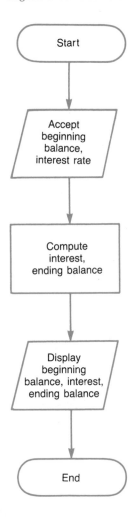

symbol for the calculation step. Notice that the logic flows from top to bottom in a straight line, which corresponds to the logic of the program.

The program in Figure 2-11 is the most complete version of the interest-calculation program. The basic logic of this program is very common in programming. The logic involves a loop that includes input, calculations, and output. The loop is terminated when a control character is entered to indicate that the end of the input data has been reached.

The flowchart for this version of the interest-calculation program is shown in Figure 2-13. This figure illustrates how a loop is expressed in a flowchart. A loop is shown by a flowline that extends from the end of the loop to its beginning. There is no separate symbol for a GOTO statement; branching from one point to another is simply indicated by a flowline. Termination of the loop is shown by a flowline leaving the flowchart symbol for the input step. This flowline is labeled to indicate that it is followed only when the end of the input data is detected (i.e., when a control character is entered.)

Figure 2-13. Flowchart of the complete interest-calculation program

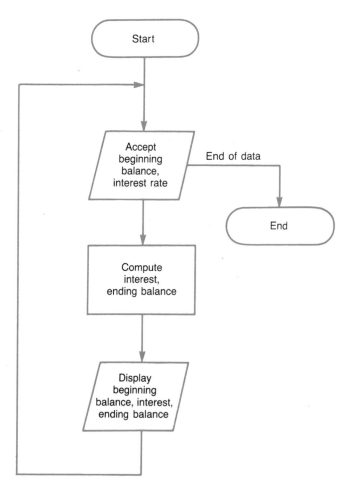

2-4 Program style

The most important objective during the programming process is to produce a program that correctly solves the required problem. The process of program testing, discussed in Chapter 1, is designed to help locate errors in a program. We will describe program testing in more detail later.

After correctness, the most important characteristic of a program is its understandability. By this we mean the qualities of the program that make it understandable or readable to others. Program understandability is important because programs are often reviewed by people other than the original programmer. For example, the programming manager may review a program to check for completeness and consistency with the problem definition. Other programmers may have to read the program to make corrections for errors that are not detected until after the program has been in use for a while. Often modifications are necessary in the program because of changing requirements. For example, payroll programs have to be modified regularly because of changing tax structures. Sometimes a program is enhanced to do more than was originally planned. In all of these situations, someone must look at the program months or even years after it was first coded. Even if the original programmer is given the task, he or she may have difficulty remembering the program's logic unless the program is easily understood.

Program style deals with those characteristics of a program that make it more understandable. Even though we have covered only a few features of the BASIC language, it is possible to begin incorporating good style into our programs. One basic rule is to use variables that symbolize the data to which they refer. For example, in the program in Figure 2-11, we use B for the beginning bank balance, R for the interest rate, I for the interest, and B1 for the ending bank balance. Long variables should be used if they are available in the version of BASIC.

Another good style rule is to use line numbers that are all the same length. This is so the statements are all aligned in the program. Usually this means using line numbers that are all three or four digits. In addition, lines should be numbered by tens to make the program easier to change.

Indentation should be used in loops and other parts of a program that we will discuss later. Such indentation helps show the organization or structure of the statements in the program. The indentation gives a visual clue to help the programmer understand the program. We will have more to say about indentation and program structure in later chapters.

Sometimes long numeric expressions are difficult to understand because of the order in which the operations are performed. When this is the case, it is often useful to include extra sets of parentheses around parts of the expression. Although these parentheses may not change the way the expression is evaluated, they often make the expression easier to understand.

Finally, remarks should be used to help explain the program. At a minimum, the program should be identified at its beginning in a REM statement and all variables that are difficult to understand should be described in REM statements. Remarks should also be used to explain complex parts of the program. Although the examples so far have been relatively straightforward, many programs involve sophisticated processing. REM statements should be used to include explanations of the processing at different points in the program.

The rules discussed here are just a few of the ways that a program can be made more understandable. As we explain other features of the BASIC language, we will give more rules for program style.

2-5 A sample problem

In this section we develop a program for a sample problem. The problem is to compute the payroll for a business. We follow the five steps of the programming process introduced in Section 1-6.

Problem definition

A program is needed to compute the gross pay, withholding tax, and net pay for each employee in a business. The program should display the results of these computations along with the employee's identification number. Descriptive phrases should be used to identify each employee's data. Figure 2-14 shows how the output should appear for one employee. (X's represent numeric data in this figure.)

Input to the program consists of each employee's identification number and his or her hours worked. There are an unknown number of employees in the business. The gross pay is computed at $6.50 per hour. The withholding tax is 18% of the gross pay. The net pay is the gross pay less the withholding tax.

Figure 2-14. Output layout for the payroll program

```
PAYROLL DATA FOR EMPLOYEE    XXX

    GROSS PAY   XXXXX
    TAX         XXXXX
    NET PAY     XXXXX
```

Program design

The algorithm that solves the problem involves accepting the input data, computing the gross pay, withholding tax, and net pay, and displaying the results. Because there are an unknown number of employees in the business, a loop is needed that repeats these steps until there is no more input data. Hence, the algorithm is basically the same as that used in other programs we have seen. We can express the algorithm as shown in Figure 2-15. The flowchart for the program is shown in Figure 2-16.

Program coding

To code the program for this problem we must determine what variables will be used for the data. We will use I for the employee's identification number, H for the hours worked, G for the gross pay, W for the withholding tax, and P for the net pay.

The program is shown in Figure 2-17. The program logic follows the algorithm in Figure 2-15 and the flowchart in Figure 2-16. The INPUT statement accepts the input data. Three LET statements are needed for the computations. The order of these statements is important. The gross pay must be computed first because it is needed in the calculation of the withholding tax. The tax must be computed before the net pay can be found. The PRINT statements display the output in the form shown earlier. The GOTO statement creates the loop. REM statements have been included with remarks that describe the program and the variables used in the program.

Program correctness

To test the program we supply input test data for which we have computed the output by hand. We then compare the output from running the program using the test data with the hand-computed output.

Figure 2-18 gives several sets of input test data and the expected output for each set. Figure 2-19 shows the input and output from running the program using the input data in Figure 2-18. As we can see, all cases give the correct results.

Program documentation

Part of the documentation for the program is included in the program in the form of remarks. The complete set of documentation for the program would include the listing of the program (Figure 2-17) and the sample run of the program (Figure

Figure 2-15. Algorithm for the payroll problem

Repeat the following until there is no more data:
    Accept the employee identification number and hours
        worked.
    Compute the gross pay, tax, and net pay.
    Display the employee identification number, gross pay,
        tax, and net pay.

Figure 2-16. Flowchart of the payroll program

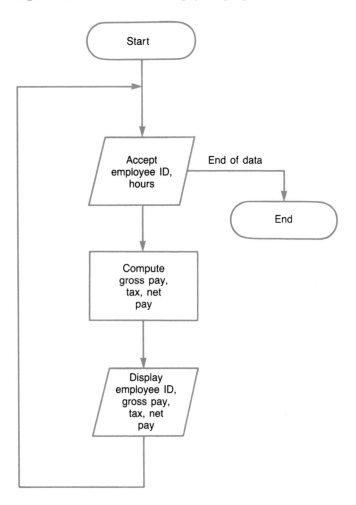

Figure 2-17. The payroll program

```
100 REM - PAYROLL PROGRAM
110 REM - VARIABLES:
120 REM        I  = EMPLOYEE ID
130 REM        H  = HOURS WORKED
140 REM        G  = GROSS PAY
150 REM        W  = WITHHOLDING TAX
160 REM        P  = NET PAY
170 INPUT I,H
180    LET G=6.5*H
190    LET W=.18*G
200    LET P=G-W
210    PRINT
220    PRINT "PAYROLL DATA FOR EMPLOYEE",I
230    PRINT
240    PRINT "   GROSS PAY",G
250    PRINT "   TAX",W
260    PRINT "   NET PAY",P
270    PRINT
280 GOTO 170
290 END
```

Figure 2-18. Input test data and expected output for the payroll program

Input Test Data		Expected Output		
Employee ID	Hours	Gross Pay	Tax	Net Pay
234	32	208	37.44	170.56
456	48	312	56.16	255.84
678	36	234	42.12	191.88

Figure 2-19. Input and output for the payroll program

```
? 234,32

PAYROLL DATA FOR EMPLOYEE      234

     GROSS PAY    208
     TAX          37.44
     NET PAY      170.56

? 456,48

PAYROLL DATA FOR EMPLOYEE      456

     GROSS PAY    312
     TAX          56.16
     NET PAY      255.84

? 678,36

PAYROLL DATA FOR EMPLOYEE      678

     GROSS PAY    234
     TAX          42.12
     NET PAY      191.88

?
```

2-19). The documentation may also include the output layout (Figure 2-14), the algorithm (Figure 2-15), the flowchart (Figure 2-16), the input test data and expected output (Figure 2-18), and other items that we will discuss later.

Review questions

1. Indicate whether each of the following is a valid or invalid constant in BASIC:
   a. −.004385
   b. 83,250
   c. 16.5%
   d. +58213
   e. 273.51E−12
   f. 8.213^8
2. Convert the following E-notation constants to simple constants:
   a. 4.23E5
   b. −8031E+2
   c. .1234E−6
   d. −5E−1

3. Convert the following simple constants to E-notation constants:
   a. −38204
   b. .0000456
   c. −10000000
   d. 7.8316

4. What is the syntax rule for a variable in BASIC?

5. Indicate whether each of the following is a valid or invalid variable in BASIC:
   a. AMT
   b. F
   c. X7
   d. 4H

6. What are the limitations on data values for the computer you are using?

7. What is the order of evaluation of the operators in a numeric expression?

8. Code a numeric expression that is equivalent to each of the following algebraic expressions:
   a. $x^2 - 2x + 3$
   b. $\dfrac{4x}{y} + \dfrac{a}{3}$
   c. $\dfrac{a - b}{a + b}$
   d. $\dfrac{\left(4 - \dfrac{x}{a + b}\right)^3}{(c - d)^2}$

9. Assume that the value of A is 2, B is 3, and C is 4. What is the value of each of the following numeric expressions?
   a. A−B+C
   b. C/A*B
   c. C+B^2
   d. A−B*C/A+B/C
   e. (A−B)*C/(A+B)/C
   f. (A−B)*(C/((A+B)/C))

10. Code a statement to compute the miles per gallon that an automobile uses given the distance traveled and the gallons used.

11. The LET statement is sometimes called an assignment statement. Why?

12. What is the effect of the following statement?
    ```
    50 LET X=X/2
    ```

13. The last statement in a BASIC program must be the _____ statement.

14. Code a statement to display the values of the variables A, B, and C.

15. How many print positions are there in a line for the computer you are using? How many print zones are there in a line? How many print positions are there in each print zone?

16. Consider the following statement:
    ```
    80 PRINT X5,A3,Z8,P,Q,R5,V
    ```
    How many lines of output are displayed when this statement is executed assuming
    a. each line contains five print zones.
    b. each line contains three print zones.

17. Code statements to display the values of the variables A, B, and C on three separate lines.

18. Code a statement to accept the values of the variables A, B, and C from the keyboard.

19. How must data be entered when an INPUT statement is executed?

20. Code a statement to branch from line number 50 to line number 100.

21. A group of statements that is repeatedly executed is called a _____.

22. How are remarks included in a BASIC program?

23. Code a statement that displays the words OUTPUT DATA followed by the values of the variables A and B.

24. What does the following statement do?
    ```
    300 PRINT
    ```

25. Why is good program style important?

Programming problems

Each of the following problems gives the requirements for a computer program. A complete BASIC program should be prepared according to the requirements. All output displayed by the program should be identified with appropriate headings or descriptive phrases. The program should be fully debugged and tested on a computer, using the test data given.

1. The annual depreciation of an asset by the straight-line method is calculated by the following formula:

$$\text{depreciation} = \frac{\text{cost} - \text{salvage value}}{\text{service life}}$$

Write a BASIC program that accepts the cost, salvage value, and service life. Then calculate the depreciation and display the result. Test the program using $13,525.00 for the cost, $1,500.00 for the salvage value, and 7 years for the service life.

2. Fahrenheit temperature is converted to Celsius temperature by the following formula:

$$C = \frac{5}{9} \times (F - 32)$$

In this formula F is the temperature in degrees Fahrenheit and C is the temperature in degrees Celsius. Write a BASIC program to accept the temperature in Fahrenheit, calculate the equivalent temperature in Celsius using this formula, and display the result. To test the program use the following Fahrenheit temperatures as input data:

$$78.4$$
$$-50$$
$$98.6$$
$$0$$
$$32$$
$$212$$

3. The present value, P, of income, I, received N years in the future is given by the formula:

$$P = \frac{I}{(1 + R)^N}$$

In this formula R is the discount rate expressed as a fraction (e.g., if the discount rate is 5%, then R is .05). Write a BASIC program that computes the present value, given the income, number of years, and discount rate, and displays the result. To test the program use the following input data:

Income	Number of years	Discount rate
$10,000	5	10%
$1,200	2	5%
$42,365	18	12.5%
$6,000	20	8%

4. In economic theory, supply and demand curves can sometimes be represented by the following equations:

$$\text{Supply: } P = A \times Q + B$$
$$\text{Demand: } P = C \times Q + D$$

In these equations, P represents the price and Q the quantity. The values of A, B, C, and D determine the actual curves.

These equations can be solved for P and Q, giving the equilibrium price and quantity for any commodity. The formulas are as follows:

$$P = \frac{C \times B - A \times D}{C - A}$$
$$Q = \frac{D - B}{A - C}$$

Write a BASIC program to calculate the equilibrium price and quantity for a product. Input to the program should be the values of A, B, C, and D. Output should be the price and quantity at equilibrium. Test the program with the following data:

Test number	A	B	C	D
1	.19	1.20	−.42	8.50
2	.5	0	.5	100
3	0	25	1	20

5. The system of linear equations

$$ax + by = c$$
$$dx + ey = f$$

has the following solution:

$$x = \frac{ce - bf}{ae - bd}$$
$$y = \frac{af - cd}{ae - bd}$$

Write a BASIC program to solve the system and to display the values of x and y. Input consists of the values of a, b, c, d, e, and f. Use the following data to test the program:

a	b	c	d	e	f
1.0	2.0	3.0	4.0	5.0	6.0
5.2	8.9	13.2	−6.3	7.2	2.1
−83.82	42.61	−59.55	14.73	5.32	−39.99
.035	−.327	1.621	.243	.006	.592

6. Several calculations are important in analyzing the current position of a company. The formulas for the calculations are as follows:

$$\text{working capital} = \text{current assets} - \text{current liabilities}$$
$$\text{current ratio} = \frac{\text{current assets}}{\text{current liabilities}}$$
$$\text{acid-test ratio} = \frac{\text{cash} + \text{accounts receivable}}{\text{current liabilities}}$$

Assume that the cash, accounts receivable, current assets, and current liabilities are available for input. Write a BASIC program to accept the data, perform the preceding calculations, and display the results. Use the following data to test the program:

Cash	10,620
Accounts receivable	5,850
Current assets	22,770
Current liabilities	14,680

7. The final score for a particular test is equal to the number of questions answered correctly minus one-fourth of the number answered incorrectly. Assume that test data available for input includes the student's identification number, number correct on the test, and number incorrect. Write a BASIC program to calculate the final score from this data and to display the results along with the input data. Use the following input data to test the program:

Student number	Number correct	Number incorrect
1	90	10
2	75	20
3	84	0
4	57	35
5	10	50
6	95	5

8. The interest and maturity value of a promissory note can be calculated as follows:

$$interest = \frac{principal \times rate \times time}{360}$$

$$maturity\ value = principal + interest$$

Write a BASIC program that accepts the loan number, principal, rate (percent), and time (days), calculates the interest and maturity value, and displays the loan number, rate (percent), time, interest, and maturity value. Note that the rate is expressed in percent for input and output purposes but must be converted to decimal form for the calculation. Thus, if the input value for the rate is 5 (meaning 5%), this must be converted to .05 for use in the calculation. The conversion from percent to decimal form must be done within the program; the input and output of the rate should be in percent. Use the program to find the interest and maturity value of loan number 1875, which is a $450 note with a rate of 6% for 60 days.

9. An approximation to the value of sin x can be computed as follows:

$$\sin x = x - \frac{x^3}{6} + \frac{x^5}{120}$$

In this formula the angle, x, must be in radians (1 radian = 59.2958 degrees). Write a BASIC program that accepts an angle in degrees and computes the sine of the angle using this equation. The program should display the angle in degrees and the value of the sine. Test the program with the following angles:

45

0

37.5

90

22

10. The payroll in a particular business is calculated as follows:

    a. Gross pay is the hours worked times the pay rate.
    b. Withholding tax is found by subtracting thirteen times the number of exemptions from the gross pay and multiplying the result by the tax rate.
    c. Social security tax is 7.05% of the gross pay.
    d. Net pay is the gross pay less all taxes.

    Write a BASIC program that accepts an employee's identification number, hours worked, pay rate, tax rate, and number of exemptions. Then the program should calculate the employee's gross pay, withholding and social security taxes, and net pay and display these results along with the employee's identification number.
    Use the following input data to test the program:

Employee number	Hours worked	Pay rate	Tax rate	Number of exemptions
1001	40	4.50	20%	3
1002	36	3.75	17 5%	4
1003	47	6.50	24%	0
1004	25	5.25	22.5%	2

11. Grade-point average is calculated by multiplying the units (credits) for each course that a student takes by the numeric grade that he or she receives in the course (A = 4.0, B = 3.0, C = 2.0, D = 1.0, F = 0.0), totaling for all courses, and dividing by the total number of units. For example, assume that a student received a C (2.0) in a four-unit course and a B (3.0) in a two-unit course. Then his or her GPA is calculated as follows:

$$\frac{4 \times 2.0 + 2 \times 3.0}{4 + 2} = 2.33$$

Write a BASIC program to calculate one student's GPA, given the units and grade in each of five courses that he or she took. Input for the program is the student's identification number and the units and numeric grade for each of the five courses. Output from the program should list the student's number, total units, and grade-point average.

Test the program with data for student number 18357, who got an A in a two-unit course, a C in a three-unit course, a D in a one-unit course, a C in a four-unit course, and a B in a three-unit course.

12. The percent correct for each part of a three-part test needs to be calculated. The number of questions in each part varies but is always less than 100. Write a BASIC program to do the necessary calculations. The first set of input is the number of questions in each of the three parts. Following this is one set of input for each student, giving the student's number followed by his or her scores on each of the three parts. The program should calculate the percent correct for each part and the percent correct on all three parts combined. Output should list for each student the student number, the number and percent correct on each part, and the total number and percent correct.

To test the program assume that Part I of the test contains 50 questions, Part II 90 questions, and Part III 40 questions. The students' results are as follows:

Student number	Part I correct	Part II correct	Part III correct
18372	37	83	28
19204	25	30	30
20013	45	87	36
21563	0	53	40

Chapter 3

Programming for decisions

If a program contains only a sequence of INPUT, LET, and PRINT statements, these statements are executed in the order in which they are written, as illustrated by the examples in the last chapter. Sometimes we wish to alter this normal sequential execution. For example, we may want the computer to select among several sequences of statements based on a particular condition or to repeat a group of statements until a condition occurs. These activities involve controlling the order of execution of the statements in a program. The BASIC statements that are used to accomplish this are called *control statements*. (The GOTO statement, discussed in the last chapter, is an example of a control statement.)

This chapter discusses control statements and program control for decision making. A *decision* involves selecting among alternative sequences of statements based on a condition that occurs during the execution of the program. For example, assume that we need to write a program that calculates the tuition for a college student based on the number of units (credits) for which the student is enrolled. If the student is taking fewer than a certain number of units (say, twelve), the tuition is calculated one way; otherwise a different calculation is used. Thus, the computer must select between two calculations based on a particular condition.

In this chapter we describe the BASIC control statements necessary for decision making and discuss related program logic. After completing this chapter you should be able to write programs that use various patterns of decision making. In the next chapter we discuss other aspects of program control.

3-1 The IF statement

The fundamental decision-making statement in BASIC is the IF statement. The syntax of this statement is as follows:

```
ln IF relational expression THEN ln
```

Following the keyword IF is a *relational expression*. Such an expression determines whether a particular relationship holds between two values. For example, A>B is a relational expression that determines whether A is greater than B. (We describe relational expressions in detail later.) Following the keyword THEN is the line number of another statement in the program. The following is an example of a valid IF statement:

```
50 IF A>B THEN 200
```

Execution of an IF statement causes the computer to evaluate the relational expression and determine whether it is true or false — that is, whether or not the relationship holds. If the expression is true, the computer branches to the statement whose number is given following the word THEN. If the condition is false, the computer does *not* branch; rather it continues with the next statement after the IF statement. In the previous example, if the value of A is greater than the value of B, the computer branches to statement 200. If A is *not* greater than B, the computer goes on to the next statement in sequence following the IF statement.

Relational expressions

A relational expression compares the values of two numeric expressions. Values can be compared to determine whether one is greater than or less than the other, whether they are equal or not equal, or whether combinations of these conditions are true. The relational expression has a *truth value* of *true* or *false* depending on the result of the comparison.

The way in which the values of the numeric expressions are compared is given by a *relational operator*. The relational operators in BASIC and their meanings are as follows:

Relational operator	*Meaning*
<	Less than
<=	Less than or equal to
>	Greater than
>=	Greater than or equal to
=	Equal to
<>	Not equal to

The simplest form of a relational expression is a constant or a variable, followed by a relational operator, and then another constant or variable. For example, the following are valid relational expressions:

```
J<K
6<=C
Q>5.6
K>=-5
A3=B4
7<>J
```

To evaluate each of these, the values of the variables and constants are compared according to the relational operator. For example, if J is 6 and K is 5, the first expression is *false*. Similarly, if both J and K are equal to 6, this expression is *false*. However, if J is 6 and K is 7, the expression is *true*.

Relational operators can be used to compare the values of complex numeric expressions. For example, the following relational expressions are valid:

```
Q>P-5.6
K+8>=-5-L
X+Y/(4.56-Z)=Z-M
(A7-I2)<>(K-5)
```

Notice that parentheses can be used to enclose part or all of either numeric expression in a relational expression.

In evaluating a relational expression containing numeric expressions, the current values of the variables are used to evaluate each numeric expression. The resulting values of the numeric expressions are then compared according to the relational operator to determine the truth value of the relational expression. If the condition specified by the relational operator is correct, the relational expression is *true*. If the condition is not correct, the relational expression is *false*. For example, consider the following relational expression:

N−3>=5

If the value of N is 10, then N-3 is 7. Because 7 is greater than 5, the relational expression is *true*. However, if N is 4, then N-3 is 1. Because 1 is not greater than or equal to 5, the expression is *false*. Finally, if N is 8, then N-3 is 5 and the relational expression is *true*.

Illustrative programs

To illustrate the use of the IF statement and relational expressions in a program, assume that we need to write a program that calculates the tuition for a college student. The input data is the student's identification number and the number of units (credits) for which the student is enrolled. The tuition is $350 if the student is taking twelve or fewer units. If the student is taking more than twelve units, the tuition is $350 plus $20 per unit for all units over twelve. The program must display the student's identification number and tuition for any valid input.

The program to accomplish this requires decision making. First the computer must accept the input data. Then the computer must examine the number of units to determine the tuition. This decision-making step can be stated as follows: If the number of units is less than or equal to twelve, the tuition is $350; otherwise the tuition is $350 plus $20 per unit for all units over twelve. In other words, the computer must select between two ways of calculating the tuition based on a comparison between the number of units and twelve. After the tuition is calculated, the computer must display the output.

The program in Figure 3-1 solves this problem. The INPUT statement accepts the student's identification number (I) and number of units (U). The IF statement then compares the number of units with twelve. If U is greater than twelve, the computer branches to statement 190. The tuition (T) is calculated at $350 plus $20 per unit for all units over twelve (U − 12). Then the output is displayed. If U is less than or equal to twelve, the computer does not branch. Instead, the computer goes on to the next statement in sequence and the tuition is set equal to $350. The purpose of the GOTO statement following statement 170 is to branch around statement 190 to the PRINT statement so that the output can be displayed.

It is important to understand why the statement GOTO 200 (line 180) is necessary in this program. Recall that the statements in a program are executed in sequence unless the sequence is broken with a branch instruction. If this GOTO statement were omitted and the number of units were less than or equal to twelve, the result would be incorrect. In this case the computer would set T equal to $350. Then, because the GOTO statement would be missing, the next statement in sequence would be statement 190. Hence, the tuition would be calculated again, this time incorrectly. The second value for the tuition would replace the first value and would be the value displayed. This situation is avoided by including the GOTO statement to branch around statement 190.

Figure 3-1. The tuition-calculation program

```
100 REM - TUITION CALCULATION PROGRAM
110 REM - VARIABLES:
120 REM      I  = STUDENT ID
130 REM      U  = NUMBER OF UNITS
140 REM      T  = TUITION
150 INPUT I,U
160   IF U>12 THEN 190
170     LET T=350
180   GOTO 200
190     LET T=350+20*(U-12)
200   PRINT "STUDENT ID:",I
210   PRINT "TUITION:",T
220 GOTO 150
230 END
```

(a) The program

```
? 1234,6
STUDENT ID:     1234
TUITION:        350
? 3456,15
STUDENT ID:     3456
TUITION:        410
? 5678,12
STUDENT ID:     5678
TUITION:        350
? 7890,12.5
STUDENT ID:     7890
TUITION:        360
?
```

(b) Input and output

This program has a loop so the processing will be repeated until no more input is supplied. If there is only one set of input data, so that a loop is not needed, the statement GOTO 150 (line 220) can be omitted.

An alternative way of writing this program is shown in Figure 3-2. In this example, the INPUT statement accepts the input and then the tuition is set equal to $350. Next the IF statement determines if the units are less than or equal to twelve. If this is the case, the computer branches around the next statement to the PRINT statement. If, however, the units are greater than twelve, the tuition is calculated at $350 plus $20 per unit over twelve. This new value of the tuition replaces the previous value. After this calculation is done, the computer goes on to the PRINT

Figure 3-2. The alternative tuition-calculation program

```
100 REM - TUITION CALCULATION PROGRAM
110 REM - VARIABLES:
120 REM      I = STUDENT ID
130 REM      U = NUMBER OF UNITS
140 REM      T = TUITION
150 INPUT I,U
160   LET T=350
170   IF U<=12 THEN 190
180     LET T=350+20*(U-12)
190   PRINT "STUDENT ID:",I
200   PRINT "TUITION:",T
210 GOTO 150
220 END
```

statement. Although this program is slightly different than the one in Figure 3-1, the output is identical for the same input.

Notice in these examples that the statements that calculate the tuition are indented. This is a common style used with the IF statement that helps the programmer see the logic of the program.

Flowcharts with decisions

In the flowchart of a program that includes decision making, a diamond-shaped symbol is used for the decision step. For example, Figure 3-3 shows the flowchart of the logic in the first tuition-calculation program (Figure 3-1). The diamond-shaped decision symbol is used for the test that determines whether the units are greater than twelve. This test is written as a question within the symbol.

Figure 3-3. Flowchart of the tuition-calculation program

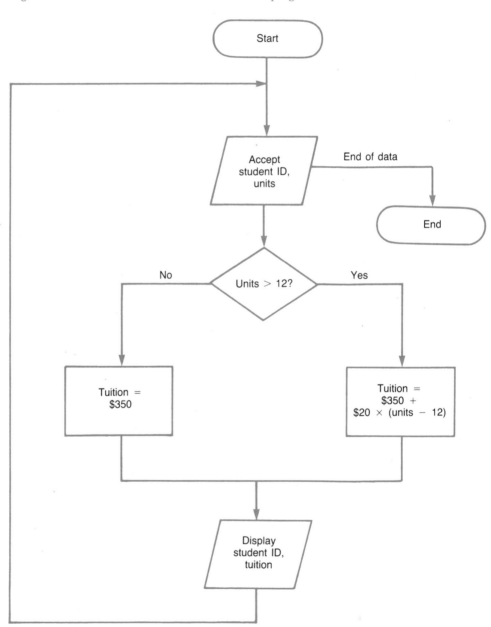

Whenever a decision symbol is used, two or more flowlines must leave the symbol. These flowlines represent the possible answers to the question asked in the symbol. The flowlines must be labeled with the answers. The decision symbol in Figure 3-3 asks whether the number of units is greater than 12; the possible answers, yes and no, are written above the flowlines leaving the symbol. By following the flowlines we can see what calculations are done for each alternative. Notice that after the calculation steps, the flowlines come together at the output step. This corresponds to the logic of the program.

Figure 3-4 is the flowchart of the logic in the alternative tuition-calculation program (Figure 3-2). This flowchart shows that, before the decision step, the tuition is set equal to $350. Then the units are tested to determine if they are less than or equal to twelve. If this is the case, the logic flows directly to the output step. If the units are not less than or equal to twelve, a new value for the tuition is calculated before going on to the output step. This logic corresponds to that of the program.

3-2 Program logic for decision making

The programs in Figures 3-1 and 3-2 use two different patterns of decision making. In this section we describe these patterns in general. First, however, we need to understand conditions and complements.

Conditions and complements

A relational expression represents a *condition* that is either true or false. For example, the condition "the number of units is greater than twelve" is represented by the relational expression $U>12$. Most conditions that involve the comparison of two values can be expressed in a relational expression.

Sometimes the logic of a program is such that the *complement* of a condition is needed. The complement is the condition that is true if the original condition is false and vice versa. For example, the complement of the condition "the number of units is greater than twelve" is the condition "the number of units is less than or equal to twelve." As another example, the complement of the condition "A is equal to B" is the condition "A is not equal to B."

For each relational operator in BASIC there is another relational operator for representing the complement. The following table lists these:

Relational operator	*Complement*
$<$	$>=$
$<=$	$>$
$>$	$<=$
$>=$	$<$
$=$	$<>$
$<>$	$=$

Thus, in BASIC the complement of the condition $U>12$ is $U<=12$. Similarly, the complement of the condition $A=B$ is $A<>B$.

Patterns of decision making

In this subsection we describe two basic patterns of decision making. We call them two-sided and one-sided decisions.

Figure 3-4. Flowchart of the alternative tuition-calculation program

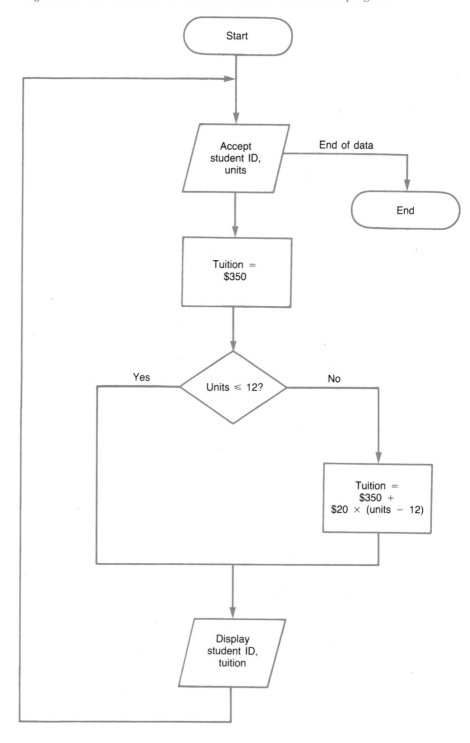

Two-sided decisions. In a *two-sided decision*, the computer selects between two alternative groups of statements based on some condition. The pattern is represented by the diagram in Figure 3-5. At the point in the program where the decision is to be made, a condition is tested for its truth value. If the condition is true, one group

Figure 3-5. The two-sided decision pattern

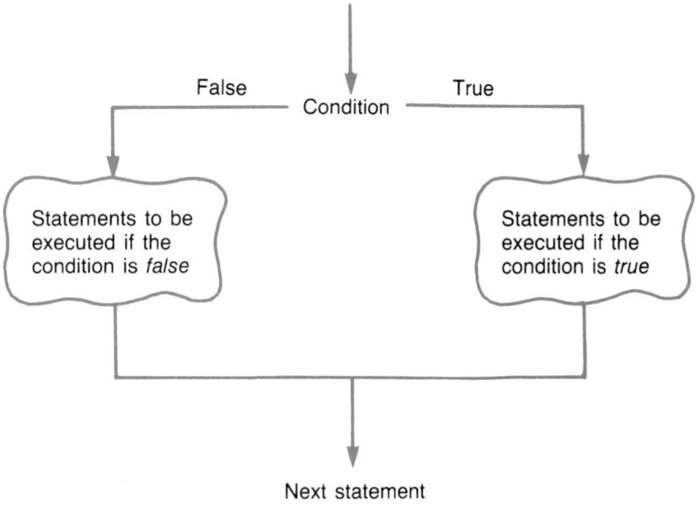

of statements is executed; if the condition is false, another set of statements is executed. We call the statements to be executed if the condition is true the *true part* of the decision, and the statements to be executed if the condition is false the *false part*. After doing either the true part or the false part (but not both) the computer continues with the next statement. We call this a two-sided decision because it has both a true part and a false part.

Another way of expressing a two-sided decision is shown in Figure 3-6. Here the true part follows the *if . . . then* line and the false part comes after the *else* line. This form shows that *if* the condition is true, *then* the true part is executed *else* the false part is executed.

Although the form in Figure 3-6 expresses very clearly the logic that we wish to use in decision making, it is not the pattern used by the IF statement. (Later, we will discuss variations of the IF statement available in some versions of BASIC that do follow this pattern.) All that the IF statement can do is branch to another statement or continue with the next statement in sequence, depending upon the truth or falsity of a relational expression. Hence, if we wish to obtain the same result as in the pattern shown in Figure 3-6, *we must branch to the true part. The false part must follow the IF statement and end with a GOTO statement that branches around the true part.* This pattern is shown in Figure 3-7.

Figure 3-6. The two-sided decision pattern

if condition *then*

else

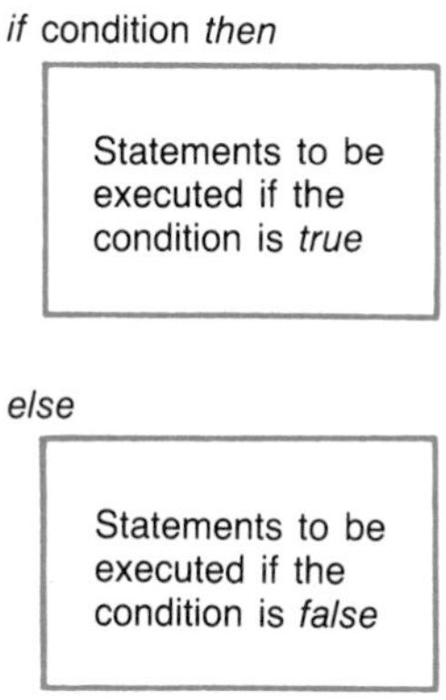

Figure 3-7. The two-sided decision pattern in BASIC

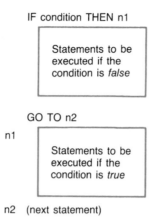

The tuition-calculation program in Figure 3-1 illustrates this approach. The decision logic in this program can be stated as follows:

> *if* the units are greater than twelve *then*
>   calculate the tuition as $350 plus $20 per unit over twelve
> *else*
>   set the tuition equal to $350

Hence, in BASIC the decision is as follows:

```
160 IF U>12 THEN 190
170    LET T=350
180 GOTO 200
190    LET T=350+20*(U-12)
200 (next statement)
```

If the condition that the number of units is greater than twelve is true, the computer branches to the second tuition calculation. If the condition is false, the computer goes on (we say that it "falls through") to the next statement in sequence. The statement GOTO 200 is necessary to branch around the true part. Notice that we have indented the true and false parts to make the decision logic easier to understand in the program.

We can usually rewrite a two-sided decision using the complement of the condition. To do this we must reverse the true and false parts. For example, the decision in the tuition-calculation program can be rewritten as follows:

```
160 IF U<=12 THEN 190
170    LET T=350+20*(U-12)
180 GOTO 200
190    LET T=350
200 (next statement)
```

The original condition was U>12. Its complement, U<=12, is used in these statements. The program with these statements produces output identical to that of the original program for the same input.

In the tuition-calculation example there is only one statement to be executed if the condition is true and one if the condition is false. In fact, there may be any number of statements in the true and false parts. For example, assume that we wish to calculate employee pay. The gross pay is $6.50 per hour for the first forty hours worked and $9.75 per hour for all time over forty hours. In addition, the withholding tax is 18% of the gross pay if forty or fewer hours are worked and 22% of the gross pay if more than forty hours are worked. The net pay is the gross pay less the withholding tax.

The program in Figure 3-8 satisfies these requirements. The program first accepts input data consisting of the employee's identification number (I) and the hours worked (H). Then the hours worked are compared with forty. If the hours are less than or equal to forty, the payroll calculations following the IF statement are performed and the computer branches to statement 240. If the hours are greater than

Figure 3-8. A payroll program

```
100 REM - PAYROLL PROGRAM
110 REM - VARIABLES:
120 REM      I  = EMPLOYEE ID
130 REM      H  = HOURS WORKED
140 REM      G  = GROSS PAY
150 REM      W  = WITHHOLDING TAX
160 REM      P  = NET PAY
170 INPUT I,H
180   IF H>40 THEN 220
190     LET G=6.5*H
200     LET W=.18*G
210   GOTO 240
220     LET G=260+9.75*(H-40)
230     LET W=.22*G
240   LET P=G-W
250   PRINT
260   PRINT "PAYROLL DATA FOR EMPLOYEE",I
270   PRINT
280   PRINT "   GROSS PAY",G
290   PRINT "   TAX",W
300   PRINT "   NET PAY",P
310   PRINT
320 GOTO 170
330 END
```

(a) The program

```
? 234,32

PAYROLL DATA FOR EMPLOYEE      234

    GROSS PAY    208
    TAX          37.44
    NET PAY      170.56

? 456,48

PAYROLL DATA FOR EMPLOYEE      456

    GROSS PAY    338
    TAX          74.36
    NET PAY      263.64

? 678,36

PAYROLL DATA FOR EMPLOYEE      678

    GROSS PAY    234
    TAX          42.12
    NET PAY      191.88

?
```

(b) Input and output

forty, the computer branches to statement 220 and performs the payroll calculations beginning there. Notice that all statements in the true and false parts of the decision are indented. After the gross pay and withholding tax are computed by one of the two methods, the net pay is computed and the output is displayed.

One-sided decisions. In a *one-sided decision,* the computer either executes one group of statements or bypasses these statements based on some condition. This pattern is represented by the diagram in Figure 3-9. If the condition is true, the true part is executed before going on to the next statement. If the condition is false, the computer bypasses the true part and goes directly to the next statement. This pattern is called a one-sided decision because there is only a true part.

The one-sided pattern can also be expressed in the form shown in Figure 3-10. The true part follows the *if . . . then* line and there is no false part. This form shows that *if* the condition is true, *then* the true part is executed.

To create the one-sided pattern with the IF statement in BASIC, *we must use the complement of the condition and branch around the true part, which follows the* IF *statement, if the complement is true.* This pattern is shown in Figure 3-11.

Figure 3-9. The one-sided decision pattern

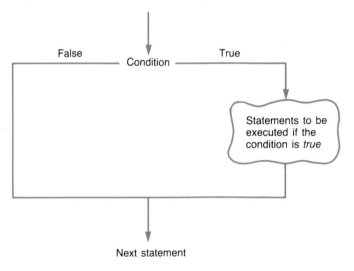

Figure 3-10. The one-sided decision pattern

if condition *then*

> Statements to be
> executed if the
> condition is *true*

Figure 3-11. The one-sided decision pattern in BASIC

IF complement of condition THEN n

> Statements to be
> executed if the
> *condition* is *true*
> (i.e. if *complement* is *false*)

n (next statement)

Figure 3-12. An alternative payroll program

```
100 REM - PAYROLL PROGRAM
110 REM - VARIABLES:
120 REM        I  = EMPLOYEE ID
130 REM        H  = HOURS WORKED
140 REM        G  = GROSS PAY
150 REM        W  = WITHHOLDING TAX
160 REM        P  = NET PAY
170 INPUT I,H
180    LET G=6.5*H
190    LET W=.18*G
200    IF H<=40 THEN 230
210      LET G=260+9.75*(H-40)
220      LET W=.22*G
230    LET P=G-W
240    PRINT
250    PRINT "PAYROLL DATA FOR EMPLOYEE",I
260    PRINT
270    PRINT "   GROSS PAY",G
280    PRINT "   TAX",W
290    PRINT "   NET PAY",P
300    PRINT
310 GOTO 170
320 END
```

The alternative tuition-calculation program in Figure 3-2 illustrates the one-sided decision. The decision logic in this program can be stated as follows:

> *if* the units are greater than twelve *then*
>   calculate the tuition as $350 plus $20 per unit over twelve

The complement of the condition "the units are greater than twelve" is "the units are less than or equal to twelve." Hence in BASIC the decision is as follows:

```
170 IF U<=12 THEN 190
180    LET T=350+20*(U-12)
190 (next statement)
```

Notice that we have indented the true part to make the decision logic easier to understand in the program.

Figure 3-12 shows an alternative version of the payroll program (Figure 3-8) that uses a one-sided decision instead of a two-sided decision. After the input is accepted, the basic payroll calculation is performed. Then the hours worked are compared with forty. If the hours are greater than forty, the payroll data is recalculated, replacing the previous data. If the hours are less than or equal to forty, these steps are bypassed. Notice that all statements in the true part of the decision are indented. Finally, the net pay is calculated and the output is displayed. The output from the program is identical to that of the previous program for the same input.

3-3 Nested decisions

Within the true or false parts of a decision-making structure may be any number or type of statements. In fact, there may be other IF statements in the true or false parts. When an IF statement is included within a set of statements that is executed depending on the condition in another IF statement, we say that there are *nested decisions*.

As an example of nested decisions, assume that the tuition charged a college student is based not only on the number of units for which the student is enrolled, but also on whether the student is a resident of the state. If the number of units is less than or equal to twelve and the student is a state resident, the tuition is $350. If the student is not a resident (and the units are less than or equal to twelve), the tuition is $800. If the number of units is greater than twelve and the student is a resident, the tuition is $350 plus $20 for all units over twelve. For a nonresident with more than twelve units, the tuition is $800 plus $45 for each excess unit.

This problem involves first deciding whether the number of units is greater than twelve and then determining whether the student is a state resident. Assume that the input data is the student's identification number (I), the number of units (U), and a residence code (R), which is 1 if the student is a state resident and 0 otherwise. A program to solve this problem is shown in Figure 3-13. After accepting the input data, the program compares U with twelve. If U is less than or equal to twelve, the computer falls through to the second IF statement. This statement checks R to determine whether the student is a state resident. If U is greater than twelve, the computer branches to statement 230 to check R. The actual tuition depends both on the number of units and on the residence code. After the tuition is calculated, the output is displayed and the loop is repeated.

Figure 3-13. The tuition-calculation program with nested decisions

```
100 REM - TUITION CALCULATION PROGRAM
110 REM - VARIABLES:
120 REM        I  = STUDENT ID
130 REM        U  = NUMBER OF UNITS
140 REM        R  = RESIDENCE CODE
150 REM        T  = TUITION
160 INPUT I,U,R
170   IF U>12 THEN 230
180     IF R=0 THEN 210
190       LET T=350
200     GOTO 270
210       LET T=800
220     GOTO 270
230     IF R=0 THEN 260
240       LET T=350+20*(U-12)
250     GOTO 270
260       LET T=800+45*(U-12)
270     PRINT "STUDENT ID:",I
280     PRINT "TUITION:",T
290 GOTO 160
300 END
```

(a) The program

```
? 2345,8,0
STUDENT ID:     2345
TUITION:        800
? 4567,13,1
STUDENT ID:     4567
TUITION:        370
? 6789,18,0
STUDENT ID:     6789
TUITION:        1070
? 8901,10,1
STUDENT ID:     8901
TUITION:        350
?
```

(b) Input and output

Notice that indentation is used in this example to show which decisions are nested and which computation belongs with which decision. This is especially important with nested decisions. The indentation gives a visual clue to the program's logic.

Within a nested decision may be other nested decisions. In fact, there may be as many nested decisions as the programmer needs. Usually, however, nesting more than one or two decisions makes the program difficult to understand.

Flowcharts with nested decisions

Figure 3-14 shows how nested decisions are depicted in a flowchart. This is the flowchart of the program in Figure 3-13. Notice that in the true part and the false part of the first decision (the decision regarding the number of units) is a second decision (the decision regarding the residence code). The nesting of the decisions shows up very clearly in the flowchart.

This flowchart also shows the use of the connector symbol (the small circle). This symbol is used when it is necessary but inconvenient to connect distant parts of a flowchart with a flowline or when a flowchart must continue onto another page. The connector symbol appears once when the flow logic leaves one part of the chart and again where the logic enters the other part. Within each set of connectors is placed an identifying letter or number. In Figure 3-14 the letter A identifies the pair of connectors. If another set of connector symbols is needed for another part of the flowchart, a different letter or symbol (such as the letter B) is used.

Case selection

A special type of nested decision, called *case selection,* involves selecting from among several cases. For example, assume that the tuition charge is based on the following schedule:

Units	Tuition
Up to 6.0	$200
6.1 to 12.0	$200 + $25/unit over 6
12.1 to 18.0	$350 + $20/unit over 12
18.1 and up	$470 + $15/unit over 18

There are four cases, depending on the number of units for which the student is enrolled. We need a program to select the appropriate case and perform the required calculations.

We can accomplish the selection process using nested decisions by first determining whether the number of units is less than or equal to six. If it is, we select the first case, and the tuition is $200. If the number of units is greater than six, we must check whether the number is less than or equal to twelve. If it is, we select the second case and the tuition is calculated appropriately. If the number of units is greater than twelve, we compare the number with eighteen. If it is less than or equal to eighteen, we select the third case; otherwise we select the fourth case.

Figure 3-15 shows the tuition-calculation program using this case-selection logic. The program selects the appropriate case by comparing U with 6, 12, and 18. After the tuition is calculated, the output is displayed. The three GOTO 260 statements are required to branch around the other cases to the PRINT statement when the first, second, or third case is selected.

This example shows one style of indentation that is used with case selection. Some programmers, however, prefer other indentation patterns.

For certain very specialized types of case selection, BASIC provides the ON-GOTO statement. We will discuss this statement later.

Figure 3-14. Flowchart of the tuition-calculation program with nested decisions

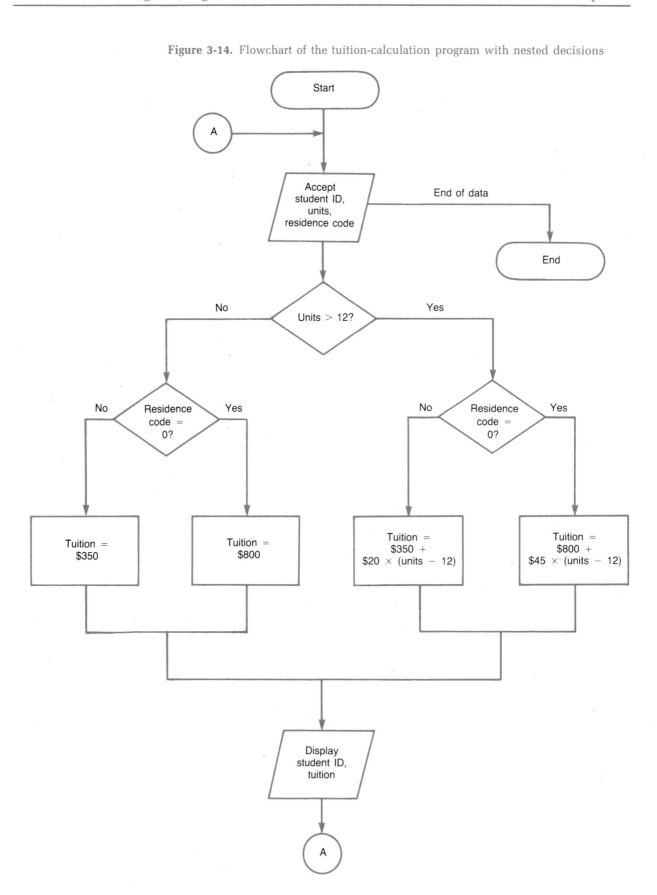

Figure 3-15. The tuition-calculation program with case selection

```
100 REM - TUITION CALCULATION PROGRAM
110 REM - VARIABLES:
120 REM        I  = STUDENT ID
130 REM        U  = NUMBER OF UNITS
140 REM        T  = TUITION
150 INPUT I,U
160   IF U>6 THEN 190
170     LET T=200
180   GOTO 260
190   IF U>12 THEN 220
200     LET T=200+25*(U-6)
210   GOTO 260
220   IF U>18 THEN 250
230     LET T=350+20*(U-12)
240   GOTO 260
250     LET T=470+15*(U-18)
260   PRINT "STUDENT ID:",I
270   PRINT "TUITION:",T
280 GOTO 150
290 END
```

(a) The program

```
? 1432,9
STUDENT ID:    1432
TUITION:       275
? 3654,16
STUDENT ID:    3654
TUITION:       430
? 5876,3
STUDENT ID:    5876
TUITION:       200
? 7098,19
STUDENT ID:    7098
TUITION:       485
?
```

(b) Input and output

Flowcharts with case selection

Case selection can be shown in a flowchart using a series of nested decisions. Alternatively, one decision symbol can be used with multiple flowlines leaving it. Each flowline represents one case and is labeled accordingly. Figure 3-16 shows how this is done in a flowchart of the program in Figure 3-15. Notice that the decision symbol gives the variable that determines which case is to be selected. The lines leaving the symbol are labeled with the possible cases. (In this figure a single line leaves the decision symbol and then splits into the four cases. Alternatively, four separate lines may come out of the decision symbol.)

3-4 A sample problem

In this section we develop a program for a sample problem that involves decision making. The problem is to compute the charges for purchases that customers make.

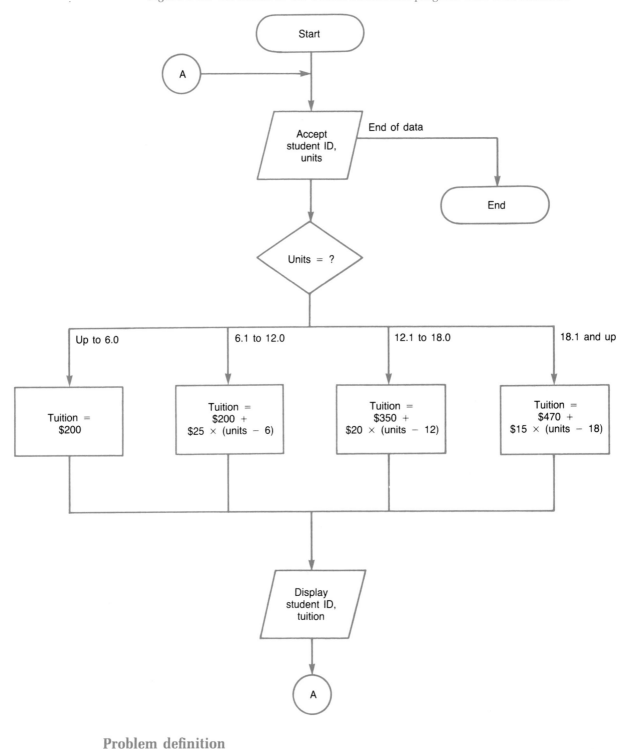

Figure 3-16. Flowchart of the tuition-calculation program with case selection

Problem definition

A program is needed to compute the purchase amount, the tax, the shipping charge, and the total due for each purchase made for a customer. The program should display the results of these computations along with the customer's number. Figure 3-17 shows how the output should appear for one customer. (X's represent numeric data in this figure.)

Figure 3-17. Output layout for the customer order program

```
CUSTOMER NUM:   XXXX
PURCHASE AMT:   XXXX
TAX:            XXXX
SHIPPING:       XXXX
TOTAL DUE:      XXXX
```

Input to the program for each customer is the customer number, the quantity ordered, and the price for each item ordered (called the unit price). There are an unknown number of customers. The purchase amount is the quantity ordered times the unit price less the discount. The discount depends on the quantity ordered. If the quantity is less than ten units, there is no discount. If the quantity ordered is ten to nineteen units, the discount is 10% of the basic purchase amount, which is the purchase amount before the discount is taken. If the quantity ordered is twenty or more units, the discount is 20% of the basic purchase amount.

The tax is 6% of the purchase amount. The shipping charge is $5 if the purchase amount is less than $100. There is no shipping charge if the purchase amount is $100 or more. The total due is the sum of the purchase amount, the tax, and the shipping charge.

Program design

The general algorithm that solves this problem can be expressed as shown in Figure 3-18. To compute the purchase amount we must first multiply the quantity purchased by the unit price and then subtract the discount. The discount depends on the quantity ordered. A nested decision is needed to find the discount because there are three cases. The shipping charge depends on the purchase amount. A simple decision (non-nested) is needed to find the shipping charge because there are only two cases. Figure 3-19 shows the flowchart for the program. The steps that compute the purchase amount and the shipping charge are specially marked in this flowchart.

Program coding

The program to solve this problem is shown in Figure 3-20. The variables used in the program are listed in REM statements at the beginning of the program. The first three variables (N, Q, and P) are for input data and the last four (A, X, S, and T) are for output data. The other two variables (B and D) are used for data that is neither input nor output. Often variables are needed in a program for non-I/O data. Such data, sometimes called temporary or internal data, usually is the result of a calculation that is needed later in the program.

The logic of the program follows the algorithm in Figure 3-18 and the flowchart in Figure 3-19. Notice that the computation of the purchase amount requires several steps including a nested decision. A simple decision is needed for the computation of the shipping charge. REM statements are included to identify each set of computations in the program.

Figure 3-18. Algorithm for the customer order problem

Repeat the following until there is no more data:
    Accept the customer number, quantity ordered, and unit price.
    Compute the purchase amount.
    Compute the tax.
    Compute the shipping charge.
    Compute the total due.
    Display the customer number, purchase amount, tax, shipping charge, and total due.

Figure 3-19. Flowchart of the customer order program

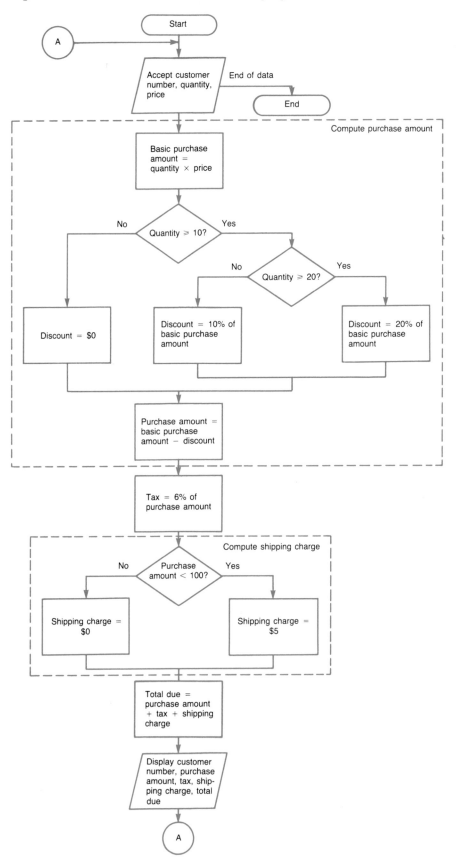

Figure 3-20. The customer order program

```
100 REM - CUSTOMER ORDER PROGRAM
110 REM - VARIABLES:
120 REM        N = CUSTOMER NUMBER
130 REM        Q = QUANTITY ORDERED
140 REM        P = UNIT PRICE
150 REM        B = BASIC PURCHASE AMOUNT
160 REM        D = DISCOUNT
170 REM        A = PURCHASE AMOUNT
180 REM        X = TAX
190 REM        S = SHIPPING CHARGE
200 REM        T = TOTAL DUE
210 INPUT N,Q,P
220    REM - COMPUTE PURCHASE AMOUNT
230    LET B=Q*P
240    IF Q>=10 THEN 270
250      LET D=0
260    GOTO 310
270      IF Q>=20 THEN 300
280        LET D=.1*B
290      GOTO 310
300        LET D=.2*B
310    LET A=B-D
320    REM - COMPUTE TAX
330    LET X=.06*A
340    REM - COMPUTE SHIPPING CHARGE
350    IF A<100 THEN 380
360      LET S=0
370    GOTO 400
380      LET S=5
390    REM - COMPUTE TOTAL DUE
400    LET T=A+X+S
410    PRINT
420    PRINT "CUSTOMER NUM:",N
430    PRINT "PURCHASE AMT:",A
440    PRINT "TAX:",X
450    PRINT "SHIPPING:",S
460    PRINT "TOTAL DUE:",T
470    PRINT
480 GOTO 210
490 END
```

Program correctness

If we have been very careful in developing the logic of the program, we can be reasonably sure it is correct. Still, we must test the program to try to locate any errors. To test a program with decisions we should test all possible cases for all decisions. For this program, we need to test cases where the quantity ordered is less than ten, between ten and nineteen, and greater than nineteen. Similarly, we need to test cases where the purchase amount is less than 100 and where it is 100 or more.

Figure 3-21 shows several sets of input test data and the expected output for each set. We can see that the different cases discussed in the previous paragraph are represented in this data. The input and output from running the program with this data is shown in Figure 3-22. As we can see, all test cases give correct results.

Program documentation

The program in Figure 3-20 contains numerous remarks that help document the program. In addition to the program description and list of variables, remarks are included at various points in the program to identify the computations being performed.

Figure 3-21. Input test data and expected output for the customer order program

Input test data			Expected output			
Customer number	Quantity ordered	Unit price	Purchase amount	Tax	Shipping	Total due
1234	9	11	99	5.94	5	109.94
2345	15	12	162	9.72	0	171.72
3456	30	1	24	1.44	5	30.44
4567	6	17	102	6.12	0	108.12
5678	20	8	128	7.68	0	135.68
6789	19	10	171	10.26	0	181.26
7890	10	7	63	3.78	5	71.78

The complete set of documentation for this program would include a listing of the program (Figure 3-20) and the input and output from running the program (Figure 3-22). The documentation may also include the output layout (Figure 3-17), the algorithm (Figure 3-18), the flowchart (Figure 3-19), the input test data and expected output (Figure 3-21), and other items that we will discuss later.

*3-5 Variations of the IF statement

All versions of BASIC allow the form of the IF statement described in Section 3-1. Some, however, permit alternative forms that may make programming easier. In this section we describe these variations of the IF statement.

The IF-GOTO statement

In some versions of BASIC, the word GOTO can replace the word THEN in the IF statement. (See Table 3-1.) We call this the IF-GOTO statement. The syntax is as follows:

```
ln IF relational expression GOTO ln
```

For example, the following IF statement conforms to this syntax:

```
50 IF A>B GOTO 200
```

The effect is the same as the basic form of the IF statement. In this example, if A is greater than B, the computer branches to statement 200; otherwise the computer continues with the next statement in sequence.

The IF-THEN statement

Some versions of BASIC allow another statement to be used in place of a line number in the IF statement. (See Table 3-2.) We call this the IF-THEN statement to distinguish it from the IF statement with a line number. The syntax is as follows:

```
ln IF relational expression THEN statement
```

* Sections marked with an asterisk describe features that are not available in some versions of BASIC.

Figure 3-22. Input and output for the customer order program

```
? 1234,9,11

CUSTOMER NUM:   1234
PURCHASE AMT:   99
TAX:            5.94
SHIPPING:       5
TOTAL DUE:      109.94

? 2345,15,12

CUSTOMER NUM:   2345
PURCHASE AMT:   162
TAX:            9.72
SHIPPING:       0
TOTAL DUE:      171.72

? 3456,30,1

CUSTOMER NUM:   3456
PURCHASE AMT:   24
TAX:            1.44
SHIPPING:       5
TOTAL DUE:      30.44

? 4567,6,17

CUSTOMER NUM:   4567
PURCHASE AMT:   102
TAX:            6.12
SHIPPING:       0
TOTAL DUE:      108.12

? 5678,20,8

CUSTOMER NUM:   5678
PURCHASE AMT:   128
TAX:            7.68
SHIPPING:       0
TOTAL DUE:      135.68

? 6789,19,10

CUSTOMER NUM:   6789
PURCHASE AMT:   171
TAX:            10.26
SHIPPING:       0
TOTAL DUE:      181.26

? 7890,10,7

CUSTOMER NUM:   7890
PURCHASE AMT:   63
TAX:            3.78
SHIPPING:       5
TOTAL DUE:      71.78

?
```

For example, the following statement may be used:

```
50 IF A>B THEN PRINT A
```

The effect is that the computer executes the statement within the IF statement if

Table 3-1. IF-GOTO statement differences

BASIC version	IF-GOTO statement available
ANS minimal BASIC	No
ANS BASIC	No
Microsoft BASIC	Yes
Applesoft BASIC	Yes
True BASIC	No
BASIC-PLUS	Yes
VAX-11 BASIC	Yes

Table 3-2. IF-THEN statement differences

BASIC version	IF-THEN statement available
ANS minimal BASIC	No
ANS BASIC	Yes
Microsoft BASIC	Yes
Applesoft BASIC	Yes
True BASIC	Yes
BASIC-PLUS	Yes
VAX-11 BASIC	Yes

the relational expression is true. If the expression is false, the statement is skipped. In the previous example, if A is greater than B, the computer displays the value of A. If A is not greater than B, the computer bypasses the PRINT statement and goes on to the next statement in sequence.

Most BASIC statements may be used in this form of the IF statement. For example, the following are valid:

```
75 IF X<Y THEN INPUT A,B,C
85 IF K=7 THEN LET K=K+1
95 IF U<=12 THEN GOTO 35
```

In each of these examples, the computer either executes the statement in the IF statement or skips it depending on whether the relational expression is true or false. If the condition is true, then after the statement in the IF statement is executed, the computer continues with the next statement in sequence unless a GOTO statement or other branching statement has been executed.

Multiple statements per line

In some versions of BASIC, multiple statements can appear on one line if they are separated by a special symbol such as a colon (:). (See Table 3-3.) For example, the following is valid in some versions of BASIC:

```
10 INPUT X,Y: LET Z=X+Y: PRINT Z
```

Table 3-3. Multiple-statements-per-line differences

BASIC version	Multiple statements per line permitted
ANS minimal BASIC	No
ANS BASIC	No
Microsoft BASIC	Yes, separated by colons (:)
Applesoft BASIC	Yes, separated by colons (:)
True BASIC	No
BASIC-PLUS	Yes, separated by backslashes (\)
VAX-11 BASIC	Yes, separated by backslashes (\)

This feature can be used in the IF-THEN statement to allow multiple statements to be executed if a condition is true. For example, consider the following statement:

```
100 IF A>B THEN LET C=A-B: PRINT C
```

In this example, if A is greater than B, the LET statement and the PRINT statement are executed. If A is not greater than B, both of these statements are bypassed.

Multiple-line statements

If a statement is too long for one line, we can continue it onto the next line by just typing beyond the end of the line. The statement will automatically continue on the next line. (Sometimes we say that the statement "wraps around" to the next line.) The RETURN or ENTER key is not pressed until all lines in the statement have been typed.

Some versions of BASIC provide a means of continuing onto the next line without typing to the end of the line. (See Table 3-4.) In some cases a key or combination of keys that indicates a line feed is typed at the end of the line to be continued. Then the statement is continued on the next line without a line number.

Table 3-4. Continuation differences

BASIC version	Continuation rules
ANS minimal BASIC	No special provisions.
ANS BASIC	Type an ampersand (&) followed by the RETURN key at the end of the line to be continued and another ampersand at the beginning of the new line.
Microsoft BASIC	Type a line feed at the end of the line to be continued. (On some computers a line feed is accomplished by holding the Ctrl key and pressing the ENTER key.)
Applesoft BASIC	No special provisions.
True BASIC	No special provisions.
BASIC-PLUS VAX-11 BASIC	Type an ampersand (&) followed by the RETURN key at the end of the line to be continued.

Using this approach, the different parts of an IF-THEN statement can be put on separate lines and indented, thus making the statement easier to read. For example, the previous IF-THEN statement may be entered as follows:

```
100 IF A>B THEN    ⟨line feed⟩
       LET C=A−B:  ⟨line feed⟩
       PRINT C     ⟨return⟩
```

A line feed is typed at the end of each of the first two lines and the RETURN or ENTER key is pressed at the end of the last line because this is the end of the statement. Notice that no line numbers are used for the second and third lines; a line number appears only with the first line. The resulting statement is easier to read than when it is typed on one line.

The IF-THEN-ELSE statement

Another variation of the IF statement that is permitted in some versions of BASIC is known as the IF-THEN-ELSE statement. (See Table 3-5.) The syntax of this statement is as follows:

$$ln \text{ IF } relational \text{ } expression \text{ THEN } \begin{Bmatrix} statement \\ ln \end{Bmatrix} \text{ ELSE } \begin{Bmatrix} statement \\ ln \end{Bmatrix}$$

Following the word THEN must be either a statement or a line number, then the word ELSE, and another statement or line number. For example, the following are valid IF-THEN-ELSE statements:

```
60 IF A>B THEN 200 ELSE 100
70 IF X<=Y THEN PRINT X ELSE PRINT Y
80 IF P=Q THEN LET C=0 ELSE 150
```

The effect of the IF-THEN-ELSE statement is that if the relational expression is true, the computer does what is indicated after the word THEN. If a line number is given, the computer branches to the indicated line; if a statement appears after the word THEN, the statement is executed. On the other hand, if the relational expression is false, the computer bypasses the THEN part and does whatever is indicated after the word ELSE. This may involve branching if a line number is given or executing the statement following the word ELSE.

Table 3-5. IF-THEN-ELSE statement differences

BASIC version	IF-THEN-ELSE *statement available*
ANS minimal BASIC	No
ANS BASIC	Yes
Microsoft BASIC	Yes
Applesoft BASIC	No
True BASIC	Yes
BASIC-PLUS	Yes
VAX-11 BASIC	Yes

To illustrate, consider the first example just given (statement 60). The effect of this statement is that if A is greater than B, the computer branches to statement 200, but if A is not greater than B, the computer branches to statement 100. In the second example (statement 70), if X is less than or equal to Y, the value of X is displayed; otherwise the value of Y is displayed. Notice that in this example, because no branching takes place, the computer goes on to the next statement in sequence after executing the appropriate PRINT statement. In the third example (statement 80), the computer either executes the LET statement or branches to statement 150, depending on whether P equals Q.

It is usually easier to read the IF-THEN-ELSE statement if the different parts of the statement are put on separate lines and indented. For example, we may write statement 70 given earlier as follows:

```
70 IF X>Y THEN
      PRINT X
   ELSE
      PRINT Y
```

The continuation rules discussed previously must be followed in entering this statement. (See Table 3-4.)

To illustrate the use of the IF-THEN-ELSE statement, consider the tuition-calculation program discussed in Section 3-1 (see Figure 3-1). We can write this program using the IF-THEN-ELSE statement as shown in Figure 3-23. Notice that if the number of units is less than or equal to twelve, T is set equal to $350; otherwise the value of T is computed by the second LET statement.

If multiple statements per line are allowed in the version of BASIC being used (see Table 3-3), then more than one statement can appear between the words THEN and ELSE and after the word ELSE in the IF-THEN-ELSE statement. Such statements must be separated by a special symbol such as a colon. For example, consider the following statement:

```
110 IF A>B THEN
       LET C=A-B:
       PRINT C
    ELSE
       LET D=B-A:
       PRINT D
```

In this example, if A is greater than B, the value of C is computed and displayed; otherwise the value of D is calculated and displayed. Notice that colons are used only between the statements after the words THEN and ELSE.

Figure 3-23. The tuition-calculation program using an IF-THEN-ELSE statement

```
100 REM - TUITION CALCULATION PROGRAM
110 REM - VARIABLES:
120 REM       I = STUDENT ID
130 REM       U = NUMBER OF UNITS
140 REM       T = TUITION
150 INPUT I,U
160    IF U<=12 THEN
          LET T=350
       ELSE
          LET T=350+20*(U-12)
170    PRINT "STUDENT ID:",I
180    PRINT "TUITION:",T
190 GOTO 150
200 END
```

Table 3-6. Nested IF-THEN-ELSE statement differences

BASIC version	*Nested* IF-THEN-ELSE *statements permitted*
ANS minimal BASIC	Not applicable
ANS BASIC	No
Microsoft BASIC	Yes
Applesoft BASIC	Not applicable
True BASIC	No
BASIC-PLUS	Yes
VAX-11 BASIC	Yes

Nested IF-THEN-ELSE statements. It is usually permissible to nest IF-THEN-ELSE statements. (See Table 3-6.) For example, the following statement may be acceptable:

```
120 IF X<Y THEN
       PRINT A
    ELSE
       IF X=Y THEN
         PRINT B
       ELSE
         PRINT C
```

In this example, A is displayed if X is less than Y, B is displayed if X equals Y, and C is displayed if X is greater than Y. Although this example is fairly straightforward, the rules can become quite complex, especially when several IF-THEN-ELSE statements are nested. In general, nesting of these statements should be avoided until the programmer becomes very familiar with the language.

The block IF statements

A few versions of BASIC provide special statements, called the block IF statements, that simplify programming for decisions. (See Table 3-7.) There are four statements in all: a special form of the IF-THEN statement, the ELSE statement, the END IF statement, and the ELSEIF statement.

Table 3-7. Block IF statement differences

BASIC version	*Block* IF *statements available*
ANS minimal BASIC	No
ANS BASIC	Yes
Microsoft BASIC	No
Applesoft BASIC	No
True BASIC	Yes
BASIC-PLUS	No
VAX-11 BASIC	No

Two-sided decisions. To form a two-sided decision, the IF-THEN, ELSE, and END IF statements are used. The syntax of these statements and their pattern of use are as follows:

```
ln IF relational expression THEN
              .
              .
              .
        statements
              .
              .
              .
ln ELSE
              .
              .
              .
        statements
              .
              .
              .
ln END IF
```

Notice that nothing comes after the word THEN in the IF-THEN statement and that line numbers are needed for the ELSE and END IF statements. Any number of statements may appear between the IF-THEN and ELSE statements and between the ELSE and END IF statements. All of these statements must have line numbers; it is not necessary to separate these statements with colons. The RETURN or ENTER key is pressed after each statement is entered. The following is an example of the use of the block IF statements:

```
110 IF A>B THEN
120    LET C=A-B
130    PRINT C
140 ELSE
150    LET D=B-A
160    PRINT D
170 END IF
```

When the computer executes a sequence of statements containing block IF statements, it first determines whether the relational expression in the IF-THEN statement is true or false. If the expression is true, the computer executes the statements between the IF-THEN statement and the ELSE statement (the true part). If the condition is false, the statements between the ELSE statement and the END IF statement (the false part) are executed. In the previous example, the computer executes the first LET and PRINT statements if A is greater than B and the second LET and PRINT statements if A is less than or equal to B. After performing either the true part or the false part, the computer continues with the next statement following the END IF statement.

Notice the role of the END IF statement. This statement marks the end of the false part of the decision. This statement is essential, because without it the computer would not know where the false part ends.

As an example of the use of the block IF statements in a program, consider the tuition-calculation program discussed in Section 3-1 (see Figure 3-1). Using block IF statements, the program can be written as shown in Figure 3-24. In this program,

Figure 3-24. The tuition-calculation program using block IF statements

```
100 REM - TUITION CALCULATION PROGRAM
110 REM - VARIABLES:
120 REM      I = STUDENT ID
130 REM      U = NUMBER OF UNITS
140 REM      T = TUITION
150 INPUT I,U
160   IF U<=12 THEN
170     LET T=350
180   ELSE
190     LET T=350+20*(U-12)
200   END IF
210   PRINT "STUDENT ID:",I
220   PRINT "TUITION:",T
230 GOTO 150
240 END
```

T is set equal to $350 if the number of units is less than or equal to twelve; otherwise the value of T is computed by the second LET statement. Notice that branching statements are not needed with the block IF statements. The computer automatically goes to the true or false part and then to the statement following END IF. In addition, it is not necessary to use the complementary condition in the IF statement. These features make these statements especially easy to use.

One-sided decisions. A one-sided decision is formed using the IF-THEN and END IF statements. The pattern is as follows:

```
ln IF relational expression THEN
            .
            .
            .
        statements
            .
            .
            .
ln END IF
```

Notice that there is no ELSE statement but that the END IF statement is required. If the relational expression is true, the computer executes the statements between the IF-THEN statement and the END IF statement and then goes on to the next statement following the END IF statement. If the expression is false, the computer bypasses these statements and goes directly to the first statement after the END IF statement.

The following statements illustrate the one-sided decision pattern:

```
200 IF A>B THEN
210    LET C=A-B
220    PRINT C
230 END IF
```

If A is greater than B, the computer executes the LET and PRINT statements. If this condition is not true, the computer skips these statements.

Nested decisions. The block IF statements can be used for nested decisions. The only restriction is that each IF-THEN statement must have a corresponding END IF statement. For example, consider the tuition-calculation program in Figure 3-13. The nested decisions in this program could be written using block IF statements as shown in the program in Figure 3-25. In this program the first END IF statement (line 220) corresponds to the second IF-THEN statement (line 180). The second END IF statement (line 280) corresponds to the third IF-THEN statement (line 240). The last END IF statement (line 290) is paired with the first IF-THEN statement (line 170). All of the END IF statements are required for the nested decision to function properly. Other patterns of nested decisions can be developed using combinations of one-sided and two-sided decisions.

Case selection. Selecting from among several cases can be done using nested decisions. Usually in such a situation all nesting occurs in the *false* parts of the decisions. For this type of nesting a special block IF statement, the ELSEIF statement, can be used. The syntax of this statement and its pattern of use are as follows:

```
ln IF relational expression THEN
            .
            .
            .
        statements
            .
            .
            .
ln ELSEIF relational expression THEN
            .
            .
            .
        statements
            .
            .
            .
ln ELSE relational expression THEN
            .
            .
            .
        statements
            .
            .
            .
ln END IF
```

Any number of ELSEIF statements may come after the IF-THEN statement. The ELSE statement is not required, but if used, it must come after the last ELSEIF statement. A single END IF statement is required at the end.

As an example of the use of the ELSEIF statement, consider the tuition-calculation program with case selection in Figure 3-15. The case-selection logic can be rewritten as shown in the program in Figure 3-26. In this program, if the condition in the IF-THEN statement is true, the computer executes the first LET statement (line 170) and then continues with the next statement following the END IF statement (line 240). If this condition is false, the computer checks the condition in the first ELSEIF statement (line 180). If this condition is true, the computer executes the second LET statement (line 190) before going on to the next statement following the END IF statement. If the condition in the first ELSEIF statement is false, the computer checks the condition in the second ELSEIF statement (line 200) and executes

Figure 3-25. The tuition-calculation program using nested block IF statements

```
100 REM - TUITION CALCULATION PROGRAM
110 REM - VARIABLES:
120 REM        I = STUDENT ID
130 REM        U = NUMBER OF UNITS
140 REM        R = RESIDENCE CODE
150 REM        T = TUITION
160 INPUT I,U,R
170   IF U<=12 THEN
180     IF R=1 THEN
190       LET T=350
200     ELSE
210       LET T=800
220     END IF
230   ELSE
240     IF R=1 THEN
250       LET T=350+20*(U-12)
260     ELSE
270       LET T=800+45*(U-12)
280     END IF
290   END IF
300   PRINT "STUDENT ID:",I
310   PRINT "TUITION:",T
320 GOTO 160
330 END
```

Figure 3-26. The tuition-calculation program using block IF statements for case selection

```
100 REM - TUITION CALCULATION PROGRAM
110 REM - VARIABLES:
120 REM        I = STUDENT ID
130 REM        U = NUMBER OF UNITS
140 REM        T = TUITION
150 INPUT I,U
160   IF U<=6 THEN
170     LET T=200
180   ELSEIF U<=12 THEN
190     LET T=200+25*(U-6)
200   ELSEIF U<=18 THEN
210     LET T=350+20*(U-12)
220   ELSE
230     LET T=470+15*(U-18)
240   END IF
250   PRINT "STUDENT ID:",I
260   PRINT "TUITION:",T
270 GOTO 150
280 END
```

the third LET statement (line 210) if this condition is true. If all conditions are false, the computer executes the LET statement following the ELSE statement.†

The block IF statements discussed in this subsection can make programming for decisions considerably easier than when other types of IF statements are used. Although they are not currently available in all versions of BASIC, their availability will probably increase in the future.

† Some versions of BASIC have a special statement called the SELECT statement that can be used for case selection in programs such as this.

3-6 The ON-GOTO statement

A statement that can be used for a special type of case selection is the ON-GOTO statement. The syntax of this statement is as follows:

```
ln ON numeric expression GOTO ln,ln,...
```

Following the word ON must be a numeric expression, then the word GOTO, and finally a list of line numbers separated by commas. For example, the following is a valid ON-GOTO statement:

```
25 ON X-3 GOTO 45,55,35
```

The effect of the ON-GOTO statement is that the computer first evaluates the numeric expression. For example, if X equals 4.7 in statement 25, $X-3$ is computed to obtain 1.7. The value of the expression is then rounded to the nearest integer (whole number). In the example, the value of the expression (1.7) is rounded to the integer 2. [Some versions of BASIC do not round the value. Instead, the fractional part is simply dropped. We say the value is *truncated.* (See Table 3-8.) If this were the case in the example, 1.7 would be truncated to get the integer 1.] Finally, the computer counts over the number of places in the list of line numbers indicated by the integer value and branches to the statement whose number appears in that place. In the example, the computer would count over two places and branch to statement 55.

As another example, consider the following statement:

```
65 ON N GOTO 45,55,55,25,45,75,75
```

In this example, the numeric expression is just the variable N. The value of N is rounded to the nearest integer. Then, if the integer value is 1 or 5, the computer branches to statement 45; if it is 2 or 3, the computer branches to statement 55; if the value is 4, the computer branches to statement 25; and if it is 6 or 7, the computer branches to statement 75.

The integer that results from rounding the value of the numeric expression must be between 1 and the number of line numbers in the list. For example, in the previous statement the value must be between 1 and 7. If the integer is less than 1 or greater than 7, an execution error occurs, causing an error message to be displayed

Table 3-8. ON-GOTO statement differences

BASIC version	Expression in ON-GOTO statement rounded or truncated
ANS minimal BASIC	Rounded
ANS BASIC	Rounded
Microsoft BASIC	Rounded
Applesoft BASIC	Truncated
True BASIC	Rounded
BASIC-PLUS	Truncated
VAX-11 BASIC	Truncated

Table 3-9. ON-GOTO statement differences

BASIC version	Result of out-of-range expression in ON-GOTO statement
ANS minimal BASIC	Execution error
ANS BASIC	Execution error
Microsoft BASIC	Continue with next statement in sequence unless expression value is less than 0 or greater than 255, in which case an execution error occurs.
Applesoft BASIC	Continue with next statement in sequence.
True BASIC	Execution error
BASIC-PLUS	Execution error
VAX-11 BASIC	Execution error

and the program to stop. [In some versions of BASIC, an error does not occur in this situation. Instead, the computer continues with the next statement in sequence after the ON-GOTO statement. (See Table 3-9.)]

The ON-GOTO statement is usually used to select one of several cases based on the value of a variable with an integer value. For example, in the tuition-calculation problem, assume that the variable C is a code indicating the amount of the scholarship that a student is to receive. If the value of C is 1, the scholarship is $100. If C is 2 or 3, the scholarship is $150. A value of 4 indicates a $300 scholarship, and a value of 5, a $400 scholarship. In this program, the following sequence of statements can be used to select the appropriate scholarship:

```
191 ON C GOTO 192,194,194,196,198
192    LET S=100
193 GOTO 199
194    LET S=150
195 GOTO 199
196    LET S=300
197 GOTO 199
198    LET S=400
199 (next statement)
```

The ON-GOTO statement branches to statement 192, 194, 196, or 198 based on the value of C. The variable S is then assigned the appropriate scholarship amount by the selected LET statement. After each LET statement (except the last, where it is not necessary), the statement GOTO 199 causes the computer to bypass the other cases and go on to the next part of the program. Notice that the LET statement for each case is indented. This is a common style that helps show the logic of the program.

As another example of the use of the ON-GOTO statement, assume that an employee's pay rate is based on the shift that the employee works. The input contains a code that indicates the shift. If the code is 0, the employee works the day shift at the rate of $6.50 per hour; if the code is 1, the employee works the evening shift at $9.75 per hour; if the code is 2 the employee works the night shift at $13.00 per hour. Figure 3-27 shows the program that computes the employee's gross pay based on this schedule. Input consists of the employee's identification number (I), hours worked (H), and shift code (S). The ON-GOTO statement selects the appropriate calculation based on the value of S. Notice that the expression $S+1$ is used in the ON-GOTO statement. The ON-GOTO statement requires an expression with a value of 1 or greater. Because S ranges from 0 to 2, we cannot use S by itself in the

Figure 3-27. A payroll program that uses the ON-GOTO statement

```
100 REM - PAYROLL PROGRAM
110 REM - VARIABLES:
120 REM       I  = EMPLOYEE ID
130 REM       H  = HOURS WORKED
140 REM       S  = SHIFT CODE
150 REM       G  = GROSS PAY
160 INPUT I,H,S
170   ON S+1 GOTO 180,200,220
180     LET G=6.5*H
190     GOTO 230
200     LET G=9.75*H
210     GOTO 230
220     LET G=13*H
230     PRINT "EMPLOYEE NUM:",I
240     PRINT "GROSS PAY:",G
250 GOTO 160
260 END
```

(a) The program

```
? 243,32,1
EMPLOYEE NUM:   243
GROSS PAY:      312
? 354,44,0
EMPLOYEE NUM:   354
GROSS PAY:      286
? 465,25,2
EMPLOYEE NUM:   465
GROSS PAY:      325
?
```

(b) Input and output

statement. Instead, we use $S+1$, which ranges from 1 to 3 and therefore satisfies the requirement of the ON-GOTO statement.

The flowchart of the program in Figure 3-27 is shown in Figure 3-28. Because the ON-GOTO statement is a special type of case selection, the flowchart uses the technique discussed at the end of Section 3-3 to show the logic.

The ON-GOTO statement can be useful in certain case-selection situations. Often, however, it cannot be used. At such times nested decisions using IF statements are required.

Review questions

1. What is the meaning of each of the following relational operators?
   a. $<=$
   b. $<>$
   c. $=$
   d. $>$
2. Code a statement that branches to statement 100 if the value of A is greater than or equal to 7.5.
3. Code a single statement that branches to statement 200 if the value of X is greater than that of Y or if the value of Y is greater than that of X.
4. Assume that the value of I is 2, J is 3, and K is 4. What is the truth value of each of the following relational expressions?
   a. $I>J$
   b. $K<=J+1$
   c. $12/I+3=J^2$
   d. $I*J<>K+2$

Figure 3-28. Flowchart of the payroll program that uses the ON-GOTO statement

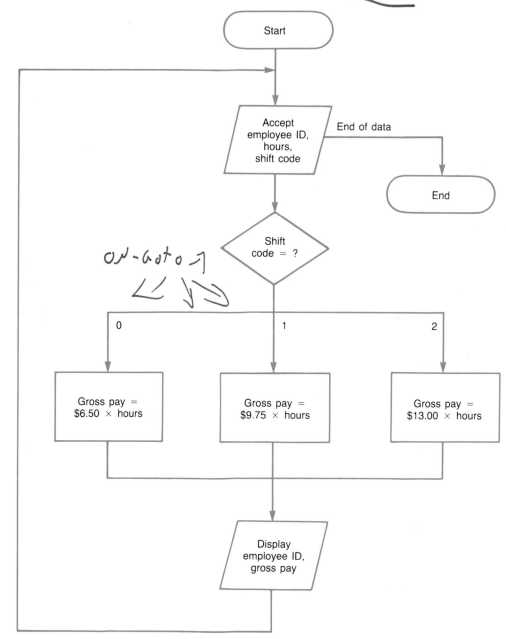

5. Consider the following statements:

```
100 IF X<Y THEN 130
110     LET Z=20
120 GOTO 140
130     LET Z=10
140 (next statement)
```

What is the value of Z after execution of these statements
a. if X is 20 and Y is 10?
b. if X is 20 and Y is 20?
6. Code a group of statements to add 5 to C if A is greater than B; otherwise add 6 to C.

7. Code a group of statements that assigns 0 to S and 1 to T if U is less than or equal to 50; otherwise assign 1 to S and 0 to T.

8. Code a group of statements that accepts and displays the values of D and E if F is not equal to 100.

9. Code a group of statements that adds the values of P and Q, assigning the result to R if I is greater than or equal to J.

10. What is the complement of each of the following conditions?
   a. A=B
   b. X<=Y
   c. P>Q
   d. S<>T

11. Code a group of statements containing one IF statement that assigns the larger of X and Y to Z. Did you use a one-sided or two-sided decision? Code another group of statements using the other approach.

12. A program pattern in which one decision is contained in another is called _____.

13. Code a group of statements that assigns 0, 1, 2, or 3 to I depending on the values of J and K as given in the following table:

		K	
		less than 5	5 or more
J	equal to 10	0	1
	not equal to 10	2	3

14. Code a group of statements that increases A by 1 if X and Y are both equal to 25, increases A by 2 if X is equal to 25 and Y is equal to 35, increases A by 3 if X is equal to 25 and Y is equal to neither 25 nor 35, and assigns 0 to A if X is not equal to 25.

15. Code a group of statements that assigns 0 to S if T is equal to 2 and U is equal to 4 and assigns 2 to S if T is not equal to 2 and U is equal to 3.

16. A program pattern which involves picking one of several alternatives is called _____.

17. Code a group of statements that assigns the value from the following table to N depending on the value of M. Assume that M can equal only 0, 1, 2, ... Do not use the ON-GOTO statement.

M	N
0	100
1 to 5	200
6, 7, or 8	300
9 or more	400

18. What variations of the IF statement are available in the version of BASIC you are using?

19. Code a single statement that branches to line 100 if the value of A is 1, 3, or 4; to line 200 if A is 2 or 5; and to line 300 if A is 6.

20. Rewrite the program in Figure 3-27 without using the ON-GOTO statement.

Programming problems

1. Commission paid to a salesperson is often based on the amount sold by the person. Assume that the commission rate is $7\frac{1}{2}\%$ if a person's sales total less than \$10,000 and 9% if sales total \$10,000 or more. The commission is calculated by multiplying the person's sales by the appropriate commission rate.

Write a BASIC program that accepts the salesperson's identification number and total sales, calculates the commission, and displays the result along with the identification number. Test the program with data for salesperson number 18735 with sales of $11,250, data for salesperson number 27630 whose sales total $6500, and data for salesperson 31084 whose sales were $10,000.

2. A telephone company's charge for long-distance calls is based not only on the distance but on the length of time of a call. Assume that between two cities the rate is $1.10 for the first three minutes or fraction thereof, and $.40 for each additional minute. Data for a customer who made calls between these two cities consists of the customer's number and length of call.

Write a BASIC program to accept the customer's number and length of call, calculate the charge, and display the customer's number, length of call, and the charge. Use the following data to test the program:

Customer number	Length of call
9606	8
9735	3
2802	2
7921	5
1509	4
5371	1

3. Write a BASIC program to find the absolute value of a number. The absolute value of x is x if x is nonnegative and $-x$ if x is negative. Input should be the number; output should give the original number and its absolute value. (Do *not* use the built-in absolute-value function.) Use the following input data to test the program:

```
  25.0
 -25.0
   0.0
 -84.6
 132.5
```

4. A real estate office employs several salespeople. At the end of each month the total value of all property sold by each salesperson is used to calculate the person's commission. If total sales exceed $600,000, the commission is $3\frac{1}{2}$% of the sales. If the sales are greater than $300,000 but not more than $600,000, the commission is 3% of the sales. Otherwise, the commission is $2\frac{1}{2}$% of the sales.

Write a BASIC program that accepts the salesperson's number and total sales, performs the necessary commission calculation, and displays the result along with the salesperson's number and total sales.

Use the following data to test the program:

Salesperson's number	Total sales
1085	$652,350
1720	$142,500
2531	$295,000
3007	$455,500
3219	$173,250
4806	$682,950
6111	$310,000
7932	$518,000

5. An electric company charges its customers 5 cents per kilowatt-hour for electricity used up to the first 100 kilowatt-hours, 4 cents per kilowatt-hour for each of the next 200 kilowatt-hours (up to 300 kilowatt-hours), and 3 cents per kilowatt-hour for all electricity used over 300 kilowatt-hours. Write a BASIC program to calculate the total charge for each customer. Input to the program consists of the customer's number and kilowatt-hours used. Output from the program should give the customer's number, the kilowatt-hours used, and the total charge. Use the following data to test the program:

Customer number	Kilowatt-hours used
1065	640
2837	85
3832	220
6721	300
8475	100

6. Write a BASIC program that finds the maximum of three numbers. Input consists of the three numbers; output should be the largest of the three. Use the following sets of input data to test the program:

        10,25,16
        17,38,41
        100,52,77
        −3,−8,−1
        0,45,−6
        −37,0,−42
        39,39,39
        14,14,8

7. Write a BASIC program to determine whether a student is a freshman, sophomore, junior, or senior based on the number of units (credits) that the student has completed. Input to the program consists of the student's number and the number of units completed.

   A student's classification is based on his or her units completed according to the following schedule:

Units completed	Classification
Less than 30 units	Freshman
30 units or more but less than 60 units	Sophomore
60 units or more but less than 90 units	Junior
90 units or more	Senior

   The output from the program should give the student's number, units completed, and the classification (FRESHMAN, SOPHOMORE, JUNIOR, or SENIOR). Use the following data to test the program:

Student number	Units completed
2352	38.0
3639	15.5
4007	29.5
4560	67.0
4915	103.5
8473	89.0

8. Write a BASIC program to evaluate the following function:

$$f(x) = \begin{cases} -x & \text{if } x < 0 \\ 1 & \text{if } x = 0 \\ 0 & \text{if } x > 0 \text{ and } x \le 10 \\ 2x & \text{if } x > 10 \end{cases}$$

   Input is the value of x; output should give the values of x and $f(x)$. Use the following data to test the program:

        38.60
        9.00
        10.00
        0.00
        −45.60
        0.01
        −0.01
        10.53

9. The basic charge for computer time is based on the number of hours of time used during the month. The schedule is as follows:

Hours used	Basic charge
0.00 to 5.00	$100
5.01 to 15.00	$100 plus $25 per hour for all time over 5 hours
15.01 and up	$225 plus $15 per hour for all time over 15 hours

A surcharge is added to the basic charge based on the priority used. The priority is indicated by a code. The surcharge is as follows:

Priority code	Surcharge
0	0
1	$50
2	$150

Write a BASIC program that accepts a customer's account number, number of hours used, and priority code. Then calculate the total charge. Display the account number and charge. Use the following data to test the program:

Account number	Hours used	Priority code
11825	3.52	0
14063	17.06	1
17185	7.93	1
19111	12.00	2
20045	5.00	1
21352	5.84	0
22841	27.94	2
23051	1.55	2
29118	15.02	0

10. Write a BASIC program to convert temperatures. If a temperature is entered in degrees Fahrenheit (F), it should be converted to degrees Celsius (C) and Kelvin (K). If a temperature is entered in Celsius, it should be converted to Fahrenheit and Kelvin. If a temperature is entered in Kelvin, it should be converted to Fahrenheit and Celsius. The following equations relate these temperature scales:

$$C = \frac{5}{9} \times (F - 32)$$
$$K = C + 273.15$$

The program should accept a code indicating the temperature scale of the input and the temperature to be converted. A code of 1 means the input temperature is in Fahrenheit, 2 means it is in Celsius, and 3 means it is in Kelvin. The program should convert the input temperatures to the equivalent temperatures in the two other scales and display the results.

Use the following input data to test the program:

Code	Temperature
1	32
2	100
3	0
3	285
2	−52
1	308

11. The results of a psychological experiment need to be analyzed. Each subject in the experiment took from one to four tests. Data available for each subject consists of the subject's identification code, the number of tests taken, and the test scores. Write a BASIC program to calculate the average test score for each subject. The output should give the subject's identification code, the number of tests taken, the score on each test, and the average score.

Use the following data to test the program:

Identification code	Number of tests taken	Test scores
408	3	17, 16, 21
519	1	24
523	2	14, 18
584	4	22, 16, 17, 14
601	1	12
677	3	25, 23, 24
701	4	17, 18, 21, 15
713	2	13, 12

12. Write a BASIC program that computes the coordinates of the point of intersection of two straight lines. Assume that the lines are given by the equations

$$y = sx + a$$
$$y = tx + b$$

where s and t are the slopes and a and b are the intercepts. In addition, determine the number of the quadrant (1, 2, 3, or 4) of the point of intersection. (If the point of intersection falls on an axis, use the lower quadrant number of the quadrants separated by the axis.)

The program should accept the values of s, a, t, and b, do the necessary computations, and display the coordinates of the point of intersection and the quadrant number. Use the following data to test the program:

s	a	t	b
18.0	6.0	30.0	6.0
2.0	8.0	-3.0	-2.0
1.0	8.0	-2.0	-22.0
3.0	-7.0	1.0	-1.0
-0.5	-3.0	2.0	-8.0

13. Input to a payroll program consists of the employee's number, year-to-date pay, base pay rate, shift code, and hours worked. Write a BASIC program to accept this data, compute the employee's gross pay, withholding tax, social security tax, and net pay, and display these results along with the employee's number.

The gross pay is found by multiplying the hours worked by the pay rate, where the pay rate is the product of the base pay rate and the shift factor. The shift factor is determined from the following table:

Shift code	Shift factor
0	1.00
1	1.25
2	1.50

The withholding tax is the product of the gross pay and the tax rate. The tax rate is found from the following table:

Gross pay	Tax rate
Less than $200.00	0
$200.00 to $349.99	8%
$350.00 to $499.99	12%
$500.00 to $699.99	15%
$700.00 or more	17.5%

The social security tax (F.I.C.A. tax) depends on the gross pay and the year-to-date pay. If the year-to-date pay is greater than or equal to $39,600, there is no social security tax. If the year-to-date pay plus the gross pay is less than or equal to $39,600, then the social security tax is 7.05% of the gross pay. If the year-to-date pay is less than $39,600, but the sum of the year-to-date and gross pay is greater than $39,600, then the tax is 7.05% of the difference between $39,600 and the year-to-date pay.

The net pay is computed by subtracting the withholding tax and social security tax from the gross pay.

Use the following input data to test the program:

Employee number	Year-to-date pay	Base pay rate	Shift code	Hours worked
1001	20,312.00	6.50	1	34.5
1002	35,888.75	5.25	0	25.0
1003	22,365.50	6.00	0	30.0
1004	39,181.25	7.25	2	38.5
1005	39,438.50	8.25	0	40.0
1006	40,465.00	10.95	2	48.0
1007	22,061.25	7.00	1	35.0
1008	39,525.00	8.00	1	40.0

14. A credit card company bases its evaluation of card applicants on four factors: the applicant's age, how long the applicant has lived at his or her current address, the annual income of applicant, and how long the applicant has been working at the same job. For each factor points are added to a total as follows:

Factor	Value	Points added
Age	20 and under	−10
	21–30	0
	31–50	20
	Over 50	25
At current address	Less than 1 year	−5
	1–3 years	5
	4–8 years	12
	9 or more years	20
Annual income	$15,000 or less	0
	$15,001–$25,000	12
	$25,001–$40,000	24
	Over $40,000	30
At same job	Less than 2 years	−4
	2–4 years	8
	More than 4 years	15

On the basis of the point total the following action is taken by the company:

Points	Action
−19 to 20	No card issued
21 to 35	Card issued with $500 credit limit
36 to 60	Card issued with $2000 credit limit
61 to 90	Card issued with $5000 credit limit

Write a BASIC program that accepts an applicant's number, age, years at current address, annual income, and years at the same job. Then the program should evaluate the applicant's credit worthiness and display the applicant's number plus a phrase describing the action taken by the company. Use the following data to test the program:

Applicant number	Age	Years at current address	Annual income	Years at same job
1234	55	10	$42,000	15
2345	18	0	$10,000	1
3456	35	2	$32,000	4
4567	22	5	$21,500	1
5678	50	1	$25,000	2
6789	31	4	$40,000	5

Chapter 4

Programming for repetition

As we know, a group of statements that is repeatedly executed is called a loop. In Chapter 2 we introduced the use of a loop to repeat the steps of a program so that more than one set of input data can be processed. We call such a loop an *input loop* because there is an input operation within it. Sometimes a loop does not contain an input operation but just processes data. We call this a *processing loop*. We will see several examples of processing loops in this chapter.

An important question when a loop is used in a program is how to *control* the loop — that is, how do we get the computer to *stop* looping. For example, consider the tuition-calculation program shown in Figure 4-1. (This is the same program shown in Figure 3-1.) The loop consists of statements 150 through 220. Notice that there is nothing in the program that stops the loop. The program will continue to loop as long as input data is supplied. When there is no more input data (i.e., when a control character is entered), the computer will stop the program.

The loop in this program is called an *uncontrolled loop* because there is no mechanism within the program to stop the repetition. As another example of an uncontrolled loop, consider the following statements:

```
10 LET K=1
20 GOTO 10
```

If these statements were in a program, the computer would continue to loop until stopped by the computer operator. Again there is nothing within this group of statements that causes the computer to stop after a period of time. Hence, this is an uncontrolled loop. Uncontrolled loops should be avoided.

A loop that has within it some way of stopping repetition is called a *controlled loop*. In this chapter we discuss programming techniques for coding controlled loops. We also describe special BASIC statements that are used for loop control. After completing this chapter you should be able to write programs that use a variety of loop-control techniques.

4-1 Controlling loops

As we have seen, the GOTO statement can be used to create a loop by branching from the end of a group of statements to the beginning. To control such a loop, we normally use an IF statement to branch out of the loop when a particular condition

Figure 4-1. The tuition-calculation program

```
100 REM - TUITION CALCULATION PROGRAM
110 REM - VARIABLES:
120 REM      I  = STUDENT ID
130 REM      U  = NUMBER OF UNITS
140 REM      T  = TUITION
150 INPUT I,U
160   IF U>12 THEN 190
170     LET T=350
180   GOTO 200
190     LET T=350+20*(U-12)
200   PRINT "STUDENT ID:",I
210   PRINT "TUITION:",T
220 GOTO 150
230 END
```

occurs. The techniques discussed in this section illustrate this approach to loop control for input loops and for processing loops.

Input loops

The program in Figure 4-1 contains an uncontrolled input loop. Each time the loop is executed, the computer accepts a new set of input data. A common technique for controlling such a loop is to use a special set of input data to indicate the end of the regular data. Each time input data is accepted, the program checks whether the special end-of-data input has been entered. If not, the program continues with the normal execution of the statements in the loop. When the end-of-data input has been entered, the program branches out of the loop.

Usually the end-of-data input contains a value for one of the variables that is not used in any other set of input data. This is called a *trailer value* or a *sentinel*. For example, in the tuition-calculation program in Figure 4-1, the input consists of the student's identification number and number of units. We could use a special identification number as a trailer value. The value would have to be one that is not used as an actual student's identification number. Then each time a set of input data is accepted we can test for this value.

We will assume that the trailer value for the tuition data is the identification number 9999. Figure 4-2 shows the program with this form of loop control. First the program accepts the identification number (I) and number of units. Then it checks the value of I. If I is *not* equal to 9999, the program continues with the next statement in sequence. If the value of I equals 9999, the program branches out of the loop to the END statement. This causes the computer to stop execution of the program. Notice that the end-of-data test comes immediately after the INPUT statement. We must check for the end of the input at this point because we do not want to process the trailer value.

When running the program in Figure 4-2, it is important to enter the trailer value correctly. Because the INPUT statement has two variables, two values must be typed each time a question mark appears on the CRT screen. This is required even with the trailer value. Thus, when the 9999 identification number is entered, we must also enter a value for the units, even though this value will not be processed. The usual procedure is to enter zero for any additional variables, but any value will do. Notice in Figure 4-2(b) that the last input consists of 9999 for the identification number and 0 for the units. The program will stop execution after this line is typed.

The program in Figure 4-2 branches to the END statement when the trailer value is detected. This causes the END statement to be executed, which stops the program. Although this approach is sometimes appropriate, there are situations where

Figure 4-2. The tuition-calculation program with the input loop controlled by a trailer-value test

```
100 REM - TUITION CALCULATION PROGRAM
110 REM - VARIABLES:
120 REM       I = STUDENT ID
130 REM       U = NUMBER OF UNITS
140 REM       T = TUITION
150 INPUT I,U
160   IF I=9999 THEN 240
170   IF U>12 THEN 200
180     LET T=350
190   GOTO 210
200     LET T=350+20*(U-12)
210   PRINT "STUDENT ID:",I
220   PRINT "TUITION:",T
230 GOTO 150
240 END
```

(a) The program

```
? 1234,6
STUDENT ID:     1234
TUITION:        350
? 3456,15
STUDENT ID:     3456
TUITION:        410
? 5678,12
STUDENT ID:     5678
TUITION:        350
? 9999,0
```

(b) Input and output

additional processing is necessary before the END statement is executed. For example, we may need to display a final output line after the trailer value is entered. Then the program would branch to a PRINT statement before going on to the END statement. Figure 4-3 shows a version of the tuition-calculation program that displays a final output line. Note that such final output or any other final processing cannot be accomplished using a control character to stop processing as in the program in Figure 4-1.

Flowcharts with input loops. In a flowchart of a program that contains an input loop controlled by a trailer-value test, the decision symbol is used for the test that terminates the loop. For example, Figure 4-4 shows the flowchart of the tuition-calculation program in Figure 4-3. The first step after the input operation is to check for the trailer value. If the student ID is 9999, the loop is terminated and the logic flows to the step that displays the final output line. Notice that the convention used in previous flowcharts for showing the end of the loop when a control character was entered (e.g., Figure 3-3) is not used in this flowchart because the loop is controlled by a trailer value.

Processing loops

A processing loop is one that is controlled by some condition of the data that is processed in the loop, not by an input value. Usually computations take place within the loop that affect the value of some variable. Each time the loop is executed, the variable is used to test whether the loop should be terminated. If the loop is properly designed, the test will eventually become true and the program will branch out of the loop.

Figure 4-3. The tuition-calculation program with a final output line

```
100 REM - TUITION CALCULATION PROGRAM
110 REM - VARIABLES:
120 REM       I = STUDENT ID
130 REM       U = NUMBER OF UNITS
140 REM       T = TUITION
150 INPUT I,U
160   IF I=9999 THEN 240
170   IF U>12 THEN 200
180     LET T=350
190   GOTO 210
200     LET T=350+20*(U-12)
210   PRINT "STUDENT ID:",I
220   PRINT "TUITION:",T
230 GOTO 150
240 PRINT "ALL DATA PROCESSED"
250 END
```

(a) The program

```
? 1234,6
STUDENT ID:    1234
TUITION:       350
? 3456,15
STUDENT ID:    3456
TUITION:       410
? 5678,12
STUDENT ID:    5678
TUITION:       350
? 9999,0
ALL DATA PROCESSED
```

(b) Input and output

As an example, consider the problem of determining the amount of time that it takes for a bank deposit to double at a given interest rate. Assume that $1000 is put into a bank at 8% interest compounded annually. This means that at the end of the first year, the interest is 8% of $1000 or $80, which is added to the original deposit to give a balance of $1080. At the end of the second year, the interest is 8% of $1080 or $86.40. The balance is then $1166.40. Thus, the interest is added to the balance at the end of each year and used in the next year's interest calculation. The problem is to write a program that displays a table of yearly interest and balance until the deposit has doubled to $2000.

Figure 4-5 shows a program that accomplishes this. There is no INPUT statement in this program because the program does not require any input data. The variable B is the bank balance; initially B is 1000. Y is a variable that counts the number of years; for the first year's calculation Y is 1. The loop consists of statements 190 through 240. The IF statement, numbered 190, stops the loop when B is greater than or equal to 2000. Within the loop, the current year's interest (I) is calculated by multiplying B by .08. The value of I is then added to B to give the new balance. (Recall from Chapter 2 that the statement LET B = B + I adds the value of I to the old value of B and assigns the result to B.) The output is then displayed and Y is increased by 1 for the next year. The GOTO statement branches back to the beginning of the loop (which is *not* the first statement in the program). The processing is repeated as long as B is less than 2000.

Notice in this program that the statements in the loop, except the first and the last, are indented. This is the style we have used in all programs that contain loops. Although this style is commonly used, some programmers prefer other styles. We will continue to use this style in our examples.

Figure 4-4. Flowchart of the tuition-calculation program

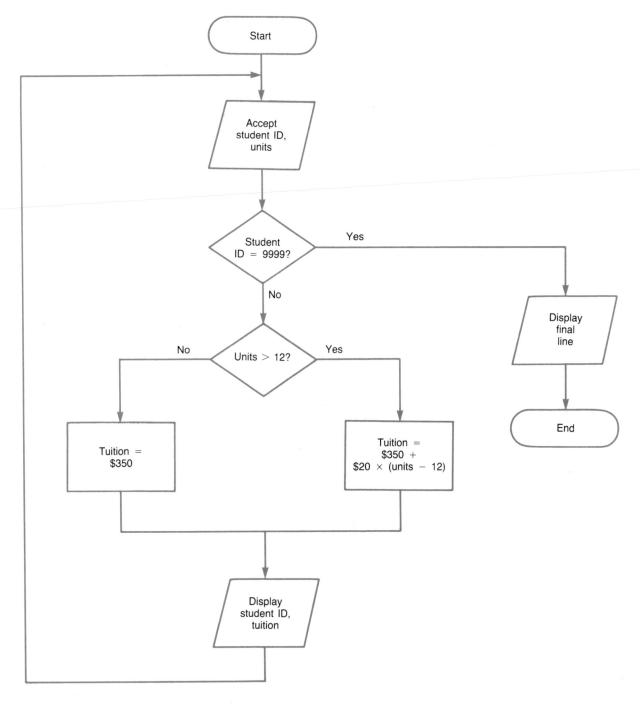

The program in Figure 4-5 shows how headings can be displayed above columns of output. The PRINT statement at line 150 causes the headings to be displayed in successive print zones. Notice that this PRINT statement is outside the loop. If it were in the loop, the headings would be displayed each time the loop is repeated.

The program also demonstrates the need for *initializing* variables, which means assigning beginning values to variables. We can never assume a variable has any known value unless we assign a value to it. Thus, in the program in Figure 4-5 we cannot assume that B equals 1000 or that Y is 1. These values must be assigned

Figure 4-5. The interest-calculation program

```
100 REM - INTEREST CALCULATION PROGRAM
110 REM - VARIABLES:
120 REM     B  = BANK BALANCE
130 REM     Y  = YEAR
140 REM     I  = INTEREST
150 PRINT "YEAR","INTEREST","BALANCE"
160 PRINT
170 LET B=1000
180 LET Y=1
190 IF B>=2000 THEN 250
200    LET I=.08*B
210    LET B=B+I
220    PRINT Y,I,B
230    LET Y=Y+1
240 GOTO 190
250 END
```

(a) The program

YEAR	INTEREST	BALANCE
1	80	1080
2	86.4	1166.4
3	93.312	1259.71
4	100.777	1360.49
5	108.839	1469.33
6	117.546	1586.87
7	126.95	1713.82
8	137.106	1850.93
9	148.074	1999
10	159.92	2158.93

(b) Output

to the variables at the beginning of the program, before the loop. If this is not done, the computer will use whatever values happen to be in the storage locations for these variables. (Most versions of BASIC initialize all variables to zero before the program is run. It is usually not a good idea, however, to assume this is the case. Even if the initial value of a variable is supposed to be zero, it should be initialized in the program.)

Flowcharts with processing loops. Figure 4-6 shows the flowchart of the interest-calculation program in Figure 4-5. The processing loop can be clearly seen. The test that determines whether the loop is to be terminated is shown in a decision symbol at the beginning of the loop. The other steps in the loop come after this decision. Notice that the headings are displayed and the balance and year are initialized before the loop is begun.

Counting loops

A special type of processing loop, called a *counting loop,* is controlled by counting the number of times that a loop is executed and branching out of the loop when the count reaches some desired number. This approach uses a variable as a *counter*. Before entering the loop, the counter is *initialized* to some beginning value. Each time the loop is executed, the value of the counter is *modified*, usually by increasing or incrementing its value by 1. Also, each time the loop is executed, the counter is *tested* to determine whether its value has exceeded some final value.

Figure 4-6. Flowchart of the interest-calculation program

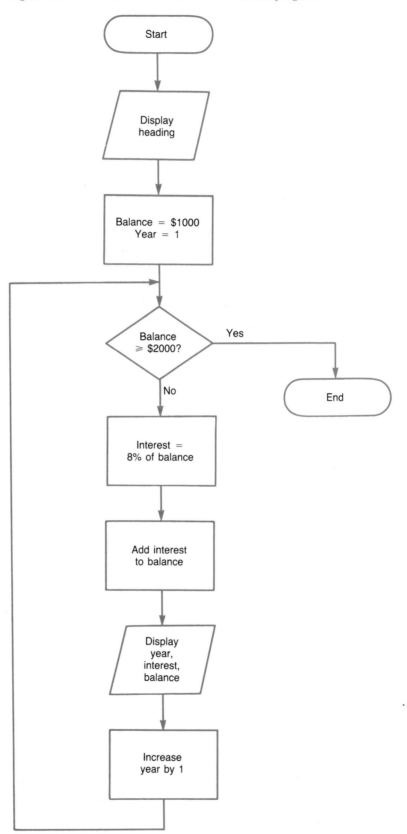

As an example, the statements in Figure 4-7 show the general form of a loop that is executed 100 times. In this example, the counter is the variable K. Initially, K is assigned the value 1. Then K is tested to see whether it exceeds 100. If this is the case, the computer branches out of the loop. If K is less than or equal to 100, the loop is executed. At the end of the loop, the value of K is increased by 1 and the loop is repeated.

Notice that the IF statement is such that the loop is terminated when K is *greater than* 100. This is necessary to ensure that the loop is executed exactly 100 times. If the IF statement were coded so that the computer branched out of the loop when the counter *equaled* 100, the loop would be executed only 99 times.

We can modify the interest-calculation program in Figure 4-5 to use this technique. Assume that we wish to display a table of interest and balance for five years. The variable Y may be used to count the number of years and, at the same time, the number of times that the loop is executed. The modified program is shown in Figure 4-8. In this program, Y is initialized to 1 in statement 180. Each time

Figure 4-7. A counting loop

```
25 LET K=1              (initialize counter)
35 IF K>100 THEN 95     (test counter)
          .
          .
          .
    statements in loop
          .
          .
          .
75    LET K=K+1         (modify counter)
85 GOTO 35
95 next statement
```

Figure 4-8. The interest-calculation program with a counting loop

```
100 REM - INTEREST CALCULATION PROGRAM
110 REM - VARIABLES:
120 REM      B  = BANK BALANCE
130 REM      Y  = YEAR
140 REM      I  = INTEREST
150 PRINT "YEAR","INTEREST","BALANCE"
160 PRINT
170 LET B=1000
180 LET Y=1
190 IF Y>5 THEN 250
200    LET I=.08*B
210    LET B=B+I
220    PRINT Y,I,B
230    LET Y=Y+1
240 GOTO 190
250 END
```

(a) The program

YEAR	INTEREST	BALANCE
1	80	1080
2	86.4	1166.4
3	93.312	1259.71
4	100.777	1360.49
5	108.839	1469.33

(b) Output

through the loop, Y is increased by 1 (statement 230). The loop is stopped when Y becomes greater than 5 (statement 190).

As another example of this form of loop control, consider the problem of finding the total and average of ten test scores. Assume that the test scores are to be entered one at a time at the keyboard and that there is no trailer value. The program must accept the data, calculate the total and average, and display the results.

One way to write the program is to use ten variables, one for each test score. Such a program, however, would be tedious to code. A better approach is to accept and process the data within a loop. Although the loop in this case contains an INPUT statement, we cannot use a trailer-value test to terminate it because there is no trailer value. However, because we know that there are exactly ten test scores, we can control the loop by counting the number of times that the loop is executed.

The program is shown in Figure 4-9. The variable T is used to accumulate the total of the test scores. Each time through the loop, the INPUT statement accepts a test score (S). The value of S is then added to T and the result is assigned to T. Notice that initially T is set equal to zero outside the loop so that, with the first execution of the loop, the first test score is added to zero. Each successive time through the loop, T is increased by the value of another test score until all ten scores have been entered and added.

The loop in this program is controlled by using the variable I as a counter. Initially, I is set equal to 1. Each time through the loop, I is increased by 1 and tested to see whether it is greater than 10. When I exceeds 10, the program branches

Figure 4-9. A program that finds the total and average of ten test scores

```
100 REM - TEST SCORE AVERAGING PROGRAM
110 REM - VARIABLES:
120 REM      S = TEST SCORE
130 REM      T = TOTAL OF TEST SCORES
140 REM      A = AVERAGE TEST SCORE
150 REM      I = COUNTER
160 LET T=0
170 LET I=1
180 IF I>10 THEN 230
190    INPUT S
200    LET T=T+S
210    LET I=I+1
220 GOTO 180
230 LET A=T/10
240 PRINT "TOTAL:",T
250 PRINT "AVERAGE:",A
260 END
```

(a) The program

```
? 85
? 92
? 77
? 54
? 89
? 100
? 72
? 78
? 82
? 53
TOTAL:        782
AVERAGE:      78.2
```

(b) Input and output

out of the loop and calculates the average by dividing T by 10. Then the output is displayed and the program terminates.

This program processes exactly ten test scores. A variation of the program is to accept the number of test scores to be processed as input before the other data is accepted. Then the program is not limited to processing exactly ten values.

The program with this modification is shown in Figure 4-10. The first INPUT statement, before the loop, accepts the number of test scores and assigns the value to the variable N. [Note that the first input data entered in Figure 4-10(b) is the number 8, which equals the number of values that follow.] The loop in this program is the same as in the previous program except for the IF statement. In the IF statement, the counter is compared with N and the loop is terminated if I is greater than the number of test scores. The average is computed by dividing T by the number of scores (N).

In these examples the testing step is at the beginning of the loop. However, this is not essential. We could put the testing step in the middle or at the end of the loop depending on the requirements of the problem. For example, Figure 4-11 shows statements for executing a loop 100 times but with the counter test at the end of the loop. Notice in this example that the loop is repeated as long as the value of the counter is *less than or equal to* 100.

We can also vary the way in which counting is done. The initial value of the counter does not have to be 1; it can be any value, depending on the problem. Nor do we need to count by ones. We can modify the counter by adding or subtracting

Figure 4-10. A program that finds the total and average of a given number of test scores

```
100 REM - TEST SCORE AVERAGING PROGRAM
110 REM - VARIABLES:
120 REM       N  = NUMBER OF TEST SCORES
130 REM       S  = TEST SCORE
140 REM       T  = TOTAL OF TEST SCORES
150 REM       A  = AVERAGE TEST SCORE
160 REM       I  = COUNTER
170 INPUT N
180 LET T=0
190 LET I=1
200 IF I>N THEN 250
210    INPUT S
220    LET T=T+S
230    LET I=I+1
240 GOTO 200
250 LET A=T/N
260 PRINT "TOTAL:",T
270 PRINT "AVERAGE:",A
280 END
```

(a) The program

```
? 8
? 91
? 78
? 85
? 100
? 73
? 66
? 91
? 75
TOTAL:         659
AVERAGE:       82.375
```

(b) Input and output

Figure 4-11. A counting loop with the testing step at the end of the loop

```
25 LET L=1                              (initialize counter)
35 first statement in loop
          .
          .
          .
      statements in loop
          .
          .
          .
75    LET L=L+1                         (modify counter)
85 IF L<=100 THEN 35                    (test counter)
95 next statement
```

any reasonable value. The test condition is determined by the initial value of the counter, how it is modified each time through the loop, and the number of times we wish to execute the loop.

Figure 4-12 gives several examples of counting loops that illustrate these variations. In part (a) of the figure, the variable M counts from 0 to 10 by 2s. The statements in this loop will be executed six times. In part (b), N is decreased or decremented each time through the loop. For this loop, N counts backward from 10 to 1. The statements in the loop will be executed 10 times. In part (c), X is increased by a fractional amount, .05, each time through the loop. X counts from 0 to 1 in increments of .05. The statements in this loop will be executed 21 times.

Figure 4-12. Examples of counting loops

```
20 LET M=0
30 IF M>10 THEN 80
          .
          .
          .
60    LET M=M+2
70 GOTO 30
80 next statement

          (a)


130 LET N=10
140 IF N<1 THEN 200
          .
          .
          .
180    LET N=N-1
190 GOTO 140
200 next statement

          (b)


240 LET X=0
250 IF X>1 THEN 290
          .
          .
          .
270    LET X=X+.05
280 GOTO 250
290 next statement

          (c)
```

Figure 4-13. Flowchart of the program that finds the total and average of ten test scores

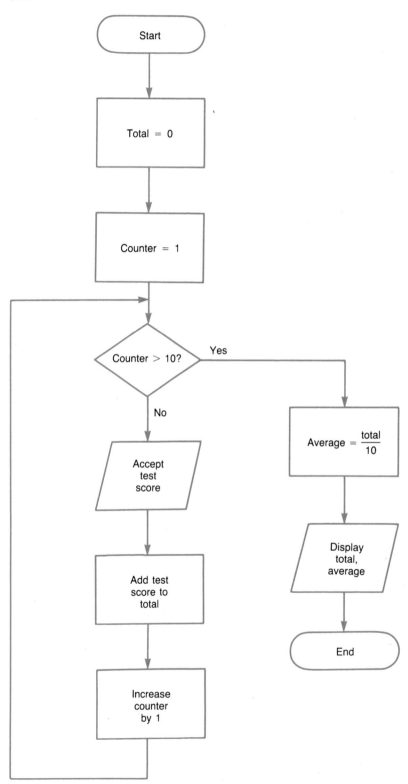

Flowcharts with counting loops. In a flowchart of a program that contains a counting loop, the steps to initialize, test, and modify the counter are shown at the appropriate points. For example, Figure 4-13 gives the flowchart of the program in Figure 4-9 that finds the total and average of ten test scores. The loop in this program is executed ten times. The flowchart shows that the counter is initialized to 1 before the loop is entered, the counter is tested to determine if it is greater than 10 at the beginning of the loop, and the counter is increased by 1 at the end of the loop. These steps correspond to those in the program.

Patterns of loop control

The discussion and examples in this section illustrate several different patterns of loop control. In all patterns the loop is repeated until some condition occurs that signals the end of the loop. The patterns vary in the placement of the end-of-loop test. Figure 4-14 summarizes the differences graphically.

Part (a) of the figure shows the basic loop pattern with the termination test in the middle of the loop. In part (b) the test is at the beginning of the loop. This pattern is called a *pretest loop*. When the test is the last step in the loop, as in part (c) of the figure, the pattern is called a *posttest loop*. All loops in programs fall into one of these patterns. The implementation of these patterns in BASIC using IF and GOTO statements is shown in Figure 4-15.

Figure 4-14. Patterns of loop control

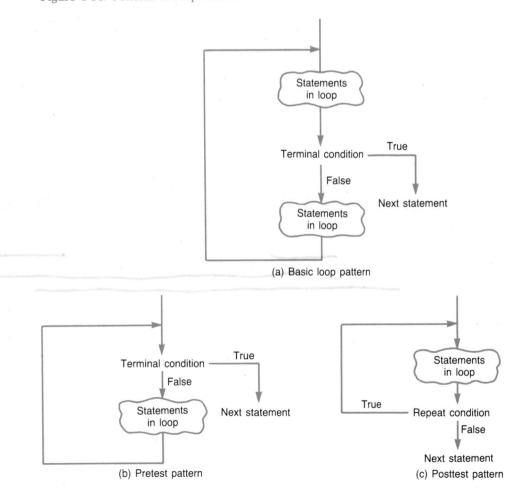

(a) Basic loop pattern

(b) Pretest pattern

(c) Posttest pattern

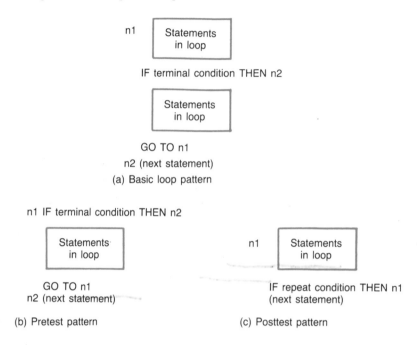

Figure 4-15. Loop control patterns in BASIC

4-2 Nested loops

Within a loop may be other loops. Such a combination is referred to as *nested loops*. (This idea is similar to that of nested decisions discussed in Chapter 3.) Any type of loop may be nested in another loop. Thus, a processing loop may be nested in another processing loop or in an input loop, and an input loop may be nested in another input loop or in a processing loop. Loops can be nested within nested loops. For example, a processing loop may be nested in another processing loop, which is nested in an input loop. There is no limit to the number of loops that can be nested.

Any of the loop patterns in Figure 4-14 may be used in nested loops. Thus, a pretest loop may be nested in another pretest loop, a pretest loop may be nested in a posttest loop, a posttest loop may be nested in a basic loop, and so forth. Any combination of types of loops and loop patterns is acceptable.

When one loop is nested within another, we think of the most encompassing loop as the *outer loop* and the loop that is nested as the *inner loop*. During execution of the program, each repetition of the outer loop causes the statements in the inner loop to be repeated as many times as the inner loop requires.

To illustrate the use of nested loops, assume that we wish to determine the amount of time it will take for a $1000 bank deposit to double at interest rates varying from 6% to 10% in 1% increments. One approach is to run the program in Figure 4-5 five times, each time using a different interest rate in the interest calculation. A better approach is to put another loop in the program that repeats the interest calculation five times each with a different rate. The resulting program is shown in Figure 4-16.

In this program, statements 180 through 240 are almost the same as statements 170 through 240 in the previous interest-calculation program. These statements include the loop that calculates the interest, accumulates the bank balance, and counts the years. This loop forms the inner loop in the program. One difference from the previous program is that the interest calculation (statement 210) uses a variable, R, for the

Figure 4-16. The interest-calculation program with nested loops

```
100 REM - INTEREST CALCULATION PROGRAM
110 REM - VARIABLES:
120 REM      B  = BANK BALANCE
130 REM      R  = INTEREST RATE
140 REM      Y  = YEAR
150 REM      I  = INTEREST
160 LET R=6
170 IF R>10 THEN 320
180    LET B=1000
190    LET Y=1
200    IF B>=2000 THEN 250
210       LET I=(R/100)*B
220       LET B=B+I
230       LET Y=Y+1
240    GOTO 200
250    LET Y=Y-1
260    PRINT "INTEREST RATE",R
270    PRINT "FINAL YEAR",Y
280    PRINT "FINAL BALANCE",B
290    PRINT
300    LET R=R+1
310 GOTO 170
320 END
```

Outer loop · Inner loop

(a) The program

```
INTEREST RATE  6
FINAL YEAR     12
FINAL BALANCE  2012.2

INTEREST RATE  7
FINAL YEAR     11
FINAL BALANCE  2104.85

INTEREST RATE  8
FINAL YEAR     10
FINAL BALANCE  2158.93

INTEREST RATE  9
FINAL YEAR     9
FINAL BALANCE  2171.89

INTEREST RATE  10
FINAL YEAR     8
FINAL BALANCE  2143.59
```

(b) Output

interest rate. The value of R is controlled by the outer loop that surrounds the inner loop. Initially, R is set equal to 6. Each time through the outer loop, R is increased by 1. The outer loop is terminated when R becomes greater than 10. Note that because R is a whole number (standing for the interest rate as a percentage), it must be divided by 100 in the interest calculation.

Another difference between this program and the previous one is that this one displays only the final results. There is no PRINT statement in the inner loop. Instead, all output is displayed after the inner loop is terminated. Notice that the variable for the year (Y) is decreased by 1 (statement 250) before the results are displayed. This is to compensate for the extra year that is added to Y just before the inner loop is terminated.

Figure 4-17. Flowchart of the interest-calculation program with nested loops

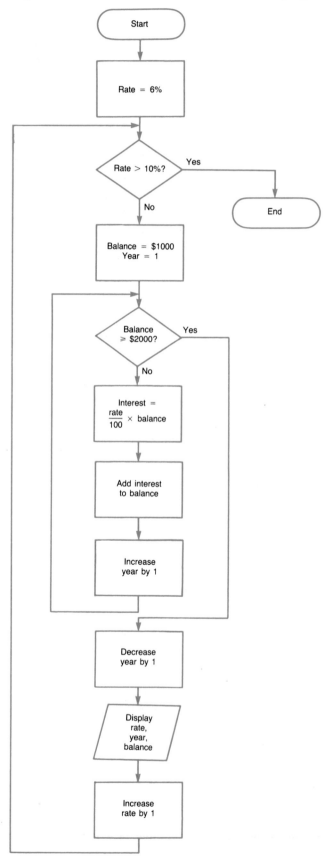

In this program, the inner loop is completely contained in the outer loop. Each time the outer loop is repeated, the inner loop is executed completely. Because the outer loop is performed five times, the inner loop is completely performed five times. Hence, the program performs the interest calculations five times, each time using a different interest rate.

This program uses indentation to show the loops and the nesting. All the statements that are in the outer loop (except the first and the last) are indented. All the statements that are in the inner loop (except the first and the last) are indented further. This style gives a visual clue to the program's organization.

We can see from this example that nested loops can be very useful. They can also be difficult to understand, especially when loops are nested within other nested loops. In general, it is best to nest no more than two or three loops so that the program's logic is not too complex.

Flowcharts with nested loops

Nested loops are shown in flowcharts by drawing one loop within another. For example, Figure 4-17 shows the flowchart of the interest-calculation program with nested loops in Figure 4-16. The flowchart clearly shows that the inner loop is completely contained in the outer loop. The conditions that terminate each loop are also shown clearly.

4-3 FOR loops

Counting loops play an important role in programming. In Section 4-1 we saw several examples of the use of counting loops. Later chapters will show more examples. Because of the importance of this type of loop, BASIC provides two special statements, the FOR statement and the NEXT statement, for control of counting loops. A loop that is controlled by these statements is called a *FOR loop*. In this section we describe the FOR and NEXT statements and discuss programming with FOR loops.

The basic steps for controlling a counting loop involve initializing a counter, testing the counter to determine whether the loop should be terminated, and modifying the counter after the statements in the loop have been executed. The program to find the total and average ten test scores in Figure 4-9 illustrated these steps. The following is the counting loop in this program:

```
170 LET I=1
180 IF I>10 THEN 230
190    INPUT S
200    LET T=T+S
210    LET I=I+1
220 GOTO 180
230 (next statement)
```

Using a FOR loop to control this loop, we can rewrite the sequence of statements as follows:

```
170 FOR I=1 TO 10 STEP 1
180    INPUT S
190    LET T=T+S
200 NEXT I
```

The first statement in this example is a FOR statement and the last is a NEXT statement. Whenever these statements are used, the statements that initialize, test, and modify the counter and the GOTO statement that repeats the loop are not needed. Instead, the FOR and NEXT statements combine these functions. Here the effect is to cause the computer to execute repeatedly the statements following the FOR statement up to the NEXT statement. The first time the loop is executed, I is assigned the value 1. On each succeeding pass through the loop, the value of I is increased by 1 unit until it exceeds 10. Then control transfers out of the loop to the statement following the NEXT statement.

The FOR and NEXT statements

The syntax of the FOR and NEXT statements and their pattern of use in a FOR loop is as follows:

```
ln FOR control variable = initial value TO limit STEP increment
      .
      .
      .
    statements
      .
      .
      .
ln NEXT control variable
```

The FOR and NEXT statements always appear in pairs; there can never be a FOR statement without a corresponding NEXT statement and vice versa. A FOR loop begins with a FOR statement, contains any number of BASIC statements, and ends with a NEXT statement. In the FOR statement the *control variable* is a variable that serves as a counter. The NEXT statement must contain the same control variable as the FOR statement. The *initial value, limit,* and *increment* in the FOR statement are each a constant, variable, or complex numeric expression. They determine how many times the loop is executed.

As an example, consider the following FOR and NEXT statements:

```
10 FOR J=1 TO 50 STEP 1
      .
      .
      .
70 NEXT J
```

The control variable is J, which is the same in the FOR statement and the NEXT statement. The initial value is 1, the limit is 50, and the increment is 1.

The effect of a FOR loop is to execute repeatedly the statements between the FOR and NEXT statements. The first time the statements are executed the control variable is assigned the initial value. Each succeeding time, when the NEXT statement is reached, the increment is added to the value of the control variable. When the value of the control variable becomes greater than the limit, the computer branches to the statement immediately following the NEXT statement.

In the previous example the control variable, J, is assigned the initial value, 1, for the first execution of the loop. When the NEXT statement is executed, the increment, 1, is added to J to make it equal to 2. Each succeeding time through the loop, J is increased by 1 until its value is greater than the limit, 50. Then the computer stops repeating the loop and goes on to the statement following statement 70 (the NEXT statement). Thus, this loop is executed exactly 50 times.

As another example, consider the following FOR loop:

```
15 FOR K=10 TO 20 STEP 3
   .
   .
   .
75 NEXT K
```

The control variable is K, the initial value is 10, the limit is 20, and the increment is 3. This loop is executed four times. The first time it is executed, K is 10. Then the control variable is incremented by 3 and assigned the value 13 and the loop is executed a second time. Next K is incremented again by 3 to get 16 and the loop is executed a third time. Then 3 is added to K to obtain 19 for the fourth repetition of the loop. After this, the increment is added to K to get 22. But because 22 is greater than the limit, 20, the loop is *not* repeated again. Instead, the computer branches to the statement following the NEXT statement.

With most FOR loops, the increment is 1. When this is the case, the word STEP and the increment can be omitted. For example, the following FOR statement is valid:

```
10 FOR J=1 TO 50
```

Because no increment is given, the computer assumes it is 1. If any increment other than 1 is needed, the STEP part must be included.

Besides constants, variables can be used for the initial value, limit, and increment. For example, the following FOR statement uses variables for the initial value and limit:

```
20 FOR K=I TO L STEP 5
```

The values of the variables when the program is run determine the initial value and limit.

When a FOR loop is used, we do *not* use separate statements to initialize, test, and modify the counter. These operations are implied by the FOR and NEXT statements. Still, the programmer must be aware of the order in which the computer performs these operations. Figure 4-18 shows the pattern that a FOR loop follows. First the control variable is initialized. Then the test is made to determine whether the control variable is greater than the limit. Next the statements in the loop are executed. Finally, the increment is added to the control variable and the loop is repeated.

Notice that this is a pretest pattern, and it is therefore possible to code a FOR loop that is never executed. For example, consider the following loop:

```
25 FOR M=A TO B
   .
   .
   .
65 NEXT M
```

If A has a value of 50 and B is 40, the initial value is greater than the limit. Hence, the loop will not be executed at all. [Some versions of BASIC use a posttest pattern for a FOR loop. (See Table 4-1.) In this case the previous loop would be executed once.]

Figure 4-18. Execution of a FOR loop

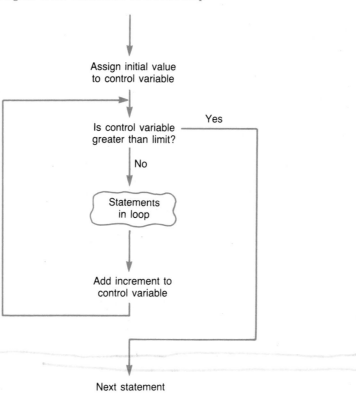

Table 4-1. FOR loop differences

BASIC version	Pretest or posttest pattern for FOR loop
ANS minimal BASIC	Pretest
ANS BASIC	Pretest
Microsoft BASIC	Pretest
Applesoft BASIC	Posttest
True BASIC	Pretest
BASIC-PLUS	Pretest
VAX-11 BASIC	Pretest

Illustrative programs

A program to find the total and average of ten test scores illustrates the use of a FOR loop. The complete program is shown in Figure 4-19. After initializing the total, T, to zero, the program accumulates the total of the ten test scores by accepting each score and adding it to the total. After the FOR loop is executed, the average is calculated and the results are displayed. (The input and output for this program are the same as in Figure 4-9.)

Figure 4-19. A program that finds the total and average of ten test scores using a FOR loop

```
100 REM - TEST SCORE AVERAGING PROGRAM
110 REM - VARIABLES:
120 REM        S = TEST SCORE
130 REM        T = TOTAL OF TEST SCORES
140 REM        A = AVERAGE TEST SCORE
150 REM        I = COUNTER
160 LET T=0
170 FOR I=1 TO 10
180    INPUT S
190    LET T=T+S
200 NEXT I
210 LET A=T/10
220 PRINT "TOTAL:",T
230 PRINT "AVERAGE:",A
240 END
```

Notice in this example that we have indented the statements between the FOR and the NEXT statements. This is a common program style that helps set off the statements in the loop so that the program is easier to understand.

There is no standard way of showing a FOR loop in a flowchart. One technique is to show explicitly the initialization, testing, and modification of the control variable. Using this technique, the flowchart for the program in Figure 4-19, which uses a FOR loop, is the same as that for the equivalent program in Figure 4-9, which does not use a FOR loop. This flowchart was given in Figure 4-13.

A modification of the program in Figure 4-19 is to accept the number of test scores to be averaged before the other data. This value determines the number of times the loop is to be executed. The program in Figure 4-20 illustrates this technique. Notice that the value of N is accepted with the first INPUT statement. N is then used as the limit in the FOR statement. (The input and output for this program are the same as in Figure 4-10.)

In Figure 4-8 we showed a program that displays the interest and balance on an original deposit of $1000 at 8% interest compounded annually for five years. The program required a counting loop and thus can be written with a FOR loop. The equivalent program with a FOR loop is shown in Figure 4-21. Notice that the value of Y is controlled with the FOR and NEXT statements. In addition, the value of this

Figure 4-20. A program that finds the total and average of a given number of test scores using a FOR loop

```
100 REM - TEST SCORE AVERAGING PROGRAM
110 REM - VARIABLES:
120 REM        N = NUMBER OF TEST SCORES
130 REM        S = TEST SCORE
140 REM        T = TOTAL OF TEST SCORES
150 REM        A = AVERAGE TEST SCORE
160 REM        I = COUNTER
170 INPUT N
180 LET T=0
190 FOR I=1 TO N
200    INPUT S
210    LET T=T+S
220 NEXT I
230 LET A=T/N
240 PRINT "TOTAL:",T
250 PRINT "AVERAGE:",A
260 END
```

Figure 4-21. The interest-calculation program with a FOR loop

```
100 REM - INTEREST CALCULATION PROGRAM
110 REM - VARIABLES:
120 REM        B = BANK BALANCE
130 REM        Y = YEAR
140 REM        I = INTEREST
150 PRINT "YEAR","INTEREST","BALANCE"
160 PRINT
170 LET B=1000
180 FOR Y=1 TO 10
190    LET I=.08*B
200    LET B=B+I
210    PRINT Y,I,B
220 NEXT Y
230 END
```

Figure 4-22. A program that finds the sum of the even integers from 2 to 20

```
10 REM - PROGRAM TO SUM THE EVEN
20 REM    INTEGERS FROM 2 TO 20
30 LET S=0
40 FOR J=2 TO 20 STEP 2
50    LET S=S+J
60 NEXT J
70 PRINT "THE SUM IS",S
80 END
```

(a) The program

```
THE SUM IS      110
```

(b) Output

variable is displayed each time through the loop. (The output for this program is the same as in Figure 4-8.)

This example illustrates the use of the control variable within the FOR loop. Whenever the control variable is used in the loop, its value depends on the initial value, the increment, and the number of times the loop has been executed. Figure 4-22 shows another program that uses the control variable within the FOR loop. This program finds the sum of the even integers from 2 to 20. In this example, the control variable, J, is used in the LET statement that calculates the sum, S. Initially, zero is assigned to the variable S. With the first execution of the loop, the initial value of the control variable (2) is added to S and the result replaces the original value of S. Thus, after the first execution of the loop, S is equal to 0 + 2 or 2. With each succeeding execution of the loop, the current value of the control variable is added to S. After the second execution of the loop, S is equal to 0 + 2 + 4 or 6. After the third execution of the loop, S is 0 + 2 + 4 + 6 or 12. This continues until, after the tenth execution of the loop, the value of S is 0 + 2 + 4 + 6 + 8 + 10 + 12 + 14 + 16 + 18 + 20 or 110. Then the control variable is incremented to a value greater than the limit and the loop is terminated.

Branching and FOR loops

Branching out of a FOR loop is allowed at any time. For example, assume that we wish to find the total and average of an unknown number of test scores. Each score is to be entered at the keyboard. The last score is zero and serves as a trailer value. If we assume that there are fewer than 100 test scores, a FOR loop that is executed

Figure 4-23. A program that finds the total and average of an unknown number of test scores

```
100 REM - TEST SCORE AVERAGING PROGRAM
110 REM - VARIABLES:
120 REM      N = NUMBER OF TEST SCORES
130 REM      S = TEST SCORE
140 REM      T = TOTAL OF TEST SCORES
150 REM      A = AVERAGE TEST SCORE
160 REM      I = COUNTER
170 LET T=0
180 FOR I=1 TO 100
190    INPUT S
200    IF S=0 THEN 230
210    LET T=T+S
220 NEXT I
230 LET N=I-1
240 LET A=T/N
250 PRINT "TOTAL:",T
260 PRINT "AVERAGE:",A
270 END
```

    (a) The program

```
? 89
? 71
? 92
? 83
? 75
? 68
? 98
? 77
? 0
TOTAL:        653
AVERAGE:      81.625
```

    (b) Input and output

100 times may be used to accept the data and total the scores. After each score is entered, however, a test for the trailer value must be made. When the trailer value is detected, the program must branch out of the FOR loop.

The program to accomplish this is shown in Figure 4-23.† Notice that after the program branches out of the loop, the number of test scores is calculated by subtracting 1 from the control variable. The value of the control variable is the last value assigned to it in the FOR loop. For each score that is accepted, the variable is incremented by 1. Thus, the control variable counts the number of input values. The trailer value is not a test score and must not be included in the count. To correct for this, the value of the control variable is reduced by 1 after the program branches out of the loop. The number of test scores is then used to calculate the average score. [Notice in the input data in Figure 4-23(b) that eight test scores are entered followed by a ninth value which is 0.]

Although it is permissible to branch out of a FOR loop at any time, branching into the middle of a FOR loop is not allowed. Thus, a GOTO statement outside a FOR loop cannot use the number of a statement in the loop.

Branching to the FOR statement itself is allowed. The program can branch to a FOR statement at any time and thus begin the loop processing. Branching to a

---

† Although this program is valid in BASIC, we will see in Chapter 6 that it violates certain principles of good program structure.

FOR statement from *outside* a FOR loop is commonly done. In general, branching to the FOR statement from *inside* the loop should not be done. If it is, the computer will reset the control variable to its initial value and restart the loop. As a consequence, the loop may never terminate.

Branching to the NEXT statement at the end of a FOR loop from inside the loop is acceptable. Occasionally this is necessary in order to bypass some of the statements in the loop and proceed directly to the modification and testing of the control variable. For example, assume that there are ten test scores to be entered. We want to find the total and average of those scores that are 60 or greater (i.e., the passing scores). The program must accept a test score and determine whether it is greater than or equal to 60. If it is, the score must be added to the total; if it is not, the program must bypass the totaling step. In addition, a count of the number of scores greater than or equal to 60 must be kept for the averaging step.

Figure 4-24 shows a program that accomplishes this. Before entering the loop the program initializes T to zero. The variable P also is initially set equal to zero. This variable is used to count the number of passing test scores (i.e., the number that are 60 or greater) and is used in the average calculation. In the FOR loop, the INPUT statement accepts a test score. The program must then check the score to determine whether it is greater than or equal to 60. If it is, the score must be added to T, and P must be increased by one. To do this, the IF statement in the loop causes the computer to bypass the LET statements if S is less than 60. Notice that the IF

Figure 4-24. A program that finds the total and average of passing test scores

```
100 REM - TEST SCORE AVERAGING PROGRAM
110 REM - VARIABLES:
120 REM        S = TEST SCORE
130 REM        P = NUMBER OF PASSING TEST SCORES
140 REM        T = TOTAL OF PASSING TEST SCORES
150 REM        A = AVERAGE OF PASSING TESTS SCORES
160 REM        I = COUNTER
170 LET T=0
180 LET P=0
190 FOR I=1 TO 10
200    INPUT S
210    IF S<60 THEN 240
220        LET T=T+S
230        LET P=P+1
240 NEXT I
250 LET A=T/P
260 PRINT "TOTAL:",T
270 PRINT "AVERAGE:",A
280 END
```

(a) The program

```
? 85
? 92
? 77
? 54
? 89
? 100
? 72
? 78
? 82
? 53
TOTAL:          675
AVERAGE:        84.375
```

(b) Input and output

statement branches to the *end* of the FOR loop (i.e., to the NEXT statement). A common mistake in this type of problem is to branch to the FOR statement. If this were done, the computer would reset the control variable to its initial value and restart the loop.

Additional FOR loop features

In a FOR statement, the initial value, limit, and increment may be any values within the limits of the computer. This means that any of these may be positive, negative, or zero (although the increment should not be zero). For example, the following FOR statement is valid:

```
30 FOR I=-10 TO 0 STEP 1
```

The first time the FOR loop for this statement is executed, the value of I is -10. Then 1 is added to I, making it -9 for the second execution of the loop. The value of I is incremented by 1 for each successive time through the loop. The last time the loop is executed, I is zero.

If the increment is negative, the FOR loop, in effect, counts backward. For example, the following FOR statement causes the value of J to be decreased by 1 each time the loop is executed:

```
40 FOR J=10 TO 1 STEP -1
```

When the increment is negative, the loop terminates when the value of the control variable is *less than* the test value. In this example, the value of J is 1 during the last execution of the loop. Then -1 is added to J, decreasing its value to zero. Because J is now less than 1, the limit, the loop is not repeated again.

The initial value, limit, and increment need not be whole numbers. For example, the following FOR statement is acceptable:

```
50 FOR X=.05 TO 1 STEP .01
```

The initial value is .05, the limit is 1, and the increment is .01. Thus the control variable, X, varies from .05 to 1 in increments of .01.

Besides constants and variables, complex numeric expressions can be used for the initial value, limit, and increment in a FOR loop. The value of any expression is evaluated at the time the FOR statement is encountered. The resulting value is then used for loop control. For example, consider the following FOR statement:

```
60 FOR Y=A TO A+B STEP 2*C
```

If A is 5, B is 20, and C is 3 when this statement is executed, the initial value of Y is 5, the limit is 25, and the increment is 6.

Nested FOR Loops

Within a FOR loop may be another FOR loop. Such a combination is referred to as *nested FOR loops*. As an example of the use of nested FOR loops, consider the problem of finding the total and average of five groups of ten test scores each. One approach would be to execute the program in Figure 4-19 five separate times. Each time, a different set of input data would be processed by the program. A better approach is to put another loop in the program to repeat the totaling and averaging statements five times. The resulting program is shown in Figure 4-25. With this program all data can be processed at one time.

Figure 4-25. A program with nested FOR loops

```
100 REM - TEST SCORE AVERAGING PROGRAM
110 REM - VARIABLES:
120 REM      C  = CLASS NUMBER
130 REM      S  = TEST SCORE
140 REM      T  = TOTAL OF TEST SCORES
150 REM      A  = AVERAGE TEST SCORE
160 REM      I  = COUNTER
170 FOR C=1 TO 5
180   LET T=0
190   FOR I=1 TO 10
200     INPUT S
210     LET T=T+S
220   NEXT I
230   LET A=T/10
240   PRINT "CLASS:",C
250   PRINT "TOTAL:",T
260   PRINT "AVERAGE:",A
270 NEXT C
280 END
```

Outer loop — lines 170 to 270
Inner loop — lines 190 to 220

(a) The program

```
? 85
? 92
? 77
? 54
? 89
? 100
? 72
? 78
? 82
? 53
CLASS:          1
TOTAL:          782
AVERAGE:        78.2
? 76
? 89
? 96
? 53
? 88
? 81
? 72
? 69
? 89
? 80
CLASS:          2
TOTAL:          793
AVERAGE:        79.3
? 100
? 79
     .
     .
     .

? 87
? 77
CLASS:          5
TOTAL:          787
AVERAGE:        78.7
```

(b) Partial input and output

In this program the first FOR statement initializes the control variable C to 1. The variable T is then assigned the value zero. The second FOR statement initializes the control variable I to 1. Next the inner FOR loop is executed. When the NEXT statement for the inner FOR loop is encountered, I is incremented. The inner loop is repeated until its control variable exceeds the limit. At that point the computer executes the statement following the NEXT statement of the inner FOR loop. In this case, the average is computed and the output is displayed. Then the NEXT statement for the outer loop is encountered, and the control variable C is incremented.

With the second execution of the outer FOR loop, the value of the variable T is reset to zero. The inner FOR statement is then encountered. This causes I to be set to 1 and the inner loop is executed ten times. Next the average is calculated and the PRINT statements are executed. Then the outer loop's control variable is incremented. This continues for a total of five times. Each time the outer loop is executed, the statements in the inner loop are performed ten times.

We can see from the example how nested FOR loops are executed. The basic rule is that each time an outer loop is performed, the inner loop is completely executed. In the previous example, the statements in the inner loop are executed a total of 50 times (5 $\times$ 10).

As another example, consider the following outline of nested FOR loops:

```
100 FOR L=11 TO 20
110   FOR M=1 TO 5
120     FOR N=2 TO 6 STEP 2
              .
              .
              .
200     NEXT N
210   NEXT M
220 NEXT L
```

In this example the innermost loop is executed three times for each execution of the intermediate loop. The intermediate loop is executed five times for each execution of the outermost loop. Because the outermost loop is executed ten times, the intermediate loop is executed a total of 50 times (10 $\times$ 5) and the innermost loop is performed 150 times (10 $\times$ 5 $\times$ 3).

Notice that the control variables of the loops in a nest are different. A unique variable must be used for the control variable of each loop in a nest of FOR loops. Also notice that each nested loop is indented beyond the loop in which it is nested. This is a common style for nested FOR loops that helps show the organization of the program.

When nested FOR loops are used, an inner loop must be completely contained within the next outer loop. Hence, the following pattern of FOR loops is invalid:

```
300 FOR I=1 TO 20
310 FOR J=1 TO 50
          .
          .
          .
400 NEXT I
410 NEXT J
```

This pattern is unacceptable because, if it is executed, the NEXT statement of the outer loop is encountered during the performance of the inner loop.

Nested FOR loops are extremely useful for manipulating certain types of data tables. We will see examples of this in Chapters 9 and 10.

4-4 A sample problem

In this section we develop a program for a sample problem that involves loop control. The problem is to compute pay for employees in a business.

Problem definition

A program is needed to compute the week's regular pay, overtime pay, and total pay for each employee in a business. The program should display the results of the computations together with the employee's identification number. Figure 4-26 shows how the output should appear for one employee. After all the output for all employees has been displayed, a line with the phrase ALL EMPLOYEE DATA PROCESSED should be displayed.

Input to the program for each employee is the employee's identification number, the number of days that the employee worked during the week (0 to 7), and the hours worked each day. The number of days worked during the week varies with each employee. Therefore, the number of data entries for the hours worked varies. To handle this, the program should accept first the employee ID and number of days. Then the program should accept the hours worked for each day that the employee worked. The number of employees is unknown. The program should stop when an employee ID of 999 is entered.

The pay is based on the total regular hours worked and the total overtime hours worked during the week. Regular hours are all hours worked up to eight in a day. Hours worked over eight in a day are overtime hours. The regular pay is 6.50 times the week's total regular hours; the overtime pay is 9.75 times the week's total overtime hours. The total pay is the sum of the regular pay and the overtime pay.

Program design

The general algorithm that solves this problem is as follows:

Repeat the following:
    Accept the employee ID and number of days worked.
    If the employee ID is 999, leave the loop.
    Accumulate the total regular hours and total overtime hours.
    Compute the regular pay, overtime pay, and total pay.
    Display the employee ID, regular pay, overtime pay, and total pay.
End of loop.
Display the final output line.

Notice that the algorithm includes an input loop. To accumulate the total regular and overtime hours, another loop is needed. This part of the algorithm can be expressed as follows:

Set the total regular hours and total overtime hours to zero.
Repeat the following for each day worked:
    Accept the hours worked.
    Add the regular hours worked to the total regular hours and the overtime
        hours worked to the total overtime hours.
End of loop.

Incorporating these steps into the previous ones gives us the complete algorithm shown in Figure 4-27.

Figure 4-26. Output layout for the payroll program

```
EMPLOYEE ID:   XXX
REGULAR PAY    OVERTIME PAY   TOTAL PAY
  XXXXX          XXXXX          XXXXX
```

Figure 4-27. Algorithm for the payroll problem

Repeat the following:
    Accept the employee ID and number of days worked.
    If the employee ID is 999, leave the loop.
    Set the total regular hours and total overtime hours to zero.
    Repeat the following for each day worked:
        Accept the hours worked.
        Add the regular hours worked to the total regular hours and the overtime hours worked to
           the total overtime hours.
    End of loop.
    Compute the regular pay, overtime pay, and total pay.
    Display the employee ID, regular pay, overtime pay, and total pay.
End of loop.
Display the final output line.

The step in which the regular and overtime hours are added to their respective totals requires a decision. If the hours worked are less than or equal to eight, all hours are added to the total regular hours. If the hours worked are greater than eight, only eight hours are added to the total regular hours and all hours over eight are added to the total overtime hours. Figure 4-28 shows the flowchart for the program with this decision.

Notice that this program involves nested loops. The outer loop is the input loop that is controlled by a trailer value test. Within the inner loop is an input operation, but this is not used to control this loop. Rather, the inner loop is executed a specific number of times and, therefore, is a counting loop.

Program coding

The program to solve this problem is shown in Figure 4-29. The variables used are listed in the REM statements at the beginning. Notice that variables are needed for the total regular hours worked (H1), total overtime hours worked (H2), and day number. This data is not used for input or output but is needed for internal calculations.

The logic of the program follows the algorithm in Figure 4-27 and the flowchart in Figure 4-28. The input loop is terminated when the employee ID (I) is equal to 999. The counting loop is controlled by a FOR statement that uses the day number (D) to count from 1 to the number of days worked (N). Within the FOR loop is a two-sided decision that adds the regular and overtime hours to their respective totals. Notice that the variables for the totals (H1 and H2) are initialized to zero before the FOR loop is entered.

Program correctness

To test this program we should test all cases for the decision and all cases for the loops. For the decision we should test the case where the hours worked in a day is less than eight, equal to eight, and greater than eight. We should also include cases where the employee worked eight or fewer hours every day of the week and where he or she worked more than eight hours every day. The input loop should be tested for the case where input data is supplied and where a trailer value is entered. The

Figure 4-28. Flowchart for the payroll program

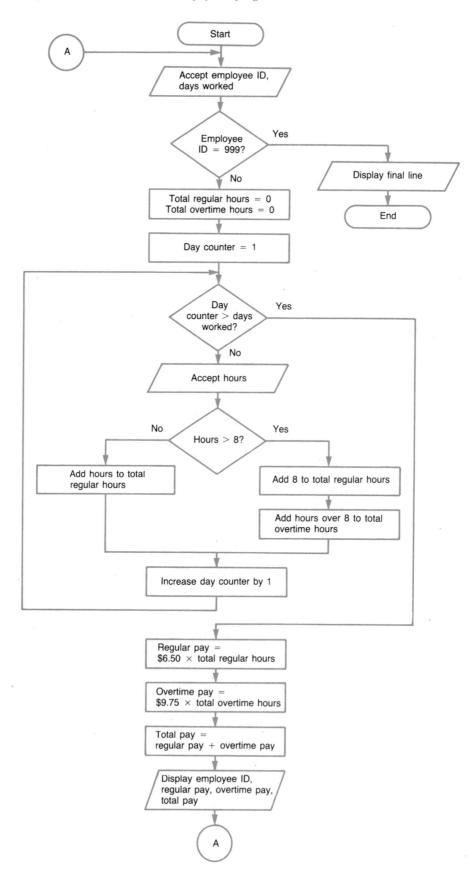

Figure 4-29. The payroll program

```
100 REM - PAYROLL PROGRAM
110 REM - VARIABLES:
120 REM        I  = EMPLOYEE ID
130 REM        N  = NUMBER OF DAYS WORKED
140 REM        H  = HOURS WORKED
150 REM        H1 = TOTAL REGULAR HOURS WORKED
160 REM        H2 = TOTAL OVERTIME HOURS WORKED
170 REM        D  = DAY NUMBER
180 REM        P1 = REGULAR PAY
190 REM        P2 = OVERTIME PAY
200 REM        P  = TOTAL PAY
210 INPUT I,N
220   IF I=999 THEN 450
230   REM - ACCUMULATE TOTAL HOURS WORKED
240   LET H1=0
250   LET H2=0
260   FOR D=1 TO N
270     INPUT H
280     IF H>8 THEN 310
290       LET H1=H1+H
300     GOTO 330
310       LET H1=H1+8
320       LET H2=H2+(H-8)
330   NEXT D
340   REM - COMPUTE PAY
350   LET P1=6.5*H1
360   LET P2=9.75*H2
370   LET P=P1+P2
380   REM - DISPLAY RESULTS
390   PRINT
400   PRINT "EMPLOYEE ID:",I
410   PRINT "REGULAR PAY","OVERTIME PAY","TOTAL PAY"
420   PRINT P1,P2,P
430   PRINT
440 GOTO 210
450 PRINT "ALL EMPLOYEE DATA PROCESSED"
460 END
```

Figure 4-30. Input test data and expected output for the payroll program

	Input test data		Expected output		
Employee ID	Number of days worked	Hours worked	Regular pay	Overtime pay	Total pay
123	4	8,11,6,9	195	39	234
234	2	4,8	78	0	78
345	0	—	0	0	0
456	3	9,12,15	156	117	273
567	7	11,3,8,13,6,2,7	273	78	351
678	1	16	52	78	130
999	0	—	—	—	—

counting loop should be tested with several values for the number of days worked including zero, one, and seven.

Figure 4-30 shows several sets of input test data and the expected output for each set. The different cases discussed in the previous paragraph are represented in this data. The input and output from running the program with this data is shown in Figure 4-31. As we can see, all test cases give the correct results.

Figure 4-31. Input and output for the payroll program

```
? 123,4
? 8
? 11
? 6
? 9

EMPLOYEE ID:    123
REGULAR PAY    OVERTIME PAY    TOTAL PAY
  195              39              234

? 234,2
? 4
? 8

EMPLOYEE ID:    234
REGULAR PAY    OVERTIME PAY    TOTAL PAY
  78               0               78

? 345,0

EMPLOYEE ID:    345
REGULAR PAY    OVERTIME PAY    TOTAL PAY
   0               0               0

? 456,3
? 9
? 12
? 15

EMPLOYEE ID:    456
REGULAR PAY    OVERTIME PAY    TOTAL PAY
  156             117             273

? 567,7
? 11
? 3
? 8
? 13
? 6
? 2
? 7

EMPLOYEE ID:    567
REGULAR PAY    OVERTIME PAY    TOTAL PAY
  273              78             351

? 678,1
? 16

EMPLOYEE ID:    678
REGULAR PAY    OVERTIME PAY    TOTAL PAY
  52               78             130

? 999,0
ALL EMPLOYEE DATA PROCESSED
```

Program documentation

The program in Figure 4-29 contains remarks to help document it. This listing of
the program along with the input and output from running the program (Figure 4-
31) should be included in the documentation. The documentation may also include

the output layout (Figure 4-26), the algorithm (Figure 4-27), the flowchart (Figure 4-28), the input test data and expected output (Figure 4-30), and other items that we will discuss later.

*4-5 WHILE loops

Some versions of BASIC provide special statements for general loop control. (See Table 4-2.) The actual statements vary with the version of BASIC, but the type of loop is usually called a *WHILE loop*. In this section we describe WHILE loops and illustrate their use for loop control.

To demonstrate the idea of a WHILE loop we will use the statements found in a common version of BASIC (Microsoft BASIC). These are the WHILE and WEND statements. The syntax of these statements and their pattern of use are as follows:

```
ln WHILE relational expression
             .
             .
             .
     statements
             .
             .
             .
ln WEND
```

Table 4-2. WHILE loop differences

BASIC version	WHILE loop syntax
ANS minimal BASIC	Not available
ANS BASIC	ln DO WHILE relational expression . . . ln LOOP
Microsoft BASIC	ln WHILE relational expression . . . ln WEND
Applesoft BASIC	Not available
True BASIC	DO WHILE relational expression . . . LOOP
BASIC-PLUS VAX-11 BASIC	ln WHILE relational expression . . . ln NEXT

The first statement, a WHILE statement, contains a relational expression. Next is a sequence of statements that is to be repeatedly executed. At the end of the loop there must be a WEND statement. For example, the following is a valid WHILE loop:

```
40 WHILE I<=10
50    PRINT I
60    LET I=I+1
70 WEND
```

The effect of the WHILE loop is to execute repeatedly the statements in the loop as long as the relational expression in the WHILE statement is true. In the above example, the PRINT and LET statements are repeatedly executed as long as I is less than or equal to 10. As soon as the relational expression becomes false, the computer branches out of the loop and continues with the next statement after the WEND statement.

A WHILE loop is a pretest loop. The pattern is shown graphically in Figure 4-32. When a WHILE statement is encountered, the computer first evaluates the relational expression. If the expression is *false,* the computer branches to the next statement following the WEND statement. If the expression is *true,* the computer executes the statements in the loop up to the WEND statement. The relational expression is evaluated again and, if true, the loop is repeated. This continues until the relational expression becomes false. Control then transfers to the statement after the WEND statement. Notice that because the expression is evaluated at the *beginning* of the loop, it is possible that the loop will not be executed at all. If the relational expression is false when the WHILE statement is first encountered, the loop will be bypassed completely.

With a WHILE loop we do not need an IF statement or a GOTO statement for loop control. The testing and looping functions are built into the WHILE and WEND statements. We can create the same effect, however, using an IF statement and a GOTO statement in a pretest pattern. To do this we must use the complement of the condition in the WHILE statement. For example, the following sequence of statements is equivalent to the WHILE loop at the beginning of this section:

```
40 IF I>10 THEN 80
50    PRINT I
60    LET I=I+1
70 GOTO 40
80 (next statement)
```

Figure 4-32. The WHILE loop

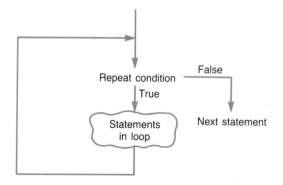

In a WHILE loop there may be any number of statements between the WHILE and WEND statements. The computer will repeatedly execute all statements while the logical expression is true. However, the WEND statement is essential. If it is omitted, the computer will not know where the end of the loop is located.

Notice in the example given earlier that we have indented the statements in the loop. Although not required, this is a common programming style that makes it easier to see the loop in a program.

Illustrative programs

We can use a WHILE loop to control any of the types of loops discussed in previous sections. Sometimes, however, the structure of the program must be modified slightly. For example, to control an input loop with a trailer-value test, we must have *two* INPUT statements. One is outside the WHILE loop and accepts the first set of input data. The other is within the WHILE loop (usually the last statement) and accepts each successive set of input data. The relational expression in the WHILE statement checks for the absence of the trailer value. Figure 4-33 shows the pattern in the tuition-calculation program (Figure 4-3). (Notice that we have used the IF-THEN-ELSE statement in this program. Usually if a version of BASIC provides WHILE loops, it also allows variations of the IF statement.)

In this program, the first INPUT statement accepts the first set of input data. The WHILE statement tests the value of I to see whether it is *not* equal to 9999, the trailer value. If this condition is true, the loop is executed. In the loop, the tuition is calculated and the output is displayed. Then the INPUT statement at the end of the loop accepts the next set of input data. The relational expression is checked again, and if true, the loop is repeated. Finally, after the last set of input data has been accepted and processed, the trailer value is entered with a value of 9999 for I. Because the relational expression is no longer true, execution continues with the next statement after the WEND statement.

The interest-calculation program in Figure 4-5 can easily be written with a WHILE loop. Because this program uses a pretest loop, we can replace the IF statement with a WHILE statement using the complement of the condition and replace the GOTO 190 statement with a WEND statement. The modified program is shown in Figure 4-34.

The program to find the total and average of ten test scores in Figure 4-9 uses a pretest counting loop. We can rewrite this program with a WHILE loop. The

Figure 4-33. The tuition-calculation program with a WHILE loop

```
100 REM - TUITION CALCULATION PROGRAM
110 REM - VARIABLES:
120 REM      I = STUDENT ID
130 REM      U = NUMBER OF UNITS
140 REM      T = TUITION
150 INPUT I,U
160 WHILE I<>9999
170    IF U<=12 THEN
          LET T=350
       ELSE
          LET T=350+20*(U-12)
180    PRINT "STUDENT ID:",I
190    PRINT "TUITION:",T
200    INPUT I,U
210 WEND
220 PRINT "ALL DATA PROCESSED"
230 END
```

Figure 4-34. The interest-calculation program with a WHILE loop

```
100 REM - INTEREST CALCULATION PROGRAM
110 REM - VARIABLES:
120 REM       B = BANK BALANCE
130 REM       Y = YEAR
140 REM       I = INTEREST
150 PRINT "YEAR","INTEREST","BALANCE"
160 PRINT
170 LET B=1000
180 LET Y=1
190 WHILE B<2000
200    LET I=.08*B
210    LET B=B+I
220    PRINT Y,I,B
230    LET Y=Y+1
240 WEND
250 END
```

Figure 4-35. A program that finds the total and average of ten test scores with a WHILE loop

```
100 REM - TEST SCORE AVERAGING PROGRAM
110 REM - VARIABLES:
120 REM       S = TEST SCORE
130 REM       T = TOTAL OF TEST SCORES
140 REM       A = AVERAGE TEST SCORE
150 REM       I = COUNTER
160 LET T=0
170 LET I=1
180 WHILE I<=10
190    INPUT S
200    LET T=T+S
210    LET I=I+1
220 WEND
230 LET A=T/10
240 PRINT "TOTAL:",T
250 PRINT "AVERAGE:",A
260 END
```

Figure 4-36. A program with nested WHILE loops

```
                   100 REM - INTEREST CALCULATION PROGRAM
                   110 REM - VARIABLES:
                   120 REM       B = BANK BALANCE
                   130 REM       R = INTEREST RATE
                   140 REM       Y = YEAR
                   150 REM       I = INTEREST
                   160 LET R=6
                   170 WHILE R<=10
                   180    LET B=1000
                   190    LET Y=1
                   200    WHILE B<2000
                   210       LET I=(R/100)*B
Outer   Inner      220       LET B=B+I
loop    loop       230       LET Y=Y+1
                   240    WEND
                   250    LET Y=Y-1
                   260    PRINT "INTEREST RATE",R
                   270    PRINT "FINAL YEAR",Y
                   280    PRINT "FINAL BALANCE",B
                   290    PRINT
                   300    LET R=R+1
                   310 WEND
                   320 END
```

result is shown in Figure 4-35. The counter is initialized outside the loop. Within the loop, the counter is incremented. The WHILE statement causes the loop to be repeated as long as the counter is less than or equal to 10.

Nested WHILE loops

A WHILE loop may be contained in another to form *nested WHILE loops*. The only restriction is that each WHILE statement must have a corresponding WEND statement. For example, the interest-calculation program in Figure 4-16 uses nested loops. This program can be rewritten with nested WHILE loops as shown in Figure 4-36. Notice that each WHILE statement has a matching WEND statement. The effect of execution is that the inner WHILE loop is completely executed for each repetition of the outer WHILE loop.

One important thing to notice in all these examples of the use of WHILE loops is the lack of GOTO statements. If IF-THEN-ELSE statements and WHILE loops are available in the version of BASIC being used, it is unnecessary to use GOTO statements. In general, this greatly reduces the complexity of programs. A program written with few or no GOTO statements is easier to understand, debug, and modify than an equivalent program written with many GOTO statements.

Review questions

1. What is the difference between an input loop and a processing loop?
2. A loop that has no way of stopping is called _____.
3. What is a trailer value?
4. Consider the following group of statements:

```
10 INPUT A,B,C
20 PRINT A,B,C
30 GOTO 10
```

These statements are supposed to form a loop that is to be repeated until the input data contains a zero for the last value. What additional statement is needed?
5. A series of numbers are to be entered at the keyboard. Code a group of statements that determines and displays how many numbers are entered up to and including the first number equal to 100.

6. Consider the program shown in Figure 4-5. Assume that statement number 190 is changed to the following:

```
190 IF B>=1500 THEN 250
```

How many years of output will be displayed by this modified program?
7. How many lines will be displayed when the following group of statements is executed?

```
100 LET J=20
110 IF J<=3 THEN 150
120    PRINT J
130    LET J=J-4
140 GOTO 110
150 (next statement)
```

8. Code a group of statements that accepts and displays 25 numbers entered at the keyboard. Do not use a FOR statement.
9. What is the difference between a pretest and a posttest loop?
10. A program pattern in which one loop is contained within another loop is called _____.
11. Consider the following program:

```
10 LET J=1
20 IF J>5 THEN 90
30    LET K=20
40    LET K=K-2
50       PRINT J,K
```

```
60   IF K>=10 THEN 40
70   LET J=J+1
80 GOTO 20
90 END
```

How many times will each of the following statements in the program be executed?

a. statement 20
b. statement 30
c. statement 40
d. statement 60
e. statement 70
f. statement 80

12. During the execution of a FOR loop, when is the control variable tested and when is it modified?

13. Rewrite the following group of statements using a FOR loop:

```
100 LET K=5
110 IF K>15 THEN 150
120   LET X=X+K
130   LET K=K+3
140 GOTO 110
150 (next statement)
```

14. Rewrite the following group of statements without using a FOR loop:

```
200 FOR L=150 TO 100 STEP -5
210   LET Y=Y+L
220 NEXT L
```

15. Code a FOR loop that displays the numbers 21, 18, 15, ... , 3 in a column.

16. How many lines are displayed by each of the following groups of statements?

a.
```
310 FOR K=1 TO 10
320   PRINT K
330 NEXT K
```

b.
```
340 FOR L=4 TO 15 STEP 2
350   PRINT L
360 NEXT L
```

c.
```
370 FOR M=9 TO -9 STEP -3
380   PRINT M
390 NEXT M
```

d.
```
400 FOR X=5 TO 7 STEP .25
410   PRINT X
420 NEXT X
```

17. How many lines are displayed by each of the following groups of statements?

a.
```
430 FOR I=1 TO 3
440   FOR J=4 TO 12 STEP 2
450     PRINT I,J
460   NEXT J
470 NEXT I
```

b.
```
480 FOR K=1 TO 9 STEP 3
490   FOR L=8 TO 2 STEP -2
500     PRINT K,L
510   NEXT L
520 NEXT K
```

c.
```
530 FOR I=10 TO 1 STEP -1
540   FOR K=100 TO 150 STEP 10
550     FOR M=1 TO 2
560       PRINT I,K,M
570     NEXT M
580   NEXT K
590 NEXT I
```

d.
```
600 FOR J=18 TO 30 STEP 3
610   PRINT J
620   FOR L=-8 TO -18 STEP -2
630     PRINT J,L
640   NEXT L
650   PRINT L
660 NEXT J
```

18. The following are the main types of loops described in this chapter:

uncontrolled	counting	nested
input	pretest	FOR
processing	posttest	

Indicate what types of loop or loops are used in each of the following groups of statements. Your answers should come from the above list. Some answers require more than one word (e.g., pretest processing loop or nested FOR loops).

a.
```
100 INPUT X
110    IF X=1 THEN 140
120    PRINT X
130 GOTO 100
140 (next statement)
```

b.
```
150 LET A=-10
160 PRINT A
170    LET A=A+1
180 IF A<=0 THEN 160
```

c.
```
190 LET Z=0
200    PRINT Z
210 GOTO 190
```

d.
```
220 FOR I=1 TO 12 STEP 3
230    PRINT I
240 NEXT I
```

e.
```
250 FOR J=1 TO 10
260    LET K=1
270    IF K>5 THEN 310
280       PRINT J,K
290       LET K=K+1
300    GOTO 270
310 NEXT J
```

f.
```
320 LET P=1000
330 IF P<50 THEN 360
340    LET P=P-.1*P
350 GOTO 330
360 (next statement)
```

19. Are WHILE loops available in the version of BASIC you are using?
20. Code a WHILE loop to display the numbers 21, 18, 15, ..., 3 in a column.

Programming problems

1. Write the program for Problem 2 or Problem 5 in Chapter 3 with the additional requirement that the program terminates when the customer number is 9999.
2. Write the program for Problem 4 in Chapter 3 with the additional requirement that the total commission for all salespeople is accumulated and displayed at the end of the regular output. Add input data with zero for the salesperson number to control the input loop.
3. Write a BASIC program to display a table for converting Fahrenheit temperature to Celsius. (See Problem 2 in Chapter 2 for the appropriate conversion formula.) The table should list the Fahrenheit temperatures from 32 to 212 degrees in two-degree increments and the equivalent of each temperature in Celsius.
4. A classic exercise in computer programming is sometimes called the "Manhattan Problem." It is based on the historical fact that in 1627 the Dutch purchased Manhattan Island from the Indians for the equivalent of $24. Did the Dutch make a good investment, or would it have been better to have deposited the original $24 in a bank at a fixed interest rate and left it for all these years?

   Assume that the original $24 used to purchase Manhattan Island was deposited in a bank that paid 3% interest compounded annually. Write a BASIC program to determine the account total at the end of 1986 (360 years later). Do not use an interest formula to calculate the amount at the end of the time period; instead, accumulate the total one year at a time.

5. Each time a ball bounces, it rises to two-thirds the height it did on the previous bounce. Assume a ball is dropped from a height of 1000 feet. Write a BASIC program that displays the height the ball rises on each bounce until it rises less than one foot. There is no input to this program.

6. A company agrees to pay one of its employees in grains of rice instead of money. The employee receives one grain on the first day, two grains the second day, four grains the third day, eight grains the fourth day, and so forth. In other words, each succeeding day the employee receives twice as many grains as he or she did the day before. The employee works for the company for 15 days.

   Write a BASIC program to determine the number of grains of rice that the employee receives on each day that he or she works. Also, accumulate the total of the rice earnings. There is no input for this program. Output should consist of 15 lines each with the day number, the number of grains received on that day, and the accumulated number of grains received to date.

7. Assume that a pair of rabbits can produce a new pair in one month's time. Each new pair becomes fertile at one month of age and begins the cycle of reproducing a new pair every month. If rabbits never die, how many pairs of rabbits are produced from a single pair in N months' time?

   If N ranges from 1 to some maximum value, then the solution to this problem creates a sequence of numbers known as the Fibonacci sequence after the Italian mathematician who first posed the problem. For $N = 1$, the value in the sequence is 1. (That is, at the end of the first month, one new pair of rabbits is produced.) For $N = 2$, the value is also 1. For any N greater than 2, the value in the sequence is the sum of the two previous values. Thus, the sequence is as follows:

Number of months	Number of pairs of rabbits
1	1
2	1
3	2
4	3
5	5
6	8
7	13
.	.
.	.
.	.

   Let N range from 1 to 24. Write a BASIC program to compute and display a table listing N and the number of rabbits produced from the original pair at the end of month N. There is no input for this program.

8. Write the program for Problem 13 in Chapter 3 with the additional requirement that the total gross pay, withholding tax, social security tax, and net pay is accumulated and displayed at the end of the regular output. Use 9999 for the employee number to control the input loop.

9. Write a BASIC program that displays a table of Fahrenheit and equivalent Celsius temperatures. The equation is given in Problem 2 of Chapter 2. The program should be designed to begin the table at any initial Fahrenheit temperature, end at any final temperature, and increment between the initial and final temperatures by any given value. Input for the program is the initial Fahrenheit temperature, the final temperature, and the increment. Use the following sets of input data to test the program:

Initial	Final	Increment
32	212	10
70	71	.1
40	30	−1
−10	0	2
0	0	0

   The program should terminate if the increment is 0.

10. The value of e^x can be found from the following infinite series:

$$e^x = 1 + x + \frac{x^2}{2!} + \frac{x^3}{3!} + \frac{x^4}{4!} + \cdots$$

$$= 1 + \sum_{i=1}^{\infty} \frac{x^i}{i!}$$

Notice that the nth term (where the first term is 1) is the previous term times $x/(n-1)$.

An approximation to the value of e^x can be computed by carrying out this summation to a finite number of terms. Write a BASIC program to approximate e^x using 6 terms in the summation. Display the approximate value of e^x. Test the program with the following values of x:

```
    1
    0
   -1
    2.7183
    5
   -5
```

11. A tabulation of exam scores is needed for the students in a class. The scores vary from 0 to 100. Write a BASIC program to determine the number of scores in the ranges 90 to 100, 80 to 89, 70 to 79, 60 to 69, and 0 to 59. Also determine the percent of the total number of test scores that fall in each range. Display all results.

    Exam scores should be accepted one at a time from the keyboard until 999 is entered. Use the following exam scores to test the program:

85	100	80	76	42	65	89
91	90	37	72	83	88	69
94	85	48	66	92	45	100
73	87	70	60	80	72	59
61	78	61	91	75	78	74
82	76	75	85	91	79	75

12. The combination of n things taken k at a time is given by the following expression:

$$\frac{n!}{k!(n-k)!}$$

Write a BASIC program that accepts the values of n and k, computes the combination, and displays the result. Use the following data to test the program:

n	k
10	3
2	1
5	2
8	6

13. A problem in timber management is to determine how much of an area to leave uncut so that the harvested area is reforested in a certain period of time. It is assumed that reforestation takes place at a known rate per year, depending on climate and soil conditions. The reforestation rate expresses this growth as a function of the amount of timber standing. For example, if 100 acres are left standing and the reforestation rate is .05, then at the end of the first year there are 100 + .05 × 100 or 105 acres forested. At the end of the second year the number of acres forested is 105 + .05 × 105, or 110.25 acres.

    Assume that the total area to be forested, the uncut area, and the reforestation rate are known. Write a BASIC program to determine the percent of the total area that is forested after 20 years. Output should give the input data plus the number of acres forested after 20 years and the percentage of the total area that this represents.

Use the following input data to test the program:

Area number	Total area	Uncut area	Reforestation rate
045	10,000	100	.05
083	1,000	50	.08
153	20,000	500	.10
192	14,000	3,000	.02
234	6,000	1,000	.01
416	18,000	1,500	.05

999 (trailer value)

14. The rate of inflation is the annual percent increase in the cost of goods and services. For example, assume that an item costs $10.00 today and the rate of inflation is 10%. Then the cost of the item in one year is $10.00 + .10 \times 10.00$ or $11.00. In two years the item will cost $11.00 + .10 \times 11.00$ or $12.10.

Write a BASIC program to find the cost of a $12.00 item in fifteen years if the rate of inflation is 2%, 3%, 4%, and so forth up to 10%. The program should display the cost after fifteen years at each inflation rate. (Hint: Use nested FOR loops.)

Also determine the overall percent increase in the cost of the item. For example, if a $10.00 item costs $18.00 after 15 years, then the percent increase is 80%; if it costs $24.00, the overall increase is 140%. Compute the overall percent increase for the $12.00 item after fifteen years at each inflation rate.

There is no input for this program. Output should list only the final result after fifteen years for each inflation rate.

Chapter 5

Input and output programming

In Chapter 2 we introduced simple input and output programming. Although such programming is sufficient for many situations, there are times when more complex I/O is required. In this chapter we describe additional input and output features of BASIC. After completing this chapter you should be able to write programs that involve complex input and output programming.

5-1 Output programming

As we know, the PRINT statement causes the values of variables to be displayed in fixed print zones. We also know that we can use the PRINT statement to display character output (words or phrases) in print zones. The PRINT statement has other capabilities. For example, we can use the PRINT statement to display output anywhere on a line, not just in fixed zones. In this section we describe this and other capabilities of the PRINT statement. We also discuss other features of BASIC that can be used for output programming.

Positioning output

On a CRT screen, there is usually a mark such as a line or a box that indicates where the next output is to be displayed. This mark is called a *cursor*. If the cursor is at a particular position on a line when an instruction is given to display some output, the output will begin at that position. We can move the cursor to different positions on a line by using certain features of the PRINT statement. This subsection describes these features.

The comma. If a comma is used in a PRINT statement to separate variables and character output, the output is displayed in fixed print zones. The effect of a comma is to move the cursor to the next print zone. For example, consider the following statement:

```
70 PRINT X,Y,Z
```

When this PRINT statement is executed, a new line is begun; the cursor is positioned on the far left of that line. Then the value of X is displayed, beginning where the cursor is positioned. (Recall that a numeric value is preceded by a blank space or a minus sign depending on whether the value is positive or negative. Thus, if X is positive, a blank will appear where the cursor is located, and the number will begin one position to the right. If X is negative, a minus sign will be displayed where the cursor is located.) After the value of X is displayed, the comma in the PRINT statement causes the cursor to be moved to the beginning of the next print zone. Then the value of Y is displayed, starting there. The second comma causes the cursor to be moved to the next print zone, where the value of Z is displayed. Thus, this statement causes the values of X, Y, and Z to be displayed in three successive print zones.

Extra commas can be used in the PRINT statement to space over print zones. Each extra comma, in effect, skips one zone. For example, the following statement displays the value of X in the second print zone and the value of Y in the fourth print zone:

```
170 PRINT ,X,,Y
```

The first comma causes the cursor to be moved to the second print zone, thus skipping the first print zone. The extra comma between the variables causes the third print zone to be skipped.

If we put a comma at the *end* of a list of variables in a PRINT statement, a new line is *not* started when the next PRINT statement is executed. Instead, the output begins on the same line as the previous output. For example, consider the following statements:

```
270 PRINT X,Y,
275 PRINT Z
```

The comma at the end of line 270 means that the value of Z will be displayed in the next print zone on the same line as the values of X and Y.

The semicolon. When commas are used in a PRINT statement, the output is widely spaced and may be difficult to read. It is possible, however, to display the output closer together. This is done by using semicolons instead of commas to separate the items in the PRINT statement. For example, consider the following statement:

```
80 PRINT X;Y;Z
```

Notice that semicolons separate the variables in the PRINT statement. Each semicolon causes the cursor to be left where it is after displaying a value, rather than being advanced to the next print zone. Thus, in this statement the values of X, Y, and Z are displayed close together, *not* in successive print zones. For example, if X is 35, Y is -27, and Z is 6.8, the output appears as follows:

```
35 -27  6.8
```

Each number is displayed with a leading blank space if it is positive or a minus sign if it is negative. Following each number is a trailing blank space.

Character output is displayed without leading or trailing blank spaces. Thus, if character output is separated by semicolons in the PRINT statement, no spaces appear between the output. For example, the statement

```
180 PRINT "STATISTICAL";"DATA"
```

results in the output

```
STATISTICALDATA
```

We can include extra spaces in this output by using spaces in the PRINT statement. Thus, if we wish to display the words STATISTICAL and DATA separated by two spaces, we can use the following statement:

```
180 PRINT "STATISTICAL ";" DATA"
```

Another approach in this case is to combine the two words in the PRINT statement as follows:

```
180 PRINT "STATISTICAL  DATA"
```

The output is the same in either case.

As another example of the use of semicolons, consider the following statement:

```
280 PRINT "AMOUNT =";A;"COUNT =";C
```

If A is 250 and C is 9, the output is as follows:

```
AMOUNT = 250 COUNT = 9
```

The extra spaces are provided in the output because numbers are always displayed with a leading space (or a minus sign) and a trailing space.

Commas and semicolons can be combined in one statement. For example, consider the following statement:

```
380 PRINT X;Y,Z
```

In this case the values of X and Y are displayed close together because a semicolon separates the variables, but Z is displayed beginning in the next print zone. If X, Y, and Z are 35, -27, and 6.8, respectively, the output appears as follows:

```
(Print Zone 1)|(Print Zone 2)
 35 -27        6.8
```

As with a comma, a semicolon at the end of a PRINT statement causes the next output to appear on the same line as the previous output. Thus, the following statements cause one line to be displayed:

```
480 PRINT X;Y;
485 PRINT Z
```

The TAB function. Occasionally we want to display the output beginning in a specific print position on the CRT screen. This can be done by using the TAB function in the PRINT statement.† The TAB function consists of the word TAB followed by a constant, variable, or more complex numeric expression in parentheses. For example, the following statement uses the TAB function twice:

```
570 PRINT TAB(10);X;TAB(20);Y
```

The effect of the TAB function is to cause the cursor to move or tabulate to the print position given in parentheses. Then output begins at that position. In the above example the value of X is displayed beginning in position 10 and Y is displayed beginning in position 20.

---

† The general concept of a function is discussed in Chapter 7.

Print positions are numbered beginning with 1 on the left. Thus, TAB(1) causes the output to begin as far to the left as possible. [In some versions of BASIC, the print positions are numbered beginning with 0. Then TAB(0) results in the leftmost output. (See Table 5-1.)]

As another example of the use of the TAB function, consider the following:

```
670 PRINT "A";TAB(6);"B";TAB(11);"C"
```

In this case the output will appear as follows:

```
A    B    C
```

The letter A is displayed in the first print position, B is displayed in the sixth print position, and C is displayed in the eleventh print position.

Notice in these examples that a semicolon is used before and after the TAB function. If commas are used instead, the cursor is moved to the next print zone whenever a comma is encountered. This usually results in output completely different from what the programmer wants.

It is not possible to move the cursor backward with the TAB function. For example, consider the following statement:

```
770 PRINT TAB(20);X;TAB(10);Y
```

After the value of X is displayed beginning in the twentieth print position, TAB(10) is encountered. This does *not* move the cursor back to print position 10 on the same line. Instead, a new line is started and the cursor is tabulated to print position 10. Then the value of Y is displayed. Thus, the output appears on two separate lines. [With some versions of BASIC, the computer ignores the TAB(10) function and displays the value of Y on the same line in the next available space. (See Table 5-1.)]

If a variable or a more complex numeric expression is used in a TAB function, the value is rounded to determine the print position. For example, if X is 5.7, TAB(X) causes the output to be displayed in the sixth print position and TAB(2*X) causes the output to begin in the eleventh print position. [With some versions of BASIC, the value of the expression is truncated rather than rounded; that is, the fractional part is dropped. Thus, if X is 5.7, TAB(X) tabulates to the fifth print position. (See Table 5-1.)]

Printer output. The rules regarding positioning output and the TAB function apply to printer output as well as to CRT screen output. With a printer, however, there is no cursor; rather there is a printing mechanism that is positioned. If the PRINT statement is available for printer output in the version of BASIC being used, the

Table 5-1. TAB function differences

BASIC version	Beginning print position	Effect of backward tab	Noninteger tab position
ANS minimal BASIC	1	New line begun	Rounded
ANS BASIC	1	New line begun	Rounded
Microsoft BASIC	1	New line begun	Rounded
Applesoft BASIC	1	Ignored	Truncated
True BASIC	1	New line begun	Rounded
BASIC-PLUS	0	Ignored	Truncated
VAX-11 BASIC	0	Ignored	Truncated

comma, semicolon, and TAB function move the printing mechanism in exactly the same way as the cursor is moved. If the LPRINT statement is used for printer output, then commas, semicolons, and the TAB function are used in this statement exactly as in the PRINT statement.

Clearing the screen

With CRT output it is often desirable to erase everything on the screen before displaying any output. This makes the screen easier to read. In many versions of BASIC this can be accomplished with a special clear screen statement. The syntax of this statement varies considerably from one version of BASIC to another. (See Table 5-2.) Here we will describe one commonly used form.

The syntax of the clear screen statement that we will describe is as follows:

```
ln CLS
```

For example, the following is a clear screen statement:

```
10 CLS
```

The effect of this statement is to erase everything on the screen and to move the cursor to the upper left-hand corner. The next output displayed in the program will begin on the top line of the screen, in the left-hand column.

Usually the clear screen statement is executed at the beginning of the program, before any input is accepted or output is displayed. We will see an example of the use of this statement in the next section.

Input prompts

In Chapter 2 we described how the INPUT statement displays a question mark to prompt the person running the program. Usually, however, we want to provide additional prompting in the form of a message that explains what input is required. For example, if a test score is to be entered, we may display the message ENTER TEST SCORE just before the appropriate INPUT statement is executed. The following statements accomplish this:

```
20 PRINT "ENTER TEST SCORE"
30 INPUT S
```

Table 5-2. Clear screen statement differences

BASIC version	Clear screen statement syntax
ANS minimal BASIC	Not available
ANS BASIC	ln CLEAR
Microsoft BASIC	ln CLS
Applesoft BASIC	ln HOME
True BASIC	CLEAR
BASIC-PLUS VAX-11 BASIC	ln PRINT CHR$(26); (May not work with all terminals.)

On the CRT screen the sequence appears as follows:

```
ENTER TEST SCORE
? 85
```

The person using the program sees the message and the question mark and types the appropriate data (85 in this example).

Another approach is to use a semicolon at the end of the PRINT statement as follows:

```
40 PRINT "ENTER TEST SCORE";
50 INPUT S
```

The effect now is that the question mark appears on the same line as the message. The sequence appears as follows on the CRT screen:

```
ENTER TEST SCORE? 85
```

In most versions of BASIC, the input prompt can be included in the INPUT statement. The syntax and rules vary somewhat from one version of BASIC to another. (See Table 5-3.) We will describe one commonly used form.

The syntax of the INPUT statement with a prompt that we will describe is as follows:

```
ln INPUT "prompt";list of variables separated by commas
```

For example, the following INPUT statement includes a prompt:

```
60 INPUT "ENTER TEST SCORE";S
```

The effect of this statement is to display the phrase enclosed in the quotation marks. Following this, a question mark is displayed on the same line, and then the computer waits for input to be entered. Thus, the effect is the same as in the previous example.

Notice that a question mark is displayed as part of the INPUT statement. Thus, a question mark should not be included in the prompt. If it is, two question marks will be shown on the CRT screen. [Some versions of BASIC do not display a

Table 5-3. INPUT statement with a prompt differences

BASIC version	Syntax and rules for INPUT statement with a prompt
ANS minimal BASIC	Not available
ANS BASIC	ln INPUT PROMPT "prompt":list ? not displayed
Microsoft BASIC	ln INPUT "prompt";list ? displayed or ln INPUT "prompt",list ? not displayed
Applesoft BASIC	ln INPUT "prompt";list ? not displayed
True BASIC	INPUT PROMPT "prompt":list ? not displayed
BASIC-PLUS VAX-11 BASIC	ln INPUT "prompt";list ? displayed

question mark when a prompt is used in an INPUT statement. In these versions, a question mark should be included in the prompt if one is desired. (See Table 5-3.)]

Constants and expressions in the PRINT statement

The PRINT statement may list variables and character output to be displayed. In addition, constants and more complex numeric expressions can be used. For example, the following PRINT statement is valid:

```
60 PRINT X;1;X+1
```

This statement causes the computer to display the value of the variable X, the constant 1, and the value of the expression X + 1. If X equals 5, the output appears as follows:

```
5   1   6
```

Any variable, constant, or numeric expression can appear in a PRINT statement. Thus, the following statements are valid:

```
160 PRINT A*B-C,.00057
260 PRINT 3.5847^3
360 PRINT 8.5E25,X/Y
460 PRINT B*(1+R)^N
```

The computer evaluates any expression, using the current values of the variables, and displays the result.

If the PRINT statement is used for printer output, the values of constants can be printed with this statement. If the LPRINT statement is used for printer output, then constants and expressions can be included in this statement.

5-2 Interactive program design

A person running a program — that is, a person who keys in input data and gets output from a program — is called a *user* of the program. A program that involves interactive processing must be easy for the user to use. Basically this is accomplished by guiding the user through the processing with messages and prompts. The user should be told what to do at each step in the program. All input data should be requested with an appropriate prompt. All output should be provided with an adequate description. It should be assumed that the user knows nothing about computers or programming and can only follow the instructions that are displayed on the CRT screen.

Figure 5-1 shows a test-score averaging program that is designed for easy use. The interactive input and output that results when the program is run is shown in Figure 5-2. The flowchart of the program is given in Figure 5-3.

This program first clears the CRT screen and moves the cursor to the upper left corner. Then the program displays a title so that the user knows which program is running. Next, a prompt is displayed requesting the number of test scores to be averaged. After the input is accepted, a message is displayed stating how many tests scores are to be entered. Notice that the input just entered (i.e., the value of N) is immediately displayed in this message. This is a common technique to remind the user of what was entered. The program then accepts the required number of test scores, computing the total as the scores are entered. After the average is computed, the total and average are displayed with appropriate descriptions.

Figure 5-1. The interactive test-score averaging program

```
100 REM - TEST SCORE AVERAGING PROGRAM
110 REM - VARIABLES:
120 REM        N = NUMBER OF TEST SCORES
130 REM        S = TEST SCORE
140 REM        T = TOTAL OF TEST SCORES
150 REM        A = AVERAGE TEST SCORE
160 REM        I = COUNTER
170 REM        R = REPETITION QUESTION RESPONSE
180 CLS
190 PRINT "TEST SCORE AVERAGING PROGRAM"
200 PRINT
210   INPUT "ENTER THE NUMBER OF SCORES TO BE AVERAGED";N
220   PRINT
230   PRINT "ENTER";N;"TEST SCORES - ONE PER LINE"
240   LET T=0
250   FOR I=1 TO N
260     INPUT S
270     LET T=T+S
280   NEXT I
290   LET A=T/N
300   PRINT
310   PRINT "THE TOTAL IS";T
320   PRINT "THE AVERAGE IS";A
330   PRINT
340   PRINT "DO YOU WANT TO AVERAGE MORE SCORES"
350   INPUT "(TYPE 1 FOR YES, 0 FOR NO)";R
360 IF R=1 THEN 200
370 PRINT
380 PRINT "END OF PROGRAM"
390 END
```

Figure 5-2. Interactive input and output for the test-score averaging program

```
TEST SCORE AVERAGING PROGRAM

ENTER THE NUMBER OF SCORES TO BE AVERAGED? 5

ENTER 5 TEST SCORES - ONE PER LINE
? 100
? 85
? 79
? 96
? 62

THE TOTAL IS 422
THE AVERAGE IS 84.4

DO YOU WANT TO AVERAGE MORE SCORES
(TYPE 1 FOR YES, 0 FOR NO)? 1

ENTER THE NUMBER OF SCORES TO BE AVERAGED? 3

ENTER 3 TEST SCORES - ONE PER LINE
? 57
? 89
? 72

THE TOTAL IS 218
THE AVERAGE IS 72.6667

DO YOU WANT TO AVERAGE MORE SCORES
(TYPE 1 FOR YES, 0 FOR NO)? 0

END OF PROGRAM
```

Figure 5-3. Flowchart of the interactive test-score averaging program

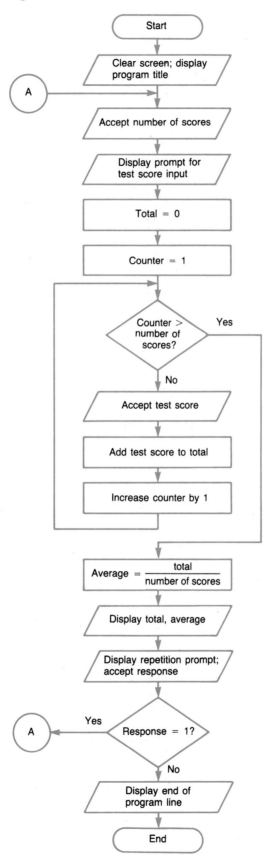

The program uses a common technique for determining whether to repeat the processing. This is shown in lines 340 through 360. The technique is to ask the user whether he or she wishes to continue. In this example the response, R, may be 1 or 0, meaning yes or no, respectively. If R equals 1, the computer branches to the beginning of the loop; otherwise a message is displayed indicating the program is finished and the END statement is executed, stopping the program.

Note that nothing is left for the user to figure out during the processing. All input is requested with an appropriate message; all output is displayed with an adequate description. Blank lines are displayed at appropriate places to make the output easier to read. The beginning and end of execution are clearly identified. All of this makes the program easier for a person to use.

This program uses certain features that may be different or not available in some versions of BASIC. These are the clear screen statement (line 180) and the INPUT statement with an input prompt (lines 210 and 350). These statements may have to be changed to run the program on some computers. However, because they are fairly common, we will use these statements in some future examples.

This program illustrates the basic principles of interactive program design. In later chapters we will see other examples of interactive programs.

5-3 The READ, DATA, and RESTORE statements

The INPUT statement is the main statement used for data input in BASIC. Its primary application is in interactive data processing. There are situations, however, where a batch of data needs to be processed. This can be done by using the INPUT statement to accept all the data from the keyboard. Another approach is to put the data in the program using a DATA statement and then to accept, or "read," the data with a READ statement. In this section we describe these statements and their use in BASIC programs.

The READ and DATA statements

The READ and DATA statements are always used together in a program. The syntax of the READ statement is as follows:

> *ln* READ *list of variables separated by commas*

For example, the following is a valid READ statement:

```
10 READ X,Y,Z
```

Notice that the syntax is the same as that of the INPUT statement with the exception of the keyword. The syntax of the DATA statement is as follows:

> *ln* DATA *list of constants separated by commas*

For example, the following is a valid DATA statement:

```
15 DATA 78,95,82
```

Any valid constants can appear in a DATA statement, including constants in E-notation.

When a READ statement is executed, data is read from a DATA statement. Each variable in the READ statement is assigned a value from a DATA statement. The data is read in sequence, left-to-right. If the READ and DATA statements just given appear in a program, then after execution of the READ statement, X is 78, Y is 95, and Z is 82.

There may be any number of DATA statements in a program, and they may be placed anywhere before the END statement. When a DATA statement is encountered during the sequential execution of a program, the computer ignores it. A DATA statement is used only when a READ statement is executed.

When there is more than one DATA statement in a program, input begins with the data in the first statement and continues sequentially through the data in the other statements. For example, consider the following statements:

```
10 READ X
11 READ Y,Z
15 DATA 78,95
16 DATA 82
```

The first READ statement reads the first value in the first DATA statement. Thus, X is assigned the value 78. Then the second READ statement is executed. Input continues where the previous READ statement left off. Thus, 95 is read and assigned to Y. Now, because there are no more values in the first DATA statement, the computer automatically goes on to the second DATA statement. Hence, the value 82 is read for Z.

When a program is executed, the computer collects all the data in sequence from the DATA statements to form a *data block*. For example, assume that a program contains the following DATA statements:

```
110 DATA 52,85.3,-69
120 DATA 35.62
210 DATA 5.5E14,.0035,0,-2.69
```

Then the data block for this program is as follows:

```
52,85.3,-69,35.62,5.5E14,.0035,0,-2.69
```

The computer reads the data from the block in sequence. It keeps track of what data has been read by using what might be imagined as a pointer to point to the next available value in the data block. Initially the pointer points to the first value. Each time a value is read, the pointer automatically advances to the next value. In this way the computer always knows where to continue reading when a READ statement is executed.

As an example, assume that the following READ statements are executed in the program with the previous DATA statements:

```
120 READ A,B
130 READ C,D,E
```

After the first READ statement is executed, A is 52 and B is 85.3. Then the pointer points to the third value (-69) in the data block. After the second READ statement is executed, C is -69, D is 35.62, and E is 5.5×10^{14}. The pointer then points to the sixth value in the data block (.0035). The next READ statement begins at that point.

If a READ statement is executed and there is no more data in the data block, an execution error occurs and the program stops. This can cause a problem in a program with an input loop containing a READ statement to read sets of data from a DATA statement where the last set contains a trailer value. For example, assume that a program contains the following statements in a loop:

```
10 READ X,Y,Z
20 IF X=999 THEN 200
```

The trailer value is the value 999 for the variable X. Each time the READ statement is executed, three values are read from the data block. The last three values must be the trailer value for X and two arbitrary values such as zeros for Y and Z. If the last two values are not included, an execution error will occur, even though the trailer value has been read.

An illustrative program

To illustrate the use of READ and DATA statements in a program, consider the tuition-calculation program discussed in Chapter 4 (see Figure 4-3). A similar program using READ and DATA statements is shown in Figure 5-4. Each time the READ

Figure 5-4. The tuition-calculation program using the READ and DATA statements

```
100 REM - TUITION CALCULATION PROGRAM
110 REM - VARIABLES:
120 REM        I = STUDENT ID
130 REM        U = NUMBER OF UNITS
140 REM        T = TUITION
150 PRINT "STUDENT ID","UNITS","TUITION"
160 PRINT
170 READ I,U
180    IF I=9999 THEN 250
190    IF U>12 THEN 220
200      LET T=350
210    GOTO 230
220      LET T=350+20*(U-12)
230    PRINT I,U,T
240 GOTO 170
250 PRINT
260 PRINT "ALL DATA PROCESSED"
270 REM - INPUT DATA
280 DATA 1001,15,1013,18,1025,8
290 DATA 1085,12,1117,20,1130,6
300 DATA 1147,3,1165,13.5,1207,11
310 DATA 1229,12.5,9999,0
320 END
```

I like ← (handwritten annotation pointing to line 260)

(a) The program

STUDENT ID	UNITS	TUITION
1001	15	410
1013	18	470
1025	8	350
1085	12	350
1117	20	510
1130	6	350
1147	3	350
1165	13.5	380
1207	11	350
1229	12.5	360

```
ALL DATA PROCESSED
```

(b) Output

statement is executed, the next two values are read from the data block. The first value read is a student's identification number and the second is the number of units. Notice that the data appears in pairs in the DATA statement and that the last pair contains the trailer value (9999) for I and an arbitrary value (0) for U.

All DATA statements are grouped together at the end of this program just before the END statement, and a REM statement is used to mark the beginning of the DATA statements. This is a common style that programmers use with DATA statements. Although DATA statements may be placed anywhere in a program, grouping them as in this example makes locating and changing the data easier.

The flowchart of this program is shown in Figure 5-5. Notice that there is no reference to the DATA statements. The flowchart shows only the logical flow in the program, not the data that the program processes.

The program in Figure 5-4 illustrates the idea of batch processing. All the data that is to be processed is prepared in a batch before the program is run. The batch of data is contained in the DATA statements. When the program is run, no interactive input is entered. The data is read from the DATA statements, and the output is produced as a batch.

The RESTORE statement

Sometimes it is necessary to move the pointer back to the beginning of the data block. This can be accomplished with the RESTORE statement. The syntax of this statement is as follows:

```
1n RESTORE
```

The effect of this statement is to restore the pointer to the first value in the data block. This is often done so that the same data can be assigned to different variables. For example, consider the following sequence of statements:

```
110 READ A,B
115 RESTORE
120 READ C,D,E
200 DATA 5,8,6
```

In this case, A and B are assigned the first two values in the data block (5 and 8). Then the RESTORE statement restores the pointer to the first value in the block. The second READ statement then reads the first two values of the data block again (5 and 8), assigning the values to C and D, and then reads the third value (6) for E.

The READ, DATA, and RESTORE statements are sometimes used to initialize a large number of variables. For example, assume that each time a loop in a program is executed, the variables L, M, and N must be initialized to 5 and the variables X, Y, and Z must be initialized to 10. This can be accomplished with six LET statements, or it can be done as follows:

```
100 READ L,M,N,X,Y,Z
110 DATA 5,5,5,10,10,10
120 RESTORE
```

These statements would be at the beginning of the loop. The first time the loop was executed, the variables would be initialized to their required values. Then the RESTORE statement would move the pointer to the beginning of the data block. Thus, the

Figure 5-5. Flowchart of the tuition-calculation program that uses the READ and DATA statements

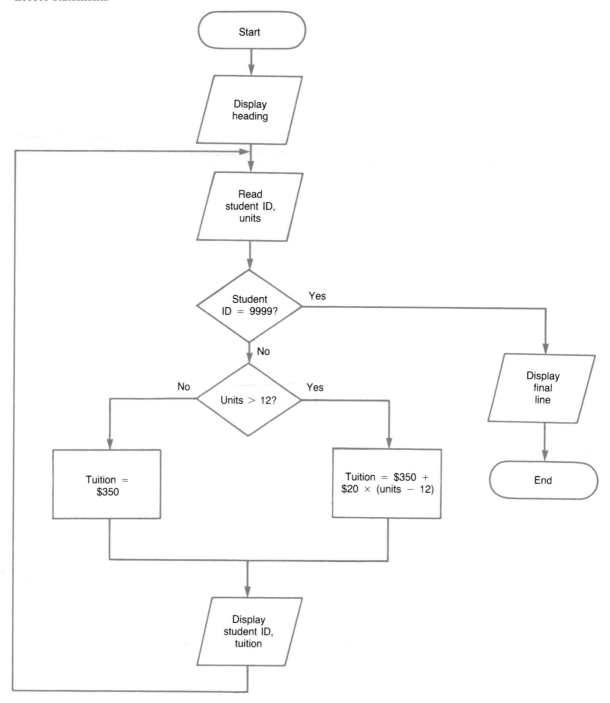

second time the loop was executed, the variables would be initialized again and the pointer would be restored. This process would continue for each execution of the loop.

5-4 A sample problem

In this section we develop a program for a sample problem that involves interactive input and output. The problem is to process customer orders for a business.

Problem definition

Each customer order received by a business includes a customer number and order information for one or more items that the customer wishes to order. The order information for each item consists of the item's number, the quantity of that item ordered, and the unit price. A program is needed to process this information for all items ordered by each customer. Processing for one customer involves computing the purchase amount for each item ordered, the total purchase amount for all items ordered, the sales tax on the total purchase amount, the shipping charge, and the total due. The program should process any number of customer orders.

The program should be interactive. The input data is the customer order information and the output is the results of processing the information. Figure 5-6 shows a sketch of how the interactive I/O should appear on the screen. At the beginning the program should display a title. Then the user should be asked for a customer number. Next the user should be asked to supply an item number, quantity ordered, and unit price. Then the item number and purchase amount should be displayed. Next the user should be asked whether more items are to be ordered. If the response to this question is yes, the program should accept another item's number, quantity, and price and proceed as before. If no more items are to be ordered, the customer number, total purchase amount, sales tax, shipping charge, and total due should be displayed. Then the user should be asked whether more customer orders are to be processed. If the response is yes, the entire sequence from the customer number entry should be repeated. If no more customer orders are to be processed, a final line that indicates the end of processing should be displayed.

The purchase amount for each item ordered is the product of the quantity ordered and the unit price. The sum of the purchase amounts for all items ordered by a customer is the total purchase amount. The sales tax is 6% of the total purchase amount. The shipping charge is $5 plus 3% of the total purchase amount. The total due is the sum of the total purchase amount, the sales tax, and the shipping charge.

Figure 5-6. Interactive input and output layout for the customer order processing program

```
CUSTOMER ORDER PROCESSING

ENTER CUSTOMER NUMBER? XXXX

ENTER ITEM NUMBER? XXX
ENTER QUANTITY ORDERED? XXXX
ENTER UNIT PRICE? XXXX

ITEM NUMBER:          XXX
PURCHASE AMOUNT:      XXXX

ARE THERE MORE ITEMS TO PROCESS
(TYPE 1 FOR YES, 0 FOR NO)? X

CUSTOMER NUMBER:        XXXX
TOTAL PURCHASE AMOUNT:  XXXX
SALES TAX:              XXXX
SHIPPING CHARGE:        XXXX
TOTAL DUE:              XXXX

ARE THERE MORE CUSTOMERS TO PROCESS
(TYPE 1 FOR YES, 0 FOR NO)? X

END OF CUSTOMER ORDER PROCESSING
```

Program design

The program that solves this problem involves processing data for any number of customers and, for each customer, processing order information for one or more items. To do this, nested loops are needed. The outer loop is repeated once for each customer; the inner loop is repeated once for each item that a customer orders.

The overall algorithm for the program, showing the outer loop, is as follows:

Clear the screen and display the program title.
Repeat the following:
    Accept the customer number.
    Process the order information for all items ordered and accumulate the total purchase amount.
    Compute the sales tax, shipping charge, and total due.
    Display the customer number, total purchase amount, sales tax, shipping charge, and total due.
    If there are no more customer orders to process, leave this loop.
End of loop.
Display the final output line.

In this algorithm the outer loop is repeated once for each customer. The inner loop is part of the step in which the order information is processed and the total purchase amount is accumulated. This step in the algorithm can be expressed as follows:

Set total purchase amount to zero.
Repeat the following:
    Accept the item number, quantity ordered, and unit price.
    Compute the purchase amount.
    Add the purchase amount to the total purchase amount.
    Display the item number and purchase amount.
    If there are no more items to order, leave this loop.
End of loop.

Incorporating these steps into the previous ones gives us the complete algorithm shown in Figure 5-7. The flowchart for the program is shown in Figure 5-8.

Program coding

Figure 5-9 shows the program that solves this problem. The variables used are listed in the REM statements at the beginning of the program. Notice that two different

Figure 5-7. Algorithm for the customer order processing problem

Clear the screen and display the program title.
Repeat the following:
    Accept the customer number.
    Set total purchase amount to zero.
    Repeat the following:
        Accept the item number, quantity ordered, and unit price.
        Compute the purchase amount.
        Add the purchase amount to the total purchase amount.
        Display the item number and purchase amount.
        If there are no more items to order, leave this loop.
    End of loop.
    Compute the sales tax, shipping charge, and total due.
    Display the customer number, total purchase amount, sales tax, shipping charge, and total due.
    If there are no more customer orders to process, leave this loop.
End of loop.
Display the final output line.

Figure 5-8. Flowchart of the customer order processing program

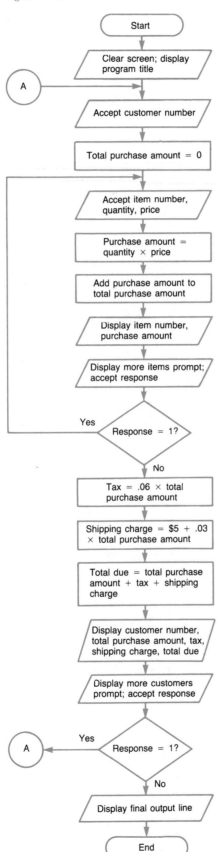

Figure 5-9. The customer order processing program

```
100 REM - CUSTOMER ORDER PROCESSING PROGRAM
110 REM - VARIABLES:
120 REM        N  = CUSTOMER NUMBER
130 REM        I  = ITEM NUMBER
140 REM        Q  = QUANTITY ORDERED
150 REM        P  = UNIT PRICE
160 REM        A  = PURCHASE AMOUNT
170 REM        T1 = TOTAL PURCHASE AMOUNT
180 REM        X  = TAX
190 REM        S  = SHIPPING CHARGE
200 REM        T  = TOTAL DUE
210 REM        R1 = MORE ITEMS QUESTION RESPONSE
220 REM        R2 = MORE CUSTOMERS QUESTION RESPONSE
230 CLS
240 PRINT "CUSTOMER ORDER PROCESSING"
250 REM - CUSTOMER PROCESSING LOOP
260 PRINT
270   INPUT "ENTER CUSTOMER NUMBER";N
280   LET T1=0
290   REM - ITEM PROCESSING LOOP
300   PRINT
310     INPUT "ENTER ITEM NUMBER";I
320     INPUT "ENTER QUANTITY ORDERED";Q
330     INPUT "ENTER UNIT PRICE";P
340     REM - COMPUTE PURCHASE AMOUNT
350     LET A=Q*P
360     LET T1=T1+A
370     PRINT
380     PRINT "ITEM NUMBER:";TAB(23);I
390     PRINT "PURCHASE AMOUNT:";TAB(23);A
400     PRINT
410     PRINT "ARE THERE MORE ITEMS TO PROCESS"
420     INPUT "(TYPE 1 FOR YES, 0 FOR NO)";R1
430   IF R1=1 THEN 300
440   REM - COMPUTE TAX
450   LET X=.06*T1
460   REM - COMPUTE SHIPPING CHARGE
470   LET S=5+.03*T1
480   REM - COMPUTE TOTAL DUE
490   LET T=T1+X+S
500   PRINT
510   PRINT "CUSTOMER NUMBER:";TAB(23);N
520   PRINT "TOTAL PURCHASE AMOUNT:";T1
530   PRINT "SALES TAX:";TAB(23);X
540   PRINT "SHIPPING CHARGE:";TAB(23);S
550   PRINT "TOTAL DUE:";TAB(23);T
560   PRINT
570   PRINT "ARE THERE MORE CUSTOMERS TO PROCESS"
580   INPUT "(TYPE 1 FOR YES, 0 FOR NO)";R2
590 IF R2=1 THEN 260
600 PRINT
610 PRINT "END OF CUSTOMER ORDER PROCESSING"
620 END
```

variables (R1 and R2) are used for the responses to the questions regarding more processing. The same variable could be used for both responses, but it is usually best to use different variables for different things so as to avoid confusion.

The program logic follows the algorithm in Figure 5-7 and the flowchart in Figure 5-8. The outer loop, which is repeated once for each customer, consists of lines 260 through 590. The inner loop, which is repeated once for each item ordered by a customer, consists of lines 300 through 430. Notice that both loops are posttest loops.

Program correctness

To test this program we need to be sure that all loops terminate properly and all calculations give the correct results. We should test the case where the customer orders only one item and the case where the customer orders several items. We should test different values for the quantity ordered and the unit price.

Figure 5-10 shows input test data and expected output. The interactive input and output from running the program with this data is shown in Figure 5-11. All test cases give the correct results.

Figure 5-10. Input test data and expected output for the customer order processing program

Customer number	Item number	Quantity ordered	Unit price	Purchase amount	Total purchase amount	Sales tax	Shipping charge	Total due
1234	987	9	11	99				
	876	15	12	180				
					279	16.47	13.37	309.11
2345	765	6	17	102				
					102	6.12	8.06	116.18
3456	654	5	3	15				
	543	19	10	190				
	432	1	21	21				
					226	13.56	11.78	251.34

Figure 5-11. Interactive input and output for the customer order processing program

```
CUSTOMER ORDER PROCESSING

ENTER CUSTOMER NUMBER? 1234

ENTER ITEM NUMBER? 987
ENTER QUANTITY ORDERED? 9
ENTER UNIT PRICE? 11

ITEM NUMBER:            987
PURCHASE AMOUNT:        99

ARE THERE MORE ITEMS TO PROCESS
(TYPE 1 FOR YES, 0 FOR NO)? 1

ENTER ITEM NUMBER? 876
ENTER QUANTITY ORDERED? 15
ENTER UNIT PRICE? 12

ITEM NUMBER:            876
PURCHASE AMOUNT:        180

ARE THERE MORE ITEMS TO PROCESS
(TYPE 1 FOR YES, 0 FOR NO)? 0

CUSTOMER NUMBER:        1234
TOTAL PURCHASE AMOUNT: 279
SALES TAX:              16.74
SHIPPING CHARGE:        13.37
TOTAL DUE:              309.11

ARE THERE MORE CUSTOMERS TO PROCESS
(TYPE 1 FOR YES, 0 FOR NO)? 1
```

(continued)

Figure 5-11. Continued

```
ENTER CUSTOMER NUMBER? 2345

ENTER ITEM NUMBER? 765
ENTER QUANTITY ORDERED? 6
ENTER UNIT PRICE? 17

ITEM NUMBER:            765
PURCHASE AMOUNT:        102

ARE THERE MORE ITEMS TO PROCESS
(TYPE 1 FOR YES, 0 FOR NO)? 0

CUSTOMER NUMBER:        2345
TOTAL PURCHASE AMOUNT: 102
SALES TAX:              6.12
SHIPPING CHARGE:        8.06
TOTAL DUE:              116.18

ARE THERE MORE CUSTOMERS TO PROCESS
(TYPE 1 FOR YES, 0 FOR NO)? 1

ENTER CUSTOMER NUMBER? 3456

ENTER ITEM NUMBER? 654
ENTER QUANTITY ORDERED? 5
ENTER UNIT PRICE? 3

ITEM NUMBER:            654
PURCHASE AMOUNT:        15

ARE THERE MORE ITEMS TO PROCESS
(TYPE 1 FOR YES, 0 FOR NO)? 1

ENTER ITEM NUMBER? 543
ENTER QUANTITY ORDERED? 19
ENTER UNIT PRICE? 10

ITEM NUMBER:            543
PURCHASE AMOUNT:        190

ARE THERE MORE ITEMS TO PROCESS
(TYPE 1 FOR YES, 0 FOR NO)? 1

ENTER ITEM NUMBER? 432
ENTER QUANTITY ORDERED? 1
ENTER UNIT PRICE? 21

ITEM NUMBER:            432
PURCHASE AMOUNT:        21

ARE THERE MORE ITEMS TO PROCESS
(TYPE 1 FOR YES, 0 FOR NO)? 0

CUSTOMER NUMBER:        3456
TOTAL PURCHASE AMOUNT: 226
SALES TAX:              13.56
SHIPPING CHARGE:        11.78
TOTAL DUE:              251.34

ARE THERE MORE CUSTOMERS TO PROCESS
(TYPE 1 FOR YES, 0 FOR NO)? 0

END OF CUSTOMER ORDER PROCESSING
```

Program documentation

The documentation for this program should include the program listing (Figure 5-9) and the interactive input and output from running the program (Figure 5-11). The documentation may also include the interactive input and output layout (Figure 5-6), the algorithm (Figure 5-7), the flowchart (Figure 5-8), the input test data and expected output (Figure 5-10), and other items that we will discuss later.

*5-5 The PRINT USING statement

With the PRINT statement, the value of a variable is displayed in a standard format determined by the computer. The programmer does not have control over how the output appears, although the output would sometimes look better in a different format. For example, columns of output usually look best if aligned on the right, and dollar amounts are usually best if displayed with two places to the right of the decimal point. These and other improvements in the output format can be made with the PRINT USING statement.

The PRINT USING statement is not available in all versions of BASIC, and its syntax varies somewhat from one version of the language to another. (See Table 5-4.) To demonstrate the idea we will use a common form. The syntax of this form is as follows:

```
ln PRINT USING "format";list of variables separated by commas
```

The following is an example of a PRINT USING statement:

```
50 PRINT USING "####   ###.###";I,T
```

The PRINT USING statement consists of the keywords PRINT and USING, followed by the *format* (also called the *image*), which must be enclosed in quotation marks. In the format, special symbols are used to describe the arrangement of the output data. Following the format is a semicolon (which may be a comma or a colon in some versions of BASIC) and then a list of variables just as in a simple PRINT statement. When the PRINT USING statement is executed, the values of the variables are displayed according to the specifications given in the format.

Table 5-4. PRINT USING statement differences

BASIC version	PRINT USING *statement syntax*
ANS minimal BASIC	Not available
ANS BASIC	ln PRINT USING "format":list
Microsoft BASIC	ln PRINT USING "format";list
Applesoft BASIC	Not available
True BASIC	PRINT USING "format":list
BASIC-PLUS	ln PRINT USING "format",list
VAX-11 BASIC	ln PRINT USING "format",list *or* ln PRINT USING "format";list

The symbols used in the format determine how the output is displayed. The rules for these symbols vary somewhat from one version of BASIC to another. (See Table 5-5.) Here we describe the rules that apply in several common versions of BASIC (Microsoft BASIC, BASIC-PLUS, VAX-11 BASIC). Similar rules apply in other versions.

Numeric output

To display a number, the # symbol is used for each digit position in the number. For example, consider the following PRINT USING statement:

```
60 PRINT USING "###";X
```

This statement tells the computer to display the value of X using the format ###. This means that the value is to be displayed in the first three print positions. If X is 128, this number is displayed at the beginning of the output line. If the value of X requires fewer than three print positions, the number is displayed so that it is aligned on the right; that is, the value is *right-justified*. For example, if X is 9, the output consists of two blank spaces and then the digit 9. When not enough print positions are provided in the format, an error occurs. In this case the % symbol is displayed, followed by the value. For example, if X is 1024, the output appears as follows:

```
%1024
```

Minus sign. If the output value is negative, a minus sign is displayed to the left of the first digit, provided there are enough print positions. Thus, if X is −4 in the previous example, the output consists of a space, the minus sign, and the digit 4. Notice, however, that if the number is positive, no plus sign is displayed.

Sometimes it is desirable to have the minus sign displayed after the number. This is accomplished by putting a minus sign after the format, as in the following example:

```
70 PRINT USING "###-";X
```

If the value to be displayed is positive, a blank space replaces the minus sign. If the value is negative, the minus sign is displayed. Thus, the value 128 is displayed as 128 followed by a blank space, and −4 appears as 4−.

Table 5-5. PRINT USING statement format differences

BASIC version	PRINT USING statement format rules
ANS minimal BASIC Applesoft BASIC	Not applicable
Microsoft BASIC BASIC-PLUS VAX-11 BASIC	Format rules are the same as described in the text.
ANS BASIC True BASIC	Rules for the # symbol and the decimal point are the same as described in the text. A minus sign on the right is not permitted. If commas are desired, they should be inserted every three digits to the left of the decimal point. If a dollar sign is desired, every character to the left of the decimal point should be a dollar sign. If asterisks are desired, every character to the left of the decimal point should be an asterisk.

Decimal point. To include a decimal point in the output, the decimal point is used in the format in the appropriate position. This is shown in the following example:

```
80 PRINT USING "###.##";Y
```

If Y is 486.37, the output consists of this number displayed in the first six print positions with a decimal point in the fourth print position. (Notice that six print positions are needed because the decimal point requires one print position.) If the value has more places to the right of the decimal point than are indicated in the format, the output is rounded. Thus, if X is 486.376, the number displayed is 486.38. When the value has fewer places to the right than indicated in the format, zeros are added to fill out the decimal positions. Thus, if Y is 486.3, then 486.30 is displayed.

Comma. If a comma is inserted *anywhere* to the left of the decimal point in the format, commas are displayed every three digits in the output. For example, consider the following statement:

```
90 PRINT USING "#,#######";Z
```

If the value of Z is 5000000, the output appears as follows:

```
5,000,000
```

Notice that two commas are displayed even though only one comma appears in the format. Each comma that is displayed requires a print position. To avoid an error, the total number of print positions to the left of the decimal point used in the output, including the commas, cannot exceed the number of positions specified to the left of the decimal point in the format. The number of positions is the number of # symbols plus one for the comma. Thus the previous statement specifies nine positions (eight # symbols plus one). Because two commas may appear in the output, any value displayed by this statement can have at most seven digits (e.g., 1,234,567).

Dollar sign. A dollar sign can be displayed immediately preceding the first digit of a number by using *two* dollar signs at the beginning of the format. For example, consider the following statement:

```
100 PRINT USING "$$##.##";P
```

If the value of P is 500, the output displayed is $500.00. If the value of P is 5, the output consists of two blank spaces and then $5.00. In effect, the double dollar sign causes one dollar sign to be displayed just ahead of the first digit in the number. Note that two dollar signs are required in the format to cause the output to be displayed as described.

A minus sign cannot be displayed before or after a dollar sign. Thus, if the value of P is negative in the previous example, an error will occur. A minus sign will be displayed on the right if the sign is used in the format. For example, the previous statement could be written as follows:

```
100 PRINT USING "$$##.##-";P
```

If P is −8, the output is displayed as $8.00 −.

Asterisk. If *two* asterisks are used at the beginning of a format, any print positions to the left of the number are filled with asterisks. The following statement illustrates this:

```
110 PRINT USING "**##.##";P
```

If P is 500, the output displayed is *500.00. If P is 5, the output appears as ***5.00. Asterisks are often used in this way to protect dollar amounts on checks from alterations. Notice that two asterisks are required in the format to cause the output to be displayed as described.

Figure 5-12 shows other examples using the special symbols described here.

Positioning output

In the examples given so far, the output has begun in the first print position. To start in a different print position, blank spaces are used at the beginning of the format. For example, the following PRINT USING statement has four blanks at the beginning of the format:

```
120 PRINT USING "    ###";X
```

This causes the first four print positions to be skipped, and the output begins in the fifth print position. Note that the TAB function cannot be used with the PRINT USING statement.

When more than one number is to be displayed on a line, the format must contain the appropriate symbols to describe the arrangement of each number with the necessary blanks to spread out the values. For example, consider the following statement:

```
130 PRINT USING "  ##   ##.##   #,###.##";A,B,C
```

This statement tells the computer to display the values of A, B, and C in the specified format. The output line contains two blanks, then the value of A in the format ##, then three spaces followed by the value of B in the format ##.##, then three more spaces and the value of C in the format #,###.##. If A is 20, B is 25.95, and C is 1482.38, the output appears as follows:

```
  20   25.95   1,482.38
```

Notice that the horizontal positioning of the output is controlled by the format, not by the punctuation in the list of variables. Commas and semicolons in the variable list have no effect on the placement of the output.

Figure 5-12. Examples of formats

Format	Value	Output
"####"	1234	1234
"####"	56	56
"####"	−789	−789
"####−"	1234	1234
"####−"	56	56
"####−"	−789	789−
"##.###"	12.345	12.345
"##.###"	12.3456	12.346
"##.###"	12	12.000
"#,###"	1234	1,234
"#,###"	56	56
"$$###"	1234	$1234
"$$###"	56	$56
"**###"	1234	*1234
"**###"	56	***56
"$$#,###.##−"	1234.56	$1,234.56
"$$#,###.##−"	−78.90	$78.90−
"**#,###.##−"	1234.56	**1,234.56
"**#,###.##−"	−78.90	*****78.90−

A semicolon can be used at the end of the list of variables. When this is done, the output from the next PRINT statement or PRINT USING statement continues on the same line. For example, the same effect as the previous PRINT USING statement can be accomplished with two PRINT USING statements as follows:

```
130 PRINT USING "  ##    ##.##";A,B;
135 PRINT USING "   #,###.##";C
```

The semicolon at the end of the first PRINT USING statement causes the output from the second PRINT USING statement to be displayed on the same line as the first statement's output.

Character output

Words or phrases that are to be displayed on the same line as the values of variables can be included in the format. Any characters that are used in the format, except for characters with special meaning such as the # symbol, are displayed exactly as they appear. For example, consider the following statement:

```
140 PRINT USING "TOTAL = ###, AVERAGE = ##.#";T,A
```

If T is 252 and A is 84, the output line appears as follows:

```
TOTAL = 252, AVERAGE = 84.0
```

An illustrative program

To illustrate the use of the PRINT USING statement in a program we will modify the interest-calculation program in Chapter 4 (Figure 4-5) to include this statement. Figure 5-13 shows the resulting program. In this program, the values of Y, I, and B are displayed in the format given in the PRINT USING statement at line 220. This format is designed to align the columns under the headings displayed by the PRINT statement at line 150. Notice that dollar signs, commas, and decimal points are used in the format in the PRINT USING statement. The program also displays a final output line with the PRINT USING statement at line 270.

Printer output

In Section 2-3 we discussed printer output, which depends on the version of BASIC. The PRINT USING statement may or may not be used for printer output, depending on the version of BASIC. If the PRINT statement can produce printer output, then the PRINT USING statement can also be used for printer output. All the format rules apply for both CRT and printer output. If, however, the LPRINT statement is used for printer output, then the LPRINT USING statement must be used instead of the PRINT USING statement for printer output. The syntax and format rules for this statement are the same as for the PRINT USING statement, with the exception that the first keyword must be LPRINT. For example, the following is an LPRINT USING statement:

```
140 LPRINT USING "TOTAL = ###, AVERAGE = ##.#";T,A
```

The result is the same as an equivalent PRINT USING statement, except the output is printed on the printer, rather than displayed on the CRT screen.

Figure 5-13. An interest-calculation program with the PRINT USING statement

```
100 REM - INTEREST CALCULATION PROGRAM
110 REM - VARIABLES:
120 REM      B  = BANK BALANCE
130 REM      Y  = YEAR
140 REM      I  = INTEREST
150 PRINT "YEAR   INTEREST   BALANCE"
160 PRINT
170 LET B=1000
180 LET Y=1
190 IF B>=2000 THEN 250
200    LET I=.08*B
210    LET B=B+I
220    PRINT USING " ##     $$##.##   $$,###.##";Y,I,B
230    LET Y=Y+1
240 GOTO 190
250 LET Y=Y-1
260 PRINT
270 PRINT USING "BALANCE DOUBLES IN ## YEARS";Y
280 END
```

(a) The program

```
YEAR    INTEREST    BALANCE

  1      $80.00     $1,080.00
  2      $86.40     $1,166.40
  3      $93.31     $1,259.71
  4     $100.78     $1,360.49
  5     $108.84     $1,469.33
  6     $117.55     $1,586.87
  7     $126.95     $1,713.82
  8     $137.11     $1,850.93
  9     $148.07     $1,999.00
 10     $159.92     $2,158.93

BALANCE DOUBLES IN 10 YEARS
```

(b) Output

Review questions

1. What is the cursor on a CRT screen?
2. Code a statement that displays the value of P in the third print zone and the value of Q in the fifth print zone. Do not use the TAB function.
3. Code a statement that displays the values of P and Q close together in the first print zone.
4. Code a statement that displays the value of P beginning in print position 5 and the value of Q beginning in print position 25.
5. Assume that the value of A is 2, B is 3, and C is 4. What output is displayed by each of the following statements? (Show the output in the exact print positions in which it appears.)
   a. 100 PRINT A,B;C
   b. 200 PRINT "DATA";A;B;C
   c. 300 PRINT A,,B;"DATA"
   d. 400 PRINT TAB(7);A;TAB(21);B,C

e. `500 PRINT A;TAB(10);"DATA"`

f. `600 PRINT 5;A*B;A-C`

6. Assume that the value of A is 2, B is 3, and C is 4. What output is displayed by the following group of statements?

```
700 PRINT A;B,
710 PRINT C;
720 PRINT "DATA"
```

7. How is the CRT screen cleared in the version of BASIC you are using?

8. Code one or two statements that display the prompt ENTER DATA and accept the values of X and Y from the keyboard.

9. Code a single statement that displays the constant 8, the value of A, and the value of 8 times A.

10. What are some ways in which an interactive program should be designed so it is easy for the user to use?

11. Code a READ statement and a DATA statement to read the values 2, 3, and 4 for the variables A, B, and C, respectively.

12. What is the value of each variable after the following group of statements is executed?

```
10 READ P,Q,R
20 READ S,T
30 DATA 8,4,7,3,6
```

13. What is the value of each variable after the following group of statements is executed?

```
10 DATA 5,7,3
20 READ X,Y,Z,V
30 RESTORE
40 DATA 2,6,4
50 READ W,U
```

14. Code a PRINT USING statement that displays the values of S, T, and U. All values should be displayed with three places to the left of the decimal point and one to the right. Two blank spaces should separate the output values.

15. Code a PRINT USING statement that displays the word AMOUNT followed by the value of A. The value of A should be displayed with five places to the left of the decimal point and two places to the right, a comma, a dollar sign, and a minus sign on the right if A is negative.

16. Assume that the value of P is 2.5, Q is 73.625, and R is 62583. What output is displayed by each of the following statements? (Show the output in the exact print positions in which it appears.)

a. `100 PRINT USING "#.#  ##.###  #####";P,Q,R`

b. `200 PRINT USING "#  ##.#  #####.##";P,Q,R`

c. `300 PRINT USING "    #,####";R`

d. `400 PRINT USING "$$#######";R`

e. `500 PRINT USING "**######";R`

f. `600 PRINT USING "CLOSE ###.##  UP ##.##";Q,P`

Programming problems

Many of the problems in previous chapters can be completed using features described in this chapter. Some suggestions are included below. Any of the problems in this or previous chapters can be completed using either the PRINT statement or the PRINT USING statement.

1. Complete the programs for Problem 2, 4, or 5 in Chapter 3 with the additional requirement that all input is requested with an appropriate prompt.

2. Complete the program for Problem 7 in Chapter 3 with the additional requirement that the output for each student is displayed in a sentence of the following form:

```
STUDENT NUMBER XXXX IS A XXXXXXXXX
```

The last word in the sentence is either FRESHMAN, SOPHOMORE, JUNIOR, or SENIOR.

3. Complete the program for Problem 9, 13, or 14 in Chapter 3 with the additional requirement that the program follow the approach to interactive design discussed in this chapter.

4. Complete the program for Problem 11 or 13 in Chapter 4 with the additional requirement that all input data is read from DATA statements.

5. The results of a questionnaire survey need to be displayed in sentence form. The input data consists of the sample identification number, the number of questionnaires processed, and the average age of the respondents. The output should appear as follows:

```
RESULTS FROM SAMPLE XXXXX
WITH XXX QUESTIONNAIRES PROCESSED,
THE AVERAGE AGE OF THE RESPONDENTS IS XX.X YEARS.
```
(Xs represent the locations of output values.)

Write a BASIC program to display the specified output from the input. Test the program using 10083 for the sample number, 253 for the number of questionnaires, and 37.3 for the average age.

6. Write a BASIC program to display your name in block letters. A sample of how the output might appear is as follows:

```
    X     XXX      X   X     X    X
    X    X   X     X   X     XX   X
    X    X   X     X   X     X    X
    X    X   X     XXXXX     X X X
    X    X   X     X   X     X    X
  X X    X   X     X   X     X   XX
   XX     XXX      X   X     X    X
```

7. A graphic representation of a student's class schedule is:

TIME	8–9	9–10	10–11	11–12	12–1	1–2	2–3	3–4
MONDAY	1	0	0	1	0	1	1	1
TUESDAY	0	1	1	1	0	0	0	0
WEDNESDAY	1	0	0	1	0	1	1	1
THURSDAY	0	1	1	1	0	0	0	0
FRIDAY	1	0	0	1	0	0	0	0

The digit 1 indicates hours when the student is in class; the digit 0 indicates hours when he or she is out of class.

Write a BASIC program that displays this graphic output. Input to the program consists of one set of data for each day with the student's schedule for that day entered as a series of ones and zeros. Use the data shown in the preceding graph to test the program.

8. Write a BASIC program to display a rectangle. Input to the program should be the lengths of the sides of the rectangle. The output should be a rectangle of the desired dimension formed from Xs. For example, if the input specifies a rectangle with sides of lengths 4 and 6, the output should appear as follows:

```
XXXXXX
XXXXXX
XXXXXX
XXXXXX
```

9. In one business the commission paid to each salesperson is based on the product line sold and the total sales. Assume that the product line is indicated by a code that can be either 5, 8, or 17. If the code is 5 or 8, the commission is $7\frac{1}{2}$% for the first $5000 of sales and $8\frac{1}{2}$% for sales over $5000. If the product-line code is 17, the commission is $9\frac{1}{2}$% for the first $3500 of sales and 12% for sales over $3500.

Write a BASIC program to determine the commission for each salesperson. Input is the salesperson's number, product-line code, and total sales. Output should be the salesperson's number, total sales, and commission with appropriate headings. Design the program to be interactive following the approach discussed in the chapter.

Use the following data to test the program:

Salesperson's number	Product-line code	Total sales
101	17	$2250
103	5	$4000
117	8	$7350
125	5	$6500
138	17	$6375
192	8	$8125
203	8	$3250
218	5	$5000
235	5	$5250
264	17	$4150
291	17	$ 750

10. Each student in a class of 15 took two examinations. A program is needed to calculate the total and average test score for each student, the total and average for the entire class on each test, and the total and average of all 30 test scores. Input to the program is each student's identification number and scores on two tests. Output should list the input data and all required totals and averages. Put the following data in DATA statements and use it to test the program:

Identification number	Score on first test	Score on second test
101	88	73
102	100	92
103	45	78
104	63	69
105	84	87
106	92	88
107	91	100
108	61	75
109	78	73
110	99	94
111	74	82
112	83	69
113	100	100
114	52	69
115	85	85

Notice that the data does not include a trailer value. The program should use a FOR loop to process exactly 15 sets of input data.

Chapter 6

Program development

In Chapter 1 we introduced the ideas of problem solving and the programming process. We used the programming process in each of Chapters 2 through 5 to solve a sample problem. In these chapters we also introduced other aspects of the process of developing computer programs, including program structure and style. Now we bring together these topics and discuss program development in detail. We present several new ideas and show how all the topics fit together in the program development process. After completing this chapter you should understand the major ideas about program development, and you should be able to apply them in developing complex programs in BASIC.

6-1 Program structure

A central concept in program development is that of program structure. The structure of a program is the way in which the instructions in the program are organized. In developing a BASIC program, the programmer builds a structure of BASIC statements. If the structure is well built, the program is correct, easy to understand, and easily modified. A poorly structured program may have errors that are difficult to detect, may be hard to read, and may be troublesome to change.

There are three basic structures of statements in a program, called *control structures:* the sequence structure, the decision structure, and the loop structure. In a *sequence structure* the statements are executed in the order in which they are written, one after the other. For example, a series of LET statements that performs some calculation is a sequence structure. A *decision structure* (also called *selection* or *alternation*) is used to decide which of two other structures is to be executed next, based on some condition. In BASIC the IF statement is used to create a decision structure. If the condition in the IF statement is true, one group of statements is executed; otherwise another set of statements is performed. In a *loop structure* (also called *repetition* or *iteration*) a group of statements is executed repeatedly until some condition indicates that the loop should be terminated. In BASIC we use a GOTO statement at the end of a set of statements to branch to the beginning and thus create a loop. The loop is controlled by checking a condition in an IF statement each time the loop is executed. The FOR and NEXT statements also form a type of loop structure.

Figure 6-1 summarizes the three basic control structures. Part (a) shows a sequence structure in which one group of statements is performed after another. In part (b) a decision structure is shown, in which one of two alternative groups of

Figure 6-1. Basic control structures

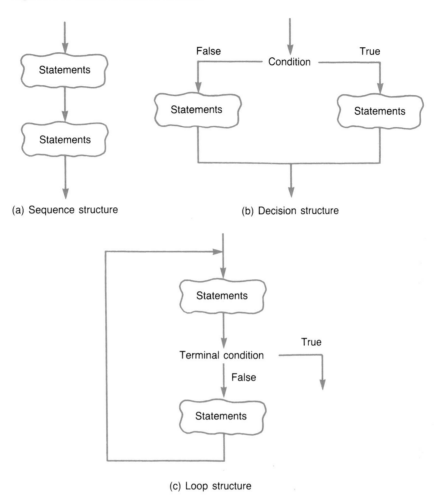

(a) Sequence structure

(b) Decision structure

(c) Loop structure

statements is executed, based on some condition. This is a two-sided decision. We can also create a one-sided decision by not executing any statements when the condition is false (see Figure 3-9). The loop structure in part (c) is such that a group of statements is executed, a terminal condition is checked, and then another group of statements is executed before the pattern is repeated. If no statements are performed in the loop before the terminal condition is checked, we have a pretest pattern [see Figure 4-14(b)]. Similarly, if the structure is such that no statements are executed after the condition is checked, the pattern is that of a posttest loop [see Figure 4-14(c)].

One characteristic common to all these structures is that there is only one way of entering each structure and only one way of leaving; that is, it is not possible to branch into the middle of any of the structures or to branch out of any structure in more than one place. We say that each structure has one *entry point* and one *exit point*. We will see that this is an important characteristic of these structures.

Within a structure we can embed any other structure that we need. This is the idea of nesting, which we discussed earlier in relation to decisions and loops. In fact, we can nest any structure within any other. For example, within a loop we may have a sequence of statements, decision structures, and other loops. Within a decision structure we may have sequences, loops, and other decisions. In terms of the diagrams in Figure 6-1, this means that we can substitute any structure for any block of statements within any structure.

We can use this idea of nesting to build a program as shown in Figure 6-2. In part (a) we start with a single block of statements. In part (b) we substitute a loop for this block. In part (c) we replace the statements at the beginning of the loop with a decision and the statements at the end with a sequence. Finally, in part (d) we nest a loop in the decision. We can continue in this manner to build more complex programs. Notice, however, that because each structure has one entry point and one exit point, the final program has only one entry point (that is, one point where execution of the program starts) and one exit point (one point where execution of the program stops).

Other control structures can appear in a program. For example, the ON-GOTO statement can be used to create a special type of selection known as a *case structure*. However, we can accomplish the same result using nested IF statements. In fact, *any* other structure can be created out of the three basic structures. This fact was proven by two computer scientists who showed that any program with a single entry point and a single exit point can be written using just the three basic control structures.† Thus, if we know how to create these structures in a programming language, we do not need any other structures.

Figure 6-2. Nested control structures

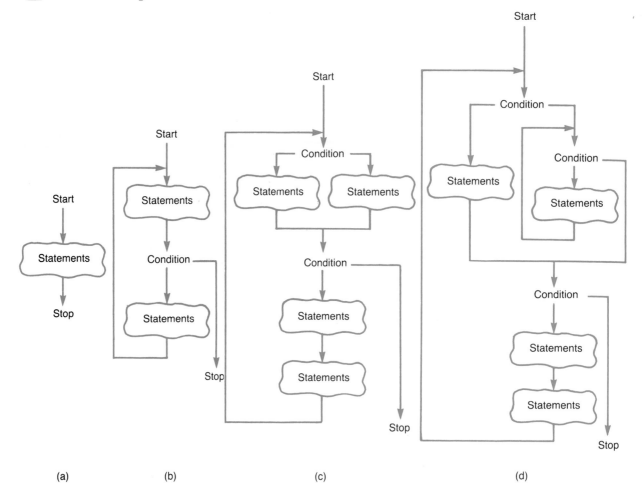

(a)   (b)   (c)   (d)

---

† C. Böhm and G. Jacopini, "Flow Diagrams, Turing Machines and Languages with Only Two Formation Rules," *Communications of the ACM,* 9, 5 (May 1966), 366–371. In proving their result, Böhm and Jacopini used a different loop structure from the one shown in Figure 6-1(c). It can be shown, however, that the general loop structure in the text can be constructed from the Böhm and Jacopini structures.

6-2 Program understandability

In Section 2-4 we discussed the importance of producing an understandable program. A program must be easily understood because people, including the original programmer, must understand it in order to correct, modify, and enhance it.

Program structure can contribute greatly to program understandability. The problem with trying to understand the logic of a complex program is that there are really two versions of the program. One is the *static version,* represented by the listing of the program on a CRT screen or on paper. The other is the *dynamic version,* which can be understood only by following the logic of the program as it is being executed. A programmer who reads a program listing is reading the static form of the program. Normally each statement is read in sequence from the top down. The dynamic version may differ from the static version because the statements are not executed in the order in which they are written. To understand a program, the programmer must read the static version but interpret it in terms of its dynamic version.

Figure 6-3 illustrates the idea of two versions of a program. In this example, many GOTO statements are used to make the static and dynamic versions very different. Part (a) gives the statements in the order in which they appear in the program listing (i.e., the static version). Part (b) shows the statements in the order in which they are executed (i.e., the dynamic version). Notice that when a GOTO statement is encountered, the next statement in the dynamic version (the statement to which the program branches) is not the same as the next statement in the static version (the next statement in sequence). When the programmer reads the listing of this program, he or she has to skip all over the program to try to understand the logic rather than just reading the program from top to bottom.

We can see from this example that one of the basic principles of producing an understandable program is to make the dynamic version of the program as close as possible to the static form. Ideally the program should execute from top to bottom just as it is read. If this were the case, however, the program would perform only a sequence of statements (that is, there would be no decisions or loops), which would not accomplish much.

The next best situation is to have the program execute from top to bottom through a sequence of basic control structures; that is, the program first executes the statements in one structure (for example, a loop), then executes the statements in the next structure (such as a decision), and so on to the end of the program. Other

Figure 6-3. Two versions of a program

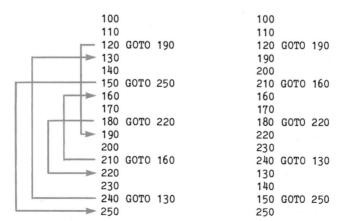

(a) The static version   (b) The dynamic version

structures may be nested in these structures, as we saw in the last section. This top-to-bottom execution using only the three basic control structures brings the dynamic version of the program as close as possible to the static form. In addition, we know that we can write any program using just these three structures.

The structure of a program can be greatly complicated by the uncontrolled use of GOTO statements. The problem with GOTO statements is that we do not always know where we came from. Although this may sound funny, it makes a lot of sense. For example, assume that we are trying to understand the conditions under which a particular statement is executed. If it is possible to branch to that statement from several different points in the program, we will not know how we got to that statement without going back to all of the GOTO statements branching to it. The logic may become even more complex if there are multiple ways to get to each of these GOTO statements. (A famous letter entitled "GO TO Statement Considered Harmful" discusses this point of view.†) Sometimes a program with lots of GOTO statements is called "spaghetti code" because lines drawn on paper for all the branches begin to look like a bowl of spaghetti. [See Figure 6-3(a).]

The ultimate improvement would be to eliminate all GOTO statements from the program. In most versions of BASIC this is not possible. GOTO statements are needed to create decision and loop structures. The patterns were shown in Figures 3-7, 3-11, and 4-15. Although these structures require the use of the GOTO statement, the logic of the program is kept at the simplest level if we use the GOTO statement only in the particular ways shown.

In some versions of BASIC, the IF-THEN-ELSE statement (or block IF statements) and WHILE loops are available. Because the former is used for decision making and the latter for loop control, we can write any program we wish using these control structures. Such a program would not have any GOTO statements. For example, Figure 4-33 showed a program that uses these structures. In general, the IF-THEN-ELSE statement (or block IF statements) and WHILE loops should be used if available instead of IF and GOTO statements. (Although it is not necessary, we may also want to use the FOR and NEXT statements for loop control.)

To summarize, the fundamental approach to producing understandable programs is to design the program so that it executes from top to bottom and uses only sequences, decisions, and loops.

6-3 Program style

Program style refers to those characteristics of a program that make it easier to read and therefore easier to understand. In previous chapters we have mentioned many style rules. The following are some that have been discussed as well as a few new ones:

1. Use meaningful variables. For example, use N for number, T for total, C for cost, and so forth. This helps the programmer remember what each name refers to. (If available, use long variables.)
2. Use line numbers of the same length. Usually this means using line numbers that are all three digits or all four digits. This helps to align the first part of each statement.

---

† Edsger W. Dijkstra, "GO TO Statement Considered Harmful," *Communications of the ACM*, 11, 3 (March 1968), 147–148. The letter begins: "For a number of years I have been familiar with the observation that the quality of programmers is a decreasing function of the density of *go to* statements in the programs they produce."

3. Assign line numbers in a logical pattern. For example, the statements in the first section of the program may be numbered between 1000 and 1990, the statements in the second section may be assigned numbers between 2000 and 2990, and so on for the other sections of the program. Number the END statement with the largest line number of the length being used (e.g., 9999). This makes it easy to refer to the END statement. Finally, number the statements by 10s so it is easy to modify the program.

4. Put all DATA statements at the end of the program and number them accordingly (e.g., with numbers between 9000 and 9990). This makes the data in the program easier to locate and modify.

5. Use parentheses in expressions to show the order of evaluation, even if they are not needed. This reduces confusion about how an expression is evaluated.

6. Indent the true and false parts of a decision and the statements in a loop. This helps the programmer see the structure of the program.

7. Use only the three basic control structures (sequences, decisions, and loops). This makes the program easiest to understand while providing the programmer with sufficient control structures for any program.

8. Do not use the GOTO statement except to create decisions and loops. This makes the static and dynamic versions of the program as close as possible. (If available, use the IF-THEN-ELSE statement or block IF statements and WHILE loops, thus avoiding the use of GOTO statements completely.)

9. Minimize the use of nested decisions and loops. The more nesting there is in a program, the more difficult the program is to understand.

Following these style rules and others that we will mention later makes the program easier to read and understand.

Using remarks

Another way of improving readability is to use remarks to explain the function of different parts of the program. We can place remarks anywhere in the program by using the REM statement. We have used some remarks in our illustrative programs, but in most cases the programs have been fairly simple and have not needed many remarks. However, as programs become more complex, remarks become much more important.

The basic function of a remark is to explain some characteristic of the program that is not immediately obvious. Often a remark is used for each important loop or decision. For example, consider the tuition-calculation program from Chapter 4 (Figure 4-3). This program is shown in Figure 6-4 without remarks. To make the program more understandable we could insert the following remarks at the beginning of the input loop:

```
145 REM - BEGIN INPUT LOOP
155 REM - LEAVE LOOP WHEN TRAILER VALUE IS ENTERED
```

Although we can get the information in these remarks from the program, the remarks make understanding the program easier. We may also put the following remark before the second IF statement in the program:

```
165 REM - CALCULATE TUITION
```

This remark describes the function of the decision structure that follows it.

A common mistake in using remarks is simply to parrot the code that follows.

Figure 6-4. The tuition-calculation program without remarks

```
150 INPUT I,U
160    IF I=9999 THEN 240
170    IF U>12 THEN 200
180      LET T=350
190    GOTO 210
200      LET T=350+20*(U-12)
210    PRINT "STUDENT ID:",I
220    PRINT "TUITION:",T
230 GOTO 150
240 PRINT "ALL DATA PROCESSED"
250 END
```

For example, consider the following sequence that might be used in the program in Figure 6-4:

```
175 REM - SET TUITION TO $350.00
180 LET T=350
```

The remark is unnecessary because it repeats the statement that follows. Another example of this unnecessary use of a remark is the following:

```
50 REM - INCREASE I BY 1
60 LET I=I+1
```

Again, the remark merely echoes the next statement.

Another common problem with the use of remarks is that a remark may state one thing but the program does something else. This may be because the programmer wrote the remark incorrectly or wrote a correct remark but incorrect code, or perhaps because the code was modified some time after the original program was written. When remarks are used, it is essential that they correctly describe the program. Otherwise, the programmer may read the remark and think that the program does one thing, when in fact it does something else. (Because of this, some programmers advocate deleting all remarks while debugging a program.)

One test that is sometimes applied to determine whether the remarks in a program are sufficient is to read just the remarks and not the code. If the basic logic of the program — but not the details — can be understood from the remarks, they are sufficient. Unfortunately, this test may lead to the inclusion of too many remarks or remarks containing too much detail. By remembering that remarks should help to explain difficult parts of the program and not simply repeat the code, we can achieve the best level of detail.

Besides describing how a program works, remarks can be used to document important information about the program. This information includes such things as who wrote the program, when it was written, what its purpose is, and what the variables in the program mean. Usually such information is put into a block of remarks at the beginning of the program. We have used simple examples of this in previous programs. Figure 6-5 shows a complete example for the tuition-calculation program. The initial remarks serve as a "preface" to the program. This example also includes remarks in the body of the program to help explain how the program works. In addition, the lines in the program have been renumbered. Notice that blank remark lines (i.e., lines with just the word REM) are used to separate groups of remarks. This helps make the remarks more readable. Blank lines may also be used to separate groups of statements in the program and thus improve the readability of the code.

Remarks are also used as points to branch to in a program. As we explained in Chapter 2, a REM statement is ignored when reached during the execution of a program. If we branch to a REM statement, the computer just goes on to the next

Figure 6-5. The tuition-calculation program with remarks

```
100 REM - TUITION CALCULATION PROGRAM
110 REM
120 REM - PROGRAMMER:  ROBERT C. NICKERSON
130 REM - DATE:  NOVEMBER 11, 19XX
140 REM
150 REM - PURPOSE:  THIS PROGRAM COMPUTES TUITION FOR EACH
160 REM             COLLEGE STUDENT BASED ON THE NUMBER OF
170 REM             UNITS THAT THE STUDENT IS TAKING.
180 REM
190 REM - VARIABLES:
200 REM       I  = STUDENT ID (INPUT/OUTPUT)
210 REM       U  = NUMBER OF UNITS (INPUT)
220 REM       T  = TUITION (OUTPUT)
230 REM
300 REM - BEGIN INPUT LOOP
310 INPUT I,U
320   REM - LEAVE LOOP WHEN TRAILER VALUE IS ENTERED
330   IF I=9999 THEN 430
340   REM - CALCULATE TUITION
350   IF U>12 THEN 380
360     LET T=350
370   GOTO 390
380     LET T=350+20*(U-12)
390   PRINT "STUDENT ID:",I
400   PRINT "TUITION:",T
410 GOTO 310
420 REM - END OF LOOP
430 PRINT "ALL DATA PROCESSED"
999 END
```

statement following the REM statement. Figure 6-6 shows an example of branching to REM statements in the tuition-calculation program. Notice that the IF statement and the GOTO statement branch to REM statements. Whether this style is used depends on the preferences of the individual programmer.

Figure 6-6. A program with branching to REM statements

```
300 REM - BEGIN INPUT LOOP
310 INPUT I,U
320   REM - LEAVE LOOP WHEN TRAILER VALUE IS ENTERED
330   IF I=9999 THEN 440
340   REM - CALCULATE TUITION
350   IF U>12 THEN 380
360     LET T=350
370     GOTO 400
380   REM
390     LET T=350+20*(U-12)
400   REM - END IF
410   PRINT "STUDENT ID:",I
420   PRINT "TUITION:",T
430 GOTO 300
440 REM - END OF LOOP
450 PRINT "ALL DATA PROCESSED"
999 END
```

6-4 Program refinement

Developing the logic of a complex program can be a difficult task. A technique that is often advocated is to develop the program through a sequence of refinement steps.

The idea is to start with a general statement of the solution and to refine this statement gradually. Each refinement should bring the program closer to the final version. The last step in the process produces the coded program. This technique is often called *stepwise refinement*.

To illustrate, consider the problem of rearranging three numbers into ascending (that is, increasing) order. This process is called *sorting*. (In a later chapter we will see how to sort large amounts of data.) We assume that the three numbers to be sorted are input data. They may be in any order initially. In the program we will refer to the numbers by the variables V1, V2, and V3. The program must accept values for V1, V2, and V3. Then it must rearrange the values so that V1 equals the smallest value, V2 is the middle value, and V3 equals the largest value. Finally, the sorted values must be displayed.

As a first step in developing the program, we write the following:

```
200 INPUT V1,V2,V3
    Sort V1, V2, and V3 into ascending order.
500 PRINT V1,V2,V3
999 END
```

This program is complete except for the second line, which is written in English, not BASIC. If we can refine this line to a set of BASIC statements that accomplishes the sorting process, the program will be complete.

One way to sort the three numbers is first to move the largest value to V3. The next largest value is then moved to V2. If this is done without destroying any of the values, V1 will be equal to the smallest value. Hence, the numbers will be sorted. For example, assume that initially the data is as follows:

$$V1 = 7$$
$$V2 = 9$$
$$V3 = 5$$

Moving the largest value, 9, to V3 results in the data being arranged into the following order:

$$V1 = 7$$
$$V2 = 5$$
$$V3 = 9$$

Moving the next largest value, 7, to V2 results in the following:

$$V1 = 5$$
$$V2 = 7$$
$$V3 = 9$$

Thus, the smallest value, 5, is automatically moved to V1. Incorporating this refinement into our program, we get the following:

```
200 INPUT V1,V2,V3
    Move largest value to V3.
    Move next largest value to V2.
500 PRINT V1,V2,V3
999 END
```

To move the largest value to V3, we first move the larger of V1 and V2 to V2, and then move the larger of V2 and V3 to V3. After doing this we move the next largest value to V2 by moving the larger of V1 and V2 to V2. Hence, the program can be refined again to the following:

```
200 INPUT V1,V2,V3
      Move larger of V1 and V2 to V2.
      Move larger of V2 and V3 to V3.
      Move larger of V1 and V2 to V2.
500 PRINT V1,V2,V3
999 END
```

To move the larger of V1 and V2 to V2, we compare V1 and V2. If V1 is larger than V2, we switch the values of V1 and V2. In effect, we are asking whether V1 and V2 are in proper sequence with respect to one another. If they are not, we switch their values. We do similar comparisons and switching for V2 and V3 and again for V1 and V2. Incorporating this refinement into the program, we obtain:

```
200 INPUT V1,V2,V3
300 IF V1<=V2 THEN 350
      Switch V1 and V2.
350 IF V2<=V3 THEN 400
      Switch V2 and V3.
400 IF V1<=V2 THEN 500
      Switch V1 and V2.
500 PRINT V1,V2,V3
999 END
```

To complete the program, we need only to include the necessary statements to switch the values of the variables. Figure 6-7 shows how the switching is done for V1 and V2. First V1 is assigned to a temporary variable, T. Then V2 is assigned to V1. Finally, the value of T is assigned to V2. Thus, the following three statements are needed to switch the values of V1 and V2:

```
310 LET T=V1
320 LET V1=V2
330 LET V2=T
```

Writing similar sets of statements for the other switching steps and including these in the program, we get the final version of the sorting program shown in Figure 6-8.

To illustrate how the program works, consider the following worst possible case:

$$V1 = 9$$
$$V2 = 7$$
$$V3 = 5$$

Figure 6-7. Switching the values of two variables

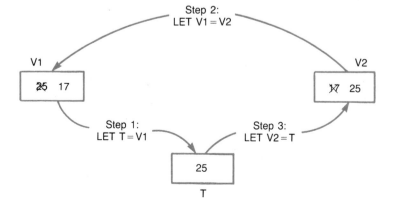

Figure 6-8. The sorting program

```
100 REM - SORTING PROGRAM
110 REM - VARIABLES:
120 REM       V1, V2, V3  = VALUES TO BE SORTED
130 REM       T  = TEMPORARY VARIABLE
200 INPUT V1,V2,V3
300 IF V1<=V2 THEN 350
310    LET T=V1
320    LET V1=V2
330    LET V2=T
350 IF V2<=V3 THEN 400
360    LET T=V2
370    LET V2=V3
380    LET V3=T
400 IF V1<=V2 THEN 500
410    LET T=V1
420    LET V1=V2
430    LET V2=T
500 PRINT V1,V2,V3
999 END
```

The data is completely out of order. After the first switch the values will be as follows:

$$V1 = 7$$
$$V2 = 9$$
$$V3 = 5$$

The larger of V1 and V2 is moved to V2. After the next switch the values will be in the following order:

$$V1 = 7$$
$$V2 = 5$$
$$V3 = 9$$

The larger of V2 and V3 is moved to V3. The effect of both switches is that the largest of all three is moved to V3. The final switch results in the following:

$$V1 = 5$$
$$V2 = 7$$
$$V3 = 9$$

The larger of V1 and V2 is moved to V2. In effect, the next largest of all three is moved to V2, and at the same time the smallest value ends up assigned to V1. Hence, the data is sorted.

This example illustrates how the technique of stepwise refinement can be applied to a problem solution. The technique allows the programmer to concentrate on small parts of the program in successively more detail. The programmer does not try to find the entire solution at once, but rather thinks about the solution in pieces. This usually makes program development easier.

6-5 The programming process

As we know, the programming process involves five activities:

1. Understand and define the problem.
2. Design the program.
3. Code the program.

4. Show that the program is correct.

5. Document the program.

In this section we describe each of these activities in detail and illustrate them with a sample problem.

The five activities in the programming process are not necessarily performed in sequence. In fact, several activities usually take place at the same time. For example, documenting begins while we are trying to understand and define the problem. Similarly, we can begin to show correctness of the program during the designing activity. The activities are listed not in the order in which they are *started* but rather in the order in which they are *finished*. For example, we cannot finish designing the program until we have finished understanding and defining the problem. However, we may start the designing activity before the first activity is completed. Similarly, final coding cannot be completed until the program design is done; showing that the program is correct cannot be completed until the coding is done; and documentation cannot be finalized until all other activities have been completed.

Problem definition

The first activity in the programming process is to understand and carefully define the problem to be solved. Frequently the most difficult step is recognizing that a problem exists for which a programmed solution is appropriate. It is usually not the programmer's responsibility, however, to recognize the need for a program to solve a problem. Most often the programmer receives a general statement of the problem, either orally or in writing, and begins the programming process from that point.

At first the programmer should try to understand the problem as a whole. What does the problem require? Usually this involves determining what output is to be produced. What data is available? Answering this question often involves determining what input data is to be processed. The programmer tries to get a general understanding of the problem as a whole without going into details about the input, the output, and the calculations.

After the programmer has a general understanding of the problem, he or she should refine the problem definition to include specific information about output layouts, input data entry, calculations, and logical operations. The refinement of the problem definition should continue until the programmer obtains sufficient detail to begin designing a solution. At a minimum the problem definition must give the following:

1. What output is to be produced and what is its layout.

2. What input data is available and how it will be entered.

3. What computations are to be performed.

4. What logical conditions affect processing.

Sometimes the programmer may have difficulty understanding a problem. When this happens, it often helps to isolate parts of the problem and work with each part separately. Another approach is to think of a simpler but similar problem and to understand it first. The programmer may get some insight from the simpler problem that helps explain the more complex problem.

Some problems cannot be solved with a computer. In mathematics some problems do not have exact solutions. Some problems may be too large for a computer or take too long to solve. Although problems that cannot be solved do not arise often, we must nevertheless be certain that it is reasonable to attempt a programmed solution.

Definition of a sample problem. To illustrate the programming process, we will consider a variation of the test-score averaging problem discussed in previous chapters.

The problem is to calculate a weighted average of three test scores for each student in a course. We assume that the best test score counts 50%, the next best score is weighted 35%, and the worst score counts only 15%. Also the corresponding letter grade must be determined based on a straight percentage scale (that is, 90% to 100% is an A; 80% to 89%, a B; 70% to 79%, a C; 60% to 69%, a D; and 59% or less, an F). Finally, the overall average score for all students in the course must be calculated.

Already we begin to understand the problem. A program is needed that produces a grade report giving the weighted average score and letter grade for each student in a class plus the overall average score for all students. The input to the program must be three test scores. In addition, there must be some way of identifying the student to whom the scores belong (such as a student identification number). The program must determine which test score is the best, which score is the worst, and which score falls in between. Then the program must apply the appropriate percentages to arrive at the average score. In addition, the program must find the grade category into which the average falls so that the appropriate letter grade can be determined. To calculate the overall average score, the program must accumulate the total of the students' average scores, count the number of students in the course, and compute the overall average by dividing the total average scores by the number of students. The program must display each student's identification number, weighted average score, and letter grade. It must also display the overall average score for all students.

We can refine the problem definition at this point to specify details about the input and output. We will assume that a batch processing program is desired and that all input data will be entered into DATA statements. For each student the following data is entered in the order listed:

> Student identification number
> Score on first test
> Score on second test
> Score on third test

To end the processing, we will assume that the last set of input contains 9999 for the student identification number and 0 for each test score.

For the output we must know the print positions in which the data is displayed. A piece of graph paper or a special form such as a *print chart* is useful in sketching the output. Figure 6-9 shows the output format for this program on a print chart.

Figure 6-9. A print chart

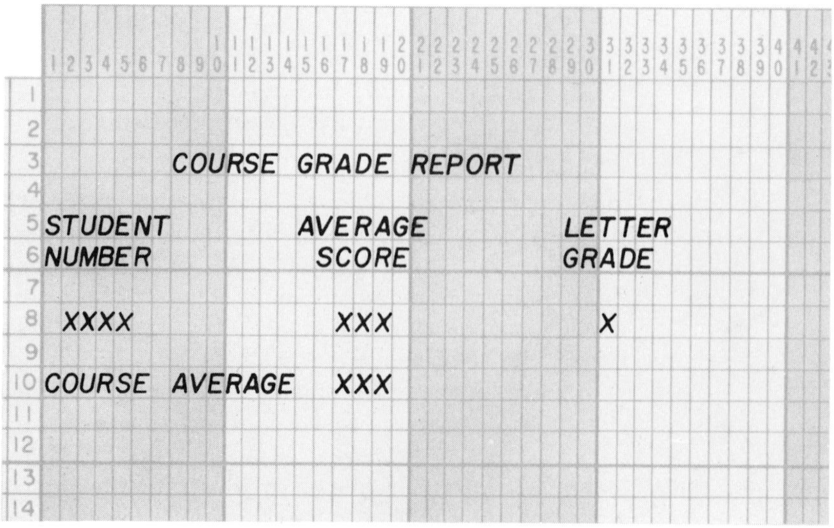

Figure 6-10. Summary of the grade-report program

Program title: Grade-report program

Purpose: This program computes the weighted average of three test scores and determines
                the appropriate letter grade for each student in a course. The program also
                determines the overall average score for all students.

Input: For each student —
                    Student identification number
                    Score on first test
                    Score on second test
                    Score on third test
                Last set of data —
                    9999 for student identification number
                    0s for tests' scores
                Data is entered in DATA statements

Output: For each student —
                    Student identification number
                    Weighted average score
                    Letter grade
                For all students —
                    Overall average score
                Output layout shown in print chart

Processing: The weighted average score for a student is determined by weighting the best test
                score 50%, the next best score 35%, and the worst score 15%. The letter grade is
                determined as follows:

Weighted average	Letter grade
90–100	A
80–89	B
70–79	C
60–69	D
0–59	F

The overall average score is the sum of the weighted average scores for all
students divided by the number of students.

The numbers across the top give the print positions. Headings are written on the
chart exactly as they are to be displayed. Variable information, such as the student's
identification number, average score, and letter grade, is indicated by Xs in the print
positions in which it is to be displayed. By sketching the output format first on a
chart such as this, it is much easier to code the necessary PRINT statements.

At this point we have a fairly good understanding of the problem. Still, we
may have to return to the problem definition later if we discover things we do not
understand. Figure 6-10 summarizes the requirements for the program that solves
the problem.

Program design

After carefully defining the problem, we can begin to design an appropriate program.
The objective is to devise a plan for a program that solves the problem. This does
not mean that the program is coded at this stage. Before coding can begin, we must
develop a solution procedure. The procedure should, of course, be correct.

As we know, a procedure for solving a problem is called an algorithm. An
algorithm is a set of instructions that, if carried out, results in the solution of a
problem. An algorithm may be represented in many forms. For example, an algorithm
may be written in English, described in mathematical notation, or expressed in a
flowchart. A recipe to bake a cake is an algorithm in a form that is understandable
to a cook. A computer program is a representation of an algorithm that can be carried
out by a computer.

During the program design activity an algorithm is developed to solve the problem. This is usually the most difficult task in the programming process, and there are many strategies that can help. It is important for the programmer to have a repertoire of algorithms upon which he or she can draw. Then, when a problem or a part of a problem requires a particular algorithm, the programmer can quickly supply the appropriate procedure.

When the algorithm is not known, the programmer must devise one. The use of stepwise refinement, discussed in the last section, can help. Besides producing the necessary algorithm, this procedure leads naturally to the use of the basic control structures in nested patterns as discussed in Section 6-1. If the programmer adheres to the basic structures during the refinement process, the final program will have a single entry point and a single exit point and will flow from top to bottom through a sequence of loops and decisions. Thus, the program refinement strategy not only helps us to devise an algorithm, but also leads to the most understandable program.

Sometimes it is difficult to devise an algorithm for a problem. When this happens, it often helps to think of a related problem and develop an algorithm for it. Another approach is to simplify the problem by discarding some of the conditions and then to develop an algorithm for the simpler version. Sometimes it is necessary to return to the problem definition to determine whether anything has been omitted. Any of these approaches may help the programmer develop an algorithm for the problem.

When developing an algorithm, the programmer must keep in mind the structure of the data. Although we have used only simple data structures so far, we can already see that we cannot develop an algorithm without knowing how the data is going to be organized. For example, we must know the characteristics of the input and output data before developing an algorithm to do the necessary processing. In later chapters we will discuss more complex data structures and see that an algorithm depends on the structure of the data. Thus, the development of an algorithm is *not* independent of the development of the data structure.

Many times the programmer develops alternative algorithms and then must select one of them. The objective is to select the best algorithm that correctly solves the problem. Which algorithm is "best," however, is often difficult to determine. The first criterion is always correctness: Does the algorithm correctly solve the problem? The second criterion is usually the understandability of the algorithm: How easy is it for a programmer to understand how the algorithm works? Another criterion that may be important is the efficiency of the algorithm: How fast will the resulting program execute and how much storage space will it occupy? In many situations the last criterion is not important. In some cases, such as when a very large problem is being solved or a small computer is being used, efficiency does matter.

Design of the program for the sample problem. To illustrate the program designing activity we continue with the development of the grade-report program. We will use the technique of stepwise program refinement discussed in the last section to derive the algorithm for this program. Recall that in this technique we start with a general statement of what the program does — that is, a general statement of the program's algorithm. Then we refine this statement gradually until we reach the final algorithm.

The most general statement of the algorithm for the grade-report program is as follows:

> Produce the grade report.

Although this is a very simple statement, it expresses what the program is to do. The next step is to determine what is necessary to accomplish this.

We know that the input data consists of a student identification number and three test scores for each student. The output is to be a report displayed on a CRT screen with headings, data for each student giving the student's weighted average score and letter grade, and a final line with the overall course average. Thus, to produce this output from the input, we can refine the general statement of the algorithm to the following:

> Display the report headings.
> Process the input data to produce the output for each student.
> Determine and display the overall average score.

The second step needs to be refined further. We know that the computer must read and process the input data in a loop until the trailer value is read. Within the loop, the computer must read a student's identification number and three test scores, evaluate the weighted average, and display the output with the appropriate letter grade. Thus, we can refine this step as follows:

> Repeat the following:
>> Read a student ID and three test scores.
>> If the student ID is 9999, leave the loop.
>> Calculate the weighted average score.
>> Determine the grade category based on the weighted average score and
>>> display the appropriate letter grade.
> End of loop.

The step to calculate the weighted average score needs further refinement. Recall that the average score is found by taking 50% of the best test score, 35% of the next best score, and 15% of the worst score. Hence, we must first determine the best score, the next best score, and the worst score. Thus, we could refine this step as follows:

> Find the best score.
> Find the next best score.
> Find the worst score.
> Compute the weighted average score.

We can easily carry out the first three steps above by simply sorting the test scores into ascending order. Then the algorithm can be expressed as follows:

> Sort the test scores into ascending order.
> Compute the weighted average score.

Because we already know a sorting algorithm for three numbers, we can use this algorithm in the first step. Thus, the refinement of the average calculation is complete (except for the final coding).

We also have to refine the step that determines the grade category and displays the output. Because there are five grade categories, we can think of this as a selection process and refine it as follows:

> Select the appropriate grade category based on the weighted average score:
>> 90–100: Display output with grade "A".
>> 80– 89: Display output with grade "B".
>> 70– 79: Display output with grade "C".
>> 60– 69: Display output with grade "D".
>> 0– 59: Display output with grade "F".

Although this does not resemble one of the three basic control structures, we know that we can code it using nested decisions.

The last step that must be refined is that of determining and displaying the overall average score. To compute this value, we must count the number of students

Figure 6-11. The algorithm for the grade-report program

```
Display the report headings.
Initialize the totals.
Repeat the following:
     Read a student ID and three test scores.
     If the student ID is 9999, leave the loop.
     Sort the test scores into ascending order.
     Compute the weighted average score.
     Accumulate the total number of students and the total average score.
     Select the appropriate grade category based on weighted average score:
          90-100:  Display output with grade "A".
          80-89:   Display output with grade "B".
          70-79:   Display output with grade "C".
          60-69:   Display output with grade "D".
           0-59:   Display output with grade "F".
End of loop.
Compute the overall average score.
Display output with the overall average score.
```

and accumulate the total of the weighted average scores. The variables used for the totals must be initialized before the input loop. The totals must be accumulated in the input loop. After the input loop is terminated, the overall average score must be computed and the final output with this average displayed.

Incorporating all the refinements discussed here, we get the complete algorithm for the grade-report program shown in Figure 6-11.

The algorithm in Figure 6-11 is written in a semi-English, semi-programming language style. This way of writing an algorithm is called *pseudocode*. Pseudocode has no rules; any written language for describing an algorithm can be thought of as pseudocode. Some programmers use an outline form; others prefer a form that looks more like a programming language. Pseudocode has many variations, and any style that works for the programmer is acceptable.

The algorithm for the grade-report program was developed with the aid of pseudocode. We could also have developed it using a flowchart. Figure 6-12 shows the flowchart for the grade-report program.

Program coding

The objective during the program coding activity is to implement the algorithm in a specific programming language. In effect, this is the last step in the program refinement. Each part of the algorithm must be translated into a group of statements. The final code will be correct if the algorithm is correct and the translation is done correctly.

A good way to begin coding is to determine what variables will be used for the input and output data. These variables and their description can be listed in REM statements. As additional variables are needed while coding, their descriptions can be added to the program.

Occasionally during the coding activity an error is discovered in the logic of the algorithm. When this happens, the programmer must redesign the program. If a serious error or misunderstanding is discovered, it may be necessary to return to the problem definition and work forward again.

During program coding, style rules, as discussed in Section 6-3, should be followed. This helps to make the program more readable and the structure more understandable. Remarks should be included as the program is coded. When the coding activity is complete, the program should be in its final form (except for the correction of possible errors).

Figure 6-12. Flowchart for the grade-report program

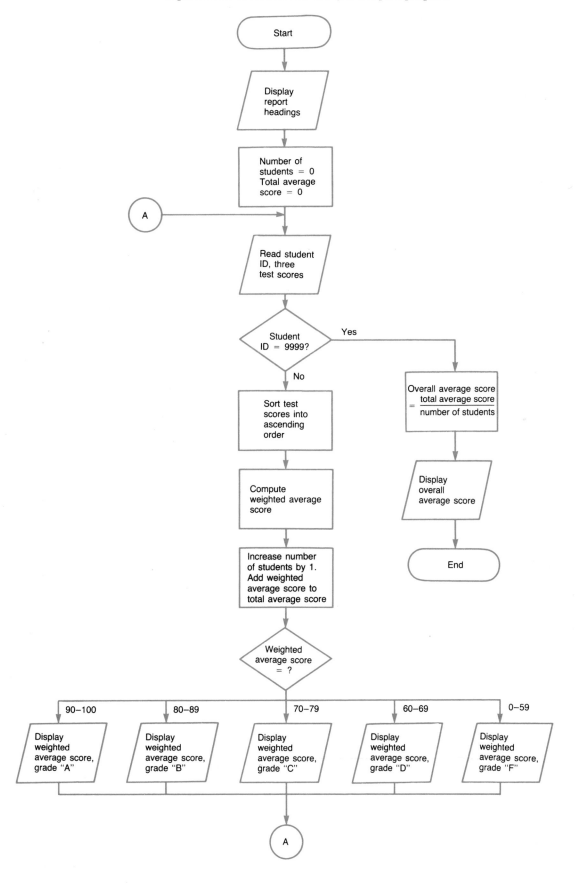

Coding of the program for the sample problem. The coding for the grade-report program is shown in Figure 6-13. The variables used in the program are listed in the REM statements at the beginning of the program. Each step in the pseudocode in Figure 6-11 or the flowchart in 6-12 is translated into one or more BASIC statements. For example, the sorting step results in twelve statements, whereas the weighted average calculation requires only one statement. Notice that the remarks in the body of the program follow closely the wording in the algorithm in Figure 6-11. This is a common approach for organizing remarks in a program. Notice also the use of introductory remarks.

Figure 6-13. The grade-report program

```
1000 REM - GRADE REPORT PROGRAM
1010 REM
1020 REM - PROGRAMMER:  ROBERT C. NICKERSON
1030 REM - DATE: NOVEMBER 18, 19XX
1040 REM
1100 REM - PURPOSE:  THIS PROGRAM COMPUTES THE WEIGHTED AVERAGE
1110 REM                OF THREE TEST SCORES AND DETERMINES THE
1120 REM                APPROPRIATE LETTER GRADE FOR EACH STUDENT
1130 REM                IN A COURSE.  THE PROGRAM ALSO DETERMINES
1140 REM                THE OVERALL AVERAGE SCORE FOR ALL STUDENTS.
1150 REM
1200 REM - VARIABLES:
1210 REM       I  = STUDENT IDENTIFICATION NUMBER (INPUT/OUTPUT)
1220 REM       S1 = SCORE ON FIRST TEST (INPUT)
1230 REM       S2 = SCORE ON SECOND TEST (INPUT)
1240 REM       S3 = SCORE ON THIRD TEST (INPUT)
1250 REM       A  = WEIGHTED AVERAGE SCORE (OUTPUT)
1260 REM       A1 = OVERALL AVERAGE SCORE (OUTPUT)
1270 REM       N  = NUMBER OF STUDENTS (INTERNAL)
1280 REM       T  = TOTAL AVERAGE SCORE (INTERNAL)
1290 REM       V  = TEMPORARY VARIABLE (INTERNAL)
2000 REM
2100 REM - DISPLAY REPORT HEADINGS
2110 PRINT "        COURSE GRADE REPORT"
2120 PRINT
2130 PRINT "STUDENT        AVERAGE        LETTER"
2140 PRINT "NUMBER          SCORE         GRADE"
2150 PRINT
2200 REM - INITIALIZE TOTALS
2210 LET N=0
2220 LET T=0
3000 REM
3100 REM - BEGIN INPUT LOOP
3110 READ I,S1,S2,S3
3120    REM - LEAVE LOOP WHEN TRAILER VALUE IS READ
3130    IF I=9999 THEN 4100
3200    REM - SORT TEST SCORES INTO ASCENDING ORDER
3210    IF S1<=S2 THEN 3250
3220      LET V=S1
3230      LET S1=S2
3240      LET S2=V
3250    IF S2<=S3 THEN 3290
3260      LET V=S2
3270      LET S2=S3
3280      LET S3=V
3290    IF S1<=S2 THEN 3410
3300      LET V=S1
3310      LET S1=S2
3320      LET S2=V
3400    REM - COMPUTE WEIGHTED AVERAGE SCORE
3410    LET A=.15*S1+.35*S2+.5*S3
```

(continued)

Figure 6-13. Continued

```
3500    REM - ACCUMULATE TOTALS
3510    LET N=N+1
3520    LET T=T+A
3600    REM - SELECT GRADE CATEGORY AND DISPLAY OUTPUT WITH GRADE
3610    IF A<90 THEN 3650
3620      REM - GRADE IS "A"
3630      PRINT I;TAB(16);A;TAB(31);"A"
3640    GOTO 3790
3650    IF A<80 THEN 3690
3660      REM - GRADE IS "B"
3670      PRINT I;TAB(16);A;TAB(31);"B"
3680    GOTO 3790
3690    IF A<70 THEN 3730
3700      REM - GRADE IS "C"
3710      PRINT I;TAB(16);A;TAB(31);"C"
3720    GOTO 3790
3730    IF A<60 THEN 3780
3740      REM - GRADE IS "D"
3750      PRINT I;TAB(16);A;TAB(31);"D"
3760    GOTO 3790
3770      REM - GRADE IS "F"
3780      PRINT I;TAB(16);A;TAB(31);"F"
3790    REM - END OF GRADE SELECTION
3800 GOTO 3100
4000 REM
4100 REM - COMPUTE AND DISPLAY OVERALL AVERAGE SCORE
4110 LET A1=T/N
4120 PRINT
4130 PRINT "COURSE AVERAGE ";A1
9000 REM
9100 REM - INPUT DATA
9110 DATA ...
       .
       .
       .
9999 END
```

The program is built from the basic control structure discussed in Section 6-1. It begins with a sequence consisting of steps to display the headings and initialize the totals. Then comes an input loop that is terminated when a trailer value is read. The loop contains a sequence of decisions for sorting, a calculation step for the average, steps to accumulate the totals, and a nested decision for the output. Finally, a sequence calculates and displays the overall average score. Style rules have been followed to make the program more readable and understandable.

There are alternative ways of accomplishing different steps in this program, depending on the language features that are available. For example, using some of the features discussed in Chapter 8, the output of the letter grade can be simplified. The programmer should be familiar with as much of the programming language as possible and use those features that make the program easiest to code and as understandable as possible.

Program correctness

In Chapter 1 we discussed the three types of errors that can occur in a program. These are syntax errors, execution errors, and logic errors. Syntax errors are detected by the computer while the program is being translated into machine language. An error message is displayed for each syntax error. To correct such errors the programmer must interpret the error message and make appropriate changes in the program.

Usually syntax errors result from the incorrect use of the programming language. Because these errors are detected by the computer, they are usually easy to correct.

Execution errors occur during the execution of the program. The program must not have any serious syntax errors in order to be executed. Thus, any execution error is the result of a condition that can be detected only during execution. Some examples of execution errors are dividing by zero, attempting to read when there is no more data in a DATA statement, and calculating a number that is too large for a variable. When such an error is detected, the computer normally stops execution of the program and displays an error message explaining the cause of the error. It is the programmer's responsibility to interpret the error message and to make the necessary correction.

If the program executes without errors, it may still not be correct. Errors may exist in the logic of the program. These are the most difficult to detect. The usual approach is to make up test data and determine by hand what output is expected from the data. Then the program is run with the test data and the actual output is compared with the expected output. If the outputs do not agree, there is an error that must be located and corrected.

A program testing procedure such as this shows only the *presence* of errors, not their *absence*. That is, the procedure can show only whether there are errors, not whether there are no errors. To show that a program is correct, we must demonstrate that under all circumstances the program produces the correct result. To do this by using test data would require running the program with all possible combinations of data and comparing the output with the expected output calculated by hand. In addition to being an enormous task, this would be senseless, because then we would have all possible outputs calculated by hand and there would be no need for a program (except, perhaps, to check our hand calculations). Thus, we need some other way of showing that the program is logically correct.

"Proving" program correctness. It is sometimes possible to show that a program is correct using a mathematical proof. This approach is usually very complex and tedious, and few programmers know what is involved. We can, however, informally "prove" a program's correctness through the stepwise refinement process. Recall that in this approach we start with a general statement of the problem and then refine the statement by determining what must be done to accomplish it. At each step in the development, we refine the statements of the previous step until we reach the coded program. To show that a program is correct, we need to demonstrate that each refinement completes the task specified at the previous step.

As an example, consider the sorting program developed in Section 6-4. The problem is to sort three numbers into ascending sequence. The first step in the refinement includes the following statement:

Sort V1, V2, and V3 into ascending order.

We assume that this is a correct definition of the problem and begin to refine it. The refinement results in the following:

Move largest value to V3.
Move next largest value to V2.

We can say that the program is correct at this point because we know that to sort the values we need only do the two steps listed above. We then refine each of these two steps separately and show that each refinement is a correct way of accomplishing the task that is being described. Thus, we can refine the preceding statements to the following:

Move larger of V1 and V2 to V3.

Move larger of V2 and V3 to V3.
Move larger of V1 and V2 to V2.

Then the program is correct at this level of refinement. We continue in this manner, showing that each successive step is a correct refinement of the previous step. Finally, we code the program, and if there are no coding errors, the coded program is logically correct.

This method of showing program correctness through stepwise refinement is a very important part of programming. Most programmers do this even though they may not think they are "proving" that the program is correct. If it is done carefully and explicitly, the chance of serious logic errors in the program is greatly reduced. Thus, the development of the program is the most important step in the programming process.

Program testing. Even if a program is developed in the manner described here, logic errors may occur. Details are often forgotten or a logical step in the development is passed over too quickly. A thorough testing of the program should be performed to force out any hidden errors. The programmer should be merciless in testing the program. Some organizations have a different programmer do the testing so that the original programmer is not tempted to overlook possible weaknesses just to finish the job. The objective of program testing is to force errors to reveal themselves.

The first tests of the program should be simple to insure that the program works in the simplest cases. Obvious errors such as misspelling of headings or non-alignment of columns can be corrected at this point. Then more complex tests can be performed.

Every statement in the program should be executed at least once and usually several times with test data. If a statement includes variables that are used for input data, test cases that represent a range of values for each variable should be provided. Testing a sequence is usually fairly simple. For example, consider the following statements from the interest-calculation program in Chapter 2 (Figure 2-11):

```
160 INPUT B,R
170 LET I=B*R
180 LET B1=B+I
```

Several different values for B and R should be supplied in testing this program. What happens if B is 0? R is 0? Both are 0? What happens if either or both B and R are large values (e.g., 1000000 for B and 1 for R)? What happens with typical values for these variables (e.g., 20000 for B and .09 for R)? Test data that represents extreme cases as well as common cases should be used.

Testing a decision is more complex. At a minimum every statement in the decision should be executed at least once using test data. This strategy, however, will not catch all obvious errors. For example, consider the following statements from the payroll program in Chapter 3 (Figure 3-8):

```
170 INPUT I,H
180 IF H>40 THEN 220
190    LET G=6.5*H
200    LET W=.18*G
210 GOTO 240
220    LET G=260+9.75*(H-40)
230    LET W=.20*G
240 (next statement)
```

To test this section of code, we might supply two sets of test data, one with the hours equal to 35 and the other with the hours equal to 45. These data would cause every statement in this sequence to be executed at least once. Nevertheless, the sequence may still be in error. For example, assume that the IF statement has been incorrectly coded as follows:

```
180 IF H>=40 THEN 220
```

Testing with only the two sets of inputs will not detect this error. We must also test the case where the hours are equal to 40.

We now have three sets of test data for this program. However, even with these data, errors may still be present. For example, the following erroneous IF statement would not be detected with these test data:

```
180 IF H>41 THEN 220
```

What we need is a test case that is just greater than 40, such as 40.1. Then this error would be detected.

We can see from this example the beginning of a general strategy for testing decisions. For this program the input value for the hours can range from zero to some reasonable limit such as eighty. We can divide this range into two subranges based on the calculations to be performed. If the hours are between zero and forty, one set of calculations should be performed. If the hours are greater than forty but less than or equal to the upper limit, another set of calculations should be carried out. Then the testing strategy is as follows: For each subrange, test the decision with the maximum and minimum values in the subrange and with some representative value within the subrange. Applying this strategy to the payroll program, we would test the program with the hours equal to 0, 35, 40, 40.1, 45, and 80. If the program works for each of these cases, we are reasonably certain that it will work for others.

In testing a loop we need to make sure that the loop repeats when required and stops when it should. Essentially, we need to test the decision that controls the loop. For an input loop that is controlled by a trailer-value test we need to provide test data that does not contain the trailer value and test data that does. For example, consider the following statements from the tuition-calculation program in Chapter 4 (Figure 4-3):

```
150 INPUT I,U
160 IF I=9999 THEN 240
```

The trailer value is the value 9999 for the variable I. We must supply test cases where I does not equal 9999 and where it does.

Sometimes with processing and counting loops we cannot control the execution of the loop using input data. For example, the interest-calculation programs in Chapter 4 (Figures 4-5 and 4-8) have no input. For such programs we must check the output to be sure it is correct. When we can control the loop with input data, we should test the program with a range of values. For example, consider the following statements from a test-score averaging program in Chapter 4 (Figure 4-20):

```
170 INPUT N
180 LET T=0
190 FOR I=1 TO N
200    INPUT S
210    LET T=T+S
220 NEXT I
230 LET A=T/N
```

The input data includes the value of N. We should test the program with extreme values for N as well as typical values. What happens if N is 1? 50? 10? Values such as these should be used when testing the program.

The testing strategies described here will not detect all errors. For example, the tests will not detect errors that might result from using invalid input data. In the previous example, the program will fail if a value of 0 is entered for N, but this case is not tested. We should make up special tests for the worst possible cases. Errors often occur at the beginning or end of processing. Hence, special tests should be made with the first and last set of input data. Tests should be made to see what happens when there is too much or too little data. The program should be run without any input data to see what happens. Every worst case that can be thought of should be tested.

Debugging. When an error is detected, the programmer must locate its cause in the program and correct it. This is the debugging process. *Testing* involves determining if errors are present; *debugging* involves finding and correcting errors.

Many errors are the result of incorrect input data. Therefore, a good practice while debugging is to display all input data immediately after it is entered. A simple PRINT statement after each INPUT or READ statement can be used for this. This is called *echo printing* and it allows the programmer to check that the desired input data has been entered or read correctly.

Another technique is to display the values of variables that are not used for input or output (i.e., internal variables). Usually this is done by putting a PRINT statement after each statement that changes the value of such a variable. This lets the programmer check the results of intermediate calculations.

A common technique is called *tracing*. The idea is to show the actual order of execution of the statements in the program. This can be done by putting a PRINT statement in each alternative of a decision and in each loop in the program. Each PRINT statement should display a simple phrase that identifies where in the program the statement is located. The resulting output allows the programmer to compare the actual execution sequence with what was expected. (Some versions of BASIC have special statements or commands for tracing execution of a program.)

Figure 6-14 shows a tuition-calculation program from Chapter 5 (Figure 5-4) with several statements changed to create errors. Additional PRINT statements have been added to help in debugging. The statement at line 175 displays a message indicating that the input loop has begun and displays the input data that is read. The statements at lines 205 and 225 display messages to indicate which alternative of the decision has been followed. We can see from the output produced by these extra statements that incorrect input data has been read in several cases and the wrong alternative has been followed in all decisions. This gives us clues about the possible errors in the program.

After a program with errors has been corrected, it should be retested. Sometimes a correction is not done correctly or a new error is introduced when a correction is made. The program should be tested any time a change is made in the program. If the program has extra PRINT statements for debugging (such as the program in Figure 6-14), these statements must be removed after all testing is completed. After these PRINT statements are removed, the program should be tested one final time.

The techniques discussed here can help detect and locate errors in a program. However, if a program has been developed by following a logical, systematic approach, errors should be at a minimum. It is the programmer's responsibility to take whatever steps are necessary to guarantee that a program is correct. A program is correct when there are no logic errors as well as no syntax and execution errors.

Correctness of the program for the sample problem. The grade-report program was developed using stepwise refinement. At each step, we were reasonably sure that the refinement correctly accomplished the task at the previous step. As a result we are now fairly confident that the program is correct. Still, we need to test the program to try to locate any errors that we may have overlooked.

Figure 6-14. A tuition-calculation program with PRINT statements for debugging

```
100 REM - TUITION CALCULATION PROGRAM
110 REM - VARIABLES:
120 REM      I  = STUDENT ID
130 REM      U  = NUMBER OF UNITS
140 REM      T  = TUITION
150 PRINT "STUDENT ID","UNITS","TUITION"
160 PRINT
170 READ I,U
175 PRINT TAB(40);"BEGIN INPUT LOOP; I=";I;"U=";U
180    IF I=9999 THEN 250
190    IF U<12 THEN 220
200      LET T=350
205      PRINT TAB(40);"U<=12 ALTERNATIVE"
210    GOTO 230
220      LET T=350+20*(U-12)
225      PRINT TAB(40);"U>12 ALTERNATIVE"
230    PRINT I,U,T
240 GOTO 170
250 PRINT
260 PRINT "ALL DATA PROCESSED"
270 REM - INPUT DATA
280 DATA 1001,15,1013,1025,8
300 DATA 1147,3,13.5,1207,11
310 DATA 1229,12.5,9999,0
320 END
```

(a) The program

STUDENT ID	UNITS	TUITION	
			BEGIN INPUT LOOP; I= 1001 U= 15
			U<=12 ALTERNATIVE
1001	15	350	
			BEGIN INPUT LOOP; I= 1013 U= 1025
			U<=12 ALTERNATIVE
1013	1025	350	
			BEGIN INPUT LOOP; I= 8 U= 1147
			U<=12 ALTERNATIVE
8	1147	350	
			BEGIN INPUT LOOP; I= 3 U= 13.5
			U<=12 ALTERNATIVE
3	13.5	350	
			BEGIN INPUT LOOP; I= 1207 U= 11
			U>12 ALTERNATIVE
1207	11	330	
			BEGIN INPUT LOOP; I= 1229 U= 12.5
			U<=12 ALTERNATIVE
1229	12.5	350	
			BEGIN INPUT LOOP; I= 9999 U= 0

ALL DATA PROCESSED

(b) Output

Generating test data for the grade-report program is much more complex than in our previous examples. The best approach is to analyze the different parts of the program separately and to design appropriate test data for each part. We can apply the decision strategy to the grade-selection algorithm in the program. We note that the grade is based on the average test score. The actual grade depends on which of the following ranges the average falls into:†

---

† Actually, the maximum value in each range should be as close to the minimum of the next range as possible (e.g., the second range should be 80–89.99). However, we will use the ranges given here to demonstrate the approach.

90–100
80–89
70–79
60–69
0–59

We must select input data for the three test scores that will generate values for the weighted average score equal to the maximum and minimum value in each range and a value in between each set of limits. This results in fifteen test cases in all.

The sorting algorithm is more complex. We note that it does not depend on whether any of the test scores are equal. Hence, for testing purposes we can assume that each score is different. Then there are six possible cases to test, based on the relative values of S1, S2, and S3. These cases are as follows:

S1 < S2 < S3
S1 < S3 < S2
S2 < S1 < S3
S2 < S3 < S1
S3 < S1 < S2
S3 < S2 < S1

We must supply input test data for each case. We can combine these six cases with the fifteen needed for the grade-selection algorithm. One additional case, with 9999 for the identification number, is needed to test the termination condition of the input loop.

A complete set of input data that satisfies these requirements is given in Figure 6-15. Tests number 2, 3, 5, 6, 8, and 9 correspond to the six cases just listed for the sorting algorithm. For each set of data, the expected output is also shown. The test data should be rearranged so that the tests are not done in any particular order (except for the trailer-value test). Then the program should be run with the data and the actual output compared with what is expected. Any discrepancy indicates an error.

The output from running the program with this data is shown in Figure 6-16. Note that the output is in a different order than the input data in Figure 6-15 because the data was rearranged when the program was run. We can see that the output is correct for all test cases. This fact, coupled with the careful development process, makes us very confident that this program is correct. Had any of the test

Figure 6-15. Input test data and expected output for the grade-report program

Test number	Input test data				Expected output	
	I	S1	S2	S3	Average	Grade
1	1001	100	100	100	100	A
2	1002	83	93	100	95	A
3	1003	70	96	90	90	A
4	1004	90	88	88	89	B
5	1005	83	73	90	85	B
6	1006	86	60	80	80	B
7	1007	78	78	80	79	C
8	1008	73	80	63	75	C
9	1009	76	70	50	70	C
10	1010	68	70	68	69	D
11	1011	80	50	50	65	D
12	1012	45	75	45	60	D
13	1013	79	48	18	59	F
14	1014	40	40	70	55	F
15	1015	0	0	0	0	F
16	9999	0	0	0	—	—
					Course average: 71.4	

Figure 6-16. Output from the grade-report program

```
                  COURSE GRADE REPORT

        STUDENT      AVERAGE      LETTER
        NUMBER        SCORE       GRADE

         1006          80           B
         1011          65           D
         1002          95           A
         1009          70           C
         1015           0           F
         1004          89           B
         1005          85           B
         1013          59           F
         1008          75           C
         1001         100           A
         1012          60           D
         1010          69           D
         1003          90           A
         1007          79           C
         1014          55           F

        COURSE AVERAGE  71.4
```

cases produced incorrect results, we would have to locate and correct the errors. We could use any of the debugging techniques discussed previously to help in this process. After any errors are corrected, the program must be run again with the test data in Figure 6-15. This must be repeated until no errors are detected.

Program documentation

Documentation of a program provides information so that others can understand how to use the program and how the program works. Documentation of how to use the program is provided mainly for people using the program to solve a particular problem. This is often called *user documentation*. It gives instructions for running the program on the computer, including what input to use and what to expect for output. Documentation on how the program works is provided for other programmers in the event that errors must be corrected or modifications in the program need to be made. This is usually called *program documentation*. In this section we are concerned with this type of documentation.

Documenting the program begins during the problem definition activity. Any written specifications of the program prepared at this stage are part of the documentation. For example, input and output data descriptions are part of the problem definition and should be included in the final program documentation. If, during program planning, pseudocode or flowcharts are prepared, they too should be included in the final documentation. Listings of the test data used and sample output should also be part of the program documentation.

This type of documentation is external to the program. Much documentation can be included in the program itself. This is the primary purpose of remarks in the program. As we have seen, remarks can be used to describe the general features of the program and the detailed logic of the algorithm. A listing of the program with appropriate remarks is an important part of the documentation.

A complete documentation package for a program might contain the following:

1. A program summary or abstract that provides a brief statement of the purpose of the program and a short description of the program's input,

output, and processing. This summary may be included as remarks in the program and may also be written or typed on a separate piece of paper or on a form.

2. Detailed descriptions of the input and output data for the program. These descriptions may include a print chart showing the output format.

3. Documentation of the program's algorithm. This documentation may include pseudocode, flowcharts, and any other description of how the program works. A written narrative of any particularly complex part of the program may be included.

4. A summary of any error messages that may be displayed. A program often includes statements that check for various errors or exceptions that are detected during execution. A message is usually displayed when such an error occurs. Although each error message should completely describe the condition that occurred, it is usually a good idea to list all error messages in the documentation and provide additional explanations of what caused each error.

5. Documentation of the testing that was done on the program. This documentation includes lists of test data used with the program and the output that resulted from each test run. These items provide information for programmers who modify the program in the future so that they can run the same tests with the modified program and check that the correct output is produced.

6. A record of any modifications that have been made in the program. A programmer who makes a change in a program should record the date, the nature of the change, and his or her name. As with the program summary, this is often included as remarks in the program.

7. The program listing. As noted earlier, the documentation must include a current listing of the program with appropriate remarks.

The complete set of documents should be bound together with a title page and a table of contents. There should be one binder for each program, and the entire library of program documentation should be the responsibility of one or more documentation librarians. If a program is changed, it is important that the documentation be updated. No programmer should ever consider his or her job done until the final documentation is prepared or appropriately modified.

Documentation of the program for the sample problem. The documentation for the grade-report program was prepared as we developed the program. This is often the case if the program development has been done in a systematic way. The programmer may have to update the documentation for any changes that occurred during the programming process and will have to prepare the final copies of all documents. These tasks, however, should be minimal if the programmer kept good documentation while preparing the program.

The complete documentation package for the grade report program might include the following:

1. The program summary (Figure 6-10)
2. The print chart (Figure 6-9)
3. The pseudocode (Figure 6-11) or the flowchart (Figure 6-12) or both
4. The list of input test data and expected output (Figure 6-15)
5. The output from running the program with the test data (Figure 6-16)
6. The program listing (Figure 6-13)

When all these documents are put together in a binder with a title page and table of contents, the programming process is complete.

6-6 Conclusion

Computer programming is a process that includes several activities. One common misconception is that programming involves only the activity of writing the program. As we have seen, however, this activity, which is called coding, is just one part of the entire programming process. When we use the word "programming," we mean the whole set of activities associated with preparing a computer program. This includes the five activities discussed in the last section.

The approach to programming emphasized in this book is commonly called *structured programming*. There is some disagreement about what is meant by structured programming; a single consensus definition does not exist. However, most people agree that structured programming involves a systematic process that results in programs that are well structured; that are easily understood, maintained, and modified; and that can be shown to be correct.

In this chapter we stressed developing programs through stepwise refinement. This approach helps us show the correctness of a program. Use of the three basic control structures leads to programs that are well structured and easy to understand and change. The style rules discussed in this chapter also aid in producing readable programs.

Structured programming should not be confused with the idea of a *structured program*. Generally, a structured program is one that uses only the three basic control structures. Producing a structured program is one of the goals of structured programming. However, structured programming is much more than this.

Structured programming is really just good programming. By following the guidelines presented in this chapter, the programmer can produce good correct programs.

Review questions

1. What are the three basic control structures in programming?
2. What type of control structure is formed by each of the following groups of statements?
   a. `100 IF A<=B THEN 120`
      `110    LET C=D`
      `120 (next statement)`
   b. `130 FOR I=1 to 10`
      `140    PRINT I`
      `150 NEXT I`
   c. `160 LET A=5`
      `170 PRINT A`
   d. `180 INPUT X`
      `190    IF X=0 THEN 210`
      `200 GOTO 180`
      `210 (next statement)`
3. Why is it important that each basic control structure have a single entry point and a single exit point?
4. What principle of good program structure is violated by the program in Figure 4-23?
5. When we read the statements in a program in the order in which they are written on paper or displayed on the CRT screen, we are reading the _____ version of the program. When we read the statements in a program in the order in which they are executed, we are reading the _____ version of the program.
6. Why can the uncontrolled use of GOTO statements make a program difficult to understand?
7. Give three rules of good program style.
8. What is wrong with the following group of statements?

```
220 REM - PRINT THE VALUES OF A, B, AND C
230 PRINT A,B,C
```

9. The process of developing a program by starting with a general statement of the problem and successively refining the statement until a program solution is obtained is called _____.

10. Consider the program shown in Figure 6-8. Assume that the input data is the numbers 8, 12, and 4. What is the value of all variables in the program after each statement is executed?

11. Which activity in the programming process is begun during problem definition but finished after all other activities are completed?

12. At a minimum, what should be determined during the problem definition activity?

13. During what activity in the programming process is the algorithm for the program developed?

14. It has been said that the most important step in the programming process is the design step. Why?

15. Program testing can show that a program is correct. True or false?

16. Assume that the value of X is a whole number that can range from 100 to 200. Design test data following the strategy discussed in the chapter that tests the following program:

```
100 INPUT X
110    IF X=0 THEN 180
120    IF X<=125 THEN 150
130       LET Y=0
140    GOTO 160
150       LET Y=1
160    PRINT Y
170 GOTO 100
180 END
```

17. What is the difference between program testing and debugging?

18. What is the purpose of program documentation?

19. What is the difference between coding and programming?

20. What is structured programming?

Programming problems

1. In the economic measurement of consumer behavior, the price elasticity of demand for a product is given by the following expression:

$$-\frac{(Q_2 - Q_1)/Q_1}{(P_2 - P_1)/P_1}$$

In this expression, Q stands for quantity sold and P for price.

If the elasticity is less than 1, the demand is said to be *inelastic*. If the elasticity equals 1, the demand is said to be *unit elastic*. If the elasticity is greater than 1, the demand is *elastic*.

Write a BASIC program to calculate the elasticity of demand for a particular product. Input is the product number and the relevant prices and quantities. Output from the program should be the product number, the elasticity of demand, and a statement of whether the demand is elastic, inelastic, or unit elastic.

Use the following data to test the program:

Product number	P_1	Q_1	P_2	Q_2
103	25.00	100	17.50	135
108	20.00	200	10.00	300
112	125.00	35	95.00	37
115	32.50	512	27.00	713
128	44.00	80	33.00	100
132	15.75	72	10.25	63
999 (trailer value)				

2. A student is placed on the dean's list of a college if his or her grade-point average (GPA) is above a certain level. The minimum GPA necessary to make the dean's list depends on the student's year in college. A freshman must have a 3.70 GPA or higher to make the dean's list. For a sophomore the minimum GPA is 3.50, and for juniors and seniors it is 3.30.

Write a BASIC program to display data for all students who are on the dean's list. Input for the program is one set of data for each student indicating the student's identification number, year in school (1 = freshman, 2 = sophomore, 3 = junior, 4 = senior), and his or her grade-point average. Output should consist of the student's number and GPA for the dean's list students only.

Use the following data to test the program:

Student number	Year	GPA
1012	2	3.61
1385	1	2.63
1472	3	3.95
1981	2	3.30
2061	4	2.91
2111	4	3.30
2385	1	3.85
2500	1	3.75
2911	2	3.50
3047	3	3.28
3568	3	3.00
3910	4	3.35
9999 (trailer value)		

3. The annual bonus paid to each employee of an organization is based on the number of years of service and the age of the employee. If the employee has 5 to 9 years of service and is between 25 and 34, the annual bonus is $200. If he or she is 35 or older, with 5 to 9 years of service, the bonus is $400. If the years of service are between 10 and 19, and the age is less than 40 years, the bonus is $400. If the employee is 40 or older, with 10 to 19 years of service, the bonus is $500. If he or she has 20 or more years of service, no matter what age, then the bonus is $600. For other employees there is no annual bonus.

Write an interactive BASIC program to determine the annual bonus for each eligible employee in the organization. Input for the program consists of each employee's identification number, age, and number of years of service. Output should include the employee's number and bonus for those employees who receive a bonus or a phrase indicating no bonus if this is the case.

Use the following data to test the program:

Employee's number	Age	Years of service
1001	38	12
1121	52	28
1305	42	16
1457	29	8
1689	29	3
1810	37	9
1925	42	20
2008	33	10
2025	24	5
2133	54	23
2485	49	19
2561	24	6
2610	33	5

4. A theater sells tickets for $5.00 and averages 100 tickets sold for each performance. At this rate the theater's cost per patron is $2.00. The theater manager estimates that for each $.25 reduction in ticket price the number of tickets sold will increase by 30 and the theater's cost per patron will increase by $.10.

Write a BASIC program to calculate and display a table listing the ticket price, the number of tickets sold, the gross revenue (ticket price multiplied by the number of tickets sold), the theater's total cost (cost per patron times number of tickets sold), and the net profit (revenue minus total cost) for each ticket price ranging from $5.00 to $3.00.

As the ticket price decreases from $5.00 to $3.00, the profit will steadily increase to a maximum and then start to decrease. Use this fact to display the phrase MAXIMUM PROFIT on the line in the table that corresponds to the greatest profit.

5. Write a BASIC program to display student grade reports. Input to the program consists of a varying number of course grades for each student. Each set of input contains a student's identification number, a course identification number, the course's units (credits), and the student's numeric course grade (equal to 4, 3, 2, 1, or 0). The input data is arranged in ascending numerical sequence by the students' identification numbers. All input data should be put in DATA statements.

The program must calculate the grade-point average (GPA) for each student. This is done by multiplying the number of units for each course by the grade, totaling for all courses, and dividing by the total number of units taken.

The output from the program should list for each student the student's identification number, the number of units and grade for each course that the student took, and the student's GPA. In addition, if the GPA is 3.5 or greater, the message HONOR LIST should be displayed. If the GPA is less than 1.5, the message PROBATION should be displayed.

Design appropriate input data that thoroughly tests the program. Note that the number of courses taken by a student varies.

6. Given the slopes, s and t, and intercepts, a and b, of two lines, that is, the lines whose equations are

$$y = sx + a$$
$$y = tx + b$$

we can compute the coordinates of the point of intersection of the lines. Write a BASIC program that does the computation and displays the name of the quadrant (FIRST, SECOND, THIRD, FOURTH) in which the point lies. If the point of intersection falls on an axis, display the name of the axis (X-AXIS or Y-AXIS). If the point of intersection is the origin, display the word ORIGIN. Include a provision in the program to check if the lines are parallel (i.e., $s = t$, $a \neq b$) or if the equations are for the same line (i.e., $s = t$, $a = b$) and display an appropriate phrase if either case holds.

Input to the program is the data identification number and the values of s, a, t, and b. Use the following data to test the program:

ID	s	a	t	b
101	2.00	8.00	−3.00	−2.00
102	4.38	4.25	−7.11	−18.92
103	.50	3.50	−.75	16.00
104	.50	0.00	−.50	0.00
105	.38	−15.79	.38	−28.35
106	.50	5.00	−.50	5.00
107	.50	5.00	−.50	−5.00
108	−5.63	28.91	6.21	14.35
109	4.87	.08	4.87	.08
110	−.50	−5.00	.50	−5.00
111	.50	−5.00	−.50	5.00
112	−.03	−16.92	1.72	24.38
113	−1.00	−4.00	−2.00	6.00

To stop processing, use a trailer value of 999 for the ID.

7. Write a BASIC program to calculate the accumulated amount of a bank deposit at any interest rate for any period of time. Input to the program is the depositor's number, the amount of his or her deposit, the interest rate the deposit earns, and the number of years that he or she leaves the deposit. The basic problem assumes that interest is compounded annually. This means that the interest earned one year is added to the deposit and multiplied by the annual interest rate to get the next year's interest. For

example, if the initial deposit is $1000, the interest rate is 5%, and the deposit is left for 3 years, then the first year's interest is $1000 × .05 = $50. At the end of the first year, the accumulated amount of the deposit is $1000 + $50 = $1050. Interest for the second year is $1050 × .05 = $52.50. The accumulated amount of the deposit at the end of the second year is $1050 + $52.50 = $1102.50. The third year's interest is $1102.50 × .05 = $55.12. Thus, the accumulated amount of the deposit at the end of 3 years is $1102.50 + $55.12 = $1157.62.

The following are the requirements for this program:

a. Accept and display the input data. Output should include appropriate titles to identify each item.

b. For each set of input data, display, below appropriate headings, the year and the accumulated amount of the deposit at the end of the year. Assume that the deposit is made at the beginning of year 1. Then the accumulated amount of the despoit at the end of year 1 is the amount of the deposit plus the interest for that year. Continue the process for the other years, making sure that the interest is compounded annually.

c. In part (b) we assumed that interest was compounded only once a year. It is possible to compound interest more frequently by incorporating a "compounding factor" into the program. This factor represents the number of times per year that interest is to be compounded. For example, a compounding factor of 4 means that interest is compounded four times per year (i.e, every 3 months). A compounding factor of 1 means that interest is compounded once per year (i.e., annually). When interest is compounded more than once a year, the interest rate used in the calculation is the annual interest rate divided by the compounding factor. For example, if the annual interest rate is 5% and the compounding factor is 4, then the interest rate used to calculate interest every 3 months is .05/4 = .0125. Interest is calculated at this rate four times a year. Each time the interest is calculated, it is added to the deposit to get a new accumulated deposit that is used for the next interest calculation. Calculate the accumulated amount of the despoit at the end of each year for each set of input data, assuming compounding factors of 2, 4, 8, and 12. Note that these compounding factors are not input data but must be generated in the program. For each compounding factor display the factor and the *final* accumulated amount of the deposit with appropriate titles. Thus, in addition to the output already described, there will be four additional lines of output for each set of data.

Use the following data to test the program:

Depositor's number	Amount of deposit ($)	Interest rate (%)	Time (years)
10851	1000.00	5	3
13751	1000.00	$4\frac{1}{2}$	3
18645	1000.00	$5\frac{1}{4}$	3
19541	50.00	$3\frac{3}{4}$	25
24712	3500.00	$6\frac{3}{4}$	10
24839	3500.00	7	10
26213	3500.00	$7\frac{1}{4}$	10
28721	3500.00	7	5

8. In a geographic area the population in each of three socioeconomic groups is increasing at a known percent per year. The current total population of the area and distribution (percent) of the population among the three groups is also known. Several things can be determined from this information, including the expected population in each group after a certain amount of time and the total population of the area.

Assume that the following data for each geographic area is available: the area code number, the current total population of the area, the percent of the current population that comprises each of the three socioeconomic groups, and the annual growth percentage rate of each group. Write a BASIC program to process these data according to the following specifications:

a. Read and display the input data with appropriate headings.

b. For each group calculate the current population and the expected population after 10 years. For example, if the current population of an area is 5000 and a group comprises 20% of that population, then the current population of the group is 1000. If the growth rate is 5%, then after one year the population of the group is 1000 + .05 × 1000 or 1050. After two years, the population is 1050 + .05 × 1050 or 1103. This continues for 10 years. Also calculate the total population of the area after 10 years and the percent of the total that each socioeconomic group comprises. Display all results with appropriate headings.

c. In part (b) we assumed that the growth rate for each group would remain constant. It may be that these growth rates are decreasing by some percent each year. Repeat the calculations for part (b), assuming the growth rate decreases by .1% per year until the growth rate reaches 2.1% or less, at which time it levels off. For example, if the growth rate this year is 2.7%, then next year it will be 2.6%. The following year it will be 2.5%. This continues until the growth rate reaches 2.1%, at which time it levels off at 2.1% for the remainder of the 10-year period. If the growth rate is currently 2.1% or less, then the rate remains unchanged for the entire 10-year period. Do this three more times, using .2%, .25%, and .35% to decrease the growth rate.

Use the data in the following table to test the program:

Code	Current total population	Distribution of current population			Annual growth rate		
		Group A	Group B	Group C	Group A	Group B	Group C
1083	14,283	35%	59%	6%	4.1%	5.2%	4.9%
1215	21,863	37%	42%	21%	5.8%	5.1%	5.9%
1371	8,460	73%	0%	27%	2.4%	0.0%	3.1%
1462	5,381	55%	41%	4%	3.7%	4.2%	4.2%
1931	12,845	90%	9%	1%	1.9%	2.2%	2.8%

9. Develop an interactive BASIC program to help reconcile your checkbook each month.

10. Develop a BASIC program to compare your expenses each month with your budget for various items (e.g., rent, food, transportation).

11. Develop a BASIC program to compute depreciation schedules for an asset using the straight-line method, the double-declining-balance method, and the sum-of-the-years'-digits method.

12. Write a BASIC program to produce a home mortgage payment schedule. Input to the program should be the amount of the loan, the monthly payment, the annual interest rate, and the number of months that the loan runs. Output should be a table that gives for each month the amount of the payment applied to the principal, the amount applied to interest, and the balance due after the payment. Yearly totals of interest paid should also be given. Assume that the first payment is due at the end of January.

13. Write the program for Problem 12 with the additional requirement that the input includes the month and year of the first payment. Then the totals for the first and last year may not necessarily represent twelve months of payments.

14. Write a BASIC program to find the definite integral of the function $f(x) = e^x$ between the limits a and b. Use the trapezoidal method described in many calculus textbooks. Input to the program should be the values of a and b. Output should be the definite integral of the function between a and b.

Chapter 7

BASIC functions

Many standard processing activities are commonly required in BASIC programs. For example, it is often necessary to find the square root of a number or to perform various trigonometric computations. In order to relieve the programmer of the responsibility of preparing the instructions necessary for such processing, BASIC supplies special built-in routines called *functions*. A function is a separate set of instructions that performs a specific task. In this chapter we describe the BASIC functions and show how they are used in programs. After completing this chapter you should be able to write BASIC programs that use functions.

The functions described here are built into the BASIC language. It is also possible for the programmer to prepare his or her own functions to do special tasks. This other type of function is discussed in Chapter 11.

7-1 General characteristics

Each BASIC function is identified by a name. We use a function in a program by coding the name of the function, usually followed by a numeric expression in parentheses. The resulting reference to the function forms a numeric expression that can be used by itself in a statement or as part of a more complex numeric expression.

The square-root function

To illustrate the general characteristics of functions, we consider the square-root function. The name of this function is SQR. We use the function by coding this name followed by a numeric expression enclosed in parentheses. We then use the combination of function name and expression in a statement in a program. For example, the following LET statement shows the use of the square-root function:

```
20 LET C=SQR(A+B)
```

In evaluating this function the computer first determines the value of the numeric expression in parentheses. Then the SQR function finds the square root of the value. For example, if A is 9 and B is 7 in the previous statement, then A + B is 16 and SQR(A + B) is 4. This value is then assigned to C by the LET statement.

The expression in parentheses may be a constant, variable, or more complex numeric expression. All the following statements are valid examples of the use of the square-root function:

```
30 LET X=SQR(Y)
40 IF Z>SQR(100) THEN 200
50 LET R=(-B+SQR(B^2-4*A*C))/(2*A)
60 IF SQR(P)<=3*SQR(Q) THEN 300
```

Note that the function cannot be used by itself but only as part of a statement. In fact, the SQR function can be used only in place of a numeric expression in a statement or as part of a more complex numeric expression. The previous statements illustrate this.

The value of the expression in parentheses must not be negative, because the computer cannot determine the square root of a negative number. In addition, only the nonnegative square root is found [e.g., SQR(16) is 4 even though $\sqrt{16}$ is ± 4].

The program in Figure 7-1 demonstrates the use of the square-root function. The input to this program is the length (L) and width (W) of a piece of carpet purchased to cover a floor. The problem is to compute the length of the side (S) of the largest square floor that can be covered by this amount of carpet. To do this, the program must first compute the area (A) of carpet purchased. This is done in statement 210. Then the square root of the area is computed in statement 220 to give the length of the side (S). Notice that because the value of A is not needed for output, statement 210 can be eliminated and statement 220 can be written as follows:

```
220 LET S=SQR(L*W)
```

Figure 7-1. A program that calculates floor dimensions

```
100 REM - FLOOR DIMENSION PROGRAM
110 REM - VARIABLES:
120 REM      L  = LENGTH OF CARPET
130 REM      W  = WIDTH OF CARPET
140 REM      A  = AREA OF CARPET
150 REM      S  = LENGTH OF SIDE OF SQUARE
200 INPUT L,W
210 LET A=L*W
220 LET S=SQR(A)
230 PRINT "THE LENGTH OF THE SIDE IS";S
999 END
```

(a) The program

```
? 10,16
THE LENGTH OF THE SIDE IS 12.6491
```

(b) Input and output

Other functions

Besides the square-root function, many other functions are available and are used in a similar fashion. The functions common to most versions of BASIC are listed in Figure 7-2. Some versions have additional functions. Notice that standard mathematical functions, such as trigonometric, logarithmic, and exponential functions, are included. Two special functions listed in Figure 7-2 — the INT and the RND functions — are discussed in detail in the next two sections.

Some functions don't follow the pattern described here. For example, the TAB function, discussed in Chapter 5, does not form a numeric expression and is used only in a PRINT statement. There are also special functions that perform operations with character data. These are called string functions and are discussed in Chapter 8.

Figure 7-2. Common BASIC functions

Function	Meaning
ABS(X)	Absolute value of X
ATN(X)	Arctangent (in radians) of X
COS(X)	Cosine of X (X must be in radians)
EXP(X)	Exponential of X (that is, e^x)
INT(X)	Largest integer less than or equal to X
LOG(X)	Natural logarithm of X (that is, ln X)
RND	Random number between 0 and 1
SGN(X)	Sign of X (that is, -1 if $X < 0$, 0 if $X = 0$, $+1$ if $X > 0$)
SIN(X)	Sine of X (X must be in radians)
SQR(X)	Square root of X
TAN(X)	Tangent of X (X must be in radians)

7-2 The integer function

A very useful function is the integer, or INT, function. This function finds the largest integer (i.e., whole number) that is less than or equal to the value of the expression in parentheses. For example, consider the following statement:

```
110 LET A=INT(B)
```

If B is 5.8, the INT function finds the largest integer that is less than or equal to 5.8. This integer is 5, which is assigned to A in the LET statement. Notice that the value is *not* rounded; the largest integer *less than or equal to* the value in parentheses is found. If the value is negative, the same rule applies. Thus, if B is -5.8 in the previous example, INT(B) is -6, the largest integer less than or equal to -5.8. The following are additional examples of the result produced by the INT function:

B	*INT(B)*
3.1	3
7	7
-6.3	-7
-10	-10
0	0
.9999	0
-4.0001	-5

Notice that the INT function does not change the value of the variable in parentheses; it merely uses the value to find the appropriate integer. For example, assume that the following PRINT statement is executed after statement 110 given earlier:

```
120 PRINT A,B
```

The value of A that is displayed will be the largest integer that is less than or equal to B, but the value of B that is displayed will be the original value of this variable. If B is 5.8, the numbers 5 and 5.8 are displayed.

As with other functions, any numeric expression can be used with the INT function. For example, the following statements are valid:

```
130 LET X=INT(2.5*Y-7.3)
140 IF M>INT(N) THEN 300
150 LET C=3.5*INT(D/E)+8.4
160 IF INT(P)*INT(Q)<=R THEN 310
```

Any expression in parentheses is first evaluated before the INT function is used. Thus, if Y is 4 in statement 130, 2.5*Y − 7.3 is 2.7 and INT(2.5*Y − 7.3) is 2, which is the value assigned to X. Note also that the INT function can be used in a statement only in place of a numeric expression or as part of a more complex expression as shown in these examples.

The INT function does not round off the value in parentheses. However, a technique called *half-adjusting* can be used if rounding is necessary. With this technique, one-half (.5) is added to the value before the INT function is used. Thus, to half-adjust the value of B and assign the result to A, we can use the following:

```
170 LET A=INT(B+.5)
```

For example, if B is 5.8, then B + .5 is 6.3 and INT(B + .5) is 6. However, if B is 5.2, then B + .5 is 5.7 and INT(B + .5) is 5. Thus, the value of B is correctly rounded with this technique. Notice that the technique works even if B is negative. For example, if B is −5.8, then B + .5 is −5.3 and INT(B + .5) is −6. Similarly, if B is −5.2, then B + .5 is −4.7 and INT(B + .5) is −5. Again, the value of B is correctly rounded.

There are many uses for the INT function. For example, Figure 7-3 shows a modification of the program in Figure 7-1 that uses the INT function. In this example we are again computing the length of a side of the largest square floor that can be covered by a certain amount of carpet. For this program, however, the length must be a whole number. Statement 230 in the program in Figure 7-3 uses the INT function to produce the desired result. Notice that we could combine statements 210, 220, and 230 and write one statement as follows:

```
230 LET S1=INT(SQR(L*W))
```

As another example, the program in Figure 7-4 calculates the number of dozens in a given number of eggs (E). After accepting the input, the program computes the number of dozens (D) by dividing E by 12. The INT function converts the result to a whole number. Then statement 220 finds the number remaining (R) after the dozens are removed. If the input value is 226 eggs, the output is 18 dozen with 10 eggs remaining.

There are many other uses of the INT function. In the next section we will see how it is used in conjunction with the RND function.

Figure 7-3. A program that calculates floor dimensions

```
100 REM - FLOOR DIMENSION PROGRAM
110 REM - VARIABLES:
120 REM        L  = LENGTH OF CARPET
130 REM        W  = WIDTH OF CARPET
140 REM        A  = AREA OF CARPET
150 REM        S  = LENGTH OF SIDE OF SQUARE
160 REM        S1 = INTEGER LENGTH OF SIDE OF SQUARE
200 INPUT L,W
210 LET A=L*W
220 LET S=SQR(A)
230 LET S1=INT(S)
240 PRINT "THE LENGTH OF THE SIDE IS";S1
999 END
```

(a) The program

```
? 10,16
THE LENGTH OF THE SIDE IS 12
```

(b) Input and output

Figure 7-4. The egg program

```
100 REM - EGG PROGRAM
110 REM - VARIABLES:
120 REM      E = NUMBER OF EGGS
130 REM      D = NUMBER OF DOZEN EGGS
140 REM      R = NUMBER OF EGGS REMAINING
200 INPUT E
210 LET D=INT(E/12)
220 LET R=E-D*12
230 PRINT "THERE ARE";D;"DOZEN WITH";R;"REMAINING IN";E;"EGGS."
999 END
```

(a) The program

```
? 226
THERE ARE 18 DOZEN WITH 10 REMAINING IN 226 EGGS.
```

(b) Input and output

7-3 Random numbers

In some computer applications uncertainty or randomness is required in a program. For example, programs that play card or dice games need to produce random output such as would result from dealing cards or rolling dice. Programs that simulate real-world situations such as manufacturing processes or ecological systems also involve uncertainty. All of these programs require the computer to produce numbers at random. In this section we see how this is done in BASIC.

A *random number* is a number that is as likely to be produced as any other number. For example, if we roll a die we get a random number (actually, a random integer) between 1 and 6, as indicated by the number of spots that are showing. If the die is fair, each integer between 1 and 6 is as likely to be produced as any other. If we want to write a program to play a dice game, we must be able to produce random integers between 1 and 6. This is accomplished by using the RND, or random number, function.

The RND function produces random numbers between 0 and 1. We say that the function *generates* random numbers. Each time the function is used, a new random number that is greater than or equal to 0 but less than 1 is generated. In most versions of BASIC, only the name of the function is required in a statement to generate a random number. For example, the following statement generates a random number and assigns it to the variable A:

```
210 LET A=RND
```

The number generated is between 0 and 1 including 0 but not including 1. Any number in this range is as likely to be generated as any other.

Some versions of BASIC require an expression in parentheses after the RND function name. (See Table 7-1.) For example, in some versions of BASIC the previous statement must be followed by a positive constant, variable, or numeric expression such as in the following example:

```
210 LET A=RND(1)
```

The effect is the same, however. We will use the more common form, without an expression, in our examples.

Table 7-1. RND function differences

BASIC version	RND function form
ANS minimal BASIC	RND
ANS BASIC	RND
Microsoft BASIC	RND
	or
	RND(X)
	$\quad$ X > 0, generate next random number
	$\quad$ X = 0, repeat previous random number
	$\quad$ X < 0, start new sequence of random
	$\quad\quad\quad\quad$ numbers
Applesoft BASIC	RND(X)
	$\quad$ X > 0, generate next random number
	$\quad$ X = 0, repeat previous random number
	$\quad$ X < 0, start new sequence of random
	$\quad\quad\quad\quad$ numbers
BASIC-PLUS	RND
VAX-11 BASIC	RND

Figure 7-5(a) shows a program that displays a list of ten random numbers using the RND function. The actual output from the program is shown in Figure 7-5(b). Notice that the numbers do not follow any pattern but appear to be entirely random.

Figure 7-5. A program that generates random numbers

```
10 FOR I=1 TO 10
20   LET A=RND
30   PRINT A
40 NEXT I
50 END
```

(a) The program

```
.204935
.229581
.533074
.132211
.995602
.783713
.741854
.397713
.709588
.67811
```

(b) Output

Generating random numbers in different ranges

Most often we are not interested in random numbers between 0 and 1 but rather numbers in some other range. The example of a dice-game program mentioned earlier illustrates this. In this case we need to generate random integers between 1 and 6. To do this we use a statement such as the following:

```
20 LET B=INT(6*RND)+1
```

This statement works as follows:

1. A random number between 0 and 1 is generated. Recall that it is possible to generate 0 but not 1. A number just less than 1 (such as .999999) can be generated.
2. The random number is multiplied by 6. This produces a random number between 0 and 6. Because RND can generate 0, 6*RND can be 0. However, because the largest value that RND can generate is just less than 1 (.999999), 6*RND cannot be 6 but at most just less than 6 (5.99999).
3. The integer part of 6*RND is found using the INT function. This gives a random integer between 0 and 5. Again, because 6 cannot be produced by 6*RND, INT(6*RND) cannot be 6.
4. The constant 1 is added to get a random integer between 1 and 6.

As an example, if RND generates .4, then 6*RND yields 2.4, INT(6*RND) is 2, and INT(6*RND)+1 is 3, which is the final result. Figure 7-6 shows a program that displays ten random integers between 1 and 6.

In general, to generate random *integers* between A and B (including A *and* B) we use the following:

    INT((B-A+1)*RND)+A

Thus, to produce random integers between 5 and 15 we use:

    INT(11*RND)+5

To generate any random number (not just an integer) between A and B (including A but not including B) we use the following:

    (B-A)*RND+A

For example, to produce random numbers between 5 and 15 we use:

    10*RND+5

Other variations can be used to produce numbers in different ranges.

Figure 7-6. A program that generates random integers between 1 and 6

```
10 FOR I=1 TO 10
20    LET B=INT(6*RND)+1
30    PRINT B
40 NEXT I
50 END
```

   (a) The program

```
2
2
4
1
6
5
5
3
5
5
```

   (b) Output

Generating different sequences of random numbers

The random numbers that are generated by the RND function are actually called *pseudorandom numbers*. This is because the numbers are not really random (as would be numbers that resulted from rolling a die) but rather only appear to be random. The numbers are generated by a formula that is built into the BASIC language. The formula requires a number, called the *seed*, to get started. If we know what the formula is and we know the value of the seed, we can predict the sequence of random numbers that will be generated.

Each time a program that uses the RND function is run on a particular computer, the same sequence of random numbers is generated. (This may not be true in all versions of BASIC.) This is because the random number generation formula does not change and the same seed is used each time the program is run. Thus, if we run the program in Figure 7-5 or the one in Figure 7-6 again, the same output will be produced. Repetition of the random number sequence is to the programmer's advantage when testing and debugging a program. However, after the program is completed, it is usually desirable to produce a different sequence of random numbers each time the program is run. To do this a new seed must be used for each run of the program. The process is usually called *seeding* the random number function. There are several ways of accomplishing this, depending on the version of BASIC. (See Table 7-2.)

The most common way of seeding the random number function is to include the RANDOMIZE statement in the program. The syntax of this statement is as follows:

```
1n RANDOMIZE
```

For example, the following is a valid RANDOMIZE statement:

```
10 RANDOMIZE
```

The statement should appear at the beginning of the program. The effect of this statement is that a new seed is used for the random number function. Thus, a new sequence of random numbers is generated. For example, the program in Figure 7-7

Table 7-2. Random number generation differences

BASIC version	To seed the random number generator
ANS minimal BASIC	Use the RANDOMIZE statement.
ANS BASIC	Use the RANDOMIZE statement.
Microsoft BASIC	Use the RANDOMIZE statement; the system will prompt the user for the seed.
	or
	Use the statement *1n* RANDOMIZE *x* where *x* is a constant, variable, or numeric expression, the value of which is the seed.
Applesoft BASIC	Use nothing; the RND function generates a new sequence of random numbers each time the program is run.
True BASIC	Use the RANDOMIZE statement.
BASIC-PLUS	Use the RANDOMIZE statement.
VAX-11 BASIC	Use the RANDOMIZE statement.

Figure 7-7. An example of the use of the RANDOMIZE statement

```
10 RANDOMIZE
20 FOR I=1 TO 10
30    LET B=INT(6*RND)+1
40    PRINT B
50 NEXT I
60 END
```

(a) The program

```
6
1
4
2
3
2
5
5
3
1
```

(b) Output

is the same as the one in Figure 7-6 except for the addition of the RANDOMIZE statement. Notice that the output shown is different from that of the previous program.

How the RANDOMIZE statement supplies a seed depends on the computer. With some computers an internal counter supplies the value for the seed. On other computers the RANDOMIZE statement displays a prompt requesting a value for the seed, as in the following example:

```
Random Number Seed (-32768 to 32767)?
```

Then the person running the program must enter a value for the seed. (It is important that a different value be entered each time the program is run; otherwise the same sequence of random numbers will be generated.)

There are a number of uses of random numbers. In the next section we will see how they are used in programs that play games. In Section 7-5 we will show how random numbers are used in programs to help teach other subjects. Finally, in Section 7-6 we will discuss simulation programs that require random numbers.

7-4 Computer games

One common use of random numbers is in programs that play games. For example, programs that play card or dice games require the use of random numbers to "deal" cards or "roll" dice. In this section we introduce the basic ideas behind such game-playing programs.

In general, a game requires two or more "players." With a computer game, one of the players is the computer program and the other player (or players) is the person at the keyboard. In some cases the computer's "play" is determined entirely by chance. This would be the situation with such games as "blackjack" or "craps." In other computer games, strategy is built into the program. For example, programs that play checkers or chess require complex strategy. Other computer games require a combination of chance and strategy. Many card-game programs, such as those that play bridge, are of this nature.

In this section we discuss only programs that play games of chance. In such a program the computer must generate a chance event. For example, dice must be "rolled" or cards "dealt." Then the game is "played" with the result of the chance event. Eventually a "winner" is determined, which may be the computer program or the person playing at the keyboard.

To illustrate this idea, consider a simple dice game. The player must first guess what the total of the next roll of a pair of dice will be. If the player guesses correctly, he or she "wins"; otherwise the player "loses." The program in Figure 7-8 shows how this is done. The flowchart of this program is in Figure 7-9. First, the player's guess, G, is accepted. Then the RND function is used twice to "roll" the dice. The total of the two rolls, T, is computed and compared with the guess. Finally, the program announces whether the player wins or loses. The actual results of playing the game several times are shown in Figure 7-10.

Although this program is relatively simple, the basic principle applies to other game-playing programs. For example, we could expand this program to include all of the rules of "craps." In addition, we could allow the player to bet different amounts and keep track of the total winnings over a period of time.

In a card game such as "blackjack" the computer must first "shuffle" a deck of cards and then "deal" the required hands. The player plays one hand and the computer plays the other. The game proceeds according to the appropriate rules until a winner can be determined.

There are many games that can be programmed. In addition to card and dice

Figure 7-8. A program that plays a simple dice game

```
100 REM - DICE GAME PROGRAM
110 REM - VARIABLES:
120 REM       G  = PLAYER'S GUESS
130 REM       D1 = ROLL OF FIRST DIE
140 REM       D2 = ROLL OF SECOND DIE
150 REM       T  = TOTAL OF ROLLS OF BOTH DICE
160 REM       R  = REPETITION QUESTION RESPONSE
200 RANDOMIZE
210 PRINT "A SIMPLE DICE GAME"
220 PRINT
230   PRINT "GUESS THE TOTAL ON THE NEXT"
240   PRINT "ROLL OF A PAIR OF DICE."
250   PRINT
260   REM - ACCEPT PLAYER'S GUESS
270   INPUT "WHAT IS YOUR GUESS";G
280   REM - ROLL DICE
290   LET D1=INT(6*RND)+1
300   LET D2=INT(6*RND)+1
310   REM - COMPUTE TOTAL OF ROLLS
320   LET T=D1+D2
330   REM - DISPLAY RESULTS
340   PRINT
350   PRINT "FIRST DIE","SECOND DIE","TOTAL"
360   PRINT D1,D2,T
370   PRINT
380   REM - DETERMINE IF PLAYER WINS OR LOSES
390   IF G=T THEN 420
400     PRINT "YOU GUESSED WRONG.  YOU LOSE."
410   GOTO 430
420     PRINT "YOU GUESSED RIGHT.  YOU WIN."
430   PRINT
440   PRINT "DO YOU WANT TO TRY AGAIN"
450   INPUT "(TYPE 1 FOR YES, 0 FOR NO)";R
460 IF R=1 THEN 220
470 PRINT
480 PRINT "END OF GAME"
999 END
```

Figure 7-9. Flowchart of the program that plays a simple dice game

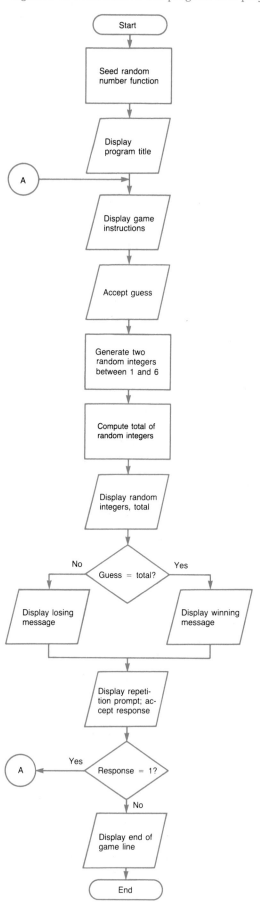

Figure 7-10. Playing the simple dice game

```
A SIMPLE DICE GAME

GUESS THE TOTAL ON THE NEXT
ROLL OF A PAIR OF DICE.

WHAT IS YOUR GUESS? 11

FIRST DIE      SECOND DIE      TOTAL
3              5               8

YOU GUESSED WRONG.  YOU LOSE.

DO YOU WANT TO TRY AGAIN
(TYPE 1 FOR YES, 0 FOR NO)? 1

GUESS THE TOTAL ON THE NEXT
ROLL OF A PAIR OF DICE.

WHAT IS YOUR GUESS? 7

FIRST DIE      SECOND DIE      TOTAL
1              6               7

YOU GUESSED RIGHT.  YOU WIN.

DO YOU WANT TO TRY AGAIN
(TYPE 1 FOR YES, 0 FOR NO)? 1

GUESS THE TOTAL ON THE NEXT
ROLL OF A PAIR OF DICE.

WHAT IS YOUR GUESS? 5

FIRST DIE      SECOND DIE      TOTAL
3              6               9

YOU GUESSED WRONG.  YOU LOSE.

DO YOU WANT TO TRY AGAIN
(TYPE 1 FOR YES, 0 FOR NO)? 0

END OF GAME
```

games, we can program a computer to play other gambling games such as roulette and keno, sports games such as football and baseball, and other games. Some of these are described in the programming problems at the end of the chapter.

7-5 Computer-assisted instruction

Another use of random numbers is in programs that help teach other subjects. Such programs are called *computer-assisted instruction*, or *CAI*, programs. CAI programs are used to help teach many subjects, including mathematics, spelling, reading, and science. In this section we introduce some basic ideas about CAI programs.

Many CAI programs are designed to provide drill and practice for the student. In such a program, a question or problem, which is chosen at random by the program, is displayed on the CRT screen. The student, who is at the keyboard, must answer the question. Then the program checks the answer to see if it is right or wrong. If the answer is right, the program goes on to the next question or problem. If the answer is wrong, the program tells the student the correct answer before going on.

To illustrate the idea of a CAI program, consider a simple program to provide drill and practice in elementary addition. The program displays five random addition problems involving the integers 0 through 9 and asks the student for the sum for each problem. The program checks the student's answer for each problem and counts how many problems the student got right and how many wrong. The program is shown in Figure 7-11 and its flowchart in Figure 7-12.

In this program, a loop is used to produce the five addition problems. In the loop, the program generates two random integers between 0 and 9 using the RND function. Then the program displays an addition problem with these numbers and accepts the student's answer. Next the student's answer is compared with the actual sum. If the answer is correct, a message is displayed and 1 is added to the count of the number of correct answers. If the answer is not correct, a different message is displayed along with the correct answer, and 1 is added to the count of the number of incorrect answers. After the loop is repeated five times, the total number of correct and incorrect answers is displayed. The results from running the program are shown in Figure 7-13.

This program is very simple, but there are many things we can do to make

Figure 7-11. A simple addition drill and practice program

```
100 REM - ADDITION PRACTICE PROGRAM
110 REM - VARIABLES:
120 REM        N1 = FIRST NUMBER
130 REM        N2 = SECOND NUMBER
140 REM        S  = SUM
150 REM        A  = STUDENT'S ANSWER
160 REM        T1 = TOTAL CORRECT ANSWERS
170 REM        T2 = TOTAL INCORRECT ANSWERS
180 REM        I  = COUNTER
200 RANDOMIZE
210 PRINT "ADDITION PRACTICE"
220 PRINT
230 PRINT "GIVE THE SUM FOR EACH PROBLEM"
240 LET T1=0
250 LET T2=0
260 FOR I=1 TO 5
270    REM - GENERATE TWO RANDOM INTEGERS (0 TO 9)
280    LET N1=INT(10*RND)
290    LET N2=INT(10*RND)
300    REM - DISPLAY ADDITION PROBLEM WITH RANDOM INTEGERS
310    PRINT
320    PRINT N1;"+";N2;"= ";
330    REM - ACCEPT STUDENT'S ANSWER
340    INPUT A
350    PRINT
360    REM - COMPUTE SUM OF RANDOM INTEGERS
370    LET S=N1+N2
380    REM - DETERMINE IF STUDENT'S ANSWER IS CORRECT
390    IF A=S THEN 440
400      PRINT "INCORRECT ANSWER"
410      PRINT "THE CORRECT ANSWER IS";S
420      LET T2=T2+1
430    GOTO 460
440      PRINT "CORRECT ANSWER"
450      LET T1=T1+1
460 NEXT I
470 PRINT
480 PRINT "TOTAL CORRECT ANSWERS:";T1
490 PRINT "TOTAL INCORRECT ANSWERS:";T2
500 PRINT
510 PRINT "END OF PRACTICE"
999 END
```

Figure 7-12. Flowchart of the simple addition drill and practice program

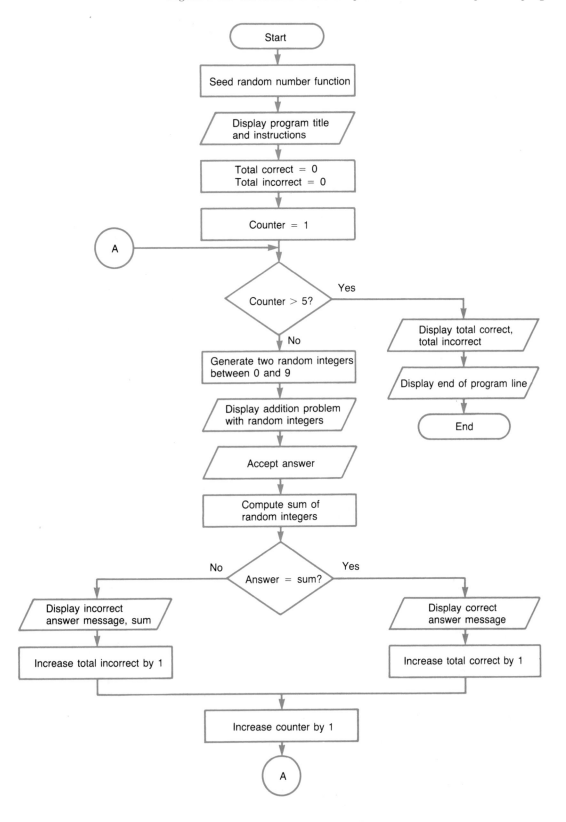

Figure 7-13. Running the simple addition drill and practice program

```
ADDITION PRACTICE

GIVE THE SUM FOR EACH PROBLEM

 8 + 0 = ? 8

CORRECT ANSWER

 5 + 2 = ? 7

CORRECT ANSWER

 2 + 8 = ? 10

CORRECT ANSWER

 5 + 4 = ? 7

INCORRECT ANSWER
THE CORRECT ANSWER IS 9

 6 + 1 = ? 7

CORRECT ANSWER

TOTAL CORRECT ANSWERS: 4
TOTAL INCORRECT ANSWERS: 1

END OF PRACTICE
```

it more sophisticated. For example, we can give the student several chances to get the correct answer before going on. We can also design the program so that problems get more difficult as the student improves. We can include subtraction, multiplication, and division problems in the program. There are many variations that can be included in a program such as this.

7-6 Computer simulation

Simulation is the technique of representing the functioning of one thing by using another. In the case of a computer simulation, we use a computer program to represent the operation of some process or system. For example, we can write a program that simulates an oil-refining process. Other examples of computer simulations are programs that simulate the service of customers at a supermarket check-out stand or at a bank window. Computer programs that play games as described in Section 7-4 are also types of simulations, and CAI programs, discussed in Section 7-5, can be thought of as simulating a teacher. In fact, we can use a computer to simulate many things, including manufacturing processes, business operations, ecological systems, spaceship flight, political situations, and economic systems.

There are several advantages to using computer simulations. For one, we can see how a system may behave without actually observing the real situation. Although the simulation cannot predict what will actually happen, it can give us some idea of the behavior of the system. We can also learn what may happen if we vary one or more of the factors that affect the system. For example, if we are simulating the customer check-out at a supermarket, we can see the effect of adding another check-out stand.

There are two basic types of simulation — *deterministic* and *stochastic* (or *probabilistic*). The difference has to do with whether or not uncertainty or randomness is incorporated into the simulation. Uncertainty is used in stochastic simulation but not in deterministic simulation. In this section we give examples of both types of simulation.

Deterministic simulation

Assume that there are currently 5000 people living on an isolated island. If the birth rate is 7% per year and the death rate 3%, what will the population of the island be after each of the next ten years? This problem involves simulating the population of the island. The birth and death rates are assumed to be fixed, hence there is no uncertainty about how many people will be born or will die each year. Thus, this is a deterministic simulation.

The program in Figure 7-14 solves the problem. The variable P represents the population, which is initially 5000. B is the number of births in a year (computed in statement 240) and D is the number of deaths (computed in statement 250). Notice that the number of births and the number of deaths have been rounded (half-adjusted). Each year the number of births is added to the population and the number of deaths is subtracted to get the new population (statement 260). The output from the program shows the year and the population at the end of the year for each of the next ten years.

Figure 7-14. A population simulation program

```
100 REM - POPULATION SIMULATION PROGRAM
110 REM - VARIABLES:
120 REM      P = POPULATION
130 REM      Y = YEAR
140 REM      B = NUMBER OF BIRTHS
150 REM      D = NUMBER OF DEATHS
200 LET P=5000
210 PRINT "YEAR","POPULATION"
220 PRINT
230 FOR Y=1 TO 10
240    LET B=INT(.07*P+.5)
250    LET D=INT(.03*P+.5)
260    LET P=P+B-D
270    PRINT Y,P
280 NEXT Y
999 END
```

(a) The program

YEAR	POPULATION
1	5200
2	5408
3	5625
4	5850
5	6084
6	6327
7	6580
8	6844
9	7118
10	7402

(b) Output

Besides using this program to answer the original question, we can use it to determine what would happen to the population if the birth or death rate were to change. For example, what would be the effect of a decreased birth rate (due, perhaps, to the introduction of family-planning techniques) or of an increased death rate (perhaps due to a new disease)? Questions such as these can be answered by slight modifications in the program.

The problem that this program solves is relatively simple and can also be solved using a method other than simulation. Such methods, called *analytic solutions*, involve using mathematical formulas. However, as the problem becomes more complex, it is less likely that there will be an analytic solution, and simulation must be used.†

This program demonstrates the basic idea of deterministic simulation. Although most programs for such simulation are more complex, they all have the characteristic that uncertainty or randomness is not used in the program.

Stochastic simulation

With stochastic simulation, random numbers are used to produce uncertainty in a program. By using the RND function we can develop stochastic simulation programs.

Programs that play games of chance as discussed in Section 7-4 are examples of stochastic simulations. For example, we can think of a program that generates a random integer between 1 and 6 as simulating the roll of a die. Similar techniques are used to simulate the shuffling of a deck of cards, the spinning of a roulette wheel, and so forth.

Besides games, we often use stochastic simulation to simulate the behavior of other types of systems. A common problem is to simulate a queuing system. A *queue* is a waiting line. For example, a queue is formed when customers wait to be checked out at a supermarket or for service by a bank teller. A *queuing system* consists of a queue plus the facility that serves the customers in the queue (for example, the supermarket checker or the bank teller). Figure 7-15 illustrates this idea. Customers arrive and go to the end of the queue. The service facility serves the first customer in the queue, who departs after being served. The queue increases in length when a customer arrives and decreases when a customer is served.

There are two main sources of uncertainty in a queuing system. One is the arrival of customers: we may not know for certain how often customers will arrive. The other is the service facility: the amount of time that it takes to serve a customer may be unknown. Because of these uncertainties, any simulation of a queuing system requires the use of randomness in the program and hence is a stochastic simulation.

The objective in simulating a queuing system is to answer questions such as the following:

1. What is the average number of customers in the queue?

Figure 7-15. A queuing system

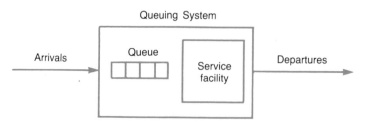

† An example of a complex deterministic simulation can be found in the book *Limits to Growth* by D. H. Meadows et al., published by Signet.

2. What is the average length of time that a customer must wait in the queue?

3. What percentage of the time will the service facility not be serving a customer (i.e., will the queue be empty)?

These questions can be answered by simulating the behavior of the queuing system.

To illustrate the technique, assume that in a five-minute period, it is equally likely that 1, 2, 3, 4, or 5 customers arrive. In addition, assume that the service facility can serve 3 customers in a five-minute period. The service facility is open five hours per day. We need to write a stochastic simulation program that determines the average length of the queue at the end of each five-minute period on each day of a five-day week.

The program that does this simulation is shown in Figure 7-16 and its flowchart in Figure 7-17. The program uses nested FOR loops. The outer loop controls the value of D, which represents the day. The inner loop controls the value of C (for "clock"), which counts the number of five-minute periods in the day. (There are 60 five-minute periods in a five-hour day.) L represents the length of the queue and T the total of

Figure 7-16. A queuing system simulation program

```
100 REM - QUEUING SYSTEM SIMULATION PROGRAM
110 REM - VARIABLES:
120 REM        D = DAY COUNTER
130 REM        L = LENGTH OF QUEUE
140 REM        T = TOTAL OF ALL QUEUE LENGTHS
150 REM        C = CLOCK COUNTER
160 REM        N = NUMBER OF ARRIVALS
200 RANDOMIZE
210 PRINT "DAY","AVE QUEUE LENGTH"
220 PRINT
230 REM - REPEAT LOOP FOR EACH DAY
240 FOR D=1 TO 5
250    LET L=0
260    LET T=0
270    REM - REPEAT LOOP FOR EACH 5 MIN PERIOD IN A DAY
280    FOR C=1 TO 60
290       LET N=INT(5*RND)+1
300       LET L=L+N
310       IF L>3 THEN 340
320          LET L=0
330       GOTO 350
340          LET L=L-3
350       LET T=T+L
360    NEXT C
370    LET A=T/60
380    PRINT D,A
390 NEXT D
999 END
```

(a) The program

DAY	AVE QUEUE LENGTH
1	1.33333
2	3.66667
3	6.21667
4	5.43333
5	3.38333

(b) Output

Figure 7-17. Flowchart of the queuing system simulation program

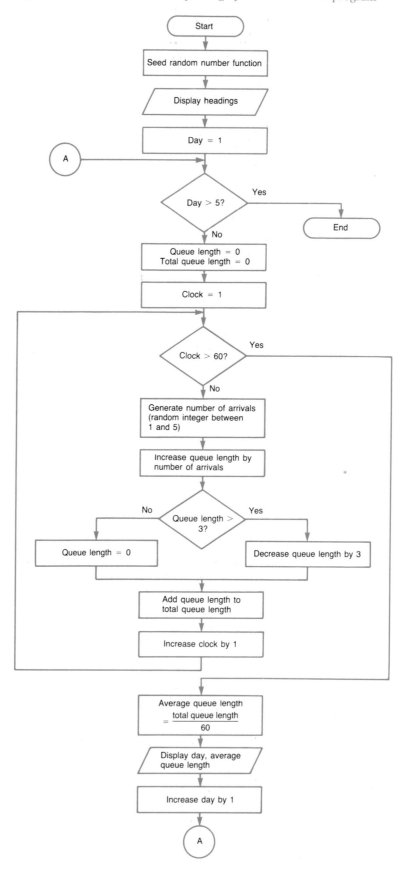

all queue lengths. At the beginning of each day, the values of L and T are set to zero.

During each five-minute period of the day, the number of arrivals (N) must be determined. Because it is equally likely that 1, 2, 3, 4, or 5 customers arrive, we need to generate a random integer between 1 and 5 for the value of N. This is done in statement 290. Then, in statement 300, N is added to L to increase the queue length by the number of arrivals. Next we reduce the queue length by the number of customers served. If there are more than 3 customers in the queue, exactly 3 customers are served (statement 340). If there are 3 or fewer customers waiting, all are served, reducing the queue length to zero (statement 320). Finally, the total of all queue lengths (T) is increased by the value of L at the end of a five-minute period (statement 350).

After each day is completed, the value of T is divided by 60 (the number of five-minute periods in the day) to obtain the average queue length (A). This is displayed along with the number of the day (D). Then the program repeats for the next day.

This program demonstrates the basic idea of stochastic simulation. The system simulated by this program is relatively simple, and in fact, there is an analytic solution to the problem of average queue length for this system; simulation is not really needed. For more complex systems, however, analytic solutions do not always exist, and simulation must be used. The technique described in this section is the basis for more complex simulations.

Review questions

1. What built-in functions are available in the version of BASIC you are using?
2. Assume that the value of A is 3, B is 4, and C is 5. What is the value of each of the following?
   a. SQR(B)
   b. SQR(A*C + 10)
   c. ABS(A − C)
   d. SGN(B − 4)
   e. SIN(12 − A*B)
   f. EXP(LOG(B − A))
3. Code a statement that is equivalent to the following algebraic equation:

$$c = \sqrt{a^2 + b^2}$$

   Use a built-in function.
4. Assume that X is 6.8, Y is 4.6, and Z is 2.1. What is the value of each of the following:
   a. INT(X)
   b. INT(Y/Z)
   c. INT(Z − X)
   d. INT(Y + .3333)
5. Code a statement that half-adjusts the value of X and assigns the result to Y.
6. Assume that S is a variable with a positive value. Code a single statement that rounds the value of S to one decimal position and assigns the result to T. For example, if the value of S is 25.578, then T should be assigned the value 25.6.
7. Code a group of statements that computes the length of a room in yards and feet, given the length in feet. For example, if the length is 17 feet, the result should be 5 yards and 2 feet.
8. What is a random number?
9. Code a BASIC statement that generates a random integer between 1 and 52.
10. Code a BASIC statement that generates random numbers between 100 and 200.
11. What does it mean to seed a random number function?

12. Code a statement to seed the random number function.
13. Think of a game not mentioned in the text. If a computer program were written to play the game, would the program determine the play by chance, by strategy, or by some combination of these?
14. What is CAI?
15. What is the difference between deterministic simulation and stochastic simulation?
16. What is a queuing system?

Programming problems

1. The economic order quantity represents the most economical quantity of inventory that should be ordered for each item in stock. The formula for calculating the economic order quantity is as follows:

$$Q = \sqrt{\frac{2 \times R \times S}{H}}$$

In this formula Q is the quantity ordered, R is the demand rate, S is the set-up or ordering cost, and H is the inventory holding cost. If C represents unit cost, the average cost per unit of inventory held is given by the following formula:

$$A = C + \frac{S}{Q} + \frac{H \times Q}{2 \times R}$$

Write a BASIC program to calculate the economic order quantity and the average cost per unit when this quantity is ordered. Input data is the inventory item number and the values of R, S, H, and C. Display the item number, economic order quantity, and average cost per unit.

Use the following data to test the program:

Item number	Demand rate	Set-up cost	Holding cost	Unit cost
12163	1025	$ 75	$ 60	$ 25
13841	500	$250	$150	$125
17213	2250	$120	$ 36	$ 10
19461	125	$450	$230	$195

2. A projectile that is fired with an initial velocity v at an angle θ reaches a maximum height h in time t given by the following formulas:

$$h = \frac{1}{2} \frac{v^2 \sin^2 \theta}{32}$$

$$t = \frac{v \sin \theta}{32}$$

The sine of an angle is found using the SIN function; the angle must be in radians. (One radian equals 57.2958 degrees.)

Write a BASIC program that accepts the values of v and θ (in degrees) and computes h and t. The program should display the values of v, θ (in degrees), h, and t. Use the following input data to test the program:

Velocity	Angle
247.38	45
100.00	72.5
360.00	0
282.61	90
75.32	25.6

3. Using the equations in Problem 2, write a BASIC program that displays a table listing the values of θ from 0 to 90 degrees in 5-degree increments along with the corresponding values of h and t. Use an initial velocity of 247.38 to test the program.

4. Write a BASIC program that converts seconds into hours, minutes, and seconds remaining. Input should be the amount of time in seconds. Output should be the number of seconds and its equivalent in hours, minutes, and seconds remaining. For example, 4372 seconds is equivalent to one hour, twelve minutes, and 52 seconds. Test the program using 28,635 seconds.

5. There are 3.281 feet in a meter and 0.3937 inches in a centimeter. Write a BASIC program that accepts a distance in feet and inches and computes and displays the equivalent distance in meters and centimeters. Give the answer in whole meters and centimeters rounded to the nearest centimeter. Test the program with the distance six feet, nine inches.

6. A classic problem in computer programming is the "automatic change-maker" problem. The problem involves determining the breakdown of a customer's change into various denominations.

   Write an interactive BASIC program that solves the automatic change-maker problem. The program should accept a customer's number, the amount of the customer's bill, and the cash payment. Then the program should display the customer's number, the amount of the bill, the payment, and the change, if any. If there is no change, an appropriate message should be displayed. Similarly, if the payment is less than the bill, a message should be displayed.

   For each transaction in which there is change, the program should display the number and kind of each denomination in the change. The total number of bills and coins should be kept to a minimum. Assume that only pennies ($.01), nickels ($.05), dimes ($.10), quarters ($.25), and one-dollar bills are available for change.

   Use the following data to test the program:

Customer's number	Customer's bill	Payment
1234	$ 3.59	$ 5.00
2345	8.00	8.00
3456	14.95	14.00
4567	21.03	25.00
5678	9.95	50.00
6789	.29	1.00

7. Write a BASIC program that finds the day of the week for any date in the twentieth century. Input to the program is the month, day, and year of any date between 1900 and 1999. The month should be numeric and the year should be two digits. For example, January 21, 1946, should be entered as 01,21,46. Output should give the day of the week for the given date (e.g., MONDAY).

   The procedure to find the day of the week is as follows. Add the year, one-fourth of the year (truncated), the day of the month, and the code for the month from the following table:

Month	Code
June	0
Sept., Dec.	1
April, July	2
Jan., Oct.	3
May	4
Aug.	5
Feb., March, Nov.	6

   If the year is a leap year (that is, if it is evenly divisible by four), the code is one less for January and February.

   From the sum subtract two and divide the result by seven. The remainder from the division is the day of the week with 0 denoting Saturday, 1 Sunday, 2 Monday, and so forth.

For example, the day of the week for January 21, 1946, is found as follows:

Year	46
1/4 of year	11
Day of month	21
Code	<u>3</u>
Subtotal	81
Subtract	<u>2</u>
Total	79

Dividing 79 by 7 gives 11 with a remainder of 2. Hence, January 21, 1946, was a Monday.

Test the program with the following dates:

October 25, 1978
March 7, 1944
December 6, 1973
April 18, 1906
January 1, 1984
February 29, 1952

8. Write a BASIC program to generate 1000 random numbers. In the program, count the number of random numbers that are between 0 and .1, between .1 and .2, between .2 and .3, and so forth. Display the counts.

9. Write a BASIC program to generate 10,000 tosses of a pair of dice. In the program, count the number of times that the dice show a total of 2, 3, 4, . . ., 12. Divide each answer by 10,000 to get an estimate of the probability that the dice will show each total. Display the results.

10. Write a BASIC program to play a simple number-guessing game. The program should generate a random integer between 1 and 100. The objective is for the player to guess what integer has been generated in as few guesses as possible. Each guess should be compared to the random integer until the correct value is entered. Keep track of the number of guesses and display this number after the random integer has been guessed.

11. Write a BASIC program to play roulette. Each spin of the wheel can be simulated by generating a random integer between -1 and 36 with -1 counting as 00. Assume that odd numbers are red and even numbers are black. The program should accept any bet and "pay off" according to the rules of the game.

12. Write a BASIC program to play the dice game "craps." The program should accept any bet and "pay off" according to the rules of the game.

13. This problem involves using arrays, which are discussed in Chapter 9. Write a BASIC program that sets up a 52-element array to represent the 52 cards of a deck. Then "shuffle" the deck by generating random integers between 1 and 52 and assigning each integer to the next element of the array. You will have to use a second array to keep track of each integer that is generated, so that the same number is not assigned to different elements of the array. Assume that the numbers 1 to 13 represent one suit, 14 to 26 represent another suit, and so forth. Then display the shuffled deck with each card's value and suit.

14. Using the program logic developed in Problem 13, write a BASIC program to play "blackjack" (or "twenty-one"). The program should accept any bet and "pay off" according to the rules of the game.

15. Write a BASIC program to assist a person in learning to subtract. The program should generate two random integers. The first random integer should be between 0 and 9. The second should also be between 0 and 9 but should be less than or equal to the first. The integers should be displayed in the form of a subtraction problem with the second integer being subtracted from the first. The answer entered at the keyboard should be compared with the correct answer computed by the program, and a message should be displayed indicating whether the answer is correct. The program should repeat for a total of ten subtraction problems and display the total number of correct and incorrect answers at the end.

16. Write a BASIC program to assist a person in learning to multiply. The program should allow the person to select the difficulty of the multiplication problems that are dis-

played. There are three levels of difficulty: problems involving multiplication of one-digit numbers, problems involving multiplication of two-digit numbers, and problems involving multiplication of three-digit numbers. The program should display ten problems of the difficulty selected, count the number of correct and incorrect answers, and display these counts.

17. Write a BASIC program like the one required in Problem 16 but with the program deciding the difficulty based on previous performance. The program should start with the easiest problems and go to more difficult ones only if the person using the program gets eight or more correct answers. If the person gets fewer than six correct answers on more difficult problems, the program should go to less difficult ones. (You may wish to include more than three levels of difficulty. For example, you can include problems that involve multiplying a two-digit number by a one-digit number, problems that do not involve carrying, etc.)

18. Assume that rabbits reproduce at the rate of 20% per month until overpopulation occurs, at which time they begin dying at the rate of 15% per month. Rabbits continue to die at this rate until their population is reduced by one-third, at which time they begin reproducing again. Write a program to simulate the rabbit population for 48 months. Assume that there are initially 1000 rabbits and overpopulation occurs when there are more than 3000 rabbits.

19. Modify the simulation program in Figure 7-16 to determine the percentage of time that the service facility is not serving a customer (i.e., that the queue is empty).

20. The simulation program in Figure 7-16 assumes that the service facility can serve exactly 3 customers in a five-minute period. Modify the program to include the assumption that the number of customers served is 2, 3, or 4 with equal likelihood.

21. Write a BASIC program to simulate a queuing system in which there are three service facilities and three queues. Design the program so that a customer goes to the end of the shortest queue. Determine the average length of time that the customer waits for service. Then modify the program so that there are three facilities but only one queue, with the customer at the front of the queue going to the next available facility. Again, determine the average amount of time that the customer waits for service.

22. Inventory is the stock of goods that a business has on hand. Assume that a business initially has 50 units in stock. Each day 1 to 5 units are sold with equal likelihood. When the stock falls below 10 units, another 50 are ordered. The order takes two, three, or four days to arrive with equal likelihood. Write a BASIC program to simulate the inventory over a period of 100 days. Display the day number, the sales for the day, the quantity on order (if any) that day, the quantity received (if any) that day, and the stock on hand at the end of the day. Assume that if there are more potential sales during the day than there is stock on hand, only the available stock is sold (i.e., the inventory cannot become negative). Also assume that any order is received at the beginning of the day, before the first sales.

Chapter 8

Strings

In many programs it is necessary to process character data—that is, data that consists of letters and symbols other than numbers. For example, input and output of character data such as a person's name and address may be required in a program. As another example, a program may have to accept character data that is entered in response to an input prompt and then analyze the data to determine what is to be done next. In BASIC, such character data is called *string data.* In this chapter we describe the features of BASIC that are used for input, output, and processing of string data. After completing this chapter you should be able to write programs that use these features.

8-1 String data

A *character string*, or simply a *string*, is a group of characters. Any character that can be stored in the computer *except* a quotation mark can be in a string. (Some versions of BASIC have provisions for including quotation marks in a string.) For example, all the following are strings:

```
ABC
X37Z$
JOHN'S
New York
1881
```

Notice that both upper and lowercase letters can be included in a string. In addition, a blank space can be part of a string because it is a character. In fact, one or more blanks without any other characters forms a string. It is also possible to have a string that does not have any characters in it. This is called a *null string* or *empty string*. Finally, notice that a string can consist entirely of numbers, as shown in the last example.

String constants

A *string constant* is a string enclosed in quotation marks. For example, the following are valid string constants:

```
"ABC"
"X37Z$"
"JOHN'S"
"New York"
"1881"
" "
""
```

Notice that a number enclosed in quotation marks is a string constant. The next-to-last example shows a string constant that consists of a single blank space. The last example has no characters between the quotation marks. This is a *null-string constant* or *empty-string constant*.

The maximum length of a string in a string constant depends on the version of BASIC. (See Table 8-1.) In some versions, the string length is limited by the maximum length of a statement; that is, the total number of characters in a statement, including any characters in a string constant, cannot exceed the limit. In other versions, strings can be no longer than a certain number of characters. In both of these cases a string can be continued onto another line. (See the discussion of multiple-line statements in Section 3-5.) In some versions of BASIC, however, a string cannot be continued onto another line. In these versions, string length is limited by the length of a terminal line.

We have already seen one use of string constants in a program. In Section 2-3 we showed how character output can be produced by enclosing the words and symbols to be displayed in quotation marks in a PRINT statement. In fact, we were using a string constant in the PRINT statement. For example, the following statement contains a string constant:

```
80 PRINT "THE ANSWER IS",X
```

Execution of this statement causes the string THE ANSWER IS to be displayed followed by the value of X. Notice that the quotation marks are not part of the string and are not displayed. We will see other uses of string constants in this chapter.

String variables

A *string variable* is a variable that is used to refer to a string. A string variable is formed from a regular variable followed by a dollar sign. For example, A$, N3$, and Z8$ are string variables. Note that A$ is a variable that identifies string data, whereas A is a variable that refers to numeric data. Both can be used in the same program.

Table 8-1. String constant differences

BASIC version	*Maximum length of a string in a string constant*
ANS minimal BASIC	Limited by maximum length of a statement (72 characters)
ANS BASIC	Limited by maximum length of a statement (depends on computer)
Microsoft BASIC	255 characters
Applesoft BASIC	255 characters
True BASIC	32,000 characters
BASIC-PLUS	Limited by length of a terminal line
VAX-11 BASIC	Limited by length of a terminal line

Table 8-2. String variable differences

BASIC version	String variable syntax
ANS minimal BASIC	A letter followed by a dollar sign
ANS BASIC Microsoft BASIC Applesoft BASIC True BASIC BASIC-PLUS VAX-11 BASIC	Any valid variable ending with a dollar sign

In most versions of BASIC any variable followed by a dollar sign forms a string variable. Some versions of BASIC, however, limit a string variable to a single letter followed by a dollar sign. (See Table 8-2.) In such versions A$ would be a valid string variable but N3$ would be invalid. If long variables are available in a version of BASIC, they can be used for string variables so long as they end with a dollar sign. For example, NAME$ is a valid string variable in some versions of BASIC. (See Section 2-1 for a discussion of long variables.)

The LET statement with string data

We can assign a string to a string variable using a LET statement. For example, the following statement assigns the string THE ANSWER IS to the string variable A$:

```
70 LET A$="THE ANSWER IS"
```

Notice in the LET statement that a string variable appears on the left of the equal sign and a string constant is on the right. After execution of this statement, the value of the string variable A$ will be the string THE ANSWER IS. We can also assign the value of one string variable to another string variable. For example, the following statement assigns the value of A$ to B$:

```
75 LET B$=A$
```

The maximum length of a string that can be assigned to a string variable depends on the version of BASIC. (See Table 8-3.) Note that in some versions of

Table 8-3. String assignment differences

BASIC version	Maximum length of a string that can be assigned to a string variable
ANS minimal BASIC	18 characters
ANS BASIC	Depends on computer
Microsoft BASIC	255 characters
Applesoft BASIC	255 characters
True BASIC	32,000 characters
BASIC-PLUS	32,767 characters, provided sufficient internal storage is available
VAX-11 BASIC	65,535 characters, provided sufficient internal storage is available

BASIC it is possible to assign strings that are longer than the maximum string constant to a string variable. This is accomplished by the use of features discussed later in this chapter.

The minimum length of a string that can be assigned to a string variable is zero characters. This is the case when we assign the null string to a string variable, as in the following example:

```
200 LET C$=""
```

String data vs. numeric data

In previous chapters we have concentrated on *numeric data*—that is, data that consists of numeric values. The types of variables that we have used to refer to numeric data are called *numeric variables*, and constants representing numeric data are called *numeric constants*. Note that a numeric variable never ends with a dollar sign and a numeric constant is never enclosed in quotation marks.

It is important to distinguish between numeric variables and string variables and between numeric constants and string constants. For example, consider the following statements:

```
210 LET X=15
220 LET X$="15"
```

The first statement assigns a numeric constant to a numeric variable; the second assigns a string constant to a string variable. Even though the characters in the constants are the same (i.e., 15), they represent different types of data. The string constant ("15") can be assigned only to a string variable, and the numeric constant (15) can be assigned only to a numeric variable. In addition, string constants and variables *cannot* be used in numeric calculations; only numeric constants and variables can be used for this purpose. Note, however, that the same letter can be used for both a numeric variable and a string variable in a program without difficulty; the dollar sign is sufficient to distinguish between the two variables.

String input and output

As we know, the value of a string can be displayed by using a string constant in a PRINT statement. We can also use a string variable in a PRINT statement. For example, consider the following statement:

```
80 PRINT A$,X
```

The effect of execution of this statement is that the value of the string variable A\$ is displayed followed by the value of the numeric variable X. If A\$ is assigned the string THE ANSWER IS, this string is displayed when this statement is executed. As many string variables as are needed can be included in a PRINT statement. In addition, string and numeric variables can be intermixed without difficulty in one PRINT statement. Thus, a statement such as the following is valid:

```
90 PRINT S,T,B$,U,C$
```

The value of a string constant or variable can be printed on paper with a printer. As discussed in Section 2-3, the approach used for printer output depends on the version of BASIC. A string constant or variable can be used with any approach, including the LPRINT statement.

We can accept a string as input data by using a string variable in an INPUT statement. For example, consider the following statement:

```
10 INPUT N$
```

When this statement is executed, a question-mark prompt is displayed on the CRT screen. A string must be entered following the question mark. In most cases, the string may be enclosed in quotation marks or the marks may be omitted. For example, the following input might be entered;

```
? JOHN
```

After the RETURN key is pressed, the computer accepts the data and assigns it to the string variable N$.

Quotation marks are optional around the string input except when the data contains a comma or when spaces to the left or right are part of the string. For example, assume that the following statement is executed:

```
20 INPUT D$
```

The string input that is to be entered is a date that begins with two spaces and ends with three spaces. In addition, a comma separates the day and the year. The data must then be enclosed in quotation marks, as shown in the following example:

```
? "  SEPT. 1, 1980   "
```

Note that quotation marks can be used even when they are not required.

We can use string variables and numeric variables in the same INPUT statement. For example, the following statement is valid:

```
30 INPUT N,N$,D$,A
```

The important thing is for the data to be entered in the same order as the variables in the INPUT statement. Thus, in this example the first and last values entered must be numbers, and the second and third values must be strings.

An illustrative program

Figure 8-1 shows an example of a program that uses string input and output. This is a simple payroll program that accepts and displays the employee's name along with other data. (This program is a variation of the one shown in Figure 2-17.) Notice that the string variable N$ is used for the input and output of the name in statements 180 and 250.

Figure 8-1. A payroll program with string input and output

```
100 REM - PAYROLL PROGRAM
110 REM - VARIABLES:
120 REM      I  = EMPLOYEE ID
130 REM      N$ = EMPLOYEE NAME
140 REM      H  = HOURS WORKED
150 REM      G  = GROSS PAY
160 REM      W  = WITHHOLDING TAX
170 REM      P  = NET PAY
180 INPUT I,N$,H
190    LET G=6.5*H
200    LET W=.18*G
210    LET P=G-W
```

(continued)

Figure 8-1. Continued

```
220    PRINT
230    PRINT "PAYROLL DATA FOR EMPLOYEE",I
240    PRINT
250    PRINT "   NAME",N$
260    PRINT "   GROSS PAY",G
270    PRINT "   TAX",W
280    PRINT "   NET PAY",P
290    PRINT
300 GOTO 180
310 END
```

(a) The program

```
? 234,JOHNSON,32

PAYROLL DATA FOR EMPLOYEE      234

     NAME        JOHNSON
     GROSS PAY   208
     TAX         37.44
     NET PAY     170.56

? 456,SMITH,48

PAYROLL DATA FOR EMPLOYEE      456

     NAME        SMITH
     GROSS PAY   312
     TAX         56.16
     NET PAY     255.84

? 678,JONES,36

PAYROLL DATA FOR EMPLOYEE      678

     NAME        JONES
     GROSS PAY   234
     TAX         42.12
     NET PAY     191.88

?
```

(b) Input and output

8-2 Comparing string data

One of the important uses of string data is in relational expressions. String constants and variables can appear on both sides of a relational operator. The result is that the string data is compared to determine the truth value of the relational expression. All six of the relational operators discussed in Section 3-1 can be used with string data. For example, the following are valid relational expressions:

```
N$="JOHN"
R$<>"YES"
X$<Y$
"A"<=B$
"WXYZ">U$
V$>="AA"
```

This section explains the meaning of such expressions.

Equal comparison

When the = or <> relational operator is used with string data, a comparison is made to determine if the data consists of identical characters in identical positions. If they do, the values are equal. If the string data is not identical, the values are not equal. For example, in the expression

```
N$="JOHN"
```

if the value of N$ is JOHN, the expression is true, but if N$ is JEAN, the expression is false.

Figure 8-2 shows an example of the use of this type of comparison in a program that determines tuition for a college student. In this example, the input consists of each student's identification number (I) and his or her state of residence (S$), which is a two-character code. Tuition is based on whether or not the student is a California resident. If the student is a California resident, the tuition is $350. Out-of-state residents pay a tuition of $800. The IF statement compares the string variable S$

Figure 8-2. A tuition-calculation program with string comparison

```
100 REM - TUITION CALCULATION PROGRAM
110 REM - VARIABLES:
120 REM       I  = STUDENT ID
130 REM       S$ = STATE OF RESIDENCE
140 REM       R$ = RESIDENCE STATUS
150 REM       T  = TUITION
160 INPUT I,S$
170    IF S$="CA" THEN 210
180      LET T=800
190      LET R$="NONRESIDENT"
200    GOTO 230
210      LET T=350
220      LET R$="RESIDENT"
230    PRINT "STUDENT ID:",I
240    PRINT "TUITION:",T
250    PRINT "STATUS:",R$
260 GOTO 160
270 END
```

(a) The program

```
? 2345,CA
STUDENT ID:    2345
TUITION:       350
STATUS:        RESIDENT
? 4567,IL
STUDENT ID:    4567
TUITION:       800
STATUS:        NONRESIDENT
? 6789,CA
STUDENT ID:    6789
TUITION:       350
STATUS:        RESIDENT
? 8901,NY
STUDENT ID:    8901
TUITION:       800
STATUS:        NONRESIDENT
?
```

(b) Input and output

with the string constant "CA", which is the code for California. The value assigned to the tuition (T) is based on whether this comparison is true or false. A string equal to the word RESIDENT or NONRESIDENT is assigned to the string variable R$ based on this comparison. The value of this string variable is displayed along with the other output. Note that we could use the <> relational operator in this example. Then the decision in the program would be as follows:

```
170     IF S$<>"CA" THEN 210
180        LET T=350
190        LET R$="RESIDENT"
200     GOTO 230
210        LET T=800
220        LET R$="NONRESIDENT"
```

All types of characters — letters, digits, and special characters including blanks — can be compared. For example, the following expression is valid:

```
I$="X3 ?5"
```

This expression is true if the value of I$ is the characters X, 3, blank, ?, and 5 in that order. As another example, the following relational expression determines if X$ is not all blanks:

```
X$<>"     "
```

Note that the string constant in this example contains all blank spaces.

Upper and lowercase letters can be compared. However, an uppercase letter is not equal to its corresponding lowercase letter. For example, consider the following relational expression:

```
N$="JOHN"
```

If the value of N$ is John, this expression is false. Only if N$ equals JOHN (i.e., all uppercase letters) is the expression true.

If the strings being compared are not the same length, the evaluation depends on the version of BASIC. (See Table 8-4.) In most versions of BASIC, strings that are not the same length are not equal. This is true even if the strings are the same except for extra blank spaces at the end of one string. For example, consider the following relational expression:

```
N$="JOHN "
```

Table 8-4. String comparison differences

BASIC version	Comparison of strings of different lengths
ANS minimal BASIC	Strings of different lengths are not equal.
ANS BASIC	Strings of different lengths are not equal.
Microsoft BASIC	Strings of different lengths are not equal.
Applesoft BASIC	Strings of different lengths are not equal.
True BASIC	Strings of different lengths are not equal.
BASIC-PLUS VAX-11 BASIC	Strings of different lengths are equal if all corresponding characters are the same except for extra blanks at the end of the longer string; otherwise the strings are not equal.

Here the string constant is JOHN with a blank space at the end. If the value of N\$ is JOHN without a blank space at the end, this expression is false. Only if N\$ is the characters J, O, H, N, and a blank, in that order, is the expression true. In some versions of BASIC, any extra blanks at the end of the longer string are ignored in the comparison. In these versions, the previous expression is true if the value of N\$ is JOHN without a blank space at the end.

When comparing string data, it is important to use only string constants and string variables. We cannot compare string data with numeric data. For example, the following relational expression is invalid because 123 is a numeric constant:

```
123=A$
```

This does not mean, however, that we cannot determine if A\$ equals 123. To do this we must make 123 a string constant by putting quotation marks around it. Hence the following relational expression is valid:

```
"123"=A$
```

Interactive program design. In Section 5-2 we discussed the design of interactive programs so that they are easy for the user to use. One common use of string comparison is in such programs to analyze the user's response to input prompts. For example, an interactive program is frequently designed so that the user is asked whether he or she wants the program to be repeated. The statement in the program to accomplish this might be something like the following:

```
340 INPUT "DO YOU WANT THE PROGRAM TO REPEAT";R$
```

When the INPUT statement is executed, the prompt is displayed followed by a question mark. Then the user must type YES or NO. The program accepts the string input and determines what to do based on the response. If the response is YES, the program must repeat. If the response is NO, the progam must end. The statements to accomplish this are as follows:

```
340 INPUT "DO YOU WANT THE PROGRAM TO REPEAT";R$
350 IF R$="YES" THEN 200
360 IF R$="NO" THEN 390
370 PRINT "PLEASE ANSWER YES OR NO."
380 GOTO 340
390 END
```

Notice that the prompt is repeated if a valid string is not entered.

Greater-than and less-than comparison

When the relational operator is $<$, $<=$, $>$, and $>=$, the evaluation of the relational expression is based on the ordering of the characters for the computer being used. This ordering is called the *collating sequence* and depends on the internal code used for the characters by the computer. Many computers use an internal code called the *American Standard Code for Information Interchange*, or *ASCII* code. There are 128 ASCII codes. The codes correspond to the numbers 0 through 127, and their numerical sequence is the collating sequence. Figure 8-3 lists the ASCII codes and the character each represents. Note that the codes 0 through 31 and 127 are for special control characters which are not normally displayed on a CRT screen.

When two characters are compared, one is less than the other if it is earlier in the ASCII collating sequence. Referring to Figure 8-3, we can see that for the

Figure 8-3. ASCII codes

ASCII	Character	ASCII	Character
0-31	(control characters)	80	P
32	(space)	81	Q
33	!	82	R
34	"	83	S
35	#	84	T
36	$	85	U
37	%	86	V
38	&	87	W
39	'	88	X
40	(	89	Y
41	)	90	Z
42	*	91	[
43	+	92	\
44	,	93	]
45	-	94	^
46	.	95	_
47	/	96	`
48	0	97	a
49	1	98	b
50	2	99	c
51	3	100	d
52	4	101	e
53	5	102	f
54	6	103	g
55	7	104	h
56	8	105	i
57	9	106	j
58	:	107	k
59	;	108	l
60	<	109	m
61	=	110	n
62	>	111	o
63	?	112	p
64	@	113	q
65	A	114	r
66	B	115	s
67	C	116	t
68	D	117	u
69	E	118	v
70	F	119	w
71	G	120	x
72	H	121	y
73	I	122	z
74	J	123	{
75	K	124	|
76	L	125	}
77	M	126	~
78	N	127	(control character)
79	O		

uppercase letters, the collating sequence is the alphabetic order. Thus, A is less than B, which is less than C, and so forth. Similarly, the collating sequence for the lowercase letters is the alphabetic order. Hence, a is less than b, which is less than c, and so on. All lowercase letters, however, come after the uppercase letters in the collating sequence. Hence, A is less than a, B is less than b, and so on. Notice that the collating sequence for the digits is the same as the numerical sequence. Thus, 0 is less than 1, 1 is less than 2, and so on, as we would expect. All digits, however, are less than all letters. Notice also that special characters appear at various positions in the collating sequence.

When two strings of several characters each are compared, the evaluation is done by comparing strings character-for-character, left-to-right. As soon as two corresponding characters are not equal to each other, the computer determines which string is the lesser on the basis of which of the unequal characters is earlier in the ASCII collating sequence. Thus, in comparing JEAN and JOHN, the computer examines the first character of each and determines that they are equal. It then compares the second character of each and determines that they are not equal. Then, because E is earlier in the collating sequence than O, the computer would indicate that JEAN is less than JOHN.

If we just consider the uppercase letters, one string is less than the other if it appears before the other in an alphabetical list. Thus, as we have just seen, the string JEAN is less than JOHN. Also, JOHN is less than MARY. Hence, the expression

        A$<"JOHN"

is true if A$ is JEAN, but false if it is JOHN or MARY.

When there are both upper and lowercase letters in the strings, the results may be different. Jean is less than John, as we would expect, but greater than JOHN because lowercase e is greater than uppercase O. Thus, in comparing alphabetic strings we have to be careful about the case of the letters in the strings. It is usually best if the letters are either all uppercase or all lowercase.

If a string contains a blank space, the blank is less than any other character. Hence, JOHN SMITH is less than JOHNNY JONES because the fifth character in the first string is a blank space, which is less than the fifth character in the second string which is an N.

A string of digits is evaluated in the same way as a string of letters. Thus, 123 is less than 456, as we would expect. But because a blank space is less than any other character, *b*9 is less than 8*b* (where *b* stands for a blank). Notice that comparing strings of digits can yield results different from those of comparing the corresponding numbers.

When a string contains a mixture of letters, digits, and special characters, the evaluation is done based on the collating sequence. For example, X37Z is less than XM7Z because the digit 3 is less than the letter M. Similarly, AB#5 is less than AB12 because the # symbol is less than the digit 1.

If one string is shorter than another and if all characters are the same up to the end of the string, the shorter string is less than the longer one. Thus, JOHN is less than JOHNNY. Note, however, that the longer string can be less than the shorter one if the characters are not the same. Thus, JOANNE is less than JOHN because the third character of JOANNE is less than the third character of JOHN. Figure 8-4 shows other examples of string comparison.

Figure 8-4. Examples of string comparison

Relational Expression	Truth Value
"ED JONES"<"ED SMITH"	True
"EDWARD JONES"<"ED SMITH"	False
"ED JONES"<"ED JON"	False
"1234">"4567"	False
"1234">" 4567"	True
" 1234">"4567"	False
"MARY"="MARY"	True
"MARY"="MARY "	False
"MARY"="MAR Y"	False
" "<>" "	True
"X37Z<>"2AY7"	True
"abc"<>"ABC"	True

Figure 8-5. A program that sorts three names

```
100 REM - NAME SORTING PROGRAM
110 REM - VARIABLES:
120 REM      N1$, N2$, N3$  = NAMES TO BE SORTED
130 REM      T$  = TEMPORARY VARIABLE
200 INPUT N1$,N2$,N3$
300 IF N1$<=N2$ THEN 350
310    LET T$=N1$
320    LET N1$=N2$
330    LET N2$=T$
350 IF N2$<=N3$ THEN 400
360    LET T$=N2$
370    LET N2$=N3$
380    LET N3$=T$
400 IF N1$<=N2$ THEN 500
410    LET T$=N1$
420    LET N1$=N2$
430    LET N2$=T$
500 PRINT N1$,N2$,N3$
999 END
```

(a) The program

```
? MARY,JOHN,JEAN
JEAN           JOHN           MARY
```

(b) Input and output

An illustrative program. One use of string comparison is to sort words or names into alphabetical order. In Section 6-4 we discussed a program that sorts the values of three numeric variables into ascending numerical order (see Figure 6-8). By substituting string variables for the numeric variables, we have a program to sort strings into ascending alphabetical order. The program, shown in Figure 8-5, accepts three strings as input. The strings may be in any order initially. Through a series of comparisons and switching of values, the strings are rearranged into the required sequence.

*8-3 Processing string data

So far we have used string data only in LET statements, for input and output, and in comparisons. String data can also be processed much as we process numeric data. In this section we describe the BASIC language elements for processing string data.

Substrings

A *substring* is a group of one or more adjacent characters in a string. For example, consider the string NEW YORK. The following are substrings of this string:

```
NEW
OR
YORK
EW YO
W
NEW YORK
```

Notice that any single character in a string is a substring and that the entire string is a substring of itself. Any group of characters that are adjacent to one another in a string also form a substring. However, if a group of characters from the string are not adjacent to each other, they do not form a substring. Thus, NOR is *not* a substring of NEW YORK, even though the characters come from the string.

In BASIC, a copy of a substring can be extracted from a string. The way this is done depends on the version of BASIC. (See Table 8-5.) The most common technique is to use functions such as LEFT$, RIGHT$, and MID$. Here we describe how these functions are used.

The form of the LEFT$ function is LEFT$(A$,N). [In some versions of BASIC the form is LEFT(A$,N).] This function extracts the leftmost N characters of the string A$. For example, if A$ is the string ABCDEF, then LEFT$(A$,3) is ABC. Notice that using this function (or any of the functions) does *not* change the value of the original string; only a copy of the substring is extracted. Thus, after the function is used in this example, A$ is still the string ABCDEF. Notice also that this function (as well as others) is not a statement by itself but must be used in a statement. The function can be used anywhere that a string variable or string constant can be used. Thus, the following statements are valid:

```
400 LET B$=LEFT$(A$,3)
410 PRINT LEFT$(A$,3)
420 IF C$=LEFT$(A$,3) THEN 500
```

The form of the RIGHT$ function is RIGHT$(A$,N). [In some versions of BASIC the form is RIGHT(A$,N).] The function extracts the rightmost N characters

Table 8-5. Substring extraction differences

BASIC version	Substring extraction
ANS minimal BASIC	Not available.
ANS BASIC	A$(M:N) — extracts the Mth through the Nth characters of A$.
Microsoft BASIC Applesoft BASIC	LEFT$(A$,N) — extracts the leftmost N characters of A$. RIGHT$(A$,N) — extracts the rightmost N characters of A$. MID$(A$,M,N) — extracts the N characters beginning with the Mth character of A$. If N is not included, all characters from the Mth through the end of the string are extracted.
True BASIC	A$(M:N) or A$[M:N] — extracts the Mth through the Nth characters of A$.
BASIC-PLUS	LEFT(A$,N) — extracts the leftmost N characters of A$. RIGHT(A$,N) — extracts the rightmost characters of A$ beginning with the Nth character. MID(A$,M,N) — extracts the N characters beginning with the Mth character of A$.
VAX-11 BASIC	LEFT(A$,N) or LEFT$(A$,N) — extracts the leftmost N characters of A$. RIGHT(A$,N) or RIGHT$(A$,N) — extracts the rightmost characters of A$ beginning with the Nth character. MID(A$,M,N) or MID$(A$,M,N) — extracts the N characters beginning with the Mth character of A$. SEG$(A$,M,N) — extracts the Mth through Nth characters of A$.

of the string A$. For example, if A$ is ABCDEF, then RIGHT$(A$,3) is DEF. [In some versions of BASIC, this function extracts the substring beginning with the Nth character of A$ through the end of A$. Then, if A$ is ABCDEF, RIGHT$(A$,3) is CDEF.]

The MID$ function extracts a substring from the middle of a string. The form of the function is MID$(A$,M,N). [In some versions of BASIC the form is MID(A$,M,N).] The function extracts the N characters from A$, beginning with the Mth character. For example, if A$ is ABCDEF, then MID$(A$,2,3) is BCD — that is, the three characters beginning with the second character in the string. A value for N may be left out, in which case the function extracts a substring beginning with the Mth character through the end of the string. Thus, if A$ is ABCDEF, then MID$(A$,2) is BCDEF. (In some versions of BASIC, a value for N is required.)

Notice that although they are convenient, we do not really need the LEFT$ and RIGHT$ functions. We can obtain the same results by just the MID$ function. For example, MID$(A$,1,3) is the same as LEFT$(A$,3) and, assuming A$ has 6 characters, MID$(A$,4,3) is the same as RIGHT$(A$,3).

Figure 8-6 shows other examples of substrings. Notice in the last example in this figure how a single-character substring can be extracted.

In the examples so far, we have used numeric constants to indicate the position of the substring. We can also use variables and expressions. For example, MID$(S$,I,J) is valid; the actual substring that is extracted depends on the values of I and J. Similarly, MID$(S$,I+2,3*I−1) is acceptable. The expressions in this example are evaluated using the current value of I, and then the indicated substring is found.

One use of substrings is to locate the position of a particular character or group of characters in a string. For example, assume that we want to know the location of the first blank space in a string named N$. This can be accomplished with the following loop:

```
150 LET I=1
160 IF MID$(N$,I,1)=" " THEN 190
170    LET I=I+1
180 GOTO 160
190 (next statement)
```

In this example the variable I is used to count through the characters in the string. I is initially set to 1, and I is incremented by 1 with each execution of the loop. In the loop, MID$(N$,I,1) extracts the Ith character in the string. When this character is a blank, the loop is terminated. Then the value of I is the position of the blank character.

We can use this procedure to rearrange a person's name. Figure 8-7 shows a program to do this. The input to the program is a name beginning with the first name, then a blank space, and finally the last name. The program locates the position of the blank space and then rearranges the name in the PRINT statement. The output is displayed with the last name first, a comma, and then the first name.

Figure 8-6. Examples of substrings

S$="WASHINGTON"	
Function	Substring
MID$(S$,3,5)	SHING
LEFT$(S$,4) } MID$(S$,1,4)}	WASH
RIGHT$(S$,3)} MID$(S$,8,3)}	TON
MID$(S$,6,1)	N

Figure 8-7. A program that rearranges a name

```
100 REM - NAME REARRANGEMENT PROGRAM
110 REM - VARIABLES:
120 REM       N$ = NAME
130 REM       I  = COUNTER
140 INPUT N$
150 LET I=1
160 IF MID$(N$,I,1)=" " THEN 190
170    LET I=I+1
180 GO TO 160
190 PRINT MID$(N$,I+1);", ";LEFT$(N$,I-1)
200 END
```

(a) The program

```
? ROBERT JOHNSON
JOHNSON, ROBERT
```

(b) Input and output

String concatenation

Concatenation is the operation of combining two strings to form one string. For example, concatenating the strings ABC and XYZ produces the string ABCXYZ. To concatenate two strings in BASIC we use the *concatenation operator*. The symbol used as the concatenation operator depends on the version of BASIC. (See Table 8-6.) The most common symbol is a plus sign (+). For example, to concatenate ABC and XYZ, we can write the following:

```
"ABC"+"XYZ"
```

On each side of the concatenation operator may be a string constant, string variable, or substring function. For example, all the following are valid uses of the concatenation operator:

```
S$+T$
U$+"1234"
"MY "+V$
MID$(U$,4,4)+LEFT$(S$,3)
RIGHT$(V$,4)+T$
```

Table 8-6. Concatenation operator differences

BASIC version	Concatenation operator
ANS minimal BASIC	Not available
ANS BASIC	&
Microsoft BASIC	+
Applesoft BASIC	+
True BASIC	&
BASIC-PLUS	+
VAX-11 BASIC	+

In each of these cases a new string is formed consisting of the string identified by the constant, variable, or substring function on the left of the operator, followed by the string identified on the right. Thus, if S\$ equals the string ABC and T\$ equals the string XYZ, then S\$ + T\$ is ABCXYZ and T\$ + S\$ is XYZABC.

It is possible to create long strings using concatenation. Whatever string is created should not exceed the maximum length of a string that can be assigned to a string variable for the version of BASIC being used. (See Table 8-3.)

String expressions

When we use a concatenation operator, we form a type of string expression. In general, a *string expression* is a string constant, string variable, substring function, or any of these combined with the concatenation operator. In addition, we can have multiple concatenations in a string expression. For example, the following is a valid string expression:

```
U$+"ABC"+MID$(T$,6,7)+S$
```

The strings identified in the expression are concatenated left-to-right. Other examples of string expressions are shown in Figure 8-8.

A string expression by itself is not a BASIC statement; rather it must be used as part of a statement. For example, we may assign the value of a string expression to a string variable with a LET statement. Thus, the following is a valid BASIC statement:

```
430 LET S$=T$+U$+V$
```

The strings identified in the string expression are concatenated, and the resulting string is assigned to S\$. We can also use a string expression in an IF statement and a PRINT statement.

As an example of the use of a string expression, consider the problem of rearranging the order of a person's name. Assume that F\$, M\$, and L\$ are string variables that identify a person's first name, middle name, and last name, respectively. The problem is to create a string consisting of the person's first name followed by a space, then the person's middle initial followed by a period and a space, and finally the person's last name. The following statement accomplishes this:

```
440 LET N$=F$+" "+LEFT$(M$,1)+". "+L$
```

Notice that we must put the period and the spaces in the proper places in the expression so that the final result is the way we want it.

Figure 8-8. Examples of string expressions

S$="WASHINGTON"	
Operation	Result
S$+" STATE"	WASHINGTON STATE
"GEORGE "+S$	GEORGE WASHINGTON
LEFT$(S$,4)+MID$(S$,5,3)+RIGHT$(S$,3)	WASHINGTON
LEFT$(S$,3)+" "+MID$(S$,5,1)+MID$(S$,8,1)+"?"	WAS IT?
MID$(S$,10,1)+MID$(S$,9,1)+MID$(S$,8,1)	NOT

String length

Occasionally when we manipulate string data, we do not know the length of a string or substring. The easiest way of obtaining this information is to use the LEN function. This function is not available in all versions of BASIC. (See Table 8-7.) The form of this function is LEN(A$). The function determines the number of characters in the string named in parentheses. For example, the following statement assigns the length of the string S$ to the numeric variable L:

```
450 LET L=LEN(S$)
```

If S$ has eight characters in the string assigned to it, L will be equal to eight after execution of this statement. The entry in parentheses may be any string expression. For example, we can use LEN(MID$(S$,5)) to determine the length of the substring beginning with the fifth character through the end of the string S$.

Table 8-7. LEN function differences

BASIC version	LEN function available
ANS minimal BASIC	No
ANS BASIC	Yes
Microsoft BASIC	Yes
Applesoft BASIC	Yes
True BASIC	Yes
BASIC-PLUS	Yes
VAX-11 BASIC	Yes

An illustrative program

To illustrate some of the string-processing features discussed in this chapter, we consider a text-analysis program. Input to the program is a line of text (i.e., a sentence). The program must count the number of blank spaces in the line and display this count.

Figure 8-9 shows a program that accomplishes this. The flowchart of this program is in Figure 8-10. The program first displays a prompt and then accepts a line of text (T$). The LEN function is used to determine the length of the line. Next a counter (C) for the number of blanks is set equal to 0. The program then enters a loop that is repeated once for each character in the line. Each time through the loop, the next character in the line is examined to determine whether it is a blank. For each blank that is found, 1 is added to the counter. After branching out of the loop, the program displays the value of the counter. Then an input prompt is used to ask whether the program is to be repeated. If the response is YES, the computer branches to the beginning of the program; otherwise execution of the program is terminated.

This program illustrates one use of the string-processing features in BASIC. There are many other interesting and practical applications of strings in computer programs. Some of these are discussed in the programming problems at the end of the chapter.

Figure 8-9. A text analysis program

```
100 REM - TEXT ANALYSIS PROGRAM
110 REM - VARIABLES:
120 REM        T$ = LINE OF TEXT
130 REM        L  = LENGTH OF TEXT
140 REM        C  = BLANKS COUNTER
150 REM        I  = LOOP COUNTER
160 REM        R$ = REPETITION QUESTION RESPONSE
200 PRINT "TEXT ANALYSIS PROGRAM"
210 PRINT
220   PRINT "TYPE A LINE OF TEXT."
230   INPUT T$
240   LET L=LEN(T$)
250   LET C=0
260   REM - COUNT BLANKS IN LINE
270   LET I=1
280   IF I>L THEN 330
290     IF MID$(T$,I,1)<>" " THEN 310
300       LET C=C+1
310     LET I=I+1
320   GOTO 280
330   PRINT "THERE ARE";C;"BLANKS IN THIS LINE."
340   PRINT
350   INPUT "DO YOU WANT TO TRY ANOTHER LINE";R$
360 IF R$="YES" THEN 210
370 PRINT
380 PRINT "END OF PROGRAM"
999 END
```

(a) The program

```
TEXT ANALYSIS PROGRAM

TYPE A LINE OF TEXT.
? NOW IS THE TIME
THERE ARE 3 BLANKS IN THIS LINE.

DO YOU WANT TO TRY ANOTHER LINE? YES

TYPE A LINE OF TEXT.
? FOUR SCORE AND SEVEN YEARS AGO
THERE ARE 5 BLANKS IN THIS LINE.

DO YOU WANT TO TRY ANOTHER LINE? YES

TYPE A LINE OF TEXT.
? THE END
THERE ARE 1 BLANKS IN THIS LINE.

DO YOU WANT TO TRY ANOTHER LINE? YES

TYPE A LINE OF TEXT.
? HELP
THERE ARE 0 BLANKS IN THIS LINE.

DO YOU WANT TO TRY ANOTHER LINE? NO

END OF PROGRAM
```

(b) Input and output

Figure 8-10. Flowchart of the text analysis program

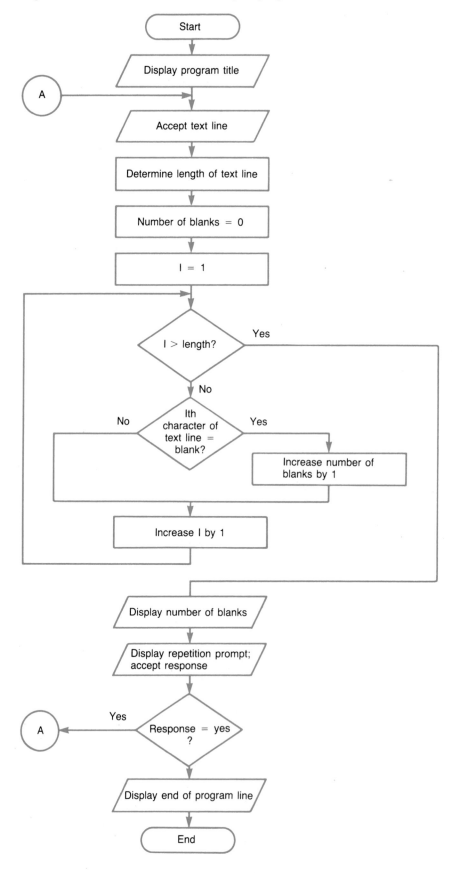

8-4 The READ and DATA statements with string data

The READ and DATA statements, discussed in Section 5-3, can be used for string input. When this is done, a string variable is used in the READ statement and a string, either with or without quotation marks, is used in the DATA statement. For example, consider the following statements:

```
140 READ N$
145 DATA JOHN
```

When the READ statement is executed, the string JOHN is read from the DATA statement and assigned to N$.

Quotation marks around the string in the DATA statement are optional unless the string contains a comma, leading spaces, or trailer spaces. For example, consider the following statements:

```
150 READ D$
155 DATA " SEPT. 1, 1980  "
```

In this case, quotation marks must be used around the string input in the DATA statement.

In some versions of BASIC, quotation marks are required around a string in a DATA statement if the string contains embedded spaces. (See Table 8-8.) In these versions, if the quotation marks are left out, any embedded spaces are removed. For example, consider the following statements:

```
160 READ N1$,N2$
165 DATA "JOHN SMITH",MARY DOE
```

In the versions of BASIC that require quotation marks when there are embedded spaces, N1$ would be JOHN SMITH with a space and N2$ would be MARYDOE without a space. Note that in versions of BASIC that do not require quotation marks in this situation, N1$ would be JOHN SMITH and N2$ would be MARY DOE, both with a space.

Both string and numeric data can be read from a DATA statement. The only restriction is that the input data and the corresponding variables be of the same type. Thus, the following statements are valid:

Table 8-8. DATA statement differences

BASIC version	Quotation marks required around a string in a DATA statement that contains embedded spaces
ANS minimal BASIC	No
ANS BASIC	No
Microsoft BASIC	No
Applesoft BASIC	No
True BASIC	No
BASIC-PLUS	Yes
VAX-11 BASIC	No

```
170 READ N,N$,D$,A
175 DATA 123,JOHN," SEPT. 1, 1980    ",25
```

The first and last variables are numeric, and the corresponding values in the DATA statement are numbers. The other variables are string variables, and strings are used for their values in the DATA statement.

*8-5 The PRINT USING statement with string output

In Section 5-5 we discussed the PRINT USING statement. This statement is used to control the format of output. In the statement, special symbols describe the arrangement of the output data. In this section we show the symbols that are used in the PRINT USING statement for string output. The symbols depend on the version of BASIC. (See Table 8-9.) Here we describe the symbols used in several common versions of BASIC (Microsoft BASIC, BASIC-PLUS, VAX-11 BASIC).

If we wish to display a string, the backslash symbol (\) is used in the format in the PRINT USING statement to mark the beginning and end of the string output. For example, consider the following statement:

```
100 PRINT USING "\  \";N$
```

The format in this statement is \   \ with two blank spaces between the backslash symbols. This causes the value of N$ to be displayed in the first four print positions. If the value of N$ is JOHN, this name is displayed at the beginning of the output line.

Notice that the backslashes mark the beginning and the end of the output. The number of characters to be displayed is determined by counting the number of spaces between the backslashes and adding two for the backslashes. Thus, in the previous example there are two spaces between the backslashes, hence four characters are displayed.

If the output string is longer than the number of characters specified in the format, only the left part of the string is displayed. For example, if N$ is ROBERT when the previous statement is executed, only ROBE is displayed. When the string is shorter than the number of characters in the form, extra spaces are added on the right. For example, if N$ is ED when the previous statement is executed, the output displayed is the string ED followed by two blank spaces.

The shortest string that can be displayed using backslashes in the format is two characters. This is because backslashes must always appear in pairs. To display

Table 8-9. PRINT USING statement format differences for string output

BASIC version	Format rules for PRINT USING statement with string output
ANS minimal BASIC Applesoft BASIC	Not applicable
Microsoft BASIC BASIC-PLUS VAX-11 BASIC	Format rules are the same as described in the text.
ANS BASIC True BASIC	The # symbol is used for string output in the format. One # symbol is used for each character position (e.g., #### is used for a four-character string).

a one-character string, the exclamation point (!) is used. For example, consider the following statement:

```
110 PRINT USING "!";N$
```

In this case, the first character in the string assigned to N$ is displayed. If N$ is JOHN, only the letter J is displayed.

We can combine string output and numeric output in the same PRINT USING statement. For example, assume that F$, M$, and L$ are equal to an employee's first name, middle name, and last name, respectively, and that S is the employee's salary. Then the following statement displays the employee's first initial, middle initial, last name, and salary:

```
120 PRINT USING "! ! \          \  $$#,###.###";F$,M$,L$,S
```

In this example we use exclamation points in the format for the initials, backslashes for the last name, and the # and other symbols for the salary.

The symbols discussed here can be used for printer output as well as CRT screen output. As discussed in Section 5-5, the PRINT USING statement or the LPRINT USING statement may be used for printer output, depending on the version of BASIC. The backslash and exclamation point are used for printed string output with either approach.

Review questions

1. What characters can be in a string?
2. Indicate whether each of the following is a valid or invalid string constant:
   a. "MY NAME IS"
   b. "Z35X19$"
   c. 853.63
   d. JOHN
   e. ""
   f. "5,280"
3. Indicate whether each of the following is a valid or invalid string variable:
   a. "A"
   b. X3
   c. M$
   d. AMT$
4. What is a null string?
5. Code a statement that assigns the string MY NAME IS to a variable.
6. Code a statement that assigns the string 12345 to a variable.
7. Code a statement that assigns the value of the string variable M$ to the string variable N$.
8. Code a statement to accept three strings from the keyboard.
9. How must string data be entered when an INPUT statement is executed?
10. Code a statement to display the values of three string variables on the CRT screen.
11. Assume that the value of A$ is AL, B$ is ALLAN, and C$ is ALFRED. What is the truth value of each of the following relational expressions?
    a. A$=B$
    b. B$<>C$
    c. C$="ALFRED "
    d. A$<B$
    e. B$<=C$
    f. A$>="AL"

12. What is the collating sequence for the version of BASIC you are using?
13. Code a group of statements that increases N by 1 if M$ equals M, decreases N by 1 if M$ equals D, and assigns 0 to N if M$ equals S.
14. A group of one or more adjacent characters in a string is called _____.
15. Assume that the value of X$ is XYZ123ABC. What is the value of each of the following?
    a. LEFT$(X$,6)
    b. RIGHT$(X$,6)
    c. MID$(X$,4,3)
    d. MID$(X$,1,4)
    e. MID$(X$,7,1)
    f. MID$(X$,1,9)
16. The operation of joining together two strings to form one string is called _____. The symbol used for this operation is _____.
17. Assume that the value of X$ is XYZ, Y$ is 123, and Z$ is ABC. What is the value of each of the following string expressions?
    a. Z$+X$
    b. X$+" "+Y$+" "+Z$
    c. Z$+"DEF"
    d. LEFT$(X$,1)+MID$(Y$,2,1)+RIGHT$(Z$,1)
18. Assume that the value of V$ is PA37Q*b*4X. (*b* stands for a blank space.) What is the value of
    a. LEN(V$)
    b. LEN(RIGHT$(V$,3))
19. Code a READ statement and a DATA statement to assign your name and date of birth to string variables.
20. Assume that your name and date of birth are assigned to string variables as in Question 19. Code a PRINT USING statement to display this data.

Programming problems

1. Write a BASIC program that accepts and displays a list of names and telephone numbers. Supply six to eight names and telephone numbers as test data for the program.
2. Write a BASIC program that accepts a name and then displays the name on a diagonal. For example, the name ROBERT should be displayed as follows:

```
R
 O
  B
   E
    R
     T
```

   Supply several names to test the program.
3. Write the program for Problem 2 or 5 in Chapter 3 with the additional requirement that the customer's name is accepted and displayed. Supply appropriate names with the test data.
4. Write the program for Problem 7 in Chapter 7 with the additional requirement that the month is entered as string data (e.g., JANUARY).
5. A market research survey gave a number of customers a choice of two brands for each of five products and asked the customers to indicate their preference. If a customer preferred the first brand over the second, his or her response was recorded as an X. If the second brand was preferred, the response was recorded as a Y.

   Write a BASIC program to analyze the results of this survey. Input to the program is each customer's code and preferences for the five products. The program should determine which customers preferred the first brand (X) for the first or second product and should display — for these customers only — the customer's code and preferences for the last three products. In addition, a count of the number of customers who preferred the first brand (X) for any of the five products should be kept and displayed at the end.

Use the following data to test the program:

Customer's code	Brand preferences
11	XYXYX
12	YYYYY
13	XXYXX
14	XYYYY
15	YYYYY
16	YYXXX
17	XYXYY
18	YYYYY
19	XXYXY
20	YYXYY

6. In a political survey a number of people were given six statements about a political candidate's involvement in illicit campaign practices. Each person was asked to indicate whether he or she felt each statement was true or false, and the responses were recorded as Ts and Fs.

Write a BASIC program to analyze these data. The program should determine the answers to the following questions:

a. What percent of the people in the survey felt that the first two statements were true and the remainder false?
b. What percent felt that all six statements were true?
c. What percent felt that all six were false?

The output should give the answers to these questions:
Use the following data to test the program:

Survey Responses

TFTFFF	TTFTFF
TTFFFF	TTFFFF
TTTTTT	TTFFFF
FFTTFF	FFFFFF
FFFFFF	TFFFFF
TTFTFT	TTTTTT
FTFTFF	TTFFFF
FFFFFF	FTFFFF
TTFFFF	FFFFFF

7. Write a BASIC program to grade a six-question multiple-choice test. Each question on the test can be answered A, B, C, D, or E. The first set of input is the correct answers. Each successive set of input consists of a student's name and his or her answers to the six questions. The program should determine the number of correct answers for each student. The output should give each student's name, his or her answers, and the number of correct answers.

Use the following data to test the program:

Correct answers: BECADC

Student's name	Student's answers
JONES	AECBDC
SMITH	BECADC
JOHNSON	EABADC
DOE	BCDEAB
ANDREWS	EDACBD
COLE	CECADC
EMERY	BEEADC

8. Write a BASIC program to compute final grades for a course. Input to the program is the student's identification number and five letter grades. In the program, convert each grade to its equivalent numerical grade according to the following table:

A+	4.3	C	2.0
A	4.0	C−	1.7
A−	3.7	D+	1.3
B+	3.3	D	1.0
B	3.0	D−	0.7
B−	2.7	F+	0.3
C+	2.3	F	0.0

The lowest of the five grades should be dropped and the remaining four should be averaged (weighted equally). Compute the numeric average and determine the final letter grade according to the following scale (where G is the numeric grade):

$$3.5 \le G \qquad A$$
$$2.5 \le G < 3.5 \qquad B$$
$$1.5 \le G < 2.5 \qquad C$$
$$0.5 \le G < 1.5 \qquad D$$
$$G < 0.5 \qquad F$$

Output from the program should give the student's identification number, numerical grade, and letter grade. Use the following data to test the program:

Student number	Grades
1015	B,C+,B+,A−,C−
1130	A,C−,C,D,D+
1426	B−,A−,B+,A+,A
1703	C,F+,D,F,D−
1933	A+,A+,A,A,A+

9. Write a BASIC program to compute the average length of the words in a line of text. Assume that the line contains only alphabetic characters and blanks. Use the following lines to test the program:

```
NOW IS THE TIME FOR ALL GOOD MEN
THE QUICK BROWN FOX JUMPED OVER THE LAZY DOG
FOUR SCORE AND SEVEN YEARS AGO
PETER PIPER PICKED A PECK
```

10. Write a BASIC program to count the number of times that the word THE occurs in a line of text. Assume that the line contains only alphabetic characters and blanks. Use the following lines to test the program:

```
THE MAN WONDERED WHETHER THE THEATER WAS THERE
THEN THE MAN THOUGHT THAT IT WAS HERE
BUT IT WAS NOT THERE
THE THE THE TITHE THE THE THE
```

11. Write a BASIC program that accepts a person's name with the last name first followed by a comma and a space, and then the first name. Then the program should rearrange and display the name with the first name first, a space, and then the last name. Use the following input data to test the program:

```
WASHINGTON, GEORGE
ADAMS, JOHN
JEFFERSON, THOMAS
MADISON, JAMES
MONROE, JAMES
```

12. A palindrome is a word, phrase, or number that reads the same forward or backward. For example, RADAR is a palindrome. Write a BASIC program that accepts a string and determines if it is a palindrome. Display the string and a statement as to whether or not it is a palindrome. Test the program with the following data:

```
RATS STAR
MOM
PALINDROME
A
11/5/11
ABLE WAS I ERE I SAW ELBA
ABABAB
1991
```

13. Write a BASIC program that accepts a title of up to 40 characters and then displays the title centered within 60-character margins. Use the following titles to test the program:

```
FUNDAMENTALS OF COMPUTER PROGRAMMING
A TALE OF TWO CITIES
MOBY DICK
MACBETH
THE HOUND OF THE BASKERVILLES
```

Do not use the TAB function in this program.

14. Write a BASIC program that accepts two words and a line of text. Then the program should create a new line by replacing every occurrence of the first word in the text with the second word. Finally, the program should display the new line. Assume that the line of text contains only alphabetic characters and blank spaces.

Use the following data to test the program:

```
THE A
NOW IS THE TIME FOR THE BEGINNING
FOX RABBIT
THE QUICK BROWN FOX JUMPED
FOUR SEVEN
FOUR SCORE AND FOUR EQUALS MORE THAN FOUR
THAT WHICH
WHICH ONE WAS IT
```

15. Write a BASIC program that right-justifies a line of text (i.e., aligns the right margin). Input to the program should be a line of no more than 40 characters including blanks. Output from the program should be the same line with the first word beginning in position one and the last word ending in position 40 (i.e., left- and right-justified). This may involve inserting extra blanks between words so that the line is properly aligned.

Make up several lines of input to test the program. There should be one test line that is exactly 40 characters in length. All other test lines should be less than 40 characters in length. There should be at least one line that is less than 30 characters in length.

16. The Roman numeral system uses the following seven symbols: M (value 1000), D (value 500), C (value 100), L (value 50), X (value 10), V (value 5), and I (value 1). The Arabic value of each symbol is shown in parentheses. The value of a Roman numeral expressed as an Arabic numeral is found by adding the Arabic value of each Roman symbol. However, if a C, X, or I is to the left of a symbol with a greater value, then the Arabic value of C, X, or I is subtracted. For example, Roman MCDLXXVI is 1476 in the Arabic system.

Write a BASIC program to convert Roman numerals to Arabic numerals. The program should accept a Roman numeral, determine the equivalent in the Arabic system, and display the Roman numeral and its Arabic equivalent.

Use the following data to test the program:

```
CMXCIX
MDCCLXVI
DCCCXXXIV
MMDCCCLXXXVIII
MCMLXXIV
MCDXLII
CCIII
MMDXXII
```

Chapter 9

Arrays

In many programs it is necessary to store and process a large amount of data. For example, we may need to process a list of 50 numbers, all of which must be available in the program at the same time. With the techniques discussed so far, it would be necessary to use a separate variable for each number in the list. Hence, we would need 50 variables for the data.

Another approach to this type of problem is to identify the entire list of data by a single variable. Then each list value is referred to by indicating its position in the list. A list of data like this is called an array. In this chapter we examine the use of arrays in BASIC. After completing this chapter you should be able to write programs that process arrays of data.

9-1 Arrays and array elements

An *array* is a group of data values that is identified in a program by a single name. An array may be thought of as a list or table of data. For example, Figure 9-1 shows an array of 10 numbers identified by the name A.

The name that refers to an array is called an *array variable*. An array variable must follow the same syntax rules as a simple variable. The array in Figure 9-1 is identified by the array variable A. We can also use variables such as A5, M9, and X as array variables. Some versions of BASIC limit array variables to a single letter. (See Table 9-1.) Long variables can be used as array variables if they are available in the version of BASIC. (See Table 2-1.) Depending on the version of BASIC, the same variable may or may not be used in a program for an array and for a nonarray value. However, using the same variable for different types of data is not a good practice — so, even if it is permitted in the version of BASIC, it should not be done.

Each value in an array is called an *array element*. In the array in Figure 9-1, the number 23.2 is an array element. Similarly, 17.5, -10.8, and so forth are each elements of the array A. There are 10 elements in this array.

In a program the elements of an array are numbered — the first element is numbered 1, the second element is numbered 2, and so forth. Figure 9-2 shows the elements of the array A and the corresponding element numbers. Element number 1 in this array is 23.2, element number 2 is 17.5, and so on up to element number 10, which is 16.2. The element numbers do not actually appear in the array, but the computer keeps track of the elements by their numbers.

In a program, we identify an array element by using the array variable

Figure 9-1. An array

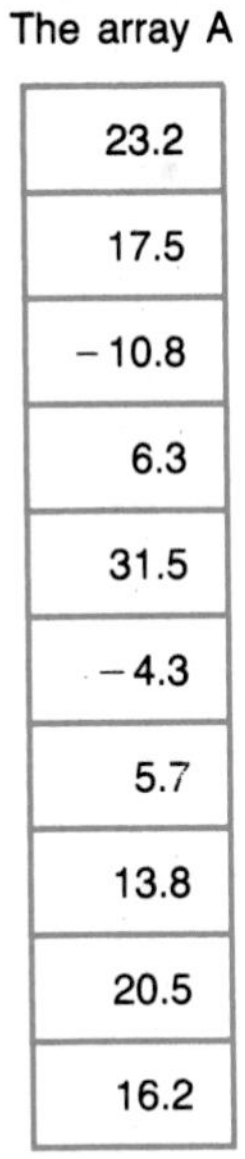

The array A

23.2
17.5
−10.8
6.3
31.5
−4.3
5.7
13.8
20.5
16.2

Table 9-1. Array variable differences

BASIC version	*Array variable syntax*
ANS minimal BASIC	A single letter
ANS BASIC Microsoft BASIC Applesoft BASIC True BASIC BASIC-PLUS VAX-11 BASIC	Any valid variable

Figure 9-2. Element numbers for an array

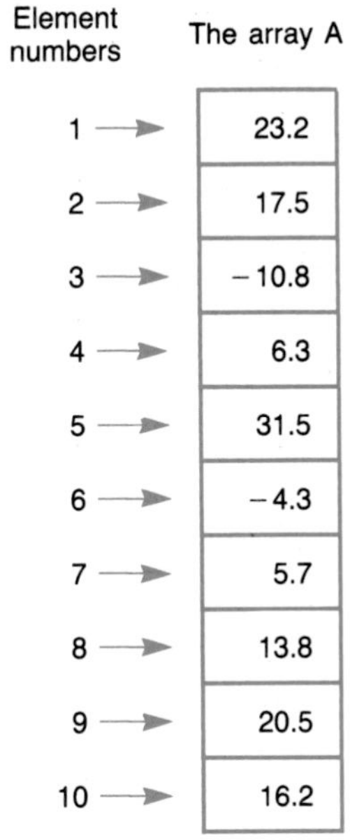

Element numbers	The array A
1 →	23.2
2 →	17.5
3 →	−10.8
4 →	6.3
5 →	31.5
6 →	−4.3
7 →	5.7
8 →	13.8
9 →	20.5
10 →	16.2

followed by the number of the element in parentheses. Figure 9-3 shows how this is done for the array A. The first element in this array is identified by A(1), the fifth element is A(5), the last element is A(10). The number in parentheses following the array variable is called a *subscript*. An array variable with a subscript is called a *subscripted variable*. A subscripted variable such as A(5) is read "A sub five."

It is important not to confuse an array element with its subscript. A subscript specifies which value in an array is being identified. The actual value is the array element. Thus, A(5) identifies the fifth value in the array A. The corresponding array element from Figure 9-3 is 31.5.

The data in an array is referred to collectively by the array variable. However, an array variable cannot be used by itself in a BASIC program. An array variable must always be followed by a subscript to identify an element of the array. A subscripted variable may be used like any other variable. Thus, subscripted variables may be used in INPUT and PRINT statements and in numeric expressions. For example, assume that X and Y identify arrays of ten elements each. Then the following statements are valid examples of the use of subscripted variables:

```
110 INPUT X(1),Y(1)
140 IF Y(5)>X(10) THEN 200
180 LET W=X(3)+X(5)+X(7)
190 PRINT W,X(7),X(5),X(3)
```

Array bounds

Although not shown in Figure 9-3, each array used in a program has an element numbered 0; that is, A(0), X(0), and Y(0) are all valid subscripted variable names. Thus, the array in Figure 9-3 has eleven elements, not ten.

Unless the programmer specifies otherwise in a program, each array has a maximum element number of 10. Thus, there are eleven elements in each array numbered 0, 1, 2, and so forth up to 10. If we do not need all eleven elements, we do not have to use them. For example, if all we need is a five-element array, we can

Figure 9-3. Subscripted variables for an array

The array A	Subscripted variables
23.2	◄─ A(1)
17.5	◄─ A(2)
− 10.8	◄─ A(3)
6.3	◄─ A(4)
31.5	◄─ A(5)
− 4.3	◄─ A(6)
5.7	◄─ A(7)
13.8	◄─ A(8)
20.5	◄─ A(9)
16.2	◄─ A(10)

use A(1), A(2), A(3), A(4), and A(5). The other elements in the array A are available but they do not have to be used.

In some versions of BASIC, the minimum element number is not automatically 0 but rather 1. Also in some versions of BASIC, the maximum element number is not automatically 10. (See Table 9-2.)

The DIM statement. If we need an array with element numbers greater than 10, we must specify the array in a DIM statement. This is called *dimensioning* the array. The syntax of the DIM statement is as follows:

```
ln DIM list of array declarations separated by commas
```

In the DIM statement, each array declaration consists of an array variable followed by a whole number enclosed in parentheses. For example, the following statement contains two array declarations:

```
100 DIM B(50),C(25)
```

The number in parentheses is *not* a subscript but rather specifies the maximum element number for the array. In this example, the elements of array B are numbered 0 to 50, and the elements for array C are numbered 0 to 25.

Notice that the number of elements in an array is one more than the number given in the array declaration. This is because of the element numbered 0. Thus, in the example just given B contains 51 elements and C has 26 elements. Even though this is the case, we commonly ignore the element numbered 0. Thus, we would regard B and C as being 50- and 25-element arrays, respectively. We will follow this practice in this book.

As many arrays as are needed can be dimensioned in a DIM statement. All arrays can be dimensioned in one DIM statement, or several statements can be used. For example, the following statements could be used in a program:

```
10 DIM Z(100)
20 DIM S(50),T(200),U(84)
30 DIM W(320),D(39)
```

Note, however, that we cannot dimension the same array in more than one DIM statement.

Table 9-2. Array bound differences

BASIC version	*Default minimum element number*	*Default maximum element number*
ANS minimal BASIC	0	10
ANS BASIC	1	None, must dimension all arrays
Microsoft BASIC	0	10
Applesoft BASIC	0	10
True BASIC	1	None, must dimension all arrays
BASIC-PLUS	0	10
VAX-11 BASIC	0	10

DIM statements may appear anywhere in a program, as long as each array is declared before it is used. Most programmers group all DIM statements together at the beginning of the program. This makes it easier to refer to the DIM statements and to check whether an array has been dimensioned.

A DIM statement is not required for an array if the maximum element number does not exceed 10. However, the DIM statement can be used even when it is not needed. Thus, if D is an array with a maximum element number of 5 and X has a maximum of 10, these arrays can be dimensioned as follows:

```
10 DIM D(5),X(10)
```

Although these array declarations are not needed, they can be used. In fact, most programmers dimension all arrays whether or not dimensioning is needed, and we will follow that practice in this book.

The OPTION BASE statement. In some versions of BASIC it is possible to specify whether the minimum element number of all arrays used in a program is 0 or 1. This is done with the OPTION BASE statement. This statement is not available in all versions of BASIC. (See Table 9-3.)

The syntax of the OPTION BASE statement is as follows:

$$ln \text{ OPTION BASE } \begin{Bmatrix} 0 \\ 1 \end{Bmatrix}$$

Following the keywords OPTION BASE must be the number 0 or 1. For example, the following is a valid OPTION BASE statement:

```
100 OPTION BASE 1
```

The effect of this OPTION BASE statement is to specify that all arrays used in the program in which the statement appears have a minimum element number of 1. If 0 were used instead of 1, all arrays would have a minimum element number of 0. Note that, for most versions of BASIC, using 0 in the OPTION BASE statement is the same as not including the statement in the program.

The OPTION BASE statement, if used, must appear before any reference to an array in the program. Thus, this statement must come before any DIM statement and before any use of a subscripted variable.

Table 9-3. OPTION BASE statement differences

BASIC version	OPTION BASE statement available
ANS minimal BASIC	Yes
ANS BASIC	Yes
Microsoft BASIC	Yes
Applesoft BASIC	No
True BASIC	Yes
BASIC-PLUS	No
VAX-11 BASIC	No

Subscripts

A subscript indicates which element of an array is being identified. As we have seen, a subscript may be a numeric constant. A subscript may also be a numeric variable. For example, A(I) is a valid subscripted variable. This is read "A sub I." The element of the array A identified by this variable depends on the value of I. For example, if the value of I is 3, the third element of the array A is identified by A(I).

The use of a variable as a subscript is a powerful technique in BASIC programming. As an example, assume that the input to a program consists of ten numbers. The program must store the numbers in an array, compute the total of the numbers, display the array data, and then display the total. The program in Figure 9-4 shows how this can be done. The program is complete except for the input and output of the array data. (Array input and output are discussed in the next section.)

At the beginning of the program is a DIM statement for the array A. The array contains ten elements (plus the element numbered 0, which is not used in the program). Processing in the program begins with the input of the array data. The total of the array elements is then found by successively adding each element to the variable T. This is accomplished in a FOR loop by using the control variable as the subscript to identify an array element. Initially the value of T is set to zero. With the first execution of the loop, the control variable I is 1 and hence the value of A(1) is added to T. The second execution of the loop causes the value of A(2) to be added to T. This continues for the remaining executions of the loop. Upon completion of the FOR loop, the value of T is $0 + A(1) + A(2) + ... + A(10)$. The program terminates after displaying the array data and the total.

In addition to constants and variables, numeric expressions can be used as subscripts. For example, $A(2*I - 1)$ is a valid subscripted variable. If I is 5, this variable refers to the ninth element of A. Any valid numeric expression can be used as a subscript.

The value of a subscript, whether a constant, variable, or more complex expression, must be between 0 and the maximum element number declared in the

Figure 9-4. An array processing program

```
100 REM - ARRAY DATA TOTALING PROGRAM
110 REM - VARIABLES:
120 REM      A = ARRAY (10 ELEMENTS)
130 REM      T = TOTAL
140 REM      I = COUNTER
200 DIM A(10)
210 REM - ACCEPT DATA FOR ARRAY
         .
         .
         .
260 REM - FIND TOTAL OF ARRAY DATA
270 LET T=0
280 FOR I=1 TO 10
290    LET T=T+A(I)
300 NEXT I
310 REM - DISPLAY ARRAY DATA
         .
         .
         .
370 REM - DISPLAY TOTAL
380 PRINT
390 PRINT "TOTAL";T
999 END
```

Table 9-4. Subscript differences

BASIC version	Round or truncate subscript
ANS minimal BASIC	Round
ANS BASIC	Round
Microsoft BASIC	Round
Applesoft BASIC	Truncate
True BASIC	Round
BASIC-PLUS	Truncate
VAX-11 BASIC	Truncate

DIM statement (or 10 if a DIM statement is not used). Thus, a subscript cannot be negative. Similarly, if A has a maximum element number of 10, A(15) is invalid.

The value of a subscript need not be a whole number. For example, A(X) where the value of X is 3.25 is acceptable. When the subscript is not a whole number, its value depends on the version of BASIC. (See Table 9-4.) In some versions the value is rounded. Thus, if X is 3.25, A(X) is interpreted as A(3), but if X is 3.75, A(X) is A(4). In other versions of BASIC any fraction in the subscript is chopped off or *truncated*. In such a case, A(X) where X is 3.75 is interpreted as A(3).

Arrays are very powerful ways of organizing and processing data in a program. We will see a number of examples of array processing in this chapter.

9-2 Input and output of array data

Several techniques can be used for input and output of array data. One technique is to list each subscripted variable in an INPUT, READ, or PRINT statement. For example, assume that B is an array with five elements. We can use the following statement to accept five input values and assign them to the elements of B:

```
110 INPUT B(1),B(2),B(3),B(4),B(5)
```

When this statement is executed, five values must be entered after the question-mark prompt. We can use the same technique with the READ statement. For example, the following READ statement reads the five values for the array B from the accompanying DATA statement:

```
110 READ B(1),B(2),B(3),B(4),B(5)
120 DATA 78,95,84,36,67
```

To display the values of B, we can use this approach in a PRINT statement as in the following example:

```
130 PRINT B(1),B(2),B(3),B(4),B(5)
```

This causes five values to be displayed on one line.

The problem with this technique is that if the array is very large, the list of subscripted variables in the INPUT, READ, or PRINT statement is quite long and tiresome to code. A better approach is to use a loop to control the input or output operation. For example, the following sequence of statements uses a FOR loop to control the input process:

```
110 FOR I=1 TO 5
120   INPUT B(I)
130 NEXT I
```

The control variable in this loop is used as a subscript for the array. With each execution of the loop, the INPUT statement is executed and a new value is accepted. Thus, with the first execution of the loop, the value of B(1) is accepted. Then the control variable is incremented and the value of B(2) is accepted during the second execution of the loop. This continues until the loop is terminated. Notice that because the INPUT statement is executed five times, five question-mark prompts are displayed. Thus, each value is entered on a separate line.

We can use this technique with a READ statement or a PRINT statement. For example, the following program segment reads the five values for B from a DATA statement and then displays the values:

```
110 FOR I=1 TO 5
120   READ B(I)
130 NEXT I
140 FOR I=1 TO 5
150   PRINT B(I)
160 NEXT I
170 DATA 78,95,84,36,67
```

The output is displayed with one value per line on five lines because the PRINT statement is in a loop that is executed five times.

Using a loop to control the input and output of array data is most useful for large arrays or when there is an unusual arrangement of the data. For example, assume that the 100 elements of an array named M are to be entered two at a time. The data can be accepted using a FOR loop that is executed 50 times, as shown in the following statements:

```
110 FOR I=1 TO 99 STEP 2
120   INPUT M(I),M(I+1)
130 NEXT I
```

The control variable I in the FOR loop ranges from 1 to 99 in steps of two. With each execution of the FOR loop, two elements of the array are accepted. The use of the control variable in the subscripts I and I+1 causes the data to be assigned to the proper subscripted variables.

As another example, consider the problem of displaying two arrays in adjacent columns. Assume that X and Y are two 20-element arrays. The following statements cause the data in the arrays to be displayed in two columns along with another column for the value of the FOR loop control variable:

```
170 FOR J=1 TO 20
180   PRINT J,X(J),Y(J)
190 NEXT J
```

If array data is to be accepted until a trailer value is entered, a looping technique must be used. For example, assume that the array named N has at most 150 elements. Each element is to be entered on a separate line. The last value entered

is a trailer value equal to zero. To accept the data, a loop must be used with a test
for the trailer value included in the loop. The following statements accomplish this:

```
110 DIM N(151)
120 LET J=1
130 INPUT N(J)
140    IF N(J)=0 THEN 180
150    LET J=J+1
170 GOTO 130
180 (next statement)
```

Notice in this example that N has a maximum subscript of 151. This is because there
can be at most 150 elements entered for N plus the trailer value. When the loop is
terminated, J is equal to the number of elements entered plus one for the trailer
value. Hence, to find the actual number of data values in the array, J must be
decreased by one.

A complete program

We can now complete the program shown in Figure 9-4. Recall that this program
finds the total of ten numbers. The program is not complete because the array input
and output are not included.

Figure 9-5 shows the program with the array input and output. The flowchart
of the program is shown in Figure 9-6. The array input is accepted using a loop.
Notice in Figure 9-5(b) that ten numbers are entered, one on each line. A loop is
also used to display the array data. The output is displayed with one element per
line.

Figure 9-5. A complete array processing program

```
100 REM - ARRAY DATA TOTALING PROGRAM
110 REM - VARIABLES:
120 REM      A = ARRAY (10 ELEMENTS)
130 REM      T = TOTAL
140 REM      I = COUNTER
200 DIM A(10)
210 REM - ACCEPT DATA FOR ARRAY
220 PRINT "ENTER ARRAY DATA"
230 FOR I=1 TO 10
240    INPUT A(I)
250 NEXT I
260 REM - FIND TOTAL OF ARRAY DATA
270 LET T=0
280 FOR I=1 TO 10
290    LET T=T+A(I)
300 NEXT I
310 REM - DISPLAY ARRAY DATA
320 PRINT
330 PRINT "ARRAY DATA"
340 FOR I=1 TO 10
350    PRINT A(I)
360 NEXT I
370 REM - DISPLAY TOTAL
380 PRINT
390 PRINT "TOTAL";T
999 END
```

(a) The program   (continued)

Figure 9-5. Continued

```
ENTER ARRAY DATA
? 23.2
? 17.5
? -10.8
? 6.3
? 31.5
? -4.3
? 5.7
? 13.8
? 20.5
? 16.2

ARRAY DATA
 23.2
 17.5
-10.8
  6.3
 31.5
 -4.3
  5.7
 13.8
 20.5
 16.2

TOTAL 119.6
```

(b) Input and output

9-3 Array-processing techniques

Arrays are one of the most powerful features of the BASIC programming language. With the proper use of loops and subscripts, extensive processing can be accomplished with just a few statements. This section illustrates several array-processing techniques. Although many of the examples may seem simple, the techniques appear often in complex array-processing programs. For the examples we assume that the arrays X, Y, and Z have 20 elements each.

Initializing an array

Often it is necessary to set each element of an array to an initial value. For example, assume that the elements of the array X must be initialized to zero, and the elements of Y and Z are each to be given an initial value of one. Then the three arrays may be initialized in one loop as follows:

```
110 FOR I=1 to 20
120    LET X(I)=0
130    LET Y(I)=1
140    LET Z(I)=1
150 NEXT I
```

Copying an array

After the data has been read for an array, we may have to copy the data into another array. As a result, the original data can be saved in one array while it is manipulated

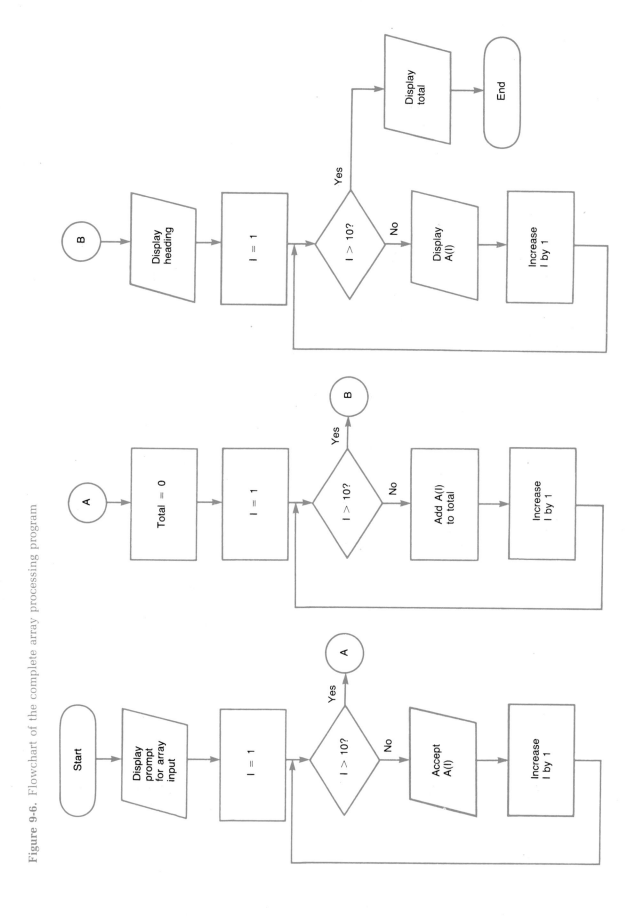

Figure 9-6. Flowchart of the complete array processing program

or modified in the other. For example, assume that data has been entered for array X. The data is copied into array Y by the following statements:

```
210 FOR J=1 TO 20
220    LET Y(J)=X(J)
230 NEXT J
```

Copying an array in reverse order

Occasionally a copy of the array data is necessary with the elements in reverse order. To do this, the first element of one array is assigned to the last element of another array, the second element of the first array is assigned to the next-to-last element of the other array, and so forth until the last element of the first array is assigned to the first element of the other array. Thus, the subscript of the first array must be incremented from 1 to the maximum, while the subscript of the second array is decremented from the maximum to 1. The following statements accomplish this for arrays X and Y:

```
310 LET J=20
320 FOR I=1 TO 20
330    LET Y(J)=X(I)
340    LET J=J-1
350 NEXT I
```

Notice that the variable J is initialized to 20 and then decreased by 1 with each execution of the FOR loop. Thus, with the first execution of the loop, X(1) is assigned to Y(20). The value of the FOR loop control variable I is then incremented to 2, while the value of J is decremented to 19. The second execution of the loop causes the value of X(2) to be assigned to Y(19). This continues until the last execution of the loop, when the value of X(20) is assigned to Y(1).

Processing corresponding elements of two arrays

Often we need to process corresponding elements of two arrays. For example, we may have to add corresponding elements of the X and Y arrays, assigning the results to the Z array. The following statements show how this is done:

```
410 FOR K=1 TO 20
420    LET Z(K)=X(K)+Y(K)
430 NEXT K
```

Counting specific values in an array

On occasion it is necessary to determine how many times a particular value occurs in an array. For example, we may wish to know the number of elements of Y that are zero. The following statements accomplish this:

```
510 LET N=0
520 FOR I=1 to 20
530    IF Y(I)<>0 THEN 550
540       LET N=N+1
550 NEXT I
```

At the end of execution of this sequence, the variable N will be equal to the number of elements of Y that are equal to zero. A similar situation occurs when we want to know the number of elements in one array that are equal to corresponding elements in a second array. For example, we may want to know how many elements of X and Z are the same. The following statements accomplish this:

```
560 LET N=0
570 FOR J=1 TO 20
580   IF X(J)<>Z(J) THEN 600
590     LET N=N+1
600 NEXT J
```

Finding the largest or smallest element of an array

Often it is necessary to locate the largest or smallest element in an array. For example, assume that it is necessary to find the smallest element in the array X. The following statements accomplish this:

"smallest"

```
610 LET S=X(1)
620 FOR L=2 TO 20
630   IF X(L)>=S THEN 650
640     LET S=X(L)
650 NEXT L
```

Initially we assume that the first element of the array is the smallest, and its value is assigned to the variable S. This value is then compared with each succeeding element to determine whether there is one smaller. If an element is smaller, its value is assigned to S, replacing the previous value. If an element is not smaller than the current value of S, this assignment is bypassed. At the end of the execution of the loop, the value of the variable S is the smallest element in the array. The same basic technique is used to find the largest element of an array.

9-4 Array searching

One common problem in data processing is to locate a specific value in a group of data. This is called *searching*. In this section we describe two algorithms for searching an array.

Sequential searching

Many situations involve searching. In the simplest case a value is given and the first occurrence of an equivalent value is to be located in an array. For example, assume that X is an array with 20 elements. The following statements search this array for the first element whose value is equal to that of V:

```
110 LET I=1
120 IF X(I)=V THEN 150
130   LET I=I+1
140 GOTO 120
150 PRINT "VALUE FOUND AT ELEMENT";I
```

135 if I >20 then 160
160 Print "value not found"
170 END

In this sequence, I is used as a subscript. Initially the value of I is 1. Each time through the loop, I is increased by 1. The loop is terminated when X(I) is equal to V. The value of I at this time is the number of the first element in X that has a value equal to V. This value of I is displayed along with an appropriate message when the loop is terminated.

The problem with this sequence of statements is that it does not take into account the case where the value of V is not in the array. We can modify the statements to display a message if the value is not found. The sequence of statements shown in Figure 9-7 accomplishes this. In this sequence the loop is terminated when X(I) equals V *or* when X(I) does not equal V but I equals 20.† The latter case occurs when we reach the end of the array without finding the value. After branching out of the loop, we must see if the value was actually found or if the loop was terminated without finding the value. If X(I) is equal to V, the value was found and the corresponding array element is displayed. If X(I) is not equal to V when the loop is terminated, the value was not found and an appropriate message is displayed.

Frequently we need to search one array and retrieve the corresponding element of another array. For example, we may wish to search array X for value V and display the corresponding value of another array, Y, when V is found. The only modification in the sequence of statements in Figure 9-7 that is necessary is that Y(I) is displayed instead of I in statement 290.

The algorithm described here is commonly used to search an array. In this algorithm we search through the array elements in sequence. This approach is called a *sequential search*. In a sequential search we begin by examining the first element of the array, then the second, then the third, and so on until the desired element is found or until we can determine that the item is not in the array.

An illustrative program. To illustrate the use of sequential searching in an actual program, consider the problem of locating the price of an item in a table. For example, Figure 9-8 shows a table of item numbers and prices. The problem is to store the pricing table in two arrays, one for the item numbers and one for the prices. Then the program must accept the item number and quantity of the item ordered, locate the item's price in the table, and compute the cost of the order by multiplying the price by the quantity. Figure 9-9 shows a program that accomplishes this. The flowchart of this program is shown in Figure 9-10.

In this program, N is the item number array and P is the array of corresponding prices. The program begins by reading the data for these arrays from DATA statements. A FOR loop with a READ statement accomplishes this. Each execution of the READ statement in the loop reads the next two values from a DATA statement and assigns

Figure 9-7. A sequential search algorithm

```
210 LET I=1
220 IF X(I)=V THEN 260
230 IF I=20 THEN 260
240    LET I=I+1
250 GOTO 220
260 IF X(I)=V THEN 290
270    PRINT "VALUE NOT FOUND"
280 GOTO 300
290    PRINT "VALUE FOUND AT ELEMENT";I
300 (next statement)
```

† In some versions of BASIC, statements 220 and 230 in Figure 9-7 may be combined into one statement as follows:

```
220 IF X(I)=V OR I=20 THEN 260
```

Figure 9-8. A pricing table

Item Number	Price
1001	$2.95
1023	$3.64
1045	$2.25
1172	$1.75
1185	$1.52
1201	$1.95
1235	$4.85
1278	$9.95
1384	$6.28
1400	$4.75

Figure 9-9. A pricing program with a sequential search

```
100 REM - PRICING PROGRAM
110 REM - VARIABLES:
120 REM        N  = ITEM NUMBER ARRAY
130 REM        P  = PRICE ARRAY
140 REM        N1 = NUMBER OF ITEM ORDERED
150 REM        Q  = QUANTITY ORDERED
160 REM        C  = COST OF ORDER
170 REM        I  = COUNTER
200 DIM N(10),P(10)
210 REM - READ ARRAY DATA
220 FOR I=1 TO 10
230    READ N(I),P(I)
240 NEXT I
250 PRINT "PRICING PROGRAM"
260 PRINT
270 INPUT "ENTER ITEM NUMBER OR 9999 TO END";N1
280    IF N1=9999 THEN 450
290    INPUT "ENTER QUANTITY";Q
300    REM - SEARCH ITEM NUMBER ARRAY
310    LET I=1
320    IF N(I)>=N1 THEN 360
330    IF I=10 THEN 360
340      LET I=I+1
350    GOTO 320
360    IF N(I)=N1 THEN 400
370      PRINT
380      PRINT "ITEM";N1;"NOT FOUND IN TABLE"
390    GOTO 430
400      LET C=P(I)*Q
410      PRINT
420      PRINT "ITEM";N1;"PRICE";P(I);"QUANTITY";Q;"COST";C
430    PRINT
440 GOTO 270
450 PRINT
460 PRINT "END OF PROGRAM"
900 REM - ARRAY DATA
910 DATA 1001,2.95,1023,3.64,1045,2.25,1172,1.75,1185,1.52
920 DATA 1201,1.95,1235,4.85,1278,9.95,1384,6.28,1400,4.75
999 END
```

(a) The program

(continued)

Figure 9-9. Continued

```
PRICING PROGRAM

ENTER ITEM NUMBER OR 9999 TO END? 1172
ENTER QUANTITY? 5

ITEM 1172 PRICE 1.75 QUANTITY 5 COST 8.75

ENTER ITEM NUMBER OR 9999 TO END? 1400
ENTER QUANTITY? 1

ITEM 1400 PRICE 4.75 QUANTITY 1 COST 4.75

ENTER ITEM NUMBER OR 9999 TO END? 1025
ENTER QUANTITY? 10

ITEM 1025 NOT FOUND IN TABLE

ENTER ITEM NUMBER OR 9999 TO END? 1438
ENTER QUANTITY? 7

ITEM 1438 NOT FOUND IN TABLE

ENTER ITEM NUMBER OR 9999 TO END? 1001
ENTER QUANTITY? 15

ITEM 1001 PRICE 2.95 QUANTITY 15 COST 44.25

ENTER ITEM NUMBER OR 9999 TO END? 985
ENTER QUANTITY? 3

ITEM 985 NOT FOUND IN TABLE

ENTER ITEM NUMBER OR 9999 TO END? 9999

END OF PROGRAM
```

(b) Input and output

the values to the next two elements of N and P. Notice that the data appears in pairs in the DATA statements. The first pair is the first item number and price, then comes the second item number and price, and so on.

After the data is read into the pricing table arrays, the program accepts an item number, N1, and quantity, Q, from the keyboard. It then searches the item number array for an element that is equal to N1. The program assumes that the item numbers are in increasing order in the array and branches out of the search loop when N(I) is either equal to N1 or greater than N1. This latter case occurs when the search has gone beyond the value of N1 in the array. (If the item numbers are not in increasing order, the greater-than-or-equal-to condition in the IF statement must be changed to an equal-to condition.) The search loop is also terminated if we reach the end of the array without finding N1 (i.e., if I equals 10). After leaving the loop, the program checks to see if N(I) equals N1. If this condition is true, P(I) is multiplied by Q to get the cost, and the result is displayed. Otherwise, a message indicating that the item was not found is displayed. Then the input loop is repeated.

Binary searching

Another algorithm for searching for an element in an array is called a *binary search*. In a binary search the array elements *must* be in ascending or descending order. We

Figure 9-10. Flowchart of the pricing program with a sequential search

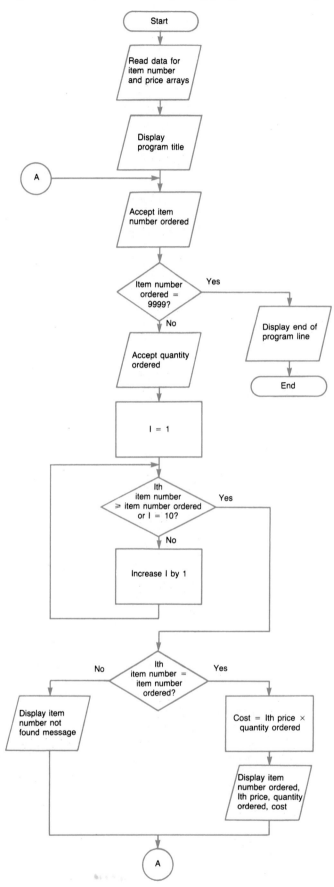

will assume that the elements of the array to be searched are in ascending order. Then with a binary search we first look at the *middle* element of the array and determine whether this is the desired element. If we have *not* found the element that we want, we determine whether it is located before or after the middle one. We then search the appropriate half of the array by examining the middle element of that half. Again we determine whether the element is the one we want or whether we should search above or below the middle element. We continue to search by examining the middle of smaller and smaller sections of the array until the desired element is found or until we can determine that the element is not in the array.

To illustrate this algorithm, assume that the 20 elements of array X are in ascending order. We wish to use a binary search to locate the element with a value equal to V. The sequence of statements shown in Figure 9-11 accomplishes this. In this sequence, B equals the number of the bottom element of the part of the array being searched and T equals the number of the top element. Initially these are 1 and 20, respectively. The number of the middle element of the part of the array being searched is computed and assigned to M in statement 330. Notice that M is calculated by dividing the sum of B and T by 2. The INT function is used to convert this result to an integer. (See Section 7-2.) Each time through the loop, we check whether X(M) equals V and branch out of the loop if this is the case. If X(M) is not equal to V, we check whether V is less than X(M). If this is the case, we let T be one less than M. If V is greater than X(M), then B is M plus 1. Then we compute a new M and repeat the process. The loop terminates either when we find the desired element, in which case the value of M is the number of the element, or when B is greater than T, in which case the element is not in the array. Figure 9-12 shows how a binary search compares with a sequential search.

For large arrays, a binary search is much faster then a sequential search. For example, if an array contains 1000 elements, then on the average a sequential search will require about 1000/2 or 500 repetitions of the loop. For a binary search, however, the loop will be repeated no more than $\log_2 1000$ or about ten times. For large arrays, the extra complexity required to program a binary search results in considerable savings in execution time of the program.

An illustrative program. We can use the binary search algorithm in the pricing program. Figure 9-13 shows the complete program. The flowchart of this program is shown in Figure 9-14. Notice that after the appropriate item is found, the cost is determined by multiplying P(M) by Q. The input and output for this program are identical to those of the sequential search program [see Figure 9-9(b)].

Figure 9-11. A binary search algorithm

```
310 LET B=1
320 LET T=20
330 LET M=INT((B+T)/2)
340    IF X(M)=V THEN 410
350    IF B>T THEN 410
360    IF V<X(M) THEN 390
370       LET B=M+1
380    GOTO 330
390       LET T=M-1
400 GOTO 330
410 IF X(M)=V THEN 440
420    PRINT "VALUE NOT FOUND"
430 GOTO 450
440    PRINT "VALUE FOUND AT ELEMENT";M
450 (next statement)
```

Figure 9-12. Sequential vs. binary search

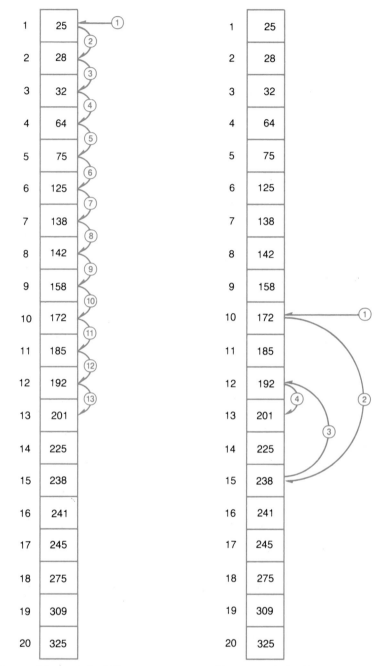

Sequential search for 201   Binary search for 201

9-5 Array sorting

Sorting is the process of rearranging a set of data into a particular order. For example, given a list of numbers, we may wish to sort the numbers into ascending or descending order. There are many times when sorted data is needed. For example, we may want to produce a list of students in a class in order by student identification number.

Figure 9-13. A pricing program with a binary search

```
100 REM - PRICING PROGRAM
110 REM - VARIABLES:
120 REM        N  = ITEM NUMBER ARRAY
130 REM        P  = PRICE ARRAY
140 REM        N1 = NUMBER OF ITEM ORDERED
150 REM        Q  = QUANTITY ORDERED
160 REM        C  = COST OF ORDER
170 REM        I  = COUNTER
180 REM        B  = BOTTOM OF ARRAY SEARCH SECTION
190 REM        T  = TOP OF ARRAY SEARCH SECTION
200 REM        M  = MIDDLE OF ARRAY SEARCH SECTION
300 DIM N(10),P(10)
310 REM - READ ARRAY DATA
320 FOR I=1 TO 10
330    READ N(I),P(I)
340 NEXT I
350 PRINT "PRICING PROGRAM"
360 PRINT
370 INPUT "ENTER ITEM NUMBER OR 9999 TO END";N1
380    IF N1=9999 THEN 600
390    INPUT "ENTER QUANTITY";Q
400    REM - SEARCH ITEM NUMBER ARRAY
410    LET B=1
420    LET T=10
430    LET M=INT((B+T)/2)
440      IF N(M)=N1 THEN 510
450      IF B>T THEN 510
460      IF N1<N(M) THEN 490
470        LET B=M+1
480      GOTO 430
490        LET T=M-1
500    GOTO 430
510    IF N(M)=N1 THEN 550
520      PRINT
530      PRINT "ITEM";N1;"NOT FOUND IN TABLE"
540    GOTO 580
550      LET C=P(M)*Q
560      PRINT
570      PRINT "ITEM";N1;"PRICE";P(M);"QUANTITY";Q;"COST";C
580    PRINT
590 GOTO 370
600 PRINT
610 PRINT "END OF PROGRAM"
900 REM - ARRAY DATA
910 DATA 1001,2.95,1023,3.64,1045,2.25,1172,1.75,1185,1.52
920 DATA 1201,1.95,1235,4.85,1278,9.95,1384,6.28,1400,4.75
999 END
```

This requires sorting if the data is not already in order. In the last section we saw that an array must be in ascending or descending order if the binary search algorithm is to be used. If the array is not in the appropriate order, it must be sorted before it can be searched.

There are many algorithms for sorting the data in an array. In this section we discuss *bubble sorting*. (This type of sorting is also called *pushdown sorting*, *interchange sorting*, and *exchange sorting*.) As we will see, bubble sorting gets its name from the fact that data "bubbles" to the top of the array.

The basic principle of bubble sorting is to compare adjacent elements of the array to be sorted. If any two adjacent elements are found to be out of order with respect to each other, they are interchanged (i.e., their values are switched). For example, assume that the array B has five elements that are to be sorted into

Figure 9-14. Flowchart of the pricing program with a binary search

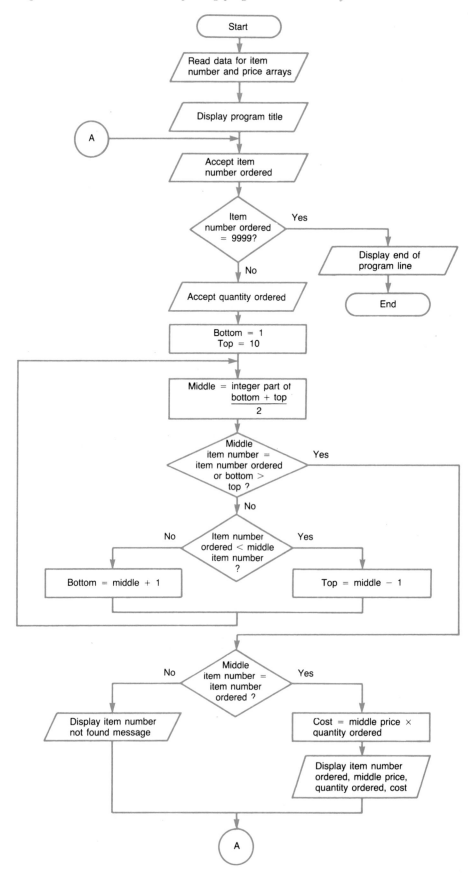

ascending order. The following loop will pass through the array once, interchanging elements that are not in the proper order:

```
110 FOR I=1 TO 4
120   IF B(I)<=B(I+1) THEN 160
130     LET T=B(I)
140     LET B(I)=B(I+1)
150     LET B(I+1)=T
160 NEXT I
```

Notice that the loop is repeated *four* times. Each time through the loop, B(I) is compared with B(I+1). Thus, the first time through the loop, B(1) is compared with B(2). Then B(2) is compared with B(3). Next B(3) and B(4) are compared. Finally, B(4) and B(5) are compared. If any two adjacent elements are not in ascending order, they are switched. (See Section 6-4 for a discussion of switching the values of two variables.) Figure 9-15 shows what takes place for a particular set of data.

This loop will cause the largest element of the array to be "pushed down" to the last position in the array. At the same time, smaller elements start to "bubble up" to the top of the array. We must now repeat the loop to cause the next largest element to be pushed to the next-to-last position in the array. The loop must then be repeated for the next-to-next largest element, and so forth. In all, this loop must be repeated four times. The last time, the smallest element will automatically appear in the first position of the array. This repeated execution of the loop can be accomplished by nested FOR loops as follows:

```
100 FOR J=1 TO 4
110   FOR I=1 TO 4
120     IF B(I)<=B(I+1) THEN 160
130       LET T=B(I)
140       LET B(I)=B(I+1)
150       LET B(I+1)=T
160   NEXT I
170 NEXT J
```

Figure 9-16 shows how the array appears after each execution of the outer loop. Notice that large values in the array are "pushed down" and small values "bubble up."

We can make the algorithm more efficient by recognizing that with each successive "pass" through the inner loop one less comparison is required. This is because once the largest element has been pushed to the end of the array, we do not need to include it in any subsequent comparisons. The same holds true for the next

Figure 9-15. Pushing the largest element to the end of an array

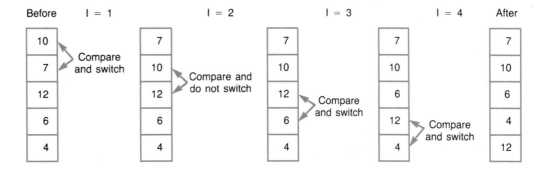

Figure 9-16. Sorting a five-element array

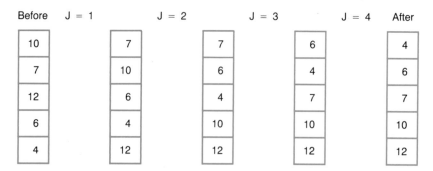

Figure 9-17. A bubble sorting algorithm

```
100 FOR K=4 TO 1 STEP -1
110    FOR I=1 TO K
120       IF B(I)<=B(I+1) THEN 160
130          LET T=B(I)
140          LET B(I)=B(I+1)
150          LET B(I+1)=T
160    NEXT I
170 NEXT K
```

largest element and so forth. The sequence of statements shown in Figure 9-17 includes this modification. Notice that the test value for the inner loop is the value of the variable K, which is the control variable for the outer loop. Initially K is 4 and the inner loop is executed four times. Then K is decremented by 1 and the inner loop is repeated only three times. We can see that K is one less for each successive time through the inner loop. Hence, one fewer comparison is carried out with each repetition of the loop.

The example so far demonstrates *ascending* order sorts. To sort an array into *descending* order, the less-than-or-equal-to condition in the IF statement must be changed to a greater-than-or-equal-to condition. The effect is that the smaller elements are pushed to the end of the array and the larger elements "bubble up" to the beginning of the array.

Bubble sorting is just one of many ways to sort an array. A number of algorithms are considerably faster than bubble sorting for large arrays. These algorithms are also more difficult to program. As the programmer finds more situations where sorting is required, other techniques should be explored.†

An illustrative program

We can use bubble sorting to sort the pricing table used in the searching examples in the previous section. This is required if a binary search is to be done and the table is not already in ascending order by item number. The only necessary modification

---

† Most textbooks on data structures include sections on sorting. A very complete reference is Donald Knuth, *The Art of Computer Programming, Vol. 3, Sorting and Searching* (Reading, Mass.: Addison-Wesley, 1973).

Figure 9-18. A program that sorts a pricing table

```
100 REM - PRICING TABLE SORTING PROGRAM
110 REM - VARIABLES:
120 REM        N  = ITEM NUMBER ARRAY
130 REM        P  = PRICE ARRAY
140 REM        I,K = COUNTERS
150 REM        T  = TEMPORARY VARIABLE
200 DIM N(10),P(10)
210 REM - READ ARRAY DATA
220 FOR I=1 TO 10
230    READ N(I),P(I)
240 NEXT I
250 REM - SORT ARRAY DATA
260 FOR K=9 TO 1 STEP -1
270    FOR I=1 TO K
280      IF N(I)<=N(I+1) THEN 350
290        LET T=N(I)
300        LET N(I)=N(I+1)
310        LET N(I+1)=T
320        LET T=P(I)
330        LET P(I)=P(I+1)
340        LET P(I+1)=T
350    NEXT I
360 NEXT K
370 REM - DISPLAY SORTED ARRAYS
380 PRINT "ITEM NUMBER ","PRICE"
390 PRINT
400 FOR I=1 TO 10
410    PRINT N(I),P(I)
420 NEXT I
900 REM - ARRAY DATA
910 DATA 1235,4.85,1278,9.95,1045,2.25,1400,4.75,1201,1.95
920 DATA 1001,2.95,1023,3.64,1185,1.52,1384,6.28,1172,1.75
999 END
```

(a) The program

```
ITEM NUMBER    PRICE

    1001        2.95
    1023        3.64
    1045        2.25
    1172        1.75
    1185        1.52
    1201        1.95
    1235        4.85
    1278        9.95
    1384        6.28
    1400        4.75
```

(b) Output

is that each time two item numbers are found out of sequence and are switched, the corresponding prices must be switched. This is done to maintain the relationship between the item numbers and prices. The program in Figure 9-18 sorts the pricing table. The flowchart of this program is shown in Figure 9-19. The input to the program consists of the data for the pricing table in any order; the output is the pricing data in increasing order by item number. Note that the statements to do the sorting could be included in the programs in Figures 9-9 and 9-13.

Figure 9-19. Flowchart of the program that sorts a pricing table

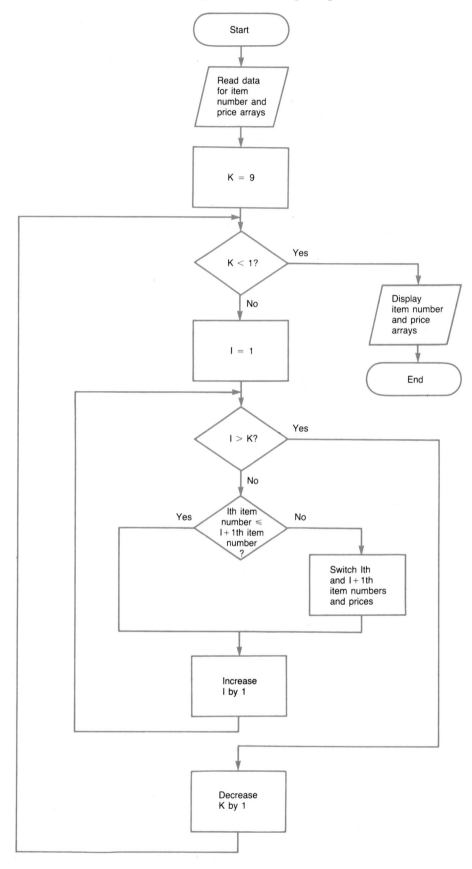

9-6 String arrays

In most versions of BASIC, an array may contain string data. (See Table 9-5.) Such an array is called a *string array*. Each element of a string array is a string. An array variable that identifies a string array is called a *string array variable*. A string array variable must end with a dollar sign. For example, A$ can be used as a string array variable. A *subscripted string variable* is a string array variable followed by a subscript in parentheses. For example, A$(1) is the first element (i.e., the first string) in the A$ array, A$(2) is the second element, and so forth. If the maximum subscript for the array is greater than ten, the array must be declared in a DIM statement. Thus, if the array A$ is to contain 20 elements, the following DIM statement must be used in the program:

```
100 DIM A$(20)
```

A subscripted string variable can be used in a string expression just like a simple string variable. For example, the following statements use subscripted string variables:

```
120 LET A$(5)=A$(4)
140 IF A$(I)="END" THEN 190
150 PRINT A$(18),A$(19),A$(20)
160 LET A$(I+2)=A$(I+1)+A$(I)
180 LET B$=MID$(A$(10),3,5)
```

Table 9-5. String array differences

BASIC version	String arrays permitted
ANS minimal BASIC	No
ANS BASIC	Yes
Microsoft BASIC	Yes
Applesoft BASIC	Yes
True BASIC	Yes
BASIC-PLUS	Yes
VAX-11 BASIC	Yes

An illustrative program

To illustrate the use of string arrays in a program, assume that the data in a group of DATA statements consists of the names of the 50 states and their corresponding populations. A program must read the data into two arrays, one for the state names and one for the populations, to create a population table. The state name array must be a string array, and the population array should be a numeric data array. Next, the program must accept a state's name as input from the keyboard. Then the population table must be searched for the corresponding state name, and the state's population must be displayed. Figure 9-20 shows a program that accomplishes this. The program is complete except for the data in the DATA statements. Notice that the string array for the state names is searched using a sequential search.

Figure 9-20. A program to look up state populations

```
100 REM - STATE POPULATION LOOK-UP PROGRAM
110 REM - VARIABLES:
120 REM      S$ = STATE NAME ARRAY
130 REM      P  = STATE POPULATION ARRAY
140 REM      N$ = STATE NAME
150 REM      I  = COUNTER
160 REM      R$ = REPETITION QUESTION RESPONSE
200 DIM S$(50),P(50)
210 REM - READ ARRAY DATA
220 FOR I=1 TO 50
230   READ S$(I),P(I)
240 NEXT I
250 PRINT "STATE POPULATION LOOK-UP PROGRAM"
260 PRINT
270 INPUT "ENTER NAME OF STATE";N$
280   REM - SEARCH STATE NAME ARRAY
290   LET I=1
300   IF S$(I)=N$ THEN 340
310   IF I=50 THEN 340
320     LET I=I+1
330   GOTO 300
340   IF S$(I)=N$ THEN 380
350     PRINT
360     PRINT N$;" IS AN INVALID STATE NAME"
370   GOTO 400
380     PRINT
390     PRINT N$;" HAS A POPULATION OF";P(I);"(THOUSANDS)"
400   PRINT
410   INPUT "DO YOU WANT TO LOOK UP ANOTHER STATE'S POPULATION";R$
420   PRINT
430 IF R$="YES" THEN 270
440 PRINT "END OF PROGRAM"
800 REM - ARRAY DATA
810 DATA ALABAMA,3890,ALASKA,400,ARIZONA,2718,ARKANSAS,2286
820 DATA CALIFORNIA,23669,COLORADO,2889,CONNECTICUT,3108
830 DATA DELAWARE,595,FLORIDA,9740,GEORGIA,5464,HAWAII,965
          .
          .
          .
940 DATA VERMONT,511,VIRGINIA,5346,WASHINGTON,4130
950 DATA WEST VIRGINIA,1950,WISCONSIN,4705,WYOMING,471
999 END
```

(a) The program

```
STATE POPULATION LOOK-UP PROGRAM

ENTER NAME OF STATE? CALIFORNIA

CALIFORNIA HAS A POPULATION OF 23669 (THOUSANDS)

DO YOU WANT TO LOOK UP ANOTHER STATE'S POPULATION? YES

ENTER NAME OF STATE? WYOMING

WYOMING HAS A POPULATION OF 471 (THOUSANDS)

DO YOU WANT TO LOOK UP ANOTHER STATE'S POPULATION? YES

ENTER NAME OF STATE? SOUTH VIRGINIA
```

(continued)

Figure 9-20. Continued

```
SOUTH VIRGINIA IS AN INVALID STATE NAME

DO YOU WANT TO LOOK UP ANOTHER STATE'S POPULATION? YES

ENTER NAME OF STATE? WASHINGTON

WASHINGTON HAS A POPULATION OF 4130 (THOUSANDS)

DO YOU WANT TO LOOK UP ANOTHER STATE'S POPULATION? NO

END OF PROGRAM
```

(b) Input and output

Review questions

1. Define each of the following terms:
   a. array
   b. array variable
   c. array element
   d. subscripted variable
2. Code a statement to specify that S and T are each 50-element arrays.
3. If an array is not specified in a DIM statement, what are the minimum and maximum element numbers for the array?
4. Code a statement to specify that the minimum element number for all arrays in the program is 1.
5. Consider the array A shown in Figure 9-1. Assume that the value of J is 4 and K is 3. What is the value of each of the following subscripted variables?
   a. A(9)
   b. A(J)
   c. A(J+K)
   d. A(J/K)
6. Code a statement that multiplies the first two elements of the array S defined in Question 2 and assigns the result to the last element of S.
7. Code a group of statements to read the data for the array S defined in Question 2 from DATA statements.
8. Code a group of statements to accept the data for the array S defined in Question 2 from the keyboard. Assume that two elements are entered after each prompt.
9. Code a group of statements to display the elements of the array S defined in Question 2 in a column in reverse order.
10. Code a group of statements to display the elements of the array S defined in Question 2 in two adjacent columns. The first column should contain the elements S(1) through S(25). The second column should contain the elements S(26) through S(50).
11. Code a group of statements to assign the numbers 1, 2, . . . , 50 to the corresponding elements of the array S defined in Question 2.
12. Code a group of statements to find the total of the odd-numbered elements of the array S defined in Question 2.
13. Consider the arrays S and T defined in Question 2. Code a group of statements to search the array S for all elements equal to R. Each time an element of S equal to R is found, display the corresponding element from the array T.
14. Code the answer to Question 13 with the modification that only the first element of the array S equal to R is to be found. If no such element is found, display an appropriate message. Use a sequential search.
15. Assume that the elements of the array S defined in Question 2 are in decreasing order. Code a group of statements that uses a binary search to search S for an element equal

to R. If such an element is found, display a message indicating this. If no such element is found, display an appropriate message.

16. Consider the sorting algorithm discussed in Section 9-5 and the five-element array, B, shown in Figure 9-15. This figure shows the order of the data in B for each value of I during the *first* execution of the sorting loop. Draw the equivalent figure for the *second* execution of the sorting loop.

17. Consider the program shown in Figure 9-18. What modification would have to be made in the program for a descending order sort?

18. An array is needed to store the names of the 30 students in a class.
    a. Code a statement to specify this array.
    b. Code a group of statements to determine how many names of students in the class begin with S.

Programming problems

1. Write a BASIC program that reads hourly temperatures for a day into a 24-element array. The first element of the array gives the temperature at 1:00 A.M., the second gives the temperature at 2:00 A.M., and so forth. Note that the thirteenth element is the temperature at 1:00 P.M. Then search the array for the maximum and minimum temperatures. Display these temperatures along with the times that they occur. Supply appropriate input data to test the program.

2. An inventory table contains information about the quantity of inventory on hand for each item stocked. Assume that there are 15 items in the inventory. The inventory table contains 15 entries, each consisting of an item number and the quantity of the item that is in stock. The data is in increasing order by item number.

   Write a BASIC program to do the following:

   a. Read the inventory table data into two arrays, one for the item numbers and one for the quantities. Then display the inventory data in columns below appropriate headings.

   b. Accept an item number, an amount received, and an amount sold. Search the inventory table for the corresponding item, using either a sequential search or a binary search. Then update the quantity on hand by adding the amount received to the amount from the table and subtracting the amount sold. Repeat this step until 9999 is entered for an item number. Be sure to account for the case where the item is not in the table.

   c. After all items have been updated, display the inventory data in columns below appropriate headings.

   Use the following data for the inventory table:

Item number	Quantity on hand
1102	100
1113	25
1147	37
1158	95
1196	225
1230	150
1237	15
1239	105
1245	84
1275	97
1276	350
1284	82
1289	125
1351	138
1362	64

Use the following data to update the inventory table:

Item number	Quantity received	Quantity sold
1230	25	100
1113	0	15
1255	16	42
1289	50	0
1405	26	5
1102	100	75
1239	25	25

3. Figure 9-21 shows the tax rate schedule used to compute income tax for a single tax-payer. The tax is based on the individual's taxable income. For example, if the taxable income is $21,500, the income tax is $2737 plus 26% of the difference between $21,500 and $18,200, or $3595.

Write a BASIC program that reads the tax rate schedule into several arrays. One approach is to use three arrays — one for the first column and two for the third column. Then the program should accept a taxpayer identification number and taxable income, compute the income tax, and display the results.

Use the following data to test the program:

Taxpayer number	Taxable income
1234	$ 17,500
1332	6,200
1424	10,201
2134	1,500
2432	47,300
3144	154,000
3223	23,350

4. Write a BASIC program to find the mean and standard deviation of the heights of the students in a class. If there are n students with heights x_i, $i = 1, \ldots, n$, the formulas for the mean and standard deviation are as follows:

Figure 9-21. Tax rate schedule

Schedule X
Single Taxpayers

Use this Schedule if you checked **Filing Status Box 1** on Form 1040—

If the amount on Form 1040, line 37 is: Over—	But not over—	Enter on Form 1040, line 38	of the amount over—
$0	$2,300	—0—	
2,300	3,400	........11%	$2,300
3,400	4,400	$121 + 12%	3,400
4,400	6,500	241 + 14%	4,400
6,500	8,500	535 + 15%	6,500
8,500	10,800	835 + 16%	8,500
10,800	12,900	1,203 + 18%	10,800
12,900	15,000	1,581 + 20%	12,900
15,000	18,200	2,001 + 23%	15,000
18,200	23,500	2,737 + 26%	18,200
23,500	28,800	4,115 + 30%	23,500
28,800	34,100	5,705 + 34%	28,800
34,100	41,500	7,507 + 38%	34,100
41,500	55,300	10,319 + 42%	41,500
55,300	81,800	16,115 + 48%	55,300
81,800	....	28,835 + 50%	81,800

$$\text{mean} = \bar{x} = \frac{\sum_{i=1}^{n} x_i}{n}$$

$$\text{standard deviation} = s = \sqrt{\frac{\sum_{i=1}^{n} (x_i - \bar{x})^2}{n}}$$

Test the program for a class of 25 students with the following heights in inches:

70	62	71	67	67
69	74	63	70	68
71	70	69	68	73
75	77	66	69	74
67	60	72	71	64

5. The results of a random survey of the households in an area of a city need to be analyzed. The data consists of the following information for each household in the area: an identification number, the annual income of the head of the household, and the number of people living in the household. The last set of data contains 9999 for the identification number. Write a BASIC program to analyze these data according to the following specifications:

a. Read the survey results into three arrays — one for the identification numbers, one for the annual incomes, and one for the number of people living in the households. Assume that there are no more than 50 households in the survey, and dimension all arrays accordingly. However, there may be fewer than 50 households, so a count of the number of households must be kept as the data is read. Finally, display the array data in columns below appropriate headings.

b. Calculate the average income and average number of people for all households. Display the results with appropriate headings.

c. Display the identification number and annual income of all households whose income is below average.

d. Determine the percent of the households in the area that have incomes below the poverty level. The poverty level depends on the number of people living in the household. If there is one person, the poverty level income is $6500. If there are two people, the poverty level is $8500. For a household with more than two people, the poverty level is $8500 plus $950 for each additional person.

   Use the following data to test the program:

Identification number	Annual income	Number of people	
1101	$10,750	3	
1020	5,250	2	
1083	8,000	5	
1141	8,500	1	
1157	14,300	4	
1235	9,000	6	
1347	10,350	7	
1508	4,350	1	
1512	6,900	3	
1513	7,600	4	
1584	8,385	2	
1631	6,300	2	
1690	17,200	4	
1742	15,350	5	
1755	5,700	1	
1759	8,300	3	
1809	10,250	1	
1853	12,500	2	*(continued)*

Identification number	Annual income	Number of people
1899	14,000	6
1903	2,500	1
1952	5,250	3
9999 (trailer value)		

6. This problem involves analyzing product sales information. Input consists of the identification number and quantity sold for each of 25 products. Write a BASIC program to do the following:

a. Read the identification numbers and quantities into two arrays. After all data has been read, display the arrays in columns below appropriate headings.

b. Calculate and display the average of the quantities sold.

c. Determine the number of products whose sales fall into each of the following categories:

> 500 or more
> 250 to 499
> 100 to 249
> 0 to 99

Display the results with appropriate headings.

d. Sort the quantity array into descending order (largest to smallest) using the bubble sort algorithm. Note that there are two arrays, although only the quantity array is to be sorted. However, whenever two elements of the quantity array are out of order and need to be switched, the corresponding identification numbers must be switched. After the array is sorted, display the two arrays in columns with appropriate headings.

e. Sort the identification number array into ascending order (smallest to largest). Again note that any exchange of elements in one array must be accompanied by an exchange of corresponding elements in the other array. After the array is sorted, display the two arrays in columns below appropriate headings.

Use the following data to test the program:

Identification number	Quantity sold
208	295
137	152
485	825
217	100
945	250
607	435
642	500
735	36
300	163
299	255
435	501
116	75
189	0
218	63
830	617
695	825
708	416
325	99
339	249
418	237
225	712
180	328
925	499
455	240
347	378

7. Merging is the process of bringing together two lists of data to form one. For example, consider the following lists of five numbers each:

List 1	List 2
2	1
3	6
5	8
8	9
10	12

When these two lists are merged, they form the following list:

Merged list

1
2
3
5
6
8
8
9
10
12

Notice that the original lists are in increasing order and so is the merged list.

Write a BASIC program to read two lists of 15 numbers each. The numbers may be in any order initially. The program should sort each list into increasing order and then merge the two lists to form one list of 30 numbers. Finally, the program should display the original two lists, the sorted lists, and the merged list.

Use the following data to test the program:

List 1	List 2
100	53
87	85
91	92
52	98
63	63
39	75
85	89
91	96
82	81
99	62
73	69
57	85
82	91
85	80
78	71

8. Write a BASIC program to read student test score data into an array, calculate the mean (average) of the test scores, tabulate the test scores, sort the test scores into descending order, and find the median (middle value) of the test scores.

Input data consists of a student's identification number and a test score for an unknown number of students. In the last set of input data the student identification number is 999. Use this trailer value to control the input process. Assume that there are no more than 99 sets of input data, and dimension all arrays accordingly.

Prepare the program according to the following specifications:

a. Read the identification numbers and the test scores into two arrays. It is necessary to count the data as it is read to get a count of the number of test scores to be processed. Finally, list below appropriate headings the data in the identification-number and test-score arrays. At the end, display a statement of the number of test scores in the data.

b. Accumulate and display the total of the test scores. Calculate and display the mean of the test scores. The mean is the average of a set of data values, which is found by dividing the total by the number of values.

c. Tabulate (count) the number of scores that fall into each of the following categories:

$$90 - 100$$
$$80 - 89$$
$$70 - 79$$
$$60 - 69$$
$$0 - 59$$

Display the results with appropriate titles.

d. Sort the test scores into descending order (largest to smallest). Display a list of the identification numbers and the test scores in descending order. Use the bubble sorting algorithm to sort the test-score data. Note that there are two arrays, although only the test-score array is to be sorted. However, when two elements of the test-score array are out of order and need to be switched, the corresponding identification numbers must be switched.

e. Determine and display the median of the test scores. The median is the middle value of a set of data. Fifty percent of the data values are greater than or equal to the median and 50% are less than or equal to the median. In order to determine the median, we must first sort the data into ascending or descending order. Then the median is the middle value of the sorted data when there is an odd number of values or the average of two middle values when there is an even number of values. Be sure to make the program sufficiently general to handle both cases.

Use the following input data to test the program:

Identification number	Test score	Identification number	Test score	Identification number	Test score
282	99	283	83	240	73
115	75	116	72	145	74
124	76	123	71	267	74
215	77	114	74	294	91
275	69	287	96	232	75
208	78	201	79	206	75
225	85	242	71	150	76
113	77	119	63	133	83
205	76	142	78	255	70
122	89	219	84	250	77
137	78	248	72	210	70
185	75	173	79	233	80
235	100	261	85	166	71
138	74	265	71	202	61
298	74	281	72	176	81
217	62	139	55	257	72
104	82	141	73	256	14
108	73	266	65	230	73
191	79	110	81	129	89

9. Each state has a two-letter abbreviation authorized by the U.S. Postal Service. For example, the abbreviation for California is CA; the abbreviation for New York is NY. (See a Zip Code directory for a complete list.)

Write a BASIC program that reads a complete table of state abbreviations and corresponding state names. Use one array for the abbreviations and another array for the names. Then display the arrays below appropriate headings. Next, accept a state abbreviation and search the table for the corresponding state's name. Display the abbreviation and the name. Repeat this part of the program until an abbreviation of XX is entered. Supply appropriate input data to test the program.

10. Write a BASIC program that reads an array of 20 names and sorts the names into alphabetical order. Each name consists of the last name, a comma, a space, and then the first name. It will be necessary to separate the names into two arrays before doing the sorting and then to reconstruct the names in the appropriate format after the sorting is completed. Display the sorted array of names. Supply an appropriate list of 20 names to test the program.

11. Write a BASIC program to score a 25-question true-false test. The first set of input consists of the correct answers to the questions. Following this is one set of input for each student with the student's number and his or her answers to the questions. The program should correct each student's answers. It should display each student's number followed by a list in adjacent columns of the correct answers, the student's answers, and an X opposite any incorrect answers. At the end of this list the program should display the percent of the answers that are correct for the student.

Use the following data to test the program:

Correct answers:	FTTTFFTFTTFTFFFFTFTTFFTFFT

Student's number	Student's answers
11301	FTTFTFTFTTTFTFFFTFTTFFFTFT
11302	FFTTTTFFTTFTTFFFTTFTFFTFFFF
11303	FTTTFFTFTTFTFFFFTFTTFFTFFT
11304	TFTTFFTFTTTFFFFFFFFTTFTTFTT
11305	TTTTFFFFTTFTFFFFTFTFFFFTFFT
11306	FFFFFFTFTTTTTFFFTFFTFTFFFF
11307	TTTFFFFTTTFTFFFFTTFTFTTFFT
11308	FTFTFTFTFTFTFTFTFTFTFTFTF
11309	TFTFTFTFTFTFTFTFTFTFTFTFT
11310	TTTTTTTTTTTTTTTTTTTTTTTTT
11311	FFFFFFFFFFFFFFFFFFFFFFFFF
11399 (trailer value)	

12. Using the data in Problem 11, write a BASIC program that determines and displays the percent of the students in the class that got each question correct. That is, determine and display the percent of the students that got the first question correct, the percent that got the second question correct, and so forth.

Chapter 10

Two-dimensional arrays and matrix operations

The type of array described in Chapter 9 is called a *one-dimensional array*. This is because we think of the data in the array as being organized in one direction, like a column (for example, see Figure 9-1). BASIC also allows two-dimensional arrays. In this chapter we examine two-dimensional arrays and their use in BASIC. We also discuss special operations for processing array data. After completing this chapter you should be able to write programs that process two-dimensional arrays.

10-1 Two-dimensional array concepts

A *two-dimensional array* is usually thought of as a table of data organized into rows and columns. Figure 10-1 shows a two-dimensional array of four rows and three columns. This data represents the test scores of four students on three different exams. For example, the data in row one represents the three test scores of student number 1. The score on the first test for this student is 91; this score is found in column 1 of row 1. In row 1, column 2, is the score of this student on the second test (78). The third test score for this student is found in row 1, column 3. Similarly, test scores for the other students are found in the other rows.

Like a one-dimensional array, a two-dimensional array is identified by an array variable. A two-dimensional array variable must follow the same syntax rules as a one-dimensional array variable. (See Table 9-1.) For example, A, S5, and Z3 are valid two-dimensional array variables. The same array variable cannot be used in

Figure 10-1. A two-dimensional array

Column numbers

	1	2	3
1	91	78	85
2	95	90	96
3	85	100	89
4	69	75	68

Row numbers

295

Figure 10-2. Subscripted variables for a two-dimensional array

Column numbers

	1	2	3
1	S(1, 1)	S(1, 2)	S(1, 3)
2	S(2, 1)	S(2, 2)	S(2, 3)
3	S(3, 1)	S(3, 2)	S(3, 3)
4	S(4, 1)	S(4, 2)	S(4, 3)

Row numbers

a program to identify both a one-dimensional array and a two-dimensional array. Thus, we cannot use A as an array variable for both types of arrays in a program.

To identify an element of a two-dimensional array, both the row number and the column number of the element must be given; that is, a subscripted variable is formed from the array variable and *two* subscripts. The subscripts are separated by commas and enclosed in parentheses. The first subscript is the row number and the second subscript is the column number. For example, assume that the array in Figure 10-1 is identified by the array variable S. Then the element in row 1, column 2, is referred to by the subscripted variable $S(1,2)$. The element in row 3, column 1, is $S(3,1)$. Figure 10-2 shows the subscripted variables for all elements in this two-dimensional array.

Two-dimensional array bounds

In the last chapter we noted that a one-dimensional array has an element numbered 0. Similarly, a two-dimensional array has a "0 row" and a "0 column." For example, in the array shown in Figure 10-2, the "0 row" contains the elements $S(0,0)$, $S(0,1)$, $S(0,2)$, and $S(0,3)$. The "0 column" has the elements $S(0,0)$, $S(1,0)$, $S(2,0)$, $S(3,0)$, and $S(4,0)$. Although these elements exist, they are not used in programming except in certain special situations.

We also noted in the last chapter that, unless we specify otherwise, the maximum element number for a one-dimensional array is 10. Similarly, for a two-dimensional array, the maximum row number is 10 and the maximum column number is 10, unless we indicate otherwise in the program.

In some versions of BASIC the minimum row number and column number is not automatically 0 but rather 1. Also in some versions of BASIC the maximum row and column number is not automatically 10. (See Table 10-1.)

If we need an array with row and column numbers greater than 10, the array must be specified in a DIM statement. For example, assume that the array T is to have 25 rows and 8 columns. The following DIM statement can be used to declare the array:

```
110 DIM T(25,8)
```

The numbers in parentheses are the maximum row number and column number, respectively. The array T in this example is said to be a "25-by-8" array.

Note that we can always use a DIM statement even if it is not needed. Thus, the following statement is valid:

```
120 DIM A(10,10)
```

In fact, most programmers declare all arrays in DIM statements, and we will follow that practice in this book.

Table 10-1. Two-dimensional array bound differences

BASIC version	Default minimum row and column number	Default maximum row and column number
ANS minimal BASIC	0	10
ANS BASIC	1	None, must dimension all two-dimensional arrays
Microsoft BASIC	0	None, must dimension all two-dimensional arrays
Applesoft BASIC	0	10
True BASIC	1	None, must dimension all two-dimensional arrays
BASIC-PLUS	0	10
VAX-11 BASIC	0	10

We can use one- and two-dimensional arrays in the same program as long as each array is identified by a different array variable. In addition, the same DIM statement can be used for both one- and two-dimensional arrays. For example, the following statement declares three arrays:

```
130 DIM X(20,20),Y(50),Z(5,100)
```

The first array is a 20-by-20 two-dimensional array, the second array is a 50-element one-dimensional array, and the third array is a 5-by-100 two-dimensional array.

If the OPTION BASE is available in the version of BASIC (see Table 9-3) it can be used to specify whether the minimum row and column number for all two-dimensional arrays is 0 or 1. In fact, if this statement is used in the program, it applies to *all* arrays in the program, both one- and two-dimensional. Thus, the statement

```
100 OPTION BASE 1
```

specifies that for all one-dimensional arrays the minimum element number is 1 and for all two-dimensional arrays the minimum row number is 1 and the minimum column number is 1.

Subscripts for two-dimensional arrays

Subscripts for two-dimensional arrays may be constants, variables, or more complex numeric expressions. For example, S(I,J) refers to the element in the "Ith" row and "Jth" column. Similarly, S(3,K + 2) refers to the element in row 3 and column K + 2. The value of each subscript must be between 0 and the maximum row and column number, respectively, specified in the DIM statement (or 10 if the DIM statement is not used). As with one-dimensional arrays, if the subscript is not a whole number, then, depending on the version of BASIC, its value is either rounded or truncated to locate the array element. (See Table 9-4.)

We can use a two-dimensional subscripted variable like any other variable. For example, all the following statements are acceptable in BASIC:

```
100 INPUT S(1,1),S(1,2),S(1,3)
130 LET A=S(I,J)+S(I,K)
160 PRINT S(X+3,2*Y-1)
190 IF S(I,3)>90 THEN 300
```

To illustrate the processing of a two-dimensional array in a program, assume that we need to find the total of all elements in the test-score array S discussed

Figure 10-3. A two-dimensional array-processing program

```
100 REM - TWO-DIMENSIONAL ARRAY DATA TOTALING PROGRAM
110 REM - VARIABLES:
120 REM       S  = TEST SCORE ARRAY
130 REM       T  = TOTAL
140 REM       I,J = COUNTERS
200 DIM S(4,3)
210 REM - READ ARRAY DATA
       .
       .
       .
270 REM - TOTAL ALL ELEMENTS OF ARRAY
280 LET T=0
290 FOR I=1 TO 4
300   FOR J=1 TO 3
310     LET T=T+S(I,J)
320   NEXT J
330 NEXT I
340 REM - DISPLAY ARRAY DATA
       .
       .
       .
460 REM - DISPLAY TOTAL
470 PRINT
480 PRINT "TOTAL OF ALL SCORES:";T
999 END
```

earlier. Figure 10-3 shows a program that does this. The program is complete except for the input and output of the array data, which we will discuss later.

In this program, the two-dimensional array is processed using nested FOR loops. The control variable of the outer loop is used as the subscript that indicates the row number. This control variable is incremented from 1 to 4. The control variable of the inner loop is used as the subscript for the column number. This control variable is incremented from 1 to 3. In the inner loop, an element of the array is added to the total (which is initially zero). For each repetition of the outer loop, the inner loop is executed three times, causing the elements of one row of the array to be added to the total. After four repetitions of the outer loop, the elements in all four rows will have been added to the total.

The loop pattern in this example is commonly used in processing two-dimensional arrays. We will see more examples of it later.

Higher-dimensional arrays

Some versions of BASIC allow arrays with more than two dimensions. (See Table 10-2.) For example, a three-dimensional array requires three subscripts, and the

Table 10-2. Multidimensional array differences

BASIC version	Maximum number of dimensions
ANS minimal BASIC	2
ANS BASIC	3
Microsoft BASIC	255
Applesoft BASIC	88
True BASIC	10
BASIC-PLUS	2
VAX-11 BASIC	32

maximum value of each subscript must be specified in a DIM statement (unless 10 is the maximum value). Similar rules apply to higher-dimensional arrays. The principles behind the processing of two-dimensional arrays that we discuss in this chapter apply also to higher-dimensional arrays.

10-2 Input and output of two-dimensional array data

Input and output of two-dimensional array data can be accomplished by listing the subscripted variables for the array in an INPUT, READ, or PRINT statement. For example, assume X is a 2-by-3 array. The following statements can be used to accept input data for X and then to display the array data:

```
10 INPUT X(1,1),X(1,2),X(1,3),X(2,1),X(2,2),X(2,3)
20 PRINT X(1,1);X(1,2);X(1,3);X(2,1);X(2,2);X(2,3)
```

The problem with this technique is that if the array is large, the list of subscripted variables will be long. The usual approach, therefore, is to use some sort of looping technique. For example, assume that the data for the 4-by-3 test score array, S, is to be entered one row at a time. The following loop can be used to accept the data:

```
100 FOR I=1 TO 4
110    INPUT S(I,1),S(I,2),S(I,3)
120 NEXT I
```

Execution of this loop causes the INPUT statement to be executed four times. Each time the statement is executed, a question-mark prompt is displayed on the CRT screen. Three test scores must be entered after each prompt. Each set of input data is stored in one row of the array.

We can use nested FOR loops for the input operation. The following statements show how this is done for the test-score array:

```
200 FOR I=1 TO 4
210    FOR J=1 TO 3
220       INPUT S(I,J)
230    NEXT J
240 NEXT I
```

In this case the INPUT statement is executed 12 times. Hence, 12 prompts are displayed on the CRT screen. Following each prompt, one test score must be entered. The first three scores entered must be the data for the first row; then the data for the second row must be entered, and so forth.

Nested FOR loops are often used to read data for a two-dimensional array using READ and DATA statements. For example, the following statements can be used to read the test-score data:

```
110 FOR I=1 TO 4
120    FOR J=1 TO 3
130       READ S(I,J)
140    NEXT J
150 NEXT I
        .
        .
        .
900 DATA 91,78,85,95,90,96
910 DATA 85,100,89,69,75,68
```

Notice that the data is recorded in the DATA statements in order by rows because this is the order in which the data is read in the nested FOR loops.

To display a two-dimensional array we can use a FOR loop. For example, the following statements display the test-score array with each row on a separate line:

```
200 FOR I=1 TO 4
210    PRINT S(I,1),S(I,2),S(I,3)
220 NEXT I
```

We can also use nested FOR loops as in the following example:

```
280 FOR I=1 TO 4
290    FOR J= 1 TO 3
300      PRINT S(I,J)
310    NEXT J
320 NEXT I
```

In this case, however, the elements of the array are displayed one per line on 12 lines.

To display a two-dimensional array with one row per line using nested FOR loops requires a special technique. Recall from Chapter 5 that a comma or a semicolon at the end of a PRINT statement causes the next value displayed to appear on the same line as the previous value. We can use this fact in the previous example to display the data in rows. We start by modifying statement 300 as follows:

```
300 PRINT S(I,J),
```

Notice that a comma has been added to the PRINT statement after the subscripted variable. Then, each time the PRINT statement is executed, the array element is displayed on the same line as the previous element, provided there is room on the line. Once a line is full, the next value is automatically displayed at the beginning of the next line. In this case, five values are displayed on each line because there are five print zones. (If a semicolon is used instead of a comma, the values are displayed closer together, and more data will appear on a line.)

This approach still does not display one row per line unless there are five elements in each row. However, by including a PRINT statement with no variables between the two NEXT statements, we obtain the desired result. This is shown in the program in Figure 10-4. In this program, the comma in the PRINT statement causes each value in a row to be displayed on the same line as the previous value. But after a complete row is displayed, the PRINT statement at line 320 causes a new line to be started. Thus, each row is displayed on a separate line.

There are other approaches to the input and output of array data, but the techniques can be quite complex. In general, it is best to use the simplest approach that causes the data to be processed in the desired order.

A complete program

We can now complete the program shown in Figure 10-3. Recall that this program finds the total of all elements in the 4-by-3 test-score array, S. To complete the program we need to include the statements necessary for the array data input and output.

The final program is shown in Figure 10-5. The flowchart of this program is

Figure 10-4. A program with two-dimensional array input and output

```
100 REM - TWO-DIMENSIONAL ARRAY INPUT AND OUTPUT PROGRAM
110 REM - VARIABLES:
120 REM        S  = TEST SCORE ARRAY
130 REM        I,J = COUNTERS
200 DIM S(4,3)
210 REM - READ ARRAY DATA
220 FOR I=1 TO 4
230    FOR J=1 TO 3
240      READ S(I,J)
250    NEXT J
260 NEXT I
270 REM - DISPLAY ARRAY DATA
280 FOR I=1 TO 4
290    FOR J=1 TO 3
300      PRINT S(I,J),
310    NEXT J
320    PRINT
330 NEXT I
900 REM - ARRAY DATA
910 DATA 91,78,85,95,90,96
920 DATA 85,100,89,69,75,68
999 END
```

(a) The program

91	78	85
95	90	96
85	100	89
69	75	68

(b) Output

in Figure 10-6. Nested FOR loops are used to read the array data from DATA statements. Nested FOR loops are also used to display the array data. The PRINT statement at line 400 displays the value of the outer FOR loop's control variable. This corresponds to the student's number. The comma at the end of this PRINT statement prevents a new line from being started. Thus, when the PRINT statement at line 420 is executed, the output is displayed on the same line as the previous output. The comma at the end of this PRINT statement causes all elements in one row of the array to be displayed on the same line. The PRINT statement at line 440 starts a new line for the next row of the array.

10-3 Processing two-dimensional arrays

As we have seen, a two-dimensional array can be processed using nested FOR loops. This is a very common technique. The control variable of the outer loop is used as one subscript for the array and the control variable of the inner loop is used as the other subscript. With an appropriate initial value, limit, and increment for each loop, part or all of the array can be processed. In this section we show several examples that use this and other techniques for two-dimensional array processing. We will use the 4-by-3 test-score array S described earlier in our examples.

```
100 REM - TWO-DIMENSIONAL ARRAY DATA TOTALING PROGRAM
110 REM - VARIABLES:
120 REM      S = TEST SCORE ARRAY
130 REM      T = TOTAL
140 REM      I,J = COUNTERS
200 DIM S(4,3)
210 REM - READ ARRAY DATA
220 FOR I=1 TO 4
230   FOR J=1 TO 3
240     READ S(I,J)
250   NEXT J
260 NEXT I
270 REM - TOTAL ALL ELEMENTS OF ARRAY
280 LET T=0
290 FOR I=1 TO 4
300   FOR J=1 TO 3
310     LET T=T+S(I,J)
320   NEXT J
330 NEXT I
340 REM - DISPLAY ARRAY DATA
350 PRINT TAB(19);"TEST SCORES"
360 PRINT
370 PRINT "STUDENT","TEST 1","TEST 2","TEST 3"
380 PRINT
390 FOR I=1 TO 4
400   PRINT I,
410   FOR J=1 TO 3
420     PRINT S(I,J),
430   NEXT J
440   PRINT
450 NEXT I
460 REM - DISPLAY TOTAL
470 PRINT
480 PRINT "TOTAL OF ALL SCORES:";T
900 REM - ARRAY DATA
910 DATA 91,78,85,95,90,96
920 DATA 85,100,89,69,75,68
999 END
```

(a) The program

```
                  TEST SCORES

STUDENT        TEST 1         TEST 2         TEST 3

1              91             78             85
2              95             90             96
3              85             100            89
4              69             75             68

TOTAL OF ALL SCORES: 1021
```

(b) Output

Initializing a two-dimensional array

Very often we must initialize all elements of an array to the same value. For example, assume we must set each element of the test-score array to zero. The following statements accomplish this:

```
110 FOR I=1 TO 4
120   FOR J=1 TO 3
130     LET S(I,J)=0
140   NEXT J
150 NEXT I
```

In this example the control variable of the outer loop is used as the row number. The outer loop is executed with the control variable incremented from one to the maximum number of rows in the array. The control variable of the inner loop is used as the column number. It is incremented from one to the maximum number of columns. Thus, for each execution of the outer loop, the inner loop causes the elements in one row to be set to zero. Because the outer loop is executed four times, once for each row, all elements of the array are set to zero by these statements.

Totaling the elements in each row or column of a two-dimensional array

Occasionally it is necessary to find the total of the elements in each row or column of an array. For example, to find the average of the test scores for each student, we must first determine the total of the elements in each row of the test-score array. This can be accomplished most easily by using a one-dimensional array of four elements, where each element is used to accumulate the total of a row. Assume that this one-dimensional array is called R. Because this array is used to accumulate totals, it must first be initialized to zero. Then the elements in each row of the test-score array are successively added to the appropriate element of the row-total array. The following statements show how this is done:

```
210 FOR I=1 TO 4
220   LET R(I)=0
230 NEXT I
240 FOR I=1 TO 4
250   FOR J=1 TO 3
260     LET R(I)=R(I)+S(I,J)
270   NEXT J
280 NEXT I
```

When execution of this sequence of statements is completed, the elements of the array R will contain the totals of the elements in each row of the test-score array.

A similar approach can be used to calculate the total of the elements of each column of the test-score array. Assume that C identifies a one-dimensional, three-element array. After setting the elements of C to zero, the following sequence of statements accumulates the total of each column of the test-score array and assigns the results to elements of the array C:

```
310 FOR J=1 TO 3
320   LET C(J)=0
330 NEXT J
340 FOR J=1 TO 3
350   FOR I=1 TO 4
360     LET C(J)=C(J)+S(I,J)
370   NEXT I
380 NEXT J
```

Notice in this example that the outer loop of the nested FOR loops controls the column number. The inner loop controls the row number and is executed four times for each execution of the outer loop. At the end of the execution of this sequence of statements, the elements of the array C will contain the correct column totals.

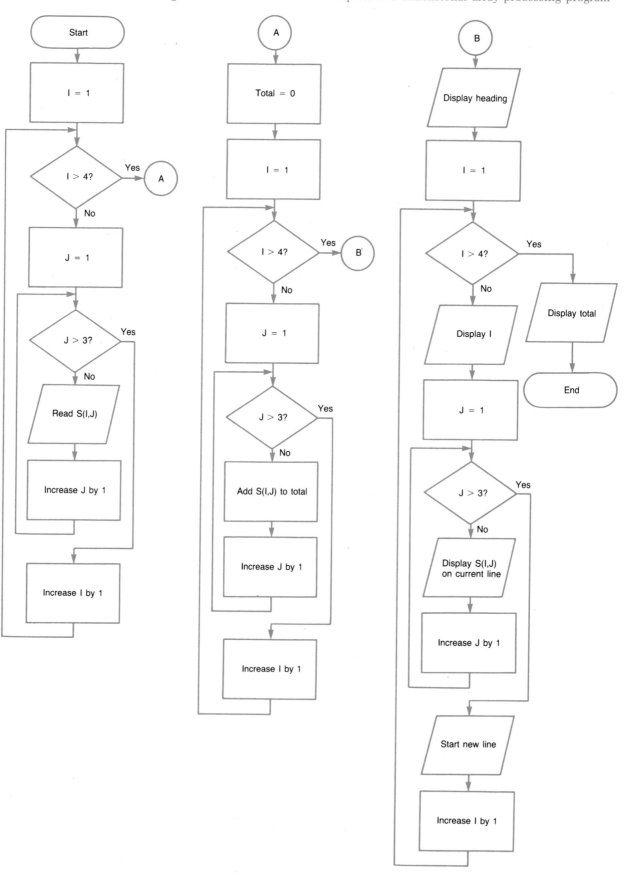

Counting specific values in a two-dimensional array

As with one-dimensional arrays, sometimes we need to determine how many times a particular value occurs in a two-dimensional array. For example, the following statements count the number of elements of the test score array that are equal to 100:

```
410 LET N=0
420 FOR I=1 TO 4
430   FOR J=1 TO 3
440     IF S(I,J)<>100 THEN 460
450       LET N=N+1
460   NEXT J
470 NEXT I
```

In this example, N, which is initially zero, is incremented by 1 each time an element of the array is equal to 100. When these statements have been executed, N will equal the number of elements of the test-score array that are equal to 100.

A more complex example involves counting the number of rows in the test-score array that have all elements equal to 100. The following statements show how this is done:

```
510 LET C=0
520 FOR I=1 TO 4
530   LET A=1
540   FOR J=1 TO 3
550     IF S(I,J)=100 THEN 570
560       LET A=0
570   NEXT J
580   IF A=0 THEN 600
590     LET C=C+1
600 NEXT I
```

In this example, the variable A is used to indicate whether or not all elements in a row equal 100. Before checking each row — that is, before the inner loop is executed — A is set equal to 1. While checking the elements in a row in the inner loop, A is set equal to 0 if any element in that row is found that is not equal to 100. After all elements in a row have been checked, the value of A is tested. If A equals 1, indicating that all elements in the row were 100, C is increased by 1. At the end of execution, C will equal the number of rows in the test-score array that have all elements equal to 100.

The variable A in this example is used to signal the presence or absence of a condition. Such a variable is called a *flag*. Often a string variable is used as a flag, and string constants such as "YES" and "NO" are used instead of 1 and 0.

Searching a two-dimensional array

To search a two-dimensional array for a specific value, we include a test for the value in the nested FOR loops. For example, assume that it is necessary to display the student number and test number for any student who scored 90 or more on any test. The following statements accomplish this:

```
610 FOR I=1 TO 4
620   FOR J=1 TO 3
630     IF S(I,J)<90 THEN 650
```

```
640        PRINT I,J
650     NEXT J
660 NEXT I
```

In this example, the PRINT statement is executed only if the student's test score is 90 or above. The current values of the control variables for each FOR loop are displayed and indicate the student number and test number, respectively.

Frequently when we search a two-dimensional array, we search one column (or row) for a specific value and use the information from the other columns (or rows). For example, assume that we wish to calculate and display the average of the second and third test scores for each student who scored 90 or above on the first test. The following statements accomplish this:

```
710 FOR I=1 TO 4
720    IF S(I,1)<90 THEN 750
730       LET A=(S(I,2)+S(I,3))/2
740          PRINT I,A
750 NEXT I
```

In the IF statement, S(I,1) refers to the first column of the Ith row of the array. Hence, each time through the loop, we check the first score to see whether it is less than 90. If this is not the case, we compute the average of the other two scores for that student and display the student's number and average.

Sorting the elements in a row or column of a two-dimensional array

We can sort the elements in one row or column of a two-dimensional array. If it is necessary to maintain the correspondence between elements in a row or column during the sorting process, then any time two elements in one row or column are switched, the corresponding elements in the other rows or columns must be switched. For example, the following sequence of statements sorts the first column of the test-score array into descending order:

```
710 FOR K=3 TO 1 STEP -1
720    FOR I=1 TO K
730       IF S(I,1)>=S(I+1,1) THEN 790
740          FOR J=1 TO  3
750             LET T=S(I,J)
760             LET S(I,J)=S(I+1,J)
770             LET S(I+1,J)=T
780          NEXT J
790    NEXT I
800 NEXT K
```

The sorting is done on the first column because the second subscript in each subscripted variable used in the IF statement is 1. The innermost loop switches all the elements of two rows if the elements in the first column are out of order with respect to each other.

10-4 An illustrative program

To illustrate some of the two-dimensional array processing techniques discussed in this chapter, consider the problem of tabulating test scores. Assume that there are

12 students in a class and each student took four tests. The problem is to count, for each test, the number of students who scored between 90 and 100, between 80 and 89, between 70 and 79, and between 0 and 69. In addition, we need the total number of test scores that fall in each range for all tests.

Figure 10-7 shows the program that accomplishes this. In this program, S is a 12-by-4 array that contains the test-score data. The rows correspond to the students and the columns correspond to the tests. The 4-by-4 array C is used to keep count of the number of test scores in each range for each test. The first row of this array is used for the number of scores between 90 and 100 on each of the four tests, the second row is used for the number of scores between 80 and 89 on each test, and so on. Finally, the four-element, one-dimensional array T is used for the total number of test scores in each range on all tests.

At the beginning of the program, the test-score data is read into the S array using nested FOR loops. Then the elements of the C array are initialized to zero.

Figure 10-7. The test-score tabulation program

```
100 REM - TEST SCORE TABULATION PROGRAM
110 REM - VARIABLES:
120 REM       S  = TEST SCORE ARRAY
130 REM       C  = ARRAY FOR COUNT OF TEST SCORES
135 REM            IN EACH RANGE FOR EACH TEST
140 REM       T  = ARRAY FOR TOTAL NUMBER OF TEST SCORES
145 REM            IN EACH RANGE
150 REM       I,J = COUNTERS
200 DIM S(12,4),C(4,4),T(4)
210 REM - READ TEST SCORE ARRAY DATA
220 FOR I=1 TO 12
230    FOR J=1 TO 4
240       READ S(I,J)
250    NEXT J
260 NEXT I
270 REM - COUNT TEST SCORES IN EACH RANGE
280 FOR I=1 TO 4
290    FOR J=1 TO 4
300       LET C(I,J)=0
310    NEXT J
320 NEXT I
330 FOR I=1 TO 12
340    FOR J=1 TO 4
350       IF S(I,J)<90 THEN 380
360          LET C(1,J)=C(1,J)+1
370       GOTO 450
380       IF S(I,J)<80 THEN 410
390          LET C(2,J)=C(2,J)+1
400       GOTO 450
410       IF S(I,J)<70 THEN 440
420          LET C(3,J)=C(3,J)+1
430       GOTO 450
440          LET C(4,J)=C(4,J)+1
450    NEXT J
460 NEXT I
470 REM - ACCUMULATE TOTAL IN EACH RANGE
480 FOR I=1 TO 4
490    LET T(I)=0
500 NEXT I
510 FOR I=1 TO 4
520    FOR J=1 TO 4
530       LET T(I)=T(I)+C(I,J)
540    NEXT J
550 NEXT I
```

(continued)

Figure 10-7. Continued

```
560 REM - DISPLAY OUTPUT
570 PRINT TAB(30);"TEST SCORE SUMMARY"
580 PRINT
590 PRINT ,"90-100","80-89","70-79","0-69"
600 PRINT
610 FOR J=1 TO 4
620   PRINT "TEST";J,
630   FOR I=1 TO 4
640     PRINT C(I,J),
650   NEXT I
660 NEXT J
670 PRINT
680 PRINT "TOTALS",
690 FOR I=1 TO 4
700   PRINT T(I),
710 NEXT I
900 REM - TEST SCORE ARRAY DATA
910 DATA 74,84,86,77,100,94,95,89
920 DATA 82,87,87,91,35,48,52,63
930 DATA 85,84,75,72,91,84,72,95
940 DATA 72,78,81,69,84,75,80,79
950 DATA 70,69,72,73,55,72,70,38
960 DATA 90,95,91,82,75,81,78,72
999 END
```

(a) The program

```
                        TEST SCORE SUMMARY

              90-100        80-89         70-79         0-69

   TEST 1        3             3             4             2
   TEST 2        2             5             3             2
   TEST 3        2             4             5             1
   TEST 4        2             2             5             3

   TOTALS        9            14            17             8
```

(b) Output

This is necessary because these elements are used to count the number of test scores in each range. Next, nested FOR loops cause the elements of the S array to be checked one at a time. Within the FOR loops, IF statements are used to determine in which range a test score falls. Once this is determined, one is added to the appropriate element of the C array.

After all elements of the S array have been checked, the totals of the counts in each range are accumulated. This is done by totaling the elements in each row of the C array. The T array is used to accumulate the totals. Notice that the elements of the T array are first initialized to zero.

The final steps in the program involve displaying the output. First, headings are displayed. Then the elements of the C array are displayed using nested FOR loops. Each column of the array is displayed on a separate line. A column of this array represents the counts of the number of test scores in each range on one test. The test number is displayed on the left by using the control variable of the outer FOR loop in a PRINT statement at the beginning of the outer loop. The elements in a column are displayed by using a PRINT statement in the inner FOR loop. A comma at the end of the PRINT statement causes the output to be displayed on one line. Because there are five print zones and a value is displayed in each zone, a new line will begin after the last value is displayed in a line. Hence, an extra PRINT statement between the two NEXT statements is not needed to start a new line. Finally, the elements of the T array are displayed at the end of the output.

10-5 Two-dimensional string arrays

In Section 9-6 we discussed one-dimensional string arrays. Versions of BASIC that allow such arrays also permit two-dimensional string arrays. (See Table 9-5.) As with all string variables, a two-dimensional string-array variable must end with a dollar sign. A two-dimensional string array must be specified in a DIM statement (unless the maximum row and column numbers are 10). For example, the following DIM statement declares an eight-by-five string array T$:

```
10 DIM T$(8,5)
```

Two-dimensional subscripted string variables can be used just like any string variable. The important thing to remember is that two subscripts are always required. The following are examples of uses of two-dimensional subscripted string variables:

```
130 LET T$(2,4)="HELP"
160 INPUT T$(I,J)
190 IF T$(K+1,3)=T$(K-1,3) THEN 300
```

Most of the techniques for processing two-dimensional numeric arrays can be adapted to two-dimensional string-array processing.

*10-6 Matrix operations

An array is sometimes called a *matrix*. In general, a matrix is a group of data that is organized into rows and columns. The two-dimensional test-score array in Figure 10-1 is organized this way and can be regarded as a matrix. A one-dimensional array is also a matrix because it can be thought of as being composed of a number of rows and *one* column.

Some versions of BASIC provide special statements and functions that perform various operations on an entire matrix. (See Table 10-3.) These are called the MAT

Table 10-3. Matrix operation differences

BASIC version	MAT *statements and functions available*
ANS minimal BASIC	No
ANS BASIC	Yes
Microsoft BASIC	No
Applesoft BASIC	No
True BASIC	Yes
BASIC-PLUS	Yes
VAX-11 BASIC	Yes

or matrix operations. The characteristics of these operations vary slightly from one version of BASIC to another. In this section we describe a common form of the matrix operations. We also note when certain characteristics of the operations are different in different versions of BASIC.

Elementary matrix operations

To illustrate the characteristics of the matrix operations, assume that S is a 4-by-3 matrix (i.e., array). If we wish to initialize all the elements of S to 0, we can write the following nested FOR loops:

```
110 FOR I=1 TO 4
120   FOR J=1 TO 3
130     LET S(I,J)=0
140   NEXT J
150 NEXT I
```

With a matrix operation, however, we can achieve the same result with one statement as follows:

```
110 MAT S=ZER
```

The effect of this statement is to set all elements of the matrix S (except the elements in the 0-row and 0-column) to zero.

The syntax of the matrix zero-initialization statement is as follows:

```
ln MAT array variable=ZER
```

The statement must begin with the keyword MAT. An array variable without a subscript must appear to the left of the equal sign. For example, the following statement sets all the elements of the matrix T to zero:

```
250 MAT T=ZER
```

The matrix zero-initialization statement illustrates the general characteristics of the matrix operations. All matrix operations accomplish in one statement what normally requires several statements. Each matrix statement begins with the keyword MAT. The matrix operation affects all elements in the matrix *except* the elements in the 0-row and 0-column. These elements are not changed by any of the matrix operations.

A matrix operation can be used with a one-dimensional or two-dimensional array. For example, assume that X is a one-dimensional array with 20 elements. The following matrix operation statement sets each element of X to zero:

```
210 MAT X=ZER
```

In general, any array that is processed by a matrix operation should be declared in a DIM statement. This is so that the number of elements affected by the operation is explicitly stated in the program. It is possible to leave out the DIM statement for some arrays when using the matrix operations. However, the rules for determining the size of the array that is used in the matrix operation are complex, and this situation should be avoided.

The matrix zero-initialization statement sets all elements of a matrix to zero. We can also set all elements to one with the matrix constant-initialization statement.

The syntax of this statement is as follows:

> *ln* MAT *array variable*=CON

For example, the following statement initializes all elements of S to one:

    120 MAT S=CON

If we wish to copy one matrix into another, we can use a matrix assignment statement. The syntax of this statement is as follows:

> *ln* MAT *array variable*=*array variable*

For example, the following statement copies the elements of X into Y:

    220 MAT Y=X

Whenever a matrix assignment statement is used, the two arrays must be the same size.

Matrix input

Input of matrix data can be accomplished with the MAT INPUT or MAT READ statements. The MAT INPUT statement accepts input data for a matrix from the keyboard. The syntax of this statement is as follows:

> *ln* MAT INPUT *list of array variables separated by commas*

For example, the following statement can be used to accept the data for the 4-by-3 test score matrix S:

    110 MAT INPUT S

When the MAT INPUT statement is executed, a question-mark prompt is displayed on the CRT screen. Following the prompt, all the data for the matrix must be entered. The data must be entered in order by rows with the elements separated by commas. For example, the data for S would be entered as follows:

    ? 91,78,85,95,90,96,85,100,89,69,75,68

The first three values are the elements for the first row; then comes the data for the second row, and so forth. Notice that data is not entered for the 0-row and 0-column because the elements in this row and column are not affected by any of the matrix operations.

We can use the MAT INPUT statement for one-dimensional array input. For example, the following statement accepts input data for the five-element array Z:

    210 MAT INPUT Z

After the question-mark prompt is displayed, all five elements of Z must be entered separated by commas.

We can list more than one array variable in a MAT INPUT statement. For example, the following statement can be used to accept input for both S and Z:

```
220 MAT INPUT S,Z
```

All data for S must be entered followed by the data for Z. We can also use the MAT INPUT statement for one- and two-dimensional string arrays. For example, assume that T$ is an 8-by-5 string array. The following statement can be used to accept input data for the array:

```
230 MAT INPUT T$
```

Each input element entered must be a string and the data must be entered in order by rows.

Matrix data can be read from DATA statements using the MAT READ statement. The syntax of the MAT READ statement is as follows:

> *ln* MAT READ *list of array variables separated by commas*

For example, the following statements can be used to read the data for the test-score matrix S:

```
120 MAT READ S
140 DATA 91,78,85,95,90,96
150 DATA 85,100,89,69,75,68
```

The data in the DATA statements is in order by rows. This is required with the MAT READ statement. Notice also that data is not provided for the 0-row and 0-column.

As with the MAT INPUT statement, the MAT READ statement can be used to read one-dimensional array data, multiple arrays, and string arrays. Thus, if Z and S are one- and two-dimensional arrays, respectively, and T$ is a string array, the following statement is valid:

```
240 MAT READ Z,S,T$
```

The corresponding DATA statements must contain all the data for Z, followed by all of the data for S, and then the string data for T$.

Matrix output

Matrix output can be displayed with the MAT PRINT statement.† The syntax of this statement is as follows:

> *ln* MAT PRINT *array variable*

For example, to display the test-score matrix S, we can use the following statement:

```
130 MAT PRINT S
```

When this statement is executed, all the data in the matrix S (except the data in the 0-row and 0-column) is displayed. Notice that there can be only one array variable

---

† Some versions of BASIC also have a MAT PRINT USING statement.

in the MAT PRINT statement. (Some versions of BASIC allow multiple array variables separated by commas or semicolons in the MAT PRINT statement.)

When there is no punctuation in the MAT PRINT statement, each element is displayed on a separate line. Thus, if S is a 4-by-3 matrix, 12 lines are displayed by the previous statement. The first three lines contain the data from the first row, then comes the data from the second row, and so forth.

To display the data in a tabular form with one row per line, the array variable in the MAT PRINT statement should be followed by a comma or a semicolon. For example, either of the following statements could be used to display the data in the array S by rows:

```
130 MAT PRINT S,
130 MAT PRINT S;
```

A comma causes the data to be displayed with one element in each print zone (i.e., five elements per line). A semicolon causes the data to be displayed as close together as possible. (In some versions of BASIC, if no comma or semicolon comes after the array variable, the data is displayed in rows as if a comma were used.)

Figure 10-8 shows a program that contains matrix input and output. The input data is read from DATA statements using a MAT READ statement. The output is displayed using a MAT PRINT statement. Notice that a comma is used to display the data with one row per line. If a semicolon were used instead of a comma, the output would be closer together.

The MAT PRINT statement can also be used to display one-dimensional arrays. For example, to display the five elements of the one-dimensional array Z on five lines, we can use the following statement:

```
230 MAT PRINT Z
```

If a comma or semicolon were used after the array variable in this statement, the data would be displayed on one line. We can also use the MAT PRINT statement to display string arrays.

Matrix input and output statements can be used in programs that do not

Figure 10-8. A matrix input and output program

```
100 REM - MATRIX INPUT AND OUTPUT PROGRAM
110 DIM S(4,3)
120 MAT READ S
130 MAT PRINT S,
140 DATA 91,78,85,95,90,96
150 DATA 85,100,89,69,75,68
160 END
```

(a) The program

91	78	85
95	90	96
85	100	89
69	75	68

(b) Output

involve other matrix operations. This can often simplify the input and output steps in a program that requires one- and two-dimensional arrays.

An illustrative program

Figure 10-7 showed a program that tabulated test scores. Several of the steps in this program can be simplified by using matrix operations. Statements 220 through 260 can be replaced by a MAT READ statement. Matrix zero-initialization statements can be used in place of statements 280 through 320 and statements 480 through 500. The output steps in statements 690 through 710 can be accomplished with a MAT PRINT statement. These modifications are shown in the program in Figure 10-9. The output from this program is the same as for the previous version of the program.

Other matrix operations

A number of matrix operations are used for various mathematical computations. To understand these operations fully, the programmer should be familiar with elementary matrix algebra. In this subsection we explain and illustrate these operations.

Besides setting the elements of a matrix to zero or one, we can also initialize a matrix to the identity matrix. An identity matrix has ones along the main diagonal and zeros elsewhere. The syntax of the matrix identity-initialization statement that accomplishes this is as follows:

```
ln MAT array variable=IDN
```

For example, to initialize the matrix X to the identity matrix, we use the following statement:

```
120 MAT X=IDN
```

Only a square matrix (i.e., a matrix with the same number of rows and columns) can be initialized to the identity matrix. Figure 10-10 shows a program that initializes and displays an identity matrix.

The corresponding elements of two matrices can be added or subtracted and the result assigned to a third matrix using special matrix statements. The syntax of the matrix addition and subtraction statements is as follows:

```
ln MAT array variable=array variable+array variable
ln MAT array variable=array variable−array variable
```

For example, to add the elements of the matrices A and B and assign the results to the matrix C, we use the following statement:

```
140 MAT C=A+B
```

Similarly, if the difference between the elements of A and B must be computed and assigned to D, we use the statement:

```
150 MAT D=A−B
```

Figure 10-11 shows a program that includes these operations. Note that whenever matrix addition or subtraction is used, the sizes of all matrices must be the same;

Figure 10-9. The test-score tabulation program using matrix operations

```
100 REM - TEST SCORE TABULATION PROGRAM
110 REM - VARIABLES:
120 REM       S  = TEST SCORE ARRAY
130 REM       C  = ARRAY FOR COUNT OF TEST SCORES
135 REM              IN EACH RANGE FOR EACH TEST
140 REM       T  = ARRAY FOR TOTAL NUMBER OF TEST SCORES
145 REM              IN EACH RANGE
150 REM       I,J  = COUNTERS
200 DIM S(12,4),C(4,4),T(4)
210 REM - READ TEST SCORE ARRAY DATA
220 MAT READ S
270 REM - COUNT TEST SCORES IN EACH RANGE
280 MAT C=ZER
330 FOR I=1 TO 12
340    FOR J=1 TO 4
350      IF S(I,J)<90 THEN 380
360        LET C(1,J)=C(1,J)+1
370      GOTO 450
380      IF S(I,J)<80 THEN 410
390        LET C(2,J)=C(2,J)+1
400      GOTO 450
410      IF S(I,J)<70 THEN 440
420        LET C(3,J)=C(3,J)+1
430      GOTO 450
440        LET C(4,J)=C(4,J)+1
450    NEXT J
460 NEXT I
470 REM - ACCUMULATE TOTAL IN EACH RANGE
480 MAT T=ZER
510 FOR I=1 TO 4
520    FOR J=1 TO 4
530      LET T(I)=T(I)+C(I,J)
540    NEXT J
550 NEXT I
560 REM - DISPLAY OUTPUT
570 PRINT TAB(30);"TEST SCORE SUMMARY"
580 PRINT
590 PRINT ,"90-100","80-89","70-79","0-69"
600 PRINT
610 FOR J=1 TO 4
620    PRINT "TEST";J,
630    FOR I=1 TO 4
640      PRINT C(I,J),
650    NEXT I
660 NEXT J
670 PRINT
680 PRINT "TOTALS",
690 MAT PRINT T,
900 REM - TEST SCORE ARRAY DATA
910 DATA 74,84,86,77,100,94,95,89
920 DATA 82,87,87,91,35,48,52,63
930 DATA 85,84,75,72,91,84,72,95
940 DATA 72,78,81,69,84,75,80,79
950 DATA 70,69,72,73,55,72,70,38
960 DATA 90,95,91,82,75,81,78,72
999 END
```

that is, the matrices that are added or subtracted and the matrix to which the result of the operation is assigned must all have the same number of rows and columns.

All elements of a matrix can be multiplied by the same value by using a matrix scalar multiplication statement. The syntax of this statement is as follows:

ln MAT *array variable=(numeric expression)*∗*array variable*

Figure 10-10. A program that displays an identity matrix

```
100 REM - MATRIX IDENTITY DEMONSTRATION PROGRAM
110 DIM X(4,4)
120 MAT X=IDN
130 PRINT "IDENTITY MATRIX"
140 MAT PRINT X;
150 END
```

(a) The program

```
IDENTITY MATRIX
 1  0  0  0

 0  1  0  0

 0  0  1  0

 0  0  0  1
```

(b) Output

The numeric expression in parentheses can be a constant, a variable, or a more complex numeric expression. (In some versions of BASIC, the parentheses are not required.) For example, to double the elements of the matrix A and assign the result to the matrix B, we can use the following statement:

```
130 MAT B=(2)*A
```

Figure 10-12 shows the effect of this statement in a program. Notice that A and B must be the same size (i.e., they must have the same number of rows and columns). The following are other examples of scalar multiplication:

```
210 MAT C=(K)*B
220 MAT D=(K+5)*C
```

Two matrices can be multiplied using a special matrix operation. Matrix multiplication does *not* involve multiplication of the corresponding elements of two matrices; rather, it involves a special form of multiplication.† Figure 10-13 shows an example of matrix multiplication. Notice that in matrix multiplication the number of columns in the first matrix must be the same as the number of rows in the second matrix (i.e., the matrices must be *conformable*). The product contains the same number of rows as the first matrix and the same number of columns as the second matrix.

The syntax of the matrix multiplication statement in BASIC is as follows:

> *ln* MAT *array variable=array variable*∗*array variable*

For example, to multiply matrices A and B and assign the result to C, we use the following statement:

```
140 MAT C=A*B
```

Figure 10-14 shows a program that includes this statement. Notice that A is a 2-by-3 matrix, B is a 3-by-2 matrix, and C is a 2-by-2 matrix.

† Most college algebra texts explain matrix multiplication in detail.

Figure 10-11. A program with matrix addition and subtraction

```
100 REM - MATRIX ADDITION AND SUBTRACTION PROGRAM
110 DIM A(2,3),B(2,3),C(2,3),D(2,3)
120 MAT READ A
130 MAT READ B
140 MAT C=A+B
150 MAT D=A-B
160 PRINT "MATRIX A"
170 MAT PRINT A,
180 PRINT "MATRIX B"
190 MAT PRINT B,
200 PRINT "MATRIX C=A+B"
210 MAT PRINT C,
220 PRINT "MATRIX D=A-B"
230 MAT PRINT D,
240 DATA 5,7,9,2,4,6
250 DATA 3,5,7,6,4,2
260 END
```

(a) The program

```
MATRIX A
 5            7            9

 2            4            6


MATRIX B
 3            5            7

 6            4            2


MATRIX C=A+B
 8           12           16

 8            8            8


MATRIX D=A-B
 2            2            2

-4            0            4
```

(b) Output

Two built-in functions process matrices — the TRN function and the INV function. The first finds the transpose of a matrix and the second finds the inverse of a matrix.

The *transpose* of a matrix is the matrix whose columns are the same as the rows of the original matrix. For example, consider the following matrix:

$$\begin{pmatrix} 2 & 4 & 6 \\ 1 & 3 & 5 \end{pmatrix}$$

The transpose of this matrix is as follows:

$$\begin{pmatrix} 2 & 1 \\ 4 & 3 \\ 6 & 5 \end{pmatrix}$$

Figure 10-12. A program with scalar multiplication

```
100 REM - MATRIX SCALAR MULTIPLICATION PROGRAM
110 DIM A(2,3),B(2,3)
120 MAT READ A
130 MAT B=(2)*A
140 PRINT "MATRIX A"
150 MAT PRINT A,
160 PRINT "MATRIX B=(2)*A"
170 MAT PRINT B,
180 DATA 5,7,9,2,4,6
190 END
```

(a) The program

```
MATRIX A
 5              7              9

 2              4              6


MATRIX B=(2)*A
 10            14             18

 4             8              12
```

(b) Output

Figure 10-13. Matrix multiplication

$$\begin{pmatrix} 2 & 4 & 6 \\ 1 & 3 & 5 \end{pmatrix} \times \begin{pmatrix} 1 & 5 \\ 4 & 2 \\ 3 & 6 \end{pmatrix}$$

$$= \begin{pmatrix} 2 \times 1 + 4 \times 4 + 6 \times 3 & 2 \times 5 + 4 \times 2 + 6 \times 6 \\ 1 \times 1 + 3 \times 4 + 5 \times 3 & 1 \times 5 + 3 \times 2 + 5 \times 6 \end{pmatrix}$$

$$= \begin{pmatrix} 2 + 16 + 18 & 10 + 8 + 36 \\ 1 + 12 + 15 & 5 + 6 + 30 \end{pmatrix}$$

$$= \begin{pmatrix} 36 & 54 \\ 28 & 41 \end{pmatrix}$$

To form the transpose of a matrix in BASIC, we use the TRN function. For example, the following statement assigns the transpose of matrix A to the matrix B:

```
130 MAT B=TRN(A)
```

This statement is used in the program in Figure 10-15.

The *inverse* of a matrix is the matrix that, when multiplied by the original matrix, yields the identity matrix. Only a square matrix (i.e., a matrix with the same number of rows and columns) can have an inverse — and then only if certain other conditions hold. In BASIC the INV function is used to form the inverse of a matrix. For example, the following statement finds the inverse of the matrix A and assigns it to the matrix B:

```
130 MAT B=INV(A)
```

Figure 10-14. A program with matrix multiplication

```
100 REM - MATRIX MULTIPLICATION PROGRAM
110 DIM A(2,3),B(3,2),C(2,2)
120 MAT READ A
130 MAT READ B
140 MAT C=A*B
150 PRINT "MATRIX A"
160 MAT PRINT A,
170 PRINT "MATRIX B"
180 MAT PRINT B,
190 PRINT "MATRIX C=A*B"
200 MAT PRINT C,
210 DATA 2,4,6,1,3,5
220 DATA 1,5,4,2,3,6
230 END
```

(a) The program

```
MATRIX A
 2              4              6

 1              3              5


MATRIX B
 1              5

 4              2

 3              6


MATRIX C=A*B
 36             54

 28             41
```

(b) Output

Figure 10-16 shows a program that uses this statement to find the inverse of a matrix and then multiplies the result by the original matrix to obtain the identity matrix.

Matrix inversion can be used to solve systems of linear equations. For example, consider the following equations:

$$2x_1 + 1x_2 = 5$$
$$3x_1 - 2x_2 = 4$$

These equations can be written in the following form:

$$\begin{pmatrix} 2 & 1 \\ 3 & -2 \end{pmatrix} \begin{pmatrix} x_1 \\ x_2 \end{pmatrix} = \begin{pmatrix} 5 \\ 4 \end{pmatrix}$$

Alternatively, if A is the 2-by-2 matrix of coefficients, X is the 2-by-1 matrix of unknowns, and B is the 2-by-1 matrix of right-hand side values, the equations can be written as follows:

$$A*X = B$$

If we multiply both sides of this equation by the inverse of A, we obtain the following:

$$INV(A)*A*X = INV(A)*B$$

Figure 10-15. A program that finds the transpose of a matrix

```
100 REM - MATRIX TRANSPOSE DEMONSTRATION PROGRAM
110 DIM A(2,3),B(3,2)
120 MAT READ A
130 MAT B=TRN(A)
140 PRINT "MATRIX A"
150 MAT PRINT A;
160 PRINT "MATRIX B=TRN(A)"
170 MAT PRINT B;
180 DATA 2,4,6,1,3,5
190 END
```

(a) The program

```
MATRIX A
 2   4   6

 1   3   5


MATRIX B=TRN(A)
 2   1

 4   3

 6   5
```

(b) Output

Figure 10-16. A program that finds the inverse of a matrix

```
100 REM - MATRIX INVERSE DEMONSTRATION PROGRAM
110 DIM A(2,2),B(2,2),C(2,2)
120 MAT READ A
130 MAT B=INV(A)
140 MAT C=A*B
150 PRINT "MATRIX A"
160 MAT PRINT A,
170 PRINT "MATRIX B=INV(A)"
180 MAT PRINT B,
190 PRINT "MATRIX C=A*B"
200 MAT PRINT C,
210 DATA 2,1,3,2
220 END
```

(a) The program

```
MATRIX A
 2             1

 3             2

MATRIX B=INV(A)
 2            -1

-3             2

MATRIX C=A*B
 1             0

 0             1
```

(b) Output

Figure 10-17. A program that solves a system of linear equations

```
100 REM - PROGRAM TO SOLVE THE SYSTEM OF
110 REM    LINEAR EQUATIONS A*X=B
120 DIM A(2,2),X(2),B(2),C(2,2)
130 REM - READ MATRIX DATA
140 MAT READ A
150 MAT READ B
160 REM - COMPUTE SOLUTION TO EQUATIONS
170 MAT C=INV(A)
180 MAT X=C*B
190 REM - DISPLAY OUTPUT
200 PRINT "MATRIX A"
210 MAT PRINT A,
220 PRINT "MATRIX B"
230 MAT PRINT B
240 PRINT "MATRIX X=INV(A)*B"
250 MAT PRINT X
260 REM - DATA FOR MATRIX A
270 DATA 2,1,3,-2
280 REM - DATA FOR MATRIX B
290 DATA 5,4
300 END
```

(a) The program

```
MATRIX A
 2              1

 3             -2


MATRIX B
 5
 4

MATRIX X=INV(A)*B
 2
 1
```

(b) Output

However, the inverse of A times A is the identity matrix, and the identity matrix times X is X. Hence, we have the following:

$$X = INV(A)*B$$

We can use this final equation to find the solution to a system of linear equations. Figure 10-17 shows a program that does this. Notice in this program that it is necessary first to assign the inverse of A to another matrix, C, and then to multiply C by B. This is because most versions of BASIC do not allow more than one matrix operation in a single statement.

The matrix operations discussed in this section can be used in a wide variety of problems. Their use can often greatly simplify complex processing steps.

Review questions

1. What are the differences between one-dimensional arrays and two-dimensional arrays?
2. Consider the two-dimensional array, S, shown in Figure 10-1. Assume that the value of I is 2, J is 3, and K is 4. What is the value of each of the following subscripted variables?
   a. S(3,2)
   b. S(K,1)
   c. S(I,J)
   d. S(I*J-4,K/2)
3. a. Code a statement to specify that X is a two-dimensional array with four rows and 20 columns.
   b. How many elements are in this array? (Do not count the elements in the "0 row" and "0 column.")
4. Consider the array X defined in Question 3. Code a statement that adds the first element of the first row of this array and the third element of the second row and assigns the result to the last element of the fourth row.
5. Code a group of statements to read data for the array X defined in Question 3. Assume the data is recorded in order by rows in DATA statements.
6. Code a group of statements to display the data in the array X defined in Question 3 with the last column on the first line, the next-to-last column on the second line, and so forth.
7. Consider the program shown in Figure 10-4. Assume that the statements at lines 220 and 230 were switched and the statements at lines 250 and 260 were switched. What output would be displayed by the resulting program?
8. Code a group of statements to initialize the elements of the array X defined in Question 3. Assign 1 to the elements in the first row of X, 2 to the elements in the second row and so forth up to the fourth row, in which the elements should be assigned the value 4.
9. Code a group of statements to determine how many corresponding elements in the first two rows of the array X defined in Question 3 are equal.
10. Code a group of statements to find the largest element in the array X defined in Question 3. Assign the value of the largest element to L.
11. Code a group of statements to search the array X defined in Question 3 for the first element in each row that is equal to the value of V. If such an element is found, display an appropriate message. If no element in a row is equal to V, display a message indicating this.
12. Code a group of statements that sorts the elements in each row of the array X defined in Question 3 into decreasing order.
13. Assume that A and B are each 10-by-4 arrays. Code a matrix operation statement to do each of the following:
    a. Initialize the elements of A to zero.
    b. Initialize the elements of B to 1.
    c. Assign the elements of B to A.
    d. Accept the elements of A from the keyboard.
    e. Read the elements of B from DATA statements.
    f. Display the elements of A in a column.
    g. Display the elements of B in 10 rows and 4 columns with the columns in separate print zones.
    h. Display the elements of B in 10 rows and 4 columns with the elements as close together as possible.
14. Assume that the following DIM statement appears in a program:

    ```
    100 DIM C(10,10),D(10,5),E(10,5),F(10,5),G(5,10),H(10,10)
    ```

    Code a matrix operation statement to do each of the following:
    a. Set C to the identity matrix.

b. Add the elements of D and E and assign the result to F.

c. Multiply each of the elements of F by 5 and assign the result to E.

d. Multiply E by G and assign the result to C.

e. Form the transpose of D, assigning the result to G.

f. Form the inverse of C, assigning the result to H.

Programming problems

1. A company sells five products with four models for each product. The following table gives the price of each model of each product:

<table>
<tr><th></th><th></th><th colspan="4">Model number</th></tr>
<tr><th></th><th></th><th>1</th><th>2</th><th>3</th><th>4</th></tr>
<tr><td rowspan="5">Product
number</td><td>1</td><td>10.50</td><td>16.25</td><td>21.00</td><td>23.75</td></tr>
<tr><td>2</td><td>4.95</td><td>5.95</td><td>6.50</td><td>6.95</td></tr>
<tr><td>3</td><td>.38</td><td>.47</td><td>.59</td><td>.62</td></tr>
<tr><td>4</td><td>8.75</td><td>8.95</td><td>9.10</td><td>9.22</td></tr>
<tr><td>5</td><td>1.52</td><td>1.75</td><td>1.95</td><td>2.25</td></tr>
</table>

Write a BASIC program to read the pricing table and store it in a two-dimensional array. Then display the pricing table with appropriate headings. Next, accept from the keyboard a customer number, product number, model number, and quantity sold. From this information calculate the sales amount for each customer by multiplying the price from the table by the quantity sold. Display the customer number, product number, model number, quantity sold, price, and sales amount.

To test the program use the data in the preceding pricing table and the following sales data:

Customer number	Product number	Model number	Quantity
10113	1	1	10
11305	5	4	35
11412	1	1	100
22516	2	3	125
11603	4	2	75
11625	4	1	65
11735	3	3	50
11895	1	3	130
11899	2	4	20
11907	5	2	82
00000 (trailer value)			

2. Data for Problem 8 of Chapter 9 consists of each student's number and score on a test. The first digit of the student's number indicates his or her year in school (1 = freshman, 2 = sophomore). A tabulation of test scores by score category for each year is needed. The score categories are 90 to 100, 80 to 89, 70 to 79, 60 to 69, and 0 to 59.

Write a BASIC program to create a two-dimensional array of five rows and two columns, where the rows represent the score categories and the columns the year in school. That is, the array should appear as follows:

	Freshman	*Sophomore*
90–100		
80–89		
70–79		
60–69		
0–59		

Tabulate the number of scores that fall into each classification. Display the results of the tabulation with appropriate headings. After the data has been tabulated, determine the total number of freshmen and the total number of sophomores who took the test. Display the result.

[*Hint:* To obtain the year in school, divide the student's identification number by 100 and use the INT function.]

Use the data for Problem 8 of Chapter 9 to test the program.

3. The data gathered from scouting a football team may be analyzed by a computer. In a simple system, assume that four characteristics of each offensive play are recorded by the scout. The characteristics are the down, the yards to go for a first down, the type of play (where 0 identifies a pass and 1 indicates a run), and the number of yards gained or lost (where a negative value indicates lost yardage). The information for each play can be recorded in one row of a two-dimensional array. The first element in the row is the down, the second element is the yards to go, the third element is the type of play, and the final element is the yards gained or lost. In all, 25 plays are to be analyzed.

Write a BASIC program to read the scouting data and store it in a two-dimensional array. Display the data in columns with appropriate headings. Then find and display the answers to the following questions:

a. What was the average yards gained per play?
b. What was the average yards gained per running play?
c. Of all running plays, what percent gained yardage, what percent lost yardage, and what percent gained zero yardage?
d. What was the average yards gained per passing play?
e. What percent of the plays were passes?
f. What percent of first-down plays were passes?
g. What percent of second-down plays were passes?
h. What percent of third-down plays were passes?
i. Of third-down plays with less than five yards to go, what percent were passes?

Use the following data to test the program:

Down	Yards to go	Play	Gain (+) or loss (−)
1	10	Run	+4
2	6	Pass	0
3	6	Pass	+8
1	10	Run	−3
2	13	Run	+8
1	10	Run	0
2	10	Pass	+8
3	2	Pass	+15
1	10	Pass	+12
1	10	Run	−15
2	25	Pass	+5

3	20	Pass	0
1	10	Run	+2
2	8	Run	+4
3	4	Run	+1
1	10	Pass	0
2	10	Run	+6
3	4	Pass	+12
1	10	Pass	0
2	10	Run	+6
3	4	Run	+2
1	10	Pass	-3
2	13	Run	-5
1	10	Run	+2
2	10	Run	-16

4. A telephone company charges varying rates for a long distance call between two cities. The rate charged depends on the time of day the call is made and how the call is placed. There is a fixed charge for the first three minutes and a charge for each additional minute or fraction thereof. The following table outlines the rate structure:

	Time of day			
How placed	*Day*	*Evening*	*Night*	*Weekend*
Direct-dialed	.79 .26	.58 .23	.52 .21	.49 .15
Station-to-station, operator assisted	.95 .30	.73 .25	.64 .24	.57 .21
Person-to-person	1.55 .52	1.55 .52	1.55 .52	1.55 .52

For any given time of day and method of placing the call, two figures are shown. The top figure represents the charge for the first three minutes or fraction thereof; the bottom figure represents the charge for each additional minute or fraction thereof. For example, a night call that is station-to-station, operator-assisted is charged $.64 for the first three minutes and $.24 for each additional minute.

Write a BASIC program to read and display the rate table. Use two two-dimensional arrays. One array should be used for the charges for the first three minutes and the other for the charges for each additional minute. Then accept from the keyboard a customer's number, a "how placed" code, a "time of call" code, and the length of call in minutes and fraction of minute. The "how placed" codes are as follows:

1 Direct-dialed
2 Station-to-station, operator-assisted
3 Person-to-person

The "time of call" codes are as follows:

1 Day
2 Evening
3 Night
4 Weekend

From this information determine the charge for each customer. Display the customer's number, the length of call, and the charge.

To test the program, use the data in the preceding rate table and the following customer data:

Customer number	"How placed"	"Time of call"	Length	
9606	1	1	3.84	
2160	3	4	2.50	
6100	2	2	3.00	
1820	3	3	4.00	(continued)

Customer number	"How placed"	"Time of call"	Length
9215	2	1	8.50
2111	1	3	6.32
1452	2	3	2.15
6658	1	2	1.05
1138	3	2	9.72
6886	2	4	6.35
3552	3	1	3.51
7111	1	4	5.75

5. Data on the age, sex, and marital status of students in the freshman class of a small college are available. Each set of data consists of a student number, age, sex (1 = male, 2 = female), and marital status (1 = single, 2 = married).

A tabulation of the number of students in different age groups for each sex and marital status is needed. The results are to be presented in the following form:

Age	Single		Married	
	Male	Female	Male	Female
18 and under				
19 or 20				
21 and over				

Write a BASIC program to create a three-dimensional array to store the tabulated data. The array should have three rows, two columns, and two levels. The subscript of an array element should indicate age group, sex, and marital status, respectively. Display the results of the tabulation in the form shown above. (If three-dimensional arrays are not available in the version of BASIC being used, created two two-dimensional arrays, one for single students and one for married students.)

From the three-dimensional array create a two-dimensional array of the number of students in each age group for each sex. Display the data in the array in an appropriate format.

Finally, from the two-dimensional array create a one-dimensional array of the number of students in each age group. Display this array data with appropriate headings.

Use the following data to test the program:

Student number	Age	Sex	Marital status	Student number	Age	Sex	Marital status
1001	19	1	1	1021	19	1	2
1002	17	2	1	1022	26	2	2
1003	18	2	1	1023	23	2	2
1004	22	1	2	1024	17	1	1
1005	20	2	2	1025	18	1	1
1006	18	1	1	1026	21	1	2
1007	27	2	1	1027	26	2	1
1008	17	2	1	1028	25	1	2
1009	17	1	1	1029	28	2	2
1010	18	2	1	1030	21	1	1
1011	19	1	2	1031	25	2	1
1012	20	2	2	1032	20	2	1
1013	17	1	1	1033	19	1	1
1014	18	1	2	1034	18	1	1
1015	18	1	1	1035	17	1	1
1016	20	2	1	1036	16	2	1
1017	23	1	1	1037	23	2	2
1018	20	2	1	1038	24	2	2
1019	25	2	2	1039	20	1	1
1020	17	2	1	1040	16	2	1

6. In the data processing department of a particular organization there are three basic job functions — Systems Analysis, Programming, and Operations. For each function there are four levels — Manager, Senior, Junior, and Trainee. Write a BASIC program that reads the job functions into a three-element, one-dimensional array and the levels into a four-element, one-dimensional array. Then create from these arrays a two-dimensional job-category array of three rows and four columns containing all possible combinations of functions and levels. For example, element (1,1) in the array should contain the following:

Systems Analysis — Manager

Finally, display the two-dimensional array in an appropriate format.

7. An airline flies between six cities. Whether or not there is a direct flight from one city to another is indicated in the following table:

To

		1	2	3	4	5	6
	1	X	D	D	X	X	D
	2	D	X	D	X	X	D
	3	X	X	X	D	X	X
From	4	X	D	X	X	D	X
	5	X	D	X	D	X	X
	6	X	D	X	X	D	X

On the left and across the top are the numbers of the cities. If there is a D at the intersection of a row and column, there is a direct flight from the city marked on the left to the city indicated at the top. An X indicates that there is no direct flight between the two cities.

The information in this table can be used to determine whether a flight pattern is possible. A flight pattern indicates the cities between which the customer wishes to fly. For example, a pattern of 1,3,4,2,6 indicates that the customer wishes to fly from city 1 to city 3, then from city 3 to city 4, then to city 2, and finally to city 6. The maximum number of cities in a flight pattern is five. If the customer has less than five cities in his or her pattern, the remaining numbers are zeros. Thus, a pattern of 6,2,0,0,0 indicates that the customer wishes to fly from city 6 to city 2 and does not wish to continue beyond that.

Write a BASIC program to read the data for the flight table. Display the table with appropriate headings. Next accept from the keyboard a customer's number and a requested flight pattern. Then determine if the customer's requested flight pattern is possible. Display the customer's number, his or her requested flight pattern, and a statement of whether or not a ticket may be issued for the desired pattern.

To test the program use the data in the previous flight table and the following customer data:

Customer number	Flight pattern
10123	1,3,4,2,6
11305	6,2,0,0,0
13427	4,2,3,2,0
18211	5,2,5,0,0
19006	3,4,2,1,2
20831	6,5,4,2,6
21475	3,2,0,0,0
22138	4,3,6,2,1
24105	1,3,4,2,4
24216	6,5,2,3,1
25009	3,4,2,5,0
00000 (trailer value)	

8. Write a BASIC program that does the following *without* using the special matrix operations.

a. Read two matrices from DATA statements. Assume that both matrices are the same size but that the size is not known when the program is written. First the program should read the number of rows and the number of columns in the matrices. Then the data for the matrices should be read. Assume that the matrices have no more than ten rows and eight columns, and dimension all arrays accordingly.
b. Compare the two matrices to determine whether they are equal; that is, determine whether the corresponding elements in the two matrices are the same.
c. If the matrices are equal, display an appropriate message, multiply one of the matrices by two, and display the result.
d. If the matrices are not equal, display an appropriate message, add the matrices, and display the result.

Use the following pairs of matrices to test the program:

$$\text{I.} \quad \begin{pmatrix} 8.35 & 6.25 \\ 7.91 & -5.32 \end{pmatrix}, \quad \begin{pmatrix} 8.35 & 6.24 \\ 7.91 & -5.32 \end{pmatrix}$$

$$\text{II.} \quad \begin{pmatrix} 1.62 & 4.35 & -2.13 & 7.62 \\ -8.35 & -12.72 & 6.51 & 8.39 \\ -1.82 & 4.21 & 7.83 & -0.71 \end{pmatrix}, \quad \begin{pmatrix} -4.71 & 5.63 & 7.81 & -1.22 \\ 17.39 & 8.42 & 5.61 & -2.22 \\ -5.81 & 3.92 & 8.35 & 1.11 \end{pmatrix}$$

9. The product of the $l \times m$ matrix A with elements a_{ik} and the $m \times n$ matrix B with elements b_{kj} is an $l \times n$ matrix C with elements c_{ij} given by the following formula:

$$c_{ij} = \sum_{k=1}^{m} a_{ik} b_{kj}$$

Write a BASIC program to read two matrices, find their product, and display the result. Do not use the special matrix operations. Test the program with the following matrices:

$$A = \begin{pmatrix} 2 & -3 & 1 \\ -5 & 6 & 4 \\ -1 & 0 & 5 \\ 3 & -2 & -4 \end{pmatrix}, \quad B = \begin{pmatrix} 7 & 0 & 3 & -4 & -2 \\ 4 & 6 & -6 & -1 & 5 \\ -5 & -3 & 1 & 2 & -7 \end{pmatrix}$$

10. Do Problem 9 using the special matrix operations.
11. Consider the following matrices:

$$X = \begin{pmatrix} 1 & 6 & 3 \\ 5 & 2 & 8 \\ 4 & 7 & 9 \end{pmatrix}, \quad Y = \begin{pmatrix} 8 & 5 & 4 \\ 7 & 9 & 1 \\ 3 & 2 & 6 \end{pmatrix}$$

Write a program to compute and display the following:
a. $3X^2 - 4XY - 2Y^2$
b. $(X - 2Y)(3X + Y)$
c. XY
d. YX
12. Consider the following matrix:

$$P = \begin{pmatrix} .5 & .25 & .25 \\ .5 & 0 & .5 \\ .25 & .25 & .5 \end{pmatrix}$$

Write a BASIC program to read and display this matrix. Then compute and display P^2, P^3, P^4, and P^5.
13. A method of solving a system of linear equations is called the Gauss elimination method. It is described in many algebra textbooks. Write a BASIC program that uses this method to solve the following system of four equations in four unknowns:

$$\begin{aligned} 1.00x_1 + 7.30x_2 + 12.60x_3 + 11.20x_4 &= 31.30 \\ 0.20x_1 - 4.74x_2 - 6.78x_3 - 36.82x_4 &= -76.82 \\ -0.20x_1 - 1.46x_2 + 0.88x_3 - 15.84x_4 &= -38.90 \\ 0.30x_1 + 2.29x_2 + 4.03x_3 + 1.79x_4 &= 6.17 \end{aligned}$$

14. Write a BASIC program that uses the technique discussed at the end of Section 10-6 to solve the system of linear equations given in Problem 13.

Chapter 11

Subroutines and user-defined functions

Sometimes, when writing a program, it is necessary to repeat a statement or group of statements at several points. For example, it may be necessary to perform the same computation several times. As another example, a set of input or output statements may have to be used at a number of points in a program. Repeating a group of statements each time they are needed can make the program tiresome to code. It would simplify program preparation if the necessary statements could be coded once and then referred to each time they are needed. The effect of referring to the statements would be the same as if the statements were placed in the program at the point where they are referenced.

This is the purpose of subroutines and functions. Subroutines and functions consist of one or more BASIC statements that can be referred to at different points in a program. Each time that a subroutine or a function is referenced, we say that it is *called*. We can call a subroutine or a function from the main part of a program, which we just call the *main program,* or from another subroutine or function. The effect of calling a subroutine or function is the same as if the statements in the subroutine or function were coded in the program at the calling point.

In this chapter we describe the programming and use of subroutines and functions. After completing this chapter you should be able to write BASIC subroutines and functions and call them in a program. We also discuss the development of large programs and the design of complex interactive programs.

11-1 Subroutines

A *subroutine* is a group of statements that can be executed from different points in a program. A subroutine begins with any BASIC statement and ends with a RETURN statement. The form of a subroutine is as follows:

```
ln first statement in subroutine
        .
        .
        .
    statements
        .
        .
        .
ln RETURN
```

For example, the following is a simple subroutine that finds the total and average of three numbers:

```
200 LET T=X+Y+Z
210 LET A=T/3
299 RETURN
```

A subroutine can begin at any statement in a program. The subroutine is identified by the *number* of the first statement in the subroutine. In the example just given, the subroutine begins at statement 200. There can be any number of statements in a subroutine. The last statement executed in a subroutine must be a RETURN statement, which just consists of the keyword RETURN. When executed, the RETURN statement causes the computer to return to the point where the subroutine is called.

As a matter of style, it is usually best to begin a subroutine with a REM statement containing a phrase that identifies the subroutine. This sets off the subroutines more clearly from the rest of the program. For example, we would code the previous subroutine as follows:

```
200 REM - TOTAL AND AVERAGE SUBROUTINE
210 LET T=X+Y+Z
220 LET A=T/3
299 RETURN
```

We can have as many subroutines as we need in a program. Each subroutine begins at a unique line number and ends with a RETURN statement. A subroutine can do any type of processing required. Often subroutines contain sets of input or output statements or statements for complex computations.

The GOSUB statement

To call a subroutine, we use a GOSUB statement. The syntax of the GOSUB statement is as follows:

```
ln GOSUB ln
```

The effect of this statement is to execute the statements in the subroutine that begin at the line number given after the keyword GOSUB. For example, to call the subroutine at line 200, we can use the following GOSUB statement:

```
140 GOSUB 200
```

The GOSUB statement causes the computer to branch to the subroutine whose number is given in the statement. Then the statements in the subroutine are executed. When the RETURN statement is reached, the computer branches back to the *next statement following* the GOSUB statement. This is illustrated in Figure 11-1. Notice that when the computer branches to a REM statement at the beginning of the subroutine, it merely continues with the next statement in sequence.

One advantage of using a subroutine is that it can be called from several points in the program; that is, we can have more than one GOSUB statement that calls the same subroutine. When a RETURN statement in a subroutine is executed, the computer branches back to the next statement following the GOSUB statement that called the subroutine. This is illustrated in Figure 11-2, in which a subroutine is called twice in a program.

Figure 11-1. Calling a subroutine

```
  ┌──── 120 GOSUB 200
  │ ┌─► 130 (next statement)
 ①│ │                    ·
  │②│                    ·
  │ │                    ·
  │ └─► 200 REM - TOTAL AND AVERAGE SUBROUTINE
  │     210 LET T=X+Y+Z
  │     220 LET A=T/3
  └──── 299 RETURN
```

We can call a subroutine from any point in a program. We can even call one subroutine from another. This situation is illustrated in Figure 11-3. All that is needed to call a subroutine is a GOSUB statement with the number of the first statement of the subroutine. When the RETURN statement of the called subroutine is reached, the computer branches back to the point where the subroutine was called.

Complete programs

All subroutines in a program are normally placed at the end of the program before the END statement. The first part of the program forms the main program that calls the subroutines. So that the subroutines are not executed in the normal sequential processing of the program, there must be a GOTO statement at the end of the main program, just ahead of the first subroutine, that branches to the END statement.

Figure 11-4 shows a complete program that includes a subroutine. The subroutine is called twice in this program. Notice the GOTO statement at line 170 that causes the computer to branch around the subroutine to the END statement.

Instead of a GOTO statement before the subroutines in a program, a STOP statement can be used. The syntax of a STOP statement is as follows:

```
ln STOP
```

Figure 11-2. Calling a subroutine more than once

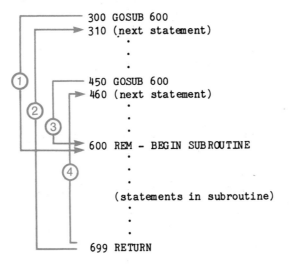

```
  ┌────────── 300 GOSUB 600
  │ ┌──────► 310 (next statement)
  │ │                    ·
  │ │                    ·
  │ │                    ·
  │ │  ┌──── 450 GOSUB 600
 ①│ │  │ ┌─► 460 (next statement)
  │②│  │ │                ·
  │ │ ③│ │                ·
  │ │  │ │                ·
  │ │  └─┼─► 600 REM - BEGIN SUBROUTINE
  │ │    │                ·
  │④│    │                ·
  │ │    │                ·
  │ │    │     (statements in subroutine)
  │ │    │                ·
  │ │    │                ·
  │ │    │                ·
  └─┴────┴── 699 RETURN
```

Figure 11-3. Calling a subroutine from another subroutine

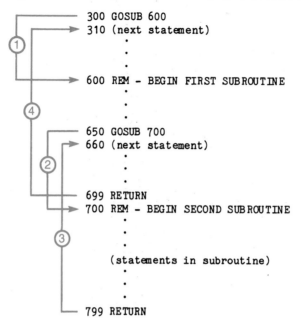

```
300 GOSUB 600
310 (next statement)
        .
        .
        .
600 REM - BEGIN FIRST SUBROUTINE
        .
        .
        .
650 GOSUB 700
660 (next statement)
        .
        .
        .
699 RETURN
700 REM - BEGIN SECOND SUBROUTINE
        .
        .
        .
(statements in subroutine)
        .
        .
        .
799 RETURN
```

Thus, in the program in Figure 11-4, the following statement can be used in place of the GOTO statement at line 170:

```
170 STOP
```

There are many uses of subroutines. In Section 11-5 we will see how they can be used in the development of large programs, and in Section 11-6 we will discuss the design of complex interactive programs using subroutines.

Figure 11-4. A program that includes a subroutine

```
100 REM - MAIN PROGRAM
110 INPUT X,Y,Z
120 GOSUB 200
130 PRINT X,Y,Z,T,A
140 INPUT X,Y,Z
150 GOSUB 200
160 PRINT X,Y,Z,T,A
170 GOTO 999
200 REM - TOTAL AND AVERAGE SUBROUTINE
210 LET T=X+Y+Z
220 LET A=T/3
299 RETURN
999 END
```

(a) The program

```
?  78,95,82
   78           95          82          255          85
?  100,84,92
   100          84          92          276          92
```

(b) Input and output

Flowcharts of programs with subroutines

If a program contains subroutines, a separate flowchart is drawn of each subroutine and a flowchart is drawn of the main program. For example, Figure 11-5 shows a set of flowcharts for the program in Figure 11-4. The flowchart of the main program

Figure 11-5. Flowchart of a main program and a subroutine

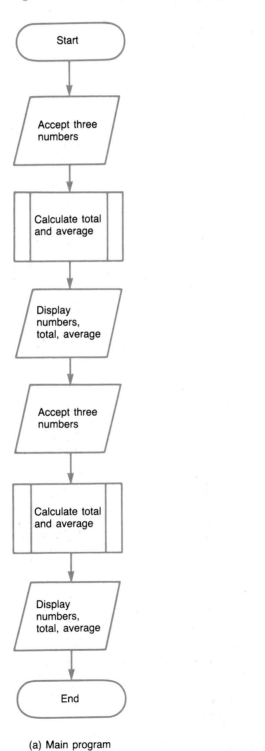

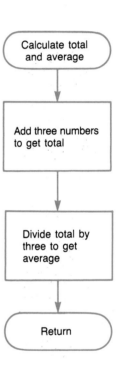

(a) Main program   (b) Subroutine

begins with a terminal-point symbol marked START and ends with one marked END. To show where a subroutine is called, a process symbol is used with a vertical line on each side. This is called a *predefined process symbol*. Within the symbol is written a phrase that identifies the subroutine. Thus, the flowchart in Figure 11-5(a) shows that the subroutine that calculates the total and average is called twice.

The flowchart of each subroutine begins with a terminal-point symbol that contains a phrase that identifies the subroutine. The flowchart ends with a terminal-point symbol marked RETURN. Between these symbols, standard flowchart symbols are used to show the logic of the subroutine. Figure 11-5(b) illustrates this technique.

For large programs there may be many subroutines and hence many flowcharts. Some subroutines may call other subroutines, in which case the predefined process symbol is used in one subroutine to show where another is called. We will see an example of this later in this chapter.

The ON-GOSUB statement

Most versions of BASIC provide the ON-GOSUB statement, which functions much like the ON-GOTO statement. (See Table 11-1.) The syntax of the ON-GOSUB statement is as follows:

```
ln ON numeric expression GOSUB ln,ln,...
```

The effect of this statement is to call one of the subroutines whose numbers are listed after the word GOSUB based on the value of the numeric expression. For example, consider the following statement:

```
250 ON K GOSUB 400,500,600,700
```

When this statement is executed, the computer calls the subroutine beginning at line 400 if the value of K is 1; it calls the subroutine at line 500 if K is 2, and so forth for the other subroutines. All the differences in the ON-GOTO statement for different versions of BASIC also apply to the ON-GOSUB statement. (See Section 3-6.)

Table 11-1 ON-GOSUB statement differences

BASIC version	ON-GOSUB *statement available*
ANS minimal BASIC	No
ANS BASIC	Yes
Microsoft BASIC	Yes
Applesoft BASIC	Yes
True BASIC	Yes
BASIC-PLUS	Yes
VAX-11 BASIC	Yes

11-2 User-defined functions

In Chapter 7 we discussed functions that are built into the BASIC language. The SQR, INT, and RND functions are examples of these. To call such a function, we use the name of the function followed by a numeric expression enclosed in parentheses. For example, the SQR function is called in the following statement:

```
130 LET X=SQR(Y)
```

A function computes a value (in this example, the square root of Y) and returns the value to the statement in which the function is called.

The DEF statement

Besides the built-in functions, a programmer can code his or her own functions and call them when needed in the program. Such a *user-defined function* is specified with a function-defining or DEF statement in the program. The syntax of the DEF statement is as follows:

```
ln DEF name(parameters)=numeric expression
```

For example, the following is a DEF statement that specifies a user-defined function:

```
100 DEF FNY(X)=3*X^2-2*X+4
```

The DEF statement begins with the keyword DEF. Following this comes the name of the function. The syntax of the name of a user-defined function depends on the version of BASIC. (See Table 11-2.) In many versions of BASIC, the name must consist of the letters FN followed by a variable. Thus, in the example just given, FNY is the function's name. Similarly, FNA, FNM7, and FNZ2 are valid function names.

Following the function name is a list of variables separated by commas and enclosed in parentheses. These variables are called the *parameters* (or *dummy arguments*) of the function. The FNY function defined previously has one parameter, X. The

Table 11-2. User-defined function name differences

BASIC version	*Function name syntax*
ANS minimal BASIC	FN*letter*
ANS BASIC	*variable*
Microsoft BASIC	FN*variable*
Applesoft BASIC	FN*variable*
True BASIC	*variable*
BASIC-PLUS	FN*variable*
VAX-11 BASIC	*variable* *or* FN*variable*

maximum number of parameters allowed depends on the version of BASIC. (See Table 11-3.) We can also define a function without a parameter. We will see later how parameters are used.

Following the parameters is an equal sign and then a numeric expression. The expression indicates what computation the function is to perform. The parameters are usually used in the expression. The expression can be any valid numeric expression in BASIC.

The DEF statement defines a function but does *not* cause it to be executed. In most versions of BASIC, a DEF statement must come before the first use of the function in the program. Most programmers put all DEF statements at the beginning of the program. When the computer reaches a DEF statement during the normal sequential execution of the program, it goes on to the next statement in sequence without doing anything. The function defined in a DEF statement is executed only when it is called.

Calling a user-defined function

A user-defined function is called in the same way that a built-in function is called: the name of the function is used, followed by a list of numeric expressions separated by commas and enclosed in parentheses. For example, consider the FNY function defined previously. The following LET statement calls this function:

```
130 LET D=FNY(E+F)
```

In this example only one numeric expression is used after the function name, but sometimes several expressions are required.

The effect of calling a function is that first the values of the expressions in parentheses are computed. Then these values are assigned to the parameters in the function. Next the expression in the function is computed, using the parameters' values. Finally, the result is assigned to the function's name and returned to the statement in which the function is called. This sequence is shown in Figure 11-6 for the FNY function. In this example, if E is 3 and F is 2, the value of the function is 69. This value is assigned to the variable D in the LET statement.

The expressions in parentheses following the function name when the function is called are called *arguments* (or *actual arguments*). The arguments can be constants, variables, or more complex numeric expressions. For example, the following are valid calls of the FNY function:

Table 11-3. User-defined function parameter differences

BASIC version	Maximum number of parameters
ANS minimal BASIC	1
ANS BASIC	No limit
Microsoft BASIC	No limit
Applesoft BASIC	1
True BASIC	No limit
BASIC-PLUS	5
VAX-11 BASIC	255

Figure 11-6. Calling a user-defined function

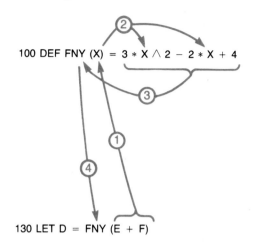

Steps:
1 Value of argument is computed and assigned to parameter.
2 Parameter value is used in expression.
3 Value of expression is computed and assigned to function name.
4 Result is returned to calling statement.

```
160 LET S=FNY(3)
170 LET T=FNY(Z)
180 LET U=FNY(3*Z+5)
```

In each case the value of the argument is assigned to the parameter of the function when the function is called.

We can call a function as many times as needed in a program. We can even call a function more than once in a single statement. In fact, we can use a function call in a program wherever a variable or a constant can be used. For example, all the following are valid uses of the FNY function:

```
190 IF FNY(G)>10 THEN 400
200 LET H=7.5*FNY(I+2)-FNY(J)
210 PRINT FNY(1),FNY(2),FNY(3)
```

Figure 11-7 shows a complete program that calls the FNY function several times.

Local and global variables

A variable that is used as a parameter in a DEF statement can also be used in the rest of the program. When this is done, there is no relationship between the parameter and the same variable elsewhere in the program. We say that the parameter is a *local variable* in the function. For example, consider the following statements:

```
100 DEF FNY(X)=3*X^2-2*X+4
        .
        .
        .
220 LET X=5
230 LET Y=FNY(6)
```

Figure 11-7. A program that includes a user-defined function

```
100 DEF FNY(X)=3*X^2-2*X+4
110 LET E=3
120 LET F=2
130 LET D=FNY(E+F)
140 LET D1=FNY(4)
150 LET D2=FNY(E)
160 PRINT D,D1,D2
999 END
```

(a) The program

69   44   25

(b) Output

In this case we set the value of X in the program to 5 and then call the FNY function with an argument of 6. This causes the value of X *in the function* to be assigned the value 6 for the purpose of evaluating the function. However, this does *not* change the value of X in the rest of the program. If we were to display the value of X after statement 230 was executed, the number 5 would be displayed.

Besides using a local variable in a function definition, we can also use other variables. These other variables are not local to the function but are used throughout the program. They are called *global variables*. For example, consider the following DEF statement:

```
110 DEF FNZ(X)=A*X^2+B*X+C
```

In this function, X is a *local* variable, but A, B, and C are *global* variables. When the function is called, the value of the argument is assigned to X. The values of A, B, and C that are used in the function evaluation are the values of these variables at the time the function is called. For example, assume that A is 3, B is 2, and C is 1 and that the following statement is executed:

```
150 PRINT FNZ(4)
```

Then the value displayed will be $3 \times 4^2 + 2 \times 4 + 1$ or 57.

(In a subroutine there are no local variables. All variables used in a subroutine are global.)

Additional user-defined function features

A function can be defined without a parameter. Then all the variables in the function definition are global. For example, consider the FNA function defined by the following DEF statement:

```
120 DEF FNA=(X+Y+Z)/3
```

This function computes the average of three values identified by the global variables X, Y, and Z. Whenever this function is called, no argument is used. For example, the following statement computes the average of X, Y, and Z, and assigns the result to A:

```
130 LET A=FNA
```

When more than one parameter is used, the parameters are separated by commas and enclosed in parentheses following the function name. For example, the FNA function just described can be defined with three parameters as follows:

```
120 DEF FNA(X,Y,Z)=(X+Y+Z)/3
```

In this case, X, Y, and Z are local variables. When the function is called, three arguments must be given. For example, to find the average of S, T, and 25, we can write the following:

```
130 LET A=FNA(S,T,25)
```

In this case, the value of S is assigned to X, the value of T is assigned to Y, and 25 is assigned to Z. These values are then used to compute the average, which is returned to the statement where the function is called.

We can define as many functions as are needed in a program. We can even define one function in terms of another. For example, the following DEF statements could be included in a program:

```
100 DEF FNS(A)=A+2
110 DEF FND(A)=A-2
120 DEF FNC(A)=2*FNS(A)+3*FND(A)
```

Then if we write the statement

```
200 PRINT FNS(5),FND(4),FNC(3)
```

the output will be the numbers 7, 2, and 13.

Functions can be useful when a complex computation needs to be carried out several times with different parameter values. However, their use is limited to computations that require only a single line. In Section 11-3 we will describe multiple-line functions that are available in some versions of BASIC.

User-defined string functions

Most versions of BASIC allow user-defined string functions. (See Table 11-4.) The name of such a function must end with a dollar sign. The result produced by a string function is a string and not a numeric value. The parameters, however, may be string variables or numeric variables.

Table 11-4. User-defined string function differences

BASIC version	User-defined string functions available
ANS minimal BASIC	No
ANS BASIC	Yes
Microsoft BASIC	Yes
Applesoft BASIC	No
True BASIC	Yes
BASIC-PLUS	Yes
VAX-11 BASIC	Yes

As an example of a user-defined string function, consider the following DEF statement:

```
200 DEF FNC$(F$,M$,L$)=F$+" "+LEFT$(M$,1)+". "+L$
```

This function creates a string consisting of a person's first name (F$) followed by the person's middle initial (the first letter of M$), and then the person's last name (L$). To call this function, arguments that are string constants or string variables must be supplied for the three parameters. For example, the following statement could be used to call the function:

```
150 LET N$=FNC$(A$,B$,"SMITH")
```

Notice that when the function is called, the result is a string, and the value must therefore be assigned to a string variable.

User-defined string functions can be extremely useful in simplifying complex string operations. The example demonstrates just one case in which a string function can be used in a program.

*11-3 Multiple-line functions

A user-defined function can only be a single line. This restriction greatly limits the type of processing that can be performed by such a function. To overcome this limitation, some versions of BASIC allow *multiple-line functions*. (See Table 11-5.) The actual form of a multiple-line function varies with the version of BASIC. In this section we describe multiple-line functions and illustrate their uses.

To demonstrate the idea of a multiple-line function we will use a form found in several common versions of BASIC (BASIC-PLUS and VAX-11 BASIC). The syntax of this form is as follows:

```
1n DEF name(parameters)
        .
        .
        .
    statements
        .
        .
        .
1n FNEND
```

For example, Figure 11-8 shows the definition of a function that finds the maximum of three numbers.

A multiple-line function begins with a DEF statement that gives the name of the function. The function name follows the same syntax as a user-defined function name (see Table 11-2) and usually consists of the characters FN followed by a variable. If the function is a string function, a dollar sign must come at the end of the name. In the example in Figure 11-8, the function name is FNM. Following the function name is the list of parameters, separated by commas and enclosed in parentheses. The maximum number of parameters is the same as for a user-defined function. (See Table 11-3.) In the example in Figure 11-8 there are three parameters, A, B, and C. Notice that the DEF statement does *not* contain an equal sign or an expression; the

Table 11-5. Multiple-line function differences

BASIC version	Multiple-line function syntax
ANS minimal BASIC	Not available
ANS BASIC	*ln* FUNCTION *name(parameters)*
	.
	.
	statements
	.
	.
	ln END FUNCTION
Microsoft BASIC	Not available
Applesoft BASIC	Not available
True BASIC	DEF *name(parameters)*
	.
	.
	statements
	.
	.
	END DEF
BASIC-PLUS	*ln* DEF *name(parameters)*
VAX-11 BASIC	.
	.
	statements
	.
	.
	ln FNEND

computation to be performed by the function is given by the statements following the DEF statement.

A multiple-line function ends with the FNEND statement. When this statement is executed, the computer returns to the point where the function is called.

Between the DEF statement and the FNEND statement can be any number of BASIC statements that perform the processing required of the function. However, one statement is required in the function. This is a LET statement that assigns a value to the *name* of the function. This statement is required because the name of the function is used to return a value to the point where the function is called. The value to be returned must be assigned to the function name at some point in the function. In the example function in Figure 11-8, statement 160 assigns a value to the function name, FNM.

Figure 11-8. A multiple-line function

```
100 DEF FNM(A,B,C)
110 LET L=A
120 IF B<=L THEN 140
130    LET L=B
140 IF C<=L THEN 160
150    LET L=C
160 LET FNM=L
170 FNEND
```

We can now understand how the function in Figure 11-8 works. The purpose of this function is to find the largest of the three variables A, B, and C. The technique used is to assume that A is the largest. The value of this variable is assigned to L. Then L is compared with B and C. If either is larger than the current value of L, the larger value is assigned to L. Finally, the value of L is assigned to the name of the function, FNM. The FNEND statement then causes the computer to return to the point in the program where the function is called.

A multiple-line function is called in the same way that a single-line function is called. For example, if we wish to find the maximum of X, Y, and 37, we can use the following statement:

```
200 LET M=FNM(X,Y,37)
```

The function is executed with the values of the arguments assigned to the parameters, and the result is returned to the calling statement.

A multiple-line function, like a user-defined function, must appear before any statement that calls the function. Usually it is best to put all functions at the beginning of the program. When the program is executed, the computer passes over all functions to reach the first executable statement in the program. A function is executed only when it is called.

All the rules about local and global variables for user-defined functions apply to multiple-line functions. The parameters are local variables in the function. All other variables are global. In the function in Figure 11-8, A, B, and C are local variables, but L is a global variable. This means that the value of L will be modified when the function is executed, which could cause problems in the program if L is used for another purpose.

There can be as many multiple-line functions in a program as needed. One function can be called from another function. The program should never branch out of a function with a GOTO or IF statement. The only way that the execution of a function should be terminated is with the FNEND statement.

Multiple-line functions can be very useful in a complex program. They can simplify programming by allowing a set of computations to be coded once and then called whenever needed.

*11-4 Subprograms

A few versions of BASIC provide a special feature that combines some of the characteristics of functions with some of the aspects of subroutines. (See Table 11-6.) This is the subprogram feature. A *subprogram* is a separate set of statements much like a multiple-line function. However, it is called by a special CALL statement.

The syntax of a subprogram is as follows:

```
ln SUB name(parameters)
     .
     .
     .
    statements
     .
     .
     .
ln END SUB
```

Table 11-6. Subprogram differences

BASIC version	Subprograms available
ANS minimal BASIC	No
ANS BASIC	Yes
Microsoft BASIC	No
Applesoft BASIC	No
True BASIC	Yes
BASIC-PLUS	No
VAX-11 BASIC	Yes

For example, Figure 11-9 shows a subprogram that finds the total and average of three numbers.

A subprogram begins with a SUB statement that contains the name of the subprogram. The name must follow the same syntax rules as those of a variable. Following the name is a list of parameters separated by commas and enclosed in parentheses. As we will see, the parameters are used both to send data to the subprogram and to return data to the point where the subprogram is called. The subprogram contains any BASIC statements necessary to perform the processing required of the subprogram. The last statement of the subprogram must be an END SUB statement. When this statement is executed, the computer returns to the point where the subprogram is called.

To call a subprogram, the CALL statement is used. The syntax of the CALL statement is as follows:

> *ln* CALL *name*(*arguments*)

The statement gives the name of the subprogram and the arguments to be assigned to the parameters of the subprogram. For example, to call the subprogram TOTAVE in Figure 11-9, we could use the following statement:

```
150 CALL TOTAVE(A,B,C,S,M)
```

When a CALL statement is executed, the values of the arguments are assigned to the parameters in the subprogram. In this example, the value of A is assigned to X, the value of B is assigned to Y, and so on. There must be the same number of arguments as there are parameters, and the arguments must be in the same order as the parameters. After the argument values are assigned to the parameters, the computer branches to the first statement in the subprogram.

The statements in the subprogram are executed until the END SUB statement is reached. Then the values of the parameters are assigned to the arguments. In the example, the value of X in the subprogram is assigned to A, the value of Y to B, and so forth. In this case, the values of A, B, and C are unchanged by the process, but the arguments S and M are assigned the new values of T and A computed by

Figure 11-9. A subprogram

```
1000 SUB TOTAVE(X,Y,Z,T,A)
1010 LET T=X+Y+Z
1020 LET A=T/3
1099 END SUB
```

the subprogram. This is how the results are returned to the point where the subprogram is called. After the parameter values are assigned to the arguments, the computer branches back to the next statement following the CALL statement. This process is summarized in Figure 11-10.

The arguments used in a CALL statement can be constants, variables, or more complex expressions. For example, the following statement could be used to call the TOTAVE subprogram:

```
250 CALL TOTAVE(A+B,35,X,T,A)
```

When an argument is not a variable, the value of the parameter is *not* returned to the program that called the subprogram. This is because a value cannot be assigned to a constant or an expression, only to a variable.

Arrays can also be used as parameters and arguments. To indicate an array parameter, parentheses are used after the array variable. For example, consider the subprogram shown in Figure 11-11. This subprogram finds the average, A, of an N-element array, X. X is an array variable because of the parentheses following the variable in the list of parameters. To call this subprogram, we must use an array variable as an argument in the CALL statement. Depending on the version of BASIC, the array variable may or may not have to be followed by parentheses. (See Table 11-7.) For example, assume we need to call the subprogram in Figure 11-11 to find the average, M, of the L-element array, D. Then in some versions of BASIC we would use the statement

```
350 CALL AVE(M,D( ),L)
```

and in other versions of BASIC we would use the statement

```
350 CALL AVE(M,D,L)
```

Depending on the version of BASIC, a subprogram may be either an *internal subprogram* or an *external subprogram*. (See Table 11-8.) An internal subprogram is

Figure 11-10. Calling and returning from a subprogram

```
  150 CALL TOTAVE(A,B,C,S,M)
  160 (next stmt)

 1000 SUB TOTAVE(X,Y,Z,T,A)
 1010 LET T=X+Y+Z
 1020 LET A=T/3
 1099 END SUB
```

(a) Calling a subprogram

```
  150 CALL TOTAVE(A,B,C,S,M)
  160 (next stmt)

 1000 SUB TOTAVE(X,Y,Z,T,A)
 1010 LET T=X+Y+Z
 1020 LET A=T/3
 1099 END SUB
```

(b) Returning from a subprogram

Figure 11-11. A subprogram with an array parameter

```
2000 SUB AVE(A,X(),N)
2010 LET T=0
2020 FOR I=1 TO N
2030   LET T=T+X(I)
2040 NEXT I
2050 LET A=T/N
2099 SUB END
```

Table 11-7. Subprogram calling differences

BASIC version	*Array argument syntax*
ANS minimal BASIC	Not applicable
ANS BASIC	*array variable*
Microsoft BASIC	Not applicable
Applesoft BASIC	Not applicable
True BASIC	*array variable*
BASIC-PLUS	Not applicable
VAX-11 BASIC	*array variable*()

placed in the program before the first reference to the subprogram. The parameters are local variables in the subprogram. All other variables are global. Thus, if the subprogram in Figure 11-11 is an internal subprogram, the variable T is a global variable, and changing its value will change the value of T elsewhere in the program.

An external subprogram is placed *after* the END statement of the program. Thus, the subprogram is a separate, distinct program. As a result, all the variables used in a subprogram are local; that is, any variable that is not a parameter can be used without affecting the same variable outside the subprogram. For example, the variable T in the subprogram in Figure 11-11 is distinct from the same variable in the main program. Changing the value of T in the subprogram does not change the value of T elsewhere.

We can use as many subprograms as needed by a program. A subprogram can be called as often as required with different arguments. We can even call one subprogram from another.

Subprograms are very useful for developing a large program. Although they are currently available only in a few versions of BASIC, we can expect their availability to increase in the future.

Table 11-8. Subprogram placement differences

BASIC version	*Internal or external subprogram*
ANS minimal BASIC	Not applicable
ANS BASIC	Internal, unless SUB statement begins with the keyword EXTERNAL, in which case the subprogram is external
Microsoft BASIC	Not applicable
Applesoft BASIC	Not applicable
True BASIC	Internal if placed before END statement of main program; external if placed after END statement of main program
BASIC-PLUS	Not applicable
VAX-11 BASIC	External

11-5 Developing large programs

In Chapter 6 we discussed several aspects of program development, including program structure, style, and understandability, and the activities in the programming process. We saw that following the guidelines in Chapter 6 resulted in programs that were well structured, easily understood, and correct.

As programs become larger, their development becomes more complex. One way of organizing a large program that helps in its development is to divide the program into sections, which are called *modules*. Each module performs some function related to the overall processing of the program. The modules for a program can be developed separately and then combined to form a complete program after all modules are finished.

Subroutines provide a convenient mechanism for modular programming. The approach is to code each module as a separate subroutine. (User-defined functions can also be used as modules, although each is limited to one line. Multiple-line functions and subprograms can also be used as modules if they are available in the version of BASIC.) Then the main program is composed of a series of calls to the subroutines. In this section we discuss this approach to program development.

An illustrative program

To illustrate this approach, consider the problem of updating a pricing table. In an example in Section 9-4 we showed a table that consisted of two ten-element arrays, one for item numbers and one for the corresponding prices (see Figure 9-8). Assume now that some of the prices in the table have changed. We need a program to make the appropriate modifications in the table — that is, to *update* the table. In addition, we want to display the table before and after the changes are made.

We can see that the program must basically do the following:

1. Read the pricing table.
2. Display the pricing table.
3. Update the pricing table.
4. Display the updated table.

Following our approach of using subroutines to modularize the program, we can code each of these steps as a separate subroutine. However, because the second and fourth steps both involve displaying the pricing table, we need only three subroutines — one to read the pricing table, one to display the table, and one to update the table. The main program calls these three subroutines in order and then calls the display subroutine again.

Assume that we have coded the three subroutines and that they begin at lines 400, 500, and 600, respectively. The main program to call the subroutines in the proper sequence is shown in Figure 11-12. Notice the simplicity of this part of the program; it is basically a sequence of four GOSUB statements. REM statements are included to document further which subroutine is called at each point.

The input and output subroutines can be coded fairly easily. Each involves a loop to read or display the elements of two arrays — one for the item numbers and one for the prices. The subroutines are shown in Figures 11-13 and 11-14. Notice that the DATA statements containing the pricing data are in the input subroutine. Although this is not required, it simplifies the process of locating these statements. The output is displayed in four columns.

The updating process has not been fully defined. Assume that new prices along with corresponding item numbers are to be entered at the keyboard. There are any number of changes that need to be made, and the input data is not entered in

Figure 11-12. The main program for the pricing-table updating program

```
100 REM - PRICING TABLE UPDATE PROGRAM
110 REM - VARIABLES:
120 REM        N  = ITEM NUMBER ARRAY
130 REM        P  = PRICE ARRAY
140 REM        N1 = NUMBER OF ITEM UPDATED
150 REM        P1 = NEW PRICE
160 REM        L  = LOCATION OF ITEM IN ARRAY
170 REM        R$ = REPETITION QUESTION RESPONSE
180 REM        I  = COUNTER
200 REM - MAIN PROGRAM
210 DIM N(10),P(10)
220 REM - CALL READ TABLE SUBROUTINE
230 GOSUB 400
240 REM - CALL DISPLAY TABLE SUBROUTINE
250 GOSUB 500
260 PRINT
270 REM - CALL UPDATE TABLE SUBROUTINE
280 GOSUB 600
290 PRINT
300 REM - CALL DISPLAY TABLE SUBROUTINE
310 GOSUB 500
399 GOTO 999
        .
        .
        .

(subroutines go here)
        .
        .
        .

999 END
```

any particular order. The updating process must repeat until the user indicates that no more prices are to be changed.

The updating subroutine must do the following:

1. Accept an item number and new price.
2. Find the corresponding item in the pricing table.
3. Make the necessary change in the pricing table.

Assume that we have a subroutine beginning at line 800 that finds the location (i.e., the element number) of a given item in the item-number array. If the item number is found, the subroutine sets the variable L to its location; otherwise, the value of L is set to zero.

We can use this item-locating subroutine in the table-updating subroutine shown in Figure 11-15. First, an item number and new price are accepted from the keyboard. Then the item-locating subroutine is called. Next the value of L is tested to determine whether it is zero. If it is, an error message is displayed; otherwise, the new price is assigned to P(L), thereby modifying the pricing table.

The only part of the program that remains to be completed is the item-locating subroutine. This subroutine searches the item-number array for a given value. We

Figure 11-13. The table-input subroutine

```
400 REM - READ TABLE SUBROUTINE
410 FOR I=1 TO 10
420   READ N(I),P(I)
430 NEXT I
490 REM - TABLE DATA
491 DATA 1001,2.95,1023,3.64,1045,2.25,1172,1.75,1185,1.52
492 DATA 1201,1.95,1235,4.85,1278,9.95,1384,6.28,1400,4.75
499 RETURN
```

Figure 11-14. The table-output subroutine

```
500 REM - DISPLAY TABLE SUBROUTINE
510 PRINT "                PRICING TABLE"
520 PRINT
530 PRINT "ITEM NUMBER","PRICE","ITEM NUMBER","PRICE"
540 PRINT
550 FOR I=1 TO 5
560   PRINT N(I),P(I),N(I+5),P(I+5)
570 NEXT I
599 RETURN
```

could use a sequential search or, if the array is in ascending order, a binary search. We will assume that the latter is not necessarily the case and search sequentially. The complete subroutine is shown in Figure 11-16. Notice that the variable L in the subroutine is assigned the subscript of the matching element if the item is found in the table; otherwise it is assigned a value of zero.

Incorporating the subroutines in Figures 11-13, 11-14, 11-15, and 11-16 into the main program in Figure 11-12 results in a complete program to update the pricing table. Sample input and output for this program is shown in Figure 11-17. Notice that three prices are updated and that the second pricing table, which is displayed after the updating takes place, includes the updated prices.

Top-down program development

One advantage of using subroutines to modularize a program is that we can develop the program in a top-down fashion. Top-down program development includes top-down design, coding, and testing.

Top-down design is similar to the idea of stepwise program refinement discussed in Section 6-4. We start by designing the overall logic of the program. Each basic operation that the program is to perform becomes a subroutine. The main program contains a series of calls to the subroutines. (There may be other statements in the main program besides those that call subroutines. For example, loop-control or decision-making statements may be needed to control the order of execution of the subroutines.) We then design each subroutine in a similar top-down fashion. Eventually we reach the point where the basic operations of the program can be coded.

One way of displaying the top-down design of a program is to draw a diagram

Figure 11-15. The table-updating subroutine

```
600 REM - UPDATE TABLE SUBROUTINE
610 PRINT "PRICING TABLE UPDATING ROUTINE"
620 PRINT
630   INPUT "ENTER ITEM NUMBER";N1
640   INPUT "ENTER NEW PRICE";P1
650   PRINT
660   REM - CALL LOCATE ITEM SUBROUTINE
670   GOSUB 800
680   IF L=0 THEN 720
690     LET P(L)=P1
700     PRINT "ITEM";N1;"UPDATED"
710   GOTO 730
720     PRINT "ITEM";N1;"NOT FOUND IN TABLE"
730   PRINT
740   INPUT "DO YOU WANT TO UPDATE MORE PRICES";R$
750 IF R$="YES" THEN 620
760 PRINT
770 PRINT "END OF ROUTINE"
799 RETURN
```

Figure 11-16. The item-locating subroutine

```
800 REM - LOCATE ITEM SUBROUTINE
810 LET L=1
820 IF N(L)=N1 THEN 860
830 IF L=10 THEN 860
840   LET L=L+1
850 GOTO 820
860 IF N(L)=N1 THEN 899
870   LET L=0
899 RETURN
```

Figure 11-17. Input and output for the pricing-table updating program

```
                    PRICING TABLE

ITEM NUMBER   PRICE        ITEM NUMBER   PRICE

   1001        2.95           1201        1.95
   1023        3.64           1235        4.85
   1045        2.25           1278        9.95
   1172        1.75           1384        6.28
   1185        1.52           1400        4.75

PRICING TABLE UPDATING ROUTINE

ENTER ITEM NUMBER? 1172
ENTER NEW PRICE? 1.95

ITEM 1172 UPDATED

DO YOU WANT TO UPDATE MORE PRICES? YES

ENTER ITEM NUMBER? 1400
ENTER NEW PRICE? 5.25

ITEM 1400 UPDATED

DO YOU WANT TO UPDATE MORE PRICES? YES

ENTER ITEM NUMBER? 1027
ENTER NEW PRICE? 3.79

ITEM 1027 NOT FOUND IN TABLE

DO YOU WANT TO UPDATE MORE PRICES? YES

ENTER ITEM NUMBER? 1001
ENTER NEW PRICE? 3.29

ITEM 1001 UPDATED

DO YOU WANT TO UPDATE MORE PRICES? NO

END OF ROUTINE

                    PRICING TABLE

ITEM NUMBER   PRICE        ITEM NUMBER   PRICE

   1001        3.29           1201        1.95
   1023        3.64           1235        4.85
   1045        2.25           1278        9.95
   1172        1.95           1384        6.28
   1185        1.52           1400        5.25
```

Figure 11-18. Structure chart for the pricing-table updating program

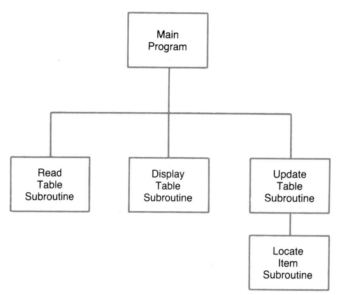

showing the relationship between the main program and the subroutines. Figure 11-18 shows such a diagram for the pricing-table updating program. This diagram is sometimes called a *structure chart*. The box at the top represents the main program. Each box below signifies a subroutine. A line connects two boxes if one part of the program calls the other. Thus, Figure 11-18 shows that the main program calls the read-table, display-table, and update-table subroutines and that the update-table subroutine calls the locate-item subroutine.

This diagram also shows how we can regard the program in terms of *levels*. At the highest level we can think of the program as the sequence of activities that takes place in the main program. If we wish, we can understand the program just at this level and not examine any of the subroutines. If we wish to understand the program at a deeper level, we can look at the subroutines that are called by the main program. Even further, we can examine the next level of subroutines, and so forth until we reach the bottom of the diagram.

A structure chart is *not* the same as a flowchart. A structure chart shows how the subroutines and the main program are related — that is, what part of the program calls what other parts. The structure chart does not show the flow of logic in any part of the program; that is the purpose of the flowchart. For each box in the structure chart, a flowchart is drawn that shows the logical flow in the part of the program that the box represents. Thus, for the program with the structure chart in Figure 11-18, five flowcharts would be drawn, one for the main program and one for each of the four subroutines. These are shown in Figure 11-19 on pages 351–355. The drawing of the flowcharts is often the last step in the top-down design before the actual coding begins.

Besides designing the program in a top-down fashion, we can also follow a *top-down coding and testing* pattern. In this approach we code the main program first. Then for each subroutine called by the main program we code a "dummy" subroutine called a *stub* that simulates, but does not actually perform, the function of the subroutine. Usually each stub just displays a line stating that the subroutine was executed. We can then run the program with the incomplete subroutines to make certain that the logic of the main program is correct. Next we follow the same procedure for the first subroutine, coding stubs for any subroutines that it calls. We

Figure 11-19. Flowcharts for the pricing-table updating program

(a) The main program   (continued)

then test the program with the completed first subroutine. This process is repeated for all subroutines until the complete program is coded and tested. The process helps isolate errors, because we are coding and testing only a part of the program at a time.

An alternative strategy is called *bottom-up coding and testing*. In this approach we design the program in a top-down fashion but then start coding and testing with the lowest-level subroutines. This requires writing programs (sometimes called *exercisers*) to call and test the subroutines. We build the program from the bottom up until we finally reach the top level, which is the main program.

Figure 11-19. Continued

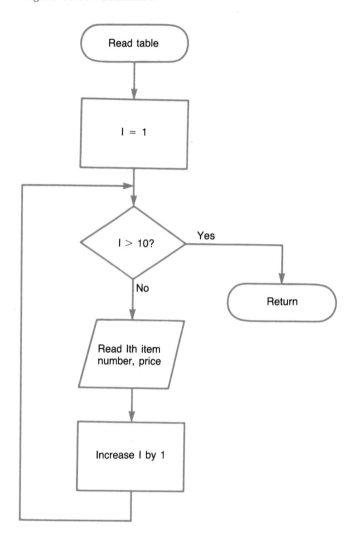

(b) The table-input subroutine

(continued)

Reusing subroutines

An advantage of using subroutines to modularize a program is that the subroutines can often be used in other programs. For example, assume that we need a program that computes the cost of an order by multiplying the quantity purchased by the price. Because we already have a subroutine to read the pricing tables and one to locate an item in the table, we can use these in an order-cost-computation program. The main program to do this is shown in Figure 11-20 on page 356. The program first reads the pricing table using the table-input subroutine. It then accepts an item number and quantity from the keyboard. Next the program uses the item-locating subroutine to find the location of the desired item in the table. The value of L is then checked to determine whether the item was found. If it was, the price for the

Figure 11-19. Continued

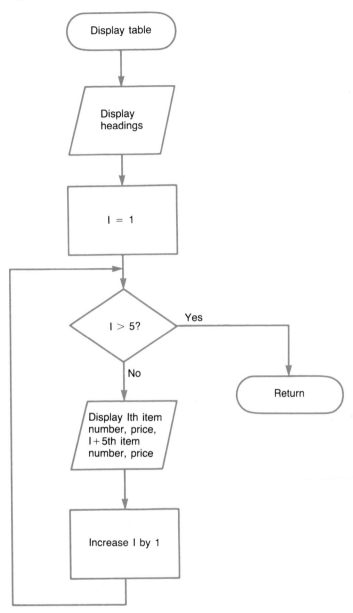

(c) The table-output subroutine   (continued)

item is multiplied by the quantity to obtain the cost, and the output is displayed. If the item was not found, an error message is displayed. This main program, together with the table-input and item-locating subroutines, forms a complete program.

The examples in this section show us that the use of subroutines has a number of advantages. In fact, most large programs are developed in the manner described here. For any complex program, the programmer should consider using the techniques in this section.

Figure 11-19. Continued

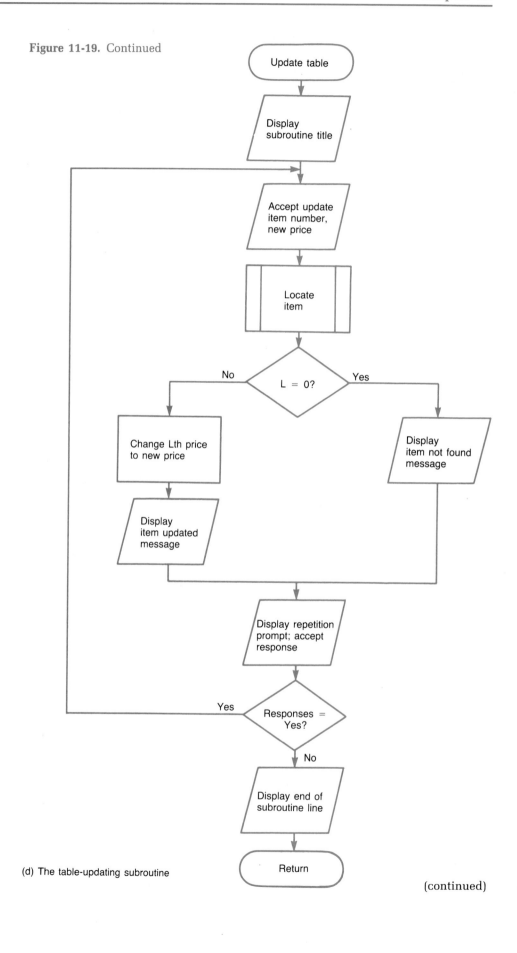

(d) The table-updating subroutine

(continued)

Figure 11-19. Continued

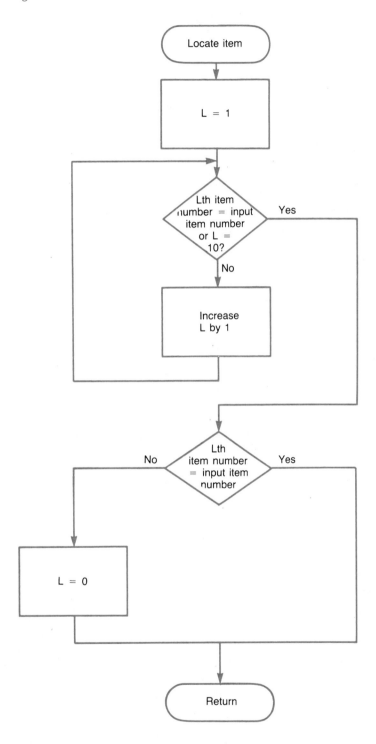

(e) The item-locating subroutine

Figure 11-20. The main program for the order-cost computation program

```
100 REM - ORDER COST COMPUTATION PROGRAM
110 REM - VARIABLES:
120 REM        N  = ITEM NUMBER ARRAY
130 REM        P  = PRICE ARRAY
140 REM        N1 = NUMBER OF ITEM ORDERED
150 REM        Q  = QUANTITY ORDERED
160 REM        C  = COST OF ORDER
170 REM        L  = LOCATION OF ITEM IN ARRAY
180 REM        R$ = REPETITION QUESTION RESPONSE
190 REM        I  = COUNTER
200 REM - MAIN PROGRAM
210 DIM N(10),P(10)
220 REM - CALL READ TABLE SUBROUTINE
230 GOSUB 400
240 PRINT "ORDER COST COMPUTATION PROGRAM"
250 PRINT
260    INPUT "ENTER ITEM NUMBER";N1
270    INPUT "ENTER QUANTITY";Q
280    PRINT
290    REM - CALL LOCATE ITEM SUBROUTINE
300    GOSUB 800
310    IF L=0 THEN 350
320      LET C=P(L)*Q
330      PRINT "ITEM";N1;"PRICE";P(L);"QUANTITY";Q;"COST";C
340    GOTO 360
350      PRINT "ITEM";N1;"NOT FOUND IN TABLE"
360    PRINT
370    INPUT "DO YOU WANT TO COMPUTE MORE ORDER COSTS";R$
380 IF R$="YES" THEN 250
390 PRINT "END OF PROGRAM"
399 GOTO 999
        .
        .
        .

(subroutines go here)
        .
        .
        .

999 END
```

11-6 Interactive program design revisited

In Section 5-2 we introduced basic principles for the design of interactive programs. Such devices as input prompts and descriptive output make a program easier for the user to use. As programs become more complex, however, other techniques are needed. In this section we describe a common approach to the design of sophisticated interactive programs.

Many programs allow the user to select which of several tasks he or she wants the program to perform. For example, a pricing program, similar to the one discussed in the last section, may let the user indicate whether the pricing table is to be displayed, whether prices are to be updated, or whether the cost of an order is to be computed. The program must be designed so that the user has complete control over which task is selected and the order in which the tasks are performed.

This type of program usually operates in the following way. First, a list of the tasks that the program can perform is displayed. This list is called a *menu*. For example, Figure 11-21 shows a menu for a pricing program. Each task in the list has a code associated with it. In the example in Figure 11-21 the codes are numbers

Figure 11-21. The menu for a pricing program

```
SELECT ONE TASK:
 1 DISPLAY PRICING TABLE
 2 UPDATE PRICES
 3 COMPUTE ORDER COSTS
 9 STOP

WHICH TASK?
```

(1, 2, 3, and 9), but letters can also be used. Notice that one of the codes (9 in this example) is used to indicate that the program should stop.

Following the menu, the program displays an input prompt which requests the code for the desired task. The user must enter one of the codes from the menu. Then the program analyzes the code to determine what is required. Usually each task is performed by a subroutine in the program. The input code is analyzed, and the program calls the appropriate subroutine. If the code indicates that execution should stop, the program displays a final output line and branches to the END statement. If an invalid code is entered, an error message is displayed and the menu is displayed again. After a task is performed by a subroutine, the program displays the menu and asks for the next task. This way the user has complete control over the computer's activities.

Figure 11-22 shows a complete pricing program that incorporates this approach. The main part of the program calls subroutines to read the pricing table, display the menu, and perform the appropriate task based on the code that is entered. The process of displaying the menu and analyzing the code is repeated until a code of 9 is entered, indicating that the program should stop.

The rest of the program consists of six subroutines to perform the various processing required of the program. The subroutines are as follows:

Line	Subroutine
2100	Display Menu
2200	Compute Order Cost
2400	Read Table
2500	Display Table
2600	Update Table
2800	Locate Item

The last four subroutines are the same as the subroutines used in the last section but with new line numbers. The order-cost computation subroutine is derived from the main part of the program shown in Figure 11-20. The menu-displaying subroutine is new to this program. The structure chart for the program is shown in Figure 11-23 on page 359. Figure 11-24 on pages 360–362 shows the flowcharts of the main program, the menu-displaying subroutine, and the order-cost computation subroutine. The flowcharts for the other subroutines are the same as those in Figure 11-19.

The input and output from running the pricing program are shown in Figure 11-25 on pages 363–364. Notice that after each task is performed, the menu is displayed again so that a new task code can be entered. The program terminates when a 9 is entered for the task code.

The program design approach described in this section is commonly used for complex interactive programs. If a program can perform many tasks and the user can select which task is to be performed, this approach should be considered.

Figure 11-22. The pricing program

```
1000 REM - PRICING PROGRAM
1010 REM - VARIABLES:
1020 REM          N = ITEM NUMBER ARRAY
1030 REM          P = PRICE ARRAY
1040 REM          T = TASK
1050 REM          N1 = NUMBER OF ITEM ORDERED OR UPDATED
1060 REM          Q = QUANTITY ORDERED
1070 REM          C = COST OF ORDER
1080 REM          P1 = NEW PRICE
1090 REM          L = LOCATION OF ITEM IN ARRAY
1100 REM          R$ = REPETITION QUESTION RESPONSE
1110 REM          I = COUNTER
1200 REM
1210 REM - MAIN PROGRAM
1220 REM
1230 DIM N(10),P(10)
1240 PRINT "PRICING PROGRAM"
1250 PRINT
1260 REM - CALL READ TABLE SUBROUTINE
1270 GOSUB 2400
1280 REM - CALL DISPLAY MENU SUBROUTINE
1290 GOSUB 2100
1300    IF T=9 THEN 1470
1310    PRINT
1320    IF T<>1 THEN 1360
1330       REM - CALL DISPLAY TABLE SUBROUTINE
1340       GOSUB 2500
1350    GOTO 1450
1360    IF T<>2 THEN 1400
1370       REM - CALL UPDATE TABLE SUBROUTINE
1380       GOSUB 2600
1390    GOTO 1450
1400    IF T<>3 THEN 1440
1410       REM - CALL COMPUTE ORDER COST SUBROUTINE
1420       GOSUB 2200
1430    GOTO 1450
1440       PRINT "INVALID TASK"
1450    PRINT
1460 GOTO 1290
1470 PRINT
1480 PRINT "END OF PROGRAM"
1499 GOTO 9999
2000 REM
2010 REM - SUBROUTINES
2020 REM
2100 REM - DISPLAY MENU SUBROUTINE
2110 PRINT "SELECT ONE TASK:"
2120 PRINT " 1 DISPLAY PRICING TABLE"
2130 PRINT " 2 UPDATE PRICES"
2140 PRINT " 3 COMPUTE ORDER COSTS"
2150 PRINT " 9 STOP"
2160 PRINT
2170 INPUT "WHICH TASK";T
2199 RETURN
2200 REM - COMPUTE ORDER COST SUBROUTINE
2210 PRINT "ORDER COST COMPUTATION ROUTINE"
2220 PRINT
2230    INPUT "ENTER ITEM NUMBER";N1
2240    INPUT "ENTER QUANTITY";Q
2250    PRINT
2260    REM - CALL LOCATE ITEM SUBROUTINE
2270    GOSUB 2800
2280    IF L=0 THEN 2320
2290       LET C=P(L)*Q
2300       PRINT "ITEM";N1;"PRICE";P(L);"QUANTITY";Q;"COST";C
2310    GOTO 2330
2320       PRINT "ITEM";N1;"NOT FOUND IN TABLE"
2330    PRINT
2340    INPUT "DO YOU WANT TO COMPUTE MORE ORDER COSTS";R$
2350 IF R$="YES" THEN 2220
2360 PRINT
```

358

(continued)

Figure 11-22. Continued

```
2370 PRINT "END OF ROUTINE"
2399 RETURN
2400 REM - READ TABLE SUBROUTINE
2410 FOR I=1 TO 10
2420   READ N(I),P(I)
2430 NEXT I
2490 REM - TABLE DATA
2491 DATA 1001,2.95,1023,3.64,1045,2.25,1172,1.75,1185,1.52
2492 DATA 1201,1.95,1235,4.85,1278,9.95,1384,6.28,1400,4.75
2499 RETURN
2500 REM - DISPLAY TABLE SUBROUTINE
2510 PRINT "                  PRICING TABLE"
2520 PRINT
2530 PRINT "ITEM NUMBER","PRICE","ITEM NUMBER","PRICE"
2540 PRINT
2550 FOR I=1 TO 5
2560   PRINT N(I),P(I),N(I+5),P(I+5)
2570 NEXT I
2599 RETURN
2600 REM - UPDATE TABLE SUBROUTINE
2610 PRINT "PRICING TABLE UPDATING ROUTINE"
2620 PRINT
2630   INPUT "ENTER ITEM NUMBER";N1
2640   INPUT "ENTER NEW PRICE";P1
2650   PRINT
2660   REM - CALL LOCATE ITEM SUBROUTINE
2670   GOSUB 2800
2680   IF L=0 THEN 2720
2690     LET P(L)=P1
2700     PRINT "ITEM";N1;"UPDATED"
2710   GOTO 2730
2720     PRINT "ITEM";N1;"NOT FOUND IN TABLE"
2730   PRINT
2740   INPUT "DO YOU WANT TO UPDATE MORE PRICES";R$
2750 IF R$="YES" THEN 2620
2760 PRINT
2770 PRINT "END OF ROUTINE"
2799 RETURN
2800 REM - LOCATE ITEM SUBROUTINE
2810 LET L=1
2820 IF N(L)=N1 THEN 2860
2830 IF L=10 THEN 2860
2840   LET L=L+1
2850 GOTO 2820
2860 IF N(L)=N1 THEN 2899
2870   LET L=0
2899 RETURN
9999 END
```

Figure 11-23. The structure chart for the pricing program

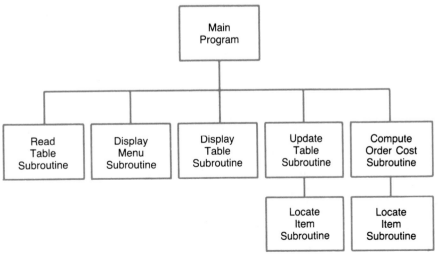

Figure 11-24. Flowcharts for the pricing program

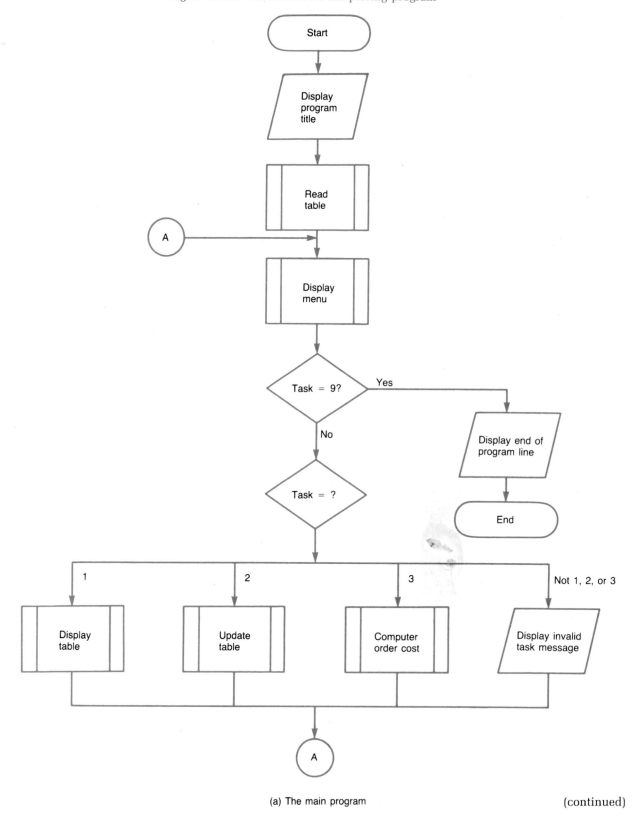

(a) The main program

(continued)

Figure 11-24. Continued

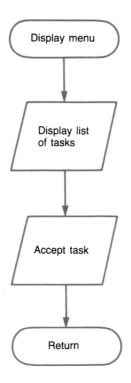

(b) The menu-displaying subroutine

(continued)

Figure 11-24. Continued

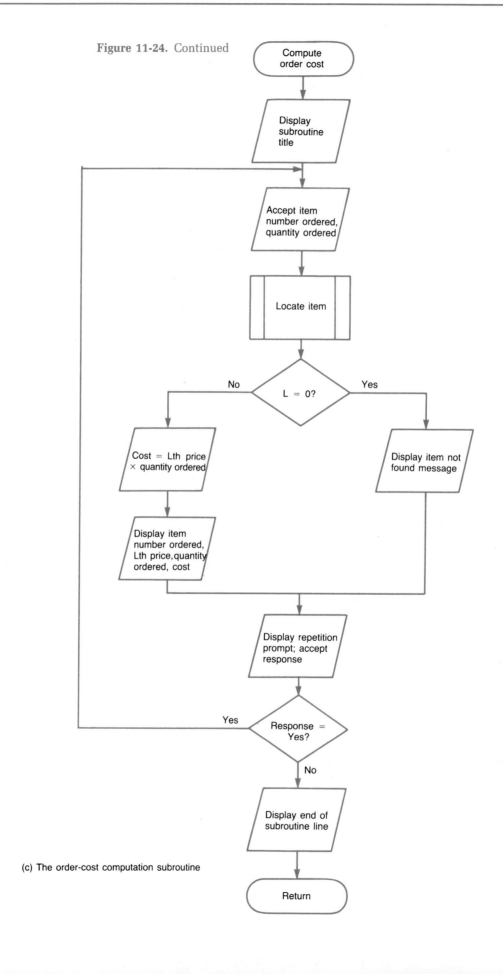

(c) The order-cost computation subroutine

Figure 11-25. Input and output for the pricing program

```
PRICING PROGRAM

SELECT ONE TASK:
 1 DISPLAY PRICING TABLE
 2 UPDATE PRICES
 3 COMPUTE ORDER COSTS
 9 STOP

WHICH TASK? 1

                 PRICING TABLE

ITEM NUMBER   PRICE      ITEM NUMBER   PRICE

   1001        2.95         1201        1.95
   1023        3.64         1235        4.85
   1045        2.25         1278        9.95
   1172        1.75         1384        6.28
   1185        1.52         1400        4.75

SELECT ONE TASK:
 1 DISPLAY PRICING TABLE
 2 UPDATE PRICES
 3 COMPUTE ORDER COSTS
 9 STOP

WHICH TASK? 2

PRICING TABLE UPDATING ROUTINE

ENTER ITEM NUMBER? 1172
ENTER NEW PRICE? 1.95

ITEM 1172 UPDATED

DO YOU WANT TO UPDATE MORE PRICES? YES

ENTER ITEM NUMBER? 1234
ENTER NEW PRICE? 5.25

ITEM 1234 NOT FOUND IN TABLE

DO YOU WANT TO UPDATE MORE PRICES? YES

ENTER ITEM NUMBER? 1235
ENTER NEW PRICE? 5.25

ITEM 1235 UPDATED

DO YOU WANT TO UPDATE MORE PRICES? NO

END OF ROUTINE

SELECT ONE TASK:
 1 DISPLAY PRICING TABLE
 2 UPDATE PRICES
 3 COMPUTE ORDER COSTS
 9 STOP

WHICH TASK? 4

INVALID TASK
```

(continued)

Figure 11-25. Continued

```
SELECT ONE TASK:
 1 DISPLAY PRICING TABLE
 2 UPDATE PRICES
 3 COMPUTE ORDER COSTS
 9 STOP

WHICH TASK? 1

                    PRICING TABLE

ITEM NUMBER    PRICE        ITEM NUMBER    PRICE

   1001        2.95           1201         1.95
   1023        3.64           1235         5.25
   1045        2.25           1278         9.95
   1172        1.95           1384         6.28
   1185        1.52           1400         4.75

SELECT ONE TASK:
 1 DISPLAY PRICING TABLE
 2 UPDATE PRICES
 3 COMPUTE ORDER COSTS
 9 STOP

WHICH TASK? 3

ORDER COST COMPUTATION ROUTINE

ENTER ITEM NUMBER? 1023
ENTER QUANTITY? 12

ITEM 1023 PRICE 3.64 QUANTITY 12 COST 43.68

DO YOU WANT TO COMPUTE MORE ORDER COSTS? YES

ENTER ITEM NUMBER? 1279
ENTER QUANTITY? 20

ITEM 1279 NOT FOUND IN TABLE

DO YOU WANT TO COMPUTE MORE ORDER COSTS? YES

ENTER ITEM NUMBER? 1278
ENTER QUANTITY? 20

ITEM 1278 PRICE 9.95 QUANTITY 20 COST 199

DO YOU WANT TO COMPUTE MORE ORDER COSTS? NO

END OF ROUTINE

SELECT ONE TASK:
 1 DISPLAY PRICING TABLE
 2 UPDATE PRICES
 3 COMPUTE ORDER COSTS
 9 STOP

WHICH TASK? 9

END OF PROGRAM
```

Review questions

1. What are the differences between subroutines and user-defined functions?
2. When a subroutine or function is referenced in a program, we say it is _____.
3. The last statement executed in a subroutine must be a _____ statement.
4. Code a statement to call a subroutine that begins at line 500.
5. What is the next statement executed after a RETURN statement is executed?
6. A subroutine can be called only from a main program. True or false?
7. What is wrong with the following program?

```
10 INPUT X
20 GOSUB 40
30 PRINT Y
40 LET Y=2*X
50 RETURN
60 END
```

8. All variables in a subroutine are _____ (global/local).
9. A program contains three subroutines beginning at lines 1000, 2000, and 3000, respectively. Code a single statement that calls the subroutine at line 1000 if the value of X is 1 or 4, the subroutine at line 2000 if X is 2 or 3, and the subroutine at line 3000 if X is 5.
10. Code a user-defined function that computes the value of A given by the following formula:

$$A = B(1 + R)^Y$$

The parameters of the function are B, R, and Y.
11. Code a statement to call the function defined in Question 10 using 1000 for B, .1 for R, and 5 for Y. Assign the result computed by the function to P.
12. The parameters of a function are _____ (global/local) variables. All other variables used in a function are _____ (global/local) variables.
13. What output is displayed by the following program?

```
10 DEF FNA(B)=A+B
20 LET A=5
30 LET B=10
40 LET A=FNA(A)
50 LET B=FNA(B)
60 PRINT A,B
70 END
```

14. Are multiple-line functions available in the version of BASIC you are using? If they are, code a multiple-line function that computes Z as follows: if X is less than Y, then Z is Y minus X; if X is greater than Y, then Z is X minus Y; if X is equal to Y, then Z is 30. Code a statement that calls this function using A and B for X and Y, respectively. The statement should assign the result computed by the function to C.
15. Are subprograms available in the version of BASIC you are using? If they are, code a subprogram to compute the sum and difference of the values of two variables. Code a statement to call this subprogram to find the sum, S1, and difference, D1, of X and Y.
16. What is meant by top-down design?
17. Draw a structure chart for the program in Figure 11-20.
18. What is meant by top-down coding and testing?
19. A list of tasks that a program can perform is called _____.
20. Consider the program shown in Figure 11-22 and the input and output for this program shown in Figure 11-25. How many times is the item-locating subroutine called during this input-and-output sequence?

Programming problems

1. The tuition charged a student at a small private college is based on the number of units (credits) that the student takes during a quarter. The tuition charge is $200 plus $25 per unit for each of the first eight units and $32.50 per unit for all units taken over eight. Write a subroutine to determine the tuition charged given the number of units.

   Write a BASIC program that accepts student data consisting of the student number, the units taken during the fall quarter, the units taken during the winter quarter, and the units taken during the spring quarter. Then, using the subroutine described in the previous paragraph, the program should calculate the tuition for each quarter. Finally, the program should display these results along with the student number.

   Use the following input data to test the program:

Student number	Fall quarter	Winter quarter	Spring quarter
1018	7.0	18.0	15.0
1205	15.0	12.5	6.0
1214	15.5	15.5	15.5
1218	8.0	7.0	5.0
1293	8.5	7.5	4.0
1304	6.0	6.0	6.0
1351	10.5	18.5	0.0
1354	0.0	15.0	6.0
0000 (trailer value)			

   (Header: *Units taken*)

2. Write a subroutine to determine the expected population of a group in ten years, given the current population and the annual growth rate. Write a BASIC program that reads population data for two socioeconomic groups in each area of a city. The input data consists of the area number, the current population and growth rate for group A, and the current population and growth rate for group B. Then the program should use the subroutine to calculate the expected population of each group in ten years. Finally, the program should display the area number, the expected population of each group, and the total expected population for the area.

   Use the following data to test the program:

Area number	Group A Current pop.	Group A Growth rate	Group B Current pop.	Group B Growth rate
001	14,500	3.5%	6,300	4.1%
002	18,251	2.3%	2,215	2.9%
003	6,205	4.0%	8,132	3.9%
004	3,738	5.4%	12,730	2.7%
005	12,100	3.0%	10,150	3.0%
000 (trailer value)				

3. Adding amounts of time expressed in hours and minutes requires special manipulation because there are 60 minutes in an hour. Write a subroutine that determines the sum of two amounts of time. For each time to be added and for the sum, two variables are needed — one for the hours and the other for the minutes.

   Write a BASIC program that reads an employee number and the time that the employee worked on each day of the week. Then the program should use the subroutine described in the previous paragraph to calculate the total time worked by the employee for the week. This requires four calls of the subroutine. Display all input data and the total of the times with appropriate headings.

Use the following data to test the program:

Employee number	Monday		Tuesday		Wednesday		Thursday		Friday	
	Hr	Min	Hr	Min	Hr	Min	Hr	Min	Hr	Min
10011	8	0	7	30	8	0	7	30	7	30
10105	7	45	7	55	6	30	5	0	8	45
10287	10	0	8	5	6	25	8	0	7	15
10289	9	45	8	0	6	10	8	30	0	0
10304	0	0	0	0	8	0	8	25	7	45
10455	6	35	8	40	0	0	0	0	11	55

4. Write the following subroutines:
   a. *Calculate charge.* This subroutine determines the total gas utility charge based on the number of gas therms used. (Gas consumption is measured in therms.) The charge is $.09 per therm for the first 200 therms, $.08 per therm for the next 300 therms, $.07 per therm for the next 500 therms, and $.065 per therm for all gas used over 1000 therms.
   b. *Display output.* This subroutine displays the customer number, the gas used in therms, and the charge for one month.

   Write a main BASIC program that reads the customer number and the gas consumed for three separate months. Then, through three calls of the first subroutine, calculate the charge for each of the three months. Display the results for each month using three calls of the second subroutine.

   Use the following data to test the program:

Customer number	Month 1	Month 2	Month 3
11825	425	172	253
13972	665	892	1283
14821	45	572	313
19213	1562	973	865
28416	200	500	1000
31082	0	300	600
99999 (trailer value)			

5. Write the program for Problem 11 in Chapter 3 using subroutines. There should be four subroutines that accept one, two, three, or four test scores, respectively; calculate the average of the number of scores accepted; and display the results. Use the data in Problem 11 of Chapter 3 to test the program.
6. Assume that F, G, and H are polynomials defined as follows:

$$F(X) = A(1) + A(2)*X + A(3)*X^2 + ... + A(N+1)*X^N$$

$$G(X) = B(1) + B(2)*X + B(3)*X^2 + ... + B(M+1)*X^M$$

$$H(X) = C(1) + C(2)*X + C(3)*X^2 + ... + C(L+1)*X^L$$

Note that the degrees of these polynomials are N, M, and L, respectively. Assume a maximum of 20 for each and dimension any arrays accordingly. Note also that the coefficient of X^I has a subscript $I+1$.

Write the following subroutines:
   a. *Read polynomial.* This subroutine reads an array A of the coefficients of a polynomial of degree N. Input data should include the degree of the polynomial followed by the coefficients. Note that a polynomial of degree N has N+1 coefficients.
   b. *Display polynomial.* This subroutine displays the array A of the coefficients of a polynomial of degree N. The coefficients should be neatly arranged and labeled.
   c. *Scalar multiply.* This subroutine multiplies a polynomial of degree N with array A of coefficients by the constant D, producing a polynomial of degree N with array C of coefficients.

d. *Add polynomials.* This subroutine adds a polynomial of degree N with coefficient array A and a polynomial of degree M with coefficient array B, producing a polynomial with coefficient array C of degree L.

Prepare a main program that uses these subroutines to do the following:

    Read F(X)
    Display F(X)
    Read G(X)
    Display G(X)
    Compute H(X) = F(X) + 2*G(X)
    Display H(X)
    Compute a new F(X) = 3*H(X)
    Display the new F(X)

Use the following to test your program:

Polynomial F(X)	Polynomial G(X)
N = 5	M = 2
A(1) = 1.0	B(1) = −7.0
A(2) = 17.6	B(2) = 3.1
A(3) = 0.0	B(3) = −1.0
A(4) = 2.0	
A(5) = −3.6	
A(6) = 1.0	

7. Problem 8 in Chapter 9 involves writing a program to process student test-score data. Rewrite this program as the following series of subroutines:

a. *Read arrays.* This subroutine reads identification numbers and test scores into two arrays. The subroutine must count the data as it is read to get a count of the number of test scores to be processed. Note that the count should not include the trailer value.

b. *Display arrays.* This subroutine displays in columns below appropriate headings the array of identification numbers and test scores.

c. *Calculate mean.* This subroutine calculates the mean of the test scores. The mean is the average of the test scores.

d. *Tabulate scores.* This subroutine tabulates (that is, counts) the number of test scores in various categories. The subroutine should determine the number of scores in each of the following categories:

                        90–100
                        80–89
                        70–79
                        60–69
                        0–59

e. *Sort scores.* This subroutine sorts the *test-score array* into descending order (largest to smallest). Be sure that the correspondence between the identification-number array and the test-score array is maintained during the sorting.

f. *Find median.* This subroutine determines the median of the test scores. The subroutine should handle both the case where there is an even number of test scores and the case where the number of scores is odd.

Write a BASIC program that uses the subroutines to process the test-score data. The program should call the subprograms in the following order:

    Read arrays
    Display arrays
    Calculate mean
    Tabulate scores
    Sort scores
    Display array
    Find median

Notice that after sorting, the arrays are displayed using the *display-arrays* subroutine. The program also requires other output operations. The mean must be displayed by the program after the *calculate-mean* subroutine is called. The tabulated data must be displayed after the *tabulate-scores* subroutine is called. The median must be displayed after the *find-median* subroutine is used. All output should be displayed with appropriate headings or descriptive comments. Use the data in Problem 8 of Chapter 9 to test the program.

8. Write a function to convert Fahrenheit temperature to Celsius temperature. The formula is given in Problem 2 of Chapter 2. Write a BASIC program that accepts a temperature in Fahrenheit, calls the function, and displays the result. Use the data in Problem 2 of Chapter 2 to test the program.

9. The present value of an amount, A, received Y years in the future is given by the following formula:

$$\text{present value} = \frac{A}{(1 + R)^Y}$$

In this formula, R is called the discount rate. Write a function to compute the present value, given an amount, discount rate, and number of years. Write a BASIC program to accept an amount, discount rate, and number of years; call the function; and display the present value. Test the program with an amount of $1000, a discount rate of 6%, and 10 for the number of years.

10. Write a BASIC program for Problem 8 in Chapter 2 using two functions, one to find the interest and the other to compute the maturity value.

11. Write a multiple-line function to find the balance in a bank account given the initial balance, the interest rate, and the number of years since the initial amount was deposited. Assume that interest is compounded annually. Write a BASIC program that accepts the initial balance, interest rate, and number of years, calls the function, and displays the balance computed by the function. Test the program with several sets of input data.

12. Write a multiple-line function to find the Nth Fibonacci number. (See Problem 7 in Chapter 4 for a description of Fibonacci numbers.) Write a BASIC program that accepts a value of N, calls the function, and displays the result. Test the program with N equal to 5, 12, 1, 25, 2, 8, and 3.

13. The factorial of a positive integer n, written $n!$, is $n \times (n - 1) \times (n - 2) \times \cdots \times 2 \times 1$. For example, 5! is $5 \times 4 \times 3 \times 2 \times 1 = 120$. Write a multiple-line function to find the factorial of a positive integer. Then write a multiple-line function that uses the factorial function to find the combination of n things taken k at a time. The combination is given by the following expression:

$$\frac{n!}{k!(n - k)!}$$

Note that the combination function calls the factorial function three times. Finally, write a BASIC program that accepts the values of n and k, calls the combination function to find the combination of n things taken k at a time, and displays the result. Use the following data to test the program:

n	k
6	3
10	9
4	1
7	2

14. Do Problem 3 using a subprogram rather than a subroutine. There are six parameters for the subprogram — two for each amount of time to be added and two for the sum.

15. Problem 10 in Chapter 3 describes a program to convert a temperature from Fahrenheit to Celsius and Kelvin, from Celsius to Fahrenheit and Kelvin, and from Kelvin to Fahrenheit and Celsius. Write a subprogram to do the required conversion. The subprogram needs four parameters: the code for the scale of the temperature sent to the subprogram, the Fahrenheit temperature, the Celsius temperature, and the Kelvin temperature. Note that the parameter used to send a temperature to the subprogram depends on the value of the parameter for the code. The other parameters are used to return the temperature in the other two scales.

Write a BASIC program that accepts the code and temperature, calls the subprogram, and displays the temperature in all three scales. Use the data in Problem 10 of Chapter 3 to test the program.

16. Do Problem 7 using subprograms rather than subroutines. Six subprograms will be needed.

17. Develop an interactive program to compute a depreciation schedule for an asset based on the straight-line method, the double-declining-balance method, and the sum-of-the-years'-digits method. The program should be designed so that the user can select the desired method from a menu. Test the program with a number of sets of input data.

18. Modify the program described in Problem 7 so that the user can select the desired task from a menu. Include the following tasks:

> Accept student identification number and test score
> Display student identification numbers and test scores
> Update test score
> Calculate mean of test scores
> Tabulate test scores
> Sort test scores
> Find median of test scores

Notice that one of the tasks is to accept a student's identification number and test score. This allows the data to be entered at the keyboard instead of being read from DATA statements. The data that is entered should be added to the end of the array, and the count of the number of students should be increased by one. There is also a task that allows the user to update (i.e., change) a test score for any student after the score has been entered.

Test all the tasks in the program, using appropriate test data.

Chapter 12

Files

In Chapter 1 we described the auxiliary storage component of a computer. (See Figure 1-1.) A common type of auxiliary storage is magnetic disk. Information is stored on the surface of the disk by the use of patterns of magnetism. Another type of auxiliary storage is magnetic tape. Magnetic patterns are also used for data storage on tape. Although both disk and tape are used for auxiliary storage, disk is the more common and we will be concerned only with it in this chapter.

One of the purposes of auxiliary storage is to store *programs* that are not currently being executed by the computer. When a program is saved (e.g., when the SAVE command is typed), the program that is currently in internal storage is stored in auxiliary storage. A program that is saved will remain in auxiliary storage until it is erased. A saved program can be retrieved from auxiliary storage as many times as necessary.

Another purpose of auxiliary storage is to store *data* that is not currently being processed by the computer. This could be data not needed immediately by the program that is executing or it could be data used by another program. Such data can be stored in auxiliary storage as long as necessary and retrieved whenever it is needed.

A collection of data that is stored in auxiliary storage is called a *data file* or simply a *file*. Files are used for several reasons. Sometimes a large amount of data needs to be processed by a program. There may be so much data that not all of it can be stored in the computer's internal storage at one time. For example, a statistical program may have to analyze a large amount of experimental data. In such a case, the data can be stored in a file and then processed by the program piecemeal.

Another reason for utilizing files is that data may have to be saved for use by a program more than once. For example, personnel data for a business has to be processed by a payroll program every time the payroll is prepared. When personnel data is stored in a file, it does not have to be reentered each time it is needed.

Finally, files can be used when several programs process the same data. For example, if student test scores are kept in a file, one program can be used to compute totals and averages for each student, another program can tabulate data for all students, and a third program can produce grade reports. We can run these programs without reentering the data for each program.

In this chapter we discuss the programming necessary for the use of files in BASIC. We describe how a file is created and how data is retrieved from a file. We also explain how to modify data in a file. After completing this chapter you should be able to write BASIC programs that process auxiliary storage files in several ways.

12-1 File concepts

Several concepts about files must be understood before we discuss file processing in BASIC. In this section we cover these concepts.

File organization

A file is a collection of data stored in auxiliary storage. Each individual data value in a file is called a *field*. For example, a file of personnel data would contain fields for each employee's name, social security number, and pay rate. Related fields are grouped together to form a *record*. For example, a personnel record would contain the fields for one employee (e.g., one employee's name, number, and rate). A *file* is a group of related records. Thus, all the personnel records, one for each employee, form the personnel file.

Figure 12-1 shows a listing of the data in an inventory file. Inventory is the stock of goods that a business has on hand. Each line in Figure 12-1 is a separate record in the inventory file. Each record contains information about one item that the business stocks. The information is contained in the fields in the records. Notice that the fields are separated by commas, just as the data values entered at a keyboard are separated by commas. (Not all types of files require commas between fields.)

The first field in each inventory record in Figure 12-1 is the item's identifying number. The second field is the item's description. The next field is the price. The last field is the stock on hand. Notice that the fields in each record are in the same order. In fact, as we will see, we must know the order of the fields in the records when we write a program to process the data in the file.

Usually, each record in a file has one field that identifies the record. This is called the *key field*. For example, in a personnel file the key field might be the employee's social security number. In the inventory file in Figure 12-1 the key field is the item number. Normally each record has a unique key field; that is, the key field in each record is different. As we will see, this helps us to retrieve specific records in the file.

The last record in the file in Figure 12-1 has 9999 in the key field. This is a trailer value used to signal the end of the file. This last record is called a *trailer record*. Notice that the other fields in the trailer record must contain some data. In this case, the item description is merely the letter X, and the price and quantity are both zero. (A trailer record is not always required with a file.)

File storage and retrieval

Physically the data in the file is stored as patterns of magnetism on a magnetic disk (or some other type of auxiliary storage). A magnetic disk is a flat round platter (like

Figure 12-1. An inventory file

```
1001 ,SCREWS, 2.95 , 15
1023 ,NAILS, 3.64 , 7
1045 ,BOLTS, 2.25 , 0
1172 ,WASHERS, 1.75 , 32
1185 ,NUTS, 1.52 , 4
1201 ,HOOKS, 1.95 , 11
1235 ,GLUE, 4.85 , 3
1278 ,CLAMP, 9.95 , 0
1384 ,HANGER, 6.28 , 12
1400 ,TAPE, 4.75 , 0
9999 ,X, 0 , 0
```

a phonograph record) made of metal or plastic and covered with a magnetic coating. (See Figure 12-2.) The surface of the disk is organized into concentric circles called *tracks* (similar to the grooves in a phonograph record). The computer stores data on a disk by recording patterns of magnetism along the tracks of the disk. It can change data that is stored on a disk by erasing the magnetic patterns and replacing them with new ones. The computer retrieves data from a disk by sensing the magnetic patterns along a track.

The fields in a record are stored in order along a track, as shown in Figure 12-2. One record is stored after another until the track is full. Then the file is continued onto the next track. Often many tracks are required to store all of the records in the file. If there is room, more than one file can be stored on a disk. Usually many files are stored on a disk.

To store data on a disk and to retrieve data from a disk, a *disk drive* is used. In a disk drive, the disk rotates at a high speed. While the disk is rotating, an *access arm* moves over it. At the end of the access arm is a *read/write head*. As the disk rotates, data can be recorded on a track by means of signals sent to the read/write head. Similarly, as the disk rotates, the data that is stored on a track can be retrieved by the read/write head. When data is recorded on the surface of a disk, any data existing in the same place is destroyed. When data is retrieved from a disk, however, the data is not destroyed.

Data that is stored in a file is retrieved one record at a time. To retrieve the

Figure 12-2. Magnetic disk storage

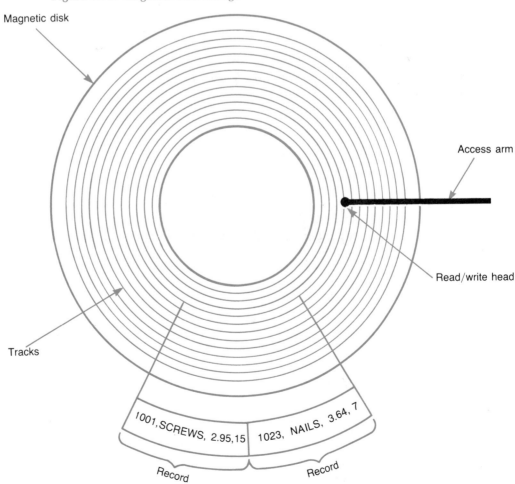

records in a file, the disk drive can position the read/write head at the first track of the file and retrieve records in sequence, moving the head from track to track. This is called *sequential access*. The disk drive can also move the read/write head forward or backward to any track and retrieve the records there without going through the records on other tracks. This is called *direct access* (or *random access*).

File types

The two types of file access — sequential and direct — correspond to two basic types of files — sequential files and random files. In a *sequential file* the records are stored in sequence, one after the other, in auxiliary storage. The records in a sequential file must be retrieved in the order in which they are stored. Thus, first the program must retrieve the first record in the file, then it must retrieve the second record, and so on. To retrieve the fifth record in the file, the program must first retrieve the first four records. Thus, the records in a sequential file are accessed sequentially.

In a *random file,* the records are identified by numbers. The first record is number 1, the second record is number 2, and so on. To retrieve a record in a random file, the program must specify the number of the desired record. For example, to retrieve the first record in the file, the program must specify that record number 1 is to be retrieved. Once the record number is given, however, that record can be retrieved without retrieval of other records in the file. For example, the program can retrieve record number 5 in the file without retrieving the first four records. Thus, the records in a random file are accessed directly.

File processing

We need to be able to do several things when we use files. One is to *create* a file; that is, we need to be able to put initial data into a file. The data that goes into a file must come from some other source. This data could be accepted from the keyboard or read from a DATA statement. It is even possible to obtain the data from another file. In any case, the data must first be brought into the computer's internal storage and then sent to the file. This is shown in Figure 12-3. Notice that *input* data must be obtained from another source and that *output* data is sent to the file. This is done one record at a time.

After a file is created, we can *access* the data in the file. As we have discussed already, this involves retrieving records from the file, one record at a time. Each record that is retrieved is processed in internal storage, and output is produced. This is shown in Figure 12-4. The *input* data is from the file and the *output* data goes to the CRT screen, the printer, or another file.

Finally, we may need to *update* the data in a file — that is, to change the data in one or more records in a file in order to bring the data up to date. Figure 12-5 shows this process. The data that describes the required updating is *input* data that comes from the keyboard, a DATA statement, or another file. The file to be updated contains data that needs to be changed. This is also *input* data, because each record to be updated must be brought into internal storage so the necessary changes can be made. After the record is updated, the *output* data for the modified file is sent to auxiliary storage.

Figure 12-3. Creating a file

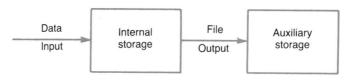

Figure 12-4. Accessing a file

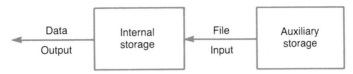

Figure 12-5. Updating a file

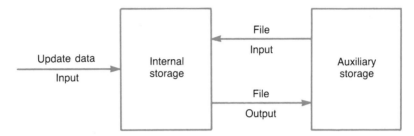

In all the situations described here, data must be transferred between the internal storage and the file in auxiliary storage. Data can be processed only if it is in the computer's internal storage. When data is brought into internal storage from a file, the process is viewed as an *input* operation. When data is sent from the internal storage to a file, the process involves an *output* operation. Input and output of file data is done one record at a time.

Notice also that a program can use more than one file. In fact, we could have several input files and several output files processed by the same program. This provides a great deal of versatility in what can be accomplished using files.

The next section describes statements for sequential file processing. Then Section 12-3 covers sequential file creation and access and Section 12-4 discusses sequential file updating. Random file processing is described in Section 12-5.

*12-2 Statements for sequential file processing

In this section we describe the statements used for sequential file processing. Almost all versions of BASIC permit sequential files. (See Table 12-1.) The syntax of the sequential file processing statements, however, varies somewhat from one version of the language to another. In this section we describe the statements used in one common version of BASIC (Microsoft BASIC).

Table 12-1. Sequential file differences

BASIC version	Sequential files permitted
ANS minimal BASIC	No
ANS BASIC	Yes
Microsoft BASIC	Yes
Applesoft BASIC	Yes
True BASIC	Yes (called "text files")
BASIC-PLUS	Yes (called "formatted ASCII files")
VAX-11 BASIC	Yes

The OPEN statement

Before a file can be processed, it must be "opened." Opening a file makes the file ready for processing. To open a file we use an OPEN statement. The syntax of this statement is as follows:

$$ln \text{ OPEN } \begin{Bmatrix} \text{"I"} \\ \text{"O"} \end{Bmatrix}, \#number, \text{"file name"}$$

For example, to open a particular file we could use the following statement:

```
100 OPEN "I",#1,"FILEX"
```

[The syntax of the OPEN statement is different in different versions of BASIC. (See Table 12-2.)]

The OPEN statement begins with the keyword OPEN. Following this must be either "I" or "O". "I" is used if the file is an input file — that is, if we are going to bring data from the file into internal storage. "O" is used in the OPEN statement if the file is an output file — that is, if we are going to send data from internal storage to the file. In the previous example, "I" was used, so the file is an input file.

Table 12-2. Sequential file OPEN statement differences

BASIC version	*Sequential file* OPEN *statement syntax*
ANS minimal BASIC	Not applicable
ANS BASIC	ln OPEN $\#number$:NAME "file name", ACCESS $\begin{Bmatrix} \text{INPUT} \\ \text{OUTPUT} \end{Bmatrix}$, ORGANIZATION SEQUENTIAL
Microsoft BASIC	ln OPEN $\begin{Bmatrix} \text{"I"} \\ \text{"O"} \end{Bmatrix}$, $\#number$, "file name" or ln OPEN "file name" FOR $\begin{Bmatrix} \text{INPUT} \\ \text{OUTPUT} \end{Bmatrix}$ AS $\#number$
Applesoft BASIC	OPEN statement not available. A sequential file is opened as follows: ln PRINT CHR\$(4);"OPEN file name"
True BASIC	OPEN $\#number$:NAME "file name", ACCESS $\begin{Bmatrix} \text{INPUT} \\ \text{OUTPUT} \end{Bmatrix}$, CREATE $\begin{Bmatrix} \text{OLD} \\ \text{NEW} \end{Bmatrix}$, ORGANIZATION TEST
BASIC-PLUS	ln OPEN "file name" FOR $\begin{Bmatrix} \text{INPUT} \\ \text{OUTPUT} \end{Bmatrix}$ AS FILE $\#number$
VAX-11 BASIC	ln OPEN "file name" FOR $\begin{Bmatrix} \text{INPUT} \\ \text{OUTPUT} \end{Bmatrix}$ AS FILE $\#number$

(Many versions of BASIC use the words INPUT and OUTPUT in the OPEN statement instead of "I" and "O".)

Next in the OPEN statement comes a # symbol (which is optional) followed by a number which identifies the *channel* that will be used to transfer data to and from the file. A channel can be thought of as a connection between internal storage and auxiliary storage. The channels are numbered 1, 2, . . ., 15. One of these numbers must be used in the OPEN statement. In the previous example we used channel number 1, but any number between 1 and 15 is acceptable. (The maximum channel number is different in different versions of BASIC.)

The reason there are several channels is that sometimes we need to open more than one file in a program. We will see an example of this when we discuss file updating. Each file must be opened with a separate OPEN statement and must use a different channel number. Thus, with channels 1 to 15, we can have at most 15 files open at one time in a program.

The final item needed in the OPEN statement is the file name. Each file that is stored in auxiliary storage must be identified by a unique name. This is because many files may be stored in auxiliary storage, and names are needed to distinguish them. A file name is one to eight characters in length and is enclosed in quotation marks in the OPEN statement. For example, the name of the file in the previous OPEN statement is FILEX. (The form of a file name may be different in different versions of BASIC.)

When an output file is opened, the computer creates a file with the given name. If a file already exists with the same name, that file is destroyed and replaced by the new file. When an input file is opened, the computer checks to see if a file with the given name exists. If the file does not exist, an execution error occurs. We must remember the name of any file we create, so that we can use the same name when we access the file. We do not, however, have to use the same channel number for a file. Thus, we can create a file using channel number 1 and access the file using channel number 2.

A file must be opened before it can be processed, but a file needs to be opened only once in a program. The OPEN statement usually appears at the beginning of the program before the input/output loop. We will see examples of this later.

The CLOSE statement

After a file has been processed, it must be "closed." Closing a file makes it no longer available for processing. The statement that accomplishes this is the CLOSE statement. The syntax of this statement is as follows:

```
ln CLOSE #number
```

Following the word CLOSE comes a # symbol (which is optional) and then a channel number for the file. For example, we close the file associated with channel number 1 with the following statement:

```
300 CLOSE #1
```

We can close more than one file at a time by using several channel numbers in a single CLOSE statement. For example, the following statement closes three files:

```
800 CLOSE #3,#8,#6
```

[The syntax of the CLOSE statement is different in different versions of BASIC.

Some versions of BASIC only allow one file to be closed in a CLOSE statement. (See Table 12-3.)]

A file needs to be closed only once in a program, after it has been processed. The CLOSE statement usually appears at the end of the program, following the input/output loop. We will see examples of this later.

The INPUT statement

To retrieve a record from a file, a special form of the INPUT statement is used. The syntax of this statement is as follows:

> *ln* INPUT *#number,list of variables*

For example, to retrieve a record from a particular file we could use the following statement:

    110 INPUT #1,K,X,P$

[The syntax of the sequential file INPUT statement is different in different versions of BASIC. (See Table 12-4.)]

In this form of the INPUT statement, the number following the # sign is the channel number for the file. This must be the same number that is given in the OPEN statement for the file. The file must be opened as an input file. In the example just given, we assume that the file was opened as file #1. Thus, we must "input" from file #1. Notice that only the channel number makes this form of the INPUT statement different from the keyboard INPUT statement.

The list of variables used in the INPUT statement must correspond to the fields in the records in the file. When we access a file, we must know how many fields there are in each record, the order of the fields, and the type of data in each field. In the example just given we assume that each record has three fields, of which the first two contain numeric data and the last contains string data. Hence, three variables are needed in the INPUT statement list — two numeric variables and a string variable, in that order. Notice that the type of the variable must correspond

Table 12-3. CLOSE statement differences

BASIC version	CLOSE *statement syntax*
ANS minimal BASIC	Not applicable
ANS BASIC	*ln* CLOSE *#number* (Each file must be closed with a separate statement.)
Microsoft BASIC	*ln* CLOSE *#number* (Multiple files may be closed with one statement.)
Applesoft BASIC	CLOSE statement not available. A file is closed as follows: *ln* PRINT CHR$(4);"CLOSE *file name*"
True BASIC	CLOSE *#number* (Each file must be closed with a separate statement.)
BASIC-PLUS	*ln* CLOSE *#number* (Multiple files may be closed with one statement.)
VAX-11 BASIC	*ln* CLOSE *#number* (Multiple files may be closed with one statement.)

Table 12-4. Sequential file INPUT statement differences

BASIC version	*Sequential file* INPUT *statement syntax*
ANS minimal BASIC	Not applicable
ANS BASIC	`ln INPUT #number:list of variables`
Microsoft BASIC	`ln INPUT #number,list of variables`
Applesoft BASIC	`ln INPUT list of variables`
	Prior to using a sequential file INPUT statement, use the statement
	`ln PRINT CHR$(4);"READ file name"`
	to specify that subsequent INPUT statements will retrieve records from the file.
	After the desired records are retrieved, use the statement
	`ln PRINT CHR$(4)`
	to specify that subsequent input will come from the keyboard.
True BASIC	`INPUT #number:list of variables`
BASIC-PLUS	`ln INPUT #number,list of variables`
VAX-11 BASIC	`ln INPUT #number,list of variables`

to the type of data in the fields; that is, a numeric variable must be used for numeric data and a string variable must be used for string data.

Each time an INPUT statement for a file is executed, the next record in the file is retrieved. Input begins with the first record in the file and proceeds sequentially through the records in the file. We cannot access records out of sequence or in reverse order.

The PRINT statement

To store a record in a file, a special form of the PRINT statement is used. The syntax of this statement is as follows:

```
ln PRINT #number,output list
```

For example, to store one record in a particular file, we could use the following statement:

```
220 PRINT #2,K;",";X;",";P$
```

[The syntax of the sequential file PRINT statement is different in different versions of BASIC. (See Table 12-5.)]

The number following the # sign in this form of the PRINT statement is the channel number for the file. This must be the same number that is given in the OPEN statement for the file. The file must be opened as an output file. Notice that only the channel number differentiates this form of the PRINT statement from the PRINT statement for CRT output.

Following the channel number is a list of the data that is to appear in one record in the file. There is one variable in this list for each field. Semicolons are used so that the fields are as close together as possible. (Commas can also be used, but

Table 12-5. Sequential file PRINT statement differences

BASIC version	*Sequential file PRINT statement syntax*
ANS minimal BASIC	Not applicable
ANS BASIC	*ln* PRINT #*number*:*output list*
Microsoft BASIC	*ln* PRINT #*number*,*output list*
Applesoft BASIC	*ln* PRINT *output list*
	Prior to using a sequential file PRINT statement, use the statement
	ln PRINT CHR$(4);"WRITE *file name*"
	to specify that subsequent PRINT statements will store records in the file.
	After the desired records are stored, use the statement
	ln PRINT CHR$(4)
	to specify that subsequent output will go to the CRT screen.
True BASIC	PRINT #*number*:*output list*
BASIC-PLUS	*ln* PRINT #*number*,*output list*
VAX-11 BASIC	*ln* PRINT #*number*,*output list*

then the fields are spread out in the record and the file requires more space on the disk.) Notice that between each variable in the PRINT statement the string "," appears. This causes a comma to be placed in the record between each field. These commas appear in the file and are necessary because the INPUT statement that accesses a record requires commas between the data. If the commas are omitted, the computer will not know where each field ends and thus cannot assign the data to the proper variables. (Some versions of BASIC do not require commas to be inserted with the PRINT statement.)

Each time a PRINT statement for a file is executed, one record is stored in the file. The first record that is stored becomes the first record in the file, the second record stored becomes the second record in the file, and so forth. Each successive record that is stored follows the previous record.

*12-3 Sequential file creation and access

Program logic for sequential file creation and access is very similar to the logic of many programs we have discussed in previous chapters. Normally, a loop is used that processes the records in the file one at a time. In this section we discuss several examples of programs that create and access sequential files.

Creating a sequential file

To illustrate the program logic for creating a sequential file, assume that we need to create the inventory file shown in Figure 12-1. Recall that this file contains information about the items that a business stocks. Each record in the file contains data about one item. Each record has four fields: the item's identifying number, the item's description, the item's price, and the stock on hand of the item. The last record is a trailer record with 9999 for the item-number field. We need a program that creates this file.

A sequential file-creation program usually stores the records in the file one at a time. First the data for a record must be obtained from some other source such as the keyboard or a DATA statement. Then the program must store the data for the record in the file. This sequence is repeated until all the records, including the trailer record, are stored in the file.

Figure 12-6 shows a program that creates the sequential inventory file from data in DATA statements. The OPEN statement in the program opens the file as an output file associated with channel number 1 and gives the file the name INVEN. The OPEN statement comes at the beginning of the program, before the input loop. The READ statement reads the data for one record from a DATA statement. Four values are read for the four fields in the record. Numeric variables are used for the item number, price, and stock on hand; a string variable is used for the item description. Notice that the values are in a different order in the DATA statement than their order in a record in the file, but this is not required. The data may be in the same or a different order. After the data for one record is read, the special form of the PRINT statement is used to store one record in the file. Notice that commas are inserted between each field in the record. This is so the data can be retrieved using the INPUT statement.

The READ and PRINT statements are repeated in a loop until the trailer record is stored in the file. The last DATA statement contains the data that is to go into the trailer record. This record must be stored in the file by the program that creates the file. The IF statement repeats the READ/PRINT loop until *after* the trailer record is read and stored. When the loop is terminated, the CLOSE statement closes the file. Notice that the OPEN and CLOSE statements are outside the loop. The file must be *opened once before* the first record in the file is processed and *closed once after* all records are processed.

Figure 12-6. A program that creates a sequential inventory file

```
100 REM - SEQUENTIAL INVENTORY FILE CREATION PROGRAM
110 REM - VARIABLES:
120 REM      N  = ITEM NUMBER
130 REM      D$ = ITEM DESCRIPTION
140 REM      P  = PRICE
150 REM      S  = STOCK ON HAND
200 OPEN "O",#1,"INVEN"
210 READ N,S,P,D$
220   PRINT #1,N;",";D$;",";P;",";S
230 IF N<>9999 THEN 210
240 CLOSE #1
900 REM - DATA FOR FILE
901 DATA 1001,15,2.95,SCREWS
902 DATA 1023,7,3.64,NAILS
903 DATA 1045,0,2.25,BOLTS
904 DATA 1172,32,1.75,WASHERS
905 DATA 1185,4,1.52,NUTS
906 DATA 1201,11,1.95,HOOKS
907 DATA 1235,3,4.85,GLUE
908 DATA 1278,0,9.95,CLAMP
909 DATA 1384,12,6.28,HANGER
910 DATA 1400,0,4.75,TAPE
911 DATA 9999,0,0,X
999 END
```

Accessing a sequential file

A program that accesses a sequential file may process all the records in the file or it may process just certain records. Figure 12-7 shows a program that illustrates the first case. This program displays a list giving the stock value for each item in the inventory file. The stock value of an item is the product of the item's price and the stock on hand of the item. One line is displayed for each record in the file except for the trailer record.

The OPEN statement in this program is the same as before, except the file is opened as an input file. The OPEN statement is at the beginning of the program, before the loop. In the loop, the special form of the INPUT statement retrieves one record from the file. All fields in the record are retrieved; variables of the appropriate type (numeric or string) are used for each field. The programmer must know the number, order, and type of each field in each record of the file so that the INPUT statement can be correctly coded.

After a record is retrieved, the stock value is computed. Then the PRINT statement displays a line on the CRT screen with the item's number, description,

Figure 12-7. A program that processes all records in a sequential inventory file

```
100 REM - STOCK VALUE LISTING PROGRAM
110 REM - VARIABLES:
120 REM        N  = ITEM NUMBER
130 REM        D$ = ITEM DESCRIPTION
140 REM        P  = PRICE
150 REM        S  = STOCK ON HAND
160 REM        V  = STOCK VALUE
200 OPEN "I",#1,"INVEN"
210 PRINT "         INVENTORY VALUE REPORT"
220 PRINT
230 PRINT "ITEM NUMBER","DESCRIPTION","STOCK VALUE"
240 PRINT
250 INPUT #1,N,D$,P,S
260    IF N=9999 THEN 300
270    LET V=P*S
280    PRINT N,D$,V
290 GOTO 250
300 CLOSE #1
999 END
```

(a) The program

```
                INVENTORY VALUE REPORT

ITEM NUMBER     DESCRIPTION     STOCK VALUE

   1001         SCREWS          44.25
   1023         NAILS           25.48
   1045         BOLTS           0
   1172         WASHERS         56
   1185         NUTS            6.08
   1201         HOOKS           21.45
   1235         GLUE            14.55
   1278         CLAMP           0
   1384         HANGER          75.36
   1400         TAPE            0
```

(b) Output

and stock value. The loop is repeated until the trailer record is retrieved. When the program branches out of the loop, the file is closed.

The program in Figure 12-7 processes all records in the file. To illustrate the case where only certain records are processed, assume that we need to display a list of the item number and description for all items in the inventory file with a stock on hand of zero. Figure 12-8 shows a program that accomplishes this.

This program has some characteristics in common with the previous one. Both programs have an OPEN statement to open the file and an INPUT statement to retrieve a record from the file. Also in both programs the input loop repeats until the trailer record is reached. There are several differences between the programs, however. One difference is that the program in Figure 12-8 does not use the price field which is contained in each input record. However, the variable for this field must still be included in the INPUT statement. This is because each execution of the INPUT statement causes a complete record to be retrieved and a variable must be provided for each field in the record. Another difference is that output is displayed only for certain records in the file. The PRINT statement is executed only if the stock on hand is not greater than zero. Notice in the output in Figure 12-8(b) that only three lines are displayed (other than the headings), even though there are more records in the file.

The program in Figure 12-8 retrieves all records in the inventory file but processes only certain ones (i.e., those with a stock-on-hand field equal to zero). All records in the file must be retrieved, because we do not know which records to process. The program must go through all the records to locate those that satisfy the required condition.

Figure 12-8. A program that processes selected records in a sequential inventory file

```
100 REM - OUT OF STOCK LISTING PROGRAM
110 REM - VARIABLES:
120 REM       N  = ITEM NUMBER
130 REM       D$ = ITEM DESCRIPTION
140 REM       P  = PRICE
150 REM       S  = STOCK ON HAND
200 OPEN "I",#1,"INVEN"
210 PRINT "THE FOLLOWING ITEMS ARE OUT OF STOCK"
220 PRINT
230 PRINT "ITEM NUMBER","DESCRIPTION"
240 PRINT
250 INPUT #1,N,D$,P,S
260   IF N=9999 THEN 300
270   IF S>0 THEN 290
280     PRINT N,D$
290 GOTO 250
300 CLOSE #1
999 END
```

(a) The program

```
THE FOLLOWING ITEMS ARE OUT OF STOCK

ITEM NUMBER    DESCRIPTION

   1045        BOLTS
   1278        CLAMP
   1400        TAPE
```

(b) Output

Searching a sequential file

A more complex sequential file-access situation involves locating a specific record in a file. For example, we may need to locate the record for a particular item in the inventory file. Usually we specify the record to be located by giving the key field for the record. Recall that the key field is the field that identifies the record. In the inventory file this is the item number. Thus, to locate a particular inventory record, we would give the number for the item whose record is to be located.

Locating a specific record in a sequential file involves searching the file until the record with the desired key field is found. The search is done by retrieving one record at a time, beginning with the first record in the file. Each time a record is retrieved, we compare its key field with the desired key. If they are the same, the search stops; otherwise we continue to the next record. The processing stops either when the desired record is found or when the end of the file is reached without its being found.

Figure 12-9 shows a sample program that involves file searching. The flowchart of the program is shown in Figure 12-10. The purpose of this program is to compute the cost of an order of a specific item by multiplying the quantity purchased by the price of the item. The interactive input and output for this program are shown in Figure 12-11.

At the beginning of the program the item number and quantity for the item

Figure 12-9. A program that searches a sequential inventory file

```
100 REM - ORDER COST COMPUTATION PROGRAM
110 REM - VARIABLES:
120 REM        N  = ITEM NUMBER
130 REM        D$ = ITEM DESCRIPTION
140 REM        P  = PRICE
150 REM        S  = STOCK ON HAND
160 REM        N1 = NUMBER OF ITEM ORDERED
170 REM        Q  = QUANTITY ORDERED
180 REM        C  = COST OF ORDER
190 REM        R$ = REPETITION QUESTION RESPONSE
200 PRINT "ORDER COST COMPUTATION PROGRAM"
210 PRINT
220 INPUT "ENTER ITEM NUMBER";N1
230    INPUT "ENTER QUANTITY";Q
240    PRINT
250    REM - SEARCH FOR ITEM IN FILE
260    OPEN "I",#1,"INVEN"
270    INPUT #1,N,D$,P,S
280      IF N=9999 THEN 310
290      IF N=N1 THEN 310
300    GOTO 270
310    CLOSE #1
320    IF N=N1 THEN 350
330      PRINT "ITEM";N1;"NOT FOUND IN FILE"
340    GOTO 410
350      IF Q<=S THEN 380
360        PRINT "INSUFFICIENT STOCK ON HAND FOR ITEM";N1
370      GOTO 410
380        LET C=P*Q
390        PRINT "ITEM";N1;D$
400        PRINT "PRICE";P;"QUANTITY";Q;"COST";C
410    PRINT
420    INPUT "DO YOU WANT TO COMPUTE MORE ORDER COSTS";R$
430    PRINT
440 IF R$="YES" THEN 220
450 PRINT "END OF PROGRAM"
999 END
```

Figure 12-10. Flowchart of the program that searches a sequential inventory file

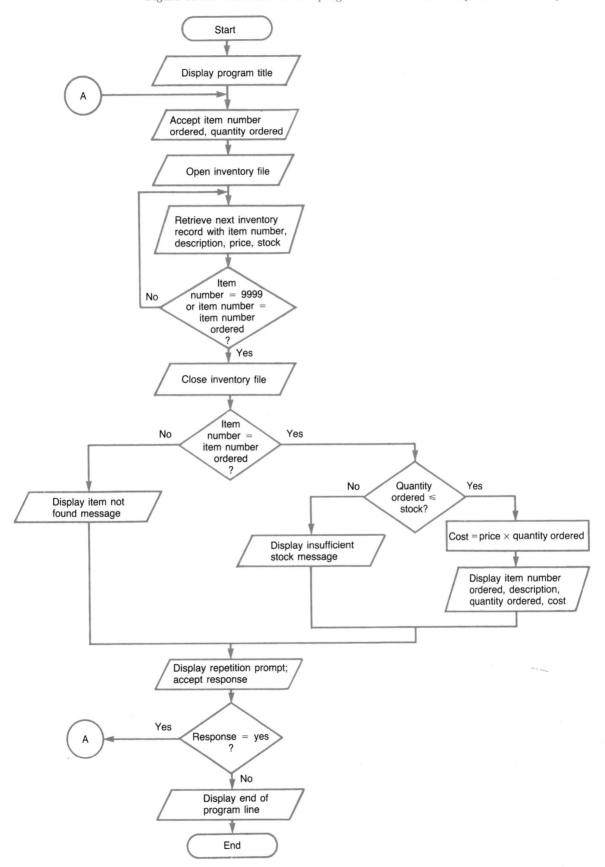

Figure 12-11. Interactive input and output for the program that searches a sequential inventory file

```
ORDER COST COMPUTATION PROGRAM

ENTER ITEM NUMBER? 1201
ENTER QUANTITY? 5

ITEM 1201 HOOKS
PRICE 1.95 QUANTITY 5 COST 9.75

DO YOU WANT TO COMPUTE MORE ORDER COSTS? YES

ENTER ITEM NUMBER? 1045
ENTER QUANTITY? 10

INSUFFICIENT STOCK ON HAND FOR ITEM 1045

DO YOU WANT TO COMPUTE MORE ORDER COSTS? YES

ENTER ITEM NUMBER? 1225
ENTER QUANTITY? 8

ITEM 1225 NOT FOUND IN FILE

DO YOU WANT TO COMPUTE MORE ORDER COSTS? YES

ENTER ITEM NUMBER? 1023
ENTER QUANTITY? 1

ITEM 1023 NAILS
PRICE 3.64 QUANTITY 1 COST 3.64

DO YOU WANT TO COMPUTE MORE ORDER COSTS? NO

END OF PROGRAM
```

ordered are accepted from the keyboard. Then the file is searched for a matching item number. First the file is opened (line 260). Then a loop is performed that searches the file. In the loop, a record is retrieved from the file (line 270). If the record is the trailer record, the loop is terminated (line 280). If the record is not the trailer record, the item number entered at the keyboard is compared with the item number from the file (line 290). If these are the same, the loop is terminated; otherwise the loop is repeated. After the loop is terminated, the file is closed (line 310).

The search loop is repeated until either the trailer record is reached or the desired item is found in the file. In the former case we know the item is not in the file, and a message indicating this is displayed (line 330). In the latter case the quantity ordered is compared to the stock on hand from the record in the file (line 350). If insufficient stock is available, a message is displayed (line 360); otherwise the cost is computed and the output is displayed (lines 380 through 400).

After the output is produced, the user is asked whether he or she wishes to repeat the processing (line 420). If more costs are to be computed, the computer branches to the beginning of the main input loop and the program is repeated.

Notice that the program closes the file after a search for an item is completed and then reopens the file when the search for a new item is begun. This must be done so that the computer begins accessing the file with the first record each time the file is to be searched. If we do not close and reopen the file, processing will continue with the next record following the last record retrieved.

In this program the records in the file are searched in order beginning with the first record in the file. This is called a *sequential search*. The search stops either when the desired record is located or when the trailer record is retrieved, indicating an unsuccessful search. If the records are sorted in increasing order by key field, an unsuccessful search can be detected before the trailer record is reached. This can be done in the program in Figure 12-9 if we change line 290 to the following:

```
290 IF N>=N1 THEN 310
```

In this case the search stops if the item number from the input file is greater than or equal to the desired item number. The greater-than condition occurs if we have gone beyond the desired item in the file without finding the item. This would occur only if the item is not in the file. Again, this approach assumes that the records are organized in increasing order by key field.

Although a sequential search is useful, it can be very slow, because each time an INPUT statement is executed, the computer must retrieve a record from the disk. Such disk access is time-consuming in comparison to other types of processing that the computer can do.

An alternative approach to file searching is to retrieve all the records in the file at one time and to store the data in internal storage. This can be done only if the file is small enough to fit in internal storage, which in many realistic situations is not possible. When it is possible, however, the file is brought into internal storage and stored in several arrays, one for each field. For example, to retrieve the ten data records from the inventory file and to store the data in four arrays, we could use the following statements:

```
200 DIM N(10),D$(10),P(10),S(10)
210 OPEN "I",#1,"INVEN"
220 FOR I=1 TO 10
230    INPUT #1,N(I),D$(I),P(I),S(I)
240 NEXT I
250 CLOSE #1
```

Once the data from the file is in internal storage in arrays, it can be searched very quickly. We can use a sequential search to search the arrays or, if the data is in increasing order by key field, a binary search. (These approaches to array searching were discussed in Section 9-4.) It is important to remember, however, that this approach works only if the file is sufficiently small to fit in internal storage.

*12-4 Sequential file updating

File updating involves changing the data in a file. For example, data in the inventory file discussed in the last section may need to be updated periodically to reflect changes in the stock on hand. To update a file, we must locate each record in the file that is to be modified. After a record is found, individual fields in the record can be changed.

Sequential file updating concepts

When updating a sequential file, we normally cannot change existing data in it. Once a sequential file is created, the data in the file usually cannot be modified. Therefore, to update a sequential file we must create a *new* (updated) file which contains all the data from the *old* (nonupdated) file after any desired changes have been made in the data. (There may be exceptions to this, depending on the version of BASIC being used.)

We call the file to be updated the *old master file* because the data in it is the main or "master" data and has not been updated (i.e., it is "old" data). The records in this file are called *old master records*. The updated file is called the *new master file*. This file contains data from the old master file that has been modified. The records in this file are called *new master records*. The data that indicates what modifications are to be made in the master file is called *transaction data* because it represents events or "transactions" that have taken place and that need to be reflected in the master file. The transaction data may be stored in a file (the *transaction file* containing *transaction records*), may be read from DATA statements, or may be entered interactively as the updating program executes.

To illustrate these concepts, assume that we need to update the stock on hand in the inventory file discussed in the last section. Updating involves subtracting the amount withdrawn from stock and adding the amount added to stock. The old master file is the inventory file. The transaction data includes the amount withdrawn and the amount added to stock for each item to be updated. For example, if the stock on hand for an item in the old master file is 7 and the transaction data indicates that the amount withdrawn for the item is 4 and the amount added is 15, then the new stock on hand is 7 minus 4 plus 15 or 18. This is the amount that would go into the new master file for this item. The new master file would be the same as the old master file except for changes such as this.

When updating a file we must have a way of determining which records are to be updated. This is usually done by including a key field in the master records to uniquely identify each record. For example, in the inventory file the key field is the item number. Each record in the inventory file has a unique value in this field. The transaction data for updating this file would have to have the values of the key fields for the records to be updated. Thus, for updating the stock on hand in the inventory file, each set of transaction data would have to include a field for the item number, the amount withdrawn from stock, and the amount added to stock. We call the key field in the master file the *master key* and that in the transaction data the *transaction key*.

One requirement for the sequential file updating algorithm that we will be discussing in this section is that the master records and the transaction data must be in *increasing* order by key field. For example, the records in the inventory file must be in increasing order by item number and the transaction data must also be in increasing order by item number. If the data is not in this order, the updating algorithm will not work. (A slight variation of the algorithm is needed if the data is in decreasing order by key field.)

Usually the transaction data does not contain transactions for each record in the old master file. In the inventory example there would be no transaction data for an item if stock was not withdrawn or added. In such a case, however, the record from the old master file must still be put in the new master file; otherwise the record would be lost from the file.

There can also be transaction data for records that do not exist in the master file. This would be the case if an error were made in the transaction data or if a corresponding record had not yet been added to the master file. If such a situation occurs, a message should be displayed indicating the condition so that corrective action can be taken.

An illustrative program

Figure 12-12 shows a program that updates the inventory file. The flowchart for this program is shown in Figure 12-13. The old master file is the file named INVEN created by the program in Figure 12-6 and shown in Figure 12-1. The records in this file are in increasing order by item number and the last record is a trailer record

Figure 12-12. A program that updates a sequential inventory file

```
100 REM - SEQUENTIAL INVENTORY FILE UPDATING PROGRAM
110 REM - VARIABLES:
120 REM        N  = MASTER RECORD ITEM NUMBER
130 REM        D$ = ITEM DESCRIPTION
140 REM        P  = PRICE
150 REM        S  = STOCK ON HAND
160 REM        N1 = TRANSACTION DATA ITEM NUMBER
170 REM        W  = AMOUNT WITHDRAWN FROM STOCK
180 REM        A  = AMOUNT ADDED TO STOCK
200 REM - OPEN OLD MASTER FILE AND NEW MASTER FILE
210 OPEN "I",#1,"INVEN"
220 OPEN "O",#2,"NEWINV"
230 REM - READ TRANSACTION DATA
240 READ N1,W,A
250 REM - RETRIEVE OLD MASTER RECORD
260 INPUT #1,N,D$,P,S
270 IF N<>9999 THEN 290
280    IF N1=9999 THEN 540
290    IF N1<>N THEN 410
300      REM - TRANSACTION KEY EQUALS MASTER KEY
310      REM - UPDATE STOCK ON HAND
320      LET S=S-W+A
330      REM - STORE NEW MASTER RECORD
340      PRINT #2,N;",";D$;",";P;",";S
350      REM - READ TRANSACTION DATA
360      READ N1,W,A
370      REM - RETRIEVE OLD MASTER RECORD
390      INPUT #1,N,D$,P,S
400    GOTO 530
410    IF N1<N THEN 480
420      REM - TRANSACTION KEY GREATER THAN MASTER KEY
430      REM - STORE NEW MASTER RECORD
440      PRINT #2,N;",";D$;",";P;",";S
450      REM - RETRIEVE OLD MASTER RECORD
460      INPUT #1,N,D$,P,S
470    GOTO 530
480      REM - TRANSACTION KEY LESS THAN MASTER KEY
490      REM - DISPLAY ERROR MESSAGE
500      PRINT "ITEM";N1;"NOT IN FILE"
510      REM - READ TRANSACTION DATA
520      READ N1,W,A
530 GOTO 270
540 PRINT #2,9999;",";"X";",";0;",";0
550 CLOSE #1,#2
900 REM - TRANSACTION DATA
901 DATA 1023,4,15
902 DATA 1172,30,0
903 DATA 1193,12,20
904 DATA 1201,0,15
905 DATA 1225,0,30
906 DATA 1235,0,0
907 DATA 9999,0,0
999 END
```

with 9999 for the item-number field. This file is opened as an input file in the updating program. The new master file is named NEWINV. It is opened as an output file. Notice that these files are associated with channel number 1 and channel number 2, respectively. When more than one file is open at a time in a program, each file must be associated with a different channel number.

The transaction data for the updating program is read from DATA statements. Each set of transaction data consists of an item number, the amount withdrawn from inventory, and the amount added to inventory. The data is in increasing order by

Figure 12-13. Flowchart of the program that updates a sequential inventory file

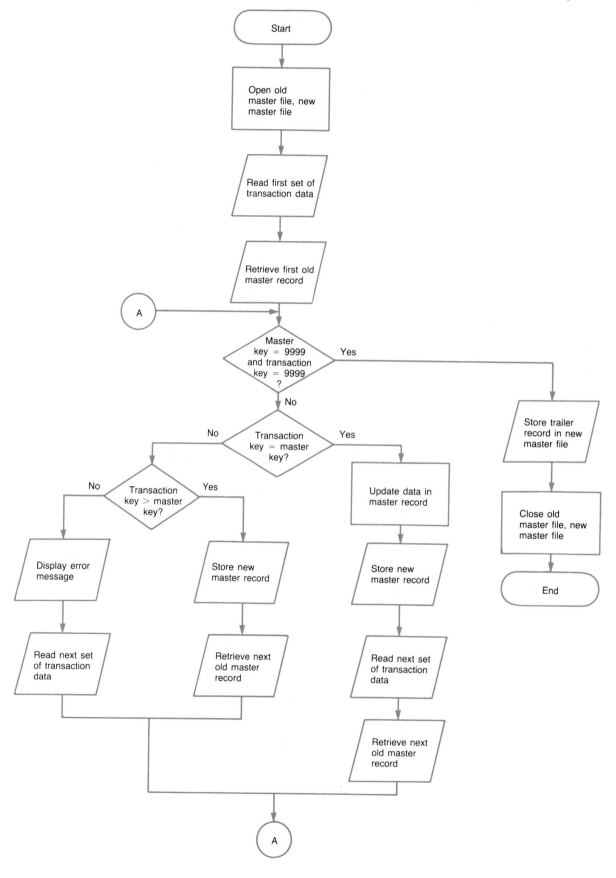

item number. The last set of transaction data contains a trailer value of 9999 for the item number.

The basic logic of the algorithm used in the program in Figure 12-12 is to read a set of transaction data and then to retrieve records from the old master file until a record is located with the same key field as that in the transaction data. When such a record is found, the data in the old master record is updated. This process is then repeated for the next set of transaction data and so forth until all sets of transaction data have been read.

The program in Figure 12-12 begins by reading one set of transaction data and retrieving one master record. In this program we must determine if the end of the transaction data and the end of the master file have been reached. The end of the transaction data is detected when the item number from the transaction data (N1) equals 9999. This is the trailer value that signals the end of this data. The end of the master file is detected when the trailer record in the master file is read. When that record is read, the item number from the master record (N) equals 9999.

The main loop in the program is repeated until the end of the master file and the end of the transaction data have been reached — that is, until N equals 9999 *and* N1 equals 9999. In the loop, a nested decision is used to determine what to do next, based on how the item numbers compare. To see how this works, assume that the item numbers in the transaction data and the records in the master file are as follows:

N1	*N*
1023	1001
1172	1023
1193	1045
9999	1172
	1185
	1201
	1235
	9999

Because the first set of transaction data is read and the first master record is retrieved before the loop is entered, N1 is 1023 and N is 1001 when the nested decision in the loop is first reached. Then the conditions in the decision and subsequent input result in the following steps with each repetition of the loop. (In the following comparisons N1 is on the left and N is on the right.)

1. 1023 > 1001:
   Store new master record (N = 1001)
   Retrieve next old master record (N = 1023)
2. 1023 = 1023:
   Update stock on hand
   Store new master record (N = 1023)
   Read next transaction data (N1 = 1172)
   Retrieve next old master record (N = 1045)
3. 1172 > 1045:
   Store new master record (N = 1045)
   Retrieve next old master record (N = 1172)
4. 1172 = 1172:
   Update stock on hand
   Store new master record (N = 1172)
   Read next transaction data (N1 = 1193)
   Retrieve next old master record (N = 1185)

    5. 1193 > 1185:

          Store new master record (N = 1185)

          Retrieve next old master record (N = 1201)

    6. 1193 < 1201:

          Display error message

          Read next transaction data (N1 = 9999)

    7. 9999 > 1201:

          Store new master record (N = 1201)

          Retrieve next old master record (N = 1235)

    8. 9999 > 1235:

          Store new master record (N = 1235)

          Retrieve next old master record (N = 9999)

After the last step is completed, both N and N1 equal 9999 and the loop is terminated.

    In this example, the end of the transaction data is reached before the end of the old master file. At that time N1 becomes 9999 and all subsequent values of N are less than this value. As a consequence, the remaining old master records are stored in the new master file. Had the end of the old master file been reached first, N would be equal to 9999 and the subsequent values of N1 would be less than this. In this case, an error message would be displayed for each of the remaining sets of transaction data.

    After the loop is terminated, a trailer record must be stored in the new master file. This is done with a PRINT statement. Then both the old master file and the new master file must be closed and the program terminated.

    The output from this program is shown in Figure 12-14. Part (a) of the figure shows the new master file that is created by the program. Notice that the stock-on-hand field in several records has been updated. (Compare this figure with the old master file in Figure 12-1.) Part (b) of the figure shows the displayed output, which indicates that two items included in the transaction data were not found in the old master file.

    A file-updating program such as this is used whenever the data in a sequential file changes. Additional statements can be included in the program to add new records to the file and to delete out-of-date records. These would be required in a complete file-maintenance program.

Figure 12-14. Output from the program that updates a sequential inventory file

```
1001 ,SCREWS, 2.95 , 15
1023 ,NAILS, 3.64 , 18
1045 ,BOLTS, 2.25 , 0
1172 ,WASHERS, 1.75 , 2
1185 ,NUTS, 1.52 , 4
1201 ,HOOKS, 1.95 , 26
1235 ,GLUE, 4.85 , 3
1278 ,CLAMP, 9.95 , 0
1384 ,HANGER, 6.28 , 12
1400 ,TAPE, 4.75 , 0
9999 ,X, 0 , 0
```

    (a) New master file output

```
ITEM 1193 NOT IN FILE
ITEM 1225 NOT IN FILE
```

    (b) Displayed output

*12-5 Random files

In this section we describe random file processing. Most versions of BASIC permit random files. (See Table 12-6.) The syntax and rules for the random file processing statements, however, vary considerably from one version of the language to another. In this section we describe the statements used in one common version of BASIC (Microsoft BASIC).

Random file concepts

As we know, records in a sequential file are processed sequentially. Whenever we use an INPUT or a PRINT statement with a sequential file we mean retrieve or store the *next* record in sequence. The computer remembers what record was last processed so it can determine what the next record is. (When a sequential file is first opened, the "next" record is the first record in the file.)

With a random file we can process records directly without going through other records in the file. In BASIC this is accomplished by identifying each record by a *record number*. The record numbers begin with 1 for the first record and increase through the file. To process a record in a random file we specify the number of the record. For example, we can tell the computer to retrieve record 5 or store record 8. We can retrieve or store any record in a random file as long as we know the record number.

Figure 12-15 shows an example of a random file. The records in this file contain data about students. Each record has a student's name and scores on three tests. Each record is identified by its record number. To put data in the file for Mary Smith we would tell the computer to store record number 2 in the file. Similarly, to get the data for James Cole we would tell the computer to retrieve record number 7 from the file.

Statements for random file processing

In this subsection we describe the BASIC statements for random file processing. Some of these statements are similar to those used for sequential file processing; others are different.

The OPEN statement. The syntax of the OPEN statement for a random file is as follows:

```
ln OPEN "R",#number,"file name",length
```

Table 12-6. Random file differences

BASIC version	Random files permitted
ANS minimal BASIC	No
ANS BASIC	Yes (called "relative files")
Microsoft BASIC	Yes
Applesoft BASIC	Yes
True BASIC	Yes (called "record files")
BASIC-PLUS	Yes (called "block I/O files")
VAX-11 BASIC	Yes (called "relative files")

Figure 12-15. A random file of student data

Record
numbers   Records

1	JOHNSON ROBERT	78	92	83
2	SMITH MARY	100	95	97
3	ANDERSON RICHARD	65	72	57
4	WILSON ALEX	73	69	78
5	DEAN BRIAN	42	56	47
6	EMERY SUSAN	91	100	92
7	COLE JAMES	75	78	73
8	GUINN DOROTHY	86	82	74
9	JONES ED	71	84	78

For example, to open a particular random file we could use the following statement:

```
100 OPEN "R",#1,"FILEA",16
```

[The syntax of the random file OPEN statement is different in different versions of BASIC. (See Table 12-7.)]

In this form of the OPEN statement the "R" indicates that the file is to be opened as a random file. It is not necessary to indicate whether the file is an input file or an output file. Opening a random file makes it both an input file and an output file.

As with a sequential file we must specify a channel number following the # symbol in the OPEN statement. (The # symbol is optional.) The channel number must be between 1 and 15. (The maximum channel number is different in different versions of BASIC.) In the previous example, channel number 1 is used for the file. We must also give the file name, which consists of one to eight characters and is enclosed in quotation marks in the OPEN statement. In the previous example, the file name FILEA is used. (The form of the file name may be different in different versions of BASIC.)

Finally, with a random file we must specify the length of each record in the file in the OPEN statement. The length is the number of characters in each record. This length must be greater than or equal to the length specified in the FIELD statement for the file. (The FIELD statement is discussed later.) In the previous example, the length of each record is 16 characters. (The length specification may be left out of the OPEN statement, in which case the computer uses a predetermined length for each record. This length may or may not be appropriate, so it is usually best to include the length specification in the OPEN statement.)

The CLOSE statement. The CLOSE statement for a random file is identical to that of a sequential file. For reference, the syntax is as follows:

```
ln CLOSE #number
```

Table 12-7. Random file OPEN statement differences

BASIC version	*Random file OPEN statement syntax*
ANS minimal BASIC	Not applicable
ANS BASIC	*ln* OPEN #*number*:NAME "*file name*",ACCESS $\begin{Bmatrix} \text{INPUT} \\ \text{OUTPUT} \\ \text{OUTIN} \end{Bmatrix}$, ORGANIZATION RELATIVE, RECSIZE VARIABLE LENGTH *length*
Microsoft BASIC	*ln* OPEN "R",#*number*,"*file name*",*length* or *ln* OPEN "*file name*" AS #*number* LEN=*length*
Applesoft BASIC	OPEN statement not available; a random file is opened as follows: *ln* PRINT CHR$(4);"OPEN *file name*,L*length*"
True BASIC	OPEN #*number*:NAME "*file name*",ACCESS $\begin{Bmatrix} \text{INPUT} \\ \text{OUTPUT} \\ \text{OUTIN} \end{Bmatrix}$, CREATE $\begin{Bmatrix} \text{OLD} \\ \text{NEW} \\ \text{NEWOLD} \end{Bmatrix}$,ORGANIZATION RECORD, RECSIZE *length*
BASIC-PLUS	*ln* OPEN "*file name*" FOR $\begin{Bmatrix} \text{INPUT} \\ \text{OUTPUT} \end{Bmatrix}$ AS FILE #*number*
VAX-11 BASIC	*ln* OPEN "*file name*" FOR $\begin{Bmatrix} \text{INPUT} \\ \text{OUTPUT} \end{Bmatrix}$ AS FILE #*number* ORGANIZATION RELATIVE

For example, to close the random file associated with channel number 1 we would use the following statement:

```
400 CLOSE #1
```

Multiple files may be closed with one CLOSE statement as in the following example:

```
700 CLOSE #5,#12
```

[The rules for the CLOSE statement may vary in different versions of BASIC. (See Table 12-3.)]

Random file record specification. To process a random file record, we must specify the fields in the record. Before a record can be stored in a random file, data must be assigned to the fields. Similarly, after a record is retrieved from a random file, we must assign the data from the fields to variables in the program. The fields in a record are specified with the FIELD statement. Data is assigned to the fields specified in the FIELD statement with the LSET and RSET statements. In doing this, the MKS$ function may be needed to convert numeric data to string data. Data in the fields specified in the FIELD statement is assigned to variables in the program with the LET statement. In doing this, the CVS function may be needed to convert string data to numeric data. In this subsection we describe these statements and functions. [The procedure for random file record specification may be different in different versions of BASIC. (See Table 12-8.)]

The fields in a record in a random file are specified with a FIELD statement. The syntax of this statement is as follows:

```
ln FIELD #number,width AS string variable,width AS string variable, ...
```

For example, the following is a valid FIELD statement:

```
110 FIELD #1,12 AS Z$,4 AS L$
```

The FIELD statement must come after the OPEN statement for the file and use the same channel number as that in the OPEN statement. We define each field in a record in the file in the FIELD statement by giving its width, which is the number of characters in the field, and a string variable that identifies the field. The width must be a numeric expression, although usually just a constant is used. In the previous example, the record consists of two fields. The first contains 12 characters and is identified by the string variable Z$. The second consists of 4 characters and is identified by L$.

Note that only string variables can be used to identify fields in the FIELD statement; numeric variables cannot be used for this purpose. In addition, the total width of all fields must be less than or equal to the length of the record given in the OPEN statement. Thus, in the previous example the total width is 12 plus 4 or 16, which must not exceed the record length in the OPEN statement for this file.

Data is assigned to the fields specified in the FIELD statement with the LSET and RSET statements. The syntax of these statements is as follows:

```
ln LSET string variable=string expression
ln RSET string variable=string expression
```

Table 12-8. Random file record specification differences

BASIC version	Random file record specification procedures
ANS minimal BASIC	Not applicable
ANS BASIC	Record is specified by items in input/output statement list
Microsoft BASIC	Record is specified as described in text
Applesoft BASIC	Record is specified by items in input/output statement list
True BASIC	Fields must be concatenated to form one string prior to storing a record. The NUM$ function is used to convert numeric data to string data. After retrieving a record, fields must be separated using substring extraction. The NUM function is used to convert string data to numeric data.
BASIC-PLUS	Record is specified as described in the text except the CVTF$ function is used to convert numeric data to string data and the CVT$F function is used to convert string data to numeric data.
VAX-11 BASIC	The same procedures as those in BASIC-PLUS may be used or the MAP statement can be used to define the fields, in which case the LSET, RSET, and data-conversion functions are not needed.

Only string variables and string expressions can be used in these statements. The following are valid LSET and RSET statements:

```
200 LSET Z$=Y$
210 RSET Z$="XYZ"
```

The effect of the LSET statement is to assign the value of the string expression to the *left* part of the field identified by the string variable and fill in any places on the right with blank spaces. (We say the data is *left-justified*.) Thus, if Y$ equals ABCDE, and the field named Z$ has a width of 12, then after the LSET statement just given is executed, Z$ will equal ABCDE followed by seven blank spaces. The RSET statement assigns the value of the string expression to the *right* part of the field and fills in any places on the left with blank spaces. (We say the data is *right-justified*.) Thus, if the field named Z$ has a width of 12, then after the RSET statement just given is executed, Z$ will equal nine blank spaces followed by XYZ.

Data must be assigned to the fields in a FIELD statement with the LSET and RSET statements. The LET, INPUT, and READ statements must *not* be used for this purpose as they will cause the variable for the field to no longer identify the field. In most cases, the LSET statement is used to assign data to fields. The RSET statement is needed only for special applications.

The FIELD statement can contain only string variables, and the LSET and RSET statements can only assign string data to string variables. If we wish to store numeric data in a field, that data must be converted to string data first. This is accomplished with the MKS$ function. This function converts a numeric value to a four-character form that can be assigned to a string variable. Usually, the function is used in an LSET statement. For example, consider the following statement:

```
220 LSET L$=MKS$(K)
```

The MKS$ function converts the value of the numeric variable K to a four-character string. This string is then assigned to the string variable L$ with the LSET statement. Note that the MKS$ function produces a four-character string, so the width of the field identified by L$ in this example should be 4.

To summarize, the procedure that must be followed to store a record in a random file is as follows:

1. Open the file.
2. Specify the fields in the records in the file in a FIELD statement.
3. Convert numeric values to strings using the MKS$ function.
4. Assign data to the fields in the FIELD statement using the LSET and RSET statements.
5. Store the records in the file. (The statement to do this is discussed later.)

We will see an example of this procedure later in a sample program.

The FIELD statement is used not only to specify the fields in a record to be stored in a random file, but also to identify the fields in a record that is retrieved from a random file. After a record is retrieved from a random file, the data in the fields can be assigned to other variables in the program with the LET statement. The LSET and RSET statements are *not* used for this purpose. For example, if Z$ identifies a field in a FIELD statement, then the following statement can be used to assign the value of this field to Y$:

```
250 LET Y$=Z$
```

Note that if the field named Z$ has a width of 12, then after this LET statement is executed, Y$ will equal the 12 characters in the field including any blank spaces.

If a field contains string data, we may not need to assign the data in the field to another variable as in the previous example. Thus, if all we wish to do is display the value of the field, we can simply use the variable that identifies the field in a PRINT statement as in the following example:

```
260 PRINT Z$
```

On the other hand, if a field contains a string that represents numeric data, then the data must be converted to numeric data and assigned to a numeric variable. To convert a string to numeric data, the CVS function is used. This function converts a four-character string to a numeric value. For example, consider the following statement:

```
270 LET K=CVS(L$)
```

The CVS function converts the value of the string variable L$ to a numeric value. This numeric value is then assigned to the numeric variable K with the LET statement. Note that the CVS function converts a four-character string to a numeric value, so the width of the field identified by L$ in this example should be 4.

To summarize, the procedure that must be followed to retrieve a record from a random file is as follows:

1. Open the file.
2. Specify the fields in the records in the file in a FIELD statement.
3. Retrieve a record from the file. (The statement to do this is discussed later.)
4. Convert string fields that represent numeric data to numeric form using the CVS function.
5. Assign data from the fields in the FIELD statement to other variables using the LET statement.

We will see an example of this procedure later in a sample program.

The random file output statement. To store a record in a random file, the PUT statement is used. The syntax of this statement is as follows:

```
ln PUT #number,record
```

For example, the following is a valid PUT statement:

```
230 PUT #1,5
```

[The syntax of the random file output statement is different in different versions of BASIC. (See Table 12-9.)]

The channel number in the PUT statement must be the same as the number used in the OPEN statement and the FIELD statement for the file. Following the channel number must be a constant or variable which gives the number of the record to be stored. Recall that records in a random file are numbered beginning with 1. The record number in the PUT statement identifies which record is to be stored. This number must be between 1 and the total number of records in the file. In the previous example, the fifth record is stored because the constant 5 is used in the statement. A variable can also be used, as in the following example:

```
230 PUT #1,R
```

The value of R in this example determines which record is stored in the file. The

Table 12-9 Random file output statement differences

BASIC version	Random file output statement syntax
ANS minimal BASIC	Not applicable
ANS BASIC	*ln* WRITE #*number*,RECORD *record:output list*
Microsoft BASIC	*ln* PUT #*number*,*record*
Applesoft BASIC	*ln* PRINT *output list*
	Prior to using a random file PRINT statement use the statement
	ln PRINT CHR$(4);"WRITE *file name*,R";*record*
	to specify that the next PRINT statement will store data in the record whose number is specified by the value of *record*.
	After the record is stored, use the statement
	ln PRINT CHR$(4)
	to specify that subsequent output will go to the CRT screen.
True BASIC	WRITE #*number*:*variable*
	Prior to using a random file WRITE statement, use the statement
	SET #*number*:RECORD *record*
	to specify that the next WRITE statement will store data in the record whose number is specified by the value of *record*.
BASIC-PLUS	*ln* PUT #*number*,RECORD *record*
VAX-11 BASIC	*ln* PUT #*number*,RECORD *record*

record number may be left out, in which case the record is stored as the next record in the file.

Before a PUT statement can be executed, the file must be opened, the FIELD statement for the file must be executed, numeric values must be converted to strings, and data must be assigned to the fields using LSET and RSET statements.

The random file input statement. To retrieve a record from a random file, the GET statement is used. The syntax of this statement is as follows:

> *ln* GET #*number*,*record*

For example, the following is a valid GET statement:

        240 GET #1,10

[The syntax of the random file input statement is different in different versions of BASIC. (See Table 12-10.)]

The channel number in the GET statement must be the same as the number used in the OPEN statement and the FIELD statement for the file. Following the channel number must be a constant or variable which gives the number of the record to be retrieved. This number must be between 1 and the total number of records in the file. In the previous example, the tenth record is retrieved, because the constant 10 is used in the statement. A variable can also be used, as in the following example:

        240 GET #1,N

The value of N in this example determines which record is retrieved from the file.

Table 12-10. Random file input statement differences

BASIC version	Random file input statement syntax
ANS minimal BASIC	Not applicable
ANS BASIC	`ln READ #number,RECORD record:list of variables`
Microsoft BASIC	`ln GET #number,record`
Applesoft BASIC	`ln INPUT list of variables`
	Prior to using a random file INPUT statement use the statement
	`ln PRINT CHR$(4);"READ file name,R";record`
	to specify that the next INPUT statement will retrieve data from the record whose number is specified by the value of *record*.
	After the record is retrieved, use the statement
	`ln PRINT CHR$(4)`
	to specify that subsequent input will come from the keyboard.
True BASIC	`READ #number:variable`
	Prior to using a random file READ statement, use the statement
	`SET #number:RECORD record`
	to specify that the next READ statement will retrieve data from the record whose number is specified by the value of *record*.
BASIC-PLUS	`ln GET #number,RECORD record`
VAX-11 BASIC	`ln GET #number,RECORD record`

The record number may be left out, in which case the next record in sequence is retrieved.

Before a GET statement can be executed, the file must be opened and the FIELD statement for the file must be executed. After the GET statement is executed, string fields that represent numeric data must be converted to numeric form and data from the fields must be assigned to other variables.

Creating a random file

When creating a random file, we must store each record in the file by specifying its record number. The records for the file may be stored in sequence or in some other order. For example, we could create a random file by first storing record number 1, then record number 2, then record number 3, and so on. Alternatively, we could first store record number 5, then record number 8, then record number 2, etc. Because the file is a random file, records can be stored in any order.

To illustrate a program for creating a random file, assume that a file of student data is needed. Each record in the file contains four fields. The first field, which is 16 characters, is the student's name. The other three fields, which are each four characters, are the scores for the student on three tests. Notice that there is no number to identify the student in the records in this file. Instead we will use the record number as the student's identifying number. (We could have student numbers in the file, but then we would need some way of associating each student number with a record number. Techniques for doing this are beyond the scope of this book.)

Figure 12-16 shows a program that creates the student data file. The name of the file that is created is STUDAT. It is associated with channel number 1 in the OPEN statement. Each record in the file contains one 16-character field and three

Figure 12-16. A program that creates a random file of student data

```
100 REM - RANDOM STUDENT DATA FILE CREATION PROGRAM
110 REM - VARIABLES:
120 REM        M$  = FIELD FOR STUDENT NAME
130 REM        T1$ = FIELD FOR FIRST TEST SCORE
140 REM        T2$ = FIELD FOR SECOND TEST SCORE
150 REM        T3$ = FIELD FOR THIRD TEST SCORE
160 REM        I   = STUDENT IDENTIFICATION NUMBER
170 REM        N$  = STUDENT NAME
180 REM        S1  = FIRST TEST SCORE
190 REM        S2  = SECOND TEST SCORE
200 REM        S3  = THIRD TEST SCORE
300 OPEN "R",#1,"STUDAT",28
310 FIELD #1,16 AS M$,4 AS T1$,4 AS T2$,4 AS T3$
320 LET I=0
330 READ N$,S1,S2,S3
340   IF N$="END" THEN 420
350   LET I=I+1
360   LSET M$=N$
370   LSET T1$=MKS$(S1)
380   LSET T2$=MKS$(S2)
390   LSET T3$=MKS$(S3)
400   PUT #1,I
410 GOTO 330
420 PRINT "STUDENT DATA FILE CREATED WITH";I;"RECORDS"
430 CLOSE #1
900 REM - DATA FOR FILE
901 DATA JOHNSON ROBERT,78,92,83
902 DATA SMITH MARY,100,95,97
903 DATA ANDERSON RICHARD,65,72,57
904 DATA WILSON ALEX,73,69,78
905 DATA DEAN BRIAN,42,56,47
906 DATA EMERY SUSAN,91,100,92
907 DATA COLE JAMES,75,78,73
908 DATA GUINN DOROTHY,86,82,74
909 DATA JONES ED,71,84,78
910 DATA END,0,0,0
999 END
```

(a) The program

```
STUDENT DATA FILE CREATED WITH 9 RECORDS
```

(b) Displayed output

fields with four characters each. Hence, there are 28 characters in each record. This record length is specified in the OPEN statement. Notice that the file is opened at the beginning of the program, before the input loop.

Following the OPEN statement is the FIELD statement. The four fields in each record are specified with the appropriate widths in this statement. A string variable is used to identify each field. The FIELD statement is at the beginning of the program, before the input loop.

The data for the new file is read from DATA statements by the READ statement. An input loop is used that terminates when the value of the student name is the word END. Each set of data that is read is stored as a record in the new file. Before the data is stored, it is assigned to the fields specified in the FIELD statement. The LSET statement is used for each assignment. Notice that the numeric test scores are converted to strings using the MKS$ function in the LSET statements. These strings are each four characters long. The variable I, which represents the student identification number, is used in the PUT statement to specify which record is to be stored. Initially I is 0. Before each record is stored I is increased by 1. Hence the records are stored in sequence: first record number 1 is stored, then record number 2, and so on. (We could have used a PUT statement without a record number, because the records are stored in sequence.) After the input loop terminates, the file is closed. Then the current value of I is displayed to give a count of the number of records stored in the file. Notice that no trailer record is stored in the file. A trailer record may or may not be used in a random file.

The displayed output for this program is shown in Figure 12-16(b). This output indicates that nine records were stored in the file. The file output for this program is the student data file shown in Figure 12-15.

Accessing a random file

A program that accesses a random file may process all the records in the file or it may process only selected records. In both cases each record that is processed is accessed by specification of its record number. If all records are to be accessed, then all record numbers must be specified in some logical order. If selected records are to be accessed, then only the numbers of those records need to be given.

Figure 12-17 shows a program that processes all records in the student data file created in the last subsection. The OPEN statement and the FIELD statement in this program are the same as in the program that created the file. Note that the record length and each field's width must be the same as when the file was created.

To retrieve a record we specify the record number in the GET statement. In this program we use I, which represents the student identification number, for the record number in the GET statement. (We could have used a GET statement without a record number because all records are retrieved in sequence.) Because we wish to process all records in the file, I must be incremented through all its values. This is accomplished with a FOR loop. In the FOR loop I is incremented from 1 to the number of records in the file. This latter value is given by the variable C. C is assigned a value of 9 at the beginning of the program because there are nine records in the file. To write a program such as this we must know how many records are in the file. (We cannot use a trailer-value test to end processing because there is no trailer record in this file.)

Within the FOR loop a record is retrieved from the random file. The CVS function is used to convert each field in the record that contains a test score to a numeric form. Then the total and average of the test scores are computed and the results, along with the student's name, are displayed. Notice that the variable that identifies the student name field in the FIELD statement is used in the PRINT statement. It is not necessary to assign this field to another variable, because we are only going to display it. Sample output from this program is shown in Figure 12-17(b). This output was produced using the student data file shown in Figure 12-15.

To illustrate the case where we wish to process selected records in a random file, assume that we need an interactive program that accesses specific records in the student data file. Input to the program is the student identification number, which, as we know, is also the record number. The program must access the desired record, determine the total and average of the test scores in the record, and display the results along with the student's name. The program must handle the case where an invalid student number is entered. Figure 12-18 shows a program that accomplishes this. The flowchart of this program is shown in Figure 12-19.

In this program a loop is repeated for each record that is processed. At the beginning of the loop a prompt is displayed and the student identification number

Figure 12-17. A program that processes all records in a random file of student data

```
100 REM - TEST SCORE ANALYSIS PROGRAM
110 REM - VARIABLES:
120 REM        M$  = FIELD FOR STUDENT NAME
130 REM        T1$ = FIELD FOR FIRST TEST SCORE
140 REM        T2$ = FIELD FOR SECOND TEST SCORE
150 REM        T3$ = FIELD FOR THIRD TEST SCORE
160 REM        C   = NUMBER OF RECORDS IN FILE
170 REM        I   = STUDENT IDENTIFICATION NUMBER
180 REM        S1  = FIRST TEST SCORE
190 REM        S2  = SECOND TEST SCORE
200 REM        S3  = THIRD TEST SCORE
210 REM        T   = TOTAL SCORE
220 REM        A   = AVERAGE SCORE
300 OPEN "R",#1,"STUDAT",28
310 FIELD #1,16 AS M$,4 AS T1$,4 AS T2$,4 AS T3$
320 REM - ASSIGN NUMBER OF RECORDS IN FILE TO C
330 LET C=9
340 PRINT "            TEST SCORE ANALYSIS"
350 PRINT
360 PRINT " STUDENT NAME    TOTAL SCORE    AVERAGE SCORE"
370 PRINT
380 FOR I=1 TO C
390    GET #1,I
400    LET S1=CVS(T1$)
410    LET S2=CVS(T2$)
420    LET S3=CVS(T3$)
430    LET T=S1+S2+S3
440    LET A=T/3
450    PRINT M$;TAB(22);T;TAB(36);A
460 NEXT I
470 CLOSE #1
999 END
```

(a) The program

```
               TEST SCORE ANALYSIS

    STUDENT NAME    TOTAL SCORE    AVERAGE SCORE

    JOHNSON ROBERT      253          84.3333
    SMITH MARY          292          97.3333
    ANDERSON RICHARD    194          64.6667
    WILSON ALEX         220          73.3333
    DEAN BRIAN          145          48.3333
    EMERY SUSAN         283          94.3333
    COLE JAMES          226          75.3333
    GUINN DOROTHY       242          80.6667
    JONES ED            233          77.6667
```

(b) Output

for the desired record is accepted from the keyboard. In the loop the program checks to see if the student number that was entered is valid — that is, if the number is between 1 and the number of records in the file. (Again, the number of records in the file is assigned to the variable C at the beginning of the program.) If a valid student number is entered, the record for that student is retrieved, the total and average of the test scores are computed, and the output is displayed. If an invalid student number is entered, an error message is displayed.

This program does not process the records in the file in any preset order. Each record is accessed directly, based on the student number that is entered. Figure

Figure 12-18. A program that processes selected records in a random file of student data

```
100 REM - TEST SCORE ANALYSIS PROGRAM
110 REM - VARIABLES:
120 REM        M$  = FIELD FOR STUDENT NAME
130 REM        T1$ = FIELD FOR FIRST TEST SCORE
140 REM        T2$ = FIELD FOR SECOND TEST SCORE
150 REM        T3$ = FIELD FOR THIRD TEST SCORE
160 REM        C   = NUMBER OF RECORDS IN FILE
170 REM        I   = STUDENT IDENTIFICATION NUMBER
180 REM        S1  = FIRST TEST SCORE
190 REM        S2  = SECOND TEST SCORE
200 REM        S3  = THIRD TEST SCORE
210 REM        T   = TOTAL SCORE
220 REM        A   = AVERAGE SCORE
230 REM        R$  = REPETITION QUESTION RESPONSE
300 OPEN "R",#1,"STUDAT",28
310 FIELD #1,16 AS M$,4 AS T1$,4 AS T2$,4 AS T3$
320 REM - ASSIGN NUMBER OF RECORDS IN FILE TO C
330 LET C=9
340 PRINT "TEST SCORE ANALYS      .OGRAM"
350 PRINT
360 INPUT "ENTER STUDENT NUMBER";I
370    IF I<1 THEN 500
380    IF I>C THEN 500
390       GET #1,I
400       LET S1=CVS(T1$)
410       LET S2=CVS(T2$)
420       LET S3=CVS(T3$)
430       LET T=S1+S2+S3
440       LET A=T/3
450       PRINT
460       PRINT "STUDENT NAME:   ";M$
470       PRINT "TOTAL SCORE:    ";T
480       PRINT "AVERAGE SCORE:";A
490    GOTO 520
500       PRINT
510       PRINT "INVALID STUDENT NUMBER"
520    PRINT
530    INPUT "DO YOU WANT TO ANALYZE MORE TEST SCORES";R$
540    PRINT
550 IF R$="YES" THEN 360
560 PRINT "END OF PROGRAM"
570 CLOSE #1
999 END
```

12-20 shows sample interactive input and output for this program using the data file in Figure 12-15 as input. Notice in Figure 12-20 that record 5 is accessed first, then record 1, and then record 8. The records in a random file can be accessed in any order.

Updating a random file

There are several differences between updating a random file and updating a sequential file. In sequential file updating a new file is created with the updated data. This is because it is usually not possible to change the data in a sequential file once the file is created. In a random file, however, data can be changed without creating a new file. This is done by retrieving the record to be changed, making changes in the data in the record, and then storing the new record in the same location in auxiliary storage from where it was retrieved. When the new record is stored, the old record

Figure 12-19. Flowchart of the program that processes selected records in a random file of student data

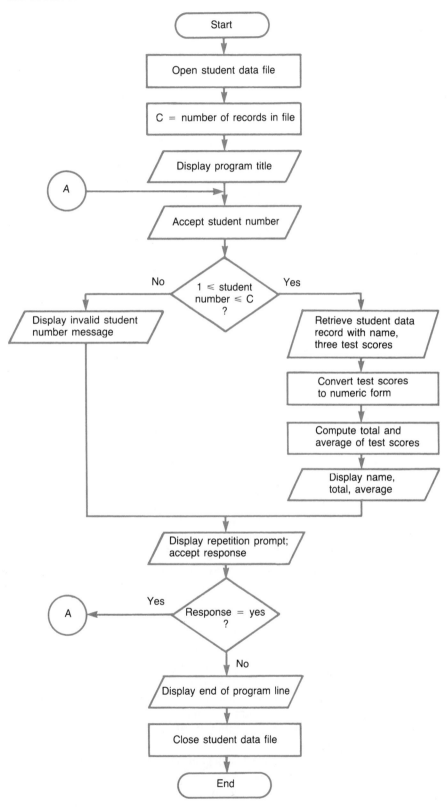

Figure 12-20. Interactive input and output for the program that processes selected records in a random file of student data

```
TEST SCORE ANALYSIS PROGRAM

ENTER STUDENT NUMBER? 5

STUDENT NAME:   DEAN BRIAN
TOTAL SCORE:    145
AVERAGE SCORE: 48.3333

DO YOU WANT TO ANALYZE MORE TEST SCORES? YES

ENTER STUDENT NUMBER? 1

STUDENT NAME:   JOHNSON ROBERT
TOTAL SCORE:    253
AVERAGE SCORE: 84.3333

DO YOU WANT TO ANALYZE MORE TEST SCORES? YES

ENTER STUDENT NUMBER? 12

INVALID STUDENT NUMBER

DO YOU WANT TO ANALYZE MORE TEST SCORES? YES

ENTER STUDENT NUMBER? 8

STUDENT NAME:   GUINN DOROTHY
TOTAL SCORE:    242
AVERAGE SCORE: 80.6667

DO YOU WANT TO ANALYZE MORE TEST SCORES? NO

END OF PROGRAM
```

is erased and therefore the file is updated. Thus, although sequential file updating requires two master files — the old master file and the new — random file updating uses only one master file.

Another difference is that in updating a sequential file the master records must be in order by key field and the transaction data must be in the same order. With random file updating these requirements are not necessary. Because the records in a random file can be accessed in any order, the records do not have to be updated in sequence. Hence, the order of the records in the file and the order of the transaction data are not important.

Figure 12-21 shows a program that updates test scores in the random file of student data created earlier. The flowchart of this program is shown in Figure 12-22. In this program the student data file, which is the master file, is opened and the fields in the records in the file are specified as in the previous programs. Updating is accomplished in a loop that is repeated for each student record to be updated. At the beginning of the loop the student number for the record to be updated is accepted from the keyboard and a check is made to determine if the student number is valid. If a valid student number is entered, updating proceeds; otherwise an error message is displayed.

In the record-updating process, the master record for the student whose number was entered is retrieved from the random file. The test scores in the record are converted to numeric form and these scores along with the student name are displayed. Then the transaction data is accepted from the keyboard and processed. Transactions for this program involve changes in scores on tests. The number of the test with a

Figure 12-21. A program that updates a random file of student data

```
100 REM - RANDOM STUDENT DATA FILE UPDATING PROGRAM
110 REM - VARIABLES:
120 REM         M$  = FIELD FOR STUDENT NAME
130 REM         T1$ = FIELD FOR FIRST TEST SCORE
140 REM         T2$ = FIELD FOR SECOND TEST SCORE
150 REM         T3$ = FIELD FOR THIRD TEST SCORE
160 REM         C   = NUMBER OF RECORDS IN FILE
170 REM         I   = STUDENT IDENTIFICATION NUMBER
180 REM         S1  = FIRST TEST SCORE
190 REM         S2  = SECOND TEST SCORE
200 REM         S3  = THIRD TEST SCORE
210 REM         N   = NUMBER OF TEST TO UPDATE
220 REM         S   = NEW TEST SCORE
230 REM         R$  = REPETITION QUESTION RESPONSE
300 REM - OPEN MASTER FILE
310 OPEN "R",#1,"STUDAT",28
320 FIELD #1,16 AS M$,4 AS T1$,4 AS T2$,4 AS T3$
330 REM - ASSIGN NUMBER OF RECORDS IN FILE TO C
340 LET C=9
350 PRINT "TEST SCORE UPDATING PROGRAM"
360 PRINT
370 REM - ACCEPT STUDENT NUMBER FOR RECORD TO UPDATE
380 INPUT "ENTER STUDENT NUMBER";I
390    IF I<1 THEN 770
400    IF I>C THEN 770
410      REM - RETRIEVE MASTER RECORD TO UPDATE
420      GET #1,I
430      LET S1=CVS(T1$)
440      LET S2=CVS(T2$)
450      LET S3=CVS(T3$)
460      PRINT
470      PRINT "STUDENT NAME:    ";M$
480      PRINT "SCORE ON TEST 1:";S1
490      PRINT "SCORE ON TEST 2:";S2
500      PRINT "SCORE ON TEST 3:";S3
510      PRINT
520      REM - ACCEPT AND PROCESS TRANSACTION DATA
530      INPUT "ENTER TEST NUMBER";N
540      PRINT
550      IF N<1 THEN 750
560      IF N>3 THEN 750
570        PRINT "ENTER NEW SCORE FOR TEST";N;
580        INPUT S
590        REM - UPDATE TEST SCORE
600        IF N>1 THEN 630
610          LET S1=S
620        GOTO 670
630        IF N>2 THEN 660
640          LET S2=S
650        GOTO 670
660          LET S3=S
670        LSET T1$=MKS$(S1)
680        LSET T2$=MKS$(S2)
690        LSET T3$=MKS$(S3)
700        REM - STORE UPDATED MASTER RECORD
710        PUT #1,I
720        PRINT
730        PRINT "SCORE ON TEST";N;"UPDATED"
740      GOTO 790
750        PRINT "INVALID TEST NUMBER"
760    GOTO 790
770      PRINT
780      PRINT "INVALID STUDENT NUMBER"
790    PRINT
800    INPUT "DO YOU WANT TO UPDATE MORE TEST SCORES";R$
810    PRINT
820 IF R$="YES" THEN 380
830 PRINT "END OF PROGRAM"
840 CLOSE #1
999 END
```

Figure 12-22. Flowchart of the program that updates a random file of student data

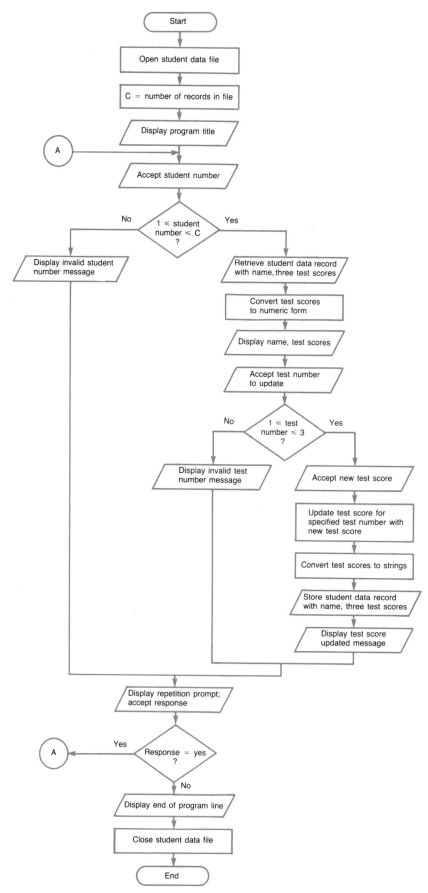

```
TEST SCORE UPDATING PROGRAM

ENTER STUDENT NUMBER? 5

STUDENT NAME:    DEAN BRIAN
SCORE ON TEST 1: 42
SCORE ON TEST 2: 56
SCORE ON TEST 3: 47

ENTER TEST NUMBER? 2

ENTER NEW SCORE FOR TEST   ? 60

SCORE ON TEST 2 UPDATED

DO YOU WANT TO UPDATE MORE TEST SCORES? YES

ENTER STUDENT NUMBER? 1

STUDENT NAME:    JOHNSON ROBERT
SCORE ON TEST 1: 78
SCORE ON TEST 2: 92
SCORE ON TEST 3: 83

ENTER TEST NUMBER? 4

INVALID TEST NUMBER

DO YOU WANT TO UPDATE MORE TEST SCORES? YES

ENTER STUDENT NUMBER? 1

STUDENT NAME:    JOHNSON ROBERT
SCORE ON TEST 1: 78
SCORE ON TEST 2: 92
SCORE ON TEST 3: 83

ENTER TEST NUMBER? 3

ENTER NEW SCORE FOR TEST 3 ? 81

SCORE ON TEST 3 UPDATED

DO YOU WANT TO UPDATE MORE TEST SCORES? YES

ENTER STUDENT NUMBER? 12

INVALID STUDENT NUMBER

DO YOU WANT TO UPDATE MORE TEST SCORES? YES

ENTER STUDENT NUMBER? 8

STUDENT NAME:    GUINN DOROTHY
SCORE ON TEST 1: 86
SCORE ON TEST 2: 82
SCORE ON TEST 3: 74

ENTER TEST NUMBER? 1

ENTER NEW SCORE FOR TEST 1 ? 93

SCORE ON TEST 1 UPDATED

DO YOU WANT TO UPDATE MORE TEST SCORES? NO

END OF PROGRAM
```

Figure 12-24. The random file of student data after updating

Record
numbers   Records

1	JOHNSON ROBERT	78	92	81
2	SMITH MARY	100	95	97
3	ANDERSON RICHARD	65	72	57
4	WILSON ALEX	73	69	78
5	DEAN BRIAN	42	60	47
6	EMERY SUSAN	91	100	92
7	COLE JAMES	75	78	73
8	GUINN DOROTHY	93	82	74
9	JONES ED	71	84	78

score to be changed is accepted from the keyboard. If this number is not valid, an error message is displayed. If it is valid, a new test score is accepted from the keyboard. Then the test score in the master record that was retrieved is updated by assigning the new test score to the variable for the test score to be changed. Next, the test scores are converted to strings and assigned to fields in the record. Note that it is not necessary to assign the student name to a field in the record because no change was made in the name field. Finally, the updated master record is stored in the direct file. Notice that the record number in the PUT statement is identified by I, which is used also in the GET statement. Because the value of I is not changed between the GET and PUT statements, the same record number is used for both input and output. Hence, the original record is destroyed when the record is stored and replaced by the new, updated record.

This program updates the student data in any order. Figure 12-23 shows the interactive I/O for the program. The student data file in Figure 12-15 was used during the updating process. Notice that the first record updated is for student number 5, then student number 1's record is updated, and finally the record for student number 8 is updated. Figure 12-24 shows the updated file that results from this processing. As we can see, the third test score in record 1 is 81, the second score in record 5 is 60, and the first score in record 8 is 93. These are different than in the original file shown in Figure 12-15 and reflect the changes resulting from the interactive execution of the program in Figure 12-23.

This program shows one approach for updating a random file. Many programs use a similar approach, but other techniques are also used. Random file updating programs can vary considerably, depending on the updating requirements.

*12-6 Chaining

Sometimes a program is too large to fit into the computer's internal storage. When this is the case, it is necessary to break the program into sections and save each section in auxiliary storage. Essentially each section becomes a separate program and is given a name when it is saved. Then execution is begun by bringing the first section of the program into internal storage and running it. At the end of the first section, a special statement is executed that brings the second section into internal storage, erasing the first section and continuing with execution. This can be repeated for as many program sections as required. The process is called *chaining*.

The statement that is used to bring in the next section of a program is the CHAIN statement. This statement is not available in all versions of BASIC. (See Table 12-11.) The syntax of this statement is as follows:

```
ln CHAIN "program name"
```

For example, to bring in a program section named SEC2, we could use the following statement:

```
830 CHAIN "SEC2"
```

Execution of this statement causes the computer to replace the program currently in internal storage with the one named SEC2. Processing then continues with the first statement in SEC2.

We can use the CHAIN statement to execute any program section that is saved. We can even return to the first section of the program and repeat it. Each program section that is brought in by the CHAIN statement replaces the current program section in internal storage. Hence, we can use the same statement numbers and variables in different program sections; the computer will treat each program section as if it were a new program.

One problem with chaining is that any *data* stored in a program section is lost when the next section is brought in. To solve this problem, we can create a file containing all the data that needs to be used by the next section just before the CHAIN statement is executed. Then the file can be accessed at the beginning of the next program section, and processing can continue without loss of data.

For example, assume that the values of the variables A, B, C, and D are determined in the first section of a program and are needed in the next section (SEC2). The following statements can then be executed at the end of the first section:

```
800 OPEN "O",#1,"FILE1"
810 PRINT #1,A;",";B;",";C;",";D
820 CLOSE #1
830 CHAIN "SEC2"
```

Table 12-11. CHAIN statement differences

BASIC version	CHAIN *statement available*
ANS minimal BASIC	No
ANS BASIC	Yes
Microsoft BASIC	Yes
Applesoft BASIC	No
True BASIC	Yes
BASIC-PLUS	Yes
VAX-11 BASIC	Yes

At the beginning of the second section we would have statements such as the following:

```
200 OPEN "I",#1,"FILE1"
210 INPUT #1,A,B,C,D
220 CLOSE #1
```

Thus, the values of A, B, C, and D would be transferred from one program section to the other by use of a file.

Chaining can be very useful in large programs, especially interactive programs involving many tasks. Each task can be stored as a separate program section and brought in as needed. This not only makes it possible to write large programs, but also simplifies the development of programs that perform many different operations.

Review questions

1. Auxiliary storage is used to store _____ and _____.
2. Give three reasons for storing data in files in auxiliary storage.
3. An individual data value in a file is called _____.
4. A group of related fields is called _____.
5. What is a key field?
6. What is a track on a magnetic disk? What is a read/write head?
7. When data is recorded on a disk, existing data is _____ (destroyed/not destroyed). When data is retrieved from a disk the data is _____ (destroyed/not destroyed).
8. Explain the difference between sequential access and direct access.
9. What is the difference between a sequential file and a random file?
10. When a file is created, the file data is _____ (input/output) data.
11. When a file is accessed, the file data is _____ (inut/output) data.
12. When a file is updated, the data in the file to be updated is _____ (input/output) data and the new, updated data for the file is _____ (input/output) data.
13. Assume that it is necessary to create a sequential file named AFILE. Each record in the file will have two fields with numeric data and two fields with string data. Code statements to do each of the following:
    a. Open the file.
    b. Store one record in the file.
    c. Close the file.
14. Assume that a sequential file named BFILE already exists. Each record in the file has one field with string data and three fields with numeric data. Code statements to do each of the following:
    a. Open the file.
    b. Retrieve one record from the file.
    c. Close the file.
15. Why is a trailer record needed in a sequential file?
16. Consider the program shown in Figure 12-9. What would happen if the OPEN statement were moved to line 195 and the CLOSE statement were moved to line 460?
17. When a file is searched beginning with the first record in the file and continuing one record at a time, the process is called _____.
18. What is the difference between data in a master file and transaction data?
19. What is the importance of the master key and the transaction key in sequential file updating?
20. Consider the sequential file updating program in Figure 12-12. In executing this program using the data shown in Figure 12-1 as input, how many times will each of the following statements in the program be executed?
    a. the statement at line 320
    b. the statement at line 390

c. the statement at line 440

d. the statement at line 520

21. Assume that it is necessary to create a random file named CFILE. Each record in this file contains three four-character fields of numeric data and one eight-character field of string data. Code statements to do each of the following:

a. Open the file.

b. Specify the fields in the records in the file.

c. Assign data to the fields in a record. Assume that the numeric data is identified by the variables W, X, and Y in the program and the string data is identified by the variable Z$.

d. Store the eighth record in the file.

e. Close the file.

22. Assume that a random file named DFILE already exists. Each record in the file has three fields. The first two fields are ten characters long and contain string data. The last field has four characters and contains numeric data. Code statements to do each of the following:

a. Open the file.

b. Specify the fields in the records in the file.

c. Retrieve the twelfth record from the file.

d. Assign the string data in the file to the variables A$ and B$ and the numeric data to the variable C.

e. Close the file.

23. What are the differences between updating a random file and updating a sequential file?

24. Consider the random file updating program in Figure 12-21 which updates the random file in Figure 12-15. For the interactive input shown in Figure 12-23, how many times will each of the following statements in the program be executed?

a. the statement at line 380

b. the statement at line 420

c. the statement at line 710

d. the statement at line 780

25. Write a statement to appear in a program named PROGX that causes a program named PROGY to be retrieved from auxiliary storage and executed.

Programming problems

1. Write a BASIC program to create a sequential file of payroll data. Each record in the file contains a field for the employee's number, employee's name, hourly pay rate, number of exemptions, and year-to-date gross pay. The records are in ascending order by employee number. Store the following data in the file:

Employee number	Employee name	Hourly pay rate	Number of exemptions	Year-to-date gross pay
1234	SMITH	7.25	2	23,528.32
1345	JONES	8.12	2	40,452.00
1456	BROWN	7.75	0	39,152.25
1567	JOHNSON	6.75	3	20,295.30
1678	ANDREWS	7.20	5	34,252.85
1789	MCDONALD	8.10	0	38,825.00
2123	WHITE	6.90	1	25,302.00
2234	KNIGHT	7.25	1	39,505.41
2345	DAVIS	12.15	6	44,505.25
2456	EMERY	6.00	3	39,025.36
2567	HOLT	7.50	0	32,250.00
2678	COLE	8.00	3	19,845.00

2. Write a BASIC program to list the payroll file created in Problem 1. Supply appropriate headings and display one line for each record in the file.

3. Write a BASIC program to display the employee number and name for each employee who has zero exemptions in the payroll file created in Problem 1.

4. Write a BASIC program to search for and display an employee's record in the payroll file created in Problem 1, given the employee's number. Test the program for several employees. Be sure to test the case where there is no matching employee number in the file.

5. Write a BASIC program to process payroll transaction data along with the payroll file created in Problem 1. Transaction data consists of the employee's number and hours worked for several employees. The data is in increasing order by employee number. The program should produce a payroll summary report. The report should list the following fields for each employee for which there is transaction data: employee number, employee name, gross pay, withholding tax, social security tax, net pay, and new year-to-date gross pay. Supply appropriate headings for the columns of output. If there is transaction data for an employee for whom there is no record in the payroll file, display the employee's number and an appropriate message. The gross pay, withholding tax, social security tax, net pay, and new year-to-date gross pay are computed as follows:

   a. Gross pay is hours times rate with "time and one-half" for all hours over 40 worked in a week.

   b. Withholding tax = 22.5% of [gross pay − (exemptions × 13.5)].

   c. Social security tax is 7.05% of gross pay. Employees are exempt from social security tax once their year-to-date gross pay exceeds $39,600.

   d. Net pay is gross pay less withholding tax and social security tax.

   e. New year-to-date gross pay is the year-to-date gross pay from the payroll file plus the current gross pay.

   Use the following transaction data to test the program:

Employee number	Hours worked
1345	35
1678	40
1789	50
1890	37
2234	42
2235	40
2456	45
2460	48
2567	20

6. Write the program in Problem 5 with the additional requirement that a new payroll file is created. The new payroll file should be the same as the old payroll file with the exception that the year-to-date gross pay is updated to the new year-to-date gross pay where appropriate. Write another program to list the new payroll file after it is created. (This can be a modified version of the program for Problem 2.)

7. Write a BASIC program to create a sequential file of test-score data. Each record in the file has two fields: an identification number field and a test-score field. The records in the file are not in any particular order. Store the data given in Problem 8 of Chapter 9 in the file.

8. Write a BASIC program to display the data in the test-score file created in Problem 7.

9. Write a BASIC program to search for and display any test score in the test-score file created in Problem 7, given an identification number. Test the program with several identification numbers. Be sure to test the case where there is no matching identification number in the file.

10. Write a BASIC program to process the data in the test-score file created in Problem 7 as follows:

    a. Accumulate and display the total of the test scores.

    b. Calculate and display the mean (average) of the scores.

   c. Determine and display the number of scores that fall into each of the following categories:

90–100
80–89
70–79
60–69
0–59

11. Write a BASIC program to create a sorted test-score file from the file created in Problem 7. The data in the sorted file should be in ascending order by identification number. [*Hint:* Retrieve all the records in the file, storing the data in two arrays in the program. Then sort the identification-number array. Finally, store the sorted data in a new file.] Write another program to display the sorted test-score file. (This can be a modified version of the program for Problem 8.)

12. Write a BASIC program to update the sorted test-score file created in Problem 11. Updating involves changing the test score in any matching record in the file to the new score given in the transaction data. Use the following transaction data to test the program:

Identification number	New test score
133	92
185	70
192	83
206	85
230	68
255	75
273	81
294	100

Write another program to list the updated file. (This can be a modified version of the program written for Problem 8.)

13. Write a BASIC program to create a random name-and-address file. Each record in the file has five fields: name, street address, city, state, and zip code. Supply a list of 10 to 20 names and addresses to store in the file.

14. Write a BASIC program to produce "mailing labels" from the records in the name-and-address file created in Problem 13. Each mailing label consists of three lines with the name on the first line, the street address on the second line, and the city, state, and zip code on the third line.

15. Write a BASIC program to display any name and address from the file created in Problem 13, given the record number. Test the program with several record numbers. Be certain to test the case where there is no record in the file.

16. Write a BASIC program to update the name-and-address file created in Problem 13. Updating involves changing the street address, city, state, or zip code but not the name. Test the program by making several changes in the file. Write another program to display the updated file. (This can be a modified version of the program written for Problem 14.)

17. Write a BASIC program to create a random budget file. Each record in the file contains three fields: the budget item, the monthly budget for the item, and the month's expense for the item. The budget items and the monthly budget for each item are as follows:

Budget item	Monthly budget
Rent	300
Utilities	50
Food	160
Clothing	45
Education	35
Entertainment	50
Transportation	65
Health care	50
Miscellaneous	50
Savings	95

Put this data in the file and initialize the month's expense field in each record to zero.

18. Write a BASIC program to update the monthly budget for any item in the budget file created in Problem 17. Updating involves changing the monthly budget for an item to a new value entered at the keyboard. Test the program by updating the monthly budget for several items.

19. Write a BASIC program to update the month's expense for any item in the budget file created in Problem 17. Updating involves adding expense amounts entered at the keyboard to the month's expense field. Any number of expense amounts can be entered for any item. Test the program by entering one or more expense amounts for all budget items.

20. Write a BASIC program to produce a report from data in the budget file updated in Problem 19. The report should list the budget item, the monthly budget for the item, the month's expense for the item, and the percent that the month's expense for the item is over or under the monthly budget for the item. The report should also give the total monthly budget for all items, the total month's expense for all items, and the percent that the total month's expense is over or under the total monthly budget.

Appendix A

Summary of BASIC

This appendix summarizes the syntax of the BASIC language described in this book. It lists the language elements that are commonly found in most versions of BASIC as well as other elements, less frequently found, that are described in the book. The marking of an element with an asterisk (*) means that it may not be available in some versions of BASIC.

The information in this appendix is given in three tables:

Table A-1: Fundamental Elements of BASIC
Table A-2: BASIC Statements
Table A-3: Built-in Functions

Each entry in Tables A-1 and A-2 describes the syntax of a language element, shows an example of its use, gives the section or sections in the text where the element is discussed, and lists any tables in the text that describe differences related to the element for different versions of BASIC. Each entry in Table A-3 gives the form of a function, the function's meaning, the text section reference, and the text table reference, if any. Some elements are listed more than once in Tables A-1 and A-2. Each listing describes a different form of the element.

The version of BASIC used with a particular computer may not include some of the elements listed in this appendix; many have additional elements not listed or may use a different syntax than that given here. The programmer must consult the appropriate reference manual for detailed information about the version of BASIC being used.

Table A–1. Fundamental elements of BASIC

Element	Syntax	Example	Section reference	Table reference
array variable	(*same as* numeric variable)	A5	9-1	9-1
concatenation operator*	+	+	8-3	8-6
constant	(*see* numeric constant, string constant)			
expression	(*see* numeric expression, relational expression, string expression)			
line number	a number within a certain range	100	1-3	1-2
numeric constant	one or more digits possibly with a decimal point and possibly preceded by a sign	25 −48.56	2-1	
numeric constant (E-notation)	a simple numeric constant followed by the letter E and an exponent (one or two digits possibly preceded by a sign)	−3.58E15 856E−8	2-1	
numeric expression	a numeric constant, variable, or function, or any group of these combined with numeric operators and possibly containing parentheses	5 X3 A+(B−2.5)*C	2-2, 7-1	2-2
numeric operator	+, −, *, /, ^	+	2-2	
numeric variable	a letter or a letter followed by a single digit	A B5	2-1	2-1
relational expression	a numeric expression followed by a relational operator followed by a numeric expression	A+B>=3.5	3-1	
relational expression	a string constant, variable, or expression followed by a relational operator followed by a string constant, variable, or expression	N$>="JOHN"	8-2	8-4
relational operator	<, <=, >, >=, =, <>	<	3-1	
string array variable	an array variable followed by a dollar sign	S$	9-6	9-5
string constant	a group of characters enclosed in quotation marks	"THE END"	8-1	8-1

Element	Syntax	Example	Section reference	Table reference
string expression*	a string constant, variable, or function, or any group of these combined with the concatenation operator	"ABC" S$ "ABC"+S$	8-3	
string variable	a numeric variable followed by a dollar sign	X5$	8-1	8-2
subscripted string variable (one dimensional)	a string array variable followed by a numeric expression enclosed in parentheses	S$(5) S$(K) S$(X+3)	9-6	
subscripted string variable (two dimensional)	a string array variable followed by two numeric expressions separated by a comma and enclosed in parentheses	T$(5,6) T$(K,X+3)	10-5	
subscripted variable (one dimensional)	an array variable followed by a numeric expression enclosed in parentheses	A(5) A(K) A(X+3)	9-1	9-4
subscripted variable (two dimensional)	an array variable followed by two numeric expressions separated by commas and enclosed in parentheses	A(5,6) A(K,X+3)	10-1	
variable	(*see* array variable, numeric variable, string array variable, string variable, subscripted string variable, subscripted variable)			

Table A–2. BASIC statements

Statement	Syntax	Example	Section reference	Table reference
CALL*	ln CALL name(arguments)	300 CALL TOT(1,2,X)	11-4	11-7
CHAIN*	ln CHAIN "program name"	480 CHAIN "PROG2"	12-6	12-11
CLOSE*	ln CLOSE #number	250 CLOSE #1	12-2, 12-5	12-3
CLS*	ln CLS	100 CLS	5-1	5-2
DATA	ln DATA list of constants	800 DATA 1,2,3	5-3, 8-4	8-8
DEF	ln DEF name(variables) = numeric expression	130 DEF FNT(A,B)=A+B	11-2	11-2, 11-3
DEF*	ln DEF name(variables) = string expression	120 DEF FNS$(A$,B$)=A$+B$	11-2	11-4
DEF/FNEND*	ln DEF name(parameters) statements ln FNEND	130 DEF FNT(A,B) 140 LET FNT=A+B 150 FNEND	11-3	11-5
DIM	ln DIM list of array declarations	100 DIM A(20),B(15,5)	9-1, 10-1	9-2, 10-1, 10-2
END	ln END	999 END	2-3	
FIELD*	ln FIELD #number,width AS string variable,...	210 FIELD #2,20 AS X$,30 AS Y$	12-5	12-8
FOR/NEXT	ln FOR control variable=initial value TO limit STEP increment statements ln NEXT control variable	300 FOR I=1 TO 20 STEP 2 310 PRINT I 320 NEXT I	4-3	4-1
GET*	ln GET #number,record	300 GET #2,R	12-5	12-10
GOSUB	ln GOSUB ln	350 GOSUB 400	11-1	
GOTO	ln GOTO ln	140 GOTO 110	2-3	
IF	ln IF relational expression THEN ln	160 IF A>B THEN 200	3-1	3-1
IF-GOTO*	ln IF relational expression GOTO ln	160 IF A>B GOTO 200	3-5	3-1
IF-THEN*	ln IF relational expression THEN statement	160 IF A>B THEN LET C=A-B	3-5	3-2
IF-THEN-ELSE*	ln IF relational expression THEN { statement / ln } ELSE { statement / ln }	160 IF A>B THEN 200 ELSE LET C=B-A	3-5	3-5, 3-6
IF-THEN/ELSE/END IF*	ln IF relational expression THEN statements ln ELSE statements ln END IF	160 IF A>B THEN 170 LET C=A-B 180 ELSE 190 LET C=B-A 200 END IF	3-5	3-7
IF-THEN/END IF*	ln IF relational expression THEN statements ln END IF	210 IF A>B THEN 220 LET C=A-B 230 END IF	3-5	3-7

420

Statement	Syntax	Example	Section reference	Table reference

IF-THEN/ELSEIF/ELSE/END IF*	ln IF relational expression THEN
	  statements
	ln ELSEIF relational expression THEN
	  statements
	  .
	  .
	  .
	ln ELSE
	  statements
	ln END IF
		240 IF A>B THEN
		250 LET E=A-B
		260 ELSEIF A>C THEN
		270 LET E=A-C
		280 ELSEIF A>D THEN
		290 LET E=A-D
		300 ELSE
		310 LET E=0
		320 END IF
			3-5	3-7

IF-THEN/ELSEIF/END IF*	ln IF relational expression THEN
	  statements
	ln ELSEIF relational expression THEN
	  statements
	  .
	  .
	  .
	ln END IF
		330 IF I<J THEN
		340 LET M=1
		350 ELSEIF I<K THEN
		360 LET M=2
		370 ELSEIF I<L THEN
		380 LET M=3
		390 END IF
			3-5	3-7

INPUT	ln INPUT list of variables	110 INPUT B,C	2-3	
INPUT*	ln INPUT "prompt";list of variables	120 INPUT "ENTER DATA";B,C	5-1	5-3
INPUT*	ln INPUT #number,list of variables	150 INPUT #1,A,B,C	12-2	12-4
LET	ln LET numeric variable=numeric expression	120 LET A=B+C	2-2	2-3
LET	ln LET string variable=string constant or string variable	220 LET S$="ABC" 230 LET S$=T$	8-1	2-3, 8-3
LET*	ln LET string variable=string expression	240 LET S$="ABC"+T$	8-3	
LPRINT*	ln LPRINT output list	130 LPRINT A,B,C	2-3, 5-1	2-5
LSET	ln LSET string variable=string expression	250 LSET X$=A$	12-5	12-8
MAT addition*	ln MAT array variable=array variable+array variable	410 MAT C=A+B	10-6	10-3
MAT assignment*	ln MAT array variable=array variable	420 MAT A=B	10-6	10-3
MAT constant initialization*	ln MAT array variable=CON	430 MAT A=CON	10-6	10-3
MAT identity initialization*	ln MAT array variable=IDN	440 MAT A=IDN	10-6	10-3
MAT multiplication*	ln MAT array variable=array variable*array variable	450 MAT C=A*B	10-6	10-3
MAT scalar multiplication*	ln MAT array variable=(numeric expression)*array variable	460 MAT B=(2)*A	10-6	10-3
MAT subtraction*	ln MAT array variable=array variable-array variable	470 MAT C=A-B	10-6	10-3

421

Table A-2. (Continued)

Statement	Syntax	Example	Section reference	Table reference
MAT zero initialization*	ln MAT array variable = ZER	480 MAT A=ZER	10-6	10-3
MAT INPUT*	ln MAT INPUT list of array variables	490 MAT INPUT A,B	10-6	10-3
MAT PRINT*	ln MAT PRINT array variable	500 MAT PRINT A	10-6	10-3
MAT READ*	ln MAT READ list of array variables	510 MAT READ A,B	10-6	10-3
ON-GOSUB*	ln ON numeric expression GOSUB ln,ln,...	260 ON K GOSUB 400,500,600	11-1	11-1
ON-GOTO	ln ON numeric expression GOTO ln,ln,...	170 ON K GOTO 100,250,200,250	3-6	3-8, 3-9
OPEN* (sequential)	ln OPEN {"I" "O"}, #number,"file name"	100 OPEN "I",#1,"ABFILE"	12-2	12-2
OPEN* (random)	ln OPEN "R",#number,"file name",length	200 OPEN "R",#2,"XYFILE",50	12-5	12-7
OPTION BASE*	ln OPTION BASE {0 1}	100 OPTION BASE 1	9-1	9-3
PRINT	ln PRINT output list	130 PRINT A,B,C	2-3, 5-1	2-4, 2-5
PRINT*	ln PRINT #number,output list	160 PRINT #2,X:",";Y	12-2	12-5
PRINT USING*	ln PRINT USING "format";list of variables	360 PRINT USING "### ###";A,B	5-5, 8-5	5-4, 5-5, 8-9
PUT*	ln PUT #number,record	270 PUT #2,20	12-5	12-9
RANDOMIZE*	ln RANDOMIZE	100 RANDOMIZE	7-3	7-2
READ	ln READ list of variables	130 READ A,B,C	5-3, 8-4	
REM	ln REM remark	100 REM – ADD TWO NUMBERS	2-3	2-6
RESTORE	ln RESTORE	150 RESTORE	5-3	
RETURN	ln RETURN	799 RETURN	11-1	
RSET*	ln RSET string variable = string expression	260 RSET Y$=B$	12-5	12-8
STOP	ln STOP	500 STOP	11-1	
SUB/END SUB*	ln SUB name(parameters) statements ln END SUB	800 SUB TOT(A,B,C) 810 LET C=A+B 820 END SUB	11-4	11-6, 11-8
WHILE/WEND*	ln WHILE relational expression statements ln WEND	270 WHILE A>B 280 LET A=A-1 290 WEND	4-5	4-2

Table A–3. Built-in functions

Function	Meaning	Section reference	Table reference
TAB(X)	Tabulate to print position X	5-1	5-1
SQR(X)	Square root of X	7-1	
ABS(X)	Absolute value of X	7-1	
ATN(X)	Arctangent (in radians) of X	7-1	
COS(X)	Cosine of X (X must be in radians)	7-1	
EXP(X)	Exponential of X (that is, e^X)	7-1	
LOG(X)	Natural logarithm of X (that is, $\ln X$)	7-1	
SGN(X)	Sign of X (that is, -1 if $X < 0$, 0 if $X = 0$, $+1$ if $X > 0$)	7-1	
SIN(X)	Sine of X (X must be in radians)	7-1	
TAN(X)	Tangent of X (X must be in radians)	7-1	
INT(X)	Largest integer less than or equal to X	7-2	
RND	Random number between 0 and 1	7-3	7-1
LEFT$(A$,N)*	Left N characters of A$	8-3	8-5
RIGHT$(A$,N)*	Right N characters of A$	8-3	8-5
MID$(A$,M,N)*	Middle N characters of A$ beginning with the Mth character	8-3	8-5
LEN(A$)*	Number of characters in A$	8-3	8-7
TRN(A)*	Transpose of matrix A	10-6	10-3
INV(A)*	Inverse of matrix A	10-6	10-3
MKS$(X)*	Convert X to a string value	12-5	12-8
CVS(A$)*	Convert A$ to a numeric value	12-5	12-8

Appendix B

System commands

This appendix describes system commands used with several versions of BASIC on common computers. Some operating procedures are also described. The versions of BASIC covered in this appendix are as follows:

Microsoft BASIC on the IBM PC
Applesoft BASIC on the Apple IIe and IIc
True BASIC on the IBM PC
BASIC-PLUS on the DEC PDP-11
VAX-11 BASIC on the DEC VAX-11

The descriptions of the commands and procedures closely parallel the discussions in the subsections entitled "Using a microcomputer" and "Using a minicomputer" in Section 1-5.

The system commands and procedures described in this appendix may or may not be the same as those used with a specific version of BASIC on a particular computer. Even if the version of BASIC and the computer are the same as one listed in this appendix, the commands and procedures may be different. The appropriate reference manual must be consulted for specific information about the version of BASIC and the computer being used.

Microsoft BASIC on the IBM PC

Booting the system

The operating system on the IBM PC is called PC DOS. To boot the system insert the operating system disk in drive A and turn on the computer. After the system has booted, the symbol

        A>

will appear on the screen.

Starting BASIC

There are two commonly used versions of BASIC on the IBM PC: Disk BASIC and Advanced BASIC. Advanced BASIC has a few more features but requires more internal storage. Either version can be used with the BASIC language features described in this book. To use Disk BASIC, type

    BASIC

To use Advanced BASIC, type

    BASICA

When the BASIC language is ready to use, the symbol

    Ok

will appear on the screen. Any of the system commands can now be entered.

Program names

A program name must be one to eight characters. Any alphabetic and numeric characters and many special characters may be used in a program name.

Examples: PROG1
          YOURPROG
          L25$8X

Retrieving an existing program

To retrieve an existing program from auxiliary storage (i.e., to copy the program from auxiliary storage into internal storage) type the command

    LOAD "*program name*"

Example: LOAD "PROG1"

Running a program

To run the program that is currently in internal storage type the command

    RUN

To stop a program while it is running hold the Ctrl key and press the Break key.

Entering a new program

To enter a new program type the command

    NEW

This erases the program that is currently in internal storage. A new program can then be entered. After the program is entered, it can be run using the RUN command.

Listing a program

To list the program that is currently in internal storage on the screen type the command

    LIST

To list the program on the printer type the command

```
LLIST
```

Saving a program

To save the program that is in internal storage (i.e., to copy the program from internal storage to auxiliary storage) type the command

```
SAVE "program name"
```

Example: `SAVE "PROG1"`

The program will be saved under the name given in the SAVE command. If a program already exists in auxiliary storage with the same name, that program will be erased and replaced with the new program.

To display the names of all the programs that have been previously saved type the command

```
FILES
```

Erasing a saved program

To erase a saved program from auxiliary storage type the command

```
KILL "program name.BAS"
```

Example: `KILL "PROG1.BAS"`

Ending BASIC

To stop using the BASIC language type the command

```
SYSTEM
```

When the system is ready, the symbol

```
A>
```

will appear on the screen. The operating system disk can now be removed and the computer can be turned off.

Applesoft BASIC on the Apple IIe and IIc

Booting the system

The operating system on the Apple IIe and IIc is called ProDOS. (Sometimes an older operating system called DOS is used with the Apple IIe.) To boot the system insert the operating system disk in the disk drive and turn on the computer. After the system has booted, a list of options will be displayed on the screen. (With DOS on the Apple IIe the list of options will not be displayed but the symbol] will appear on the screen.)

Starting BASIC

To use Applesoft BASIC type B when requested by the system after the list of options. When the BASIC language is ready to use, the symbol

]

will appear on the screen. (With DOS on the Apple IIe this step is not necessary. The] symbol appears after the system has booted.) Any of the system commands can now be entered.

Program names

A program name must be one to thirty characters. Any characters except a comma may be used in a program name. A blank space may also be used. The name must begin with an alphabetic character.

Examples: `PROG1`
`YOUR PROG`
`L25$8X`

Retrieving an existing program

To retrieve an existing program from auxiliary storage (i.e., to copy the program from auxiliary storage into internal storage) type the command

`LOAD program name`

Example: `LOAD PROG1`

Running a program

To run the program that is currently in internal storage type the command

`RUN`

To stop a program while it is running hold the CONTROL key and press the letter C. If the program is waiting for input data to be entered, the RETURN key must be pressed after the CONTROL key and C are pressed.

Entering a new program

To enter a new program type the command

`NEW`

This erases the program that is currently in internal storage. A new program can then be entered. After the program is entered, it can be run using the RUN command.

Listing a program

To list the program that is currently in internal storage on the screen type the command

`LIST`

To list the program on the printer type the commands

```
PR#1
LIST
```

After the program is listed on the printer type the command

```
PR#0
```

Saving a program

To save the program that is in internal storage (i.e., to copy the program from internal storage to auxiliary storage) type the command

```
SAVE program name
```

Example: `SAVE PROG1`

The program will be saved under the name given in the SAVE command. If a program already exists in auxiliary storage with the same name, that program will be erased and replaced with the new program.

To display the names of all the programs that have been previously saved type the command

```
CATALOG
```

Erasing a saved program

To erase a saved program from auxiliary storage type the command

```
DELETE program name
```

Example: `DELETE PROG1`

Ending BASIC

To stop using the BASIC language type

```
RUN STARTUP
```

When the system is ready, the list of options will appear on the screen. (With DOS on the Apple IIe this step is not necessary.) The computer can now be turned off and the operating system disk can be removed.

True BASIC on the IBM PC

Booting the system

The operating system on the IBM PC is called PC DOS. To boot the system insert the operating system disk in disk drive A and turn on the computer. After the system has booted, the symbol

```
A>
```

will appear on the screen.

Starting BASIC

To use True BASIC type

    HELLO

When the BASIC language is ready to use, the symbol

    Ok.

will appear in the bottom part of the screen. Any of the system commands can now be entered in this part of the screen.

Program names

A program name must be one to eight characters. Any alphabetic and numeric characters and many special characters may be used in a program name.

Examples: PROG1
          YOURPROG
          L25$8X

Retrieving an existing program

To retrieve an existing program from auxiliary storage (i.e., to copy the program from auxiliary storage into internal storage) type the command

    OLD *program name*

Example: OLD PROG1

The program will appear in the top part of the screen.

Running a program

To run the program that is currently in internal storage type the command

    RUN

To stop a program while it is running hold the Ctrl key and press the Break key.

Entering a new program

To enter a new program type the command

    NEW

This erases the program that is currently in internal storage. A new program can then be entered in the top part of the screen. After the program is entered, it can be run using the RUN command.

Listing a program

The program that is currently in internal storage always appears in the top part of the screen. To list the program on the printer type the command

        LIST

Saving a program

To save the program that is in internal storage (i.e., to copy the program from internal storage to auxiliary storage) type the command

        SAVE *program name*

Example: SAVE PROG1

The program will be saved under the name given in the SAVE command. If a program already exists in auxiliary storage with the same name, an error will occur. To replace an existing program in auxiliary storage with the program in internal storage type the command

        REPLACE *program name*

Example: REPLACE PROG1

To display the names of all the programs that have been previously saved type the command

        FILES

Erasing a saved program

To erase a saved program from auxiliary storage type the command

        UNSAVE *program name*

Example: UNSAVE PROG1

Ending BASIC

To stop using the BASIC language type the command

        BYE

When the system is ready, the symbol

        A>

will appear on the screen. The operating system disk can now be removed and the computer can be turned off.

BASIC-PLUS on the DEC PDP-11

Logging in

The operating system on the DEC PDP-11 is called RSTS. (Other operating systems may be used.) To log in, you first may have to press certain keys on the keyboard or type the word HELLO. Then the word

> User:

will appear on the screen. Following this, type your account number. Next the word

> Password:

will appear on the screen. Following this, type your password. After logging in, the word

> Ready

will appear on the screen.

Starting BASIC

BASIC-PLUS is ready to use after you log in; no additional steps are needed. Any of the system commands can be entered immediately after logging in.

Program names

A program name must be one to six characters. Any alphabetic and numeric characters may be used in a program name. The name must begin with an alphabetic character.

Examples: PROG1
          YOURPR
          L258X

Retrieving an existing program

To retrieve an existing program from auxiliary storage (i.e., to copy the program from auxiliary storage into internal storage) type the command

> OLD *program name*

Example: OLD PROG1

Running a program

To run the program that is currently in internal storage type the command

> RUN

To stop a program while it is running hold the CTRL key and press the letter C.

Entering a new program

To enter a new program type the command

> NEW *program name*

Example: NEW PROG1

This erases the program that is currently in internal storage. A new program can then be entered. After the program is entered, it can be run using the RUN command.

Listing a program

To list the program that is currently in internal storage on the screen type the command

    LIST

To list the program on the printer the LIST command may be used or another command may be required, depending on the actual computer system being used.

Saving a program

To save the program that is in internal storage (i.e., to copy the program from internal storage to auxiliary storage) type the command

    SAVE

The program will be saved under the name given in the NEW command. If a program already exists in auxiliary storage with the same name, an error will occur. To replace an existing program in auxiliary storage with the program in internal storage type the command

    REPLACE

To display the names of all the programs that have been previously saved type the command

    CAT

Erasing a saved program

To erase a saved program from auxiliary storage type the command

    UNSAVE *program name*

Example: UNSAVE PROG1

Ending BASIC

No steps are needed to stop using BASIC.

Logging out

To log out, type

    BYE

The system will respond with the word

    Confirm:

Following this, type the letter Y.

VAX-11 BASIC on the DEC VAX-11

Logging in

The operating system on the DEC VAX-11 is called VMS. (Other operating systems may be used.) To log in, you may first have to press certain keys on the keyboard. Then the word

```
Username:
```

will appear on the screen. Following this, type your account number. Next the word

```
Password:
```

will appear on the screen. Following this, type your password. After logging in, the symbol

```
$
```

will appear on the screen.

Starting BASIC

To use VAX-11 BASIC type

```
BASIC
```

When the BASIC language is ready to use, the word

```
Ready
```

will appear on the screen. Any of the system commands can now be entered.

Program names

A program name must be one to nine characters. Any alphabetic and numeric characters may be used in a program name. The name must begin with an alphabetic character.

Examples: PROG1
          YOURPROG
          L258X

Retrieving an existing program

To retrieve an existing program from auxiliary storage (i.e., to copy the program from auxiliary storage into internal storage) type the command

```
OLD program name
```

Example: OLD PROG1

Running a program

To run the program that is currently in internal storage type the command

```
RUN
```

To stop a program while it is running hold the CTRL key and press the letter C.

Entering a new program

To enter a new program type the command

```
NEW program name
```

Example: `NEW PROG1`

This erases the program that is currently in internal storage. A new program can then be entered. After the program is entered, it can be run using the RUN command.

Listing a program

To list the program that is currently in internal storage on the screen type the command

```
LIST
```

To list the program on the printer the LIST command may be used or another command may be required, depending on the actual computer system being used.

Saving a program

To save the program that is in internal storage (i.e., to copy the program from internal storage to auxiliary storage) type the command

```
SAVE
```

The program will be saved under the name given in the NEW command. If a program already exists in auxiliary storage with the same name, an error will occur. To replace an existing program in auxiliary storage with the program in internal storage type the command

```
REPLACE
```

To display the names of all the programs that have been previously saved type the command

```
EXIT
```

When the $ symbols appears on the screen type the command

```
DIR
```

After the names have been displayed, type the command

```
BASIC
```

Erasing a saved program

To erase a saved program from auxiliary storage type the command

    UNSAVE *program name*

Example: UNSAVE PROG1

Ending BASIC

To stop using the BASIC language type the command

    EXIT

When the system is ready, the symbol

    $

will appear on the screen.

Logging out

To log out, type

    LOGOUT

Answers to selected review questions

Chapter 1

1. input device, output device, internal storage, processor, auxiliary storage
3. input device: keyboard
   output devices: CRT, printer
5. internal storage, processor
7. magnetic disk, magnetic tape
9. The instructions in the program are stored in internal storage. Each instruction is brought from internal storage to the processor, where it is analyzed by the control circuits. The control circuits send signals to the other units based on what the instruction tells the computer to do.
11. A machine-language program needs no translation in order to be executed. A high-level-language program must first be translated into machine language before it can be executed.
13. Application software consists of programs to solve specific problems (e.g., keep track of sales, determine a rocket velocity). System software consists of general programs that help make the computer easier to use (e.g., a compiler or interpreter).
15. In batch processing all data that is to be processed is gathered together in a batch and then processed by the computer (e.g., monthly credit card statement preparation). With interactive processing, each piece of data is entered directly into the computer and processed before the next data is entered (e.g., automatic teller systems for bank deposits and withdrawals by the customer).
17. Most versions of BASIC vary somewhat. If a program is written in one version of BASIC, it generally cannot be processed as if it were written in a different version without some modification.
19. line number (may be optional in some versions of BASIC)
21. A constant is a fixed data value in a program. A variable is a name that is used to refer to data that can change in a program.
23. System commands tell the computer what to do when processing a program. They are not part of the BASIC language.
25. Program testing involves the following steps: make up test data; determine the expected output if the program is run with the test data; run the program with the test data; compare the actual output with the expected output.
27. An algorithm is a set of steps that, if carried out, results in the solution of a problem.
29. coding

Chapter 2

1. a. valid
   c. invalid
   e. valid
2. a. 423000
   c. .0000001234

3. a. $-3.8204E4$
   c. $-1E7$
5. a. invalid (unless long variables are permitted)
   c. valid
7. exponentiation
   multiplication and division
   addition and subtraction
8. a. `X^2-2*X+3`
   c. `(A-B)/(A+B)`
9. a. 3
   c. 13
   e. $-.2$
11. The LET statement is sometimes called an assignment statement because it causes a value to be assigned to a variable (i.e., stored in the storage location identified by a variable).
13. END
15. Answer depends on computer being used.
16. a. 2
17. `70 PRINT A`
   `80 PRINT B`
   `90 PRINT C`
19. There must be one value for each variable in the INPUT statement. The values must be separated by commas.
21. loop
23. `60 PRINT "OUTPUT DATA",A,B`
25. Good program style helps make a program more understandable and readable for a human.

Chapter 3

1. a. less than or equal to
   c. equal to
3. `150 IF X<>Y THEN 200`
4. a. false
   c. true
5. a. 20
7. `100 IF U<=50 THEN 140`
   `110    LET S=1`
   `120    LET T=0`
   `130 GOTO 160`
   `140    LET S=0`
   `150    LET T=1`
   `160 (next statement)`
9. `100 IF I<J THEN 120`
   `110    LET R=P+Q`
   `120 (next statement)`
10. a. `A<>B`
   c. `P<=Q`
11. Two-sided approach:
   `100 IF X>Y THEN 130`
   `110    LET Z=Y`
   `120 GOTO 140`
   `130    LET Z=X`
   `140 (next statement)`
   One-sided approach:
   `100 LET Z=X`
   `110 IF X>Y THEN 130`
   `120    LET Z=Y`
   `130 (next statement)`

```
13. 100 IF J=10 THEN 160
    110    IF K<5 THEN 140
    120       LET I=3
    130    GOTO 200
    140       LET I=2
    150 GOTO 200
    160    IF K<5 THEN 190
    170       LET I=1
    180    GOTO 200
    190       LET I=0
    200 (next statement)
15. 100 IF T=2 THEN 140
    110    IF U<>3 THEN 160
    120       LET S=2
    130 GOTO 160
    140    IF U<>4 THEN 160
    150       LET S=0
    160 (next statement)
17. 100 IF M<>0 THEN 130
    110    LET N=100
    120 GOTO 200
    130 IF M>5 THEN 160
    140    LET N=200
    150 GOTO 200
    160 IF M>8 THEN 190
    170    LET N=300
    180 GOTO 200
    190    LET N=400
    200 (next statement)
19. 50 ON A GOTO 100,200,100,100,200,300
```

Chapter 4

1. An input loop is controlled by some characteristic of the input data. A processing loop is controlled by some characteristic of the data processed in the loop.
3. A trailer value is an input value that is used to signal the end of the data.
5.
```
10 LET C=0
20 INPUT N
30    LET C=C+1
40 IF N<>100 THEN 20
50 PRINT C
```
7. five
9. In a pretest loop, the test to terminate the loop is the first step in the loop. In a post-test loop, the test to repeat the loop is the last step in the loop.
11. a. 6
    c. 30
    e. 5
13.
```
100 FOR K=5 TO 15 STEP 3
110    LET X=X+K
120 NEXT K
```
15.
```
190 FOR I=21 TO 3 STEP -3
200    PRINT I
210 NEXT I
```
16. a. 10
    c. 7
17. a. 15
    c. 120
18. a. input loop
    c. uncontrolled loop
    e. pretest counting loop nested in a FOR loop
19. Answer depends on computer being used.

Chapter 5

1. The cursor is a mark (line or box) on the screen that indicates where the next output is to be displayed.
3. `110 PRINT P;Q`
5.
```
              11111111112222222222333333333   print
     12345678901234567890123456789012345678   position
```

   a. 2   3   4
   c. 2   3   4 DATA
   e. 2   DATA
7. Answer depends on computer being used.
9. `200 PRINT 8,A,8*A`
11. `100 READ A,B,C`
    `110 DATA 2,3,4`
13. X = 5
    Y = 7
    Z = 3
    V = 2
    W = 5
    U = 7
15. `210 PRINT USING "AMOUNT $$#,###.##-";A`
16.
```
              1111111111222   print
     123456789012345678912   position
```

   a. 2.5 73.625   62583
   c.   62,583
   e. ***62583

Chapter 6

1. sequence structure, decision structure, loop structure
2. a. decision
   c. sequence
3. Because each basic control structure has a single entry point and a single exit point, any structure can be nested in any other structure and the result has a single entry point and a single exit point.
5. static; dynamic
7. Any three of the rules listed at the beginning of Section 6-3 are an adequate answer.
9. stepwise refinement
11. documenting the program
13. during the program design activity
15. false
17. Program testing is the process of determining if there are errors in a program. Debugging is the process of locating and correcting errors once their presence has been determined.
19. Coding involves preparing the instructions for a program in a specific programming language. Programming is the whole set of activities associated with preparing a computer program.

Chapter 7

1. Answer depends on computer being used.
2. a. 2
   c. 2
   e. 0
3. `100 LET C=SQR(A^2+B^2)`
4. a. 6
   c. −5
5. `110 LET Y=INT(X+.5)`
7. `130 LET Y=INT(F/3)`
   `140 LET F1=F-Y*3`
9. `150 LET Y=INT(52*RND)+1`

11. To seed a random number function means to start a new sequence of random numbers for the function.
13. Answer depends on game.
15. Stochastic simulation involves uncertainty, whereas deterministic simulation does not.

Chapter 8

1. Any characters except quotation marks can be in a string.
2. a. valid
   c. invalid
   e. valid
3. a. invalid
   c. valid
5. `100 LET M$="MY NAME IS"`
7. `120 LET N$=M$`
9. String data input may be entered with or without surrounding quotation marks unless the string contains a comma or significant leading or trailing spaces, in which case quotation marks around the string are required.
11. a. false
    c. false (true in some versions of BASIC)
    e. false
13.
```
150 IF M$<>"M" THEN 180
160    LET N=N+1
170 GOTO 230
180 IF M$<>"D" THEN 210
190    LET N=N-1
200 GOTO 230
210 IF M$<>"S" THEN 230
220    LET N=0
230 (next statement)
```
15. a. XYZ123
    c. 123
    e. A
17. a. ABCXYZ
    c. ABCDEF
18. a. 8
19.
```
240 READ N$,D$
250 DATA GEORGE,"JAN. 1, 1960"
```

Chapter 9

1. a. An array is a group of data values identified in a program by a single name.
   c. An array element is a value in an array.
3. Minimum element number = 0
   Maximum element number = 10
   (Some versions of BASIC may be different.)
5. a. 20.5
   c. 5.7
7.
```
120 FOR I=1 TO 50
130    READ S(I)
140 NEXT I
```
9.
```
180 FOR I=50 TO 1 STEP -1
190    PRINT S(I)
200 NEXT I
```
11.
```
240 FOR I=1 to 50
250    LET S(I)=I
260 NEXT I
```
13.
```
310 FOR I=1 TO 50
320    IF S(I)<>R THEN 340
330       PRINT T(I)
340 NEXT I
```

15.
```
450 LET B=1
460 LET T=50
470 LET M=INT((B+T)/2)
480   IF S(M)=R THEN 550
490   IF B>T THEN 550
500   IF R>S(M) THEN 530
510     LET B=M+1
520     GOTO 470
530     LET T=M-1
540 GOTO 470
550 IF S(M)=R THEN 580
560   PRINT "VALUE NOT FOUND"
570 GOTO 590
580   PRINT "VALUE FOUND"
590 (next statement)
```

17. Change the IF statement to the following:
```
280 IF N(I)>=N(I+1) THEN 350
```

18. a. `100 DIM N$(30)`

Chapter 10

1. A one-dimensional array can be thought of as organized in one direction such as a column. One subscript is needed to identify an element. A two-dimensional array can be thought of as organized in two directions such as rows and columns. Two subscripts are required to identify an element.

2. a. 100
   c. 96

3. a. `100 DIM X(4,20)`

5.
```
120 FOR I=1 TO 40
130   FOR J=1 TO 20
140     READ X(I,J)
150   NEXT J
160 NEXT I
```

7.
```
91   90   89
78   96   69
85   85   78
95  100   68
```

9.
```
280 LET C=0
290 FOR J=1 TO 20
300   IF X(1,J)<>X(2,J) THEN 320
310     LET C=C+1
320 NEXT J
```

11.
```
400 FOR I=1 TO 4
410   LET J=1
420   IF X(I,J)=V THEN 460
430   IF J=20 THEN 460
440     LET J=J+1
450   GOTO 420
460   IF X(I,J)=V THEN 490
470     PRINT "VALUE NOT FOUND"
480   GOTO 500
490     PRINT "VALUE FOUND"
500 NEXT I
```

13. a. `610 MAT A=ZER`
    c. `630 MAT A=B`
    e. `650 MAT READ B`
    g. `670 MAT PRINT B,`

14. a. `690 MAT C=IDN`
    c. `710 MAT E=(5)*F`
    e. `730 MAT G=TRN(D)`

Chapter 11

1. A subroutine consists of more than one line, must contain a RETURN statement, is called by a GOSUB statement, and is usually placed at the end of a program. A user-defined function consists of a single line, is defined by a DEF statement, is called as part of a numeric expression, and is placed at the beginning of the program.
3. RETURN
5. The next statement executed after a RETURN statement is executed is the statement following the GOSUB statement that called the subroutine containing the RETURN statement.
7. There is no statement to terminate execution before the subroutine. Between statements 30 and 40 must be either a GOTO statement to branch to the END statement or a STOP statement.
9. `100 ON X GOSUB 1000,2000,2000,1000,3000`
11. `150 LET P=FNA(1000,.1,5)`
13. `10          20`
15.
```
1000 SUB SUMDIF(S,D,A,B)
1010 LET S=A+B
1020 LET D=A-B
1030 END SUB

500 CALL SUMDIF(S1,D1,X,Y)
```
17.

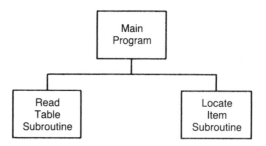

19. a menu

Chapter 12

1. programs; data
3. a field
5. A key field is a field that identifies a record in a file.
7. destroyed; not destroyed
9. In a sequential file the records are stored in sequence, one after the other, in auxiliary storage. The records must be retrieved in the order in which they are stored. In a random file the records are identified by numbers. Records in a random file can be retrieved in any order by specifying the numbers of the desired records.
11. input
13. a. `100 OPEN "O",#1,"AFILE"`
    b. `200 PRINT #1,A;",";B;",";X$;",";Y$`
    c. `300 CLOSE #1`
15. A trailer record is needed in a sequential file so that the end of the file can be detected.
17. a sequential search
19. The records in the master file and the transaction data must be in the same order (either increasing or decreasing) by key field for sequential file updating. The updating algorithm is based on locating matching master and transaction keys. When the keys match, updating takes place.
20. a. 4
    c. 6

21. a. `100 OPEN "R",#1,"CFILE",20`
   b. `110 FIELD #1,4 AS A$,4 AS B$,4 AS C$,8 AS D$`
   c. `200 LSET A$=MKS$(W)`
      `210 LSET B$=MKS$(X)`
      `220 LSET C$=MKS$(Y)`
      `230 LSET D$=Z$`
   d. `240 PUT #1,8`
   e. `300 CLOSE #1`

23. In random file updating, data in a file is changed without creating a new file, whereas with sequential file updating, a new file is created with the updated data. In random file updating the master records and transaction data may be in any order, whereas with sequential file updating the data must be in order by key field.

24. a. 5
   c. 3

25. `400 CHAIN "PROGY"`

Index

ABS function, 212 (fig.), 423 (tbl.)
Accepting input, 13
Accessing a file, 374
  random file, 402–404
  sequential file, 382–383
Access arm, 373
Actual argument, 336
Algorithm, 25, 189–190
Alternation, 176
American National Standard
  BASIC. *See* ANS BASIC
  minimal BASIC. *See* ANS minimal BASIC
American National Standards Institute. *See* ANSI
American Standard Code for Information Interchange. *See* ASCII
Analytic solution, 226
ANS BASIC, 10, 10 (tbl.)
ANSI, 10
ANS minimal BASIC, 10, 10 (tbl.)
Applesoft BASIC, 10 (tbl.), 426–428
Apple IIc, 10 (tbl.), 426–428
Apple IIe, 3 (fig.), 10 (tbl.), 426–428
Application software, 8
Argument
  of a multiple-line function, 342
  of a subprogram, 343, 344
  of a user-defined function, 336–337
Array, 260. *See also* Two-dimensional array
  bounds, 262–265. *See also* Two-dimensional array bounds
    differences, 263 (tbl.)
  element, 260. *See also* Two-dimensional array element
  input and output, 266–269. *See also* Two-dimensional array input and output
  processing. *See also* Two-dimensional array processing
    binary searching, 275–277
    copying, 269–271
      in reverse order, 271
    counting specific values, 271–272
    finding largest or smallest element, 272
    initializing, 269
    processing corresponding elements of two arrays, 271
    sequential searching, 272–275
    sorting, 278–284
  string, 285–287
  as subprogram parameter and argument, 344
  subscript, 262, 265–266

variable, 260, 418 (tbl.). *See also* Two-dimensional array variable
    differences, 261 (tbl.)
ASCII, 242–243, 243 (fig.)
Assignment, 40. *See also* LET statement
ATN function, 212 (fig.), 423 (tbl.)
Auxiliary storage, 2 (fig.), 5, 371

BASIC, 9–10
  function, 210, 212 (fig.), 423 (tbl.). *See also* entry under function name
  program, 11
  statement. *See* Statement; entry under statement name
BASIC-PLUS, 10 (tbl.), 430–432
Batch processing, 9
Beginner's All-purpose Symbolic Instruction Code. *See* BASIC
Binary searching of an array, 275–277
Block IF statements, 90–94
  case selection, 93–94
  differences, 90 (tbl.)
  nested decisions, 92–93
  one-sided decision, 92
  syntax, 91, 92, 93
  two-sided decision, 91–92
Booting a microcomputer system, 18
Bottom-up coding and testing, 351
Bounds. *See* Array bounds
Branching, 47
Bubble sorting, 279
Bug, 24
Built-in function. *See* BASIC function

CAI, 221–224
Calling
  a function, 329, 336–377
  a multiple-line function, 342
  a subprogram. *See* CALL statement
  a subroutine, 329. *See also* GOSUB statement; ON-GOSUB statement
CALL statement, 342, 343, 420 (tbl.)
  array argument in, 344
    differences, 345 (tbl.)
  syntax, 343
Case selection, 77–79
  flowchart, 79, 80 (fig.)
  using block IF statements, 93–94
  using ON-GOTO statement, 96–97
    flowchart, 97, 98 (fig.)
Case structure, 178
Cathode ray tube. *See* CRT

Central processing unit, 2 (fig.), 3 (figs.), 4 (fig.), 5
Chaining, 410–412
CHAIN statement, 411–412, 420 (tbl.)
  differences, 411 (tbl.)
  syntax, 411
Channel, 377
  number, 377, 394
Character
  output, 49–52, 171. *See also* String data, input and output
  string, 234
Clear screen statement, 151
  differences, 151 (tbl.)
  syntax, 151
CLEAR statement, 151 (tbl.)
CLOSE statement
  random file, 394–395, 420 (tbl.)
    syntax, 394
  sequential file, 377–378, 420 (tbl.)
    differences, 378 (tbl.)
    syntax, 377
Closing a file, 377
CLS statement, 151, 420 (tbl.)
  syntax, 151
Coding a program. *See* Program coding
Collating sequence, 242
Comma
  in a MAT PRINT statement, 313
  in a PRINT statement, 42, 147–148, 300
Comment. *See* Remark
Compilation, 8, 16
Compiler, 8, 16
Complement of a condition, 69
Computer, 1–6
  game, 218–221
  program. *See* Program
  programming language, 7–8
  simulation. *See* Simulation
Computer-assisted instruction. *See* CAI
CON. *See* MAT constant-initialization statement
Concatenation, 248–249
  operator, 248, 418 (tbl.)
    differences, 248 (tbl.)
Condition, 69
Conformable matrices, 316
Connector symbol, 25, 27 (fig.)
Constant, 12, 418 (tbl.). *See also* String constant
  E-notation, 31–32
  simple, 30–31
Continuing a statement, 87–88
  differences, 87 (tbl.)
Controlled loop, 105
Control statement, 64
Control structure, 176–177, 178
  nested, 177–178
Control variable in a FOR statement, 122–123
Correctness of a program. *See* Program correctness
COS function, 212 (fig.), 423 (tbl.)
Counter, 110, 112

Counting loop, 110–117
  flowchart, 116 (fig.), 117
CPU. *See* Central processing unit
Creating a file, 374
  random file, 400–402
  sequential file, 380–381
CRT, 2, 3 (figs.)
Cursor, 147
CVS function, 398, 423 (tbl.)

Data, 1, 8–9
  block, 157. *See also* DATA statement
  file, 371
DATA statement, 156–158, 420 (tbl.)
  with array data, 266, 299–300
  with matrix data, 312
  with string data, 253–254
    differences, 253 (tbl.)
  syntax, 156
Debugging a program. *See* Program debugging
DEC
  PDP-11, 10 (tbl.), 430–432
  VAX-11, 4 (fig.), 10 (tbl.), 433–435
Decision, 64. *See also* Case selection
  nested, 75–79
  one-sided, 74–75
  program logic for, 66–68, 69–75
  structure, 176, 177 (fig.)
  symbol, 25, 27 (fig.)
  two-sided, 70–74
DEF statement
  for a multiple-line function, 340–341, 341 (tbl.), 420 (tbl.)
    syntax, 340
  for a user-defined function, 335–336, 420 (tbl.)
    syntax, 336
  for a user-defined string function, 340, 420 (tbl.)
Design. *See* Program design
Deterministic simulation, 225–226
Digital Equipment Corp. *See* DEC
Dimensioning an array, 263
  two-dimensional array, 296–297
DIM statement, 263–264, 420 (tbl.)
  syntax, 263
  for a two-dimensional array, 296–297
Direct access, 374
Disk, 4 (fig.), 5, 372–373
  drive, 3 (figs.), 4 (fig.), 5, 373
Displaying output, 14
Documentation. *See* Program documentation
Documenting a program. *See* Program documentation
DO WHILE statement, 137 (tbl.)
Dummy argument, 335
Dynamic version, of a program, 179

Echo printing, 199
Element. *See* Array element
ELSEIF statement, 90, 93, 421 (tbl.)
  syntax, 93

ELSE statement, 90, 91, 93, 420 (tbl.), 421 (tbl.)
  syntax, 91, 93
Empty string, 234
Empty-string constant, 235
END DEF statement, 341 (tbl.)
END FUNCTION statement, 341 (tbl.)
END IF statement, 90, 91, 92, 93, 420 (tbl.), 421 (tbl.)
  syntax, 91, 92, 93
END statement, 15, 41, 420 (tbl.)
  syntax, 41
END SUB statement, 343, 422 (tbl.)
  syntax, 342
E-notation constant, 31–32
  for input, 46
  for output, 44
ENTER key, 18, 87, 88
Entry point, 177
Error, 24
Exchange sorting, 279
Execution error, 24
Execution of a program. See Program execution
Exerciser, 351
Exit point, 177
EXP function, 212 (fig.), 423 (tbl.)
Exponentiation, 34, 35, 36
Expression, 13, 418 (tbl.). See also Numeric expression; Relational expression; String expression
External subprogram, 344, 345

False part of a decision, 71
Field, 372
FIELD statement, 395, 396, 397, 398, 420 (tbl.)
  syntax, 396
File, 371, 372. See also Random file; Sequential file
  name, 276, 277, 393, 394
  organization, 372
  processing. See Accessing a file; Creating a file; Searching a sequential file; Updating a file
Flag, 305
Floating-point notation, 34
Floppy disk, 5
Flowchart, 25, 26
  of case selection, 79, 80 (fig.)
    using ON-GOTO statement, 97, 98 (fig.)
  of complete programs, 52–54
  of a decision, 68–69, 68 (fig.), 70 (fig.)
    nested decisions, 77, 78 (fig.)
  of a loop, 53, 54 (fig.)
    counting loop, 116 (fig.), 117
    FOR loop, 125
    input loop, 107, 109 (fig.)
    nested loops, 120 (fig.), 121
    processing loop, 110, 111 (fig.)
  of a program with subroutines, 333–334, 333 (fig.)
  of a simple program, 52, 53 (fig.)

  symbols, 25–26, 27 (fig.), 68–69, 77, 333–334
Flowline, 25, 27 (fig.)
FNEND statement, 341–342, 341 (tbl.), 420 (tbl.)
  syntax, 340
FOR loop, 121–131
  additional features of, 129
  branching and, 126–129
  differences, 124 (tbl.)
  flowchart, 125
  FOR and NEXT statements, 122–124
  nested, 129–131
Format. See PRINT USING statement format
FOR statement, 121, 122–124, 129, 420 (tbl.)
  syntax, 122
Function. See BASIC function; Multiple-line function; User-defined function
FUNCTION statement, 341 (tbl.)

Game. See Computer game
Generating a random number. See Random number generation
GET statement, 399–400, 420 (tbl.)
  differences, 400 (tbl.)
  syntax, 399
Global variable, 338, 342, 345
GOSUB statement, 330–331, 420 (tbl.)
  syntax, 330
GOTO statement, 14–15, 47–48, 420 (tbl.)
  in decision logic, 66, 71–72
  for a loop, 47–48
  and program understandability, 180
  syntax, 47

Half-adjusting, 213
Hard disk, 5
Hardware, 5–6
Heading, 51
High-level language, 8
HOME statement, 151 (tbl.)

IBM Personal Computer (PC), 3 (fig.), 10 (tbl.), 424–426, 428–430
Identity matrix, 314
IDN. See MAT identity-initialization statement
IF-GOTO statement, 84, 420 (tbl.)
  differences, 86 (tbl.)
  syntax, 84
IF statement, 64–66, 420 (tbl.)
  in case selection, 77–79
  in decisions, 66–68, 70–75
  in loops, 105–118
  in nested decisions, 75–77
  syntax, 64
  variations, 84–94
IF-THEN-ELSE statement, 88–90, 420 (tbl.)
  differences, 88 (tbl.)
  nested, 90
  syntax, 88
IF-THEN statement, 84–86, 420 (tbl.)

IF-THEN statement (continued)
  block IF form, 90, 91, 92, 93, 420 (tbl.),
      421 (tbl.)
    syntax, 91, 92, 93
  differences, 86 (tbl.)
  syntax, 84
Image, 167
Increment in a FOR statement, 122–123,
    129
Indentation
  case selection, 77, 96
  decision, 68, 77
  FOR loop, 125, 131
  loop, 48, 108, 121
  program style, 55, 181
Initializing a variable, 109
Initial value in a FOR statement, 122–123,
    129
Inner loop, 118–119
Input
  data, 2, 17 (fig.)
  device, 2, 2 (fig.)
  loop, 105, 106–107
    flowchart, 107, 109 (fig.)
  prompt. See Prompt
Input/output symbol, 25, 27 (fig.)
INPUT statement, 13, 45–46, 421 (tbl.)
  for array input, 266, 267, 268, 299
  with a prompt, 151–153, 421 (tbl.)
    differences, 152 (tbl.)
    syntax, 152
  random file, 400 (tbl.)
  sequential file, 378–379, 421 (tbl.)
    differences, 379 (tbl.)
    syntax, 378
  with string data, 238
  syntax, 45
Integer, 212
  function, 212–214
Interactive processing, 9
  program design, 153–156, 356–364
Interchange sorting, 279
Internal storage, 2 (fig.), 5
Internal subprogram, 344–345
International Business Machines Corp. See
    IBM
Interpretation, 8, 16
Interpreter, 8, 16
INT function, 212–214, 212 (fig.), 423 (tbl.)
Inverse of a matrix, 318
INV function, 318–319, 423 (tbl.)
I/O device, 3
Iteration, 176

Keyboard, 2, 3 (fig.), 18
Key field, 372
Keyword, 12
KILL command, 19

Language. See Computer programming lan-
    guage; High-level language; Machine
    language; Natural language
LEFT function, 246 (tbl.)
LEFT$ function, 246, 246 (tbl.), 423 (tbl.)
Left-justifying, 397

LEN function, 250, 423 (tbl.)
  differences, 250 (tbl.)
LET statement, 14, 39–41, 421 (tbl.)
  differences, 41 (tbl.)
  with string data, 236–237, 421 (tbl.)
    differences, 236 (tbl.)
  syntax, 39
Limit in a FOR statement, 122–123, 129
Limitation on data values, 34
Line feed, 87, 88
Line number, 11, 39, 418 (tbl.)
  differences, 11 (tbl.)
  in a GOTO statement, 47
  in a GOSUB statement, 330
  in an IF-GOTO statement, 84
  in an IF statement, 64–65
  in an IF-THEN-ELSE statement, 88–89
  in an ON-GOTO statement, 95
  in an ON-GOSUB statement, 334
  program style, 55
  in a subroutine, 330
LIST command, 19, 22
LLIST command, 19
ln. See Line number
LOAD command, 18–19
Local variable, 337–338, 342, 345
LOG function, 212 (fig.), 423 (tbl.)
Logging in, 20
Logging out, 22
Logic. See Program logic
  error, 24
Long variable, 33–34
Loop, 47, 105
  controlled, 105
  control patterns, 117–118
  counting, 110–117
  FOR, 121–131
  input, 105, 106–107
  nested, 118–121
  processing, 105, 107–110
  uncontrolled, 105
  WHILE, 137–141
Loop structure, 176, 177 (fig.)
LOOP statement, 137 (tbl.)
LPRINT statement, 45, 151, 421 (tbl.)
LPRINT USING statement, 171
LSET statement, 395, 396–397, 421 (tbl.)
  syntax, 396

Machine language, 7–8
Magnetic disk. See Disk
  drive. See Disk drive
Magnetic tape. See Tape
  drive. See Tape drive
Mainframe computer, 4 (fig.), 6
Main program, 329, 331
  flowchart, 333–334
Mass storage, 5
Master
  file, 388
  key, 388
  record, 388
MAT
  addition statement, 314–315, 421 (tbl.)
    syntax, 314

assignment statement, 311, 421 (tbl.)
  syntax, 311
constant-initialization statement, 310–311, 421 (tbl.)
  syntax, 311
identity-initialization statement, 314, 421 (tbl.)
  syntax, 314
MAT INPUT statement, 311–312, 422 (tbl.)
  syntax, 311
MAT PRINT statement, 312–313, 422 (tbl.)
  syntax, 313
MAT PRINT USING statement, 317*n*
MAT READ statement, 312, 422 (tbl.)
  syntax, 312
multiplication statement, 316, 421 (tbl.)
  syntax, 316
scalar multiplication statement, 315–316, 421 (tbl.)
  syntax, 315
subtraction statement, 314–315, 421 (tbl.)
  syntax, 314
zero-initialization statement, 310, 422 (tbl.)
  syntax, 310
Matrix, 309
  input. *See* MAT INPUT statement
  inversion. *See* Inverse of a matrix; INV function
  multiplication, 316, 318 (fig.). *See also* MAT multiplication statement
  operation, 309–310. *See also* entry under MAT statement name
    differences, 309 (tbl.)
  output. *See* MAT PRINT statement
  transposition. *See* Transpose of a matrix; TRN function
Memory. *See* Internal storage
Menu, 356–357
Microcomputer, 3 (figs.), 6
  running a BASIC program on, 18–20, 21 (fig.)
Microsoft BASIC, 10 (tbl.), 424–426
MID function, 246 (tbl.)
MID$ function, 246 (tbl.), 247, 423 (tbl.)
Minicomputer, 4 (fig.), 6
  running a BASIC program on, 20–23, 23 (fig.)
Minimal BASIC. *See* ANS minimal BASIC
MKS$ function, 397, 423 (tbl.)
Module, 346
Monitor, 2
Multidimensional array, 298–299
  differences, 298 (tbl.)
Multiple-line function, 340–342
  argument, 342
  calling, 342
  differences, 341
  parameter, 340
  syntax, 340
Multiple-line statement, 87–88
Multiple statements per line, 86–87
  differences, 87 (tbl.)

Natural language, 7
Nested control structures, 177–178
Nested decisions, 75–79
  flowchart, 77, 78 (fig.)
  using block IF statements, 92–93
Nested FOR loops, 129–131
Nested IF-THEN-ELSE statements, 90
  differences, 90 (tbl.)
Nested loops, 118–121, 129–131
  flowchart, 120 (fig.), 121
Nested WHILE loops, 141
NEW command, 19, 22
New master file, 388
New master record, 388
NEXT statement, 121, 122–124, 420 (tbl.)
  syntax, 122
  with a WHILE statement, 137 (tbl.)
Null string, 234
  constant, 235
Numeric constant, 237, 418 (tbl.). *See also* Constant
Numeric data, 237
Numeric expression, 34, 418 (tbl.)
  differences, 39 (tbl.)
  evaluating complex, 35–39
  in a LET statement, 39
  in an ON-GOTO statement, 95
  program style, 55
  in a relational expression, 65–66
  simple, 34–35
Numeric operator, 34–35, 418 (tbl.)
  order of evaluation, 36
Numeric variable, 237, 418 (tbl.). *See also* Variable

Object program, 16, 17 (fig.)
OLD command, 21
Old master file, 388
Old master record, 388
One-dimensional array, 295. *See also* Array
One-sided decision, 74–75
  using block IF statements, 92
ON-GOSUB statement, 334, 422 (tbl.)
  differences, 334 (tbl.)
  syntax, 334
ON-GOTO statement, 95–97, 422 (tbl.)
  differences, 95 (tbl.), 96 (tbl.)
  syntax, 95
Opening a file, 374
OPEN statement
  random file, 393–394, 422 (tbl.)
    differences, 395 (tbl.)
    syntax, 393
  sequential file, 376–377, 422 (tbl.)
    differences, 376 (tbl.)
    syntax, 376
Operator. *See* Concatenation operator; Numeric operator; Relational operator
Operating system, 8
OPTION BASE statement, 264, 422 (tbl.)
  differences, 264 (tbl.)
  syntax, 264
  for two-dimensional arrays, 297
Outer loop, 118–119

Output data, 2, 17 (tbl.)
Output device, 2, 2 (tbl.)

Parameter
 of a multiple-line function, 342
 of a subprogram, 343, 344
 of a user-defined function, 336–337
PDP. *See* DEC, PDP-11
Pointer in a data block, 157
Positioning output, 147–151
 with a PRINT USING statement, 170–171
Posttest loop, 117, 117 (fig.), 118 (fig.)
Predefined process symbol, 334
Pretest loop, 117, 117 (fig.), 118 (fig.)
 FOR loop, 123, 124 (fig.)
 WHILE loop, 138, 138 (fig.)
Primary storage, 5
Printer, 2, 3 (figs.), 4 (fig.)
 output, 44–45, 150–151
  differences, 45 (tbl.)
Print chart, 188–189
Printout, 2
Print position, 42, 43 (fig.)
PRINT statement, 14, 42–45, 422 (tbl.)
 for array output, 266, 267, 300
 for character output, 49–52
 comma in, 147–148
 constants and expressions in, 153
 differences, 43 (tbl.)
 positioning output, 147–151
 printer output, 44–45, 150–151
 random file, 399 (tbl.)
 semicolon in, 148–149
 sequential file, 379–380, 422 (tbl.)
  differences, 380 (tbl.)
  syntax, 379
 with string data, 237
 syntax, 42
 TAB function in, 149–150
PRINT USING statement, 167–172, 254–255, 422 (tbl.)
 differences, 167 (tbl.)
 printer output, 171
 syntax, 167
PRINT USING statement format, 167
 character output, 171
 differences, 168 (tbl.)
 numeric output, 168–170
 positioning output, 170–171
 string data, 254–255
  differences, 254 (tbl.)
Print zone, 42, 43 (fig.), 147, 148
Probabilistic simulation, 225
Problem definition, 26–27, 187
Processing loop, 105, 107–110
 flowchart, 110, 111 (fig.)
Processor, 2 (fig.), 5
Process symbol, 25, 27 (fig.)
Program, 1, 6–8
 BASIC, 11
 coding, 26, 28, 192, 204
 correctness, 26, 28, 195–199
 debugging, 24, 199
 design, 26, 27–28, 189–190

 for interactive processing, 153–156, 356–364
 development. *See* Programming process; Top-down program development
 documentation, 26, 28, 202–203
 execution, 6–7
  of a BASIC program, 13–16, 17 (fig.)
 flowchart. *See* Flowchart
 logic
  for decision making, 66–68, 69–75
  for loop control, 117–118
 name, 18, 19, 21, 22
 refinement, 183–186. *See also* Stepwise refinement
 repetition, 47–48
 structure, 176–178
 style, 54–55, 180–181
  for decisions, 68
  for loops, 48, 108, 125
  for subroutines, 330
 testing, 24, 197–199
 translation, 16, 17 (fig.)
 understandability, 179–180
Programmer, 6
Programming, 1, 204
 language. *See* Computer programming language
 process, 26–28, 186–187
Prompt, 46, 151–152
Proving program correctness, 196–197
Pseudocode, 192
Pseudorandom number, 217
Pushdown sorting, 279
PUT statement, 398–399, 422 (tbl.)
 differences, 399 (tbl.)
 syntax, 398

Queue, 226
Queuing system, 226

Random access, 374
Random file, 374
 accessing, 402–404
 creating, 400–402
 differences, 393 (tbl.)
 record specification, 395–398
  differences, 396 (tbl.)
 statements for processing, 393–400
 updating, 404–410
RANDOMIZE statement, 217–218, 422 (tbl.)
 differences, 217 (tbl.)
 syntax, 217
Random number, 214
 generation of, 214–215
  in different ranges, 215–216
  in different sequences, 217–218
   differences, 217 (tbl.)
READ statement, 156–158, 422 (tbl.)
 for array input, 266, 299
 random file, 400 (tbl.)
 with string data, 253–254
 syntax, 156
Read/write head, 373

Record, 372
  number, 393
  specification. *See* Random file record
    specification
Refinement. *See* Program refinement; Step-
    wise refinement
Relational expression, 64, 65–66, 418 (tbl.)
  with string data, 239–245
Relational operator, 65, 418 (tbl.)
  complement, 69
Remark, 48–49. *See also* REM statement
  differences, 50 (tbl.)
  program style, 55
  special form, 49
  use of, 181–183
REM statement, 13, 48–49, 422 (tbl.)
  branching to, 142–143
  program style, 55
  syntax, 48
Repetition, 176
REPLACE command, 22
Report, 2
RESTORE statement, 159–160, 422 (tbl.)
  syntax, 159
RETURN
  key, 18, 20, 87, 88
  statement, 329–330, 422 (tbl.)
    syntax, 329
RIGHT function, 246 (tbl.)
RIGHT$ function, 246–247, 246 (tbl.), 423
    (tbl.)
Right-justifying, 168, 397
RND function, 212 (fig.), 214–215, 423 (tbl.)
  differences, 215 (tbl.)
Rounding. *See* Half-adjusting
RSET statement, 395, 396–397, 422 (tbl.)
  syntax, 396
RUN command, 19, 21
Running a BASIC program
  on a microcomputer, 18–20, 21 (fig.)
  on a minicomputer, 20–23, 23 (fig.)

SAVE command, 19, 22
Searching
  an array, 272
    binary, 275–277
    comparison of techniques, 277, 278 (fig.)
    sequential, 272–275
    two-dimensional array, 305–306
  a sequential file, 384–387
Secondary storage, 5
Seeding the random number function, 217
SEG$ function, 246 (tbl.)
Selection, 176
Semantics, 7
Semicolon
  in a MAT PRINT statement, 313
  in a PRINT statement, 148–149
Sentinel, 106
Sequence structure, 176, 177 (fig.)
Sequential access, 374
Sequential file, 374
  accessing, 381–383
  creating, 380–381

differences, 375 (tbl.)
  searching, 384–387
  statements for processing, 375–380
  updating, 387–392
Sequential searching
  of an array, 272–275
  of a file, 386
SET statement, 399 (tbl.), 400 (tbl.)
SGN function, 212 (fig.), 423 (tbl.)
Simple constant, 30–31
Simulation, 224–225
  deterministic, 225–226
  stochastic, 225, 226–229
SIN function, 212 (fig.), 423 (tbl.)
Software, 8
Sorting, 184
  an array, 278–284
    two-dimensional array, 306
Source program, 16, 17 (fig.)
SQR function, 210–211, 212 (fig.), 423 (tbl.)
Square-root function, 210–211
Statement, 11–12, 420–422 (tbl.). *See also*
    entry under statement name
Static version of a program, 179
Stepwise refinement, 184
Stochastic simulation, 225, 226–229
STOP statement, 331–332, 422 (tbl.)
  syntax, 331
Storage location, 12
String, 234. *See also* Character output;
    String data
  array, 285–287
    differences, 285 (tbl.)
  array variable, 285, 418 (tbl.)
  assignment, 236–237
    differences, 236 (tbl.)
  concatenation. *See* Concatenation
  constant, 234–235, 418 (tbl.)
    differences, 235 (tbl.)
  data, 234, 237
    comparing, 239–245
      differences, 241 (tbl.)
    input and output, 237–238. *See also*
      Character output
    LET statement with, 236–237
    vs. numeric data, 237
    PRINT USING statement with, 254–255
    processing, 245–252
    READ and DATA statements with,
      253–254
  expression, 249, 419 (tbl.)
  length, 250
  function, 246–247. *See also* User-defined
    string function; entry under function
    name
  variable, 235–236, 419 (tbl.)
    differences, 236 (tbl.)
Structure. *See* Case structure; Control structure;
    Decision structure; Loop structure;
    Program structure; Sequence structure
  chart, 350
Structured program, 204
Structured programming, 204
Stub, 350

Style. *See* Program style
Subprogram, 342–345
    argument, 343, 344
    calling, 343, 344
    differences, 343 (tbl.)
    parameters, 342, 343, 344
    placement, 344–345
        differences, 345 (tbl.)
    syntax, 342
Subroutine, 329–330
    calling, 329, 330–331, 334
    complete programs, 331–332
    flowchart, 333–334
    syntax, 329
Subscript, 262, 265–266
    differences, 266 (tbl.)
    two-dimensional array, 296, 297–298
Subscripted string variable, 285, 419 (tbl.)
    two-dimensional array, 309
Subscripted variable, 262, 419 (tbl.)
    two-dimensional array, 296, 297–298
SUB statement, 343, 422 (tbl.)
    syntax, 342
Substring, 245–248
    extraction, 246–247
        differences, 246 (tbl.)
Syntax, 7
    error, 24
System
    command, 18, 21
    software, 8
SYSTEM command, 19

TAB function, 149–150, 423 (tbl.)
    differences, 150 (tbl.)
TAN function, 212 (fig.), 423 (tbl.)
Tape, 5
    drive, 4 (fig.), 5
Terminal, 2, 4 (fig.), 20
Terminal point symbol, 25, 27 (fig.)
Test data. *See* Program testing
Testing a program. *See* Program testing
Time-sharing, 9
Top-down coding and testing, 350–351
Top-down design, 348–350
Top-down program development, 348–351
Tracing, 199
Track, 373
Trailer
    record, 372
    value, 106
        with an INPUT statement, 106–107
        with READ and DATA statements,
            157–158
Transaction
    data, 388
    file, 388
    key, 388
    record, 388
Transferring control, 47
Translation. *See* Program translation
Transpose of a matrix, 317
TRN function, 318, 423 (tbl.)
True BASIC, 10 (tbl.), 428–430
True part of a decision, 71

Truncation, 95, 266
Truth value, 65
Two-dimensional array, 295–296. *See also*
        Matrix operation
    bounds, 296–297
        differences, 297 (tbl.)
    element, 296
    input and output, 299–301
    processing
        counting specific values, 305
        initializing, 302–303
        searching, 305–306
        sorting, 306
        totaling elements, 303
    subscript, 296, 297–298
    variable, 295
Two-sided decision, 70–74
    using block IF statements, 91–92

Uncontrolled loop, 105
Understandability. *See* Program
        understandability
UNSAVE command, 22
Updating a file, 374
    random file, 404–410
    sequential file, 387–392
Updating a table, 346
User, 153
User-defined function, 335–336
    additional features, 338–339
    argument, 336–337
    calling, 336–337
    local and global variables, 337–338
    parameter, 335–336
        differences, 336 (tbl.)
User-defined function name, 335
    differences, 335
User-defined string function, 339–340
    differences, 339 (tbl.)
User documentation, 202

Variable, 12–13, 12 (fig.), 32–34, 419 (tbl.).
        See also Array variable; String array
        variable; String variable; Subscripted
        string variable; Subscripted variable
    differences, 33 (tbl.)
    program style, 55
VAX. *See* DEC, VAX-11
VAX-11 BASIC, 10 (tbl.), 433–435
Version of BASIC, 9, 10 (tbl.)

WEND statement, 137–139, 422 (tbl.)
    syntax, 137
WHILE loop, 137–141
    differences, 137 (tbl.)
    nested, 141
    syntax, 137
    WHILE and WEND statements, 137–139
WHILE statement, 137–139, 422 (tbl.)
    syntax, 137
WRITE statement, 399 (tbl.)

ZER. *See* MAT zero-initialization statement
Zone. *See* Print zone